Dictionary of Youth Justice

Dictionary of Youth Justice

Edited by
Barry Goldson

WILLAN
PUBLISHING

Published by

Willan Publishing
Culmcott House
Mill Street, Uffculme
Cullompton, Devon
EX15 3AT, UK
Tel: +44(0)1884 840337
Fax: +44(0)1884 840251
e-mail: info@willanpublishing.co.uk
website: www.willanpublishing.co.uk

Published simultaneously in the USA and Canada by

Willan Publishing
c/o ISBS, 920 NE 58th Ave, Suite 300,
Portland, Oregon 97213-3786, USA
Tel: +001(0)503 287 3093
Fax: +001(0)503 280 8832
e-mail: info@isbs.com
website: www.isbs.com

First published 2008

ISBN 978-1-84392-293-3 paperback
      978-1-84392-294-0 hardback

British Library Cataloguing-in-Publication Data

A catalogue record for this book is available from the British Library

Project managed by Deer Park Productions, Tavistock, Devon
Typeset by Pantek Arts Ltd, Maidstone, Kent
Printed and bound by TJ International Ltd, Padstow, Cornwall

Contents

List of entries

List of contributors

Rob Allen, Director, International Centre for Prison Studies, King's College London.

Peter Ashplant, Senior Performance Adviser, Youth Justice Board.

Kerry Baker, Research Officer, Centre for Criminology, University of Oxford.

Sue Bandalli, Visiting Lecturer in Law, University of Birmingham.

Tim Bateman, Senior Policy Development Officer, Nacro.

Gwyneth Boswell, Director of Boswell Research Fellows and Visiting Professor, School of Allied Health Professions, University of East Anglia.

Anthony Bottoms, Emeritus Wolfson Professor of Criminology, University of Cambridge and Professorial Fellow in Criminology at the University of Sheffield.

Julian Buchanan, Professor of Criminal and Community Justice, North East Wales Institute of Higher Education.

Lol Burke, Senior Lecturer in Criminal Justice, Liverpool John Moores University.

Elizabeth Burney, Senior Research Associate, University of Cambridge.

Spike Cadman, Senior Policy Development Officer, Nacro.

Rob Canton, Professor of Community and Criminal Justice, De Montfort University, Leicester.

Stephen Case, Lecturer in Criminology, University of Wales, Swansea.

Roy Coleman, Lecturer in Criminology and Sociology, University of Liverpool.

Steve Collett, Chief Officer of the National Probation Service, Cheshire and Honorary Senior Research Fellow, University of Liverpool.

Gary Craig, Professor of Social Justice, University of Hull.

Adam Crawford, Professor of Criminology and Criminal Justice, University of Leeds.

Sheena Doyle, Independent Social Care Consultant, Liverpool.

Mark Drakeford, Professor of Social Policy, University of Cardiff and Special Adviser, Welsh Assembly Government.

Tina Eadie, Senior Lecturer in Community and Criminal Justice, De Montfort University, Leicester.

Rod Earle, Associate Lecturer in Criminology, Open University and Researcher, London School of Economics and Political Science.

Karen Evans, Senior Lecturer in Sociology, University of Liverpool.

Roger Evans, Professor of Socio-legal Studies, Liverpool John Moores University.

Finola Farrant, Senior Lecturer in Criminology, University of the West of England.

Julia Fionda, Senior Lecturer in Law, University of Southampton.

Alan France, Professor of Social Policy Research, Loughborough University.

Loraine Gelsthorpe, Reader in Criminology and Criminal Justice, University of Cambridge.

Peter Gill, Interim Head of Service, Wrexham Youth Offending Service.

Barry Goldson, Professor of Criminology and Social Policy, University of Liverpool.

John Graham, Director, Police Foundation.

Patricia Gray, Principal Lecturer in Criminal Justice, University of Plymouth.

Chris Greer, Lecturer in Criminology, City University, London.

Kevin Haines, Reader in Criminology and Youth Justice, University of Wales, Swansea.

Diane Hart, Principal Officer, Children in Public Care Unit, National Children's Bureau.

Keith Hayward, Senior Lecturer in Criminology, University of Kent.

Neal Hazel, Senior Lecturer in Criminology, Salford University.

Harry Hendrick, Associate Professor of History, University of Southern Denmark.

Richard Hester, Senior Lecturer in Youth Justice Studies, Open University.

Ross Homel, Professor of Criminology, Griffith University, Brisbane.

Mike Hough, Professor of Criminal Policy, King's College London.

Sue Howarth, Acting Deputy Head of Service, Oxfordshire Youth Offending Service.

Anthea Hucklesby, Senior Lecturer in Criminal Justice, University of Leeds.

Gordon Hughes, Professor of Criminology, Cardiff University.

Sally Ireland, Senior Legal Officer (Criminal Justice), JUSTICE.

Janet Jamieson, Senior Lecturer in Criminology, Liverpool John Moores University.

Laura Janes, Solicitor and Legal Officer for Children, Howard League for Penal Reform.

Laura Kelly, Doctoral Research Student, University of Liverpool.

Paul Kelly, Independent Youth/Criminal Justice Learning and Development Adviser and Researcher, Manchester.

Hazel Kemshall, Professor of Community and Criminal Justice, De Montfort University, Leicester.

Dave King, Senior Lecturer in Sociology, University of Liverpool.

Paula Lavis, Policy and Knowledge Manager, YoungMinds.

Marian Liebmann, Independent Restorative Justice Trainer and Consultant, Bristol.

Jo Lipscombe, Honorary Research Fellow, School for Policy Studies, University of Bristol.

Christina Lyon, Queen Victoria Professor of Law, University of Liverpool.

Lesley McAra, Senior Lecturer in Criminology, University of Edinburgh.

Fergus McNeill, Senior Lecturer, Glasgow School of Social Work, Universities of Glasgow and Strathclyde.

Geoff Monaghan, Senior Policy Development Officer, Nacro and Chairperson, National Association for Youth Justice.

Linda Moore, Lecturer in Criminology, University of Ulster.

Robin Moore, Senior Research Officer, Ministry of Justice.

John Muncie, Professor of Criminology, Open University.

Mike Nellis, Professor of Criminal and Community Justice, Glasgow School of Social Work, Universities of Glasgow and Strathclyde.

Tim Newburn, Professor of Criminology and Social Policy, London School of Economics and Political Science and President, British Society of Criminology.

David O'Mahony, Reader in Law, Durham University.

Kaushika Patel, Senior Lecturer in Community and Criminal Justice, De Montfort University, Leicester.

Lisa Payne, Principal Policy Officer, National Children's Bureau.

Jo Phoenix, Reader in Sociology, Durham University.

Jane Pickford, Senior Lecturer in Law and Criminology, University of East London.

Harriet Pierpoint, Lecturer in Criminology and Criminal Justice, University of Glamorgan.

Christine Piper, Professor of Law, Brunel University.

Kathryn Pugh, Head of Policy and Innovation, YoungMinds.

Ken Roberts, Professor of Sociology, University of Liverpool.

Barbara Russell, Service Manager for Foster Care, NCH Wessex Community Projects.

Phil Scraton, Professor of Criminology, Queen's University, Belfast.

Michael Shiner, Lecturer in Social Policy, London School of Economics and Political Science.

Joe Sim, Professor of Criminology, Liverpool John Moores University.

David Smith, Professor of Criminology, Lancaster University.

Roger Smith, Professor of Social Work Research, De Montfort University, Leicester.

Anna Souhami, Lecturer in Criminology, University of Edinburgh.

Peter Squires, Professor of Criminology and Public Policy, University of Brighton.

Mike Stein, Research Professor of Social Work, University of York.

Martin Stephenson, Professor of Social Inclusion Strategy, Nottingham Trent University.

Nigel Stone, Senior Lecturer in Criminology, University of East Anglia.

Mike Thomas, Head of Youth Offending Services, West Sussex and Chairperson, Association of Youth Offending Team Managers.

Sue Thomas, Senior Policy Development Officer, Nacro Cymru.

Roy Walker, Manager, Sutton Place Safe Centre, Hull.

Sandra Walklate, Eleanor Rathbone Professor of Sociology, University of Liverpool.

Charlotte Walsh, Lecturer in Law, University of Leicester.

Beth Weaver, Doctoral Research Student, Glasgow School of Social Work, Universities of Glasgow and Strathclyde.

Colin Webster, Reader in Criminology, Leeds Metropolitan University.

David Weir, Director of Community Services, Youth Justice Agency of Northern Ireland.

Dick Whitfield, former Chief Officer of Probation, Kent.

Bill Whyte, Professor of Social Work Studies in Criminal and Youth Justice, University of Edinburgh.

Brian Williams, formerly Professor of Community Justice and Victimology, De Montfort University, Leicester. Brian died tragically on 17 March 2007.

Howard Williamson, Professor of European Youth Policy, Glamorgan University and Member, Youth Justice Board.

Carolyne Willow, National Co-ordinator, Children's Rights Alliance for England.

Joe Yates, Principal Lecturer in Criminology, Liverpool John Moores University.

The above list of contributors shows the position that they held at the time of writing.

Acknowledgements

The compilation and editing of this volume – which represents the work of almost 100 authors and comprises more than 300 entries – obviously would not have been possible without the support and assistance of many colleagues.

Many thanks, therefore, to Brian Willan and the staff at Willan Publishing, not only for their impeccable professionalism but also for their enthusiastic encouragement and support for the project. Thanks, too, to each of the reviewers commissioned by Willan who offered detailed and considered comment in respect of the original proposal and the initial list of entries.

It has been a privilege to work with each and all of the contributing authors who, despite being busy and pressed for time, managed to retain good humour and observe tight deadlines throughout.

Special thanks to two people. To John Muncie for his wise counsel derived from experience of similar projects and to Sonia McEwan for her excellent organizational skills and administrative support.

Together we offer the book to the research, policy, practice and student communities in the hope that it might help to clarify and contextualize the complex and ever-changing world of contemporary youth justice.

Introduction – Making sense of youth justice

More than two decades have passed since Robert Harris and David Webb (1987: 7–9) observed that the '[youth justice] system is riddled with paradox, irony, even contradiction ... [it] exists as a function of the child care and criminal justice systems on either side of it, a meeting place of two otherwise separate worlds'. Nothing has occurred in the meantime to obviate the complexity and contestation to which Harris and Webb allude. If anything, the 'paradoxes', 'ironies' and 'contradictions' are even more conspicuous and, in some jurisdictions at least, the distance between child welfare and youth justice is as great, if not greater, than it has ever been.

This short introductory chapter aims to sketch the contours within which contemporary youth justice is located and to define core sources of complexity. By referring to the dynamic and ever-changing nature of youth justice, to differentiated forms of 'justice', to both the potential and the limitations of comparative analysis and to the major reforms and transformations that characterize contemporary systems in the UK, the challenging task of *making sense of youth justice* will become apparent. It is within this context that the Dictionary has been conceived, and the chapter will conclude by summarizing its rationale and purpose.

A CONSTANTLY MOVING IMAGE

According to Nikolas Rose (1989: 121), 'childhood is the most intensively governed sector of personal existence' (see also McGillivray 1997). If children *per se* are so closely governed, therefore, it is almost certain that those who offend adult sensibilities, transgress normative boundaries and/or breach the criminal law – the 'disorderly', the 'anti-social', 'young offenders' – are governed more closely still. That said, the various means by which children and young people are governed and/or youth justice is delivered are neither uniform nor static. Rather, both informal and formal modes of governance – and youth justice interventions more particularly – are characterized by distinctive and dynamic impulses transmitted through ever-changing organizational forms.

It follows, therefore, that certain juvenile/youth justice systems tend to privilege *welfare* approaches (rooted in inquisitorial, adaptable, informal, needs-oriented and child-specific processes), as distinct from orthodox *justice*-based responses (derived from adversarial, fixed, formal, proportionate and offence-focused priorities). In other systems the converse applies and classical justice imperatives prevail – including, in some cases, explicitly retributive/punitive elements – while a third typology of youth justice systems attempt to broker a difficult balance – a hybrid fusion – comprising a combination of welfare, justice and/or punitive dimensions. Furthermore, the extent to which youth justice systems prioritize 'welfare' or 'justice' or attempt to establish hybrid fusions is *temporally* and/or *spatially* contingent. In other words, policy responses and practice formations not only change over time (the temporal dimension) but they also vary *between* jurisdictions and, in some cases, *within* jurisdictions (spatial dimensions).

DIFFERENTIAL JUSTICE

If youth justice systems are dynamic configurations that are ever in flux – changing over time and across space – then it follows that the organizational frameworks, statutes and policies, modes and methods of intervention and the practices of 'justice' that underpin them will also vary. Perhaps the clearest expression of such variation or 'differential justice', centres around the age of criminal minority or criminal responsibility. This relates to the age at which a child or young person is held to be fully accountable in criminal law: the point at which an 'act' of 'deviant transgression' might be formally processed as a 'criminal offence'. There is extraordinary variation in the age of criminal minority/responsibility between youth justice systems across Europe, as elsewhere in the world. For example, in Scotland the age of criminal responsibility is 8; in England and Wales, Northern Ireland and Australia it is 10; in Canada, the Republic of Ireland, the Netherlands and Turkey it is 12; in France it is 13; in New Zealand, Germany, Italy, Spain and Japan it is 14; in Denmark, Finland, Norway and Sweden it is 15; and in Belgium and Luxembourg it is 18 (Goldson and Muncie 2006a; Muncie and Goldson 2006). As stated, there is equal dissonance in the range of responses to children and young people depending on the extent to which youth justice systems emphasize welfare, justice, diversion, informalism, prevention, intervention, rights, responsibilities, restoration, remoralization, retribution or even starkly punitive imperatives.

In short, youth justice is uncertain. Governments, formal administrations, judicial bodies and correctional agencies 'choose' to govern 'deviant' children and young people in accordance with widely divergent ideological perspectives, political calculations, judicial conceptualizations and operational strategies. In this way, policies and practices are constantly in motion, and similar 'acts' can elicit quite different responses. Children's experiences of 'justice' are defined and differentiated in accordance with time and place. Indeed, Muncie and Hughes (2002: 1) – not unlike Harris and Webb above – have argued that 'youth justice is a history of conflict, contradictions, ambiguity and compromise … [it] tends to act on an amalgam of rationales, oscillating around and beyond the caring ethos of social services and the neo-liberal legalistic ethos of responsibility and punishment'.

THE COMPLEXITIES OF COMPARATIVE YOUTH JUSTICE

Given the ever-changing and differentiated nature of youth justice, many academic researchers, policymakers, practitioners and students are increasingly becoming interested in comparative analysis (Muncie and Goldson 2006). By comparing national and international youth justice systems it is assumed that greater understanding will follow. Furthermore, the interest in transnational youth justice is often accompanied by a growing demand in policy and practitioner communities to discover 'what works' and to emulate 'best practice'.

While comparative analysis, and the study of international youth justice, offers enormous potential, it is often imagined and/or presented in oversimplified forms and its complexity tends to be missed. At the most rudimentary level two quite different assumptions commonly prevail (in the UK at least) with regard to conceptualizing key trends in international youth justice. The first assumption is intrinsically pessimistic. It conceives a hegemonic 'culture of control' (Garland 2001) within which the special status of childhood is diminishing; welfare protectionism is retreating; children are increasingly 'responsibilized' through processes of 'adulteration'; children's human rights are systemically violated; and the global population of young people in penal custody continues to grow. This way of seeing situates England and Wales (just behind the USA) at the vanguard of a burgeoning wave of authoritarianism and punitivity that is sweeping uniformly across the 'advanced' democratic world. The second assumption idealizes international (especially specific west European and Australasian) jurisdictions. It infers a sense of continual advance towards penal tolerance, child centredness and progressive human rights compliance. Within this frame of reference, England and Wales and the USA are conceived as being conspicuously out of step with the liberal progressiveness that is said to typify other youth justice systems. Such binary classification is oversimplified, however, and it neglects the complexities and nuances that prevail *between* and *within* comparative youth justice systems. Furthermore, even when comparative analyses transcend crude penal severity/lenience dichotomies, their methodologies and scope often remain constrained.

International statistical comparisons of the operation of juvenile/youth justice systems are now routinely gathered by various government agencies and research institutes. Whatever their value, such processes are often dogged with problems. Comprehensive data are not always easy to recover or to interpret and, even when data exist they do not necessarily lend themselves to straightforward comparability, for three key reasons. First, the definition, codification and recording of 'crime' vary between jurisdictions. Second, discrete jurisdictions have developed different systems for categorizing and processing 'young offenders'. For example, what is classified as 'penal custody' in one country may not be in others, even though the regimes and the practices of secure detention may be similar (Pitts and Kuula 2006). Furthermore, as noted, significant variations exist across the world in relation to the ages of criminal responsibility. Consequently, not all jurisdictions collect the same data on the same age groups and populations of children and young people and few, if any, appear to do so in the same time periods. Third, linguistic, cultural and socio-legal differences mean that such terms as 'minor', 'juvenile', 'child' and 'young offender' are defined and operationalized in different ways.

Similarly, despite their interest and benefits, several attempts to unravel national and international differences rarely go much beyond describing the development, powers and procedures of particular national jurisdictions (for example, Bala *et al.* 2002; Winterdyk 2002; Tonry and Doob 2004). This pays scant regard to the actual translation and transmission of statute via the varying (discretionary) practices of youth justice. Indeed, it can even be argued that the national is an inadequate unit of comparative analysis in that it conceals, or at least obfuscates, local and/or regional differences *within* jurisdictions. For sure, neoliberal economics, conservative politics and policy transfer may well serve to create some standardized and homogenized global responses to youth offending but, paradoxically, 'international' youth justice is also significantly 'localized' through national, regional and local enclaves of difference (Muncie 2005; Goldson and Muncie 2006a; Hughes and Follett 2006). In many countries it is difficult to prioritize national developments above widely divergent regional differences, most evident in sentencing disparities (justice by geography). In short, once it is recognized that variations *within* nation-state borders may be as great, or even greater, than some differences *between* them, then the problems associated with taking the national (let alone the international and the global) as the basic unit for understanding policy shifts and processes of implementation become apparent (Crawford 2002; Stenson and Edwards 2004; Edwards and Hughes 2005).

CONTEMPORARY YOUTH JUSTICE IN THE UK

The UK is, of course, the site of three separate youth justice jurisdictions: England and Wales, Northern Ireland and Scotland and, in recent years, each has been characterized by major reform and substantial changes in law, policy and practice.

Such change has been most evident in England and Wales, the largest of the three jurisdictions. Since the election of the first New Labour government in May 1997, the youth justice system has been radically transformed. In fact, contemporary developments in law and policy have formulated the most radical overhaul of the youth justice system in England and Wales since the inception of the first juvenile courts in 1908 (Goldson 2007). In particular, the Crime and Disorder Act 1998, the Youth Justice and Criminal Evidence Act 1999, the Anti-social Behaviour Act 2003 and the Criminal Justice and Immigration Bill (that is before Parliament at the time of writing) have introduced, or will introduce, a multitude of new legal processes, court orders and statutory powers. Indeed, the entire youth justice apparatus in England and Wales has been radically restructured and expanded via the statutory establishment of new national and local infrastructures. At the national level, an executive non-departmental public body, the Youth Justice Board, was established in 1998. At the local level, since 2000, social services authorities, education authorities, the Probation Service, the police and regional health authorities have been statutorily required to form multi-agency 'youth offending teams' (YOTs) and some 155 YOTs – substantially sized inter-agency organizations – have been established in England and Wales.

In Northern Ireland, youth justice reform was a key element of the *Criminal Justice Review* – initiated in 1998 and published in 2000 – that informed the provisions of the Justice (Northern Ireland) Act 2002, the legislation at the root of substantial change and system reconfiguration. In some key respects the pattern of developments in Northern Ireland – although on a quite dissimilar scale – has mirrored those in England and Wales. A new 'Youth Justice Agency' has taken over the responsibilities of the Juvenile Justice Board for Northern Ireland and multi-agency teams have been formed. However, in other respects youth justice in Northern Ireland has defined a distinctiveness through an ambitious and wide-ranging youth conferencing model and a significantly reduced reliance on penal custody.

Perhaps Scotland comprises the most stable youth justice system in the UK, primarily defined by the children's hearing system. The hearings developed out of the recommendations of an influential committee in 1964, chaired by one of Scotland's most senior judges, Lord Kilbrandon. The hearings, which were first operationalized in 1971, were provided with statutory footing by the Social Work (Scotland) Act 1968 and, subsequently, by the Children (Scotland) Act 1995. More recently, however, legislative developments – including the Criminal Justice (Scotland) Act 2003 and the Anti-Social Behaviour (Scotland) Act 2004 – represent signs that youth justice in Scotland is perhaps moving closer to the model found in England and Wales: new systems of police warnings and restorative cautions have been introduced; parenting orders have been implemented; the 'fast tracking' of 'persistent young offenders' and youth courts have been piloted; electronic monitoring has been extended; the availability of secure accommodation has been increased; national practice standards have been imposed; and an emphasis on 'anti-social behaviour' has also become evident. This has prompted leading Scottish youth justice analysts to question whether long-established welfarist traditions are facing a state of 'crisis' (Whyte 2003; McAra 2006).

In sum, each of the youth justice jurisdictions in the UK has been subject to substantial change and significant expansion in recent years. Youth justice is now conceived as an increasingly important area, not only in broader criminal justice and crime and disorder reduction discourses but also in policy and practice debates with regard to child welfare, youth services, health, community development, urban regeneration, education and employment (Goldson and Muncie 2006b).

USING THE DICTIONARY

It is apparent – even from a schematic overview of the constantly changing nature and form of youth justice systems; of core inter-jurisdictional differences; of the complex nature of comparative analysis; and of the major reforms that have impacted in the three UK jurisdictions in recent years – that *making sense of youth justice* presents formidable challenges. The Dictionary is designed to equip the reader to meet such challenges. The entries explicitly address the historical, legal, theoretical, organizational, policy, practice, research and evidential contexts within which 'modern' youth justice in the UK and beyond is located. A hundred years have passed since the inception of the first juvenile courts, yet the pace and reach of contemporary reform, together with the volume of growth in national and international youth justice systems, are unprecedented. In this sense the publication of the Dictionary is particularly timely.

The entries cover a spectrum of theoretical orientations and conceptual perspectives ranging from 'abolitionism' to 'zero tolerance'. They address explicitly the key statutory provisions and policy and practice imperatives in each of the three UK jurisdictions. Each entry is written by an expert in the respective field, and all entries follow a standardized format, beginning with a short definition, followed by the main substance of the entry and concluding with a concise list of key texts and sources including, where relevant, website references. Carefully organized cross-referencing, together with a detailed index, will assist readers to make the connections between and across entries.

The Dictionary is a key resource for lecturers and students involved with the Foundation Degree in Youth Justice, together with those teaching and studying undergraduate and postgraduate courses in criminology, criminal justice, sociology, social policy, law, socio-legal studies, community justice, social work, youth and community work and police studies. Furthermore, the book is designed to meet the needs of a substantially expanded population of policymakers, managers and practitioners (including staff training officers, youth justice officers, social workers, probation officers, police officers, teachers and education workers, health professionals, youth workers, drug and alcohol workers and juvenile secure estate staff). Taken together, it is hoped that what follows will prove invaluable to readers seeking to make sense of the complexities and challenges that characterize contemporary youth justice.

Barry Goldson

ABOLITIONISM

> Abolitionism contends that penal institutions have failed to contain crime and to protect the public and that, therefore, they should be abolished and replaced with a system of confinement that would be used only as a last resort. In their place, alternatives to custody should be developed, based on social justice, inclusion and reparation.

The theoretical, political and policy starting point for abolitionists is the recognition that penal institutions for juveniles are themselves social problems that not only have a minimal impact on crime but also inflict serious harm and damage on individual young prisoners, their families and communities. The issue of child deaths in custody is an example of this point. In addition, these institutions fail to offer psychological comfort to the victims of crime or their relatives, and fail to protect the wider public from further victimization when the young prisoner is eventually released. Abolitionists would argue that the youth justice system, and the penal institutions which underpin that system, are indefensible and socially harmful. They would maintain that liberal reforms have done little to challenge the brutal and punitive nature of the current system of juvenile confinement and that these reforms have overwhelmingly been incorporated into the system, thereby legitimating its further expansion.

Abolitionists advocate a range of interventions and strategies designed to challenge, contradict and transform both the terms of the current debate around youth justice and the policies pursued with respect to juvenile offenders. First, at an ideological level, youth crime should be considered against the crimes committed, and the social harms generated, by the anti-social behaviour and criminality of the powerful. Thus, while youth crime as conventionally defined can have a negative impact on individuals and communities, abolitionists argue that these very public actions are easily targeted and criminalized by the state, while the detrimental and damaging activities of the powerful, often carried out in the world of the private – the home, the state institution, the boardroom – can be equally, and often more devastating, than the activities of young people. Abolitionists, therefore, argue that the debate about crime, deviance and anti-social behaviour should be extended to include not only the public criminality of powerless young people but also the private criminality of powerful older people. The small number of murders committed by young people, compared with the many deaths at work caused by violations of health and safety legislation, is an example of this argument.

Secondly, abolitionists reject the positivist determinism that underpins much of the debate around youth crime, which implicitly and explicitly equates social deprivation with criminality. This position neglects the crimes committed by young people from more affluent backgrounds, whose activities are often labelled as 'high jinks'. Nonetheless, abolitionists *would* argue for the abolition of the major social divisions – social class, gender, 'race', age, sexuality and ability/disability – that scar the landscape of the contemporary social order. These divisions, and the structures of power which underpin them, particularly state power, are key elements in how crime is constructed and responded to and are central to the subversion of ideas around individual and collective social justice.

Thirdly, at a policy level, abolitionists argue for a moratorium on the construction of penal institutions for young people, for the closure of many existing institutions and for the development of well funded, radical alternatives to custody built on the discourses of welfare and social inclusion as opposed to the punitive, retributive discourses that currently prevail and that legitimate the drive to build yet more prisons for juvenile offenders. Furthermore, the culture of masculinity which underpins the systemic violence that dominates daily life in many institutions for juvenile offenders would be radically transformed and replaced by a range of empathic and supportive policies and interventions for the minority of young offenders who need to be confined.

Fourthly, abolitionists argue that the scope of the criminal law and the criminalization processes that follow from the mobilization of the law as a response to social problems, should be curtailed in the context of a drastic and democratizing overhaul of both sentencing policy and the judiciary. This, in turn, would underpin a radical shift from the neoliberal, authoritarian emphasis on retribution and punishment to welfare and rehabilitation for children and young people. Reactive and reactionary policies, such as anti-social behaviour orders, would be abolished, while preventative, welfare-oriented, socially inclusive policies and services would be proactively developed and extended.

Abolitionism has not been without its critics. For conservatives and liberals, abolitionists are too idealistic and utopian and simply want to tear down the prison walls and let dangerous offenders walk free. Abolitionists argue that what is needed in political and criminal justice debates is *more* not *less* idealism and utopianism. Furthermore, while there are some individuals who are clearly dangerous in terms of the crimes they have committed (for example, those who have engaged in sexual violence towards women), abolitionists maintain that they have *not* advocated that such individuals should walk free but that they should be held in a system of confinement very different from the system that currently prevails. They also point out that the criminal justice system does little to protect women from male violence, as the official criminal statistics, victimization surveys and self-report surveys indicate.

For abolitionists such as Angela Davis, abolitionism has failed to think about the role of anti-racist struggles in delivering a radically transformed penal system. This point has become particularly important in the context of an emerging penal-industrial complex, in the privatization of criminal justice and in the detention of increasing numbers of minority ethnic boys, girls, men and women, including juveniles, in penal institutions that are designed not to control crime but to defend and reproduce a globalized, and deeply divided, international social order.

In conclusion, abolitionists argue that the current levels of juvenile incarceration are unsustainable in terms of the financial and human costs they generate. Therefore a radical change of philosophy, policy and practice is needed if these costs are to be curtailed, human rights protected and public safety ensured.

Joe Sim

Related entries

Alternatives to custody; Children in custody; Criminal responsibility; Custody-free zones; Decarceration; Decriminalization; Deaths in custody; Informalism; Social harm.

Key texts and sources

Davis, A. (2003) *Are Prisons Obsolete?* New York, NY: Seven Stories Press.

Goldson, B. and Coles, D. (2005) *In the Care of the State? Child Deaths in Penal Custody in England and Wales.* London: Inquest.

Mathiesen, T. (2000) *Prison on Trial.* Winchester: Waterside Press.

Sim, J. (2005) 'Abolitionism', in E. McLaughlin and J. Muncie (eds) *The Sage Dictionary of Criminology* (2nd edn). London: Sage.

Sudbury, J. (2004) 'A world without prisons: resisting militarism, globalized punishment and empire', *Social Justice*, 31: 9–30.

See also the websites of Inquest (**www.inquest.org.uk**) and No More Prison (**www.alternatives2prison.ik.com**).

ABSOLUTE DISCHARGE

> Absolute discharge is a disposal available to the youth court in criminal cases where – having taken into account the circumstances relating to the offence or the offender – punishment is considered inexpedient.

An absolute discharge does not qualify as a conviction and so it does not need to be disclosed, although it will appear as part of the offender's record in any subsequent criminal proceedings (Powers of Criminal Courts (Sentencing) Act 2000, ss. 12–15). The number of absolute discharges has shown an enormous increase over the last ten years – 645 in the youth court in 1995, 3,060 in 2005. The use of this disposal calls into question the appropriateness of prosecution in such cases. The Crown Prosecution Service (CPS) is bound by the *Code for Crown Prosecutors* to consider triviality, the likely outcome and public interest before proceeding with a prosecution. One reason for the increase may be the constraints on the CPS in following its own guidelines as a consequence of the reprimand and final warning scheme in the Crime and Disorder Act 1998, restricting the discretion to divert trivial cases or those where there has been a previous conviction. Additionally, the impact of the mandatory referral order on the youth court's options may mean that, in essence, if the only other disposal available besides absolute discharge is referral to the youth offender panel, the former may be deemed to be more appropriate.

Sue Bandalli

Related entries

Conditional discharge; Referral orders; Reprimands and final warnings; Youth Justice and Criminal Evidence Act 1999.

Key texts and sources

See the Office of Public Sector Information's website (**http://www.opsi.gov.uk/acts/acts2000/20000006.htm**) for the text of the Powers of Criminal Courts (Sentencing) Act 2000.

ACCEPTABLE BEHAVIOUR CONTRACTS (ABCs)

> Acceptable behaviour contracts (ABCs) or agreements (ABAs) are non-statutory and formally 'voluntary' written agreements between young people, their families and 'relevant authorities', that specify particular behaviour or activities that the named person should refrain from.

The central features of the government's anti-social behaviour strategy that bear directly on acceptable behaviour contracts (ABCs) include the principle of early intervention (ensuring that youthful anti-social behaviour does not lead to more serious and persistent criminality); the principle of public reassurance (ensuring that problems are seen to be dealt with swiftly, before they escalate); and the principles of community, accountability and responsibility (the idea that behaviour is made accountable to community norms while communities are supported in asserting standards of acceptable behaviour). To this end, many local authorities and crime and disorder reduction partnerships followed Islington (where ABCs were first employed) in establishing ABC schemes. By April 2002 there were over 170 schemes operating in 39 different police force areas (Bullock and Jones 2004).

Although not legally binding, ABCs are intended to be cheap, quick, flexible, informal and consensual responses to anti-social behaviour committed by young people, but they can also be used for adults. They are brought into play prior to a consideration of full anti-social behaviour order (ASBO) proceedings and for lower levels of anti-social or disorderly behaviour or for cases involving younger children. ABCs are instituted for periods of six months and are reviewed regularly while in force but can be extended. The consequences of breaching an ABC can include the commencement of full ASBO proceedings or, in cases where the ABC is brought by, or managed on behalf of, a registered social landlord, the beginning of eviction proceedings.

Bullock and Jones' (2004) evaluation of the Islington ABC initiative concluded that ABCs provided a popular and generally effective way of reducing anti-social behaviour. They went on to make a number of recommendations for improving the ABC operation, including the adoption of better evidence gathering and selection criteria; more effective partnership working, information sharing and scheme monitoring; and ensuring that support is available to help make sure that any contracts that are arranged are seen through to a successful conclusion.

Other research (Squires and Stephen 2005), however, has raised a number of critical concerns about ABCs. There are questions about just how voluntary and consensual the contracts really are when an ASBO, or the threat of eviction, is used as the leverage to secure agreements. Such issues open up broader questions about the spuriously 'contractual' nature of the means by which anti-social behaviour is managed (Crawford 2003) and the entitlements to 'welfare rights' obtained (Flint and Nixon 2006). The threat of evicting a whole family may appear a substantial sanction to place on the shoulders of a 12-year-old. Approximately half the contracts in the Squires and Stephen research were imposed on young people with clinically diagnosed personality disorders but for whom social support was lacking. Contracts were drafted entirely negatively – things you must not do – but were short on positive statements and shorter still on entitlements, opportunities or supportive resources. More generally, the ABC can be seen as part of a further and more pre-emptive net-widening process (Brown 2004).

On 28 August 2007, the Home Secretary, Jacqui Smith, launched new government guidance advising practitioners on the 'best use' of ABCs and called on the police and local authorities 'across the country' to use them more 'to nip anti-social behaviour in the bud' (Youth Justice Board 2007c).

Peter Squires

Related entries

Anti-social behaviour (ASB); Anti-social behaviour orders (ASBOs); Early intervention; Net-widening.

Key texts and sources

Brown, A.P. (2004) 'Anti-social behaviour, crime control and social control', *Howard Journal of Criminal Justice*, 43: 203–11.

Bullock, S. and Jones, B. (2004) *Acceptable Behaviour Contracts: Addressing Antisocial Behaviour in the London Borough of Islington. Home Office Online Report* 02/04 (available online at http://www.homeoffice.gov.uk/rds/pdfs2/rdsolr0204.pdf).

Crawford, A. (2003) 'Contractual governance of deviant behaviour', *Journal of Law and Society*, 30: 479–505.

Flint, J. and Nixon, J. (2006) 'Governing neighbours: anti-social behaviour orders and new forms of regulating conduct in the UK', *Urban Studies*, 43: 939–55.

Squires, P. and Stephen, D.E. (2005) *Rougher Justice: Anti-social Behaviour and Young People.* Cullompton: Willan Publishing.

Youth Justice Board (2007c) 'Government launches new guidance on the use of acceptable behaviour contracts' (available online at http://www.yjb.gov.uk/en-gb/News/newAcceptableBehaviourContractsguidance.htm?area=Corporate).

ACTION PLAN ORDERS (APOs)

An action plan order (APO) is a community sentence created by the Crime and Disorder Act 1998. It is available for any 'juvenile' (10–17-year-old) who has been convicted of an offence that the court considers serious enough to merit a community sentence. The order is intended to provide a 'short, intensive, individually tailored response to offending behaviour and associated risks' (Youth Justice Board 2004a: para. 8.37).

Guidance issued by the Youth Justice Board, together with the National Standards for Youth Justice Services, provides advice to courts and youth offending teams (YOTs) on the operation of the action plan order (APO). This guidance concerns the procedure at court when the order is made; the requirements that may be included in the order; the role of the responsible officer; liaison with victims; variation and discharge arrangements; and appeals and breach proceedings. Subsequent guidance (Youth Justice Board

2004b) reflects a number of changes, including the introduction of drug treatment and drug testing.

Before imposing an APO, the court is required to consider the circumstances that have contributed to the child's/young person's offending and to attempt to ensure that the 'action plan' addresses those circumstances with a view to preventing reoffending. The order is imposed for three months, and the court will appoint a 'responsible officer' from the local YOT who will co-ordinate the programme/requirements of the 'action plan'; supervise the child/young person as he or she completes the order; and alert the court if there is any 'failure to comply'.

The specific requirements of an APO may include any combination of:

- participation in activities;
- attendance at offence-focused groupwork;
- attendance at an attendance centre;
- staying away from specified places;
- monitored school attendance;
- reparation, either to the victim of the offence or to the community as a whole; and/or
- attendance at a review hearing at the youth court.

Schedule 24 of the Criminal Justice Act 2003 amends provisions of the Powers of Criminal Courts (Sentencing) Act 2000 to allow for drug treatment and, where appropriate, drug testing to be included as requirements in an APO (or supervision order). Drug treatment and/or drug testing requirements are supposedly targeted at children/young people who have – or who are thought to be 'at risk' of developing – drug problems. The court may also impose a parenting order on the parents of a young person subject to an APO.

If the child/young person 'fails to comply' with the order, at most two warnings within the period of the order may be issued before breach proceedings are activated that involve the child/young person being returned to court. Breach proceedings can be taken at any stage of the order (regardless of the length of time it has to run).

The APO is premised on the concept of intensive early intervention as a means of 'nipping offending in the bud'. As such it is open to the same critiques that are levelled at other early intervention initiatives, including the labelling effect and the potentially counterproductive tendencies that early intervention can invoke. If the relevant provisions of the Criminal Justice and Immigration Bill 2006–7 to 2007–8 are implemented, the APO will be replaced – along with the curfew order, the attendance centre order, the exclusion order and the supervision order – with the single 'menu-based' youth rehabilitation order.

Barry Goldson

Related entries

Crime and Disorder Act 1998; Criminal Justice and Immigration Bill 2006–7 to 2007–8; Early intervention; Powers of Criminal Courts (Sentencing) Act 2000; Restorative justice; Sentencing framework; Specific sentence reports (SSRs); Supervision orders.

Key texts and sources

Ashford, M., Chard, A. and Redhouse, N. (2006) *Defending Young People in the Criminal Justice System.* London: Legal Action Group.
Youth Justice Board (2004a) *National Standards for Youth Justice Services.* London: Youth Justice Board (available online at http://www.yjb.gov.uk/Publications/Scripts/prodView.asp?idproduct=155&eP=PP).
Youth Justice Board (2004b) *Guidance Document: Action Plan Order Drug Treatment and Testing Requirement as Part of an Action Plan Order or Supervision Order* (available online at http://www.yjb.gov.uk/en-gb/practitioners/CourtsAndOrders/Disposals/ActionPlanOrder/).
See also the Home Office's *Police: Action Plan Orders – Full Guidance (the Crime and Disorder Act)* (available online at http://police.homeoffice.gov.uk/news-and-publications/publication/operational-policing/action_plan_order1.pdf) and the Youth Justice Board's Disposals: Action Plan Order (available online at http://www.yjb.gov.uk/en-gb/practitioners/CourtsAndOrders/Disposals/ActionPlanOrder/).

ACTUARIALISM

> Actuarialism encapsulates an approach to crime control that dispenses with deeper concerns about the origins of offences in favour of 'risk minimization' (Feeley and Simon 1994). It has become increasingly influential in the formal youth justice process.

The appeal of actuarialism reflects broader social trends associated with the idea of the 'risk society' (Beck 1992). In youth justice, there has been a shift from concerns about the motivation and well-being of offenders to a preoccupation with measurement and the prediction of *future* risk. Quasi-scientific means of quantifying the likelihood of future offending are now in place (using assessment tools such as Asset and Onset), and disposals often rely on surveillance and the containment of those who are identified as posing a threat (tagging, tracking and the Intensive Supervision and Surveillance Programmes, for example).

The government has also instigated a number of similar initiatives in the wider policy context. For example, 'Every Child Matters' initiated a scheme to generate shared information on all children that could provide an 'early warning' of problems, including potential offending, and 'preventive' programmes have targeted those identified as 'at risk' of offending (for example, youth inclusion programmes and youth inclusion and support panels). The courts now have a range of powers to impose orders prospectively, ostensibly to prevent future offending. These include anti-social behaviour orders, dispersal orders, child safety orders and parenting orders.

However, the use of predictive tools to justify actuarial practice has a number of crucial limitations. First, they are crude and incorporate the problem of applying *generalized* probabilities to *individual* children and young people. For exam-

ple, Asset is found to be, at best, only 70 per cent accurate in estimating the risk of reoffending. Thus, selection processes are arbitrary, interventions incorporate inherent unfairness and individuals are 'labelled' without justification. Secondly, because predictions are based on subjective judgements and are often inaccurate, there will be substantial numbers of 'false positives' – individuals wrongly identified as potential (re)offenders. Thirdly, the process of identifying and acting against individuals on the basis of their putative future behaviour is divisive and exclusive. It also threatens the rights of young people, who do not have to be proven offenders to incur intrusive interventions. Fourthly, interventions based on actuarial assessments have little impact on crime rates (France *et al.*, 2004), suggesting that they are based on an unsound premise.

Major concerns thus emerge: on the one hand, actuarial justice is based on speculative assumptions about the nature of risk and risk management while, on the other, the increasing dominance of this perspective compromises inclusive early-intervention strategies.

Roger Smith

Related entries

Administrative criminology; Assessment framework; Early intervention; Managerialism; Risk factors; Risk management.

Key texts and sources

Beck, U. (1992) *Risk Society*. London: Sage.
Feeley, M. and Simon, J. (1994) 'Actuarial justice: the emerging new criminal law', in D. Nelken (ed.) *The Futures of Criminology*. London: Sage.
France, A., Hine, J., Armstrong, D. and Camina, M. (2004) *The On Track Early Intervention and Prevention Programme: From Theory to Action*. London: Home Office.
Smith, R. (2006) 'Actuarialism and early intervention in contemporary youth justice', in B. Goldson and J. Muncie (eds) *Youth Crime and Justice: Critical Issues*. London: Sage.

ADMINISTRATIVE CRIMINOLOGY

> Administrative criminology is the term used to describe the emergence and rise of a form of criminological analysis and criminal justice response that prioritizes prevention, assesses and reduces risk and manages those considered criminal, deviant or anti-social.

Jock Young (1999: 45) states that administrative criminology 'explains crime as the inevitable result of a situation where the human state of imperfection is presented with an opportunity for misbehaviour'. Its priority is to establish mechanisms to 'restrict such opportunities' and to develop policies of crime prevention that minimize risk and reduce the potential for crime and anti-social behaviour. It is 'concerned with managing rather than reforming' and 'does not pretend to eliminate crime (which it knows is impossible) but to minimise risk' (Young 1999: 46). Thus it 'separate[s] out the criminal from the decent citizen, the troublemaker from the decent shopper and minimise[s] the harm that the addict or the alcoholic can do to themselves rather than proffer any 'cure' or transformation'.

Also significant is the underlying assumption that individuals make rational choices to conform or deviate from laws, regulations and conventions. No consideration is given to the social, cultural, political or material contexts in which laws are made or conventions established. They are taken for granted as appropriate and necessary to maintain discipline, order and stability. From petty infringement to grave crime, the objective is prevention. James Q. Wilson (1983) considered that theorizing about the causes and contexts of crime had contributed little to dealing with its reality and consequences. He prioritized the full spectrum of behaviours that threaten societal order and community stability, from unkempt neighbourhoods and low-level misdemeanours to burglary, robbery and casual assaults. Effective policing and penal policy should apply a zero-tolerance approach to all behaviour perceived as a threat, using punishment as a deterrent.

The identification of criminogenic risk factors, serving as a kind of early warning system, is a significant element in the methodology of youth crime prevention. Once the young person is identified as being 'at risk' of involvement in deviant or criminal behaviour, risk management interventions follow. For state institutions committed to crime reduction, targeting problem individuals, families and communities is a rational proposition. It offers the veneer of prevention and reduction without addressing the complexities of causation and context. Further, responsibility for crime reduction extends to *all* state institutions. Education, health and welfare services are expected to integrate preventive measures into policies and practices and, collectively, to adopt multi-agency strategies that are responsive to risk-oriented behaviour.

Risk reduction appeals because it is 'an inescapable part of the human condition' and 'the basic ingredient of social co-operation' (Hudson 2003: 45). The 'social contract is that individuals cede some of their freedom to governments in return for a greater level of security than they could provide for themselves'. Being a transactional process it is actuarial. Hudson notes that risk assessment and management are a 'fundamental, virtually definitionally entailed feature of criminal justice'. In defining 'crime' and enforcing laws 'backed by penal sanctions', the intended outcome 'is to make crime less likely: to reduce the risk of crime'. Criminal justice has always been concerned with identifying and managing perceived risks and, while they 'might not be able to be eliminated, they can be kept within reasonable levels, and can be reduced where they can be anticipated' (2003: 46). Governance hinges on the delicate and contested social contract between the introduction of tighter social controls to manage risk and the maintenance of liberty in a 'free society'.

Risk management in youth justice is predicated on predictability – that a rational, evidence-based calculus can be used instrumentally to assess accurately future misbehaviour and criminality. The rationale for crime prevention and early intervention strategies appeals to common sense (if ill-disciplined behaviour goes unchecked it will escalate), to liberal interventionism (the best interests of the young 'offender' alongside public interest) and to conservative interventionism (penal sanctions disciplining the individual while deterring others).

Thus it is not difficult to appreciate why the public-protection rhetoric that is central to stronger controls on young people's movements, to burgeoning street and community surveillance, to the banking of DNA, to the introduction of identity cards, and so on, has gained popular appeal. If the 'threat' is exceptional then the rules and conventions of pre-emption must adapt to meet the danger and to control the risk. While self-evident in responding to the media-led campaigns to impose preventive sanctions on potential as well as convicted sex offenders, it has extended to the low-level regulation of an unlimited range of less damaging behaviours.

In the UK the 1997 New Labour government based its commitment to early interventionism and crime prevention on several interconnected factors. It claimed there existed a 'tolerance' of a whole range of anti-social, unacceptable and threatening behaviours; an 'excuse culture' infecting caring agencies, not least youth work and youth justice; a youth justice system hopelessly out of date and out of touch with reality; an underemphasis on the interests and needs of victims; and an overcommitment to the care and rights of young offenders. On this basis, the Crime and Disorder Act 1998 was introduced in England and Wales. While complex and wide ranging in scope, civil injunctions directly connected to criminal justice sanctions (e.g. age-specific curfews, anti-social behaviour orders and parenting orders) established the foundation of a new, preventive direction that, despite rhetorical claims to be progressive and protectionist, proved to be punitive and net-widening. The consequences for children and young people have been severe, with a marked increase in their criminalization and imprisonment solely on the grounds that they breach civil injunctions, the terms of which are often impossible to sustain.

Phil Scraton

Related entries

Actuarialism; Crime and disorder reduction (CDR); Crime prevention; Early intervention; Left realism; Risk factors; Risk management.

Key texts and sources

Hudson, B. (2003) *Justice in the Risk Society*. London: Sage.
Walters, R. (2003) *Deviant Knowledge: Criminology, Politics and Policy*. Cullompton: Willan Publishing.
Wilson, J.Q. (1983) *Thinking about Crime*. New York, NY: Basic Books.
Young, J. (1999) *The Exclusive Society*. London: Sage.

ADOLESCENCE

'Adolescence' is a stage in the life course, usually referring to the years between 12 and 18, which is said to separate 'childhood' from 'adulthood'.

The popular use of the term 'adolescence' dates from the late nineteenth century and is found primarily in urban industrial societies where the 'transition' between childhood and adulthood continues for years after 'puberty' (the beginning of sexual maturity) and always precedes fully acknowledged adult status, which is normally achieved through education, employment and marriage and/or leaving the family of origin. This is in contrast to many non-industrial contexts where progress from childhood to adulthood is marked by a *rites de passage* (or *ritual*) leading to a more rapid assumption of adult responsibilities.

Adolescence is often defined in terms of a fixed physiological/psychological identikit that locked young people into a model of 'transition', characterized by what was known as 'storm and stress', associated with the American psychologist, G.S. Hall (1844–1924), who is sometimes said to have 'created' the modern concept of adolescence. The theory of 'storm and stress' claims that 'teenagers' face a number of developmental tasks/difficulties involving, for example, identity crises, conflict relationships with parents and other authority figures, becoming sexually responsible, resisting the 'drift' into juvenile delinquency and adjusting to the demands of the labour market. In general, adolescents are portrayed as physiologically and psychologically prone to deviance, emotional volatility, rebelliousness and irresponsibility and, therefore, to be in 'need' of supervision and discipline. Although over the years numerous sociological/psychological surveys have shown this portrait to be a travesty of the experiences of the great majority of young people, there is still a popular tendency, especially in the media and the government (drawing upon vulgarized models of biological/psychological development), to see young people as constituting a 'social problem' (around which there often arises a 'moral panic').

Social scientists, however, in considering the nature of adolescence, increasingly pay less attention to physiological/psychological factors (without denying their relevance in particular circumstances during the adolescent period), preferring instead to focus on social determinants. The apparent trauma of the 'transition' is now frequently referred to as a 'myth', and the idea of 'transition' itself is regarded as largely a 'social construction'. In opposition to the popular view of young people as *inherently* unstable and threatening, it is argued that the 'bio-political' influence of the 'storm and stress' approach serves to legitimate the so-called immutable psychological and physiological characteristics when in fact the true condition of adolescence has its basis in the organization of the social relations of industrial societies. Where gender and ethnicity are concerned, it has long been recognized that social and cultural factors are important in accounting for 'difference' between social groups. But it is only relatively recently that 'age' has been accorded the same status. Many contemporary researchers now believe that, if we are to understand adolescence properly, it is necessary to recognize the influence of the aforementioned social relations, which originate in a variety of specific 'structures', notably those emanating from within employment, education, medicine, family, law, social security and, not least, from within the overarching configuration of 'age hierarchies'.

Harry Hendrick

Related entries

'Adulteration'; Demonisation; Mental health and young offenders; Moral panic.

Key texts and sources

Cohen, P. (1997) *Rethinking the Youth Question.* Basingstoke: Macmillan.

Davis, J. (1990) *Youth and Generation in Modern Britain: Images of Adolescent Conflict.* London: Athlone Press.

Graham, P. (2004) *The End of Adolescence.* Oxford: Oxford University Press.

Hendrick, H. (1990) *Images of Youth: Age, Class and the Male Youth Problem, 1880–1920.* Oxford: Clarendon Press.

Mizen, P. (2004) *The Changing State of Youth.* Basingstoke: Palgrave Macmillan.

'ADULTERATION'

'Adulteration' refers to the *unravelling* of those processes of youth justice that were hitherto based on the recognition that children and young people should be dealt with separately and differently from adult offenders, in recognition of age-related differences in levels of capacity, competence, responsibility and maturity.

The foundational element of youth justice is that children who offend deserve to be treated in a way that recognizes their vulnerability, immaturity, reduced capacity and lack of full awareness of the consequences of their behaviour. Throughout the twentieth century, numerous procedures, rules and powers were developed and practised to reflect such an approach. However, since the 1980s there has been a fundamental reversal of this logic when applied to young offenders. A series of legislative changes, major judicial decisions and reformulations of guidance to practitioners have produced a 'blindness' towards the limited responsibility of the child offender (Fionda 1998). Political expediency and a recurring demonization of young people in many jurisdictions have resulted in a redefinition of the nature of childhood and a growing tendency to move towards an 'adulteration' of youth justice policy and practice.

Such developments have been most evident in the USA in the widespread dismantling of special court procedures that had been in place for much of the twentieth century to protect young people from the stigma and formality of adult justice. Since the 1980s (but beginning in Florida in 1978), most states expanded the charges for which juvenile defendants could be tried as adults in criminal courts (the so-called juvenile court waiver), lowered the age at which this could be done, changed the purpose of juvenile codes to prioritize punishment and resorted to more punitive penal regimes. A renewed emphasis on public safety (rather than a child's best interests) has also meant that confidentiality has been removed in most states, with the names of juvenile offenders made public and in some cases listed on the Internet. In many states, children below the age of 14 and as young as 7 can have their cases waived by the juvenile court and can be processed as if they were adult. By the early twenty-first century, 46 states could require juvenile court judges to waive jurisdiction over minors, and 29 states had enacted laws that do not allow certain cases to be heard in a juvenile court at all. As a result, around 200,000 children under 18 are processed as adults each year (Fagan and Zimring 2000; Snyder 2002).

Such pressures to treat children and young people as fully responsibilized adults are also evident in the UK. The principle of *doli incapax* – which, for many centuries, had protected 10–14-year-olds from the full rigours of adult justice – was abolished by the Crime and Disorder Act 1998. The Home Secretary announced that it no longer reflected the fact that 'children aged between 10 and 13 were plainly capable of differentiating between right and wrong' (Bandalli 2000). In the New Labour reforms of the late 1990s, established and successful means of ensuring informality and maximum diversion from criminal justice processing were replaced by formal warnings and early intervention initiatives. Maximum penalties were raised for certain offences, thereby drawing more children into the adult court system as a result of 'grave crimes' provisions. The creation of secure training units allowed for the imprisonment of children as young as 12. The result has been dramatic increases in the numbers of children prosecuted and incarcerated.

As in adult justice, it appears to be increasingly assumed that child offending is a product of free will and volition and that all offenders should be made fully accountable for their actions. In turn this places pressure on any progressive age-specific interventions in favour of an adult-style retribution.

John Muncie

Related entries

Criminalization; Criminal responsibility; Demonization; Grave offences; Secure training centres (STCs); Punitiveness; Responsibilization.

Key texts and sources

Bandalli, S. (2000) 'Children, responsibility and the new youth justice', in B. Goldson (ed.) *The New Youth Justice.* Lyme Regis: Russell House.

Fagan, F. and Zimring, F. (2000) *The Changing Borders of Juvenile Justice: Transfer of Adolescents to the Criminal Court.* Chicago, IL: University of Chicago Press.

Fionda, J. (1998) 'The age of innocence? The concept of childhood in the punishment of young offenders', *Child and Family Law Quarterly*, 10: 77–87.

Snyder, H. (2002) 'Juvenile crime and justice in the United States of America', in N. Bala et al. (eds) *Juvenile Justice Systems: An International Comparison of Problems and Solutions.* Toronto: Thompson.

ALL WALES YOUTH OFFENDING STRATEGY

The *All Wales Youth Offending Strategy* is a policy document setting out the way in which the youth justice system in Wales will aim to prevent offending by young people and respond to young people who have committed offences.

The *All Wales Youth Offending Strategy* is a joint policy statement produced by the Welsh Assembly Government and the Youth Justice Board. The genesis of this policy needs to be seen in the context of devolution and the tensions of governance that followed. Justice, including justice for minors, is not a devolved responsibility. Constitutionally, the Home Office (a department of the Westminster government) retains responsibility for the youth justice system in England and Wales. In practice, much of this responsibility is discharged through the Youth Justice Board, which promulgates youth justice policy, advises both the Home Secretary and youth offending teams (YOTs) on effective practice, sets targets for YOTs and monitors their performance. Thus these activities of the Youth Justice Board apply equally to YOTs in Wales as they do in England. However, the framework of youth justice services in Wales differs from that in England. While YOTs exist in both countries, the funding arrangements and array of local services involved in the prevention of offending differ. Moreover, within the context of devolution, there is a distinct and growing Welsh policy framework within which Welsh YOTs must work. Notable among these Welsh policies is 'Extending entitlement' (the Welsh equivalent of 'Youth matters' in England), which sets out 10 universal 'entitlements' for all young people in Wales – including those embroiled with the criminal justice system. The *All Wales Youth Offending Strategy*, therefore, is designed to assist YOTs and other services to find a coherent path through the tensions between the Westminster government and the Youth Justice Board, on the one hand, and the Welsh Assembly Government, on the other. Thus the strategy incorporates the aims of the Youth Justice Board amd the policies of the Welsh Assembly Government.

As in England, therefore, the prevention of offending remains the primary objective of youth offending services in Wales, as the following extract from the 'Foreword', makes clear:

When a young person gets into trouble then everyone suffers – their family, their community and the young person themselves. Whenever we can prevent offending there is a benefit for us all, too. This Strategy sets out the way to make this happen in Wales. It starts from the basic principle that the best way to stop young people offending is to prevent it from happening in the first place. The more we can stop young people entering the criminal justice system, the more we reduce the risk of them getting into even worse trouble in the future. When a child or young person does offend, there need to be effective ways of dealing with them in the community. Sometimes custody will be a necessity. But it really does need to be a last resort. Locking up children and young people almost always stores up worse trouble for the future – creating new victims and more serious harm. We have to break that cycle and this strategy shows what can be done, and needs to be done in Wales, to help make that happen (Welsh Assembly Government/Youth Justice Board 2004).

As this extract also makes clear, however, in Wales, for children, custody '*really does* need to be a last resort' (emphasis added) – a statement intended as a clear demarcation between policy and practice in Wales and England. This policy approach is further demarcated by the way in which the Welsh strategy avers talk of the responsibilization of young people, characteristic of the English approach, and instead emphasizes the responsibility of all those providing services to children to do so in a manner that promotes positive growth. To state this policy difference starkly: in Wales young people have entitlements and adults have responsibilities.

There are further distinctive features of the *All Wales Youth Offending Strategy*. The strategy is clearly embedded within 'Extending entitlement', and both these strategies are explicitly drawn from the United Nations Convention on the Rights of the Child. There is clear recognition that a range of social factors are often linked to offending behaviour by young people. Thus the response to young people who commit offences and to the more general prevention of offending by young people is based on the principle of 'Children first' – that is, the needs of young people and the social causes of offending are the primary targets of intervention; responding directly to the offence(s) committed is a secondary consideration. In practice, therefore, preventing offending and responding to those young people who have committed offences are based on the provision of services to young people that tackle disadvantage and that promote social and educational inclusion.

Kevin Haines

Related entries

Children First; Extending Entitlement (National Assembly for Wales); Welsh Assembly Government.

Key texts and sources

Welsh Assembly Government/Youth Justice Board (2004) *All Wales Youth Offending Strategy.* Cardiff: Welsh Assembly Government and Youth Justice Board.

ALTERNATIVES TO CUSTODY

Alternatives to custody are community-based schemes to which the courts can refer young offenders rather than imprison them, whether awaiting trial or following conviction. These are usually advocated in a deliberate attempt to avoid the negative impact of custody on a child.

Custodial institutions have always been a feature of the youth justice system throughout the UK. Even before specialized juvenile institutions were developed in the first half of the nineteenth century, young offenders were still imprisoned (together with adults). The public and policymakers have always felt the need to lock up children as a serious punishment and as a method of social control, and custody rates suggest that such a practice is more popular than ever. Nevertheless, the arguments for not doing so are well established. Evidence suggests that imprisonment does not prevent offending, places children at risk of self-harm or in danger from others, and interrupts any positive ties with their home community. Moreover, the United Nations Convention on the Rights of the Child commits all signatories (including the UK) to using child custody only as a 'last resort'.

Consequently, academics and policymakers have been searching for community-based alternatives to custody. This has become all the more urgent in recent years as the prison system reaches full capacity and the negative effects on young inmates are intensified. In England and Wales, the Youth Justice Board (YJB) (2005c) sees the development of such alternative sanctions as the way forward: 'The YJB is committed to developing community-based alternatives in which sentencers have sufficient confidence that their proportionate use of custody for children and young people progressively falls and the average daily number in custody is reduced.'

The National Audit Office concurred with this strategy in its 2004 report on youth justice, arguing that increasing the credibility and effectiveness of high-tariff community sentences is the best way to reduce the numbers of children in prison. Since 2001, the primary high-tariff alternative to a prison sentence developed in England and Wales has been the Intensive Supervision and Surveillance Programme (ISSP). The intensity of the supervision has been seen as a 'positive punishment', while the surveillance and restrictions on the offender's movements have offered social control. Moreover, support workers can develop the child's positive relationships in the community and the child is able to continue with existing (or renewed) education, training or employment.

Other countries have developed similar schemes for supervision and surveillance in the community. Canada has developed an almost identical model to the ISSP. In Italy, police supervision is used as an alternative to short-term custody. In this scheme, the young person is required to report to the station on a very regular basis so as to control movement. In a similar intensive scheme in the Netherlands, parents are obliged to participate and all members of the family sign a contract committing to observe conditions.

Often incorporated into such intensive supervision schemes is the use of curfews, which are becoming increasingly popular across jurisdictions. These offer an alternative to institutional custody by allowing the courts to impose what is effectively imprisonment in the offender's own home for specified hours, usually at night or whenever the child is deemed most at risk of offending. Countries imposing curfews on young offenders include the USA, Belgium, France, England and Wales, Scotland and four states in Australia. Electronic monitoring (or 'tagging') is now an increasingly common element of any alternative provision to custody for a child, often tied to either curfews or intensive supervision. Again, this allows an element of punishment through the inconvenience caused and through the 'shame' of having to wear a tag, and it offers social control without the most damaging effects of imprisonment. In addition to England, Wales and Scotland, electronic tagging has recently been introduced in several countries, including the USA, France, Canada, Australia, Sweden, the Netherlands and Singapore.

The imprisonment of children has sometimes been defended because it is said to break ties with any negative influences at home. In view of this, some countries have developed schemes to remove the child from home, but not to place him or her in institutional custody. This may involve sentencing the child to abide by the care of another member of his or her family (for example, Czech Republic and Spain) or to therapeutic or intensive foster care (for example, Greece) specifically as an alternative to custody. This is somewhat similar to the idea of 'secure foster care' that has featured recently in policy debates in England and Wales. In addition, some countries have developed institutions for delivering intensive supervision, but which are deliberately non-custodial (for example, closed education centres in France). At this point, however, any difference from custody is very thin: although the children are not locked up, they are compelled to attend (and sometimes stay overnight) on threat of imprisonment.

It is important to realize that the current search for alternatives to custody mirrors concerns that have emerged at various times over the past 200 years of youth justice. For example, in the mid-nineteenth century the reformatory movement looked to develop an alternative to punitive imprisonment based on intensive religious education, domestic training and childhood play in large children's homes (both custodial and non-custodial). In the mid-twentieth century, most approved schools were open institutions used as a non-custodial alterna-

tive to Borstals, run on more welfarist principles. However, as a word of warning, it is worth noting that such 'open' institutions still suffered with many of the same problems as 'closed' prisons, including abuse and child death scandals.

Neal Hazel

Related entries

Abolitionism; Children in custody; Curfew orders; Decarceration; Electronic monitoring; Fostering; Intensive Supervision and Surveillance Programme (ISSP).

Key texts and sources

Goldson, B. (2002a) 'New punitiveness: the politics of child incarceration', in J. Muncie et al. (eds) *Youth Justice: Critical Readings*. London: Sage.

Hazel, N. (in press) *Cross-national Scoping Review of Policy and Practice in Juvenile Justice*. London: Youth Justice Board.

Lobley, D. and Smith, D. (2007) *Persistent Young Offenders: An Evaluation of Two Projects*. Aldershot: Ashgate.

McNeill, F. (2006) 'Community supervision: context and relationships matter', in B. Goldson and J. Muncie (eds) *Youth Crime and Justice: Critical Issues*. London: Sage.

Youth Justice Board (2005c) *Strategy for the Secure Estate for Children and Young People: Plans for 2005/06 to 2007/08*. London: Youth Justice Board.

See also Papers to the European Society of Criminology Working Group on Juvenile Justice (2004) (available online at **www.esc-eurocrim-org/ workshops.shtml**).

ANOMIE THEORY

Anomie refers to a breakdown of social norms or a lack of moral regulation. An important concept in the classical writings of Emile Durkheim, it is Robert K. Merton's later formulation that has had a major influence in the study of crime, delinquency and deviance.

Merton's theory of anomie was first published in 1938 and later expanded in 1957 and 1968. Now often depicted as the main example of *strain-*

type theories, his general argument was that particular sociocultural conditions can produce a pressure or strain on members of certain sections of a society to behave in a non-conforming or deviant fashion just as other conditions can induce conforming behaviour.

The particular sociocultural conditions that Merton is concerned with are where the culture and the social structure are in conflict. This can occur when the 'culturally defined goals' of a society and the 'institutional means' for achieving them have become dissociated. Where a society has a disproportionate accent on goals with little or no moral constraints on the means of achieving them, a situation of anomie exists. Merton argued that this situation was characteristic of American society, where the accumulation of wealth was held out as the goal to be achieved above all else. Moreover, this was the goal to which everyone should aspire, and no one was barred from the possibility of success. In reality, Merton pointed out, the legitimate means by which to achieve material success were actually limited and differentially available, depending on a person's location in the social structure.

In response to this state of anomie, Merton proposed that there were four deviant 'modes of adaptation'. The one that has been seen as most relevant to the study of youth crime and delinquency has been that of 'innovation', which Merton sees as the characteristic mode of adaptation of those at the bottom of American society. In this section of society the emphasis on material success has been absorbed, but the access to the legitimate means of achieving such success is severely limited. The goal is pursued using whatever appears likely to be most effective, irrespective of its legitimacy.

Much of criminology from the mid-twentieth century onwards focused on explaining the delinquency of young men. One of the criticisms that was levelled at Merton was that

he overlooked the most obvious feature of such behaviour – namely, its group character. The attempts of Albert Cohen and others to revise and extend Merton's ideas to take this into account provided the basis for the development of subcultural theory. Merton was also criticized for accepting the picture of the class distribution of crime shown by official statistics and thereby over-predicting lower-class crime and underestimating white-collar crime. With the rise of feminism in criminology, Merton's theory was found to be wanting in its inability to address the most obvious aspect of crime and delinquency: its gendered distribution.

Despite these criticisms, anomie theory remains 'one of the most plausible attempts' (Downes and Rock 2007: 121) to explain the high levels of crime and delinquency found in affluent, mass-consumption societies with high levels of inequality.

Dave King

Related entries

Left realism; Subcultural theory.

Key texts and sources

Adler, F. and Laufer, W.S. (eds) (2000) *The Legacy of Anomie Theory*. New Brunswick, NJ: Transaction Publishers.

Clinard, M.B. (ed.) (1964) *Anomie and Deviant Behaviour*. New York, NY: Free Press.

Cohen, A.K. (1965) 'The sociology of the deviant act: anomie theory and beyond', *American Sociological Review*, 30: 5–14.

Downes, D. and Rock, P. (2007) *Understanding Deviance: A Guide to the Sociology of Crime and Rule-breaking* (5th edn). Oxford: Oxford University Press.

Merton, R.K. (1968) *Social Theory and Social Structure*. New York, NY: Free Press.

ANTI-SOCIAL BEHAVIOUR (ASB)

Anti-social behaviour (ASB) has been generically defined as involving nuisance, incivility, disorderly or offensive and/or 'pre-criminal' (often youthful) behaviour, which cumulatively undermine the quality of life of the wider community or which cause, or are likely to cause, 'harassment, alarm or distress' to people.

Despite the rather generic and imprecise definition of anti-social behaviour (ASB) given above, the clear majority of enforcement actions – by the police and crime and disorder reduction partnerships (CDRPs) – to tackle problems of ASB involve cases in which the behaviour is already criminal. In this light it is probably now most accurate to describe ASB as an 'enforcement opportunity': the opportunity to bring new enforcement powers to bear upon a wide range of individuals for behaviour that ranges from the illegal, offensive and harmful to the distressing and disrespectful.

It may be unusual for a single politician, let alone a prime minister, to be so closely identified with a specific policy agenda but, on occasion, Tony Blair came very close to claiming authorship of the entire ASB agenda (Squires 2006). In fact, it is possible to trace several distinct paths towards the present focus on ASB in contemporary crime and disorder policy (Burney 2005; Squires and Stephen 2005). However, what may well be most remarkable about the concept is the way in which these separate strands have coalesced as a set of concerns and the speed with which they have become adopted, not just in policy circles but also in popular consciousness and language.

The problems of ASB reflect a series of concerns involving a loss of civic responsibility, a pessimism about the growing 'incivilities' of modern life and the residualization of a public service culture, especially in the most deprived, divided and excluded communities. Putative solutions for residential ASB problems first appeared in the Housing Act 1996, where 'public authorities' had a greater leverage by virtue of their social housing management responsibilities. The 'left realist' criminological perspective, with its focus on victimization, hidden and under-reported rates of offending and the cumulative impact of criminal harm in already-deprived neighbourhoods, gave licence to a collective community interest in addressing the nuisance behaviours that appeared to make so many people's lives a misery. Such ideas merged seamlessly with the discourse on 'zero tolerance' that was also gaining popularity. Finally, at the centre of these concerns lay the, always deeply symbolic, problem of youth.

The problems attributed to young people are always deeply symptomatic of wider problems of society, and matters were no different regarding the ASB question. Since the James Bulger murder in 1993, there had been a marked hardening of attitudes towards young people in trouble. The liberal treatment of young offenders and policies to divert young people from court or custody came to be seen as dangerously complacent responses and, following the publication of the Audit Commission's *Misspent Youth* report in 1996, the incoming New Labour government committed itself to a major overhaul of the youth justice system based on notions of early intervention – to 'nip youth offending in the bud'. As Jack Straw (Home Secretary) put it in the Foreword to *No More Excuses*, the 1997 New Labour white paper on the reform of youth justice, the aim was to 'break the links between (youthful) anti-social behaviour and crime'.

This focus on youth and delinquency connected the discourse on ASB with an older psychological preoccupation with youthful 'anti-social personality disorders', seen as precursors of an adult criminal career, and the idea of 'pre-delinquency'. Yet, although the phenomenon of ASB rapidly became associated with disorderly and nuisance behaviour by young people, this was not how the government initially described the purpose of the new anti-social behaviour orders (ASBOs) introduced in 1998. Neither does it reflect the initial guidance on ASBOs provided to local authorities by the Home Office in 1998. Notwithstanding this, an early endorsement for the targeting of ASB enforcement measures on young people came in a Home Office review of ASBOs in 2002. The report argued that young people 'were often perceived as the cause of many anti-social behaviour problems' and that they were able to indulge in this behaviour 'in the full knowledge that there were few criminal sanctions that could touch them' (Campbell 2002: 2). In other words, ASB identified the existence of a supposed 'enforcement deficit', especially so in respect of troubling behaviour by young people.

Legislation to give effect to new powers to tackle ASB came in s. 1(1) of the Crime and Disorder Act 1998, which established the original ASBO. ASB enforcement powers soon underwent significant changes, however, evolving, expanding and developing very rapidly. In 2002, ss. 64 and 65 of the Police Reform Act allowed the courts to attach an ASBO to a criminal conviction and established the 'interim ASBO', which might be agreed by a court – on application from the relevant authorities (the police, CDRPs, social landlords) – until such time as a full hearing for an order might be held. In the same year, the Home Office published new guidance on non-statutory acceptable behaviour contracts (ABCs). ABCs had been first pioneered in the London Borough of Islington in 1999 to address nuisance behaviour by younger children (even aged under 10) or less serious and pre-criminal ASB (Bullock and Jones 2004).

In 2003, the Anti-social Behaviour Act, following a white paper, *Respect and Responsibility: Taking a Stand against Anti-social Behaviour* (Home Office 2003d), consolidated and extended the range of enforcement powers in the government's ASB arsenal to include closure notices for disorderly or noisy premises or those in which drug dealing occurred; dispersal orders to disperse and remove groups of people (aged under 16) believed to be causing intimidation, harassment, alarm or distress to members of the community; graffiti removal orders; parenting orders (for the parents of anti-social young people); and, perhaps most peculiarly of all, remedies for persons whose homes were 'overwhelmed' by the high hedges of their inconsiderate neighbours.

Finally, reflecting the social contract philosophy of the 2003 white paper with its emphasis on duty and responsibility, 2006 saw the launch of the 'Respect' action plan (http://www.homeoffice. gov.uk/documents/respect-action-plan), emphasizing civic responsibility, community empowerment and cohesion to tackle the stubbornly resistant causes of ASB in families, classrooms and the community at large. The action plan was populated with such phrases as: 'The only person who can start the cycle of respect is you', 'Give respect – get respect', and 'Respect cannot be learned, purchased or acquired it can only be earned'. The assumption implicit in the slogans seemed to be that such 'respect' and 'disrespect' issues, and the behaviour to which they were related, were constructed almost entirely as questions of choice and personal motivation. The solution for ASB, notwithstanding complex dilemmas about the very variable perceptions of behaviour construed as 'anti-social', was thereby reconstituted as a type of 12-step programme that the virtuous or committed might choose to ascend (at times prompted by the threat of enforcement sanctions).

It is immediately obvious that the 'Respect' agenda – and the problem of ASB to which it was construed as a response – is very broadly drawn indeed, encompassing civic renewal, personal morality and the elimination of criminal and public nuisances. In place of the old liberal caution that people cannot be made good, by law, New Labour sought to achieve a sea change in public attitudes and behaviour – by exhortation, moral and community rearmament and the selective use of new sanctions and enforcement powers. There were those who argued that, by drawing such attention to the problem of ASB, New Labour had promised too much, raised public aspirations and bitten off more than it could chew such that, ultimately, disappointment about the limits to what government could achieve would set in (see, for example, Tonry 2004). Despite the fact that British Crime Survey data have recently described a decline in concerns about ASB (although young people 'hanging about' still featured as a primary concern), this may still be the case.

Nevertheless, what is already the most significant aspect of the ASB issue – and what is likely to be its most important legacy – is the way in which ASB has been the foundation upon which a whole new range of hybrid and semi-criminal enforcement powers have been brought into being. Across a wide range of government action against problems of crime and disorder – from the management of sex offenders, the surveillance of terrorists, criminal asset recovery, to ASB management itself – loosely defined 'offences', streamlined due process, peremptory evidential scrutiny, pre-emptive criminalization and inclusive net-widening define the contours of a new approach to crime control and security management. Ironically, the very factors that led critics to question the focus on ASB as a crime and disorder strategy – the imprecise definitions, its relativity and flexibility, its low-key and, at times, almost routine nature, not forgetting its close relation to youthful misbehaviour in public – are precisely the keys to its greatest utility.

Peter Squires

Related entries

Acceptable behaviour contracts (ABCs); Anti-social behaviour orders (ASBOs); Crime and Disorder Act 1998; Crime and disorder reduction (CDR); Early intervention; Net-widening; Respect (government action plan); Responsibilization.

Key texts and sources

Bullock, S. and Jones, B. (2004) *Acceptable Behaviour Contracts: Addressing Antisocial Behaviour in the London Borough of Islington. Home Office Online Report* 02/04. London: Home Office (available online at **http://www.homeoffice.gov.uk/rds/pdfs2/rdsolr 0204.pdf**).

Burney, E. (2005) *Making People Behave: Anti-social Behaviour, Politics and Policy: The Creation and Enforcement of Anti-social Behaviour Policy.* Cullompton: Willan Publishing.

Campbell, S. (2002) *A Review of Anti-social Behaviour Orders. Home Office Research Study* 236. London: Home Office Research, Development and Statistics Directorate (available online at **http://www. homeoffice.gov.uk/rds/pdfs2/hors236.pdf**).

Home Office (2003d) *Respect and Responsibility: Taking a Stand against Anti-social Behaviour.* London: Home Office (available online at **http://www.archive2.official-documents.co.uk/ document/cm57/5778/5778.pdf**).

Squires, P. (2006) 'New Labour and the politics of anti-social behaviour', *Critical Social Policy*, 26: 144–68.

Squires, P. and Stephen, D.E. (2005) *Rougher Justice: Anti-social Behaviour and Young People.* Cullompton: Willan Publishing.

Tonry, M. (2004) *Punishment and Politics: Evidence and Emulation in English Crime Control Policy.* Cullompton: Willan Publishing.

ANTI-SOCIAL BEHAVIOUR ACT 2003

The Anti-social Behaviour Act 2003 expanded and developed the government's anti-social behaviour management strategy and led the way to the establishment of the 'Respect' task force and a 'Respect' action plan launched in 2006.

The Anti-Social Behaviour Act 2003 was preceded by a white paper, *Respect and Responsibility: Taking a Stand against Anti-social Behaviour* (Home Office 2003d), which clearly articulated the nature of the contract of disciplined citizenship at the heart of New Labour's orderly vision of modern social democracy (Stephen 2006). The government's aims were particularly ambitious, declaring the need for a 'cultural shift … to a society where we respect each other, our property and our shared public spaces' (Home Office 2003d: 6). The catalogue of anti-social behaviours specifically mentioned was long and diverse: from 'noisy neighbours' to 'drunken "yobs" taking over town centres', although it was never intended to be exhaustive. Anti-social behaviour powers were meant to be flexible and responsive, to be more concerned with the (perceptions of) harm and distress that resulted, than with the precise proscription of (harmful) activities (as in conventional criminal law prohibitions).

The Act consolidated and extended the range of anti-social behaviour enforcement powers. Those of most direct relevance to young people included dispersal orders and curfews (to disperse and remove groups of people aged under 16, believed to be causing intimidation, harassment, alarm or distress to members of the community);

graffiti removal orders; parenting orders (for the parents of anti-social young people); and new age limits on air weapon possession. In addition, the Act introduced closure notices to tackle disorderly or noisy premises or those in which drug dealing took place.

The 2003 Act and the 'Respect' agenda were very broadly framed, embracing civic renewal, personal morality and the elimination of certain criminal and public nuisances (O'Malley and Waiton 2004).

Peter Squires

Related entries

Anti-social behaviour (ASB); Dispersal orders; Fixed-penalty notices (FPNs); Parenting contracts; Parenting orders; Penalty notices for disorder (PNDs).

Key texts and sources

Home Office (2003d) *Respect and Responsibility: Taking a Stand against Anti-social Behaviour.* London: Home Office.

Home Office (2006f) *Respect Task Force and Action Plan 2006.* London: Home Office (available online at **http://www.homeoffice.gov.uk/documents/ respect-action-plan**).

O'Malley, C. and Waiton, S. (2004) *Who's Anti-social? New Labour and the Politics of Antisocial Behaviour.* London: Institute of Ideas (available online at **http://www.instituteofideas.com/publications/ index.html#occasional**).

Stephen, D.E. (2006) 'Community safety and young people: 21st century homo sacer and the politics of injustice', in P. Squires (ed.) *Community Safety: Critical Perspectives on Policy and Practice.* Bristol: Policy Press.

See the Office of Public Sector Information's website (**http://www.opsi.gov.uk/acts/acts2003/20030038. htm**) for the text of the Anti-social Behaviour Act 2003.

ANTI-SOCIAL BEHAVIOUR ORDERS (ASBOs)

Anti-social behaviour orders (ASBOs) were introduced in s. 1(1) of the Crime and Disorder Act 1998. It is a civil order (lasting a minimum of two years) available from the magistrates' court containing specific provisions concerning the future behaviour of the person named intended to prevent 'harassment, alarm or distress' being caused to members of the wider community.

Although the anti-social behaviour order (ASBO) rapidly came to be seen as a specific response to youth nuisance, the government had originally suggested that young people (aged 10–16) were not intended to be the chief recipients of the new orders. All this was to change, however, as the ASBO moved to the forefront of the government's efforts to manage youth crime and disorder more effectively, to reassure the public and to streamline youth justice enforcement processes. By the end of 2005, over 40 per cent of ASBOs had been issued in respect of persons aged under 18, while concern was growing regarding the government's anti-social behaviour management strategy – in particular that up to 50 per cent of ASBOs were being breached (National Audit Office 2006).

Key areas of concern, shared by lawyers, academics and community safety practitioners alike, regarding the ASBO have included the vague nature of the circumstances that might occasion the granting of an order; questions of due process, evidence and standards of proof (Chakrabarti 2006); the fact that ASBO proceedings are exempted from the normal non-disclosure arrangements relating to young people in court; the question as to whether ASBOs really were a 'last resort' (Millie *et al.* 2005); the high rate of breaches of ASBOs; and, finally, whether the ASBO contributed to a counterproductive net-widening process for young people in trouble (Squires and Stephen 2005).

Peter Squires

Related entries

Anti-social behaviour (ASB); Crime and Disorder Act 1998; Criminalization; Governance; Individual support orders (ISOs); Net-widening; Responsibilization.

Key texts and sources

Chakrabarti, S. (2006) 'ASBO-mania: from social and natural justice to mob rule.' BIHR lunchtime lecture, January (available online at **http://www.liberty-human-rights.org.uk/publications/3-articles-and-speeched/asbomania-bihr.PDF**).

Millie, A., Jacobson, J., McDonald, E. and Hough, M. (2005) *Anti-social Behaviour Strategies: Finding a Balance* (ICPR and Joseph Rowntree Foundation). Bristol: Policy Press.

National Audit Office (2006) *Tackling Anti Social Behaviour: Report by the Comptroller and Auditor General* (HC 99 Session 2006–2007, 7 December). London: Home Office.

Squires, P. and Stephen, D.E. (2005) *Rougher Justice: Anti-social Behaviour and Young People.* Cullompton: Willan Publishing.

See also ASBOwatch's website (**http://www.statewatch.org/asbo/ASBOwatch.html**). See the Office of Public Sector Information's website (**http://www.opsi.gov.uk/acts/acts1998/19980037.htm**) for the text of the Crime and Disorder Act 1998.

ANTI-SOCIAL BEHAVIOUR (SCOTLAND) ACT 2004

The Anti-social Behaviour (Scotland) Act 2004 introduces a number of measures aimed at tackling anti-social behaviour in Scotland. These include: the extension of anti-social behaviour orders to children aged between 12 and 15 years, the introduction of parenting orders and new police powers to disperse groups. The Act also enables the electronic monitoring of children under the age of 16 as a direct alternative to secure accommodation.

Anti-social behaviour orders (ASBOs) were first introduced by the Crime and Disorder Act 1998 and were available for people aged 16 or over in Scotland. Although now extended to children between the ages of 12 and 15, breach of orders for this age group (which constitutes a criminal conviction) cannot be punished by imprisonment. In Scotland, local authorities have the lead role in seeking ASBOs, along with registered social landlords. Where children (aged 12–15) are involved, the principal reporter is required to arrange a children's hearing to seek advice on whether an ASBO is necessary, and the sheriff court is required to take that advice into account before granting an order. There has been limited take-up of the new provisions to date. By the end of 2006 there had been four ASBOs for 12–15-year-olds, no parenting orders and only 13 dispersal zones had been created.

Lesley McAra

Related entries

Anti-social behaviour orders (ASBOs); Children's hearing system; Crime and Disorder Act 1998; Sheriff courts.

Key texts and sources

DTZ Consulting and Research and Heriot-Watt University (2006) *Use of Anti-social Behaviour Orders in Scotland: Report of the 2005/06 Survey* (available online at **http://www.scotland.gov.uk/Publications/2006/11/28153603/0**).

See the Office of Public Sector Information's website (**http://www.opsi.gov.uk/legislation/scotland/acts2004/20040008.htm**) for the text of the Anti-social Behaviour (Scotland) Act 2004.

APPEAL

An appeal is the process by which a defendant can challenge the court's decision by reference to a higher court. The prosecution also has a more limited right of appeal.

Children and young people under the age of 18 enjoy the same rights of appeal as adults. For the large majority whose cases are heard in the youth court, appeal is made to the Crown court and is largely unrestricted, providing that a notice of intent is lodged within 21 days of sentence. The powers of the Crown court are wide:

it may confirm, reverse or vary any part of the decision of the youth court. Where appeal is against sentence, the Crown court may increase the sentence of the lower court, provided that it does not exceed the maximum penalty that could have been imposed at the original hearing. While this power is used relatively infrequently, it has been suggested, nonetheless, that it can act as a disincentive to taking advantage of what is otherwise a relatively generous system of appeal from the youth court.

For the smaller numbers of young people tried in the Crown court, the right to appeal is heavily circumscribed and can only proceed with the leave of the court of appeal or the permission of the trial judge. More than two thirds of applications are turned down and, where permission is granted, the criteria governing the court's decision-making are significantly tighter than those which pertain to appeal from the youth court. An appeal against conviction will only succeed if the finding of guilt was unsafe. An appeal against sentence will only result in a variation of the original disposal if the higher court determines that the penalty was clearly excessive or wrong in principle.

The number of young people sentenced to custody fell dramatically, from 7,700 to 1,400, in the ten years from 1981. While a broad range of factors no doubt contributed to the decline, the impact of appeals was not insignificant. In the seven years following the introduction of statutory restrictions on imposing custodial sentences against young people, the incidence of appeal rose sharply and, in more than half of all cases, resulted in the substitution of a shorter or a non-custodial disposal. Increases in sentence represented less than 1 per cent of the total.

From the early 1990s, by contrast, custody for children grew substantially but, as the severity of sentencing increased, the proportion of custodial sentences imposed in the youth court that were appealed declined, from 13 per cent in 1993 to 7.3 per cent three years later. Nevertheless where appeal was pursued, success rates remained relatively high: in 1996, for instance, 44 per cent of appeals against detention in a young offender institution led to a shorter custodial term or the substitution of a community penalty. Sentence was increased in just two cases.

On the basis of past experience, the active promotion of appeal in appropriate cases by youth justice staff might, as part of a broader strategy, have considerable potential to contribute to a reduction in the numbers of young people deprived of their liberty.

Tim Bateman

Related entries

Bail; Crown courts; Sheriff courts.

Key texts and sources

Ashford, M., Chard, A. and Redhouse, N. (2006) *Defending Young People in the Criminal Justice System* (3rd edn). London: Legal Action Group.

Nacro (2006a) *Appeals against Conviction and Sentence in the Youth Justice System. Youth Crime Briefing.* London: Nacro.

Nacro (2006b) *Reducing Custody: A Systematic Approach. Youth Crime Briefing.* London: Nacro.

APPROPRIATE ADULT

The role of the appropriate adult is defined by the Police and Criminal Evidence Act 1984 codes of practice. The presence of the appropriate adult is required during police questioning and the other key stages of police detention of a juvenile. The appropriate adult – who can be a parent or guardian, social worker or other responsible adult aged 18 years or over not employed by the police – is there to assist and advise the juvenile, and the juvenile can consult privately with the appropriate adult at any time.

The presence of an appropriate adult is required when a suspect, who appears to be under the age of 17 years, is informed of his or her rights, cautioned, interviewed or asked to provide or sign a written statement under caution or record of interview, subject to an identification procedure or given a reprimand or final warning. An appropriate adult must also be present when a urine or non-intimate sample is taken. The presence of an appropriate adult, of the same sex as the juvenile, is also required when the suspect is intimately or strip searched, unless the suspect indicates that he or she would prefer otherwise. The appropriate adult has certain rights: to consult with the suspect privately if requested by the juvenile; to request legal advice on behalf of the juvenile; and to consult the custody record. An appropriate adult may decide whether or not to agree to a police interpreter and to interrupt or delay the juvenile's rest period and participate in representations to the custody officer when the suspect's detention is reviewed. The role of the appropriate adult in the police interview is defined as follows:

> If an appropriate adult is present at an interview, they shall be informed: they are not expected to act simply as an observer; and the purpose of their presence is to: advise the person being interviewed; observe whether the interview is being conducted properly and fairly; facilitate communication with the person being interviewed
>
> (Home Office 2006b: Code C, para. 11.17).

The concept of the appropriate adult developed from the *Confait* case in which three youths were wrongly convicted of murder. The subsequent Fisher Inquiry (1977) found that the police had broken the administrative directions accompanying the Judges' Rules, which required that, as far as practicable, young and mentally disordered suspects could only be interviewed in the presence of their parents, guardians or other independent persons of the same sex. The subsequent Royal Commission on Criminal Procedure (1981) made a number of recommendations, including that, in the case of displayed vulnerability, specifically that of youth or of mental disorder, an appropriate adult, of either sex, should be present during the police investigation process. This recommendation was endorsed in the Police and Criminal Evidence Act 1984 (PACE) codes of practice. Since the creation of this role, it has been subject to a number of revisions in some of the

subsequent editions of the codes and in the Crime and Disorder Act 1998.

In the revised codes of practice (Home Office 2005e, 2006d), a number of categories of people have been excluded from acting as appropriate adults. The main ones are solicitors and independent custody visitors; people who have received admissions; people who are suspected of involvement in or are victims or witnesses of the offence in question; and estranged parents if the juvenile objects to their presence.

The Crime and Disorder Act 1998 extended the appropriate adult's role to include being present at a reprimand or final warning. It also required local authorities to ensure the provision of appropriate adults for juveniles and provided that it was youth offending teams' (YOTs) duty to co-ordinate their provision. YOT workers started to provide appropriate adult services and, increasingly so, volunteers. A postal survey of YOT managers in 2000 found that volunteers were used as appropriate adults in 50 per cent of their areas (Pierpoint 2004). This move followed various calls for the use of volunteers as appropriate adults by, for example, the Audit Commission and Home Office Appropriate Adult Review Group. Arguments made in favour of using volunteers, some more convincingly than others, have related to the potentially increased availability of appropriate adults, cost and time saving accrued to YOTs, the notion of good citizenship and improved police–community relations (see Pierpoint 2004, 2006).

The appropriate adult has been subject to a number of official reviews over the years, such as those by the Home Office Appropriate Adult Review Group in 1995, the Home Office and Cabinet Office as part of their review of PACE in 2002, the National Appropriate Adult Network in 2006, and empirical research (see, for example, Pierpoint 2004, 2006). The main criticisms made by the various reviews and by academics have been as follows:

- The treatment of 17-year-olds as adults and the fact that they are not required to be accompanied by an appropriate adult.
- The difficulties and delays in obtaining appropriate adults.

- The ambiguity and contradictory nature of the definition of the appropriate adult in the PACE codes.
- The lack of contribution in police interviews by some appropriate adults and the different practices of parents, social workers and volunteers in the role.
- The lack of a national policy and guidance for appropriate adult services.

Now some guidance does exist in the form of the Youth Justice Board's National Standards for Youth Justice (2004) (which provide for the minimal level of service required by those working in the delivery of youth justice services) and the National Appropriate Adult Network, a registered charity and company working to promote best practice in appropriate adult work (the network published standards on recruitment, retention, training and service delivery in 2005). In March 2007, the Home Office announced a public consultation exercise to look at the potential to review PACE. The consultation paper refers to the scope to develop a regional or national approach for appropriate adults and seeks suggestions on how to raise their input and improve the quality of contact with suspects.

Harriet Pierpoint

Related entries

Arrest and decision-making process; Justice (Northern Ireland) Act 2002; Police and Criminal Evidence Act 1984 (PACE); Remand management; Reprimands and final warnings; Restorative cautioning; Youth Justice Agency; Youth offending teams (YOTs).

Key texts and sources

Home Office (2005e) *Police and Criminal Evidence Act 1984* (s. 60(1)(a), s. 60A(1) and s. 66(1)) *Codes of Practice A-G 2005 Edition.* London: HMSO (available online at **http://police.homeoffice. gov.uk/operational-policing/powers-pacecodes/ pace-code-intro/**).

Home Office (2006d) *Police and Criminal Evidence Act 1984* (s. 66(1)) *Codes of Practice C and H July 2006.* London: HMSO (available online at **http://police.homeoffice.gov.uk/operational- policing/powers-pace-codes/pace-code-intro/**).

Pierpoint, H. (2004) 'A survey on volunteer appropriate adult services', *Youth Justice*, 4: 32–45.

Pierpoint, H. (2006) 'Reconstructing the role of the appropriate adult in England and Wales', *Criminology and Criminal Justice: The International Journal*, 6: 219–38.

See the Office of Public Sector Information's website (**http://www.opsi.gov.uk/acts/acts1998/1998 0037.htm**) for the text of the Crime and Disorder Act 1998.

ARREST AND DECISION-MAKING PROCESS

In youth justice, an arrest involves taking a child into custody. The arrest is made by an authorized person, normally a police officer, where specified grounds laid down in statute are met. Such grounds usually comprise suspicion of committing an offence; breaching bail; or responding to an arrest warrant previously issued by a court.

A warrant for arrest issued by a court gives the police power to make that arrest and take the subject into police detention. More complex is arrest on suspicion of committing an arrestable offence (listed in Schedule 1A of the Police and Criminal Evidence Act 1984 (PACE) as variously amended). A person may be arrested where the officer believes that there are reasonable grounds to suspect that he or she is in the act of committing, or is about to commit, an offence; has committed the offence; or has conspired, attempted, aided and abetted another to commit an offence. The 'citizen's arrest' is now restricted to indictable-only offences. An arrest can be made in relation to a non-arrestable offence (one which might otherwise be dealt with only by summons) for one or more of a list of reasons that make up the general arrest conditions. These are contained in PACE, s. 25 and are largely related to situations where there is doubt about identity and address, or to prevent injury or indecency.

On arrest, the child or young person may be taken to a police station in accordance with the procedures and rights contained in the PACE codes of practice. In conflict with international children's rights conventions, young people aged 17 are dealt with in exactly the same way as adults. Alternatively, the arresting officer may issue a form of bail requiring the child or young person to attend a police station at a later date. This is often known as street bail. On arrest, or as soon as possible thereafter, the child or young person (and an appropriate adult) should be told of the reason for arrest.

The police investigation and other procedures must be completed within time limits and may involve interview and identification procedures, such as fingerprinting, photographing and taking intimate samples. Procedures now include the routine taking of DNA samples, which may be retained even where the child or young person is released without charge (by 2007 it was estimated that there are over 100,000 innocent children whose DNA is retained). At the conclusion of investigations where the grounds for charge are met, the process moves to decision-making about the outcome.

On arrest subject to a warrant or for breach of bail, the child or young person is brought before the next available court. After arrest for a suspected offence and any further investigation or interrogation – if it is determined that there would be a realistic prospect of conviction if the case was prosecuted in a criminal court – a decision is made whether to charge or otherwise dispose of the matter by way of diversion. The decision-making process is the responsibility of the police and the Crown Prosecution Service (CPS). Advice and information can be sought – often during a period of police bail – from the youth offending team and specialists, such as mental health professionals and social services. The system is not identical across all three UK jurisdictions and what follows primarily pertains to England and Wales.

Historically, the police were solely responsible for decision-making but, more recently, the CPS is involved in all but the more minor matters. In many cases the decision will be made without delay, but there has been an increase in the use of police bail in order to facilitate further assessment and consultation. This is commonly the case where consideration is being given to a final warning.

The main options available to the police are no further action (for very trivial matters or where evidence is insufficient), reprimand, final warning or charge. In some areas, informal action might be agreed and recorded on local systems. A form of police informal restorative action is also being piloted in specified areas. Conditional warnings may be introduced as provided by the Criminal Justice and Immigration Bill 2006–7 to 2007–8. If implemented, the conditional warning will differ from the adult conditional caution in that it will not be available, perversely, where there has been any previous conviction.

The latest guidance on final warnings (Home Office 2006) has the potential effect of increasing diversionary action, allowing for informal action; warnings for breach of anti-social behaviour orders; and warnings where a previous court outcome was a conditional discharge. The guidance also acknowledges that consistency and parity are problematic, with wide variations in diversion rates across the country. Further lack of parity, and sometimes discrimination, occurs with regard to race and ethnicity. Of all those dealt with, some black and minority ethnic groups are more likely to be prosecuted (than diverted), with significant variations around the country.

Decision-making is informed by a process that has developed over time, particularly since final warnings replaced cautions. This is based largely on an assessment 'score' determined by the seriousness of the offence, aggravating and mitigating factors and offending history. CPS codes (2004) and legal guidance detail how the public interest is considered and set out approaches for specific groups, such as 'mentally disordered offenders' and children living in children's homes. The latter guidance was developed in response to excessive prosecution for behaviour that would not normally be criminalized.

There are concerns that too many children and young people are prosecuted for minor offences or for first offences, where diversion would be more suitable and effective in preventing further offending. The large number of children being drawn into the system is mainly a result of the intolerant and inflexible nature of the final warning scheme, 'nipping in the bud' interventionist policies and, to an extent, targets to 'narrow the justice gap', which require the police formally to process more recorded offences.

Geoff Monaghan

Related entries

Appropriate adult; Assessment framework; Bail; Caution; Crown Prosecution Service (CPS); Diversion; Police and Criminal Evidence Act 1984 (PACE); Net-widening; 'Race' and justice; Reprimands and final warnings.

Key texts and sources

Crown Prosecution Service (2004) *The Code for Crown Prosecutors*. London: CPS.

Home Office (2006g) *The Final Warning Scheme* (Circular 14/06). London: Home Office.

Nacro (2006d) *Out of Court – Making the Most of Diversion for Young People (Recent Developments). Youth Crime Briefing*. London: Nacro.

For the Police and Criminal Evidence Act 1984, see **http://www.statutelaw.gov.uk/legResults.aspx?LegType=All+Legislation&title=police+and+criminal+evidence+act&searchEnacted=0&extentMatchOnly=0&confersPower=0&blanketAmendment=0&TYPE=QS&NavFrom=0&activeTextDocId=1871554&PageNumber=1&SortAlpha=0.**

The CPS's legal guidance, *Youth Offenders*, is available online at **http://www.cps.gov.uk/legal/section4/chapter_b.html#01.**

ASSESSMENT FRAMEWORK

> Assessment primarily relates to identifying the causes of youth offending in order to inform intervention. Assessment involves the systematic collation, analysis and application of information relating to the child's/young person's circumstances and offending behaviour. Assessment frameworks have been introduced to provide a consistent range of information by using standardized formats accompanied by guidance.

Asset

In the youth justice context, the principal assessment framework is Asset. In 1999 the Youth Justice Board (YJB) commissioned the then Probation Studies Unit (PSU) at Oxford University to design Asset. This followed the involvement of the PSU in the design of the 'ACE' assessment tool for use in relation to adult offenders (piloted from 1993 by the Probation Service). During 1999, Asset was piloted in selected youth offending team (YOT) areas and was redesigned twice in the process. Between January and April 2000, the YJB promoted a national training programme for practitioners in the use of Asset. Since that time, however, there has been no further centrally co-ordinated direct training for youth justice practitioners in the use of Asset, although there have been 'training for trainers' events to stimulate a 'cascading' approach. Additionally, YOTs have organized 'in-house' training for newly recruited staff.

Since its inception, Asset documentation has developed into a portfolio of assessment 'profiles' and accompanying guidance for their use, comprising the following:

- Introduction.
- Core profile guidance.
- Core profile.
- Risk of serious harm guidance.
- Risk of serious harm profile.

- What do you think? guidance.
- What do you think? profile.
- Intervention guidance.
- Intervention.
- Final warning profile guidance.
- Final warning profile.
- Bail profile guidance.
- Bail profile.
- Appendices.

The 'Asset core profile' is the 'key' document. It comprises a section to collate background information on the child/young person including personal information; previous offending; offence analysis; age at onset of offending; and other 'static criminogenic factors' (which cannot be changed). Additionally, information is collected in respect of 12 'domains' that comprise 'dynamic criminogenic factors' (that are susceptible to change). The 'core profile' also has sections for positive factors and 'screening' for risk of vulnerability and serious harm to others. The 12 'domains' are as follows:

- Living arrangements.
- Family and personal relationships.
- Education, training and employment.
- Neighbourhood.
- Lifestyle.
- Substance use (including nicotine and alcohol).
- Physical health.
- Emotional and mental health.
- Perception of self and others.
- Thinking and behaviour.
- Attitudes to offending.
- Motivation to change.

Each 'domain' is scored on a scale of 0–4 and the total score (maximum 48) is taken as an indicator of the risk of reoffending. The 'domains' are composed of questions related to risk, with an evidence box to support/explain the assessment/conclusions.

Any 'domain' attracting a score of 2 should be explicitly addressed in the 'intervention plan'. For example, a score of 2 in the 'emotional and mental health domain' should lead to the use of a more detailed 'screening questionnaire interview for adolescents' (SQIfA), which in turn

may lead to fuller assessment by a mental health professional using the 'screening interview for adolescents' (SIfA).

The 'risk screening' sections are for assessing either 'vulnerability' (risk of harm *from others* and/or self and/or events and circumstances) or risk of serious harm *to others*. The 'final warning profile' is an abbreviated form of 'core profile'. 'What do you think?' is a self-administered questionnaire for completion by children and young people. Although different in structure from the 'core profile', it covers broadly the same areas. 'Bail profile' has a different structure, focusing on the grounds available to a court to deny bail although, naturally, there is a degree of overlap with the 'core profile'. The 'bail profile' also has a specific section addressing the issue of vulnerability in the case of 15–16-year-old boys at risk of detention in the juvenile secure estate.

The first two years' use of Asset were evaluated by the Centre for Criminology at Oxford University (CCOU – previously the PSU) (Baker *et al.* 2003; Baker 2005).

Onset

The emphasis on prevention and early intervention in youth justice policy and practice has also resulted in the development – by the CCOU at Oxford – of the Onset assessment framework. Intended for use with children and young people 'on the cusp' of offending, there are clear parallels and intersections with Asset and the same 'domains' and scoring systems apply. Onset also has sections for 'positive factors', vulnerability and risk of serious harm.

Asset and Onset

Comments, feedback and queries from youth justice practitioners on the use of Asset and Onset have centred around the following:

- Whether there is a standard, commonly held interpretation of the allocated scores. In some cases, adherence to the 'guidance' appears to be limited when practitioners are completing the 'profiles'. The latest version of 'core profile guidance', however, provides explicit examples and explanation of the meaning that might be attributed to each score.

- The 'risk skew' that both Asset and Inset have arguably produced, which may lead to practitioners over-concentrating on 'managing risk', to the detriment of promoting and nurturing protective factors. In this respect Onset – in having a 'positive factors' evidence box alongside that for 'risk factors' in each 'domain' – is perhaps more 'user friendly' and balanced.

- At a broader level, whether the use of such assessment frameworks inhibits professional practitioner judgement and discretion and leads to an overly mechanistic 'tick-box' approach to practice, with disproportionate attention attached to performance targets and statistical returns as distinct from the individual needs of children and young people (Baker 2005).

Thus far, the comments and observations from the YOT inspectorate have tended to focus on questions of practitioner training and completion rates.

Common Assessment Framework

In a move to establish uniform standards across the broader range of children's services, and as part of the 'Every child matters' initiative, the Department for Education and Skills has introduced the Common Assessment Framework (CAF) for children whose welfare needs require safeguarding and promoting. Strictly speaking this only applies to England – as social care is a devolved responsibility for the Welsh Assembly Government, which intends to introduce a comparable framework in Wales.

Because research and practice experience has confirmed that the 'risk' and 'protective' factors for child 'offenders' and children 'in need' closely intersect and mirror each other, a closer relationship between the various assessment frameworks, if not a merging, might be anticipated. Notwithstanding this, the relationship of the CAF to Asset and Onset portfolios was initially unclear. More recently, however, this position has been clarified, and the YJB has now issued guidance for YOT practitioners on the use of Asset and Onset alongside the CAF.

Nevertheless, the impression of a degree of 'distance' between the youth justice frameworks and the CAF remains. It is possibly less than helpful that, at the time of devising Asset, there was apparently limited communication between the YJB and the Department of Health, which was compiling the 'Assessment framework for children in need and their families' – the predecessor to CAF.

Spike Cadman

Related entries

Actuarialism; Dangerousness; Early intervention; Every Child Matters (ECM); Protective factors; Risk factors; Risk management; Vulnerability.

Key texts and sources

Baker, K. (2005) 'Assessment in youth justice: professional discretion and the use of Asset', *Youth Justice*, 5: 106–22.

Baker, K. *et al.* (2003) *The Evaluation of the Validity and Reliability of the Youth Justice Board's Assessment for Young Offenders: Findings from the First Two Years of the Use of ASSET.* London: Youth Justice Board.

Asset documentation is available online at http://www.yjb.gov.uk/en-gb/practitioners/Assessment/Asset.htm. Common Assessment Framework documentation is available online at http://www.everychildmatters.gov.uk/deliveringservices/caf/. Onset documentation is available online at https://www.yjb.gov.uk/en-gb/practitioners/Assessment/Onset.htm.

ATTENDANCE CENTRE ORDERS

An attendance centre order may be imposed on a child/young person who has been found guilty of any offence for which an adult may be punished by a sentence of imprisonment, or who has 'failed to comply' with a previous court order (including non-payment of a fine).

Attendance centre orders were first introduced in the Criminal Justice Act 1948. They are available in all three UK jurisdictions, although there is some variation in practice between them. The orders do not require the consent of the 'offender', and the maximum number of hours that the court can impose is 36 for those aged 16–20 and 24 hours for those aged under 16. The minimum number of hours is 12, except in the case of a child under the age of 14 if the court is of the opinion that 12 hours would be excessive.

When a child/young person is made subject to an attendance centre order, he or she is required to report to the 'attendance centre' as instructed. In England and Wales, attendance centres are often in school buildings, and children and young people are normally required to attend on Saturday mornings. In Northern Ireland all 'community service projects' are used as attendance centres. The hours of attendance will usually be completed over a number of months through planned sessions of up to 2 hours at a time.

The order seeks to punish through restriction of liberty (leisure time); offer a disiplined learning environment; provide occupation guidance and instruction to assist the development of self-discipline, skills and interests; and develop social skills through structured activity. Children and young people will often take part in 'offence-focused' groups that aim to encourage an understanding of their offending and how to prevent further offending. Many attendance centres – particularly in England and Wales – also provide guidance on physical fitness and expect children and young people to participate in physical exercise. Children and young people may also be expected to do 'reparation' work, usually tidying up around the attendance centre (school) or similar work in the 'community'.

In England and Wales, National Standards for Youth Justice Services require youth offending teams to 'have an effective system in place for ensuring that enforcement action is taken promptly whenever there is non-compliance with an Attendance Centre Order' (Youth Justice Board 2004a: para. 8.56). If the relevant provi-

sions of the Criminal Justice and Immigration Bill 2006–7 to 2007–8 are implemented, the attendance centre order will be replaced – along with the curfew order, action plan order, exclusion order and supervision order – with the single 'menu-based' youth rehabilitation order.

Attendance centre orders in England and Wales are often managed by police officers. The emphasis on discipline, physical fitness and exercise recalls Borstal regimes and 'short, sharp, shock' imperatives. This also raises questions in relation to gender and particular constructions of masculinity. In Northern Ireland there is greater official emphasis on providing a 'safe' educational environment in community service projects staffed by social workers, teachers and youth workers (Youth Justice Agency 2007).

Barry Goldson

Related entries

Criminal Justice and Immigration Bill 2006–7 to 2007–8; Criminal Justice (Children) (Northern Ireland) Order 1998; Powers of Criminal Courts (Sentencing) Act 2000; Sentencing framework; Youth Justice Agency.

Key texts and sources

Youth Justice Agency (2007) *Attendance Centre Orders: A Guide for Young People and their Carers*. Belfast: Youth Justice Agency (available online at **http://www. youthjusticeagencyni.gov.uk/community_services/ court_services/**).

Youth Justice Board (2004a) *National Standards for Youth Justice Services*. London: Youth Justice Board (available online at **http://www.yjb.gov.uk/ Publications/Scripts/prodView.asp?idproduct= 155&eP=PP**).

See also the Youth Justice Board's document, *Disposals: Attendance Centre Order* (available online at **http://www.yjb.gov.uk/en-gb/practitioners/Courts AndOrders/Disposals/AttendanceCentre Order/**).

AUDIT COMMISSION

> The Audit Commission is an independent public body responsible for ensuring that public money is used economically, efficiently and effectively in the areas of local government, housing, health and criminal justice.

The Audit Commission was set up in 1983 to audit and inspect local government, health and criminal justice organizations and to make recommendations for improving performance. A small section of the commission is responsible for undertaking national studies, which aim to improve specific aspects of public services through independent, authoritative analyses of national evidence and local practice. In the field of youth justice, the commission has published two highly influential studies: *Misspent Youth* (Audit Commission 1996) and *Youth Justice 2004* (Audit Commission 2004).

Misspent Youth established that the existing system for dealing with youth crime was inefficient and ineffective, with services failing both young offenders and their victims. It identified four key shortcomings: long delays in the processing of offenders through the courts; too much of the £1 billion spent on dealing with youth crime being taken up by processing and administration rather than directly addressing offending behaviour; poor co-ordination between the agencies working with young offenders; and little being done to prevent young people from offending in the first place. To remedy these shortcomings, the commission made a number of recommendations, including setting targets to reduce delays; addressing offending behaviour through improvements in community supervision; setting up multi-agency partnerships; and targeting evidence-based prevention programmes in high-risk areas.

Reducing costs and improving efficiency and effectiveness, the three key concerns of the Audit Commission, became the driving forces of reform. As with other public services, youth justice became subject to the new 'managerialism', with its emphasis on devising plans, setting targets, measuring performance and reviewing progress. This new discourse was subsequently enshrined in the Crime and Disorder Act 1998, which incorporated many of the Audit Commission's recommendations and now forms the bedrock of the new youth justice system in England and Wales and has had significant influence in other jurisdictions.

Six years later, with less than four years to bed down, the Audit Commission subjected the reforms to renewed scrutiny. In its report, *Youth Justice 2004*, it identifies a number of improvements, particularly a big reduction in delays – the target to halve the time from arrest to sentence for persistent young offenders was reached very soon after the new legislation was enacted – and a more effective structure for delivering youth justice through a national Youth Justice Board (YJB) that oversees 155 local, multi-agency youth offending teams (YOTs) in England and Wales. It also commends the adoption of a new statutory aim – the prevention of offending and reoffending – and cites evidence to show that offenders are now less likely to offend on bail, more likely to receive an intervention and are more likely to make amends for their wrongdoing.

While it concludes that the new system is a considerable improvement on the old one, it also draws attention to a number of shortcomings, including too many minor offences taking up valuable court time and too many offenders being remanded and sentenced to custody. The report highlights in particular the alarming rise in the proportion of black and 'mixed race' young people remanded in custody – an increase of 50 per cent in two years – and the relative ineffectiveness of intensive supervision and surveillance programmes in reducing the use of custody.

Many of these shortcomings have since been highlighted by others. The ex-chairperson of the YJB, Professor Rod Morgan, publicly bemoaned the silting up of the youth courts with minor offenders and the rise in the juvenile prison population (*Guardian* 19 February 2007), while the Home Affairs Committee of Inquiry has recently reported on the issue of the increasingly disproportionate number of young black people passing through the criminal justice system (Home Affairs Committee Inquiry 2007).

But one concern, the severe lack of knowledge among the public about YOTs and what they do and their lack of confidence in the youth justice system as a whole, has yet to be politically acknowledged or effectively addressed.

On the whole, *Youth Justice 2004* steers clear of suggesting major changes, but it does list a number of ways in which the reforms could be improved. Most interestingly, it recommends that the courts could be much more cost-effective if they focused their resources primarily on the most serious and persistent offenders, with the Crown Prosecution Service being used to divert minor offenders from court; and that current efforts to reduce the use of custody should be enhanced through a number of measures, including improving magistrates' confidence in community-based alternatives; providing more feedback to high custody areas on the costs and the effectiveness of custody and community alternatives; and shifting from a vertical sentencing tariff to a more horizontal or 'sloping' tariff. In effect, the Audit Commission is endorsing the diversion orthodoxy while simultaneously approving the new reforms.

Youth Justice 2004 also sets out a number of ways in which the needs of young offenders could be better met, which effectively endorses the imperative of the welfare principle and underlines the importance of switching more resources to prevention, as originally recommended in *Misspent Youth*. This time, however, it carefully costs the political pressure to deliver improved outcomes in the short term at the expense of long-term investment in preventive services, showing how annual savings of up to £1 billion could be made if mainstream agencies, such as schools and health services, took full and effective responsibility for preventing offending by young people.

John Graham

Related entries

Diversion; Early intervention; Fast-tracking; First-time entrants; Managerialism; 'Race' and justice; Youth justice plans.

Key texts and sources

Audit Commission (1996) *Misspent Youth*. London: Audit Commission.
Audit Commission (2004) *Youth Justice 2004: A Review of the Reformed Youth Justice System*. London: Audit Commission.
Guardian (2007) 'A temporary respite: jailing young people in ever larger numbers is not the answer to tackling youth crime', 19 February.
Home Affairs Committee Inquiry (2007) *Young Black People and the Criminal Justice System*. London: House of Commons Home Affairs Select Committee.

AUTHORITARIANISM

Authoritarianism refers to the mobilization of state power to promote regulation and to secure hegemony through repressive political and criminal justice agendas.

In a lecture delivered to the civil liberties organization, the Cobden Trust, in London in 1979, Stuart Hall noted how a drift to a 'law-and-order society' or an 'authoritarian state' had gathered pace during the 1970s, particularly in the UK and the USA. He argued that criminal law was being turned to, not simply to control 'criminality' but to contain disorder and political opposition. This 'criminalization', he argued, is a powerful weapon of the state because it constructs public fear and mobilizes the public's support and consent in the development of repressive state practices. 'Crime' is used to prepare the ground for a general exercise of legal restraint and political control. Neither did he consider this move to a 'more disciplinary, authoritarian kind of society' to be a short-term affair. This process he referred to as *authoritarian populism*, thereby capturing a sense of how the securing of repressive policies is not always dependent on overtly coercive means.

The politicization of the law-and-order agenda has continued unabated since the 1970s (Scraton 1987). Political parties regularly enter 'bidding wars' to reveal their 'tough' credentials to the electorate, whether this is expressed in the Conservative dogma that we must 'condemn more and understand less' or the Labour discourse of 'no more excuses' and being 'tough on crime and tough on the causes of crime'. More police and more prisons, coupled with the political will and resources to support law enforcement, combine to increase the amount of recorded crime. Christie (1993) has argued that there is always an unlimited well of unrecorded crime to be tapped and, the more techniques of mass surveillance and zero-tolerance policing increase, the more likely it is that further 'crime' will be discovered. The 'problem of crime' becomes a self-perpetuating industry while always providing a useful function in legitimating repressive state practices. Between 1997 and 2006, New Labour created over 700 new criminal offences and launched hundreds of anti-crime initiatives.

Typically it has been children and young people who have borne the brunt of this authoritarian climate. Their 'crimes' usually occur in the most *visible* of public places – the street, the shopping centre, the football ground, outside schools. The past decade has been notable for the targeting of disorder, via dispersal orders, curfews, anti-social behaviour orders, parenting orders and so on, coupled with an expansion of the use of juvenile custody. It is a climate driven by processes of 'child demonization' and the 'ideological whiff of child-hate' (Haydon and Scraton 2000).

John Muncie

Related entries

Criminalization; Critical criminology; Demonization; Moral panic; Politicization; Punitiveness; Respect (Government Action Plan); Zero tolerance.

Key texts and sources

Christie, N. (1993) *Crime Control as Industry.* London: Routledge.
Hall, S. (1980) *Drifting into a Law and Order Society.* London: Cobden Trust.
Haydon, D. and Scraton, P. (2000) '"Condemn a little more, understand a little less": the political context and rights implications of the domestic and European rulings in the Venables–Thompson case', *Journal of Law and Society,* 27: 416–48.
Scraton, P. (ed.) (1987) *Law, Order and the Authoritarian State.* Milton Keynes: Open University Press.

B

BAIL

Bail is the releasing of a person suspected or charged with an offence while awaiting the outcome of an investigation, trial, sentence or appeal. If young people are refused bail, they are either detained by the police or remanded in custody by the courts, depending on the stage the case has reached.

Both the police and the courts make bail decisions. Police decisions are governed by the Police and Criminal Evidence Act 1984 and court decisions by the Bail Act 1976. However, in practice, the law is similar for both police and court decisions. The police are able either to bail defendants or detain them until the next available court hearing. In cases where the police refuse bail, young people should be transferred to local authority accommodation unless it is impractical to do so or no secure accommodation is available. In reality, young people are rarely moved out of police custody and, while not breaching the letter of the law, this practice clearly contravenes its spirit and results in vulnerable young people being detained in police custody.

Most bail decisions are taken when defendants are legally 'innocent', and it is for this reason that they are of paramount importance to perceptions of fairness and legitimacy of the criminal justice process and are a significant indicator of civil liberties. Bail decisions are also important because of their impact on the penal remand population, on subsequent decisions (including pleas and sentencing) and on defendants and their families.

Bail decisions attempt to predict future behaviour and consequently are open to a considerable degree of error. The aim of remand decisions is to minimize the risks to victims and the public while respecting the rights of young people. Concerns are heightened with regard to young people because they are a more risky group in terms of their behaviour on bail while also being vulnerable because of their age. Domestic and international conventions and legislation recognize young people's vulnerability and provide that young people should only be remanded in custody as a last resort when all other options have been considered and for the minimum length of time. Accordingly, remand decisions for young people should always be the least restrictive and intrusive option.

The options open to decision-makers for young people are unconditional bail; conditional bail (including bail supervision and support and/or electronically monitored curfews); bail intensive supervision and surveillance programmes (bail ISSPs); remand to local authority accommodation (with or without conditions); court-ordered secure remands; and custodial remands. There is a general lack of remand accommodation and this often results in young people who are remanded to local authority accommodation being placed at home. While this may be expedient for the local authority, it does not comply with the courts' wishes or deal with the risks the courts believe the young people pose. It also tends to undermine the credibility of this remand option.

The law provides a presumption in favour of bail in most circumstances. More recently, however, the remand process has altered as a result of the agendas to 'rebalance' the criminal justice process in favour of the 'law-abiding majority' and to 'narrow the justice gap'. These have resulted in bail being more difficult to obtain and non-compliance being dealt with more punitively, which has arguably impacted on young people disproportionately. A major general concern has been the problem of offending while on bail, which has been regarded as making a significant contribution to the overall crime problem. Young people have been identified as the main contributors to this problem, some of them being dubbed as 'bail bandits' by the press. Despite widespread acceptance that the problem exists, there is a lack of systematic evidence, no agreement about how to measure it and no routinely collected data to quantify it. The second area of concern is the number of defendants who fail to attend court hearings. The Audit Commission (2004) highlighted this problem, estimating that 15 per cent of defendants fail to attend court and stressing the costs involved in terms of time and money. Various measures have been used to increase court attendance rates, including conditions to report to police stations the day before the next court hearing and bail supervision and support schemes.

High rates of offending while on bail and failure to attend court hearings undermine the credibility of the remand process and the criminal justice process more generally. Human rights considerations and the size of the prison population mean that it is not feasible to remand in custody all defendants who pose risks. An alternative is to use conditional bail, which restricts defendants' movements in order to reduce bail risks. Both the police and the courts have the power to attach conditions to bail with which defendants are obliged to comply. There is no legal guidance about which conditions may be used, although they should relate to the grounds on which unconditional bail is refused. In practice, a limited range of conditions are used, including residence, curfew, exclusion zones and 'no contact' conditions. More stringent conditions have been introduced recently specifically for young people, including bail ISSP, electronic monitoring and bail supervision and support, in an attempt to ensure compliance and to decrease the use of custodial remands. Nevertheless, conditions significantly restrict the movements of legally 'innocent' young people and increase the likelihood that they will breach conditions, potentially raising the numbers remanded in custody. Concerns also exist about the purpose, effectiveness and necessity of conditional bail, especially in the light of its increased use and variations in its application between courts.

Custodial remand rates vary between courts, and this raises questions about the consistency and fairness of remand decision-making. There is also evidence that both police and court remand decisions vary for different groups of suspects/defendants and that suspects/defendants from minority ethnic groups are less likely to be bailed. A significant minority of young people who are remanded in custody are later acquitted or receive non-custodial sentences. This suggests that some custodial remands are unnecessary although, potentially, some young people have non-custodial sentences imposed because they have already spent time in custody on remand.

Anthea Hucklesby

Related entries

Bail Act 1976; Bail information schemes; Bail supervision and support (BSS); Police and Criminal Evidence Act 1984 (PACE); 'Race' and justice; Remand; Remand fostering; Remand management.

Key texts and sources

Audit Commission (2004) *Youth Justice 2004: A Review of the Reformed Youth Justice System.* London: Audit Commission.

Cavadino, P. and Gibson, B. (1993) *Bail: The Law, Best Practice and the Debate.* Winchester: Waterside Press.

Goldson, B. (2002b) *Vulnerable Inside: Children in Secure and Penal Settings.* London: Children's Society.

Goldson, B. and Jamieson, J. (2002a) 'Community bail or penal remand? A critical analysis of recent policy developments in relation to unconvicted and/or unsentenced juveniles', *British Journal of Community Justice*, 1: 63–76.

Hucklesby, A. (2002) 'Bail in criminal cases', in M. McConville and G. Wilson (eds) *The Handbook of the Criminal Justice Process.* Oxford: Oxford University Press.

Moore, S. and Smith, R. (2001) *The Pre-trial Guide: Working with Young People from Arrest to Trial.* London: Children's Society.

Thomas, S. and Hucklesby, A. (2004) *Key Elements of Effective Practice – Remand Management.* London: Youth Justice Board (available online at **http://www.yjb.gov.uk/Publications/Scripts/prodView.asp?idProduct=112&eP=PP**).

BAIL ACT 1976

The Bail Act 1976 (as amended) is the major piece of legislation governing the operation of the remand process.

The Bail Act 1976 applies to young people in the same way it does to adults. In most cases, it enshrines a presumption in favour of bail. Consequently, young people have a right to bail unless certain exceptions apply. The main grounds for the refusal of bail are that young people may abscond, commit offences on bail or interfere with witnesses. Other less commonly used grounds exist, which significantly include the welfare of a child or young person.

The Bail Act has been amended considerably and this has resulted in bail becoming more difficult to obtain for some defendants – namely, those who have allegedly committed serious offences or offences on bail. The presumption in favour of bail is reversed if the court believes that a young person was on bail when he or she committed the alleged offence(s). In these circumstances, defendants are refused bail unless the court believes there is no significant risk of further offences being committed.

When bail is refused, young people are remanded in custody either to local authority accommodation, secure accommodation or prison. Custodial remands are for seven days after the first hearing and for up to 28 days thereafter. Bail can be unconditional or conditional. Conditions can be attached to bail on similar grounds to those which enable bail to be refused. These conditions range from residence and banning conditions to bail intensive supervision and surveillance programmes and electronically monitored curfews. Breaching conditions is not an offence but results in young people being returned to court, whereas failure to attend court hearings is an offence.

Anthea Hucklesby

Related entries

Bail; Remand.

Key texts and sources

Corre, N. and Wolchover, D. (2004) *Bail in Criminal Proceedings* (3rd edn). Oxford: Oxford University Press.

Hucklesby, A. (2002) 'Bail in criminal cases', in M. McConville and G. Wilson (eds) *The Handbook of the Criminal Justice Process*. Oxford: Oxford University Press.

Thomas, S. and Hucklesby, A. (2004) *Key Elements of Effective Practice – Remand Management*. London: Youth Justice Board (available online at **http://www.yjb.gov.uk/Publications/Scripts/prodView.asp?idProduct=112&eP=PP**).

See also the Crown Prosecution Service's publication, Bail (available online at **http://www.cps.gov.uk/legal/section14/chapter_l.html**).

BAIL INFORMATION SCHEMES (BISs)

Bail information schemes (BISs) provide independently verified information to the courts during remand hearings in an attempt to raise the likelihood that defendants are granted bail, thus diverting them from custodial remands and, consequently, reducing the prison remand population.

The lack of information available to the courts during remand hearings has been a concern since the 1960s, and bail information schemes (BISs) are an attempt to address this. There are two types of schemes: court-based schemes (which usually work with defendants appearing in court for the first time) and prison-based schemes (which deal with defendants already remanded in custody). Traditionally, these schemes have provided information only in support of bail. Potentially, this meant BIS staff could uncover information that suggested defendants posed serious risks but that they were not required to disclose this to the courts. More recently, however, concerns about the potential risks posed by certain defendants have meant that BISs are expected to divulge both positive and negative information in relation to remand decisions. This may militate against the objective of reducing custodial remands but it increases the quality and quantity of available information to the courts, thus increasing the likelihood that remand decisions are fully informed as well as raising the credibility of the schemes.

The idea of BISs was imported from the USA, and the first scheme was set up in the 1970s. Following this, the Home Office funded eight pilot schemes for adults in the mid-1980s. The aim of these schemes was to provide the Crown Prosecution Service (CPS) with verified, factual and favourable information about defendants that was relevant to the issue of bail. The schemes were deemed to be successful because at least some defendants were granted bail who would otherwise have been remanded in custody.

The schemes diverted defendants from custodial remands in several ways: by affecting CPS decisions to object to bail; by influencing defence decisions to apply for bail; and by strengthening bail applications by the defence. As a result, BISs were extended nationally but began to decline in the mid to late 1990s when ring-fenced funding was withdrawn and other youth justice and probation tasks took priority. A report relating to adult courts suggested that provision of bail information had reduced markedly and, in some areas, had disappeared (Drakeford *et al.* 2001). Currently, a bail information 'pathfinder project' is running in Yorkshire and Humberside.

BISs do not exist in the same way in youth courts as they do in adult courts, although national standards require youth offending teams (YOTs) to provide the service. The standards require YOTs to assess young people using bail Asset and to provide this information to the CPS. There are, however, no formal schemes. Instead, information is provided by generic YOT workers in response to requests from defence solicitors or the CPS, or as a result of sharing known information about the young person's circumstances. Additionally, bail information is provided as part of the assessment process for bail supervision and support schemes. This appears to have increased the information available to the courts, to have speeded up decision-making and enabled more appropriate remand decisions to be made.

Anthea Hucklesby

Related entries

Assessment framework; Bail; Crown Prosecution Service (CPS); Diversion; Remand; Remand fostering; Remand management.

Key texts and sources

Drakeford, M., Haines, K., Cotton, B. and Octigan, M. (2001) *Pre-trial Services and the Future of Probation.* Cardiff: University of Wales Press.
Lloyd, C. (1992) *Bail Information Schemes: Practice and Effect. Research and Planning Unit Paper 69.* London: Home Office.
Thomas, S. and Hucklesby, A. (2004) *Key Elements of Effective Practice – Remand Management.* London: Youth Justice Board (available online at **http://www.yjb.gov.uk/Publications/Scripts/prod View.asp?idProduct=112&eP=PP**).

BAIL SUPERVISION AND SUPPORT (BSS)

Bail supervision and support (BSS) is a condition of bail. It can be defined as the provision of services (intervention and support) designed to assist young people awaiting trial or sentence to comply with bail requirements.

Bail supervision and support (BSS) has three primary aims: to reduce custodial remands, to increase attendance at court and to reduce offending on bail. The ways in which schemes operate vary considerably. Accordingly, the components of BSS packages are not uniform but often include an assessment; three or four meetings a week; referrals to specialist services; meetings with mentors; and the provision of accommodation. Ensuring that young people attend court and other appointments by providing reminders and transport often plays a significant role in the work undertaken. This illustrates a key concern about BSS which relates to whether they encourage young people to be passive recipients of assistance rather than active participants. This is only apparent when support is removed suddenly at the end of the remand period.

BSS is one of the statutory services youth offending teams (YOTs) are required to provide under the Crime and Disorder Act 1998. Between 1999 and 2002, the Youth Justice Board funded 144 YOTs to provide BSS. The evaluation of the schemes, while not robust methodologically, suggested that BSS enables the courts to receive a higher quantity and a better quality of information about defendants, diverts some defendants from custodial remands and improves court attendance rates. Schemes for adults have also been shown to be effective in that they target appropriate referrals, but there is less evidence about their impact on court attendance rates or custodial remands. However, the long-term effectiveness and the nature of the work undertaken will always be compromised by the relatively short periods of time young people are subject to BSS and because interventions stop suddenly.

Concerns continue about the possibility of net-widening: some defendants would have been bailed in any event without recourse to BSS. Indeed, a significant proportion of young people assessed for BSS are not at risk of custody. As the young people are legally 'innocent', issues have also been raised about the intrusive nature of some interventions and about potential human rights violations. Of particular concern is that some interventions appear to have stepped over the crucial boundary between dealing with offending-related behaviour and behaviour linked to the specific *alleged* offence(s). Additionally, there is some unease about the schemes setting defendants up to fail as a result of the stringent requirements they are obliged to comply with, despite the unsettled and relatively chaotic lives many young offenders lead.

The ring-fenced funding of BSS for young people came to an end in 2002 and, although provision continues in some areas, it is often not in the same form and is usually part of a generic court service. While this may be a pragmatic response to resourcing issues and the priority provided to post-sentence work, it is likely to result in the demise of BSS over time as other areas of work are prioritized. Furthermore, effective BSS is provided by dedicated specialists and is proactive, and this is unlikely to occur when it is not prioritized or separately funded.

Anthea Hucklesby

Related entries

Bail; Diversion; Net-widening; Remand; Remand fostering; Remand management; Youth offending teams (YOTs).

Key texts and sources

Drakeford, M., Haines, K., Cotton, B. and Octigan, M. (2001) *Pre-trial Services and the Future of Probation.* Cardiff: University of Wales Press.

Moore, S. and Smith, R. (2001) *The Pre-trial Guide: Working with Young People from Arrest to Trial.* London: Children's Society.

Thomas, S. (2005b) *National Evaluation of Bail Supervision and Support Schemes Funded by the Youth Justice Board for England and Wales from April 1999 to March 2002.* London: Youth Justice Board (available online at **http://www.yjb.gov.uk/ Publications/Scripts/prodView.asp?idProduct= 273&eP**).

BEHAVIOUR AND EDUCATION SUPPORT TEAMS (BESTs)

Behaviour and education support teams (BESTs) are multi-agency teams intended to bring together a complementary mix of professionals from the fields of health, social care and education. They were first introduced in 2002 in targeted areas. The aim of a BEST is to promote emotional well-being, positive behaviour and school attendance, by identifying and supporting those with, or at risk of developing, emotional and behavioural problems.

Behaviour and education support teams (BESTs) aim to work with children aged 5–18, their families and schools to intervene early and to prevent problems developing further. Each BEST works in partnership with a cluster of primary schools and one or two secondary schools, selecting schools with high proportions of pupils with, or 'at risk' of developing, emotional, behavioural and/or attendance problems.

Typically, a BEST consists of at least four or five professionals from a range of education, social care and health disciplines. This may include some of the following: behaviour support staff; clinical psychologists; education welfare officers; educational psychologists; health visitors; primary mental health workers; school nurses; social workers/family support workers; and speech and language therapists. As well as providing direct interventions with individuals, families, groups and the schools as a whole, BESTs are also supposed to provide an important liaison and referral role to other more specialized services, such as youth offending teams (YOTs), Connexions and specialist health services, as required.

A number of positive outcomes have been reported, including improvements in child and family well-being, and subsequent improvements in attendance, behaviour and, ultimately, attainment; improved access to services, particularly specialist services, for parents and schools; the acquisition of new skills and strategies for school staff in managing behavioural and emotional difficulties; and the sharing of interdisciplinary knowledge and skills among BEST practitioners.

While some of these outcomes might have had an indirect effect on reducing offending, there appears to have been little specific, direct offence-focused work with young people. Few links have been found between BESTs and the youth justice sector and, while there was some police representation, BESTs were much more likely to have members from education welfare, educational psychology and social services. None of the BESTs that were evaluated contained staff from YOTs (Hallam 2007).

While general funds remain available for behaviour and attendance initiatives such as BESTs, there is no longer any specific ring-fenced funding. A standard successful model does not seem to have emerged and the work is to be absorbed into schools.

Martin Stephenson

Related entries

Partnership working; School exclusion; School non-attendance.

Key texts and sources

Hallam, S. (2007) 'Evaluation of behavioural management in schools: a review of the Behaviour Improvement Programme and the role of behaviour and education support teams', *Child and Adolescent Mental Health* (forthcoming).

Halsey, K., Gulliver, C., Johnson, A., Martin, K. and Kinder, K. (2005) *Evaluation of Behaviour and Education Support Teams. Research Report* RR706. London: DfES.

See also the Department for Education and Skills' document, *Behaviour and Education Support Teams Working in Partnership* (available online at http://www.dfes.gov.uk/best/).

BIFURCATION

Bifurcation is a criminal justice policy for targeting the more severe sanctions on the most serious offenders and for making use of less severe sanctions for all other offenders.

The term 'bifurcation' was first used by Anthony Bottoms in 1977 and further discussed in 1980. At that time Bottoms was writing about the actual trend in sentencing practice and the emerging Home Office policy of sentencing *dangerous* offenders to longer terms of imprisonment while simultaneously giving shorter prison sentences to offenders not deemed to be dangerous – the implication being that sentencing was polarizing or bifurcating to the extent that the longer sentences were even longer and the shorter sentences even shorter than would otherwise have been the case. Official support for this policy was predicated on the penal crisis of the time: there was a record prison population of 42,000 inmates, and this sentencing policy was seen as a pragmatic response to the problem. Bottoms went further, however, by arguing that bifurcation in penal policy could extend to the prison–community sentence dichotomy – that prison should be reserved for serious offenders (those posing a threat to society) while other offenders should be given community sentences. This was, in fact, the official policy thrust behind the Criminal Justice Act 1991, which did produce a bifurcation in sentencing and an actual decline in the prison population. This effect was, however, short lived, and the now infamous 'prison works' speech in 1993 by the then Home Secretary, Michael Howard, signalled a changing political climate that has brought about an unabated populist punitiveness and a prison population (including many minor property offenders) of over 80,000 in 2008.

Much of the above applies to the adult criminal justice system and not specifically to juveniles. John Pitts (1988), however, argued that bifurcation existed in the juvenile justice policy and practice of the 1970s. In the case of young people, policies of bifurcation could be seen not only in terms of the custody–community supervision dichotomy but also in respect of institional 'care'. Thus policies at the time directed certain young people (some of whom were offenders but others were institutionalized for a variety of social or educational reasons) into a range of institutional provision while others were dealt with in the community.

Both Bottoms and Pitts seem to agree on some of the key features and problems with bifurcation. The first difficulty is deciding down which route of the bifurcated options an individual should be sent. For example, what constitutes a dangerous offender or someone who presents a risk to the public, and who should receive a prison sentence or a longer prison sentence or, indeed, a community sentence? Such decisions may be (and be perceived as) harsh (unjust) or abitrary and potentially open to (political) interference. There are few absolutes in this area of decision-making, which may change over time. Secondly, policies of bifurcation seem to be pursued partly for pragmatic reasons (in response to a penal crisis) and partly for financial reasons (custody is expensive), especially when compared with the range of community options. Thirdly, bifurcation policies tend not to work in practice because sentencers primarily respond to the 'get tough' part of a message (which says simultaneously 'get tough' and 'get soft') and because this message also has the tendency to lead those responsible for community sentences to 'toughen' them up to make them more attractive to sentencers, often at the cost of their rehabilitative value. Finally, bifurcation illustrates the extent to which criminal justice policy is vulnerable to political vicissitudes. Thus bifurcation policies are rarely, if ever, rooted in criminological thinking but owe much more, as noted, to political concerns of a pragmatic or financial nature.

Kevin Haines

Related entries

Community justice; Criminal Justice Act 1991; Politicization; Punitiveness; Tariff.

Key texts and sources

Bottoms, A. (1977) 'Reflections on the renaissance of dangerousness', *Howard Journal of Penology and Crime Prevention*, 16: 70–96.
Bottoms, A. and Preston, R. (1980) *The Coming Penal Crisis*. Edinburgh: Scottish Academic Press.
Cavadino, M. and Dignan, J. (2002) *The Penal System: An Introduction* (3rd ed). London: Sage.
Pitts, J. (1988) *The Politics of Juvenile Crime*. London: Sage.
Snacken, S. and Beyens, K. (1994) 'Sentencing and prison overcrowding', *European Journal on Criminal Policy and Research*, 2: 84–99.

BIND OVER

Bind over refers to specified powers the courts have to require a person to fulfil certain conditions, on pain of forfeiting a sum of money for failing to do so.

Three powers of bind over are currently available in England and Wales. First, both the magistrates' courts and the Crown court may bind a person over to keep the peace, even in the absence of a criminal conviction. A sum of money is specified, which can be forfeited if the person does not keep the peace for the period required by the court. Under the Powers of Criminal Courts (Sentencing) Act 2000 (s. 150), the magistrates' courts and Crown court may bind over the parent or guardian of a person under 18 (who is convicted of an offence) to take proper care of him or her and exercise proper control over him or her, and to ensure that he or she complies with any community sentence that the court has passed, entering into a recognizance of up to £1,000.

The Crown court has an additional power to bind over a convicted offender to come up for judgment. Conditions are set which if broken, will result in the offender being sentenced for the offence and forfeiting the recognizance. There is no longer a power to bind over a person to be of good behaviour (see *Hashman and Harrup* v. *UK*).

Sally Ireland

Related entries

Criminal Justice Act 1991; Parental bind overs.

Key texts and sources

Home Office (2003b) *Bind Overs: A Power for the 21st Century.* London: Home Office.
See the Office of Public Sector Information's website (http://www.opsi.gov.uk/acts/acts2000/20000006.htm) for the text of the Powers of Criminal Courts (Sentencing) Act 2000.

BOOT CAMPS

Boot camps are American shock incarceration regimes for adults and juveniles that emphasize discipline and physical training in a military-style environment. They are generally restricted to non-violent or first-time offenders.

The origins of the boot camp lie in survival training for US military personnel during the Second World War. They were introduced in the USA from 1982 (first in Georgia and Oklahoma) in response to prison overcrowding and in a belief that short periods of retributive punishment would change or deter 'offending behaviour'. Originally aimed at adult offenders, the juvenile justice system did not immediately adopt boot camps because of questions about their appropriateness for young people. However, as the population of juveniles in prison increased sharply, correctional officials began to turn to boot camps as a way of delivering a 'short, sharp, shock' to less serious, usually first-time, juvenile offenders and as providing an alternative to longer periods of penal confinement. By the mid-1990s the US federal government and about two thirds of the 50 states were operating some 120 boot camp programmes, run by a mixture of public and private bodies.

Sentences in boot camps generally range from 90 to 180 days. Typically, detainees face pre-dawn starts, enforced shaved heads, silent regimes, military discipline, no access to the media and a rigorous (and abusive) atmosphere for 16 hours a day. These techniques are designed to promote fear, degradation, humiliation, discipline and 'respect for authority', in order to impose total compliance.

Such regimes have consistently failed to live up to correctional expectations and the deterrent effect of military training has proved negligible. In fact, some researchers have found that boot camp 'graduates' are more likely to be rearrested or rearrested more quickly than other offenders. The authoritarian atmosphere has denied access to effective 'treatment', and there have been occasional lawsuits from inmates claiming that elements of the programme are dangerous and life threatening. Significantly, they have had no impact on prison populations. Indeed, the enduring popularity of boot camps appears to rely more on an emotive nostalgia for some mythical orderly past than on any measure of effectiveness. Moreover, boot camps tend to be more labour intensive and more expensive to operate, particularly if used as an alternative to probation or a community-based programme. For black youths (who represent the vast majority of the juveniles sentenced to boot camps in America) as well as for those with emotional, behavioural or learning problems, degrading tactics appear particularly inappropriate and damaging.

The boot camp, as described above, is quintessentially American. The idea of 'shock incarceration', though, has appeared in other jurisdictions. In the UK, for example, detention centre regimes, particularly in the early 1980s, were explicitly geared to delivering a 'short, sharp, shock'. In the following decade the idea was revived when the UK's first 'boot camp' was opened in 1996 at Thorn Cross Young Offender Institution in Cheshire. But instead of a military-based regime, this institution employed a 'high intensity' mixture of education, discipline and training. A second camp, opened at the Military Corrective Training Centre in Colchester in 1997, promised a more spartan American-style regime. However, the notion of handing 'offenders' over to a military authority provoked an avalanche of complaints from virtually all sides of the criminal justice system. Eventually pressure from the Prison Service – on grounds of cost, if not effectiveness and/or human rights violations – was successful in shutting down the Colchester camp barely 12 months after its opening and when only 44 offenders had gone through its regime. The high-intensity training regime at Thorn Cross endured even though evaluations of its effectiveness have been mixed. In general it appears to have had no positive effect on the prospect of reconviction per se, although reoffenders are recorded as having committed fewer offences. The latter has been attributed to education, employment, mentoring, resettlement and throughcare programmes rather than to Thorn Cross's military drill components.

The heyday of boot camps now appears to be over. In the USA, North Dakota, Colorado, Georgia and Arizona all abandoned boot camps in the 1990s after mounting allegations of abuse and negligible effects on recidivism. In 2005, 14-year-old Martin Lee Anderson was killed by drill instructors at Bay County Boot Camp in Panama City, Florida. The subsequent outcry led to the closure of Florida's five state-run boot camp facilities for juvenile offenders. Nevertheless the idea of 'military training' remains a popular political soundbite (as witnessed by the suggestion by the Scottish National Party in 2006 that it reopen the Airborne Initiative based at Braidwood House in Carluke, Lanarkshire, as an alternative to prison for repeat offenders aged 18–25). In the USA private operators continue to run punitive programmes for juveniles, often paid for by parents seduced by the promise of a 'quick-fix solution' and the hope of 'scaring kids straight'.

John Muncie and Barry Goldson

Related entries

Detention centres; Punitiveness.

Key texts and sources
Farrington, D., Ditchfield, J., Hancock, G., Howard, P., Jolliffe, D., Livingston, M. and Painter, K. (2002) *Evaluation of Two Intensive Regimes for Young Offenders. Home Office Research Study 239.* London: Home Office.
National Institute of Justice (2003) *Correctional Boot Camps: Lessons from a Decade of Research.* Washington, DC: US Department of Justice.
Parent, D.G. (1995) 'Boot camps failing to achieve goals', in M. Tonry and K. Hamilton (eds) *Intermediate Sanctions in Over-crowded Times.* Boston, MA: Northeastern University Press.
Simon, J. (1995) 'They died with their boots on: the boot camp and the limits of modern penality', *Social Justice,* 22: 25–48.

BORSTALS

Borstals are penal regimes for young people with an emphasis on physical labour, moral reformation and discipline, backed by corporal punishment.

The Gladstone Committee of 1895 proposed the concept of a *training* prison for young people in order to separate those aged 16–21 from adults. The prison commissioner, Sir Evelyn Ruggles-Brise (1857–1935), established the first institution in Borstal, near Rochester in Kent in 1902. Statutory recognition of this new form of penal 'treatment' was provided in the Prevention of Crime Act 1908. The second Borstal was opened at the site of a former reformatory school at Feltham, Middlesex in 1911. The first purpose-built Borstal, Lowdham Grange, opened in 1931.

The Borstal system was heralded as a major liberal breakthrough. The separation of young prisoners (under 21-year-olds) from adults – in specially designated closed institutions – was seen as a significant step towards the retraining of the young offender. In the prevailing spirit of individual rehabilitation, Borstal 'trainees' could be held on a semi-indeterminate basis of between one and three years. Release was dependent on professional assessments of 'behavioural improvement'. The regime was based on strict discipline, hard work, drill and corporal punishment, designed, in the words of Ruggles-Brise, to promote 'industrious labour' and 'respect for authority'. It was directed specifically at young people who were thought to display 'criminal habits and tendencies' or those associating with 'persons of bad character' but who were, none the less, believed to be redeemable. The 'incorrigible' were explicitly excluded from Borstal and sent to prison. On release the 'trainee' was placed on a period of licensed supervision of at least six months.

From the outset, Borstals attracted criticism for instituting periods of confinement (of up to three years) for offences that would not ordinarily attract more than six months' detention. However it was also claimed that Borstals had a remarkable initial success in preventing reoffending. The first survey in 1915 reported reconviction rates as low as 27–35 per cent. The Criminal Justice Act 1961 reduced the minimum age for Borstal training to 15, made it easier to transfer young people from approved schools and integrated Borstals into the prison system. This integration meant that the training component declined and their regimes became yet more punitive. The role of Borstal as an alternative to prison was undermined, and it was turned instead into a primary punitive institution that acted as a funnel into the prison system. As a result, younger children and young people with less serious offences were increasingly subject to 'tougher punishment' (as graphically represented in Roy Minton's 1979 film, *Scum*). The reconviction rate (which had stayed at 30 per cent throughout the 1930s) increased to 70 per cent in the 1970s, suggesting that Borstal accentuated the forms of behaviour

it was designed to suppress. In 1982 Borstals were renamed youth custody centres and, in 1988, were included in a wider network of young offender institutions.

John Muncie and Barry Goldson

Related entries

Alternatives to custody; Children in custody; Corporal punishment; Detention centres; Intermediate treatment (IT); Young offender institutions.

Key texts and sources
Behan, B. (1958) *Borstal Boy*. New York: Berkeley Windhover. Hood, R. (1965) *Borstal Re-assessed*. London: Heinemann. Radzinowicz, L. and Hood, R. (1990) *The Emergence of Penal Policy*. Oxford: Clarendon Press.

BRITISH CRIME SURVEY (BCS)

The British Crime Survey (BCS) is a large sample survey of the general public in England and Wales. It provides estimates of the extent of crime committed against individuals and their personal property. Because it is able to estimate the extent of unreported crime as well as reported and recorded crime, it provides an invaluable index of crime trends.

The British Crime Survey (BCS) was set up in 1982 as a complementary measure of crime. It relies on large population samples of adults in England and Wales who are asked directly whether they have been the victim of crime over the last 12 months. The BCS provides a count of crime that includes *unreported* offences and reported offences that have gone *unrecorded*. As the survey's methodology has been fairly stable over time, it is thought to provide an index of crime trends that in some ways is better than police statistics.

However, the BCS also has limitations. Its estimates of crime levels are based on samples and are thus subject to sampling error. Not everyone selected for interview agrees to take part, and thus there is scope for sample bias. Equally, not everyone who has been the victim of a crime will choose to provide details to an interviewer. By definition, it excludes 'victimless crimes' and those crimes committed against organizations (for example, fraud) and environmental crimes. Despite these limitations, the survey is thought by government statisticians and by academic criminologists to provide a better guide to crime trends than police statistics. All are agreed, however, that, taken together, the two sources of information provide a better picture of crime than could be obtained from either series alone.

The BCS has provided a reasonably comprehensive account of crimes against individuals and their property since 1982. There have been similar surveys in both Scotland and Northern Ireland. The BCS was modelled in part on the US National Crime Victimization Survey, which began in the 1970s. The first sweep of the survey was conducted in early 1982, with a nationally representative sample of 10,905 respondents in England and Wales.

Following the first BCS, the survey was repeated in 1984, 1988 and 1992. It was then conducted in alternate years until 2000, when the sample size doubled – to about 20,000. In 2001 it moved to being a continuous 'rolling' annual survey with 40,000 interviews conducted throughout the year. One reason for the increased sample size was to provide more reliable measures of different forms of violent crime. Another was the perceived need for numerical 'performance indicators' relating to levels of public confidence in the police in each of the 43 police force areas in England and Wales. The much larger sample size allows tolerably precise survey estimates for overall household and personal crime at individual police-force level.

The BCS not only collects information about crime but also asks people about their experience of, and attitudes towards, the police and other parts of the criminal justice system. The survey is one of the main sources of information about public ratings of the police in England and Wales.

Mike Hough

Related entries

Crime statistics; Fear of crime; Victimization.

Key texts and sources

Hough, M. and Maxfield, M. (2007) *Surveying Crime in the 21st Century*. Cullompton: Willan Publishing.

Smith, A. (2006) *Crime Statistics: An Independent Review (Carried out by the Crime Statistics Review Group for the Secretary of State for the Home Department, November 2006)*. London: Home Office (available online at **http://www.homeoffice. gov.uk/rds/pdfs06/crime-statistics-independent-review-06.pdf**).

Walker, A., Kershaw, C. and Nicholas, S. (2006) *Crime in England and Wales, 2005/06*. Home Office Statistical Bulletin 12/06. London: Home Office (available online at **http://www.homeoffice. gov.uk/rds/pdfs06/hosb1206.pdf**).

BULGER

On 12 February 1993, James Bulger – a 2-year-old child – was murdered on a railway-siding in Bootle, north Liverpool. Subsequently, two 10-year-old children were convicted of his murder. Beyond the profound tragedy of the case, it was cynically exploited by politicians and the media and it had an extraordinary symbolic and institutional impact on youth justice discourse and policy.

The two boys convicted of the murder of James Bulger were sentenced in November 1993. In Preston Crown Court, Judge Morland commented that the boys 'cunning and very wicked' behaviour had resulted in 'an act of unparalled evil and barbarity', before imposing indeterminate custodial sentences on each boy. In his report to the Home Secretary, the judge recommended a tariff of 8 years. The Lord Chief Justice, however, advised the Home Secretary that, in his opinion, the minimum period of detention should be 10 years, and the Home Secretary, having made his own assessment, increased the tariff further to 15 years. Appeals and counter-appeals followed and, in all, ten judges were involved. The trial itself made no concessions to the age of the defendants, and the two 10-year-old children were fully exposed to the formality of the Crown court process; the bewigged and robed legal professionals; the presence of a full jury; and, perhaps most significantly, the gaze of the world's media (Morrison 1997).

The significance of the 'Bulger case' – in influencing the mood and trajectory of subsequent youth justice policy in England and Wales – can hardly be overstated, and it was particularly important in three principal and interrelated ways.

First, it created and/or consolidated a powerful sense of anxiety concerning youth crime that was exploited by politicians and the media. In this sense it epitomized conditions of 'moral panic' and 'folk devilling'.

Second, it provided a platform for the systematic demonization of the two 10-year-olds. Once they had been convicted, their names and photographs were published, and the concept of 'evil', which had been introduced by the trial judge himself, coloured the reporting which amounted to an 'outpouring of outrage and hatred against the boys' (Davis and Bourhill 1997). On 25 November after the trial had concluded, the pages of the mass-circulation tabloid newspapers were almost exclusively dedicated to its coverage. The *Daily Mirror's* headline castigated the two children as 'Freaks of nature'; the *Daily Star's* front page posed the question 'How do you feel now you little bastards?'; and the *Sun* proclaimed that the 'Devil himself couldn't have made a better job of two fiends'. The case was hailed as the ultimate expression of a pervasive and deepening wave of moral degeneracy and child lawlessness. In this

respect, it was not just two boys who were on trial; rather, the shadow of suspicion was cast over *childhood* itself (Scraton 1997b).

Third, by exploiting – if not manufacturing – public anxieties and emphasizing 'evil' and corrosive moral malaise, politicians promised to introduce ever-more repressive youth justice policies and to offer confident assurances that they would reinstall discipline, decency, standards and order.

The Bulger case served to concretize a percolating harshness in the governance of youth crime. The Criminal Justice and Public Order Act 1994 introduced privately managed child jails – secure training centres – for the routine incarceration of children aged 12–14; the doubling of the maximum sentence of detention in young offender institutions; and the extension of the s. 53 provisions of the Children and Young Persons Act 1933 (empowering the courts to sentence 10–13-years-olds to lengthy periods of custody). Furthermore, despite a change of government in 1997, the legacy of 'toughness' endured. A white paper, ominously entitled *No More Excuses – a New Approach to Tackling Youth Crime in England and Wales*, was published in November 1997 setting out the wide-ranging provisions of the Crime and Disorder Act 1998.

The manner in which the state treats some of its most vulnerable and disadvantaged citizens – young offenders – reveals much about the very core of society itself. The exploitation of an atypical case and the political posturing that underpins contemporary youth justice policy in England and Wales evidence a society in which the rights of children and the imperatives of justice – both social and criminal – are seriously compromised.

Barry Goldson

Related entries

Criminal Justice and Public Order Act 1994; Demonization; Moral panic; Politicization; Tariff.

Key texts and sources

Davis, H. and Bourhill, M. (1997) '"Crisis": the demon-isation of children and young people', in P. Scraton (ed.) 'Childhood' in 'Crisis'? London: UCL Press.

Goldson, B. (1998) 'Re-visiting the "Bulger case": the governance of juvenile crime and the politics of punishment – enduring consequences for children in England and Wales', Juvenile Justice Worldwide, 1: 21–2.

Morrison, B. (1997) As If. London: Granta.

Scraton, P. (ed.) (1997b) 'Childhood' in 'Crisis'? London: UCL Press.

C

CAPITAL PUNISHMENT

Capital punishment is often referred to as the 'death penalty'. Methods of execution that have been used around the world in recent times include electrocution, hanging, lethal injection, shooting, beheading and stoning. The death penalty for juveniles appears to have been abandoned in most, if not all, countries of the world.

The first execution of a juvenile offender on record was in 1642 when Thomas Graunger lost his life in Plymouth Colony, Massachusetts. It was not until 2005, however, that the death penalty was abolished in all states of the USA for those under the age of 18 at the time of their offence. This followed a Supreme Court ruling.

While 69 countries and territories retain the death penalty as a sentence, according to Streib (2003), the death penalty for juvenile offenders has almost been universally abolished. In large part this is thought to be due to the express provisions of the United Nations Convention on the Rights of the Child and several other international treaties and agreements. That said, since 1990, 'juvenile offenders' are known to have been executed in eight countries: China, the Democratic Republic of Congo, Iran, Pakistan, Yemen, Nigeria, Saudi Arabia and the USA. Furthermore, following the execution of three people in less than a week in Iran in 2005 – for crimes committed when they were children, including one who was still a child – Amnesty International urged the Iranian government to abolish capital punishment in respect of juveniles. In addition to the inhumanity of capital punishment in itself, Hood

(2002) has argued that studies have consistently failed to find any convincing evidence that the death penalty deters crime any more effectively than other punishments. Furthermore, crime figures from countries that have abolished the death penalty fail to show any negative effects.

In England, Scotland and Wales, the death penalty for murder was formally abolished in 1969. It remained theoretically available in Northern Ireland until the passing of the Northern Ireland (Emergency Powers) Act 1973. The death penalty remained on the statute book for high treason and piracy, and it was not until 10 December 1999 – International Human Rights Day – that the government ratified the 'Second Optional Protocol' to the International Covenant on Civil and Political Rights, thus totally abolishing capital punishment in Britain.

The abolition of capital punishment should not be taken to mean that children and young people do not lose their lives in penal custody, however. Between July 1990 and November 2007, for example, 30 children died in prisons and private jails in England and Wales (Goldson and Coles 2005).

Barry Goldson

Related entries

Deaths in custody; United Nations Convention on the Rights of the Child (UNCRC).

Key texts and sources

Amnesty International (2005) 'Public statement: Iran continues to execute minors and juvenile offenders' (available online at http://www.amnestyusa.org/document.php?lang=e&id=80256DD400782B84802570460056CF81).

Goldson, B. and Coles, D. (2005) *In the Care of the State? Child Deaths in Penal Custody in England and Wales.* London: Inquest.

Hood, R. (2002) *The Death Penalty: A World-wide Perspective.* Oxford: Clarendon Press.

Streib, V.L. (2003) 'The juvenile death penalty today: death sentences and executions for juvenile crimes, January 1973–September 2003' (available online at http://www.deathpenaltyinfo.org/article.php?scid=27&did=203#execsus).

See also the Death Penalty Information Centre's website (http://www.deathpenaltyinfo.org/article.php?scid=27&did=203#execsus).

CARE ORDERS

A care order is a court order made to safeguard a child by imposing on a local authority the duty to take the child into its care for the duration of the order. If necessary, the authority may remove the child from his or her family and parents for this purpose.

Care orders are currently imposed in England and Wales under s. 31 of the Children Act 1989 and, in Northern Ireland, under s. 50 of the Children (Northern Ireland) Order 1995. Only a local authority or the National Society for the Prevention of Cruelty to Children can apply for such an order, which is made by a civil court in the family justice system, and no order can be made in relation to a child aged 17 or over. The thinking has been that these provisions should provide the only legal route – other than through a penal order for detention imposed by a criminal court – by which the state can remove children from their homes against the wishes of their parents. After the implementation of the Crime and Disorder Act 1998, the court briefly had the power to impose a care order when a child breached a child safety order imposed on him or her, but this received criticism and has been repealed.

The sole criterion for the court to apply is whether 'the child concerned is suffering, or is likely to suffer, significant harm', and that this is either attributable to the care being given by parents or to the child being 'beyond parental control'. It is possible, therefore, that a child's offending might contribute to a finding of significant harm. It is also the case that children in care may commit offences: it is now known that there are similar background characteristics of children who need protection and children who offend. For example, a Youth Justice Board report in 2004 found that 11.5 per cent of all young offenders are, or have been, 'looked-after' children – that is, they were either subject to a care order or were being voluntarily looked after by the local authority.

However, this connection in practice between child protection and youth justice is very different from the legal situation that pertained when the 'offence condition' for a care order was introduced by the Children and Young Persons Act 1969. This provision had sought to remove the difference in treatment between young offenders and children who had been abused or neglected by allowing a 'welfare' response to offending. This option was never made a requirement and became the focus of controversy until it was repealed by the Children Act 1989 (Bottoms and Kemp 2006: 140–4). A similar option continues to operate in Scotland where children's hearings can use compulsory measures of supervision in relation to children who offend and supervision can include a residence requirement. However, unlike care orders, these do not give the local authority parental responsibility.

Christine Piper

Related entries

Children Act 1989; Children and Young Persons Act 1969; Children's hearing system; Family Proceedings Court; Justice (Northern Ireland) Act 2002; Juvenile Justice Centre; Looked-after children (LAC); Net-widening; Safeguarding; Welfare.

Key texts and sources

Bottoms, A. and Kemp, V. (2006) 'The relationship between youth justice and child welfare in England and Wales', in M. Hill et al. (eds) *Youth Justice and Child Protection.* London: Jessica Kingsley.

Diduck, A. and Kaganas, F. (2006) *Family Law, Gender and the State: Text, Cases and Materials* (2nd edn). Oxford: Hart Publishing (ch. 17).

See the Office of Public Sector Information's website (http://www.opsi.gov.uk/acts/acts1989/Ukpga_19 890041_en_1.htm#tcon) for the text of the Children Act 1989. The National Society for the Prevention of Cruelty to Children's bibliography is available online at http://www.nspcc.org.uk/ Inform/OnlineResources/ReadingLists/Historical PerspectiveOnChildrenInCare/HistoryOfChildre nInCare_asp_ifega26170.html.

CAUTION

A police caution is a formal warning given to an adult or juvenile as an alternative to prosecution. It is normally used for first-time offenders committing less serious offences. A caution is citable in court as part of an offender's criminal history.

In England and Wales the police can dispose of cases using alternatives to prosecution that include no further action, informal warnings or cautions, even when they have detected an offence and have sufficient evidence to prosecute. The conditions for a caution are sufficient evidence for a conviction, a full admission of guilt and consent to a caution for an adult and parental consent for a juvenile.

Police cautions have been used since the inception of organized police forces, but there was a significant increase in the use of formal cautions, particularly for juveniles, in the 1980s and 1990s. This was driven by the Children and Young Persons Act 1969 and Home Office circulars on cautioning (14/85, 59/90, 18/94, 30/05). The aim was to divert young people from court in order to avoid the stigmitization and labelling said to be consequent on a court appearance. Juveniles should only be prosecuted as a last resort. New Labour's Crime and Disorder Act 1998 replaced the juvenile caution with a system of reprimands and final warnings that was implemented in 2000.

The opposite presumption applied to adults: they were normally prosecuted unless they were 'at risk' (for example, elderly or mentally disordered). More recently, the Criminal Justice Act 2003 introduced an adult 'conditional caution' requiring rehabilitation or reparation. The decision to caution conditionally lies with the Crown Prosecution Service, leaving the police with discretion to give 'simple' adult cautions.

There is a paucity of cautioning research focused on juvenile cautioning. Early research explored the significant differences in cautioning rates between forces, leading to accusations of 'justice by geography' (Ditchfield 1976; Laycock and Tarling 1985). It also focused on the 'net-widening' thesis: juveniles were being cautioned when previously they would have been dealt with by informal warnings or no further action. Tutt and Giller (1987) argued that the increased numbers both prosecuted and cautioned from 1980 to 1985 could only be accounted for by net-widening, given the fall in the juvenile population. More recent research has focused on the impact of Home Office circulars on policy and practice (Evans and Wilkinson 1990; Evans and Ellis 1997). This found that, despite Home Office attempts to encourage greater consistency, significant differences in caution rates between and within police forces remain and are best explained by the differential use of pre-court disposals.

One of the remarkable features of police cautions is that they appear to work in preventing reoffending, particularly in contrast to court disposals. *Home Office Statistical Bulletin 8/94* found that 85 per cent of those cautioned in 1985 and 1988 were not convicted of a 'standard list' offence within two years of their caution. This has to be treated with care because reconviction rates are not the same as reoffence rates.

Roger Evans

Related entries
Children and Young Persons Act 1969; Crime and Disorder Act 1998; Crown Prosecution Service; Diversion; Justice by geography; Net-widening; Reprimands and final warnings; Restorative cautioning.

Key texts and sources

Ditchfield, J.A. (1976) *Police Cautioning in England and Wales*. London: HMSO.

Evans, R. and Ellis, R. (1997) *Police Cautioning in the 1990s. Home Office Research Findings* 52. London: Home Office.

Evans, R. and Wilkinson, C. (1990) 'Variations in police cautioning policy and practice in England and Wales', *Howard Journal of Criminal Justice*, 29: 155–76.

Home Office (1994) *The Criminal Histories of those Cautioned in 1984, 1988 and 1991. Home Office Statistical Bulletin* 8/94. London: Home Office.

Laycock, G. and Tarling, R. (1985) 'Police force cautioning: policy and practice', *Howard Journal*, 24: 81–92.

Tutt, N. and Giller, H. (1987) 'Manifesto for management: the elimination of custody', *Justice of the Peace*, 151: 200–2.

CAUTION PLUS

The term 'caution plus' is used to describe an intervention accompanying a police caution and is mainly used for juveniles.

Caution plus consists of individually tailored packages of intervention aimed at addressing offences and offence behaviour in order to reduce reoffending, often including some form of reparation. Evans and Wilkinson (1990) found that, in 1987, around half of the 42 police forces in England and Wales had some form of caution plus. This proportion had risen slightly by the mid-1990s (Evans and Ellis 1997). The majority of forces said that the availability of caution plus increased the likelihood of a decision to caution, although it is supposed to be an addition to, not a condition of, a caution. The police role in relation to caution plus is often limited to referring cases to schemes run by youth justice services.

Caution plus schemes, such as those of Northamptonshire, were cited as examples of good practice in the 1996 Audit Commission report, *Misspent Youth*. The 1997 government white paper, *No More Excuses*, suggested that caution plus should be used as a model for the proposed final warning scheme and this is what

has happened as 'change programmes' aimed at reducing reoffending now accompany final warnings. The research evidence suggests that the effectiveness of final warnings in terms of reducing reoffending is the same with and without a 'change programme', however. The introduction of 'conditional cautions' for adults in the Criminal Justice Act 2003 is modelled on the new final warning scheme for young offenders.

Roger Evans

Related entries

Caution; Reparation; Reprimands and final warnings; Restorative cautioning.

Key texts and sources

Evans, R. and Ellis, R. (1997) *Police Cautioning in the 1990s. Home Office Research Findings* 52. London: Home Office.

Evans, R. and Wilkinson, C. (1990) 'Variations in police cautioning policy and practice in England and Wales', *Howard Journal of Criminal Justice*, 29: 155–76.

See the Office of Public Sector Information's website (**http://www.opsi.gov.uk/ACTS/en2003/2003en44.htm**) for the text of the Criminal Justice Act 2003.

CHILD ABUSE

Child abuse is a generic term used to describe a range of actions or omissions that are likely to be injurious to, or to compromise, a child's development, health or safety. While child abuse is generally instigated by adults, the underlying abuse of 'power' can also take place between children. It can take different forms and may include sexual abuse, physical abuse, emotional abuse and neglect. One or more of these categories of abuse may be present together or individually in a single episode or over a period of time.

What constitutes child abuse continues to vary and broaden due to changes in societal values and cultural expectations, implying that 'child abuse' is, at least in part, a 'social construction'. Its existence in the UK has been openly acknowledged since the 1800s. The term 'child abuse' came into common use in the 1980s, and understandings of child abuse have been affected by international developments and by numerous UK inquiries into child deaths and into professional practice in protecting children (for example, Maria Colwell in 1974; the Short Inquiry of 1984; Jasmine Beckford in 1985; the Cleveland Inquiry of 1988; Kimberley Carlisle and Tyra Henry in 1987; and, most recently, the Victoria Climbie Inquiry of 2003). The findings of these and other inquiries have informed and contributed to the legislation and guidance in the UK in relation to the definitions of abuse and the processes of protecting children from physiological and/or psychological maltreatment, within/between families, within institutions, by strangers and by peer groups.

The legislative frameworks and government-issued guidance has similarly revisited and refined definitions of abuse, agency scope and practice. Contemporary law, guidance, definitions and practice principally stem from the Children Acts 1989 and 2004, and the Adoption and Children Act 2002, alongside the government's 'Working Together' guidance issued in 1991, 2000 and, most recently, in 2006.

The current threshold for compulsory intervention in family life due to child abuse is reasonable cause to suspect that a child 'is suffering, or is likely to suffer, significant harm' (Children Act 1989, ss. 31(2)(b) and 47(1)(b)). Harm is defined as 'ill treatment' (sexual, physical or mental), 'impairment of health' ('physical or mental health') or 'impairment of development' ('physical, intellectual, emotional, social or behavioural'). The significance of any harm is guided by a comparison 'with that which could reasonably be expected of a similar child' (s. 31(9)). Such a decision is a matter for multi-agency assessment, taking into account each child's individual circumstances and the currently accepted 'norms' of childhood developmental trajectories.

Many children who come to the attention of the youth justice system have experience of, or have previously experienced (witnessed, heard, been subject to), abusive situations or events. Every youth justice worker should be familiar with his or her role and responsibilities relating to child abuse disclosure and consequent intervention. These are contained in local Safeguarding Children Board policies and procedures.

Sue Howarth

Related entries

Children in custody; Corporal punishment; Safeguarding; 'Schedule one' offenders; Sex Offender register; Victims.

Key texts and sources

Corby, B. (2000) *Child Abuse: Towards a Knowledge Base*. Milton Keynes: Open University Press.

HM Government (2006) *Working Together to Safeguard Children: A Guide to Interagency Working to Safeguard and Promote the Welfare of Children*. London: HMSO.

Munro, E. (2002) *Effective Child Protection*. London: Sage.

See also the National Society for the Protection of Cruelty to Children's website (http//www.nspcc.org.uk/). Every Child Matters is available online at http//www.everychildmatters.gov.uk/.

CHILD AND ADOLESCENT MENTAL HEALTH SERVICES (CAMHS)

Child and Adolescent Mental Health Services (CAMHS) refers to the range of services available in a specific area that provide help and treatment for children and young people who are experiencing various mental health difficulties.

Child and Adolescent Mental Health Services (CAMHS) is not a specific service but a framework to describe how mental health services for children and young people are provided across a range of primary and specialist services. These services are not necessarily within the NHS but can be purchased and provided by a range of agencies.

There has been some variation and misunderstanding regarding what CAMHS is and the types of services it provides. All four countries in the UK refer to 'Comprehensive CAMHS'. This term is used to cover all people and agencies that provide a service that contributes to the mental health of a child or young person. This includes those services whose main activity does *not* necessarily involve providing mental health services (including GPs, teachers and social workers) and those services whose main activity *does* involve the provision of mental health services (the full range of mental health professionals). Another definition that has been widely used refers to CAMHS as *only* including mental health professionals. This is referred to as 'Specialist CAMHS'.

The concept of CAMHS was first described in the now seminal report *Together We Stand* (Williams and Richardson 1995). This describes a four-tiered system, as follows:

- *Tier 1*: universal services provided by those who are not mental health specialists (including GPs, health visitors, youth offending team workers).
- *Tier 2*: services provided by professionals working in primary care (youth offending team workers may also be located here and/or at tier 3, depending upon their expertise and particular local service arrangements).
- *Tier 3*: specialist multidisciplinary teams who deal with more severe, complex and persistent problems (for example, mental health in-reach teams).
- *Tier 4*: highly specialized services (for example, inpatient units, including secure forensic units).

There have been some misconceptions about the tiered model. Some erroneously believe that a child enters at tier 1 and works up whereas, in reality, he or she may simultaneously require services from different tiers. Furthermore, workers at tier 1 might be supported by professionals at tiers 2 or 3, including youth offending team workers who may be located at different tiers.

Despite processes of political devolution and jurisdictional specificities, all four countries of the UK still refer to the tiered model in their CAMHS policy documents. There has been some variation in how this framework has been developed and applied across the UK, but it has created a common language for describing and commissioning services.

The 'Comprehensive CAMHS' model is everyone's business and should be available for every child and young person with mental health difficulties. Many young people in the youth justice system have significant mental health needs, and they require the range of services as much as, or even more than, other identifiable groups of young people. However, for various reasons, many young people cannot or do not access the services they need.

Paula Lavis

Related entries

Every Child Matters; Mental health and young offenders; Secure accommodation; Safeguarding; Youth Matters.

Key texts and sources

Department of Health (2006a) *Promoting the Mental Health and Psychological Well-being of Children and Young People: Report on the Implementation of Standard 9 of the National Service Framework for Children, Young People and Maternity Services.* London: Department of Health (available online at **http://www.dh.gov.uk/assetRoot/04/14/06/79/04140679.pdf**).

Scottish Executive (2005) *The Mental Health of Children and Young People: A Framework for Promotion, Prevention and Care.* Edinburgh: Scottish Executive (available online at **http://www.headsupscotland.co.uk/documents/Framework_24Oct05.pdf**).

Welsh Assembly Government (2005) *National Service Framework for Children, Young People and Maternity Services in Wales.* Cardiff: Welsh Assembly Government.

Williams, R. and Richardson, G. (1995) *Together We Stand: The Commissioning, Role and Management of Child and Adolescent Mental Health Services: An NHS Health Advisory Service (HAS) Thematic Review.* London: HMSO.

See also the 2006 Bamford Review of mental health and learning disability in Northern Ireland (A Vision of a Comprehensive Child and Adolescent Mental Health Service) (available online at **http://www.rmhldni.gov.uk/**).

CHILD POVERTY

Child poverty refers to those children (under the age of 18) who experience the deprivations of poverty.

There is no universally agreed definition of poverty, for either adults or children. Early researchers understood poverty as the lack of physical provisions for sustaining life. More recently, however, conceptions of poverty have shifted from absolute terms to relative terms. Poverty is now defined in relation to citizenship and whether individuals can participate in, and contribute to, the life of their community. This view of poverty, or 'social exclusion', defines impoverished individuals as those whose lack of material, cultural and social resources exclude them from 'the minimum acceptable way of life' in the society to which they belong. In this respect, contemporary definitions of poverty recognize not just material deprivation or income but also the impact that lack of material resources has in relation to individuals' activities, patterns of life and access to the full benefits of being a member of any particular society.

Since the 1980s, policymakers, politicians and researchers in the UK have focused increasingly on child poverty, not least because the UK has consistently had the highest rate of child poverty in Europe – regardless of the specific methodology by which child poverty is measured. By the late 1990s, the Luxembourg Income Survey ranked the UK as having the third highest rate of child poverty across the 'developed' world. Despite the New Labour government's 'historic pledge' to end child poverty by 2020, current statistics for the UK make grim reading (Unicef 2007). In 2006, the government reported that there were still 2.4 million children living in poverty in the UK. Anti-child poverty campaign groups have contested this figure, however, claiming that the national statistics conceal both the depth of poverty many children experience and the variations across regions, and that recent government drives to 'lift children out of poverty' have only benefitted those who fell just below the poverty line.

Fundamental to understanding what child poverty means is recognizing both the deleterious effects that poverty has on children's outcomes (for example, poor educational attainment, poor health, low income as adults, high rates of criminalization, disproportionate prospects of imprisonment) and that children's experience of impoverishment is different from the adult experience. Recent qualitative studies confirm that children will often seek to protect their parents from the effects of poverty through self-denial and moderation of their needs and wants. More importantly, however, children also develop their own survival strategies to cope with the deprivations of poverty, just as they will develop their own strategies for maintaining social acceptance and inclusion – albeit in ways that are circumscribed by their material and social privations. The importance of recognizing child poverty and its impact in the context of youth justice cannot be overstated.

Jo Phoenix

Related entries

Every Child Matters; Social exclusion; Social inclusion.

Key texts and sources

Ridge, T. (2002) *Childhood Poverty and Social Exclusion: From a Child's Perspective*. Bristol: Policy Press.

Unicef (2007) *Child Poverty in Perspective: An Overview of Child Well-being in Rich Countries*. Florence: UNICEF.

See also the Child Poverty Action Group's website (http://www.cpag.org.uk) and the Joseph Rowntree Foundation's 'Child poverty' website (http://www.jrf.org.uk/child-poverty/).

CHILD PROSTITUTION

> Child prostitution refers to the involvement of children (those aged under 18 years) in the commercial exchange of sex for money.

Children and young people's involvement in prostitution is conditioned by many of the same factors that condition adult women's involvement in prostitution – namely, children and young people can be exploited, coerced and compelled into selling sex for money and, like adults, children and young people may become involved through the force of social and economic necessity, drug and alcohol problems, and the aggregate effects of poverty, marginalization and social exclusion. It is important, however, to distinguish between child prostitution and the sexual exploitation of children and young people. The sexual exploitation of children and young people encompasses everything from child pornography to the exchange of sex for non-financial gain, such as lifts in cars, accommodation, mobile telephones and so on. The majority of children in prostitution, as defined above, are 14–17-year-olds and, therefore, calling their activities 'child' prostitution is something of a misnomer. These young people, who often find themselves without families, education, employment or training, are vulnerable to the exploitative activities of others and/or also find themselves in positions whereby selling sex for money is seen as less risky than other (criminogenic) survival activities.

In March 2000, the Department of Health and the Home Office jointly issued *Safeguarding Children Involved in Prostitution* (*SCIP*). *SCIP* advised that the involvement of children in prostitution is not a simple matter of offending; rather, it is an indication that a young person could be 'at risk' of significant harm if not already suffering from abuse. As such, *SCIP* informed agencies of their statutory obligation to: (1) treat these children as victims (and not offenders); (2) safeguard and promote their welfare; (3) work together to create 'exit strategies'; and (4) use the full force of the criminal law against those who exploit and coerce young people in the course of their involvement in prostitution. Importantly, *SCIP* and all subsequent policy reforms have not decriminalized prostitution for the under 18-year-olds.

One of the principal problems associated with policy and practice reform is that the social and economic realities of many young people's lives are not fully recognized and taken into account. Young people, whose economic and social instability is accentuated by exclusion from the labour market and welfare benefits system and further compounded by policy responses that criminalize them, are, in key respects, victims of abuse. A second difficulty of such reform is that a 'persistent returners' clause was retained, wherein it is claimed that not all young people in prostitution are necessarily victims of coercion and some are involved voluntarily. For these young people criminal justice intervention is deemed appropriate. With that, two very different – and perhaps incompatible – modes of intervention and regulation coexist (child protection and youth justice), creating enormous problems for the young people themselves and for those who work with them.

Jo Phoenix

Related entries

Child abuse; Criminal Justice (Scotland) Act 2003; Decriminalization; Dispersal orders; Safeguarding; Street crime; Zero tolerance.

Key texts and sources

Melrose, M., Barrett, D. and Brodie, I. (1999) *One Way Street? Retrospectives on Childhood Prostitution*. London: Children's Society.

Pearce, J. with Williams, M. and Galvin, C. (2002) *It's Someone Taking a Part of You*. London: National Children's Bureau.

Phoenix, J. (2002) 'Youth prostitution policy reforms: new discourse, same old story', in P. Carlen (ed.) *Women and Punishment: A Struggle for Justice*. Cullompton: Willan Publishing.

Phoenix, J. (2003) 'Rethinking youth prostitution: national provision at the margins of child protection and youth justice', *Youth Justice*, 3: 152–68.

Van Meeuwen, A., Swann, S., McNeish, D. and Edwards, S.S.M. (1998) *Whose Daughter Next? Children Abused through Prostitution*. Ilford: Barnardo's.

CHILD SAFETY ORDERS (CSOs)

Created by s. 11 of the Crime and Disorder Act 1998, child safety orders (CSOs) are made in the family proceedings court on application from a local authority in relation to a child under the age of 10 who has satisfied one of the four necessary preconditions: the child has done something that would constitute an offence if he or she were over 10; his or her behaviour was such as to suggest the child was at risk of offending; the child's behaviour was disrupting and harassing to local residents; or the child has breached a local curfew.

Once imposed – possibly in conjunction with a parenting order – a child safety order (CSO) requires that the child comply with certain conditions (such as avoiding specified places or attending particular courses) for up to 12 months. Requirements should be tailored to address the behaviour that led to the CSO being imposed in the first place.

The government describes CSOs as serving a dual purpose: to ensure that the child concerned is receiving adequate *care* and that the child is being properly *controlled*. Child safety and community safety are thus conflated. This has led to criticism of CSOs on the basis that they are unnecessary in terms of child care/protection (given the powers to protect children that already exist under the Children Act 1989) and that they are ultimately a control measure, with the child welfare presentation comprising little more than a disingenuous 'smokescreen'.

A further problem with CSOs is that they blur the distinction between children who are legally criminally responsible and those who are not. This is compounded by the fact that England and Wales has one of the lowest ages of criminal responsibility in western Europe. By targeting the under-10s the rationale, apparently, is that criminal tendencies will be 'nipped in the bud'. CSOs also fudge the distinction between children who have actually offended and those who have not, yet, while technically a civil order, CSOs impose on their subjects control measures akin to a criminal order. The child may find him or herself monitored by the same youth offending team that monitors children who *have* offended, leading to the danger that the child may start to see him or herself as 'criminal' or, indeed, that others may view the child in this way.

The CSO might be said to exemplify a prevalent trend in youth justice policy and practice, moving away from criminal offending towards a more all-embracing concern with behaviour that causes offence. Furthermore, the fact that CSOs may be directed at children who are seen to be *at risk* of offending is indicative of another key movement in modern youth justice policy towards actuarialism and pre-emptive intervention.

Charlotte Walsh

Related entries

Actuarialism; Crime and Disorder Act 1998; Criminalization; Criminal responsibility; Curfew; Early intervention; Parenting orders.

Key texts and sources

Home Office (2000) T*he Crime and Disorder Act Guidance Document: Child Safety Order*. London: Home Office (available online at http://www.homeoffice.gov.uk/documents/guidance-child-curfew?view=Binary).

House of Commons (1998) *The Crime and Disorder Bill [HL] [Bill 167 of 1997–1998]: Youth Justice, Criminal Procedures and Sentencing*. London: House of Commons.

Piper, C. (1999) 'The Crime and Disorder Act 1998: child and community "safety"', *Modern Law Review*, 62: 397–408.

Walsh, C. (1999) 'Imposing order: child safety orders and local child curfew schemes', *Journal of Social Welfare and Family Law*, 21: 135–49.

See the Office of Public Sector Information's website (http://www.opsi.gov.uk/acts/acts1998/19980037.htm) for the text of the Crime and Disorder Act 1998, ss. 11, 12 and 13 (as amended by s. 60 of the Children Act 2004).

CHILDREN ACT 1908

The Children Act 1908 established a separate juvenile court, made the death penalty illegal for those under 16 years of age and enacted, re-enacted or extended a wide range of measures to protect children.

The Children Act 1908 is best remembered for establishing a juvenile court for England, Wales, Scotland and Northern Ireland. This was the culmination of a long-standing concern that there should be a forum for processing children and young people that was separate from the adult courts. The aim of those responsible for the 1908 Act was that children who offend should be reformed, not punished, and that all effort should be made to ensure that children were dealt with in ways that did not put them in contact with adult offenders. Therefore imprisonment was abolished for children under the age of 14 and restricted for those aged 14 and 15.

The juvenile court dealt with matters relating to childcare/welfare as well as offending by children. In Scotland, reforms were introduced in the 1960s, but elsewhere the dual role of the court lasted for almost a century, being replaced in England and Wales with the introduction of the youth court (and a separate family proceedings court) following the implementation of the Children Act 1989 and the Criminal Justice Act 1991.

The 1908 Act also included measures in relation to foster parents, prosecutions for child cruelty, the regulation of the employment of children, remand, industrial schools and much more. It also confirmed the common law right to use 'reasonable and moderate chastisement' in disciplining children and left the age of criminal responsibility at 7.

Christine Piper

Related entries

Capital punishment; Corporal punishment; Criminal responsibility; Juvenile courts; Welfare; Youth courts.

Key texts and sources

Buckley, H. and O'Sullivan, E. (2006) 'The interface between youth justice and child protection in Ireland', in M. Hill et al. (eds) *Youth Justice and Child Protection*. London: Jessica Kingsley.
Morris, A. and Giller, H. (1987) *Understanding Juvenile Justice*. London: Croom Helm (ch. 1).
Stewart, J. (1995) 'Children, parents and the state: the Children Act 1908', *Children and Society*, 9: 90–9.

CHILDREN ACT 1989

The Children Act 1989 provided a new legal framework and new legal concepts for the protection of children, the provision of services for children, the supervision of child-related activities and the resolution of disputes over children's upbringing in England and Wales.

The Children Act 1989 was introduced as a comprehensive new legal framework – omitting only revised provisions for adoption – for regulating child and family issues. It was a response to several separate problems: difficulties in the care system about parental autonomy and social work powers arising from various 'scandals' in the 1970s and 1980s; arrangements for children on the separation or divorce of their parents; the need to incorporate rights for children; and the administrative imperative to amalgamate separate systems of public and private law and legal process. The focus was on the limits of state power and court involvement, as well as the role and extent of parental duties, responsibilities and powers. The Act was designed to protect children while encouraging parental responsibility for them and for resolving disputes over their upbringing. Children as 'offenders' are not afforded a specifically high profile within the provisions of the Children Act 1989. Moreover, the 'separation' of children as *victims* and children as *offenders* was institutionalized by the separation of the civil (childcare) and criminal (youth justice) functions of the juvenile court, and the establishment of family proceedings courts (Children Act 1989) and youth courts (Criminal Justice Act 1991).

Section 105(1) of the Act confirmed the under 18-year-old to be a 'child' in line with the United Nations Convention on the Rights of the Child, which the UK government ratified in 1991, the year most of the Children Act provisions were implemented and when the jurisdiction of the youth court was raised to include 17-year-olds by the Criminal Justice Act 1991. Further, s. 1 of the Children Act 1989 restated that the welfare of the child must be paramount in all decisions regarding the child's upbringing. It also added a 'welfare checklist', which includes 'the ascertainable wishes and feelings of the child concerned (considered in the light of his age and understanding)'.

Section 2 introduced a new concept of parental responsibility. The aim, feeding into a prevalent political ideology, was to emphasize responsibility over rights such that parental responsibility held by a mother or married father can never be 'lost' (except by death, adoption or the majority of the child) – even if the parents separate or if the child is in care or custody. The thrust of the Act was to give priority to parental responsibility and autonomy while, at the same time, giving the local authority (and also the police) clearer powers to protect children. Section 31 consequently introduced a new test for the making of a care order by a court: that 'the child concerned is suffering, or is likely to suffer, significant harm' and that the harm is the result of the care given by the parent, or that the child is 'beyond parental control'. This has been interpreted as a strict test. The focus is on risk of significant harm, not risk of offending, and is a test that no longer provides clear encouragement for the use of care or supervision orders in relation to a child who has offended.

There are also several sections of the Act which, since the case bought by the Howard League for Penal Reform in 2002 (*The Howard League for Penal Reform* v. *The Secretary of State for the Home Department and the Department of Health* – the 'Munby judgment'), are now accepted as relevant to all children, including children who are detained in Prison Service establishments and other secure accommoda-

tion. In particular, ss. 17 and 47 of the Children Act 1989 apply.

Section 17 introduced a new concept of the child 'in need' and imposed a duty on the local authority 'to safeguard and promote the welfare' of such children in its area. The hope was that a wider range of services would be provided without the 'stigma' of social work intervention. Schedule 2 of the Act also imposes the specific duty to 'take reasonable steps' to reduce the need to bring, *inter alia*, 'criminal proceedings against such children'. There has, however, been criticism of the low priority given to that duty. The Youth Justice Board web page, referring to s. 17, states:

> *It can be argued that all young people who offend or at risk of offending meet these criteria and should therefore be considered as vulnerable children in need. In reality this does not happen and YOTs [youth offending teams] must seek to develop protocols and local working agreements to ensure that young people are able to access the services they are entitled to under the Act.*

Under s. 47 of the Act the local authority has a duty to make inquires as to whether it ought to take action to safeguard a child's welfare. This duty is activated by one of several criteria, including: the child is in police protection; has contravened a ban imposed by a curfew notice; or that the local authority has 'reasonable cause to suspect' that the child is at risk of 'significant harm'.

Further, s. 20 of the Children Act 1989 requires the local authority to provide accommodation for children if certain conditions apply and, specifically in relation to those aged 16 and over, the local authority must provide such accommodation if it considers that the child's welfare is 'likely to be seriously prejudiced if they do not provide him with accommodation'. Children provided with accommodation by the local authority under s. 20 – and those subject to a care order under s. 31 of the Children Act 1989 – are 'looked-after children'. The key problems highlighted by research and practice experience have been the low standards of educational achievement and the higher-than-average incidence of offending by – and criminalization of – such children. There is also major concern that there is insufficient care planning, foster placements and support for young people leaving prison.

Christine Piper

Related entries

Care orders; Children in custody; Family proceedings court; Looked-after children (LAC); Munby judgement; Safeguarding; Secure accommodation; Welfare.

Key texts and sources

Bainham, A. (2005) *Children – the Modern Law* (3rd edn). Bristol: Family Law (ch. 2).

Nacro (2002b) *Looked After Children and Youth Justice: Anomalies in the Law*. Youth Crime Briefing. London: Nacro.

See the Office of Public Sector Information's website (http://www.opsi.gov.uk/acts/acts1989/Ukpga_19 890041_en_1.htm) for the text of the Children Act 1989. R (on the application of the Howard League for Penal Reform) v. The Secretary of State for the Home Department [2002] EWHC 2497 is available online at http://www.bailii.org/ew/cases/EWHC/Admin/2002/2497.html. The Youth Justice Board's document, Accommodation: Children Act 1989, is available online at http://www.yjb.gov.uk/engb/practitioners/Accommodation/LegislationandResponsibilities/ChildrenAct1989/.

CHILDREN ACT 2004

The Children Act 2004 set up a new framework for the provision of services to and for children and young people, applying separate provisions for England and Wales. In particular, it imposes new safeguarding duties and encourages interagency co-operation, as well as new duties and powers relating to family proceedings in Wales and to private fostering.

The Children Act 2004 is a vital part of the 'refocusing' initiative aimed to engineer a conceptual and organizational shift from a narrow focus on child protection to a broader preventative approach to policy and practice, implemented through support for the family and the 'child in need' (Department of Health 1998). The Act was preceded by an important consultation paper – *Every Child Matters* (Department for Education and Skills 2003) – which was itself prompted, at least in part, by the inquiry on the death of Victoria Climbié.

Every Child Matters stated that:

The Government's aim is for every child, whatever their background or their circumstances, to have the support they need to:

- *Be healthy*
- *Stay safe*
- *Enjoy and achieve*
- *Make a positive contribution*
- *Achieve economic well-being.*

The Children Act 2004 incorporated these outcomes in s. 10. A subsequent publication – *Change for Children in the Criminal Justice System* (Home Office 2005) – stated that the 'key focus' of the youth justice system is on the second and fourth of the above outcomes, and 'offending' is contrasted with making 'positive contribution'.

The rationale for the Act's provisions is that interagency co-operation, more flexible funding possibilities and increased communication and data sharing will lead to an improvement in provision for children 'at risk'. The Act, therefore, includes lists of statutory partners in this project, and the youth offending team (YOT) is included. For example, the YOT is one of the seven partners of the children's services authority (local authority) listed in s. 10(4) of the Act, all of whom 'must co-operate with the authority in the making of arrangements' as specified, 'with a view to improving the well-being of children' in relation to the five 'Every Child Matters' outcomes. Sections 11 and 28 (for England and Wales, respectively) also impose the duty to ensure that services and statutory responsibilities 'are discharged having regard to the need to safeguard and promote the welfare of children', a duty that applies to numerous agencies, including YOTs. To these ends, a children's services authority and any of their relevant partner agencies may provide staff, goods, services, accommodation or other resources.

The local YOT and the governor of any prison that holds children must also be represented on the local safeguarding boards set up by s. 13 of the Children Act 2004 to replace area child protection committees. These boards are mandated to co-ordinate steps to safeguard children's welfare and so should include within their remit the welfare of children already in the youth justice system.

The duty to achieve the five outcomes for children is to be implemented through children's trust partnerships to provide services, using, if necessary, pooled resources and joint commissioning. Prior to the Children Act 2004, developments in relation to reducing youth offending included preventative programmes organized by multi-agency youth inclusion support panels for children aged 8–12 and 13–18, run as part of the Youth Justice Board's 'Prevention programme'. Such initiatives gained additional funding in 2005 and also drew on grants from the Children's Fund (established in the Department for Education and Skills in 2000). This fund is due to be phased out by 2008 when children's trusts should be established in all local authority areas.

The role of the local YOT and the children's trust will therefore be crucial. The statutory guidance notes that YOTs will have 'an important role to play' in the trusts in delivering services relevant to existing statutory duties (HM Government 2005: para. 1.16) and that they can also 'jointly commission and pool budgets with other partners for the benefit of children at risk of offending and those involved in the youth justice system' (para. 2.51). Whether this achieves more or less for children who have offended remains to be seen. The results of phase one of an evaluation of the relationship between YOTs and the developing trusts suggest a varied, complex and changing picture with uncertainty as to how YOTs will align with, or be integrated in, children's services and criminal justice agencies. Potentially of importance is that the annual Youth Justice Plan will need to be aligned with the Children and Young People's Plan, but research on pilot, 'pathfinder' trusts has shown differences in policy emphases and in definition of 'need', as well as the composition of trusts.

The Children Act 2004 also established a Children's commissioner for England and restated the functions of the commissioners for the other countries of the UK. The broad policy context for the most important provisions of this Act derives from the social inclusion agenda of the New Labour government and the 'cross-cutting reviews' it set up in 2000–01. Specifically, the Children at Risk Review (HM Treasury 2001) aimed 'to establish the key outcome targets for children's services' whereby actuarial calculations of 'risk' were used to justify early intervention policies. In this sense, offending has been afforded a high level of policy priority.

In the context of 'investing in children', the core aim of the Children Act 2004 is to increase the possibilities of effectively directing appropriate resources to children over a wide range of services, both targeted and universal. This explicit investment agenda may, as Ruth Lister argues, 'represent a politically astute discourse for politicians to use in a culture unsympathetic to children' (2005: 455). However, the rationale is conditional and the child who does not accept the opportunities offered or who does not respond positively to an intervention designed to reduce the risk of (re)offending may well be treated more severely subsequently by other agencies, notably the courts.

Christine Piper

Related entries

Children's commissioners; Children's trusts; Every Child Matters (ECM); Looked-after children (LAC); Munby judgement; Safeguarding; Youth-justice plans.

Key texts and sources

Department for Education and Skills (2003) *Every Child Matters.* London: DFES.

Department of Health (1998) *Working Together to Safeguard Children: New Government Proposals for Inter-agency Cooperation* (consultation paper). London: HMSO.

HM Government (2005) *Statutory Guidance on Inter-agency Co-operation to Improve the Wellbeing of Children: Children's Trusts.* London: DfES.

HM Treasury (2001) *Children at Risk: Cross-cutting Review.* London: HM Treasury.

Lister, R. (2005) 'Investing in the citizen-workers of the future', in H. Hendrick (ed.) *Child Welfare and Social Policy*. Bristol: Policy Press.

Smith, D. (2006b) *Social Inclusion and Early Desistance from Crime*. Report 12. Edinburgh: Centre for Law and Society, University of Edinburgh.

See the Office of Public Sector Information's website (**http://www.opsi.gov.uk/acts/acts2004/20040031. htm**) for the text of the Children Act 2004.

CHILDREN AND FAMILY COURT ADVISORY AND SUPPORT SERVICE (CAFCASS)

The Children and Family Court Advisory and Support Service (CAFCASS) was established under s. 11 of the Criminal Justice and Court Services Act 2000, which was brought into force on 1 April 2001. CAFCASS is a service that is only available in, and applicable to, England.

The Children and Family Court Advisory and Support Service (CAFCASS) is prescribed under s. 12 of the Criminal Justice and Court Services Act 2000 as having certain functions in relation to any family proceedings brought before the courts of England in which the welfare of children (other than those ordinarily resident in Wales to whom other statutes establishing a differently named and constituted service apply) is of concern. These functions relate to safeguarding and promoting the welfare of the children; to giving advice to any court about any application made to it in such proceedings; to making provision for the children to be represented in such proceedings; and, finally, to providing information, advice and other support for the children and their families.

CAFCASS was formed from the union of the old divorce court welfare service (which had the duty of providing reports to court under s. 7 of the Children Act 1989 in cases arising from parental disputes over the futures of their children) and the former Guardian ad Litem and Reporting Officer panels (which had responsibility for providing reports to court in care and supervision order proceedings under Part IV of the Children Act 1989; in adoption proceedings, originally under the Adoption Act 1976 but now under the Adoption and Children Act 2002; and in parental order applications under s. 30 of the Human Fertilization and Embryology Act 1990). For the first two years following its establishment, CAFCASS, or 'the Service' as it is referred to now in statutes (see, for example, the Children and Adoption Act 2006), experienced difficulties both in the recruitment of staff (following the departure of many experienced personnel as a result of the amalgamation) and in responding to the demands placed upon it (as a result of the rising numbers of cases going before the courts under both s. 8 and Part IV of the Children Act 1989). This was the subject of much comment in academic journals and in the national press by concerned judges.

In addition to providing reports to the court (which must be based on what the CAFCASS officer believes to be in the best interests of the child in all the types of proceedings referred to above), the Service has recently been charged – under extensive amendments to ss. 11 and 16 of the Children Act 1989 by the Children and Adoption Act 2006 – with the onerous tasks of assessing the risks to children and with monitoring the contact between children and parents where such has proved difficult in the past for a variety of reasons.

Christina Lyon

Related entries

Children Act 1989; Criminal Justice and Court Services Act 2000; Family proceedings court.

Key texts and sources

See the Office of Public Sector Information's website for the texts of the Adoption and Children Act 2002 (**http://www.opsi.gov.uk/acts/acts2002/2002 0038.htm**), the Children Act 1989 (**http://www. opsi.gov.uk/acts/acts1989/Ukpga_19890041_en_1. htm**), the Children and Adoption Act 2006 (**http://www.opsi.gov.uk/acts/acts2006/20060020. htm**) and the Criminal Justice and Court Services Act 2000 (**http://www.opsi.gov.uk/acts/acts2000/ 20000043.htm**).

CHILDREN AND YOUNG PERSONS ACT 1933

The Children and Young Persons Act 1933 aimed 'to consolidate certain enactments relating to persons under the age of eighteen years' and so re-enacted and revised measures relating to the protection and employment of children generally, and to criminal proceedings in particular.

While much of this large and important piece of legislation has since been repealed or re-enacted, many sections of the Children and Young Persons Act 1933 have been in force until relatively recently and some sections are still valuable law.

Section 1 of the Act is still the statutory basis for the offence of child cruelty, which applies to those over 16 who commit this offence against those under 16. While this provision is crucial in child protection, it can also lead to the prosecution of a 16–17-year-old minor. A similar ambiguity is found in relation to persons convicted of an offence listed in the first schedule of the Act (a 'Schedule 1' offender). Such persons are placed on a register held by the local authority of persons who are a 'risk to children'. Paradoxically, while the intention is to protect children, anyone over 10 may be listed and be subject to scrutiny from social services and other agencies for life as there is no review mechanism.

Section 44 of the Act is also still very important for children and young people in court proceedings because it provides that the court 'shall have regard to the welfare of the child or young person' who comes before it. This principle now also applies to the Crown Prosecution Service. This is a weak welfare principle in comparison with the 'paramouncy principle' in the Children Act 1989, which states that the child's welfare must be the determining factor in the court's decision about a child's upbringing. The duty to 'have regard to' means that, providing consideration has been given to the interests of the child or young person, the youth, magistrates' and Crown courts can legally give precedence to other interests such as the need to protect the public and to prevent reoffending. Nevertheless, that provision and the further arrangements in the 1933 Act for dealing with children in juvenile courts were important in stressing the need for the separate and different treatment of children. Further, s. 53 of the Act was intended to restrict the use of longer periods of detention only to those who had committed murder and a very small number of 'grave' crimes. The current version (in ss. 90–91 of the Powers of Criminal Courts (Sentencing) Act 2000) has, in comparison, much wider powers.

Section 39 also remains in force and empowers the court to restrict the identification of a child who is involved in proceedings as a defendant, victim or witness (Dodd 2002). Section 45 of the Youth Justice and Criminal Evidence Act 1999, when implemented, will replace this provision in relation to the reporting of criminal proceedings involving those under 18. Reporting has recently been a high-profile issue in relation to the trial of young offenders and has been dealt with in practice directions issued by the Lord Chief Justice in 2000 and 2006. The welfare ethos of the 1933 Act thus contrasts with the current emphasis on 'naming and shaming'.

Christine Piper

Related entries

Children and Young Persons Act 1963; Juvenile court; Grave offences; Powers of Criminal Courts (Sentencing) Act 2000; 'Schedule one' offenders; Welfare.

Key texts and sources

Dodd, M. (2002) 'Children, the press – and a missed opportunity', *Child and Family Law Quarterly*, 103.
See **http://www.swarb.co.uk/acts/1933CaYPAct.shtml** for the text of the Children and Young Persons Act 1933. *Practice Direction: Trial of Children and Young Persons in the Crown Court, 16 February 2000* is available online at **http://www.dca.gov.uk/ypeople fr.htm**.

CHILDREN AND YOUNG PERSONS ACT 1963

> The Children and Young Persons Act 1963, which is mainly applicable to England and Wales, constituted the government's legislative response to the (1960) *Report of the Home Office Departmental Committee on Children and Young Persons* (the Ingleby Report).

As the fiftieth anniversary of the publication of the Ingleby Report approaches, two provisions of the Children and Young Persons Act 1963 stand out in retrospect as of special importance. The first concerns the age of criminal responsibility – that is, the minimum age at which a child may be charged with a criminal offence. The Ingleby Report had recommended that, in England and Wales, this age should be raised from 8 (at which it had been fixed by the Children and Young Persons Act 1933) to 12, with the possibility of a further rise to 13 or 14 'at some future date'. However, in the first draft of the 1963 Bill, the then Conservative government included no proposal to raise the age.

At the committee stage in the House of Lords debates, Baroness Barbara Wootton, a leading social scientist and a juvenile court magistrate, successfully moved an amendment raising the age of criminal responsibility to 12 but, subsequently, in the House of Commons and at the government's instigation, a compromise age of 10 was enacted. These short-term parliamentary manoeuvres nevertheless produced a result of enduring significance because the age of criminal responsibility has, in England and Wales, remained unchanged at 10 since 1963.

A second major provision of the 1963 Act concerned preventive work. The Ingleby Committee had noted with regret that, under the Children Act 1948, local authorities had no clear legal responsibility to undertake preventive work with families where there was a possibility that a child or children might have to be received into care. Hence, there were no funds to support such activities. Post-Ingleby discussions widened and strengthened the committee's original recommendation, and s. 1 of the 1963 Act gave local authorities (both in England and Wales and in Scotland) the powers they had long lobbied for: 'It shall be the duty of every local authority to make available such advice, guidance and assistance as may promote the welfare of children by diminishing the need to receive children into or keep them in care…or to bring children before a juvenile court.'

Although this specific legislative section was repealed in 1980, the preventive principle it embodied remains as a key component of contemporary child-care policy.

Anthony Bottoms

Related entries

Children and Young Persons Act 1969; Criminal responsibility.

> **Key texts and sources**
>
> Home Office (1960) *Report of the Home Office Departmental Committee on Children and Young Persons* (Cmnd 1191). London: HMSO.
> Packman, J. (1975) *The Child's Generation: Child Care Policy from Curtis to Houghton*. Oxford: Blackwell.
> Wootton, B. (1978) *Crime and Penal Policy: Reflections on Fifty Years' Experience*. London: George Allen & Unwin (ch. 9).

CHILDREN AND YOUNG PERSONS ACT 1969

> The Children and Young Persons Act 1969 is the most welfare-oriented legislation ever enacted with regard to the treatment of juvenile offenders in England and Wales. However, significant sections of the Act were never brought into force, and some provisions that were implemented proved to be very controversial in the 1970s.

The publication of the Ingleby Report in 1960 (see Children and Young Persons Act 1963) was the catalyst for a prolonged period of debate about juvenile justice policy in England and

Wales because powerful voices in the Labour Party and the social work profession regarded Ingleby's policy approach as too cautious.

In 1965, the incoming Labour government published a short white paper, *The Child, the Family and the Young Offender*, proposing a more welfare-oriented juvenile justice system. Among other things, this white paper suggested the abolition of the juvenile courts, mirroring (though with important differences of detail) the parallel proposals of the Kilbrandon Committee in Scotland (1964). In England and Wales, the proposed abolition of juvenile courts proved to be politically very controversial. A second white paper, *Children in Trouble*, was therefore published in 1968, retaining juvenile courts but, within this framework, rebalancing the system to give substantially more emphasis to welfare considerations. This policy approach was then passed into law in the Children and Young Persons Act 1969.

As with many UK statutes, the 1969 Act contained a section stating that the various sections of the Act would only come into force when so ordered by the relevant Secretary of State. In the case of the 1969 Act, there was a substantial difference between the Act as it reached the statute book and the Act as actually brought into force.

The original provisions of the Act are of two main types: those relating to *procedures* and those relating to *treatment*. As regards procedures, the Act created a court procedure termed 'care proceedings', which, to be successful, required proof of each of two separate issues: first, a basic 'ground for care' – which could be, for example, parental neglect of the child, non-attendance at school or the commission of a criminal offence; and, secondly, a requirement that the child or young person 'is in need of care or control which he is unlikely to receive unless the court makes an order' (s. 1(2)). (This second requirement was an early version of the 'no non-beneficial order' principle). As regards juveniles charged with criminal offences, the original version of the Act provided: (1) that no one under 14 should be prosecuted, but care proceedings using the 'offence ground' could be brought for persons aged 10 or over (10 remaining as the age of criminal responsibility);

and (2) that, while prosecutions could be mounted for some young persons aged 14 and under 17, there would be restrictions on prosecution even for this older age group, and care proceedings would normally be the preferred procedure for them. Thus the Act, in its original formulation, intended care proceedings to become the majority procedure for offence-based cases and the only procedure for non-offence-based cases.

However, the Labour government lost power in 1970 and the incoming Conservative Home Secretary decided not to implement compulsory care proceedings for under-14s charged with offences, nor to place any restrictions on prosecution for 14–17-year-olds. Thus, in practice, while care proceedings under the 1969 Act were implemented for non-offence cases, they became a dead letter for offence cases.

In considering the treatment provisions of the Act, one must distinguish between treatments available after successful care proceedings and treatments available after a prosecution. Analogously to the 1968 Scottish reforms, only two principal treatments were available after care proceedings: the supervision order and the care order (an order placing the child or young person in the care of the local authority until he or she reached the age of 18). Custodial sentences were not available after care proceedings. Since care proceedings were intended to be the main way of bringing offence-based cases before the juvenile court, it follows that the framers of the 1969 Act envisaged a substantial reduction in the use of custodial sentences.

The Conservative Home Secretary did bring into force the Act's provisions relating to the availability of the care order and the supervision order. Custodial sentences also remained available for older juveniles found guilty of an offence, but the former 'approved school order' was discontinued.

The care order, however, proved to be deeply unpopular with many juvenile court magistrates in the 1970s. Making an approved school order on a young offender had guaranteed that he or she would be sent to residential accommodation but, under a care order, the local authority had full discretion as to the placement of the child or young person. The small number of offence-based cases where local authorities placed the child in his or her own home became highly symbolic – in the 1970s – of a power struggle between magistrates and local authority social services departments (SSDs). One effect of this was that, in offence cases for older juveniles, courts used care orders less and custody more – a very paradoxical effect, given the Act's original intention markedly to reduce the use of custodial institutions for juvenile offenders.

Subsequently, from about 1980, social work academics (led by a group from Lancaster University; see Thorpe *et al.* 1980) began to cast doubts on the care order on different grounds from the magistrates – namely, its ineffectiveness in reducing offending behaviour. Its use in criminal cases therefore declined further in the 1980s, and it was abolished as an available sentence in offence cases by the Children Act 1989.

The Children and Young Persons Act 1969 has left little enduring trace on the youth justice system of England and Wales. However, one important indirect effect is worth noting. Because of the welfare orientation of the Act, its framers envisaged a substantial transfer of responsibilities for young offenders from the Probation Service to Social Services Departments (who have responsibility for the delivery of child welfare and child protection services). This policy (together with other changes to the probation service) resulted by the mid-1980s in SSDs becoming, in most areas, the lead agency for youth justice. Within SSDs there was then an increasing tendency to create specialist 'youth justice teams', sometimes with secondments from other agencies (including probation), and these youth justice teams became the forerunners of the youth offending teams created by the Crime and Disorder Act 1998. Had the 1969 Act not projected SSDs into a prominent role in youth justice provision, matters might well have turned out very differently.

Anthony Bottoms

Related entries

Care orders; Children's hearing system; Criminal responsibility; Intermediate treatment (IT); Juvenile courts; Net-widening; Supervision orders; Welfare.

Key texts and sources

Bottoms, A.E., McClean, J.D. and Patchett, K.W. (1970) 'Children, young persons and the courts – a survey of the new law', *Criminal Law Review*, 368–95.
Morris, A. and Giller, H. (1987) *Understanding Juvenile Justice.* London: Croom Helm (chs 3 and 4).
Thorpe, D.H., Smith, D., Green, C.J. and Paley, J.H. (1980) *Out of Care: The Community Support of Juvenile Offenders.* London: George Allen & Unwin.

CHILDREN FIRST

'Children First' refers to the principle that the way in which the criminal justice system should respond to young people who have committed offences is in terms of their status as *children*, and not as *offenders*.

Principally derived from the United Nations Convention on the Rights of the Child (UNCRC), the term 'Children First' is now commonly found in the titles of local, national and international policy documents concerning children in such fields as health, education, social services and, more generally, human/children's rights. This usage is very much *rights* based and, consequently, emphasizes the principle of the *best interests of the child*, often linked to the rights of children to participate in making decisions that affect their lives. It is rare to find Children First in policy and related documents that pre-date 2000 (reflecting the recent growth of the international children's rights movement) but even rarer to find Children First statements in policies concerning young people who offend.

Children First was first used in respect of young people and their treatment by the criminal justice system by Haines and Drakeford (1998). Their use of this term was not principally intended to draw on the children's rights framework (although it is entirely consistent with the UNCRC) but to articulate a philosophy for working with children in the criminal justice system. Children First was also intended to be an alternative to the predominance, which grew during the 1980s, of focusing on and responding to the offence rather than the child in the context of the realities of children's social situations and the emerging trend in the 'responsibilization' (Goldson 2001; see also Home Office 1997a) of youth, which justified ever increasing punitiveness in responding to youth offending.

The 'responsible child' who has failed or, worse, wilfully neglected to take advantage of the multiple opportunities modern society makes available, is the target of much contemporary youth justice policy. Children First challenges the idea that children are just younger versions of responsible adults and asserts the importance of putting the child back into youth justice policy and practice. Thus children should be treated differently and distinctly from adults. Some of the distinctive features of this approach include a recognition of the child's cognitive and emotional stage of development; an aversion to responding to the offence in isolation from the child's social circumstances; an allied aversion to interventions based on criminogenic need; and an assertion that interventions with children should be pro-social, based on promoting and encouraging positive outcomes (not just trying to control young people or punishing them) – thus ensuring that services are provided to children in a responsive and appropriate manner such that blocked opportunities are unblocked and 'opportunity' and 'choice' become reality not just rhetoric.

For the most part, Children First is just an idea and not one that has taken much hold in youth justice policy or practice domestically or internationally. There are, however, some exceptions. On the international stage, following the UNCRC, both the Council of Europe and the European Network of Ombudsmen for Children advocate separate systems for juveniles and adults. While both retain some sense of the responsibility of young people for their actions, they argue that this should be separate from the criminalization of youth and that retribution has no place in the youth justice system, which should, instead, focus on the rights of the child, rehabilitation and reintegration. Children First is more firmly enshrined in youth justice policy in Wales.

Kevin Haines

Related entries

All Wales Youth Offending Strategy; Children's human rights; Extending Entitlement (National Assembly for Wales); United Nations Convention on the Rights of the Child (UNCRC).

Key texts and sources

Cross, N., Evans, J. and Minkes, J. (2003) 'Still children first? Developments in youth justice in Wales', *Youth Justice*, 2: 151–62.
Goldson, B. (2001) 'The demonisation of children: from the symbolic to the institutional', in P. Foley et al. (eds) *Children in Society: Contemporary Theory, Policy and Practice*. Basingstoke: Palgrave.
Haines, K. and Drakeford, M. (1998) *Young People and Youth Justice*. Basingstoke: Macmillan.
Home Office (1997a) *No More Excuses: A New Approach to Tackling Youth Crime in England and Wales*. London: HMSO.

CHILDREN IN CUSTODY

'Children in custody' refers to prisoners under the age of 18, often known as 'juveniles'. In the UK, 'custody' comprises a variety of locked institutions: young offender institutions, secure training centres and secure children's homes (in England and Wales); young offender institutions and secure accommodation (in Scotland); and young offenders centres and the juvenile justice centre (in Northern Ireland).

The practice of detaining children in specialist forms of custody in the UK can be traced back to the establishment of the first penal institution exclusively for children at Parkhurst Prison for boys in England in 1838. Since that time a range of policy initiatives, statutory developments and carceral experiments have created and sustained a panoply of custodial institutions, including reformatories, industrial schools, Borstals, approved schools, remand centres, detention centres, training schools, youth custody centres, young offender institutions, secure units and secure training centres. Even if the stock and flow of child imprisonment varies across time and place

– often contingent upon the political vagaries of youth justice policy – ultimately, penal institutions retain a permanent foothold within national and international youth justice systems.

A range of international human rights standards, treaties, rules and conventions apply to children in custody. The United Nations Rules for the Protection of Juveniles Deprived of their Liberty (the JDL Rules) and the United Nations Convention on the Rights of the Child (UNCRC), both adopted by the United Nations in 1990, are particularly important. The primary purpose of such instruments is to mediate the use of custodial institutions for children and, when used, to safeguard the rights and needs of child prisoners. Article 37(b) of the UNCRC, for example, provides that the detention of children in custody should only be applied as 'a measure of last resort and for the shortest appropriate period of time'. Despite such rights-based protective provisions, however, some youth justice jurisdictions continue to place significant numbers of children in custody.

In the UK in recent years, youth justice law, policy and practice have taken a punitive turn, particularly in England and Wales where greater use of custody for children is made than in most other industrialized democratic countries in the world. Such penal practice has generated a consistent stream of critique from a wide range of authoritative sources, including international human rights bodies; parliamentary committees; independent inquiries; state inspectorates; academic research; penal reform organizations; and children's human rights agencies. Despite the weight and authority of such critique, however, successive governments since 1993 – both Conservative and New Labour – have continued to pursue a 'tough' line with regard to youth justice policy.

Much of the concern that centres around children in custody derives from the particular vulnerabilities of child prisoners. Throughout the world, child prisoners are routinely drawn from some of the most disadvantaged, damaged and distressed families, neighbourhoods and communities. Poverty, family discord, public care, drug and alcohol misuse, mental distress, ill-health, emotional, physical and sexual abuse,

self-harm, homelessness, isolation, loneliness, circumscribed educational and employment opportunities, and the most pressing sense of distress and alienation are defining characteristics of children in custody. In the UK, research has revealed that approximately half of children held in custody at any given time have been, or remain, involved with social services departments and other welfare agencies and a significant proportion have biographies scarred by adult abuse and violation. In 2001, a major review of the educational needs of children in custody in England and Wales by Her Majesty's Chief Inspector of Prisons and the Office for Standards in Education found that 84 per cent of child prisoners had been excluded from school; 86 per cent had regularly not attended school; 52 per cent had left school aged 14 years or younger; 29 per cent had left school aged 13 years or younger; and 73 per cent described their educational achievement as 'nil'. In short, the combination of poverty and structural exclusion, neglect by welfare, education and health agencies, and a 'tough' policy climate renders such children profoundly vulnerable.

The vulnerabilities of children in custody are often compounded by the very experience of detention itself. Indeed, the conditions and treatment typically endured by child prisoners routinely violate their emotional, psychological and physical integrity. It is widely recognized that bullying is particularly problematic. The most obvious expression of bullying is physical assault. Child prisoners are also exposed to many other forms of 'bullying', however, including sexual abuse, verbal abuse, psychological abuse, extortion and theft, and lending and trading cultures – particularly in relation to tobacco – involving exorbitant rates of interest that accumulate on a daily basis. Moreover, in 2006, a major independent inquiry led by Lord Carlile of Berriew exposed problematic yet routine practices in custodial facilities holding children in England and Wales, including the use of physical restraint, solitary confinement and strip searching. High rates of self-harm among child prisoners, together with the deaths of 30 children in penal institutions in England and Wales between 1990 and 2007, raise the most serious questions regarding children in custody.

The humanitarian critique of child imprisonment is compounded by the enormous fiscal expense incurred by placing children in custody and by the spectacular failings of custodial institutions when measured in terms of crime reduction and community safety. In 2003–4, for example, child imprisonment in England and Wales cost £293.5 million and, in October 2004, a Parliamentary Select Committee reported that reconviction rates stood at 80 per cent with regard to released child prisoners.

The combination of the provisions of international human rights instruments, burgeoning human rights concerns, the damaging consequences of placing children in custody, the huge expense of child imprisonment and the minimal positive return in creating a safer society has led many leading criminological commentators to advocate the implementation of reductionist and abolitionist strategies.

Barry Goldson and John Muncie

Related entries

Abolitionism; Children's human rights; Deaths in custody; Juvenile Justice Centre; Secure accommodation; Secure training centres; United Nations Convention on the Rights of the Child (UNCRC); United Nations Rules for the Protection of Juveniles Deprived of their Liberty; Vulnerability; Young offender institutions.

Key texts and sources

Carlile, A (2006) The Lord Carlile of Berriew QC *An Independent Inquiry into the Use of Physical Restraint, Solitary Confinement and Forcible Strip Searching of Children in Prisons, Secure Training Centres and Local Authority Secure Children's Homes.* London: Howard League for Penal Reform.

Goldson, B. (2002b) *Vulnerable Inside: Children in Secure and Penal Settings.* London: Children's Society.

Goldson, B. and Coles, D. (2005) *In the Care of the State? Child Deaths in Penal Custody in England and Wales.* London: Inquest.

Miller, J. (1991) *Last One Over the Wall: The Massachusetts Experiment in Closing Reform Schools.* Columbus, OH: Ohio State University Press.

Muncie, J. and Goldson, B. (eds) (2006) *Comparative Youth Justice: Critical Issues.* London: Sage.

CHILDREN (LEAVING CARE) ACT 2000

The Children (Leaving Care) Act 2000 was introduced in England and Wales in October 2001. Its main aims are to delay young people's transitions from care until they are prepared and ready to leave; to strengthen the assessment and planning process; to provide better personal support for young people aftercare; and to improve the financial arrangements for care leavers.

Research studies carried out in the different UK jurisdictions since the mid-1990s showed the high risk of social exclusion for young people leaving care. They also highlighted the failure of the existing discretionary child welfare and social policy framework in improving outcomes for care leavers, as well as the wide variations in the level and quality of leaving-care services.

The New Labour government, in its response to the *Children's Safeguards Review* (HM Government 1998), committed itself to legislate for new duties for care leavers. The proposed changes, detailed in the consultation document, *Me, Survive, Out There?* (Department of Health 1999), were to build on Labour's modernization programme for children's services in England. This included the Quality Protects initiative, introduced in England in 1998, which provided central government funding linked to specific service objectives and performance indicators. Objective 5 was to 'ensure that young people leaving care, as they enter adulthood, are not isolated and participate socially and economically as citizens'. Also in England, wider government initiatives to combat social exclusion (including the introduction of the Connexions Service and initiatives to tackle youth homelessness, underachievement in education and employment, and teenage parenthood) were intended to impact on care leavers.

Against this background, the Children (Leaving Care) Act 2000 was introduced in England and Wales in October 2001. The main provisions include needs assessment and pathway planning; the appointment of personal advisers; assistance with education and training up to the age of 24;

financial support for young people 'looked after' and those who have left care at 16 and 17, administered by the local authority (also applicable in Northern Ireland and Scotland); maintenance in 'suitable accommodation'; and a duty to keep in touch by the 'responsible authority'.

Research carried out since the Act was implemented shows an increased take-up of further education linked to improvements in financial support; increased provision of supported accommodation; a strengthening of needs assessment and pathway planning; more formalized interagency work; and improved funding for leaving-care teams. However, there is also evidence of continued territorial injustices – geographical variations in the funding of services and financial support for care leavers. Official data show poor educational outcomes for care leavers in comparison with young people not in care. But these normative outcome measures fail to recognize young people's family and socio-economic backgrounds and the progress made by many young people, given their very poor starting points.

Mike Stein

Related entries

Children (Leaving Care) Act 2000; Connexions; Looked-after children (LAC); Social exclusion.

Key texts and sources

Department of Health (1999) *Me, Survive, Out There? New Arrangements for Young People Living in and Leaving Care.* London: DoH (available online at **http://www.dh.gov.uk/en/Publications andstatistics/Publications/PublicationsPolicyAnd Guidance/DH_4010312**).

Department of Health (2001) *Children (Leaving Care) Act 2000: Regulations and Guidance.* London: DoH.

HM Government (1998) *The Government's Response to the Children's Safeguards Review.* London: HMSO (available online at **http://www.archive. official-documents.co.uk/document/cm41/4105/ 4105.htm**).

Stein, M. (2004) *What Works for Young People Leaving Care?* Ilford: Barnardo's.

See HMSO's website (**http://www.uk-legislation. hmso.gov.uk/acts/acts2000/00035-b.htm**) for the text of the Children (Leaving Care) Act 2000.

CHILDREN (SCOTLAND) ACT 1995

The Children (Scotland) Act 1995 provides the legal basis for the current operation of the Scottish children's hearing system. It also introduced major reforms to Scots law relating to children, including new provisions in respect of parental responsibilities and rights, 'looked-after children', child protection and adoption.

The Children (Scotland) Act 1995 marks the culmination of a series of reviews relating to child care law and to the practice and principles of the children's hearing system (including the Orkney and Fife inquires). Although restating some elements of the Social Work (Scotland) Act 1968, the 1995 Act has made changes to the ethos of the hearing system and its relationship with the courts.

The Act sets out three principles that should frame decision-making by the courts and the hearing system:

1. The child's welfare should be paramount (with one principal exception, see below).
2. The child's views should be taken into account as far as practicable, with due regard to age and maturity.
3. No requirement or order should be made unless it is considered better for the child than doing nothing.

The exception to the first of these principles is where the child is considered to present a risk of serious harm to others. In such cases the court, the hearing or a local authority is permitted to set aside the welfare principle for the purpose of public protection. This represents a major shift away from the Kilbrandon philosophy (with its emphasis on the child's best interests) which frames the hearing system.

The Act strengthens the powers of the courts over the hearings process in two main ways. First, the sheriff court is empowered to review referral grounds in past decisions where new evidence is brought forward. If none of the original grounds is established in relation to this evidence, the sheriff may terminate a supervision requirement with immediate effect. Secondly, the sheriff is now able to substitute his or her decision for that of the hearing in cases that are appealed. (Formerly appealed decisions were returned to the hearing for further consideration.)

Aside from the hearing system, the Act sets out a range of provisions in respect of parenting, adoption law and child protection (including child protection, assessment and exclusion orders). Importantly, it specifies a range of parental responsibilities/rights, including a responsibility to safeguard the child's health, development and welfare, and to provide direction and guidance appropriate to the stage of development. All responsibilities cease at the age of 16 except for the responsibility to provide guidance, which terminates at the age of 18.

Finally, the Act defines a category of 'looked-after children' (those under the care of the local authority, subject to child protection arrangements or otherwise under supervision via the hearings) and sets out a range of local authority duties towards them, including safeguarding their welfare; providing services that are normally supplied to children cared for by their own parents; and paying due regard to the child's religious, racial, cultural and linguistic background.

Lesley McAra

Related entries

Children's hearing system; Looked-after children (LAC); National Objectives and Standards for Scotland's Youth Justice Services; Sheriff courts; Welfare.

Key texts and sources

Edwards, L. and Griffiths, A. (2006) *Family Law* (2nd edn). Edinburgh: W. Green/Sweet & Maxwell.

See the Office of Public Sector Information's website (http://www.opsi.gov.uk/acts/acts1995/Ukpga_19 950036_en_1.htm) for the text of the Children (Scotland) Act 1995.

CHILDREN'S COMMISSIONERS

Children's commissioners, or ombudsmen, are official, independent champions for children and young people. They are there to promote the rights, interests and voices of children in issues that affect them.

The first children's ombudsman was established in Norway in 1981. It took a further 20 years for the first UK children's commissioner to come into office in Wales. Despite ratifying the United Nations Convention on the Rights of the Child (UNCRC) in 1991, the UK government has always displayed an equivocal attitude to the concept of children's rights. Indeed, in the UK the children's commissioners posts have developed as much in response to the opportunities presented by political devolution as they have to the United Nations Committee on the Rights of the Child recommendations, service failures identified in a number of public inquiries and persistent campaigning by children's rights advocates. The result is that there are four distinct children's commissioner offices in the UK, with different powers and priorities and varying levels of autonomy and authority.

The Children's Commissioner for Wales was appointed in 2001 in response to an inquiry into systematic, historical abuse in a number of children's homes in North Wales. As originally envisaged, the commissioner's duties responded to the overriding need to protect children from harm – especially those living away from home – and so they focused on the operation of complaints and whistle-blowing procedures, and on making arrangements for children's advocacy.

In 2001, the First Minister for Northern Ireland announced proposals for a children's rights commissioner in response to similar developments in other European nations. The following year, Scotland's Education, Culture and Sport Committee published a report that recommended that an independent commissioner be established to co-ordinate, monitor and promote issues affecting children and young people. It was inevitable that England would have to set up its own office, and this took place in 2005 as part of the development of the 'Every Child Matters' programme.

The legislation establishing each of the commissioner posts varies considerably, leading to disparities in the scope, power and influence of the commissioners and their offices. Part V of the Care Standards Act 2000 set up the post in Wales. The role, however, was enlarged in the Children's Commissioner for Wales Act 2001 and associated regulations. Both Northern Ireland and Scotland passed legislation in 2003 – respectively, the Commissioner for Children and Young People (Northern Ireland) Order and the Commissioner for Children and Young People (Scotland) Act. Part 1 of the Children Act 2004 established the Office of the Children's Commissioner for England.

Wales, Northern Ireland and Scotland share a general function for their commissioners – to promote the rights and interests of children. England's commissioner is there to promote awareness of the views and interests of children, arguably a lesser role, though he is also obliged to have regard to the UNCRC. The English commissioner is expected to report on how well services are supporting children in England to meet the five outcomes established under the 'Every Child Matters' programme.

All the commissioners have a power to research and publish reports on issues that they believe are important to the welfare and interests of children and young people. Reviewing and commenting on youth justice follow the pattern of the devolution settlement. Scotland and Northern Ireland concentrate on their own distinct systems. England and Wales work within a common legislative framework but highlight the impact this legislation has on local service provision and the indigenous population of children and young people. Powers to undertake independent inquiries and investigate specific cases differ from nation to nation, and no commissioner is allowed to investigate matters that are already subject to legal proceedings or official inquiries.

The commissioners in Northern Ireland and Wales can carry out reviews into services provided to children and young people by public authorities, including, in the case of Wales, any action of the Welsh Assembly Government that may impact on the welfare of children and young people. The Northern Ireland commissioner has the unique power to initiate legal proceedings, which he used in 2004 when he applied for a judicial review of the way in which the Northern Ireland Office had consulted on the introduction of anti-social behaviour orders.

Both the Wales and Scotland commissioners must review all law, policy and practice that affects children and young people, while the Northern Ireland commissioner may assess the adequacy of law, policy and practice. England's commissioner has no such duty in law. In Scotland, the commissioner's office has introduced a child impact assessment template to assist them to analyse new areas of policy or legislation and to measure these against the articles of the UNCRC. Northern Ireland and England plan to do something similar. It is likely that the continuing failures of the youth justice system to comply with UNCRC requirements will receive an increasing amount of attention through child impact analysis.

Children's commissioners have no true mandate if they fail to involve and consult with children and young people, and each UK commissioner is required by legislation to do so. In England and Scotland, they are under a duty to make sure they consult with harder-to-reach groups of children, such as those in custody or those caught up in the youth justice system. In practice, the commissioners in Wales and Northern Ireland do the same.

The four commissioners may initiate investigations and can require evidence and documents and, with the exception of Scotland, have a right of entry. This could allow a commissioner to demand entrance to an institution, including custodial establishments, about which he or she may have grave concerns. However, only the Northern Ireland and Wales commissioners have complex and limited powers to investigate individual complaints, normally only when all other avenues of complaint have been exhausted.

Children's commissioners in the UK have to juggle a number of competing interests – the often incompatible views and voices of children themselves, those who work with them, their parents and carers, the media and the government – and revert attention to their core business: raising our awareness of children's rights and ensuring that these rights are respected.

Lisa Payne

Related entries

Children Act 2004; Children's human rights; Comparative youth justice; Every Child Matters; Extending Entitlement (National Assembly for Wales); United Nations Committee on the Rights of the Child; United Nations Convention on the Rights of the Child (UNCRC).

Key texts and sources

See the Office of Public Sector Information's website for the texts of the Care Standards Act 2000 (**http://www.opsi.gov.uk/acts/acts2000/20000014. htm**), the Children Act 2004 (**http://www.opsi.gov. uk/acts/acts2004/20040031.htm**), the Children's Commissioner for Wales Act 2001 (**http://www. opsi.gov.uk/ACTS/acts2001/20010018.htm**) and the Commissioner for Children and Young People (Northern Ireland) Order 2003 (**http://www.opsi. gov.uk/SI/si2003/20030439.htm**). See HMSO's website (**http://www.uk-legislation.hmso.gov.uk/ legislation/scotland/acts2003/20030017.htm**) for the text of the Commissioner for Children and Young People (Scotland) Act 2003.

The Children's Commissioner for England's website is at **https://www.childrenscommissioner.org/**, the Children's Commissioner for Wales at **http://www. childcom.org.uk/english/index.html**, the Northern Ireland Commissioner for Children and Young People at **http://www.niccy.org/** and Scotland's Commissioner for Children and Young People at **http://www.sccyp.org.uk/**.

CHILDREN'S HEARING SYSTEM

The children's hearing system is the Scottish system for dealing with children who offend and/or are in need of care and protection. The system is predominantly welfarist in orientation and involves ordinary members of the public in decision-making (via a lay panel).

The children's hearing system was enabled by the Social Work (Scotland) Act 1968 and implemented in 1971. It is based on the Kilbrandon philosophy (named after the chairman of the committee set up to review Scottish juvenile justice in the early 1960s). According to this philosophy, the problems of children who are involved in offending or who are in need of care and protection (as a consequence of such factors as victimization from sexual or violent offending or parental neglect) stem from the same source – namely, failures in the 'normal' upbringing process and/or broader social malaise. The philosophy advocates early and minimal intervention based on the needs of the child, with the best interests of the child to be paramount in decision-making. Contact with the institutions of juvenile justice should be as destigmatizing as possible, a central principle being to avoid the criminalization of children.

Children can be referred to the hearing system from birth until the age of 15 inclusive on a range of non-offence grounds (see below) and from the age of 8 to 15 on offence grounds (8 currently being the age of criminal responsibility in Scotland). Any agency and/or person can make a referral but, in practice, the highest proportion of referrals comes from the police. While most offenders aged 16 to 17 are dealt with in the adult court system, the courts do have the power (little used) to remit such cases back to the hearings system for advice or disposal. Importantly, the Crown reserves the right to prosecute certain cases in the criminal courts: those involving the most serious crimes (such as rape or homicide) and certain specified motor vehicle offences (where the child is aged 15 and the offence involves a penalty of disqualification from driving). In practice, such prosecutions are extremely rare (around 140 in a typical year, a high proportion of which are remitted back to the hearing system for disposal).

A characteristic feature of the children's hearing system is the separation of the judgment of evidence from the disposition of a case. The former lies in the hands of the reporter, whose principal task is to investigate referrals and to decide if there is a prima facie case that one of the statutory grounds of referral to the system has been met *and* whether the child is in need of compulsory measures of care. (Reporters are employed by the Scottish Children's Reporter Administration, under the authority of the Principal Reporter for Scotland.) There are currently 12 grounds for referral:

1. being beyond the control of any relevant person
2. falling into bad associations or exposed to moral danger
3. likely to suffer unnecessarily or be impaired seriously in his [*sic*] health or development due to lack of parental care
4. a child in respect of whom any of the offences mentioned in Schedule 1 of the Criminal Procedure (Scotland) Act 1995 have been committed (sex offence or one involving cruelty to children)
5. is or is likely to become a member of the same household as a child in respect of whom any of the above Schedule 1 offences have been committed
6. is or is likely to become a member of the same household as a person who has committed any of the above offences
7. is or is likely to become a member of the same household as a person in respect of whom an offence under sections 1 to 3 of the Criminal Law (Consolidation) (Scotland) Act 1995 (incest and intercourse with a child by a step-parent or person in position of trust) has been committed by a member of that household
8. failed to attend school regularly without reasonable excuse
9. committed an offence
10. misused alcohol or any drug whether or not a controlled drug within the meaning of the Misuse of Drugs Act 1971
11. misused a volatile substance by deliberately inhaling its vapour other than for medicinal purposes
12. is being provided with accommodation by a local authority under section 25 of the Children (Scotland) Act 1995, or is the subject of a parental responsibilities order obtained under section 86 of that Act and, in either case, his behaviour is such that special measures are necessary for his adequate supervision in his interest or the interests of others.

The principal task of a hearing is to consider the measures to be applied. Before a hearing can take place, both the child and his or her parents have to accept the grounds for referral (in the case of an offender there has to be an admission of guilt). If the grounds are disputed, the case is referred to the sheriff court for a proof hearing. Participants at a standard hearing are the lay panel, who are the principal decision-makers (panels comprise three members drawn from the wider panel in each local authority area and must include at least one man and one woman); the child and his or her parents; the reporter (to advise on legal and procedural matters and to record the reasons for the decision); a social worker (to provide expert advice and assessment); and, where relevant, a range of other professionals (for example, a teacher, psychologist or psychiatrist). While the child and/or his or her parents can be accompanied by a lawyer (or indeed another supporter, including a 'safeguarder'), no legal aid was available for this in the early years of the system. (As a result of the ruling in *S* v. *Miller*, legal aid is now available in cases where there is a risk that the child will lose his or her liberty or where the child is unable to participate effectively in the hearing – for example, due to lack of maturity.)

The hearing aims at participatory and consensual decision-making. The main disposal available to the panel is a supervision requirement, which may include a residential component and which ensures statutory social work supervision based on the needs of the child. Supervision requirements normally last up to one year but are subject to review and can be extended up until the child's eighteenth birthday. Hearings decisions can be appealed to the sheriff court (in the first instance) and the sheriff has the power to substitute his or her decision for that of the hearing.

Although welfarist principles continue to underpin the hearing system, a number of changes have been made over the past decade. The first signs of change were introduced by the Children (Scotland) Act 1995, which enabled reporters and panel members to place the principle of risk above that of best interests in cases where the child was considered to present a risk of serious harm to others. Policy transformation, however, has gained momentum in the wake of political devolution as successive ministers in the Scottish Executive have gradually embraced the 'New Labour' crime agenda. In particular, reform has been driven by increased concern about the capacity of the hearing system to tackle effectively the problems posed by persistent offending and perceived increases in anti-social behaviour. A raft of new institutional structures and bureaucratic procedures have been grafted on to the extant system, including multi-agency youth justice teams (with responsibility for the direction and implementation of policy); pilot fast-track hearings (now abandoned in the wake of an unfavourable evaluation); pilot youth courts (for 16–17-year-old persistent offenders and some 15-year-old offenders who would otherwise have been dealt with in the sheriff summary court); a range of restorative justice initiatives (such as pre-hearing diversion to reparation and mediation and police restorative cautioning); new national standards that set out targets in respect of timescales and reductions in the number of persistent offender referrals; and new specialist programmes for offenders based on 'What Works' principles.

Commentators on the system have expressed concerns that the new changes will undermine key elements of the Kilbrandon philosophy and make the system less rather than more effective. Research on the impact of hearings intervention on young people has generally highlighted the extreme vulnerability of serious and persistent offenders (see, for example, Waterhouse *et al.* 1999). Indeed, there is robust evidence from the

Edinburgh Study of Youth Transitions and Crime that a minimal intervention/maximum diversionary approach is likely to be the most effective in tackling persistent serious offending and that the children's hearing system, *as currently implemented*, may be damaging to young offenders in the longer term (McAra and McVie 2007).

Lesley McAra

Related entries

Children (Scotland) Act 1995; Criminalization; Looked-after children (LAC); Normalization; Persistent young offenders; Sheriff courts; Social Work (Scotland) Act 1968; Welfare.

Key texts and sources

McAra, L. (2006) 'Welfare in crisis? Youth justice in Scotland', in J. Muncie and B. Goldson (eds) *Comparative Youth Justice: Critical Issues.* London: Sage.

McAra, L. and McVie, S. (2007) 'Youth justice? The impact of system contact on patterns of desistance from offending', *European Journal of Criminology*, 4: 315–45.

Waterhouse, L., McGhee, J., Loucks, N., Whyte, B. and Kay, H. (1999) *The Evaluation of the Children's Hearings in Scotland. Volume 3. Children in Focus.* Edinburgh: Scottish Executive Central Research Unit.

See the Office of Public Sector Information's website (http://www.opsi.gov.uk/acts/acts1995/Ukpga_19 950036_en_1.htm) for the text of the Children (Scotland) Act 1995.

CHILDREN'S HUMAN RIGHTS

The Convention on the Rights of the Child sets out the human rights of children. This comprehensive treaty was adopted by the United Nations in 1989 and ratified by the UK government in 1991.

Human rights came of age following the Second World War, with the creation of the United Nations and the adoption of the Universal Declaration of Human Rights in 1948. They are derived from the concept of natural rights, which had evolved over the previous two centuries – that individuals have inalienable rights simply because they are human and that these are not contingent on behaviour or social circumstance.

The concept of children's human rights, as distinct from those of adults, began to carry momentum in the early twentieth century. Janusz Korczak is often credited as being one of the founders of the modern children's rights movement. A Polish Jew, he devoted his adult life to supporting poor and orphaned children, helping them to run a newspaper and encouraging democratic education. He stayed with the children when their orphan house was moved to the Jewish ghetto and he died with them at Treblinka concentration camp. His book, *The Child's Right to Respect* (1992), published 10 years before his death, explained: 'We learn very early in life that big is more important than little ... Small is equated with ordinary and uninteresting. Little people mean little wants, little joys and sorrows.'

Eglantine Jebb, the founder of Save the Children, was the first to codify rights for children. She drafted the Declaration of the Rights of the Child in 1923, and this was adopted by the League of Nations the following year. This short declaration set out for the first time adult obligations towards children. Its preamble urged: 'mankind owes to the child the best that it has to give.' The declaration was accepted by the newly formed United Nations and updated in 1959.

Unlike declarations, human rights treaties place legal obligations on the governments that ratify them. By the time the United Nations adopted the Convention on the Rights of the Child (UNCRC) in 1989, it had already adopted five other core human rights treaties: the International Convention on the Elimination of All Forms of Racial Discrimination (1965); the International Covenant on Economic, Social and Cultural Rights; the International Covenant on Civil and Political Rights (both adopted in 1966); the Convention on the Elimination of All Forms of Discrimination against Women (1979) and the Convention against Torture and Other Cruel, Inhuman or Degrading Treatment or Punishment (1984). All these treaties apply to young human beings but none makes provision for the unique developmental needs and the particular susceptibility of children to exploitation and mistreatment.

The UNCRC brings together existing economic, social and cultural and civil and political rights, as well as introducing tailor-made human rights for children – for example, the child's right to have his or her best interests as a primary consideration in all actions concerning him or her; the right to have contact with both parents; the right to rest and play; the right to protection from all forms of violence in all settings; the right for the child's views to be taken seriously in all matters affecting him or her; and the right to education that helps the child develop fully with respect for his or her own human rights and the rights of others. As well as placing detailed obligations on ratifying states, the UNCRC embodies a vision of childhood characterized by happiness, respect, dignity, equality and fulfilment for every child. Reflecting the sentiments of Korczak writing nearly eight decades before, the Council of Europe's Deputy Secretary General, Maud de Boer-Buquicchio, explained in 2005: 'Children are not mini-persons with mini-rights, mini-feelings and mini-human dignity. They are vulnerable human beings with full rights which require more, not less protection [than adults].'

Carolyne Willow

Related entries

Children's commissioners; United Nations Committee on the Rights of the Child; United Nations Convention on the Rights of the Child (UNCRC); United Nations Standard Minimum Rules for the Administration of Juvenile Justice; Vulnerability.

Key texts and sources

de Boer-Buquicchio, M. (2005) Conference speech by the Deputy Secretary General of the Council of Europe, Berlin, 21 October, 'Raising children without violence' (available online at **http://www.coe.int/t/e/SG/SGA/documents/speeches/2005/ZH_21102005_Berlin.asp#TopOfPage**).

Korczak, J. (1992) *The Child's Right to Respect*. New York: University Press of America.

See also the following websites: the Council of Europe Commissioner for Human Rights (http://www.coe.int/t/commissioner/default_EN.asp); the Child Rights Information Network (http://www.crin.org); the Children's Rights Alliance for England (http://www.crae.org.uk); the Office of the United Nations High Commissioner for Human Rights (http://www.ohchr.org/english/); and, for the United Nations Convention on the Rights of the Child, http://www.unhchr.ch/html/menu3/b/k2crc.htm.

CHILDREN'S TRUSTS

Children's trusts are local strategic partnerships that bring together statutory and other (private and voluntary sector) bodies that plan, commission and provide services to children and young people in that area.

Children's trusts are an English initiative, forming part of the 'Every Child Matters' developments. The trusts are a response to the government's concern that the various agencies and services that have an impact on the lives of children and young people fail to work together to a clear and common set of aims.

Section 10 of the Children Act 2004 provides the legislative framework within which children's trusts operate. It introduces a reciprocal duty on a children's services authority (local authority) and named partners to 'promote cooperation to improve the well-being of children' in relation to the five outcomes for children and young people. These outcomes are most commonly expressed as being healthy, staying safe, enjoying and achieving, making a positive contribution and achieving economic well-being.

A children's services authority should comprise local authority education and children's social services, as well as local government services that have an impact on children, such as housing or play and recreation. Since trusts are a fairly new phenomenon, however, the initial focus has been on bringing together local authority education and children's social services. The relevant partners to the children's services authority are the police, the probation board, the youth offending team (YOT), strategic health authority and primary care trust, Connexions staff and the Learning and Skills Council for England. 'Other' unspecified partners may include the voluntary and community sector or schools. The partner agencies and the children's services authority can establish and maintain a pooled fund and/or pooled resources (defined as staff, goods, services, accommodation or other resources).

The government has referred to the 'duty to co-operate' as a 'children's trust approach' to working in an integrated way at local level. The first task of the children's services authority and its partners is to develop strategic-level joint commissioning and planning of children's services across the board. In order to support that work, the government has issued guidance on children and young people's plans and a framework on joint commissioning. However, the children's trust guidance makes it clear that, in time, the government expects this concept of partnership working to run through all levels of activity right down to 'front line' staff and to lead to integrated, multi-agency service provision.

Research from the children's trusts 'pathfinder areas' shows that, in 2006, only 30–49 per cent of the children's trusts had YOT involvement in joint planning and commissioning, and only 5 out of the 31 surveyed had pooled budgets. The Youth Justice Board has designated six areas as 'demonstration sites' (Essex, Hammersmith and Fulham, Leicester City, Northumberland, Stoke-on-Trent and Wessex) to test out the developing relationships of YOTs and children's trusts.

Children's trust arrangements are the responsibility of, and report to, the local authority in the persons of the director of children's services and an elected member (local councillor) with responsibility for children's services. Each local authority must have children's trust arrangements in place by 2008.

Lisa Payne

Related entries

Children Act 2004; Connexions; Every Child Matters (ECM); Partnership working; Safeguarding; Youth Matters; Youth offending teams (YOTs).

COGNITIVE-BEHAVIOUR PROGRAMMES

A cognitive-behaviour programme is a structured programme, usually delivered in a groupwork setting, intended to help offenders identify and change habits of thought (cognition) that are associated with an increased risk of offending behaviour.

Although the term itself has become widely used only since the early 1990s, the basic principles of cognitive-behavioural work with offenders were set out in Britain in the late 1970s by Philip Priestley, James McGuire and their colleagues. They argued that work with offenders should focus on developing their social skills and problem-solving capacities, in an approach that was educative rather than therapeutic. It was to follow a coherent curriculum but be flexible enough to reflect offenders' different learning styles and the variety of their problems. Their ideas became influential in the groupwork that developed in the Probation Service from the early 1980s. At the same time a similar approach began to be used in the groupwork of many 'intermediate treatment' projects with juvenile offenders, in which the focus was on offending and factors closely associated with it, rather than on vaguely defined needs and problems that might have nothing to do with the young people's offending.

Approaches with a more explicit cognitive-behavioural label were given impetus by the appearance of research evidence that suggested that this way of working was one of the features shared by successful programmes. Some of this evidence, much of it from psychological criminologists in Canada, was new; some was based on a critical analysis of earlier research. The result was a rejection of the belief that 'nothing works', which had been a dominant influence since the mid-1970s. A particularly influential programme was 'Reasoning and rehabilitation', devised in Canada by Robert Ross and implemented in an adapted form in the Mid-Glamorgan Probation Service. By the late 1990s the Home Office was sufficiently persuaded by the evidence in favour of cognitive-behavioural work to begin to encourage the approach in all programmes for offenders, and this view was shared by the Correctional Services Accreditation Panel when it was established in 1999 to assess the value of programmes.

Cognitive-behavioural programmes have not achieved the status of one of the best ways of working with juvenile offenders as they have with adults. This is probably fortunate, since the results of the programmes in the Probation Service have been disappointing. It has proved much more difficult to implement the approach successfully on a large scale than in a well resourced local project like that in Mid-Glamorgan. Despite this – and the criticism that cognitive-behavioural work is too focused on the supposed deficiencies of individual offenders and neglects the social and economic context of their lives – it still has the potential to inform constructive practice. Shorn of the psychological language that many have found unhelpful, cognitive-behavioural programmes can be seen simply as a systematic way of putting into practice much of what social work with young offenders has always tried to do: to help them think before acting and to understand the connections between how they think (and how they feel) and how they behave.

David Smith

Related entries

Evaluative research; Groupwork; Intermediate treatment; What Works.

Key texts and sources

Hollin, C.R. and Palmer, E.J. (eds) (2006) *Offending Behaviour Programmes: Development, Application and Controversies.* Chichester: Wiley.

McGuire, J. (ed.) (1995) *What Works: Reducing Reoffending.* Chichester: Wiley.

Priestley, P., McGuire, J., Flegg, D., Hemsley, V. and Welham, D. (1978) *Social Skills and Personal Problem-solving: A Handbook of Methods.* London: Tavistock.

See also the website of the Cognitive Centre Foundation UK (**http://www.cognitivecentre.com/home.htm**).

COMMUNITY HOMES WITH EDUCATION (CHEs)

Community homes with education (CHEs) were large children's establishments which developed from the approved schools tradition to provide accommodation with education for 'difficult' and 'disturbed' children.

Community homes with education (CHEs) derived from the approved schools tradition, which they replaced when approved schools were swept away by the changes created by the Children and Young Persons Act 1969. They were intended for the most 'difficult' and 'disturbed' children who, it was felt, would benefit from being placed away from home to somewhere where their social, emotional and educational needs could be met.

CHEs were usually large institutions located some distance from the nearest town and, indeed, from the local authority responsible for them. Most provided year-round care with holiday periods at home, while other young people were placed there as weekly boarders. The homes looked after children in house blocks or dormitory-style accommodation. Staffing levels were generally low. Heads of homes and their senior staff were generally experienced, but often other staff were relatively inexperienced and saw this as a route into more 'formal' social work.

Education provision was often rudimentary and vocationally focused, with an emphasis on sport and fresh air. The homes' size and location meant that, perhaps unfairly, there was an 'out of sight, out of mind' attitude towards CHEs, although, equally, many young people thrived in such an environment. The staff worked hard to meet the children's wide range of behavioural, emotional and social needs but often had to struggle to access the resources and support required to do so. Most CHEs were phased out by the local authorities during the 1980s as social work practice changed and the limitations of placing children and young people in large residential establishments were recognized.

Roy Walker

Related entries

Children and Young Persons Act 1969; Secure accommodation.

Key texts and sources

Burton, J. (1993) *The Handbook of Residential Care.* London: Routledge.

Kahan, B. (1994) *Growing Up in Groups.* London: HMSO.

COMMUNITY JUSTICE

Community justice aims to involve members of the community in one or more aspects of criminal and youth justice, often in an informal way, in order to allow crimes and disputes to be dealt with locally by those directly involved.

Drawing upon the ideas of American communitarian writers such as Karp and Clear (2002), community justice is a vague and elastic concept. While benign in many ways – for example, in its rejection of remote, bureaucratic authority and its preference for settling offences and disputes locally – it is also open to abuse. Many of its advocates support deprofessionalizing criminal and youth justice, which can involve the replacement of state services by voluntary and/or profit-making agencies or substituting informal discussion for processes that normally involve ways of protecting human rights, such as legal representation for defendants.

Examples of experiments with community justice include community reparative boards in Vermont, USA, circles of support and accountability for offenders released from prison in Canada and England, and community justice centres such as those in the USA and the UK (Williams 2005). These experiments have arisen from dissatisfaction with existing criminal/youth justice arrangements, which are seen as too remote and alienating, insensitive to local people's concerns and too preoccupied with dealing with crimes as isolated incidents rather than with the underlying symptoms of community problems (Berman and Mansky 2005). Many supporters of the community justice movement in the USA are also motivated by a desire to see a reduction in the use of youth and adult custody, although they tend not to be very open about this. Providing services and programmes for young people in deprived areas through the justice system is seen as a way of creating healthier communities and preventing crime – but many question whether this is best done through the criminal justice system (Green 2002).

The North Liverpool Community Justice Centre is an example of an experiment in implementing community justice in England. Initially imposed by central government (unlike its predecessors in the USA), it nevertheless achieved some local support and provided a venue for a range of facilities under one roof. Its resident judge was empowered both to deal with minor anti-social behaviour and to sit as a Crown court judge. This provided a greater degree of continuity for victims and defendants than a conventional criminal court and meant that people needing services from related agencies could obtain these on the spot when they attended court. The judge was appointed by an unusual process that involved local community representatives, and he set up mechanisms for consultation with local communities about which crimes and other problems should receive priority attention. He also put mechanisms in place to enable him to monitor offenders' compliance with court, orders much more closely than is normally the case and to call them back to court, either to hold them to account for breaches of such orders or to praise them when they achieved compliance. Formal, written court reports were often dispensed with, being replaced by a kind of case conference prior to each day's court hearings. Before the results of evaluative research on this pilot project had been released, it was announced that ten similar courts were to be set up. While the stated aim of the experiment was to increase community participation and confidence in criminal justice, it is not known to what extent the latter aspiration was achieved (see the government's 'Community justice' website, which reproduces ministerial speeches but which remains silent about evaluation results). Some observers were critical of the rather marginal role accorded to victims of crime in the community justice centre, and others argued that the local community as a whole had never been brought on board (Williams 2005).

As with so many initiatives involving the use of the word 'community', community justice seems a good idea in principle but everything depends upon how it is implemented. Community justice centres have achieved a degree of popular support in the USA but, there, they are often the outcome of a lengthy period of local planning. They bring new resources to run-down areas, not just local outreach centres for criminal justice agencies. Elsewhere in the USA, however, community reparative boards were introduced in order to increase citizen participation in criminal justice, mainly dealing with minor crime in predominantly rural areas. Participation is a condition of probation, and offenders are required to meet a board of three to five local volunteers who negotiate a contract with them, which often includes reparation and has to be complied with over the following 90 days. Victims can take part. They rarely do so, however, but are usually told when the offender complies with or breaches the contract. This system does involve local people in criminal justice and it may reduce the use of custodial sentences for minor offences. It may also create opportunities for board members to patronize or even humiliate offenders. This suggests that community justice is not necessarily empowering for offenders or victims of crime.

These ideas have influenced the youth justice system in England and Wales – for example, the introduction of referral orders arose partly from communitarian ideology. Under a referral order, young offenders are required to take part in a panel meeting with local community volunteers, and the aim is to reach agreement on an enforceable contract, often involving elements of restorative justice. In most parts of the country the level of victim involvement has been relatively low.

Brian Williams

Related entries

Community safety; Informalism; Mediation; Referral orders; Reparation; Restorative justice; Victims.

Key texts and sources

Berman, G. and Mansky, A. (2005) 'Community justice centres: a US–UK exchange', *British Journal of Community Justice*, 3: 5–14.

Green, S. (2002) 'The communitarian hi-jacking of community justice', *British Journal of Community Justice*, 1: 49–62.
HM Government (2007) *Community Justice* (available online at **www.communityjustice.gov.uk**).
Karp, D.R. and Clear, T.R. (eds) (2002) *What is Community Justice? Case Studies of Restorative Justice and Community Supervision.* London: Sage.
Williams, B. (2005) *Victims of Crime and Community Justice.* London: Jessica Kingsley.
See also the government's 'Community justice' website (**www.communityjustice.gov.uk**).

COMMUNITY PAYBACK

Community payback is indirect reparation, or unpaid work of benefit to the community, undertaken as punishment for an offence.

The community payback scheme was announced, in April 2001, by the then Prime Minister, Tony Blair, as one of a raft of initiatives intended to deal with 'yob culture' by compelling adjudicated offenders to make reparation to the community through activities such as removing graffiti or picking up litter. The scheme was adopted by the National Probation Service during 2005 for adult offenders subject to the unpaid work requirements of a community order. Similarly, the National Standards for Youth Justice Services require youth offending teams to provide access to a range of structured activities – such as repairing damage or environmental improvement – to support community payback where victims do not wish to receive any form of direct reparation. The activities should 'encourage change of attitude, confidence building and community reintegration for the young offender'.

In reality, existing legislation already provided for various forms of unpaid work for young people in trouble, through final warning interventions, reparation orders, requirements of supervision or community punishment orders. In this sense community payback was something of a 'rebranding', fitting with the punitive spirit informing youth justice policy development at the time. The initiative can be seen as a response to public anxieties about anti-social behaviour and disorder. It was, accordingly, an explicit requirement of the scheme that the benefits of unpaid work should be visible, allowing 'the local community to see that young offenders have made reparation for their behaviour'.

Tim Bateman

Related entries

Community punishment orders (CPOs); National Standards for Youth Justice Services; Reparation; Reparation orders.

Key texts and sources

Youth Justice Board (2004a) *National Standards for Youth Justice Services.* London: Youth Justice Board.

COMMUNITY PUNISHMENT AND REHABILITATION ORDERS (CPROs)

The community punishment and rehabilitation order (CPRO), previously known as the combination order, is only available for offenders aged 16 or 17 who have been convicted of an imprisonable offence in the Crown, magistrates' or youth courts. It requires the offender to complete between 12 and 36 months of 'rehabilitation', alongside 40–100 hours of unpaid work in the community.

The community punishment and rehabilitation order (CPRO) was introduced by the Criminal Justice Act 1991 and is now regulated within the Powers of the Criminal Courts (Sentencing) Act 2000 and is, in essence, the marriage between the community punishment order (CPO) and the community rehabilitation order (CRO).

In effect the CPRO is a combination of the CPO and CRO but with two distinct differences. The CRO element has a minimum length of 12 months (as distinct from a straight CRO's minimum length of 6 months) in order to accommodate the 12-month period allowed for the completion of community punishment. In addition, the maximum length of the CPRO is 100 hours, compared with the 240 hours for a straight CPO, to ensure that the CPRO as a sentence is not overburdened.

Within the youth justice sector the CPRO is considered to be a higher 'tariff' disposal primarily reserved for serious and persistent offenders. It can have additional requirements – such as a curfew order, a fine or a compensation order – attached to it. If too many requirements are added, however, compliance will be difficult to achieve for a young offender. The CPRO also fulfils the individual aims of the CPO and the CRO where rehabilitation, retribution and reparation are combined within a single disposal.

When considering such a sentence the courts need to remain mindful of the seriousness of the offence and whether it reaches the 'so serious' threshold. If so, the courts also need to assess whether its imposition would:

- secure the rehabilitation of the offender;
- protect the public from harm; and
- prevent further offending.

The maturity of the young person also needs to be communicated to the court in the pre-sentence report.

The commencement, monitoring and supervision of the CPRO fall to the local youth offending team (YOT). The YOT is required to supervise the CRO element of the order and – normally with the assistance of the Probation Service – to arrange appropriate unpaid work in the community for the CPO element.

The monitoring and supervision of the order are governed by the strict directives of the National Standards for Youth Justice Services. However, the practical arrangements of monitoring and enforcing compliance are determined at a local level. In many cases concerning non-compliance, the YOT is responsible for instigating and prosecuting breach proceedings at court, whereby the Probation Service is required to provide evidence of (non)compliance with the CPO element of the order.

Kaushika Patel and Rob Canton

Related entries

Community payback; Community punishment orders (CPOs); Community rehabilitation orders (CROs); Criminal Justice Act 1991; Criminal Justice and Court Services Act 2000; Powers of Criminal Courts (Sentencing) Act 2000; Rehabilitation; Reparation.

Key texts and sources

Bottoms, A., Gelsthorpe, L. and Rex, S. (2002) *Community Penalties, Change and Challenges.* Cullompton: Willan Publishing.

Brownlee, I. (1998b) *Community Punishment: A Critical Introduction.* London: Longman.

The National Standards for the Supervision of Offenders in the Community are available online at **http://www.probation.homeoffice.gov.uk/files/pdf/national_standards.pdf**. The National Standards for Youth Justice Services are available online at **http://www.yjb.gov.uk/Publications/Resources/Downloads/NatStandYJS2004.pdf**.

COMMUNITY PUNISHMENT ORDERS (CPOs)

The community punishment order (CPO) – previously known as the community service order – is available in the Crown, magistrates' and youth courts for offenders aged 16 and 17 who have been convicted of an imprisonable offence. It requires the offender to undertake 'unpaid work' for the benefit of the community for no less than 40 hours and no more that 240 hours over a period of 12 months.

The community punishment order (CPO) was first introduced as the community service order under the provisions of the Criminal Justice Act 1972 and it is now regulated within the Powers of the Criminal Courts (Sentencing) Act 2000.

The aims of the order are to restrict the young offender's liberty by regulating his or her leisure time. However, the CPO is also recognized for its reparative and rehabilitative elements – of 'payback' to the community via unpaid work (reparation) and the opportunities this is thought to provide for the offender to learn new skills (rehabilitation). The type of unpaid work available varies from area to area but normally includes such activities as domestic chores for disabled and older people, gardening and maintaining community amenities. The type and place of work allocated to a young person will be determined via a 'risk assessment' undertaken by the youth offending team (YOT) using the Asset document. The CPO requires the young person to undertake unpaid work in blocks of time – usually a full day a week. As far as possible the times at which the young person is required to work must not conflict with his or her observation of any religious practice or interfere with paid employment or education.

The commencement, monitoring and enforcement of the CPO are all subject to the National Standards for Youth Justice Services. In the case of young offenders who are subject to a CPO and no other orders, the supervision is normally undertaken by the Probation Service, which is required to provide the work placements, supervise compliance by the young person and instigate and prosecute any breaches in the youth court. However, in cases where the young person is subject to a CPO in addition to another court order, the Probation Service will provide any evidence of non-compliance to the YOT with the expectation that breach proceedings and prosecution of breach will be managed by the YOT.

Kaushika Patel and Rob Canton

Related entries

Community payback; Community punishment and rehabilitation orders (CPROs); Reparation.

Key texts and sources

Bottoms, A., Gelsthorpe, L. and Rex, S. (2002) *Community Penalties, Change and Challenges.* Cullompton: Willan Publishing.

Brownlee, I. (1998b) *Community Punishment: A Critical Introduction.* London: Longman.

The National Standards for the Supervision of Offenders in the Community are available online at **http://www.probation.homeoffice.gov.uk/files/pdf/national_standards.pdf**. The National Standards for Youth Justice Services are available online at **http://www.yjb.gov.uk/Publications/Resources/Downloads/NatStandYJS2004.pdf**.

COMMUNITY REHABILITATION ORDERS (CROs)

The community rehabilitation order (CRO) is a community sentence of not less than 6 and not more than 36 months duration, which can be imposed on any person aged 16 or 17 who has been convicted by the court.

The community rehabilitation order (CRO) (previously known as the probation order, as provided by the Powers of the Criminal Courts Act 1973) was originally introduced as an order of the court made 'instead of sentencing' the defendant. The Criminal Justice Act 1991, which brought the youth court into being, made the probation order into a sentence in its own right rather than an alternative to a sentence. It was later incorporated into the Powers of the Criminal Courts (Sentencing) Act 2000 and was subsequently renamed the community rehabilitation order.

Where a CRO is being considered, the courts need to take account of the maturity of the young person, the offence(s) committed and the type and level of intervention required. The CRO is available in the Crown, magistrates'and youth courts for any offence, imprisonable or not, with the exception of those offences for which a sentence is fixed by law. Such an order can only be imposed where the courts are satisfied that:

- the offence(s) is/are serious enough to warrant such a disposal as directed in the Criminal Justice Act 1991, s. 6(1);
- the order is intended to secure the rehabilitation of the offender; or
- the imposition of such an order will protect the public from harm from the offender or prevent him or her from reoffending.

There are a number of additional requirements that can be attached to a CRO where the court feels they are appropriate to prevent reoffending and/or protect the public. The type of addi-

tional requirements that can be attached will be dependent on the particular circumstances of the offender and/or the seriousness of the offence. The most commonly used additional requirement is to comply with an intensive supervision and surveillance programme, which is usually reserved for serious offences or those young people at risk of a custodial sentence.

The supervision of the CRO falls to the youth offending team. However, any young person subject to a CRO who turns 18 during the period of the order will normally have the supervision of his or her order transferred to the Probation Service. At the initial meeting a supervision plan is drawn up defining the purpose, objectives and desired outcomes of supervision, together with the frequency of contact, which is governed by the National Standards for Youth Justice Services. The requirements under the national standards to attend appointments can also be seen as a means of restriction of liberty.

Kaushika Patel and Rob Canton

Related entries

Community punishment and rehabilitation orders (CPROs); Intensive Supervision and Surveillance Programme (ISSP); Menu-based sentencing; Probation; Rehabilitation.

Key texts and sources

Bottoms, A., Gelsthorpe, L. and Rex, S. (2002) *Community Penalties, Change and Challenges.* Cullompton: Willan Publishing.
Brownlee, I. (1998b) *Community Punishment: A Critical Introduction.* London: Longman.
The National Standards for the Supervision of Offenders in the Community are available online at **http://www.probation.homeoffice.gov.uk/files/ pdf/national_standards.pdf**. The National Standards for Youth Justice Services are available online at **http://www.yjb.gov.uk/Publications/ Resources/Downloads/NatStandYJS2004.pdf**.

COMMUNITY SAFETY

Community safety is a term used to describe a local, multi-agency partnership approach to the reduction of crime and disorder and the fear of crime and, more expansively, the promotion and achievement of public safety by communities. By its very nature it defies neat compartmentalization either linguistically or organizationally.

Community safety emerged in the UK in the 1980s among several metropolitan authorities as a *local* government strategy that sought to move beyond the traditionally police-driven agenda of formal crime prevention. It gained nationwide institutional recognition in the Morgan Report, *Safer Communities: The Local Delivery of Crime Prevention through the Partnership Approach*, emanating from the Home Office in 1991. Apart from seeking to involve other 'social' agencies in both crime prevention and public safety promotion, community safety policy and practice have also made more ambitious claims both to generate greater participation and possibly leadership from all sections of the community (largely geographically defined) and to target social harms from all sources in the locality (not just those classifiable as 'crimes'). Logically, crime and disorder reduction and crime prevention are subsets of community safety, rather than its defining features. Community safety, like the related notions of 'community policing', 'community justice' and 'community crime prevention', has achieved a growing policy salience in recent decades across many neoliberal, late-modern societies. However, as a formal mode of the local 'community governance' of crime, disorder and safety it has, to date, been most pronounced institutionally in the UK (Hughes 2007).

The precise meaning of community safety – like 'crime prevention' and 'crime and disorder reduction' – will always remain the subject of intense debate, not least because 'crime' is socially and historically contingent. Few academic commentators would dissent from the starting point that there is no universally accepted definition of either community safety or crime prevention (Hughes 1998). However, for the purposes of government and governance, it tends to be associated in the UK with public actions aimed at a broad range of 'volume' crimes and – increasingly since the Crime and Disorder Act 1998 – 'disorder' and acts of 'anti-social behaviour' in specific localities and communities. Furthermore, the emphasis is often focused on crime and disorder associated with young people, both as offenders and, to a lesser extent, as victims. Across both the routine day-to-day work of community safety partnerships and embedded in their longer-term strategies it is striking that the 'problem' of young people 'hanging around' and causing 'trouble' has been a persistent area of concern. Indeed it is rare to find a local partnership that does not prioritize the reduction of anti-social behaviour by young people as one of its key strategic objectives.

At the more rhetorical level, community safety is a form of *both* crime prevention and public safety promotion *and* policing in the broadest sense that aspires to involve the participation of community members alongside formal agencies of the local state and quasi-formal voluntary and private agencies (Johnston and Shearing 2003). In reality, research to date indicates that community safety 'work' is both 'owned' and driven by local government and police-dominated crime and disorder reduction partnerships (CDRPs) or community safety partnerships, set up under the terms of the Crime and Disorder Act 1998 in England and Wales (similar developments are evident in Scotland and Northern Ireland). As the institutional manifestations of community safety, CDRPs appear to sit closer to the ambition of the new public management discourse than to the politics and practice of community activism.

There remain striking tensions – perhaps contradictions – between the *social inclusionary* rhetoric and aspirations of community safety and the *social exclusionary* potential of crime and disorder reduction and repressive criminality prevention. According to a growing number of criminologists (see, for example, Johnston and Shearing 2003; Hughes 1998, 2007), governmental logics such as 'community safety', 'crime prevention' and 'security' all necessarily involve political and normative – and not just technological and administrative – questions, despite the pretensions of the new so-called 'crime sciences' and 'What Works' experimentalists. In accord with the famous distinction of the sociologist Charles Wright Mills, the concerns over prevention, fear and safety are both 'private troubles' for many individuals and 'public issues' related to the very structure and dominant processes at work in specific social structures. The potency – instrumental and symbolic – of debates about crime and community safety, and policies designed respectively to reduce and increase their prevalence, is difficult to ignore. Perhaps the greatest challenge for community safety is getting the balance right between local democratic control (and ownership of both the problems and solutions to *fear of crime* and perceived lack of public safety) and the contribution of the expert administration to the management and solution of these pressing public issues. In this context it is crucial to emphasize that community safety, like security, often becomes a metaphor for much wider moral and political questions about justice, social order and the 'good society'.

Gordon Hughes

Related entries

Community justice; Crime and Disorder Act 1998; Crime and disorder reduction (CDR); Crime prevention; Governance; Social harm; Victimology.

Key texts and sources

Crawford, A. (2007) 'Crime prevention and community safety', in M. Maguire *et al.* (eds) *The Oxford Handbook of Criminology*. Oxford: Oxford University Press.

Hughes, G. (1998) *Understanding Crime Prevention: Social Control, Risk and Late Modernity*. Buckingham: Open University Press.

Hughes, G. (2007) *The Politics of Crime and Community*. Basingstoke: Palgrave.

Johnston, L. and Shearing, C. (2003) *The Governance of Security*. London: Sage.

COMPARATIVE YOUTH JUSTICE

Comparative youth justice is a relatively new field in youth justice studies designed to assess the degree of convergence and divergence between systems of juvenile and youth justice worldwide. Recent interest in this area has been driven in part by the pragmatic concern of discovering 'best practice' and in part by theoretical concerns for assessing the impact of globalization and localization on fundamental shifts in national juvenile justice.

There are few rigorous comparative analyses of youth justice. In many respects this is not surprising. Comparative research is fraught with difficulties. The classification and recording of crime differ, and different countries have developed different judicial systems for defining and dealing with young offenders. What is classified as penal custody in one country may not be in others, though regimes may be similar. Not all countries collect the same data on the same age groups and populations. None seem to do so within the same time periods. Linguistic differences in how the terms 'minor', 'juvenile', 'child' and 'young person' are defined and translated into practice further hinder any attempt to ensure a sound comparative base. Typically, most international texts (for example, Winterdyk 2002) focus more on describing the powers and procedures of particular national systems and less on exploring the relevance of global, national and local contexts. Further, they have rarely ventured outside examinations of western (in particular Anglophone) systems of juvenile justice (for an exception, see Friday and Ren 2006).

To date, the more evaluative and critical comparative studies have been directed at processes of internationalization and globalization, and have brought attention to three key issues:

1. The varying degree of compliance and non-compliance with international children's rights conventions in national systems (Abramson, 2006).

2. The processes whereby certain policies and practices are transferred from one jurisdiction to another (Newburn and Sparks 2004).
3. The significance of economic and political globalization in the apparent shifts in crime control and juvenile justice from welfare to justice and to authoritarian and managerialized systems (Muncie 2005).

Since the early 1990s many countries have used the United Nations Convention on the Rights of the Child to improve protections for children and have appointed special commissioners or ombudspersons to champion children's rights. Yet implementation has often been half-hearted and piecemeal. The pressure to ratify the convention is both moral and economic. It may be the most ratified of all international human rights directives, but it is also the most violated. In many countries it seems clear that it is possible to claim an adherence to the principle of universal rights while simultaneously pursuing policies that exacerbate structural inequalities and punitive institutional regimes. 'Cultural difference' and localized political contingencies preclude meaningful adoption of international agreements. Little attention has been given to the extent to which *legal globalization* itself is a concept driven by western notions of 'civilized' human rights. Rights agendas may simply act to bolster western notions of individuality and freedom while implicitly perpetuating imperial and post-colonial notions of a barbaric and authoritarian 'global east' or 'global south'. (Muncie, 2005).

It has also become commonplace for nation-states to look worldwide in efforts to discover 'what works' in preventing crime and to reduce reoffending. Much of this analysis relies on tracing the export of penal – usually punitive – policies from the USA to other advanced industrial economies. However, it is also clear that international youth justice has also been informed by potentially contra-penal trajectories, such as those derived from the import of restorative justice conferencing pioneered in New Zealand and Australia. Such multiple and contrasting lines of 'policy emulation' cast doubt on any notion of homogenized policy transfer. Analyses on an international level are

also in danger of losing sight of the role of 'local agency' in the formulation and implementation of specific policies (Newburn and Sparks 2004). Detailed empirical examination of policymaking in different countries can reveal important differences in substance and significant differences in the processes through which policy is reformed and implemented. These lines of inquiry suggest that policy transfer is rarely direct and complete but is partial and mediated through national and local cultures, which are themselves changing at the same time. In policy terms, the logic of assuming we can learn 'what works' from others is certainly seductive. It implies rational planning and an uncontroversial reliance on a 'crime science' that is free of any political interference. But it also assumes that policies can be transported and are transportable without cognizance of localized cultures, conditions and the politics of space.

Nevertheless, comparative analysis has revealed some remarkable – and apparently uniform – shifts in many western systems such that, since the 1960s, penal welfarism has been undermined by the development of forms of neoliberal or 'justice'-based forms of governance (Muncie and Goldson 2006). As a result, less emphasis is being placed on the social contexts of crime and measures of state protection and more on prescriptions of individual/family/community responsibility and accountability. Welfarism has been increasingly critiqued for encouraging welfare-dependent citizens, overloading the responsibilities of the state and undermining the ability of individuals to take responsibility for their own actions. In juvenile justice this has been reflected in the re-establishment of various 'justice'-based, responsibilization and retributive strategies as the driving forces of modern juvenile justice reform. Numerous authors have remarked on the impact these processes have had on a growing homogenization of criminal justice across western societies, driven in particular by the spread of punitive penal policies from the USA. But comparative analysis also reveals widespread disparities between jurisdictions, particularly in rates of juvenile custody (Muncie 2005; Muncie and Goldson 2006). This suggests that any explanations of relative penal severity or leniency must also be mindful of regional and local cultural sensibilities.

It is certainly true that issues of globalization, transnationalization, policy transfer and localization are gradually being addressed and evaluated, but the extent to which different countries do things differently, how and why such difference is maintained, and why and how selective policies can be successfully transferred still remain under-researched.

John Muncie

Related entries

Children's human rights; Council of Europe; Crime statistics; Punitiveness; United Nations Convention on the Rights of the Child (UNCRC); Welfare; What Works.

Key texts and sources

Abramson, B. (2006) 'Juvenile justice: the "unwanted child"', in E. Jensen and J. Jepsen (eds) *Juvenile Law Violators, Human Rights and the Development of New Juvenile Justice Systems*. Oxford: Hart Publishing.

Friday, P. and Ren, X. (eds) (2006) *Delinquency and Juvenile Justice Systems in the Non-western World*. Monsey, NY: Criminal Justice Press.

Muncie, J. (2005) 'The globalisation of crime control: the case of youth and juvenile justice', *Theoretical Criminology*, 9: 35–64.

Muncie, J. and Goldson, B. (eds) (2006) *Comparative Youth Justice: Critical Issues*. London: Sage.

Newburn, T. and Sparks, R. (eds) (2004) *Criminal Justice and Political Cultures: National and International Dimensions of Crime Control*. Cullompton: Willan Publishing.

Winterdyk, J. (ed.) (2002) *Juvenile Justice Systems: International Perspectives* (2nd edn). Toronto: Canadian Scholars Press.

COMPENSATION

Compensation is financial recompense paid to a person who has suffered loss or damage, including the victim of a criminal offence or a civil wrong. In a criminal justice context it can refer to a sum of money ordered by a court to be paid by a convicted offender to the victim of the crime. It can also refer to money paid from public funds under a government scheme to provide recompense where litigation is impracticable or inappropriate.

A criminal court may make a compensation order against an offender under the Powers of Criminal Courts (Sentencing) Act 2000, requiring him or her to pay compensation for any personal injury, loss or damage resulting from the offence or any other offence taken into consideration in determining sentence, or to make payments for funeral expenses or bereavement in respect of a death resulting from any such offence (excluding road motor-vehicle accidents).

Where a child or young person under the age of 16 is convicted of an offence, the Powers of Criminal Courts (Sentencing) Act 2000, s. 137 provides that the court shall order that the compensation be paid by the parent or guardian of the child or young person, unless it is satisfied that the parent or guardian cannot be found or that it would be unreasonable to make an order for payment in the circumstances of the case. For young people aged 16 and 17, there is no presumption that the order will be made against the parent or guardian but the court retains the power to do so. This responsibility can apply to a local authority with parental responsibility for the child or young person. The parent or guardian should be heard before the order is made, unless he or she has failed to attend court when required to do so. In Scotland, compensation is governed by the Criminal Procedure (Scotland) Act 1995, ss. 249–253.

The Serious Organized Crime and Police Act 2005 (s. 144 and Schedule 10) has also created 'parental compensation orders'. Currently only in force in some areas, these are civil compensation orders made by a magistrates' court on the application of a local authority against the parent or guardian of a child under 10 years of age in respect of property taken, lost or damaged by that child.

The Criminal Injuries Compensation Authority is the agency that compensates victims of violent crime. The rates are set by Parliament in a tariff, subject to additions in some situations for financial loss. In Northern Ireland the relevant agency is the Compensation Agency. Victims of miscarriages of justice may, in specified circumstances, claim compensation under the Criminal Justice Act 1988, s. 133. An additional scheme to compensate victims of miscarriages of justice, the discretionary or 'ex gratia' scheme, was halted by a ministerial statement in April 2006.

Sally Ireland

Related entries

Community punishment and rehabilitation orders (CPROs); Fines; Parental compensation orders (PCOs); Reparation; Reparation orders.

Key texts and sources

See the Office of Public Sector Information's website for the texts of the Criminal Justice Act 1988 (http://www.opsi.gov.uk/acts/acts1988/Ukpga_19880033_en_1.htm), the Criminal Procedure (Scotland) Act 1995 (http://www.opsi.gov.uk/acts/acts1995/Ukpga_19950046_en_1.htm), the Powers of Criminal Courts (Sentencing) Act 2000 (http://www.opsi.gov.uk/acts/acts2000/20000006.htm) and the Serious Organized Crime and Police Act 2005 (http://www.opsi.gov.uk/acts/acts2005/20050015.htm).

See also the website of the Criminal Injuries Compensation Authority (http://www.cica.gov.uk).

CONDITIONAL DISCHARGE

A conditional discharge is a disposal available to the youth court in criminal cases where, having taken into account the circumstances relating to the offence or the offender, punishment is deemed inexpedient. It is an order discharging the defendant subject to the condition that he or she commits no further offence during a stated period, not exceeding three years.

A conditional discharge may be used in circumstances similar to an absolute discharge where the latter is deemed to be too lenient or where it is felt that the child needs to realize that, if there are any criminal proceedings in the future, he or she will not be treated as a first offender. The defendant must consent to being conditionally discharged and the court must explain to him or her that, if he or she commits a further offence within the stated period, he or she will be liable to be sentenced not only for the new offence but also for the offence for which he or she is receiving the conditional discharge (Powers of Criminal Courts (Sentencing) Act 2000, ss. 12–15). If the child reoffends and is sentenced for the original offence, the conditional discharge ceases to have any effect. The court may, however, allow the conditional discharge to continue and sentence only for the second offence. A conditional discharge does not qualify as a conviction and, as such, it does not need to be disclosed, although it will appear as part of the young offender's record in any subsequent criminal proceedings. This disposal does not preclude a reprimand or warning under the Crime and Disorder Act 1998 and it is a useful provision designed to operate as a deterrent against future offending, while minimizing the consequences of criminalization.

The use of conditional discharges has dramatically declined over the last ten years – 22,278 in the youth court in 1995 but only 8,914 in 2005. One reason for this reduction is the constraints imposed on the youth court by the reprimand and warning scheme in the Crime and Disorder Act 1998, whereby a court can impose a conditional discharge on a young person who has received a warning within the previous two years only in exceptional circumstances. The concern is that the decline in the availability and use of this disposal has led to up-tariffing, leading ultimately to an increase in more punitive measures, particularly custodial sentences.

Sue Bandalli

Related entries

Absolute discharge; Arrest and decision-making process; Reprimands and final warnings.

Key texts and sources

See the Office of Public Sector Information's website (http://www.opsi.gov.uk/acts/acts2000/20000006. htm) for the text of the Powers of Criminal Courts (Sentencing) Act 2000.

CONNEXIONS

Connexions is a service for 13–19-year-olds that was introduced throughout England and that absorbed the Careers Service in 2001.

Connexions was given two principal responsibilities: to deliver careers information, advice and guidance to all 13–19-year-olds (the remit of the former Careers Service); and to reduce the size of the group who were not in education, employment or training (NEET).

Connexions had two major successes. First, brand recognition was established rapidly – before the service was a year old, nearly all young people recognized the name. Secondly, high levels of satisfaction were expressed by the young people who used the service. However, from its inception Connexions was beset by two major problems. First, the service was never given sufficient funds to meet all its obligations. An assessment in 2004 found that Connexions would need around 15,000 front-line professional staff in order to deliver in full; at that time just 7,722 were in post. The universal service –

providing career guidance, advice and information to all 13–19-year-olds – was the casualty.

Second, it became apparent that hauling down the size of the NEET group was not a sensible priority target. In some ways the NEET category was too narrow because it excluded many young people who were at risk of unemployment, offending and reoffending, and other problems. In other ways the category was too broad. Young people who became temporarily NEET while they explored their options did not necessarily need any assistance. For others (with family responsibilities or multiple problems), neither education, training nor employment was always suitable in the short term.

Wales and Scotland never adopted the Connexions model. They introduced all-age careers services that are believed (by all interested parties in Wales and Scotland) to be working satisfactorily. In 2006 the government announced that England's Connexions' funding and responsibilities would be transferred to the children's trusts that were being established within local authorities. The Connexions' brand-name could continue to be used, but the national organization would disappear.

Ken Roberts

Related entries

Behaviour and education support teams (BESTs); Children (Leaving Care) Act 2000; Children's trusts; Mentoring; New Deal for Young People; Positive Activities for Young People (PAYP); Youth Matters; Youth offending teams (YOTs).

Key texts and sources

Furlong, A. (2006) 'Not a very NEET solution: representing problematic labour market transitions among early school-leavers', *Work, Employment and Society*, 20: 553–69.

Instance, D., Rees, G. and Williamson, H. (1994) *Young People Not in Education, Training or Employment in South Glamorgan*. Cardiff: South Glamorgan Training and Enterprise Council.

Yates, S. and Payne, M. (2006) 'Not so NEET? A critique of the use of NEET in setting targets for interventions with young people', *Journal of Youth Studies*, 9: 329–44.

Connexions' website is at **www.connexions.gov.uk**.

CONTESTABILITY

Contestability theory was developed in the early 1980s (Baumol *et al.* 1982) but came to prominence following the government review of the correctional services carried out by Patrick Carter (2003). It is based on the notion that, in order to act competitively and be innovative, monopoly providers need to be exposed to the threat of competition to deliver 'best value'.

Contestability is often seen as a form of privatization, but its proponents argue that it refers to a situation where public service providers face a credible threat of competition from the voluntary, not-for-profit and private sectors. The development of services is facilitated through the commissioning of contracts to a 'mixed economy' of providers.

At present, there are commissioning arrangements in the youth justice system for custodial accommodation, with the current mixed economy of young offender institutions, secure training centres and secure children's homes. Equally, the voluntary sector provides some 52 per cent of youth inclusion programmes. The introduction of contestability into public services has been at the forefront of government plans to restructure the Prison and Probation Services. It is in the Prison Service that the concept has been most widely applied through the process of market testing. Public sector prisons have competed (sometimes successfully) against private contractors. The National Probation Service has, in the past, commissioned a range of services through its partnership arrangements with other agencies. Until the creation of the National Probation Service in 2001, most probation areas were spending significant amounts of money in the community and voluntary sector, having been set a target to commit 8 per cent of their resource budgets during the late 1990s in this way.

The introduction of private (for profit) companies into the criminal justice arena, on the other hand, is a relatively new development, but there has already been significant current private sector involvement in the delivery of both operational (for example, electronic monitoring) and corporate services (for example, facilities, IT and estate management). Under the current plans the commissioning of offender services is to be transferred from the 42 local probation boards to 9 regional offender managers. Probation areas will become providers and will have to bid for contracts against the private, voluntary and community sectors to deliver services (many of which they currently hold statutory responsibility for). It is also clear, however, that probation boards will also be expected to commission services themselves at the local level – usually referred to as 'subcontracting'. Initially 'interventions' appear most vulnerable to contestability, although it is envisaged that eventually all aspects of supervision will be opened up to the market. This is in marked contrast to the commissioning role of the Youth Justice Board (YJB), which is limited to the secure estate. The commissioning of services of youth offending teams (YOTs) as a whole, or any of the component service elements, is the responsibility of the YOT itself.

Contestability is seen as having the potential to bring positive outcomes, both in terms of increased innovation and diversity in service delivery. From this perspective, public sector services are viewed as costly, unresponsive and overly bureaucratic. The introduction of competition is seen as a lever to increase efficiency and to reduce costs. It is also seen as an acknowledgement of the variety of organizations and interventions required to meet the demands of an increasingly complex criminal justice system.

Critics of contestability, on the other hand, argue that it has the potential to add layers of bureaucracy and expense and could lead to the fragmentation of service delivery and the skills that underpin it at community level. This could undermine current arrangements for the management of high-risk offenders that rely on highly developed, co-ordinated and integrated relationships between the partner agencies. Competition may drive down costs to a level that, while meeting short-term goals, produces services of a lesser quality. Larger organizations in the private sector can 'cherry pick' services or can deliver services as 'loss leaders', thereby reducing competition in real terms and resulting in the provision of public services that are reliant on a small, but influential, number of providers.

There are considerable costs involved in commissioning, contract specification, monitoring and management that are likely to divert attention from front-line activity with offenders. In its response to the plans, the YJB claimed that having to negotiate local agreements indivdually would destabilize services. Despite the enthusiasm shown by the government, the benefits of contestability remain largely unproven. For example, formal commissioning has not affected a significant step change in the quality of the juvenile secure estate and has tied the YJB into long-term arrangements with private providers.

Lol Burke and Steve Collett

Related entries

Juvenile secure estate; Managerialism; National Offender Management Service (NOMS); Probation Service; Youth offending teams.

Key texts and sources

Baumol, W.J., Panzar, J.C. and Wilig, R.D. (1982) *Contestable Markets and the Theory of Industry Structure.* New York, NY: Harcourt Brace Jovanovich.

Burke, L. (2005) *From Probation to the National Offender Management Service: Issues of Contestability, Culture and Community Involvement.* London: National Association of Probation Officers.

Carter, P. (2003) *Managing Offenders, Reducing Crime: A New Approach.* London: Home Office.

Hough, M., Allen, R. and Padel, U. (eds) (2006) *Reshaping Probation and Prisons: The New Offender Management Framework.* Bristol: Policy Press.

Wargent, M. (2006) 'Contestability: is the model for NOMS "fit for purpose"?', *Vista,* 9: 162–68.

CORPORAL PUNISHMENT

> Corporal punishment is not defined in any of the UK statutes providing for the defence of 'reasonable chastisement' (England, Wales and Northern Ireland) or 'justifiable assault' (Scotland) to be raised in relation to any charge of assault of a child. Instead, the courts will examine 'punishment to the body of the child' in the context of its severity, which then determines the type of assault charged by the prosecuting authorities.

Since the nineteenth century, the UK courts have allowed a defence of 'reasonable chastisement' (England, Wales and Northern Ireland) or 'justifiable assault' (Scotland) to be raised by parents (or anyone else acting in the place of parents) who administered corporal punishment to a child. The defence was later given statutory effect in s. 1(7) of the Children and Young Persons Act 1933 and in s. 12(7) of the Children and Young Persons (Scotland) Act 1937. Amendments to UK education law have removed the ability of teachers to claim the right to use the defence pursuant to powers delegated by parents.

In England and Wales, s. 58 of the Children Act 2004 limits the defence of 'reasonable chastisement' to cases of the most trivial form of assault (that is, common assault under s. 39 of the Criminal Justice Act 1988), which might comprise, for example, 'moderate' smacks where 'only transient harm' is caused. The defence is no longer available for more serious charges of assault (including assault occasioning actual bodily harm under s. 47 of the Offences against the Person Act (OAPA) 1861; causing grievous bodily harm under s. 18 of the 1861 Act; wounding with intent under s. 20 of the 1861 Act; or cruelty to persons under 16 contrary to s. 1 of the Children and Young Persons Act 1933). The Law Reform Miscellaneous Provisions (Northern Ireland) Order 2006, purported by Article 2 to apply s. 58 of the Children Act 2004 to Northern Ireland, was challenged by the Northern Ireland Commissioner for Children and Young People before the High Court in Northern Ireland.

In Scotland, s. 51 of the Criminal Justice (Scotland) Act 2003 offers greater protection to children and provides that, where parents claim that physical punishment was carried out in exercise of a parental right, then in determining any question as to whether what was done was 'a justifiable assault' (and thus as providing a defence to any charge of assault) a court must have regard to the factors listed by the European Court of Human Rights in *A* v. *UK*. Such factors include:

the nature of what was done; the reason for it; the circumstances in which it took place; its duration and frequency; any effect (whether physical or mental) which it has had on the child; the child's age; and the child's personal characteristics including sex and state of health at the time the thing was done (s. 51 (1))

and 'to such other factors as it considers appropriate in the circumstances of the case' (s. 51(2)). The section also provides that blows to the head, shaking, the use of an implement and punishment of a child aged 16 and over are prohibited (s. 51(3) and (4)).

Christina Lyon

Related entries

Boot camps; Borstals; Child abuse; Detention centres; Safeguarding.

Key texts and sources

Lyon, C. (2000) *Loving Smack or Lawful Assault: A Contradiction in Human Rights and Law*. London: Institute for Public Policy Research.

See the Office of Public Sector Information's website for the texts of the Children Act 2004 (http://www.opsi.gov.uk/acts/acts2004/20040031.htm), the Criminal Justice Act 1988 (http://www.opsi.gov.uk/acts/acts1988/Ukpga_19880033_en_1.htm), the Criminal Justice (Scotland) Act 2003 (http://www.opsi.gov.uk/legislation/scotland/acts2003/20030007.htm) and the Law Reform (Miscellaneous Provisions) (Northern Ireland) Order 2006 (http://www.opsi.gov.uk/si/si2006/06em1945.htm).

See also the Children are Unbeatable Alliance's website (http://www.childrenareunbeatable.org.uk/).

CORPORATISM

> Corporatism refers to a general tendency towards the centralization of policy and greater government intervention. In youth justice, the aims of a corporatist approach are to reduce conflict among professional and other interest groups, to promote interagency co-operation and to encourage consensus on aims and values.

In 1989 John Pratt identified corporatism as the 'third model' of juvenile justice and argued that it, rather than the much debated welfare and justice models, was becoming the dominant model in England and Wales. Corporatism was characterized by the blurring of boundaries between agencies and professional groups, in the interests of policy coherence. An early example was the juvenile liaison bureau in Northampton, in which social workers, police officers, probation officers and others worked together in the interests of diverting juvenile offenders from prosecution and in designing community-based programmes of intervention. The approach came largely from initiatives by social work and other practitioners who saw it as an effective means of achieving desirable policy aims, particularly diversion and a greater use of community-based measures at the expense of custody. By the end of the 1980s it was strongly supported by central government as a means of improving efficiency and promoting a sense of common purpose. It was, however, criticized by such commentators as Stan Cohen (1985), who worried that the erosion of distinctions between agencies would encourage net-widening and lead to the incorporation of welfare agencies into an essentially repressive agenda. It was also viewed sceptically by advocates of a *justice* approach, who criticized the shift of power (from courts meeting in public and operating according to known rules) to agencies with no formal constitutional basis (which met in 'private' and against whose decisions there was no appeal).

Civil servants in the Home Office were impressed by the success of youth justice workers in promoting diversion and reducing the use of custody during the 1980s, and they encouraged the development of a similar kind of corporate approach in the adult criminal justice system. This approach was interrupted by the punitive populism of Michael Howard's period as Home Secretary (1993–7) but was revived under the Labour government elected in 1997, with a commitment to modernizing the system and 'joining up' policies. The creation of the Youth Justice Board in September 1998 is perhaps the clearest indication of the government's enthusiasm for a classic corporate approach, and this was supported by the creation of youth offending teams (YOTs) and the statutory requirement in the Crime and Disorder Act 1998 for agencies involved in youth justice to work in partnership with each other.

The renewal of a corporatist approach, especially in the form of YOTs, led to a re-emergence of arguments for and against it. Critics worried that a concern with the welfare of young people would be forgotten in the YOTs' prioritization of offending over other problems; supporters argued that YOTs gave interagency working a more stable institutional form than it had ever had before. What is certain is that interagency working now takes place in a context set by central government policy, rather than resulting from local practitioner initiatives, and in that sense it is more thoroughly corporatist.

David Smith

Related entries

Crime and Disorder Act 1998; Managerialism; Net-widening; Partnership working; Systems management; Youth Justice Board (YJB); Youth offending teams (YOTs).

Key texts and sources

Burnett, R. and Appleton, C. (2004) *Joined-up Youth Justice: Tackling Youth Crime in Partnership*. Lyme Regis: Russell House.

Cohen, S. (1985) *Visions of Social Control: Crime, Punishment and Classification*. Cambridge: Polity Press.

Pratt, J. (1989) 'Corporatism: the third model of juvenile justice', *British Journal of Criminology*, 29: 236–54.

COUNCIL OF EUROPE

The Council of Europe is a pan-European organization set up in 1949 to create unity between its 46 member states by defending human rights, parliamentary democracy and the rule of law. It is distinct from the European Union but works closely with it.

The Council of Europe is the continent's oldest political organization, with 46 member states. Its constitutional text is the European Convention on Human Rights, which is legally enforced by the European Court of Human Rights. After the fall of the Berlin Wall, the council expanded considerably, and its main functions today are to assist central and eastern European countries, including the Russian Federation, in consolidating political, legal and constitutional reforms and developing continent-wide agreements on social and legal practices.

The council is divided into three main pillars: the Parliamentary Assembly (which comprises elected representatives); the Committee of Ministers (made up of national foreign ministers); and the Congress of Local and Regional Authorities. Its main work is undertaken by expert committees that draft recommendations and conventions that are then adopted by the Council of Ministers.

The council first addressed the issue of youth justice in 1987. At the forefront of this recommendation is the requirement to respect existing international norms and standards. Primarily this refers to the European Convention on Human Rights and the United Nations Convention on the Rights of the Child, but it also refers to other United Nations conventions – on juveniles deprived of their liberty (the Havana Rules), the administration of juvenile justice (the Beijing Rules) and on the prevention of juvenile delinquency (the Riyadh Guidelines). It sets out a strategy based on minimum intervention and welfare principles that encourage diversion from prosecution, addressing the needs of offenders and only using incarceration as a last resort. In 1988 it passed a second recommendation on juvenile delinquency among young people from migrant families that stressed the importance of promoting the social integration of young migrants by addressing exposure to intolerance and discrimination, cultural conflicts and lack of family support.

Fifteen years later, in 2003, the council revisited the role of juvenile justice in the wake of increasing concerns about violence and drug-related offending and the emergence in some European countries of a more punitive approach towards young offenders. Concerns were also raised about the efficiency and effectiveness of existing juvenile justice systems and confusion about their purpose – are they there to punish, to deter or to help? Developments in research were simultaneously questioning the validity of minimum intervention, and experimentation with alternative approaches, such as restorative justice and intensive, community-based support and supervision, were offering new and potentially more effective ways of addressing juvenile crime.

In reappraising its recommendation from 1987, the Council endorsed a number of its key principles, such as the requirement that juveniles receive at least the same level of procedural safeguards as adults. But influenced largely by developments in England and Wales, it recommended a number of new principles, such as the need to respond quicker, earlier and more consistently to offending behaviour and to include an element of reparation to victims and their communities. It also recommended extending responsibility for offending behaviour to the parents of young offenders and treating young adults as juveniles where their level of maturity warranted it. In practice, despite the efforts of the Council of Europe, European juvenile justice has no common vision or purpose around which a consensus could be built. Whether this is desirable or not is another matter.

John Graham

Related entries

Children First; Children's human rights; Comparative youth justice; European Convention on Human Rights (ECHR); United Nations Convention on the Rights of the Child (UNCRC); United Nations Guidelines for the Prevention of Juvenile Deliquency; United Nations Rules for the

Protection of Juveniles Deprived of their Liberty; United Nations Standard Minimum Rules for the Administration of Juvenile Justice.

Key texts and sources

Council of Europe (1987) *Social Reactions to Juvenile Delinquency* (Recommendation R (87) 20). Strasbourg: Council of Europe.
Council of Europe (2003) *New Ways of Dealing with Juvenile Delinquency and the Role of Juvenile Justice* (Recommendation R (2003) 20). Strasbourg: Council of Europe.

COURT OFFICERS

In the context of the youth justice system, a court officer is normally a member of a youth offending team, whose duty it is to represent the youth justice service in the youth court and/or the Crown court.

A youth offending team (YOT) court officer might provide information to the court on bail and sentencing arrangements, such as information on the contents of bail supervision and support, community sentences and intensive supervision (with or without electronic monitoring/tagging). In cases where the court is considering its remand and/or sentencing options, the YOT court officer might also provide information on the availability of places in the juvenile secure estate (and other non-secure residential establishments) and address such issues as vulnerability. In addition to this they may need to advise on court reports and, when necessary, provide updates on progress in respect of particular cases. In summary, court officers, as described by the Youth Justice Board, are 'the face of the YOT for magistrates'.

In most YOTs, court officers also have a responsibility for ensuring that reports (especially pre-sentence reports) are properly prepared in line with the National Standards for Youth Justice Services, although technically this is the responsibility of the YOT manager. While it is possible for the YOT to be represented in court by any of its qualified staff, it is becoming the norm for the court officer post to be regarded as a specialist function. Arrangements for the relationship between the courts and YOTs are governed by 'service agreements' and 'protocols', examples of which are provided by the Youth Justice Board (2006f) (along with guidance on good practice) and can be found on its website.

The practice of court officers is governed, to some extent, by the Key Element of Effective Practice (KEEP) 'The swift administration of justice'. One of the stated Key Indicators of Quality is that 'YOTs should ensure that the production of reports does not result in unnecessary delays'. The KEEP was derived from concerns raised in the Audit Commission report, *Misspent Youth* (1996; see also Jones 2001), which reported on the effects of delays on the youth justice system and recommended that they should be substantially reduced.

Richard Hester

Related entries

Bail information schemes (BISs); National Standards for Youth Justice Services; Remand Management; Youth offending teams (YOTs).

Key texts and sources

Audit Commission (1996) *Misspent Youth*. London: Audit Commission.

Jones, D. (2001) 'Misjudged youth: a critique of the Audit Commission's reports on youth justice', *British Journal of Criminology*, 41: 362–80.

Youth Justice Board (2006f) *Courts and Orders* (available online at **http://www.yjb.gov.uk/en-gb/ practitioners/CourtsAndOrders/**).

See also the Youth Justice Board's Key Elements of Effective Practice: Swift Administration of Justice (available online at **http://www.yjb.gov.uk/ Publications/Scripts/prodView.asp?idproduct= 47&eP**).

The Youth Justice Board's website is at **http://www.yjb.gov.uk/**.

CRIME AND DISORDER ACT 1998

> The Crime and Disorder Act 1998 was passed by the New Labour government to provide 'root and branch' reforms of the youth justice system. The provisions of the Act apply to pre-trial, trial and sentencing procedures, as well as to the establishment of the anti-social behaviour order.

Throughout the 1990s, while in opposition, New Labour pledged to overhaul the youth justice system. After its election to government in 1997, it published no less than five consultation papers setting out detailed proposals for reform. *Tackling Youth Crime* (September 1997) proposed reforms to the way in which youth crime is dealt with and punished by criminal justice agencies; *Getting to Grips with Crime* (September 1997) examined the role of community and criminal justice agencies in tackling youth crime; *New National and Local Focus on Youth Crime* (October 1997) proposed a new management system for the delivery of youth justice services; *Tackling Delays in the Youth Justice System* (September 1997) proposed ways of speeding up the process from arrest to sentencing; and *A Quiet Life* (September 1997) proposed the anti-social behaviour order. A white paper containing a range of further proposals followed in November 1997 (*No More Excuses: A New Approach to Tackling Youth Crime in England and Wales*).

The government held that, by implementing a rigorous preventive strategy on youth crime, it would ultimately offset later incidences of adult crime. The strategy, therefore, involves a package of measures that builds on New Labour's pledge to be 'tough on crime, tough on the causes of crime'. Its multifarious provisions follow the themes of *Tackling Youth Crime* – namely, to encourage young people to take responsibility for their offending behaviour; to alleviate the causes of crime through intensive and early intervention; and to prevent youth crime by tackling early signs of troublesome behaviour. The new youth justice system that emerged from these reforms was to be managed and implemented by partnership arrangements – primarily youth offending teams (YOTs) – as well as by local communities and local government.

The Crime and Disorder Act 1998 provides an overriding aim for all practitioners involved in tackling youth crime to *prevent offending* (s. 37). This statutory principal aim was designed to ensure that *all* the agencies involved were clear about the purpose of their joint endeavours in relation to young offenders. Although the section itself is bereft of detail as to how such 'prevention' work was to be achieved, the government produced guidance (Home Office *et al.* 1998b) in terms of fulfilling the aim comprising six key – if disparate – objectives:

1. The swift administration of justice so that every young person accused of breaking the law has the matter resolved without delay.
2. Confronting young offenders with the consequences of their offending, for themselves and their family, their victims and the community and helping them to develop a sense of personal responsibility.
3. Intervention which tackles the particular factors (personal, family, social, educational or health) that put the young person at risk of offending and which strengthens 'protective factors'.
4. Punishment proportionate to the seriousness and persistence of the offending.
5. Encouraging reparation to victims by young offenders.
6. Reinforcing the responsibilities of parents.

The detailed provisions of the Crime and Disorder Act 1998 itself are similarly disparate in terms of their approach to youth crime prevention. The child safety order (s. 11) aimed at young children under 10 (that is, under the minimum age of criminal responsibility) is more directly 'preventative' in that it allows the YOT to intervene where a child's behaviour may fit within criminal definitions (although cannot be prosecuted as such at this age), breaches a local curfew (s. 14) or is 'anti-social'. Coupled with this order, and many of the sentences established under the Act for convicted offenders, a parenting order is created by s. 8 which supplements previous orders applicable to the parents of con-

victed offenders under the Criminal Justice Act 1991. This new order combines requirements of parents tailored to their individual situation with compulsory attendance at parenting classes run by a local authority. The introduction of the anti-social behaviour order (s. 1) may also be viewed as part of the series of crime prevention measures, since it was the government's view that anti-social behaviour in young people may be a precursor to criminal behaviour, although critics have denied the order's rehabilitative potential.

The provisions aimed at tackling reoffending include the reprimands and warnings scheme, which effectively places the cautioning process on a statutory footing. This scheme provides for young persons who admit guilt to their first criminal charge to be reprimanded by a police officer. On a second (or more serious first charge), the young person may additionally be referred to the YOT for any necessary rehabilitative intervention in the form of a 'warning'. Both reprimands and warnings are single opportunities to avoid a criminal conviction and, in that sense, reflect the previous Home Office guidance issued in 1994, stating that repeat cautioning was to be avoided.

Much of the previous sentencing legislation on young offenders was left untouched, but new forms of community and custodial penalties were added to the options available to the youth courts. The various custodial penalties that had pre-existed were consolidated into the detention and training order (Crime and Disorder Act 1998, s. 73), which allows for half the sentence to be served in an institution appropriate to the offender's age and the other half to be served in the community under supervision. The order combines the elements of the previous secure training order with detention in a young offender institution, although the government reduced the minimum age at which custodial sentences can apply to young people to the age of 10. Existing community sentences were supplemented by a short action plan order (which adds little to the existing supervision order), the drug treatment and testing order and a restorative justice-based reparation order.

Despite the wide-ranging nature of these reforms and the government's pledge to implement a 'new' youth justice process, critics of the Crime and Disorder Act 1998 concur in arguing that it merely repackaged many pre-existing approaches and did not offer a clear move away from the previous administration's focus on punitive measures (see Brownlee 1998a; Fionda 1999; Goldson 1999; Morris and Gelsthorpe 2000). Subsequently, many of the sentencing provisions of the 1998 Act have been consolidated within the Powers of the Criminal Courts (Sentencing) Act 2000.

Julia Fionda

Related entries

Crime and disorder reduction; Criminal Courts (Sentencing) Act 2000; Early intervention; No More Excuses; Partnership working; Youth Justice Board; Youth offending teams (YOTs).

Key texts and sources

Brownlee, I. (1998a) 'New Labour – new penology? Punitive rhetoric and the limits of managerialism in criminal justice policy', *Journal of Law and Society*, 25: 313–25.

Fionda, J. (1999) 'New Labour, old hat: youth justice and the Crime and Disorder Act 1998', *Criminal Law Review*, 36–47.

Fionda, J. (2005) *Devils and Angels: Youth, Policy and Crime*. Oxford: Hart Publishing.

Goldson, B. (ed.) (1999) *Youth Justice: Contemporary Policy and Practice*. Aldershot: Ashgate.

Home Office, Lord Chancellor's Department, Attorney General's Office, Department of Health, Department for Education and Employment and Welsh Office (1998b) *Youth Justice: The Statutory Principal Aim of Preventing Offending by Children and Young People*. London: Home Office.

Morris, A. and Gelsthorpe, L. (2000) 'Something old, something borrowed, something blue, but something new? A comment on the prospects for restorative justice under the Crime and Disorder Act 1998', *Criminal Law Review*, 18–30.

See the Office of Public Sector Information's website (http://www.opsi.gov.uk/acts/acts1998/19980037.htm) for the text of the Crime and Disorder Act 1998.

CRIME AND DISORDER REDUCTION (CDR)

At its simplest and most tautological, crime and disorder reduction (CDR) is any measure, or variety of measures, aimed at reducing acts of crime and disorder. In the UK 'crime reduction' has become associated chiefly with targeted and relatively short-term situational and policing measures put in place by a variety of local agencies in line with central government performance targets. 'Disorder reduction' is less often clearly defined in its own terms but, in governmental terms, it is largely synonymous with the campaign against anti-social behaviour (often of young people).

It is important to note that the term 'crime *and disorder* reduction' (CDR) is a relatively new policy goal for both the police and other 'partners' in local crime control and youth justice. It is now institutionalized in the policy field, not only in the work of youth offending teams but, also, more broadly, through local community safety strategies and local multi-agency community safety partnerships – formally known in England (but not Wales) as 'crime and disorder reduction partnerships'. CDR is a meeting point of both rational scientific, preventive adaptations and problem-solving, and of potentially irrational, symbolic 'acting out' measures of repression and exclusion (Garland 2001). In other words this new policy mandate (of CDR) sees the confluence of two uneasy policy 'bedfellows' – that of the new public management and that of moral communitarianism (Hughes 2007). This policy confluence of two seemingly different discourses or ideologies is important to recognize, since it illustrates a more generalizable and crucial lesson for criminologists – namely, that developments in local crime control and youth justice are not necessarily coherent and internally consistent.

Crime reduction has a close affinity to targeted crime prevention and is focused largely on routine, volume crimes (such as theft and burglary) and on achieving national reductive targets. On the other hand, disorder reduction is meant to encapsulate efforts to control 'sub-criminal' acts of incivility and anti-social behaviour. Mistakenly and counter-logically, politicians and policymakers often view CDR as being synonymous with the wider policy mandate of community safety. However, it is more logical to suggest that CDR is – or, rather, should be viewed as – a subset of the broader goal of community safety.

Crime reduction came to prominence in government circles in the UK with the publication of a set of Home Office evaluation reviews of 'what works' in reducing crime in 1998. Owing much to a USA-based 'scientific' review of what works in crime prevention by Sherman *et al.* (1997), these findings – derived from a Home Office-based administrative criminology – gained support from the New Labour government and resulted in the rolling out of a national (and seemingly research driven and evidence led) Crime Reduction Programme (CRP) (1999–2002) across a number of chosen sites in England and Wales. The three-year CRP, managed from the Home Office, was intended to build on the Crime and Disorder Act 1998 and to 'harness' the activities of new local crime and disorder reduction partnerships. The CRP was also intended to achieve maximum impact for money spent, allowing such positive impact to be progressively improved. The programme hoped to: promote innovation; to generate a significant improvement in knowledge about effectiveness and cost effectiveness; and to encourage the 'mainstreaming' of 'best practice'. As Stenson and Edwards (2004: 225) note: 'At worst this may pressure local policy makers towards a naïve emulation of measures that in very different settings have, it is claimed, been shown to have "worked".' According to many academic researchers involved in this programme of 'evidence based' crime reduction, however, it failed to live up to its promise, not least due to problems of implementation and to the imperative for ministers to get 'quick' wins – at times turning 'evidence-based policy' into 'policy-based evidence'.

Follett (2006) has noted that there are two crucial assumptions underpinning the discourse of crime reduction: first, that crime cannot be prevented but merely reduced – in other words, crime is viewed pragmatically as an inevitable part of everyday life; and, secondly, cost effectiveness is pivotal to judging success, failure and/or 'what works'. In other words, crime reduction is associated with an economic calculus of 'what works'. Its advantage for policymakers and politicians alike is that it is seemingly less 'fluffy' than either crime prevention and/or community safety, which are both notoriously difficult to 'measure' in terms of outcomes. Crime reduction measures, therefore, hold the promise of being subject to 'before and after' experimental evaluations, thus being both scientifically measurable and capable of informing cost-effective outcomes. However, as an instance of evidence-based policy, crime reduction runs the risk of being dominated by counting solely that which is easily measurable.

Disorder reduction is rarely ever spoken of in isolation from CDR. Rather, 'disorder reduction' is almost universally translated by policymakers, politicians and most academic researchers alike as 'anti-social behaviour' reduction and management. In terms of specific policy and practice initiatives, 'disorder reduction' – recoded as a crusade against the 'anti-social' (youth) – may be characterized as an uneasy mixture of the following:

- Techniques of 'rational' risk management.
- Responsibilizing strategies targeted at individuals, families and communities.
- Emotive and symbolically reassuring 'zero tolerance' policing of the 'anti-social' and 'disorderly' (often drawing on popular, mass-'mediated' fears of the dangerous and predatory 'outsiders').

It would appear there is a dominant national UK trend towards the punitive exclusion of specific categories of youth (often the most marginalized and already 'outcast' young people), together with both damaged and damaging adults. In this current conjuncture, it is hard to deny that the discourse and practices of anti-social behaviour control, carry potentially worrying long-term consequences for the rights of targeted 'risky' populations. At the same time, when we examine practices in depth and *in situ* in their specific 'geo-historical' contexts, the landscape is far from tidy and even in character. Compromise, contestation, even resistance, are all present in the institutional realities of the local implementation and delivery of crime and disorder reduction-qua-community safety strategies targeted at the persistent 'youth problem'. As a site of governance, partnership work in the UK around 'anti-social' youth thus remains 'unstable', and the actions of key actors are to varying degrees 'unpredictable'. Furthermore, despite the central government project to roll out a common approach to youth CDR across the country, the uneven development of policy and practice in distinct localities (with their own specific cultures and traditions of crime control and safety) should not be underestimated by social scientists. As Muncie and Hughes (2002: 16) concluded in their overview of the changing and competing modes of youth governance under neoliberal conditions at the end of the twentieth century: 'No reading of the future can ever be clear. The logics of welfare paternalism, justice and rights, responsibilization, remoralization, authoritarianism and managerialism will continue their "dance" and new spaces for resistance, relational politics and governmental innovation will be opened up.'

A similarly nuanced reading of the uneven local developments around the management of anti-social behaviour in the name of CDR may be necessary.

Gordon Hughes

Related entries

Anti-social behaviour (ASB); Community justice; Community safety; Crime and Disorder Act 1998: Crime prevention; Governance; Managerialism; Net-widening; Partnership working; Politicization; Prolific and other priority offenders (PPOs) strategy; Youth and policing; Zero tolerance.

Key texts and sources

Crawford, A. (2007) 'Crime prevention and community safety', in M. Maguire *et al.* (eds) *The Oxford Handbook of Criminology*. Oxford: Oxford University Press.
Follett, M. (2006) 'Crime reduction', in E. McLaughlin and J. Muncie (eds) *The Sage Dictionary of Criminology*. London: Sage.

Garland, D. (2001) *The Culture of Control: Crime and Social Order in Contemporary Society*. Oxford: Oxford University Press.
Hughes, G. (2007) *The Politics of Crime and Community*. Basingstoke: Macmillan.
Muncie, J. and Hughes, G. (2002) 'Modes of youth governance: political rationalities, criminalisation and resistance', in J. Muncie et al. (eds) *Youth Justice: Critical Readings*. London: Sage.
Sherman, L.W., Gottfredson, D.C., MacKenzie, D.L., Eck, J., Reuter, P. and Bushway, S. (1997) *Preventing Crime: What Works, What Doesn't, What's Promising. Research in Brief*. Washington, DC: National Institute of Justice.
Stenson, K. and Edwards, A. (2004) 'Policy transfer in local crime control: beyond naïve emulation' in T. Newburn and R. Sparks (eds) *Criminal Justice and Political Cultures: National and International Dimensions of Crime Control* Cullompton: Willan Publishing.

CRIME PREVENTION

Crime prevention concerns any action taken, or measure employed, by public or private actors aimed at the prevention of damage caused by acts defined in law as criminal. Common to all forms of crime prevention is a future orientation rather than the reactive orientation of traditional criminal justice.

Viewed in its broadest sense, crime prevention, like, for example, the notion of social control, has been around as long as humans have sought to protect their property from threat and themselves from harm to their well-being. None the less, as a formal feature of modern crime control systems, it is more helpful to plot the rise of crime prevention since the latter decades of the twentieth century. In turn, it was during these decades that we also witnessed an ever increasing output of criminological writing and research aimed at classifying – largely for governmental purposes – the major types of crime prevention techniques and strategies and their seeming effectiveness or otherwise (Hughes 1998; Tilley 2005; Crawford 2007).

The international 'growth industry' and 'import-export' trade in practical advice and policy knowledge about crime prevention techniques and strategies (associated with 'evaluation' research) has witnessed the rise of several key definitions and typologies of crime prevention. In turn, these have had an uneven but important impact in changing policy and practice both in formal crime control systems and in the routine activities of citizens and their efforts to protect themselves prudentially (a variant of responsibilization). Crime prevention research is thus a striking example of what may be termed 'policy criminology' and the development of new governmental *savoir* arising out of social scientific inquiry and policy entrepreneurship (Hughes 2007).

Arguably, the most influential means of classifying crime prevention is that based on the distinction between *social* (or 'community' based) and *situational* techniques and strategies of prevention.

Social crime prevention

Social crime prevention is focused chiefly on changing social environments, including the nature of communities in which 'criminals' and victims live and in trying to change the motivations of offenders. It is centrally concerned with causation or aetiology, both in the short and long term. Social crime prevention and its allied measures, therefore, tend to prioritize the development of schemes and initiatives aimed at deterring potential or actual offenders from future offending. Its focus is on 'people' and 'places' and, in particular, on young people 'at risk' (socially and psychologically). In intellectual terms it is associated with what may be termed a causative and social criminological imagination. Typical instances of this social logic of crime prevention are the development of schemes for potential or actual young offenders and educational initiatives targeted at teaching young people about the risks of drug taking and carrying knives. Given the concern to address the social causes and longer-term processes behind both the criminalization and victimization of people in particular places and communities, it is difficult to demonstrate 'success' and evidence

about 'what works' in performance management terms around measurable targets. This has been seen as the Achilles heel of community-based, social crime prevention measures that policy entrepreneurs in both the USA and UK have been keen to emphasize. This critique of the 'old' causative criminology – of which social crime prevention has been a key component – underpins to a large extent the rise to prominence since the 1980s of situational crime prevention and what may be more accurately described as its 'anti-social' criminology (Hughes 2007) rather than Garland's (2001) 'new criminologies of everyday life'.

Situational crime prevention

Situational crime prevention is chiefly concerned with opportunity reduction and focuses on 'places' and 'products' rather than 'people' *per se*. It assumes that most crime is about choices made by selfish but rational actors who calculate risk in a profit-and-loss fashion. The 'criminal' in this anti-social crime science mentality is effectively amoral, asocial 'economic man'. Practically, situational crime prevention has been associated with the production and evaluation of many of the everyday, taken-for-granted techniques of prevention, from 'traffic calmers', CCTV systems of surveillance to product security devices. It has the merit of being focused on the here-and-now and offering practical solutions to 'design out' crime opportunities. It offers a view of the 'social' as simple: 'opportunity makes the thief' and, in turn, lack of opportunity unmakes the thief. Since the 1980s it has been especially associated with Home Office administrative criminology led by R.V. Clarke and, of late, is associated with the so-called 'crime sciences' (Tilley 2005). Whatever its conceptual, policy and political flaws (Hughes and Edwards 2005; Hughes 2007), it is arguably one of the most influential forms – practical and commonsensical – of criminological governmental *savoir* in late-modern societies.

Youth crime prevention

Youth crime prevention has tended to be associated with social crime prevention rather than situational crime prevention and has been criticized by supporters of situational crime prevention and proponents of rational choice theory for its 'fluffy' nature and unproven testable successes. It has also been criticized for the tendency to be 'soft' on offenders when compared with the seemingly 'tough' preventive orders associated with repressive crime prevention measures epitomized in the UK by the anti-social behaviour order and other excluding measures. Nevertheless, there is also a long history of diversion, mediation and restoration in local youth justice practices which, whatever their limitations and dangers, have potential (and at times proven capacity) in terms of both reducing offending and avoiding the resort to custodial penalization.

Despite the attempts by 'administrative' government-sponsored criminologies to provide a science of crime prevention, it is important to recognize that it is a capacious signifier that defies neat and unproblematic definition. It is increasingly recognized by social scientists that crime prevention is rarely mere technique or a matter of choosing a 'toolkit' – despite the continuing allure of such apparent context-free 'silver bullets' as CCTV and risk assessment technologies. Rather, crime prevention is embedded in social contexts and is never devoid of political and normative freight, as is evident in the ongoing debates on community safety and crime and disorder reduction in the context of the policies, practices and politics of local crime control.

Gordon Hughes

Related entries

Actuarialism; Administrative criminology; Community safety; Crime and disorder reduction (CDR); Evaluative research; Social harm.

Key texts and sources

Crawford, A. (2007) 'Crime prevention and community safety', in M. Maguire et al. (eds) *The Oxford Handbook of Criminology*. Oxford: Oxford University Press.
Garland, D. (2001) *The Culture of Control: Crime and Social Order in Contemporary Society*. Oxford: Oxford University Press.
Hughes, G. (1998) *Understanding Crime Prevention: Social Control, Risk and Late Modernity*. Buckingham: Open University Press.
Hughes, G. (2007) *The Politics of Crime and Community*. Basingstoke: Macmillan.
Hughes, G. and Edwards, A. (2005) 'Crime prevention in context', in N. Tilley (ed.) *Handbook of Crime Prevention and Community Safety*. Cullompton: Willan Publishing.
Tilley, N. (ed.) (2005) *Handbook of Crime Prevention and Community Safety*. Cullompton: Willan Publishing.

CRIME (SENTENCES) ACT 1997

The Crime (Sentences) Act 1997 can be viewed as one of a 'matrix of provisions to facilitate and increase the criminalization of children' in the 1990s (Bandalli 2000: 81).

Bandalli (2000) suggests that the provisions of the Crime (Sentences) Act 1997 were a major factor in the criminalization of children in the 1990s. The 1997 Act extended electronic tagging to children and young people aged under 16 years of age as part of a curfew order; allowed judges and magistrates to lift reporting restrictions in cases concerning young defendants; permitted the application of a community sentence for offences that would not otherwise reach the community disposal threshold in cases where a young person had committed a series of previous petty offences and/or not paid fines; and allowed convictions incurred while aged 17 or under to be taken into account when imposing the criteria for the application of new mandatory sentences for 18-year-olds and over.

Jane Pickford

Related entries

Criminalization; Electronic monitoring; Naming and shaming; Tariff.

Key texts and sources

Bandalli, S. (2000) 'Children, responsibility and the new youth justice', in B. Goldson (ed.) *The New Youth Justice*. Lyme Regis: Russell House.

Cadman, S. (2005) 'Proportionality in the youth justice system', in T. Bateman and J. Pitts (eds) *The RHP Companion to Youth Justice*. Lyme Regis: Russell House.

Dugmore, P. and Pickford, J. (2006) *Youth Justice and Social Work*. Exeter: Learning Matters.

See the Office of Public Sector Information's website (**http://www.opsi.gov.uk/ACTS/acts1997/1997043.htm**) for the text of the Crime (Sentences) Act 1997.

CRIME STATISTICS

Crime statistics are published information on crime and on responses to crime. Frequently, the expression 'crime statistics' is used to refer to a range of official, government publications.

Statistical information on offending in England and Wales is readily available from a range of official data sources. However, each source does not always tell the same story, and the figures can be read in a variety of ways, depending upon what they purport to show.

The Home Office publishes criminal statistics and sentencing statistics annually, providing a breakdown of detected offending and disposals imposed (whether pre-court or following a court conviction). Until relatively recently, these stastistics suggested a significant decline in youth crime since the early 1990s, with detected offending falling by more than a quarter between 1992 and 2002. At the same time, however, responses to youth offending were becoming more interventionist and punitive, leading to higher levels of criminalization. So, over the same period, the proportion of youth cases leading to prosecution – as opposed to a pre-court measure such as a caution, reprimand or final warning – rose from one in four to almost one in two. More recent figures appear to paint a different picture, however. Detected youth offending appears to have increased each year since 2003, while diversion from prosecution has also risen.

Care should be applied before taking these apparent trends at face value, however, since detected crime represents a relatively small percentage of the total. Just 27 per cent of crimes reported to, and recorded by, the police are 'cleared up'. Moreover, for a variety of reasons, around half of criminal incidents are never brought to police attention, because they are considered insufficiently serious, because there is no loss involved or because the victim has no confidence that reporting the matter will result in property being returned or the offender caught. Conversely, the expansion in private insurance cover tends to inflate the number of relatively minor incidents that find their way into official police statistics, since making a claim is dependent on reporting the offence.

Information on victimization is accordingly used to supplement police data, with both published, in a single volume, under the title *Crime in England and Wales*. The *British Crime Survey* (BCS) reports annually on self-reported experiences of victimization and is generally thought to provide a more accurate overview of the true extent and nature of offending, but still has significant shortcomings as a data source. The survey excludes children below 16 years of age, omits individuals – such as the homeless or those in custody – not resident in 'normal households' and does not capture 'victimless', corporate or retail crime.

Crime statistics are not only problematic in terms of incomplete data, however, but they are also plagued by shifting constructions – over time and place – of 'crime' itself. For instance, the age of criminal responsibility – which at 10 in England and Wales is one of the lowest in Europe – imposes a relatively arbitrary definition on youth crime. Similarly, statistical data are vulnerable to changes in statute, policy or practice: shifts in crime statistics are just as likely to reflect systemic modifications in responses to young people in trouble as they are to reveal actual changes in patterns of offending.

If such complexities confirm the problems of reaching an objective statistical picture of the total volume of offending, a critical engagement with statistical sources – taking due account of the limitations and relevant contextual considerations – is necessary if misleading interpretations of crime statistics are to be avoided. There are, for instance, grounds for supposing that the apparent recent increases in youth crime and the fall in the rate of prosecution shown in the data for recorded crime should not be taken at face value. There are good reasons to question whether youth crime suddenly began to rise from 2003 onwards. In the first place, such a trend is not consistent with other data sets. Self-reported offending by young people, as captured by the government's *Offending, Crime and Justice Survey*, is relatively stable; police recorded data and the BCS (although they do not distinguish youth offending from crime committed by adults) both show falls in crime since 2003. At the same time, Home Office research suggests that reoffending by children already known to the youth justice system also may have declined.

Secondly, the unequal distribution in the rise in detected and recorded youth crime ought to give pause for thought. While the overall increase in officially recorded youth crime from 2002 to 2005 was 14.8 per cent, that for girls was 35.6 per cent and that for children below the age of 15 years was 72.6 per cent. It seems unlikely that populations that have historically not accounted for a high proportion of youth offending should be responsible for such a disproportionate rise at the current juncture.

There is, in any event, a readily available alternative account. During 2002, the point from which the apparent rise is evident in the figures, the government set a target to increase the number of 'offences brought to justice'. As a consequence, the police have an incentive to deal formally with incidents that would previously have met with an informal response (and thus go unrecorded). Any shift in practice would particularly affect those populations who might hitherto have benefited from higher levels of informal responses – young people rather than adults and, more specifically, girls and younger children. At the same time, a particular impact would be felt at the 'front end' of the system. Young people who commit serious offences or who have several previous offending episodes would have in any event have been processed formally prior to the introduction of the 'offences brought to justice' target. The greatest scope for changed practice is with those young people who have no, or a limited, antecedent offending history. Increased

formality with such children would inevitably result in a relative rise in the use of reprimands and final warnings.

The pattern displayed in the figures is, in other words, exactly that which might be anticipated as a consequence of attempts to meet a government-imposed target rather than being reflective of increases in offending by girls and younger children.

Tim Bateman

Related entries

British Crime Survey (BCS); Comparative youth justice; Self-reported offending; Victimization.

Key texts and sources

Bateman, T. (2006a) 'Youth crime and justice: statistical "evidence", recent trends and responses', in B. Goldson and J. Muncie (eds) *Youth Crime and Justice: Critical Issues*. London: Sage.

Nacro (2007) *Some Facts about Children and Young People who Offend – 2005. Youth Crime Briefing*. London: Nacro.

Pitts, J. and Bateman, T. (2005) 'Youth crime in England and Wales', in T. Bateman and J. Pitts (eds) *The RHP Companion to Youth Justice*. Lyme Regis: Russell House.

CRIMINAL ANTI-SOCIAL BEHAVIOUR ORDERS (CRASBOs)

The criminal anti-social behaviour order (CRASBO) is identical in all respects to a free-standing anti-social behaviour order (ASBO) but it is made by the court in *addition* to a conviction for a criminal offence. Despite its name, the CRASBO is still a civil order intended to prevent 'harassment, alarm or distress' being caused to members of the wider community by specifying certain behaviours and actions from which the person named in the order must refrain.

Sections 64 and 65 of the Police Reform Act 2002 confirmed the increasing role that anti-social behaviour management was coming to play at the heart of the government's crime and disorder and public reassurance strategies (Burney, 2005). Section 64 allowed the court to impose an anti-social behaviour order (ASBO) in addition to a criminal conviction (criminal anti-social behaviour order or CRASBO).

Supporters of the anti-social behaviour management approach to crime and disorder issues have stressed the value of spelling out in court the social impact of the harmful or nuisance behaviour to be avoided while also providing a potentially quick and effective remedy. However, for critics, the CRASBO shares many of the shortcomings of the ASBO, with more besides, not least their net-widening and up-tariffing potential (Rowlands 2005).

CRASBOs are imposed on a range of persistent petty 'offenders', including substance misusers, beggars, street drinkers, prostitutes and shoplifters (Safer London Committee 2005), thereby exposing them to the risk of unnecessary and potentially counterproductive imprisonment. It is suggested that the government is only achieving its ASBO targets by resorting to increasing numbers of CRASBOs, and one consequence of this is a growing number of orders being breached (ASBO Concern 2005).

Peter Squires

Related entries

Anti-social behaviour (ASB); Anti-social behaviour orders (ASBOs); Criminalization; Net-widening.

Key texts and sources

ASBO Concern (2005) *ASBOs: An Analysis of the First Six Years.* London: ASBO Concern (available online at http://www.asboconcern.org.uk/).

Burney, E. (2005) *Making People Behave: Anti-social Behaviour, Politics and Policy.* Cullompton: Willan Publishing.

Rowlands, M. (2005) *The state of ASBO Britain – the Rise of Intolerance.* European Civil Liberties Network (available online at http://www.ecln.org/).

Safer London Committee (2005) *Street Prostitution in London.* London: Greater London Authority.

See the Office of Public Sector Information's website (http://www.opsi.gov.uk/acts/acts2002/20020030.htm) for the text of the Police Reform Act 2002.

CRIMINALIZATION

Derived from labelling theory, criminalization refers to the institutionalized processes that define and classify specific behaviours and acts as 'criminal'. In youth justice it relates to processes that formally transform 'children' into 'young offenders'.

Criminalization is optional. There is no preordained imperative for governments and state agencies to process particular forms of children's behaviour as 'crime' and to respond to the perpetrators of such behaviour as 'criminals'. Rather, those who exercise power 'choose' *both* to criminalize *and* to apply the processes of criminalization differentially. In other words, formal intervention, regulation, control and punishment are administered selectively, unevenly and inconsistently *within* and *between* youth justice systems.

Within youth justice systems, research and practice experience reveal that criminalization is mediated through the structural relations of class, 'race' and gender. Children and young people growing up in the most disadvantaged and distressed families, neighbourhoods and communities are disproportionately exposed to formal intervention and criminalization (White and Cunneen 2006). Black and minoritized children and young people endure unfavourable discriminatory treatment at every discrete stage of the youth justice process (Goldson and Chigwada-Bailey 1999; Webster 2006). Girls and young women are far more likely to be criminalized for particular behaviours than boys and young men (Gelsthorpe and Sharpe 2006).

Between youth justice systems, the age of criminal responsibility is the clearest indicator of differential criminalization. This is arbitrarily fixed and varies significantly between different jurisdictions. Thus, by way of illustration, the transgressive behaviour of children is formally processed as 'crime', and the same children are held to be fully culpable 'criminals', at age 8 in Scotland (although the impact of this is mediated – at least in part – by the children's hearing system); 10 in England and Wales, Northern

Ireland and Australia; 12 in Canada, the Republic of Ireland, the Netherlands and Turkey; 13 in France; 14 in Germany, Italy, Spain and Japan; 15 in Denmark, Finland, Norway and Sweden; and 18 in Belgium and Luxembourg. Behaviour formally classified as 'crime' is contingent, therefore, in accordance with the age at which 'criminal responsibility' is ascribed.

Criminalization is the antithesis of 'diversion' and runs counter to the primary thrust of international human rights standards, treaties, rules and conventions. Furthermore, the contemporary policy emphasis on early intervention, the consolidating conflation of 'anti-social behaviour', 'disorder' and 'crime', and the net-widening processes that this invokes all threaten to intensify modes of child criminalization. This is inconsistent with research findings and practice experience confirming the efficacy of strategically applied diversion (Kemp *et al.* 2002). It is also contrary to evidence from countries where the age of criminal responsibility is substantially higher than it is in the three UK jurisdictions and where 'it can be shown that there are no negative consequences to be seen in terms of crime rates' (Dunkel 1996: 38).

The criminalization of children is not only ethically problematic, applied in discriminatory forms, counterproductive (when measured in terms of crime prevention and community safety) and inimical to international human rights obligations, but it also imposes substantial strain on youth justice systems. On 26 January, 2007, Professor Rod Morgan resigned as Chairperson of the Youth Justice Board (YJB). In an open letter distributed widely, Morgan explained that the youth justice system in England and Wales is being 'swamped'. He drew particular attention to, and expressed his frustration about, 'the numbers of children and young people being criminalised and ... the growth in the number of relatively minor offenders being prosecuted'. In August 2007, the YJB's annual report was published. The report refers to 'miss-

ing data for 2005/06' in respect of 'first-time entrants' to the youth justice system. Despite the missing data, however, the available statistics reveal that in a single year no fewer than 97,329 children 'entered' the youth justice system in England and Wales for the 'first time' (Youth Justice Board 2007d: 23). The bloated nature of the modern youth justice system in England and Wales is an inevitable consequence of child criminalization and a policy obsession with early intervention that has endured for over a decade.

Barry Goldson

Related entries

Comparative youth justice; Criminal responsibility; Diversion; Early intervention; Gender and justice; Informalism; Labelling theory; Net-widening; 'Race' and justice; Social harm.

> **Key texts and sources**
>
> Dunkel, F. (1996) 'Current directions in criminal policy', in W. McCarney (ed.) *Juvenile Delinquents and Young People in Danger in an Open Environment*. Winchester: Waterside Books.
>
> Gelsthorpe, L. and Sharpe, G. (2006) 'Gender, youth crime and justice', in B. Goldson and J. Muncie (eds) *Youth Crime and Justice: Critical Issues*. London: Sage.
>
> Goldson, B. and Chigwada-Bailey, R. (1999) '(What) justice for black children and young people?', in B. Goldson (ed.) *Youth Justice: Contemporary Policy and Practice*. Aldershot: Ashgate.
>
> Kemp, V., Sorsby, A., Liddle, M. and Merrington, S. (2002) *Assessing Responses to Youth Offending in Northamptonshire*. Research Briefing 2. London: Nacro.
>
> Webster, C. (2006) '"Race", youth crime and justice', in B. Goldson and J. Muncie (eds) *Youth Crime and Justice: Critical Issues*. London: Sage.
>
> White, R. and Cunneen, C. (2006) 'Social class, youth crime and justice', in B. Goldson and J. Muncie (eds.) *Youth Crime and Justice: Critical Issues*. London: Sage.
>
> Youth Justice Board (2007d) *Annual Report and Accounts, 2006/07*. London: HMSO.

CRIMINALIZATION OF SOCIAL POLICY

The criminalization of social policy is a thesis that maintains that one of the most notable outcomes of processes of 'joined up' governance, multi-agency frameworks and crime reduction partnerships is that the rubric of various agencies of social and public policy has become imbued with responsibilities for crime control.

In England and Wales, a preoccupation with incivilities as well as crime, has not only opened the door to a range of new legislative initiatives but has also helped to draw numerous aspects of social and public policy – including housing, income support, race relations, youth work, family support, education, employment, urban planning and nursery education – into a broader criminal justice agenda. Partnerships have drawn together a range of social and public policy agencies specifically around the issue of crime (Crawford 1997). Most notably in response to the death of 8-year-old Victoria Climbié, in 2000, the Laming Inquiry eventually recommended that *every* child in England be given an ID number to track when they became known to state agencies – not only to education and social services but also to police and youth offending teams.

The practices and discourses of 'early intervention' have made it possible to identify 'new' 'risk conditions' and behaviours ripe for 'prevention'. In 2006, Louise Casey, the government's 'Respect Tsar', announced that extra resources for local government would be dependent on their commitment to crack down on 'yobbish behaviour'. In these examples, issues of child protection and urban regeneration appear to be merged with those of crime prevention. In a broader sense the thesis also intimates that fundamental social issues – related to poverty, education and unemployment, for example – have become progressively marginalized and redefined as matters of law and order (Stenson 2000).

Government funding for welfare services or urban regeneration programmes also appears to be increasingly dependent on there being some assumed crime prevention pay-off. Intervening to 'nip crime in the bud' intensifies the processes of scrutiny and surveillance to which children and families are subjected and subverts the protective/care ethos of family services. Moves to allow a wider range of bodies (including resident groups, parish councils and community panels) to initiate civil proceedings also allow for an expansion of the means through which criminalization can eventually be secured. When social inclusion work is grafted on to the operations of the youth justice system – rather than remaining independent with no formalized connections to the police, courts or corrections – then it has been effectively criminalized.

Criminal law is being increasingly turned to for the resolution of social problems. But an obsession with risk factors and evidence-based analysis fails to address the complex inter-related problems of poverty, racism, urban degeneration and social inequality which provide the context for much anti-social behaviour (Muncie 2004). Reform in these areas may be primarily legitimated in the name of public protection, opportunities, support and community empowerment, but it also raises the prospect that 'social deficiencies are being redefined as "crime problems" which need to be controlled and managed rather than addressed in themselves' (Crawford 1997: 230).

John Muncie

Related entries

Anti-social behaviour (ASB); Crime and disorder reduction; Crime prevention; Criminalization; Governance; Net-widening; Partnership working; Respect (government action plan); Social harm.

Key texts and sources

Crawford, A. (1999) *The Local Governance of Crime: Appeals to Community and Partnership.* Oxford: Oxford University Press.
Muncie, J. (2004) *Youth and Crime.* (2nd ed) London: Sage.
Stenson, K. (2000) 'Crime control, social policy and liberalism', in G. Lewis *et al.* (eds) *Rethinking Social Policy.* London: Sage.

CRIMINAL JUSTICE ACT 1982

> The Criminal Justice Act 1982 restricted the criteria for custodial disposals and transformed Borstals into youth training centres. It also created the specified activities order as a high-tariff community disposal that was later to become a direct alternative to custody under the Criminal Justice Act 1988.

Following the Conservative government's initial enthusiasm for youth custody – as witnessed in the ill-fated experiment with the militaristic-style 'short, sharp, shock' introduced in 1980 – it is arguable that the Criminal Justice Act 1982 contributed towards a trend of lowering the numbers of young offenders who were sent into custody, which was clearly in evidence by the middle of the decade (Rutherford 2002b). Over the period of the mid-1980s, the number of custodial disposals fell significantly, while Home Office circulars in the 1980s officially encouraged the use of cautions for young offenders (Home Office 1985). Additionally, the Conservative governments of the 1980s provided local authorities with funds to set up intermediate treatment schemes and programmes for young offenders as alternatives to custody. Section 1(4) of the Criminal Justice Act 1982 (as amended by s. 123(3) of the Criminal Justice Act 1988) stated that a custodial sentence should not be imposed unless:

> (i) the young person has a history of failure to respond to non custodial penalties and is unwilling or unable to respond to them; or (ii) only a custodial sentence would be adequate to protect the public from serious harm from him; or (iii) the offence of which he has been convicted or found guilty was so serious that a non custodial sentence for it cannot be justified.

Jane Pickford

Related entries

Alternatives to custody; Criminal Justice Act 1988; Supervision orders.

Key texts and sources

Home Office (1985) *The Cautioning of Offenders* (Circular 14/85). London: Home Office.
Pickford, J. (ed.) (2000) *Youth Justice: Theory and Practice*. London: Cavendish Publishing.
Pitts, J. (1988) *The Politics of Juvenile Crime*. London: Sage.
Rutherford, A. (2002b) *Growing Out of Crime: The New Era*. Winchester: Waterside Press.

CRIMINAL JUSTICE ACT 1988

> The Criminal Justice Act 1988 restricted the criteria for the use of custodial disposals for young offenders (beyond that provided by the Criminal Justice Act 1982). Under the 1988 Act, custodial disposals were to be imposed as a last resort for the most serious and dangerous young offenders only. The Act also renamed custodial facilities for young offenders as 'young offender institutions'.

Section 123(3) of the Criminal Justice Act 1988 (which amended s. 1(4) of the Criminal Justice Act 1982) stated that a custodial sentence should not be imposed unless:

> (i) the young person has a history of failure to respond to non custodial penalties and is unwilling or unable to respond to them; or (ii) only a custodial sentence would be adequate to protect the public from serious harm from him; or (iii) the offence of which he has been convicted or found guilty was so serious that a non custodial sentence for it cannot be justified.

The restricted penal criteria provided by the Criminal Justice Act 1988 arguably further consolidated a trend towards non-custodial disposals that started earlier in the 1980s. Commentators have argued that this tendency was given further impetus by a number of factors that came together by the mid to late 1980s, including official Home Office sanctioning of the use of multiple cautions; youth justice practitioners' proactive development of diversionary schemes (including the development in some local teams of an early form of 'caution plus' interventions for repeat non-serious offenders); government funding for localized intermediate treatment schemes (of which there were over 100 at the peak of this initiative – many of which operated as direct alternatives to custody); and a growing acceptance among magistrates at that time of the damaging impact on the young person of a custodial disposal (Goldson 1997; Fionda 2005).

Jane Pickford

Related entries

Alternatives to custody; Custody-free zones; Criminal Justice Act 1982; Justice; Supervision orders.

Key texts and sources

Dugmore, P. and Pickford, J. (2006) *Youth Justice and Social Work*. Exeter: Learning Matters.

Fionda, J. (2005) *Devils and Angels: Youth Policy and Crime*. Oxford: Hart Publishing.

Gelsthorpe, A. and Morris, A. (1994) 'Juvenile justice, 1945–1992', in M. Maguire *et al.* (eds) *The Oxford Handbook of Criminology*. Oxford: Clarendon Press.

Goldson, B. (1997) 'Children in trouble: state responses to juvenile crime', in P. Scraton (ed.) *'Childhood' in 'Crisis'?* London: UCL Press.

See the Office of Public Sector Information's website (http://www.opsi.gov.uk/acts/acts1988/Ukpga_19 880033_en_1.htm) for the text of the Criminal Justice Act 1988.

CRIMINAL JUSTICE ACT 1991

The Criminal Justice Act 1991 established a statutory model for sentencing youths and adults based on the notion of proportionality. The Act also introduced reforms specific to young offenders that amounted to a consolidation of a trend away from custodial disposals for all but the most serious and/or persistent young offenders.

The Criminal Justice Act 1991 was the culmination of several years of policy reform led by the then Home Secretary, Douglas Hurd. The Act proposed new arrangements for young people relating to remand, and community disposals were strengthened. Significantly, there was an expansion of the upper age limit in the 'youth court' (previously the 'juvenile court') to include 17-year-olds. Further, the Act emphasized parental responsibilities in relation to young people who come before the courts. More robust pre-sentence reports (PSRs) replaced social inquiry reports, and the production of a PSR became a statutory requirement where a youth faced a custodial or high-tariff community disposal. Restrictions were placed on considering the whole of a defendant's offending history when sentencing, and a strict system of financial calculation was imposed in the form of 'unit fines'. Section 95 provided a statutory responsibility to 'avoid discriminating against any person on the ground of race or sex or any other improper ground' and introduced statistical monitoring of the criminal justice system with a view to identifying any areas of disproportionate treatment and/or discrimination.

A twin-track or bifurcated approach to all offenders (both young people and adults) was first mooted in a consultation paper entitled *Punishment, Custody and the Community* (Home Office 1988). Fionda (2005) suggests that this paper clearly favoured the extended use of community disposals and the minimal use of custodial sentences. Twin approaches were discussed: track A (custody) should only be used for serious and dangerous offenders, while track B (strengthened non-custodial disposals) should be used where penal detention was necessary to protect the public. Community disposal responses were regarded as particularly suitable for young offenders who, when compared with adult offenders – the consultation paper observed – were more 'likely to grow out of crime' (Home Office 1988: 15). It is arguable that part of the motivation behind this dual-pronged approach was linked to concerns about the escalating cost of the criminal justice system and, in particular, the cost of custodial disposals. A hint of the birth of the managerial approach to youth crime is evident in the rationale behind this bifurcated agenda.

The doctrine of proportionality was introduced in statutory form by the Criminal Justice Act 1991. This was viewed as a pivotal principle based on the philosophy of just deserts, as outlined in the white paper published the year before the Act was passed (Home Office 1990). A duty was placed on sentencers to take account of the severity of the offence(s) and to impose a disposal that was 'directly related to the seriousness of the offence' (Home Office 1990). Fionda (2005: 142) argues that previous legislation had led to a confusion among sentencers as to which of the conventional principles of sentencing (rehabilitation, retribution, incapacitation or deterrence) they should prioritize. The Criminal Justice Act 1991 shunned this 'pick and mix' style of justice, moving 'from an "a la carte" cafeteria to a "prix fixe" system … where proportionality is the leading determinant for sentencing' (Fionda 2005: 142).

The Criminal Justice Act 1991 introduced measures directly targeted at young offenders. Significantly these included reducing the maximum custodial sentence in a young offender institution to 12 months (excluding very serious offences that were covered by s. 53 of the Children and Young Persons Act 1933 – now covered by the 'grave crimes' procedures, ss. 90 and 91 of Powers of the Criminal Courts (Sentencing) Act 2000); raising the minimum age that a young person could be sentenced to custody punishment to 15; expanding community sentences for 16 and 17-year-olds (probation, community service and combination orders available as high-level community disposals for this age group); and creating a duty on local authorities to develop new remand arrangements (including remand fostering) for 15 and 16-year-olds.

With regards to parental responsibility, in essence the Act placed statutory duties on parents and carers of children under 16 and, at the discretion of the court, for parents/carers of 16 and 17-year-olds. Specifically, s. 56 required parents/carers to attend court, s. 57 placed a duty on parents/carers to pay any financial penalties imposed on the young person (under the newly introduced 'unit fine' system that imposed strict criteria for calculation) and s. 58 created a parental bind over (up to a value of £1,000) whereby a parent/carer would be obliged to surrender a set amount to the court should he or she fail to exercise proper care and control over his or her child. Section 58 was expanded by the Criminal Justice and Public Order Act 1994, which further extended the bind over provisions to include a parental bind over to ensure their child's compliance with a community order.

The Act represented a fusing of various approaches and philosophies (Pickford 2000; Fionda 2005). While it was arguably imbued with classicist notions of proportionality, in youth justice terms it also appears to move towards ideas of welfarism in relation to non-serious offenders, elements of which can be viewed as part of the development of the bifurcation strategy witnessed over the 1980s. Muncie (2004: 272) alleges that by the late 1980s, principles of welfare and/or justice had somewhat dissolved into a 'developing corporatist strategy which removed itself from the wider philosophical arguments of welfare and punishment … The aim was not necessarily to deliver "welfare" or "justice" but rather to develop the most cost-effective and efficient way of *managing* the delinquent problem'. Causational issues were largely ignored when applying this approach, and traditional youth justice was 'reconceptualised as a delinquency management service' (Muncie 2004: 272).

Jane Pickford

Related entries

Alternatives to custody; Bifurcation; Gravity factors; Just deserts; Juvenile courts; Proportionality; Youth courts.

Key texts and sources

Fionda, J. (2005) *Devils and Angels: Youth Policy and Crime.* Oxford: Hart Publishing.

Home Office (1988) *Punishment, Custody and Community* (Cm 424). London: Home Office.

Home Office (1990) *Crime, Justice and Protecting the Public* (Cm 965). London: Home Office.

Muncie, J. (2004) *Youth and Crime* (2nd edn). London: Sage.

Pickford, J. (ed.) (2000) *Youth Justice: Theory and Practice.* London: Cavendish Publishing.

See the Office of Public Sector Information's website (http://www.opsi.gov.uk/ACTS/acts1991/Ukpga_19910053_en_1.htm) for the text of the Criminal Justice Act 1991.

CRIMINAL JUSTICE ACT 1993

> The Criminal Justice Act 1993 introduced major changes, abandoning some of the principles of proportionality enshrined in the Criminal Justice Act 1991. There was particular controversy about the restrictions sentencers faced when considering the previous offending histories of defendants and the rigid nature of the unit fine system. Both these provisions were abolished by the 1993 Act, which also stated that offences committed while on bail should be regarded as an aggravating factor when deciding appropriate disposals.

The provisions of the Criminal Justice Act 1991 regarding proportionality were not well received by some magistrates, who believed that their discretionary powers to sentence the offender (rather than the offence) had been severely curtailed. The popular press reflected this discontent, and the Conservative government was accused of being 'soft' on crime. Media stories about young offenders who were allegedly being treated 'softly' by the youth justice system swayed public and political opinion towards an era of 'getting tough' on youth criminality and a punitive backlash developed (Goldson 1997). The case involving the murder of 2-year-old James Bulger by two 10-year-old boys was pivotal and led to a 'moral panic' and the demonization of children and young people (Scraton 1997b).

In many respects the Criminal Justice Act 1993 was a response to such populist currents and, as Rutherford (1995: 58) noted, 'rapidly drafted legislation during 1993 shot great holes in the Criminal Justice Act 1991'.

Jane Pickford

Related entries

Bulger; Criminal Justice Act 1991; Demonization; Proportionality.

Key texts and sources

Dugmore, P. and Pickford, J. (2006) *Youth Justice and Social Work*. Exeter: Learning Matters.
Fionda, J. (2005) *Devils and Angels: Youth Policy and Crime*. Oxford: Hart Publishing.
Goldson, B. (1997) 'Children in trouble: state responses to juvenile crime', in P. Scraton (ed.) *'Childhood' in 'Crisis'?* London: UCL Press.
Rutherford, A. (1995) 'Signposting the future of juvenile justice policy in England and Wales', in Howard League for Penal Reform (ed.) *Child Offenders UK and International Practice*. London: Howard League.
Scraton, P. (ed.) (1997b) *'Childhood' in 'Crisis'?* London: UCL Press.
See the Office of Public Sector Information's website (**http://www.opsi.gov.uk/ACTS/acts1993/Ukpga_19930036_en_1.htm**) for the text of the Criminal Justice Act 1993.

CRIMINAL JUSTICE ACT 2003

> The Criminal Justice Act 2003 largely concerned adult justice measures although particular sections also apply to young offenders. Most notably, the Act introduced new provisions regarding custody for those convicted of certain ('specified') sexual or violent offences who are judged by the court to be 'dangerous'. The Act also contains provisions regarding individual support orders; amendments relating to parenting and referral orders; and a number of other miscellaneous provisions regarding young offenders.

The Criminal Justice Act 2003 provided magistrates and judges with increased sentencing powers in respect of young people who commit 'specified' violent or sexual offences. The 'specified' violent and sexual offences are listed in Schedule 15 of the Act and include 65 violent offences and 88 sexual offences. The impact of these changes is, therefore, potentially far reaching. Significantly for young offenders, robbery is listed as a specified offence, and so an assessment of dangerousness should be undertaken even if the violence or threat thereof was minimal. The additional sentencing powers include the extended sentence and the indeterminate sentence for the protection of the public.

A young person would fall into the 'extended sentence' category if he or she commits a violent or sexual offence for which an adult might receive a custodial disposal of 2 years or more and the court deems that there is a significant risk of serious harm to the public. In such circumstances the young person might be sentenced to extended detention, which involves a licence extension of up to 8 years for a sexual offence and 5 years for a violent offence. Young offenders who fall within the 'indeterminate sentence' category are those who have committed a violent or sexual offence carrying a maximum penalty of 10 years or above for an adult.

The Act also allowed courts to impose individual support orders (ISOs) on 10–17-year-olds as an additional order for a young person subject to an anti-social behaviour order (ASBO). The ISO is applied for by a local authority and is intended to provide support for people subject to ASBOs to prevent further behaviour of the type that led to the ASBO being imposed.

Additionally, the Criminal Justice Act 2003 removed the previous restriction that a parenting order could not be made alongside a referral order. Both can now run in tandem. It also added new provisions into the Powers of Criminal Courts (Sentencing) Act 2000 requiring a parent/carer to attend referral order panel meetings and allowing panels to refer parents to court for non-compliance. The court can then impose a parenting order for non-cooperation.

Other material provisions in the Criminal Justice Act 2003 impacting on youth justice include the following:

- The amendment of the Police and Criminal Evidence Act 1984 to allow the police to detain someone aged 14 or above after charge to test for Class A drugs.
- The presumption of privacy is removed where a post-conviction ASBO is made.
- The introduction of a drug-testing condition which can now be included as part of an action plan or supervision order.
- The use of a generic term of 'youth community order' to cover community based disposals for young offenders.

- Youth offending teams now have to be compliant with risk assessments required under multi-agency public protection arrangements.
- The extended admissibility of 'bad character' in criminal proceedings.
- A minimum sentence of 3 years for young people aged 16 and above who are found in possession of firearms (though there has been recent political pressure to extend this).

It is notable that the statutory purposes of sentencing set out in s. 142 of the Criminal Justice Act 2003 do not apply to children and young people, though parts of the sentencing framework and thresholds do. However, the thresholds for community and custodial sentences remain largely unchanged. Section 148 of the 2003 Act retains the proportionality test (introduced by the Criminal Justice Act 1991) that the offending must be 'serious enough' to warrant a community sentence, and s. 152 – regarding custodial disposals – preserves the phrase that the offending must be 'so serious' that no alternative disposal can be justified. However, as Fionda (2005) points out, if a young person does not consent to a community order or a drugs test, he or she could in any event find him or herself being made subject to custody, in negation of the standard of just deserts.

Jane Pickford

Related entries

Dangerousness; Detention for public protection (DPP); Individual support orders (ISOs); Mandatory sentences; Parenting orders; Sentencing framework.

Key texts and sources

Dugmore, P. and Pickford, J. (2006) *Youth Justice and Social Work*. Exeter: Learning Matters.

Fionda, J. (2005) *Devils and Angels: Youth Policy and Crime*. Oxford: Hart Publishing.

Gibson, B. (2004) *Criminal Justice Act 2003: A Guide to the New Procedures and Sentencing*. Winchester: Waterside Press.

See the Office of Public Sector Information's website (http://www.opsi.gov.uk/acts/acts2003/20030044. htm) for the text of the Criminal Justice Act 2003.

CRIMINAL JUSTICE AND COURT SERVICES ACT 2000

The Criminal Justice and Court Services Act 2000 removed powers regarding the length of custody to be served by young people who commit serious offences from the Home Secretary to the judiciary. Further, the Act eradicated the rule that a reprimand or final warning must be given at a police station. It also renamed certain sentences applicable to 16 and 17-year-olds and restated their purposes: probation became 'community rehabilitation', community service became 'community punishment' and a combination order became a 'community punishment and rehabilitation order'.

The European Court of Human Rights in R v *Bulger* ruled that sentencing should be left to judges to decide and recommendations should not be overruled by politicians. (The two boys convicted of James Bulger's murder were originally sentenced to 8 years by the trial judge. This was raised to 10 years by the Lord Chief Justice and then to 15 years by Michael Howard, the then Home Secretary.) The sentencing of children and young people convicted of 'grave crimes' is now set by the Lord Chief Justice on a recommendation of the trial judge. The Criminal Justice and Court Services Act 2000 put this ruling on to a statutory footing.

The amendment allowing reprimands and final warnings to be imposed at locations other than the police station has provided an opportunity for 'restorative cautioning' and informal 'conferences' to occur in places more conducive to mediation processes. A range of persons concerned can then be invited to take part, including victims, parents and other interested professionals (Crawford and Newburn 2003).

The Criminal Justice and Court Services Act 2000 also allows for parents of truants to be fined or imprisoned for up to 3 months for failing to 'cause' a young person to attend school.

Jane Pickford

Related entries

Community rehabilitation orders (CROs); Community punishment orders (CPOs); Community punishment and rehabilitation orders (CPROs); Tariff.

Key texts and sources

Crawford, A. and Newburn, T. (2003) *Youth Offending and Restorative Justice: Implementing Reform in Youth Justice.* Cullompton: Willan Publishing.
Pickford, J. (ed.) (2000) *Youth Justice: Theory and Practice.* London: Cavendish Publishing.
See the Office of Public Sector Information's website (http://www.opsi.gov.uk/acts/acts2000/20000043.htm) for the text of the Criminal Justice and Court Services Act 2000.

CRIMINAL JUSTICE AND IMMIGRATION BILL 2006–7 TO 2007–8

The Criminal Justice and Immigration Bill 2006–7 to 2007–8 contains provisions that, if implemented, will lead to substantial changes to the youth justice system in England and Wales. The Bill received its first reading in Parliament on 26 June 2007 and its second reading on 23 July 2007. It was carried over into the 2007–8 Parliamentary session.

The principal youth justice provisions contained in the Criminal Justice and Immigration Bill include: purposes of sentencing in the youth justice system; anti-social behaviour measures; a youth conditional caution (for 16–17-year-olds); extension to referral orders; youth default orders; a generic youth rehabilitation order; and violent offender orders.

The Bill states that the prevention of offending is the principal aim of any sentence with regard to a child or young person. This brings sentencing in line with the principal statutory aim of the wider youth justice system as provided by the Crime and Disorder Act 1998. In addition to this principal aim, the Bill requires the courts to have regard to other factors when passing sentence, including: the protection of the public; the making of reparation by 'young offenders' to victims; the reform and rehabilitation of young offenders; and the punishment of young offenders. The court must also have regard to the welfare of children and young people in accordance with s. 44 of the Children and Young Persons Act 1933.

The Criminal Justice and Immigration Bill contains several provisions with regard to anti-social behaviour, including statutory one-year reviews of anti-social behaviour orders for under 18-year-olds and greater use of individual support orders.

A new pre-court disposal is proposed – the youth conditional caution – that is intended to reduce the number of young people (aged 16 and 17) being taken to court for low-level offences. It will be available in cases where the young person has not previously been convicted of an offence, admits guilt and consents to the caution. The caution is available for use by the police and the Crown Prosecution Service (CPS), and the 'conditions' might include a fine and/or an attendance requirement (possibly involving completion of a specified activity up to a maximum 20 hours). The conditions must be approved by the CPS and, if the young person fails to comply, the CPS reserves the right to prosecute for the original offence.

The Bill also proposes to extend the circumstances in which a court may impose a referral order: where the child/young person has previously been bound over to keep the peace, has received a conditional discharge or has one previous conviction but did not receive a referral order.

There are also provisions for the introduction of a 'youth default order' that will enable a court to impose a curfew requirement, an attendance centre requirement or – if the young person is aged 16 to 17 – an unpaid work requirement in lieu of an unpaid fine. The length of the new order will be determined in accordance with the amount left to pay on the fine.

Perhaps the most significant youth justice provisions of the Bill relate to the proposed youth rehabilitation order (YRO), a new generic community sentence that will be the standard community-based disposal for the majority of children and young people sentenced. The YRO represents a more individualized 'risk' and 'needs'-based approach to community sentencing, enabling greater choice from a 'menu' of available requirements. It will replace a number of existing orders including the action plan order, the attendance centre order, the community punishment order, the community rehabilitation order, the community punishment and rehabilitation order, the curfew order, the drug treatment and testing order, the exclusion order, and the supervision order. A 'menu' of requirements that the court might attach to a YRO includes:

- activity
- attendance centre
- curfew
- drug testing (for children aged 14 or over)
- drug treatment
- education
- electronic monitoring
- exclusion
- extended activity – either intensive supervision and surveillance and/or intensive fostering (for persistent or serious offenders who are over the custody threshold)
- local authority residence
- mental health treatment
- programme
- prohibited activity
- residence (for young people aged 16–17)
- supervision
- unpaid work (for young people aged 16–17).

There are no restrictions proposed on the number of times a child/young person can be sentenced to a YRO. Indeed, the courts are expected to use the YRO on multiple occasions, adapting the 'menu' of requirements as appropriate. The length of a YRO cannot exceed 3 years and, if the YRO includes intensive supervision and surveillance, it cannot be imposed for less than 12 months.

The Bill further proposes to introduce a 'violent offender order' – a new civil order designed to protect the public from the risk of serious violent or psychological harm in respect of a convicted offender who has served a custodial sentence of at least 12 months' duration for certain 'specified offences'. It is proposed that this order will apply for a minimum of 2 years and will contain prohibitions, restrictions and other conditions the court might consider necessary in order to protect the public. A breach of the order will comprise a criminal offence punishable by a fine or a further term of custody. The police will be required to apply for a violent offender order through a multi-agency public protection arrangement on the basis of the risk the child/young person is thought to present at the time the application is made to the court.

The youth justice system in England and Wales has comprised a site of radical reform and turbulent change since the inception of the Crime and Disorder Act 1998. The Criminal Justice and Immigration Bill 2006–7 to 2007–8 promises to introduce further sweeping changes. At a time when there is increasing concern about the number of children and young people entering the youth justice system at the 'shallow end', and the stubbornly large population of child prisoners at the deeper end, it remains to be seen what impact the Bill might make. One immediate problem, however, is that the Bill is conspicuously silent with regard to the continued treatment of 17-year-olds as 'adults' for the purposes of bail and remand.

Barry Goldson

Related entries

Menu-based sentencing; Rehabilitation; Referral orders; Reparation; Sentencing framework.

Key texts and sources

Ministry of Justice (2007) 'Criminal Justice and Immigration Bill' (news release) (available online at **http://www.justice.gov.uk/news/newsrelease 260607c.htm**).

See **http://www.publications.parliament.uk/pa/pa bills/200607/criminal_justice_and_immigration. htm** for the text of the Criminal Justice and Immigration Bill 2007.

CRIMINAL JUSTICE AND POLICE ACT 2001

The Criminal Justice and Police Act 2001 allows electronic tagging to be used as a condition of bail for children aged 12 or over, including young suspects who are remanded into local authority accommodation (s. 23AA). Further, s. 130 permits a remand into custody or secure accommodation of a young person. Additionally, the Act extends the age limit for local child curfews (a civil order) to under 16s and allows such orders to be imposed on an area as well as on an individual. The Act also introduced 'on the spot' penalties for designated street/public offences applicable to any perpetrators aged 10 or over.

The Criminal Justice and Police Act 2001 reformed the powers of judges and magistrates when considering questions of bail or remand. A young suspect can now be refused bail if the court decides that certain criteria are satisfied (it is noteworthy that s. 130 does not use the phrase 'persistent' offender, a concept favoured by previous legal provisions). Factors to weigh in the balance include: whether there is any evidence (including the new alleged matter) of 'repeatedly' offending while on bail; whether the young person presents a risk of commission of imprisonable offences; and/or whether there is a need for a custodial/secure remand in order to protect the public from serious harm. Prior to the Criminal Justice and Police Act 2001, a court could only deprive a young person of his or her liberty while on remand if this was the only measure that could protect the public from serious harm. This legislation, therefore, increases the courts' powers to deprive a young person of his or her liberty while he or she is being processed by the courts, prior to any finding of guilt. Indeed, Goldson (2006c: 144) argues that the Act represents 'penological irrationality and indifference to the welfare of child remand prisoners'.

Jane Pickford

Related entries

Electronic monitoring; Local child curfew schemes (LCCSs); Remand.

Key texts and sources

Goldson, B. (2002b) *Vulnerable Inside: Children in Secure and Penal Settings.* London: Children's Society.

Goldson, B. (2006c) 'Penal custody: intolerance, irrationality and indifference', in B. Goldson and J. Muncie (eds) *Youth Crime and Justice: Critical Issues.* London: Sage.

Smith, R. (2003) *Youth Justice: Ideas, Policy, Practice.* Cullompton: Willan Publishing.

See the Office of Public Sector Information's website (http://www.opsi.gov.uk/acts/acts2001/20010016. htm) for the text of the Criminal Justice and Police Act 2001.

CRIMINAL JUSTICE AND PUBLIC ORDER ACT 1994

The Criminal Justice and Public Order Act 1994 introduced a series of reforms in respect of custodial penalties available to the courts in sentencing young offenders. In particular, the Act introduced a new custodial penalty – the secure training order – for children aged between 12 and 15.

The Criminal Justice and Public Order Act 1994, passed by the Conservative government, contained a disparate series of provisions on evidence, sentencing and public order. Part I of the Act focuses on custodial sentences for young offenders and created a new custodial order for offenders aged 12–15 – the secure training order (ss. 1–15). Part I also doubled the maximum period of detention available to sentencers in the youth courts (s. 17); and extended the custodial sentencing provisions (provided by s. 53 of the Children and Young Persons Act 1933 for children aged 10–14 convicted in the Crown court of a serious offence (s. 16)). Each of these provisions aimed to encourage greater severity in sentencing and the wider use of custodial penalties, particularly for children under the age of 14.

This represented something of a U-turn in youth justice policy. The Criminal Justice Act 1991 had set out a sentencing framework for the courts that placed restrictions on the use of custody. Indeed, custodial sentences had been dismissed as 'an expensive way of making bad people worse' (Home Office 1990). However, by 1994 a series of events prompted a more hardline approach. There is little doubt that the government was, in part, reacting to the murder of James Bulger by two 10-year-olds in 1993 which, for some, symbolized the greater capacity of younger children for violent behaviour. However, the 'new punitiveness' was also a campaign by a politically weak government to gain popularity (Goldson 2002a) and was a manifestation of increasing frustration on the part of some practitioners and policymakers at previous administrations' 'liberal' approach to youth crime (Home Affairs Committee 1993). In 1993, therefore, the then Home Secretary, Michael Howard, pledged to 'crack down on youth crime' (Goldson 1997).

The most controversial aspect of the Criminal Justice and Public Order Act 1994 provisions was the creation of secure training centres (STCs) as a new form of custodial institution for children aged 12–14 inclusive. Four STCs were the first prisons to be entirely built and run privately – under the aegis of the Home Office – in preference to local authority-managed secure accommodation, as originally proposed by the Home Affairs Committee (1993). Furthermore, this was the first time in many decades that children as young as 12 could be sentenced to custody for non-'grave crimes'. Pressure groups and commentators saw these 'child jails' (Howard League 1994) as a retrograde step that would undermine the attempts of earlier legislation to focus on community penalties aimed at a more rehabilitative approach. Moreover, early evaluations of the STCs were critical of the regimes' capacity to educate offenders and address their offending behaviour (Hagell *et al.* 2004).

Julia Fionda

Related entries

Bulger; Grave offences; Secure training centres (STCs).

Key texts and sources

Goldson, B. (1997) 'Children in trouble: state responses to juvenile crime', in P. Scraton (ed.) *'Childhood' in 'Crisis'?* London: UCL Press.

Goldson, B. (2002a) 'New punitiveness: the politics of child incarceration', in J. Muncie *et al.* (eds) *Youth Justice: Critical Readings.* London: Sage.

Hagell, A., Hazel, N. and Shaw, C. (2004) *Evaluation of Medway Secure Training Centre.* London: Policy Research Bureau (available online at http://www.homeoffice.gov.uk/rds/pdfs/occ-medway.pdf).

Home Affairs Committee (1993) *Juvenile Offenders* (Sixth Report) (HAC 441-I). London: HMSO.

Home Office (1990) *Crime, Justice and Protecting the Public* (Cm 965). London: Home Office.

Howard League (1994) *Child Jails: The Case against Secure Training Orders.* London: Howard League for Penal Reform.

See the Office of Public Sector Information's website (http://www.opsi.gov.uk/acts/acts1994/Ukpga_19940033_en_2.htm#mdiv16) for the text of the Criminal Justice and Public Order Act 1994.

CRIMINAL JUSTICE (CHILDREN) (NORTHERN IRELAND) ORDER 1998

The Criminal Justice (Children) (Northern Ireland) Order 1988 set the framework for the development of the youth justice system in Northern Ireland by introducing the youth court, the Juvenile Justice Board and the Juvenile Justice Centre Order.

The Children (Northern Ireland) Order 1995 had been a landmark in separating care and justice issues previously addressed by the juvenile court system. The Criminal Justice (Children) (Northern Ireland) Order 1998 continued this process of separation by establishing the youth court (a criminal court sitting for the purposes of processing charges against children). 'Child'

is defined as a person under 17 (subsequently raised to 18), and the age of criminal responsibility is set at 10. The order sets out the processes to be observed if a child is arrested and detained and defines the powers of the youth court.

The Criminal Justice (Children) (Northern Ireland) Order 1998 also created the Juvenile Justice Board (JJB), the precursor to the present Youth Justice Agency. Furthermore, the order made provision to give the JJB responsibility for the Juvenile Justice Centre and attendance centres, and the power to 'give effect to schemes for the prevention of offending by children'.

The Juvenile Justice Centre and the Juvenile Justice Centre order (JJCO) replaced training schools and the training school order. While the training school order had comprised a residential response to a child's offending, school non-attendance or being beyond parental control, the JJCO imposed a determinate period of detention for children who had *seriously* or *persistently* offended. An order could extend from 6 months to 2 years, with half being spent in custody and half under the supervision of a probation officer in the community.

The attendance centre order, as implemented by the JJB, provides an individually tailored programme of between 12 and 24 hours contact for each child. It has moved away from the traditional Saturday group attendance model and places greater emphasis on intervention rather than activity.

Prevention services are similarly individualized for children identified as being 'at risk' of offending and address individual, educational, family and community 'risk' factors. There is some anxiety that services for children perceived as being 'at risk' of offending and those for children known to have offended are not sufficiently distinct.

The Criminal Justice (Children) (Northern Ireland) Order 1998 was substantially augmented by the Justice (Northern Ireland) Act 2002.

David Weir

Related entries

Justice (Northern Ireland) Act 2002; Juvenile Justice Centre; Youth Justice Agency.

CRIMINAL JUSTICE (SCOTLAND) ACT 2003

A key aim of the wide-ranging Criminal Justice (Scotland) Act 2003 is to enhance public protection in respect of sexual and violent offenders. The Act established the Risk Management Authority and introduced a new court disposal: the order for lifelong restriction. The Act also contained a multitude of further provisions with a direct bearing on youth justice.

Part 1 of the Criminal Justice (Scotland) Act 2003 implements the principal recommendations of the MacLean Committee (set up in January 1999 to review the sentencing and management of serious violent and sexual offenders). The Act established the Risk Management Authority (RMA), a non-departmental public body whose role is to ensure the effective assessment and minimization of risk. In undertaking this role it is required to compile information about services in Scotland; to carry out/commission research; to pilot new initiatives; to develop guidelines and national standards; and to approve and review plans for the management of risk in individual cases. Membership of the RMA is at the discretion of Scottish ministers.

The Act also established the order for lifelong restriction (OLR), an incapacitative court disposal available for both adults and children on conviction in the High Court for a serious sexual or violent offence (other than murder).

Before an OLR can be made, a risk assessment report must be provided which shows that, *on the balance of probabilities*, the person, if at liberty, is likely to seriously endanger the lives, or the physical or psychological well-being, of members of the public. The Act also increases imprisonment terms for the possession/distribution of indecent photographs of children, widens the scope of extended sentences (available for sexual and violent offences) to include abduction and criminalizes people trafficking for the purpose of prostitution.

Furthermore, the Act contains a raft of other provisions that clarify procedures relating to the custody and detention of children (by including young offender institutions among the places to which certain specified children aged 14 or over may be remanded) and those relating to the physical punishment of children (in particular where punishment involves a blow to the head, shaking or the use of an implement). In addition the Act introduced new rights for victims of crime (including child victims); constituted specialist drugs courts; enabled interim anti-social behaviour orders; extended the power to apply for anti-social behaviour orders to registered social landlords; and made amendments to a number of non-custodial court disposals.

While the the Criminal Justice (Scotland) Act 2003 contains a number of measures that may serve to enhance victim support and child protection (especially those relating to people trafficking and the chastisement of children), the principal components of Part 1 reflect the general trend in post-devolution criminal justice policy in Scotland away from penal welfarism and towards more actuarial forms of justice and increased punitiveness. One major concern is that the new provisions might undermine the rights of child offenders. Indeed, the OLR could be open to challenge under Article 5 of the European Convention on Human Rights, which states that the only lawful detention of a minor is for the purpose of educational supervision or for the purpose of bringing him or her before the competent legal authority.

Lesley McAra

Related entries

Actuarialism; Punitiveness; Risk factors; Risk management.

CRIMINAL RESPONSIBILITY

Criminal responsibility (or criminal minority) refers to the age at which a child may be arrested, prosecuted, tried and, if found guilty, may receive a disposal from a criminal court for an offence.

The age of criminal responsibility in England and Wales is 10, fixed by the Children and Young Persons Act 1963. Below that age a child is irrebuttably presumed to be *doli incapax*, or incapable of evil, and any 'offending' behaviour by him or her would have to be addressed through other means: either by the provision of non-coercive services by the local authority or through care proceedings under the Children Act 1989. Above the age of 10, the child is subject to the provisions of the substantive criminal law in the same way as adults. If the child is proved by the prosecution to have committed the *actus reus* (the physical part) with the necessary *mens rea* (the required state of mind) and has no defence, then he or she is liable to be found guilty and his or her criminal record begins. The principle of subjectivity, which focuses on what is in the mind of the particular 'offender' and which is fundamental to the criminal law, should make a child's lesser ability to understand or foresee consequences a material issue in determining his or her *mens rea*, but childhood as such is not directly relevant.

There has been much discussion about whether 10 is an appropriate age to hold a child responsible for 'offending'. Historically, the trend has been to raise the age of criminal responsibility, and it was set at the current level in 1963. Attempts in the Children and Young Persons Act 1969 to raise it to 12 and then 14 were never implemented. Certainly since the mid 1990s there has been government action to increase the criminal responsibility of children rather than decrease it, by the abolition of the presumption of *doli incapax* for those aged 12–14 in the Crime and Disorder Act 1998. Before this the prosecution had to prove that a child knew what he or she was doing was *seriously wrong* and not merely naughty, in addition to other aspects of criminal liability.

The argument in favour of the low age of criminal responsibility is that the criminal law is a response that recognizes the rights of the victim and community, acknowledging harm caused and punishing and/or rehabilitating the offender with the aim of preventing further criminal behaviour. In this way, the youth justice system can be perceived to be a platform from which to deliver services aimed at 'nipping offending in the bud'. From this perspective, the earlier that intervention occurs, the better, and this is justified as being in the child's 'best interests'. This is the approach of the present government as enunciated in the 1997 white paper, *No More Excuses*.

The argument in favour of raising the age of criminal responsibility proceeds from a view of the criminal law as a very blunt instrument to use in solving social problems. Criminal liability is premised on the principle of autonomy – that each person is a responsible being and chooses to act in a particular way. However, children are clearly not fully 'autonomous', and there are few areas of law and policy that allow them to make decisions for themselves, particularly under the age of 14.

The use of the criminal law has numerous undesirable consequences for children, including the perfunctory attention given to the substantive criminal law in children's cases; the inappropriateness of much criminal procedure, both in the police station and in the courtroom; the range of disposals available (some of which are disproportionate to the offence); and the inappropriate use of custodial sentences. Additionally, there are other less direct consequences of contact with the youth justice system, such as the damaging effects of labelling and negative social reaction; the acquisition of a criminal record and its effect on a child's life chances; and the ineffectiveness of many youth justice interventions, particularly custody, to curb reoffending.

Child psychologists question whether children, especially those aged 10–14, fully understand the consequences or possible gravity of their actions in a way that makes them autonomous, responsible subjects in criminal law. The approach envisaged in the United Nations Standard Minimum Rules for the Administration of Juvenile Justice (the Beijing Rules) is to consider whether the child meets the moral and psychological requirements of criminal responsibility that are dependent on his or her capacity to discern and understand. Fixed too low and the notion of responsibility becomes meaningless. There should be a closer relationship between criminal responsibility and other social rights and responsibilities. The lack of children's autonomy is readily recognized in other areas – for example, the way the law treats children in connection with voting (18), owning land (18) and purchasing alcohol (18).

The United Nations Committee on the Rights of the Child has twice recommended (in 1995 and 2002) that the age of criminal responsibility be raised in accordance with the UK government's obligations under the United Nations Convention on the Rights of the Child. A recent report of the committee (United Nations Committee on the Rights of the Child 2007) indicates that an age of criminal responsibility below 12 is not internationally acceptable. The ages of criminal responsibility in England and Wales (10), Northern Ireland (10) and Scotland (8) are among the lowest, not only in Europe but also in the world (Muncie and Goldson 2006). There is no indication of any movement towards complying with the recommendation in any of the UK jurisdictions.

Sue Bandalli

Related entries

Children and Young Persons Act 1963; Children and Young Persons Act 1969; Children's human rights; Comparative youth justice; Criminalization; Crime and Disorder Act 1998; Labelling theory; No More Excuses; United Nations Committee on the Rights of the Child; United Nations Standard Minimum Rules for the Administration of Juvenile Justice.

Key texts and sources

Bandalli, S. (2000) 'Children, responsibility and the new youth justice', in B. Goldson (ed.) *The New Youth Justice*. Lyme Regis: Russell House.

Fionda, J. (2005) *Devils and Angels: Youth Policy and Crime*. Oxford: Hart Publishing (ch. 2).

Muncie, J. and Goldson, B. (2006) *Comparative Youth Justice: Critical Issues*. London: Sage.

United Nations Committee on the Rights of the Child (2007) *General Comment No. 10: Children's Rights in Juvenile Justice*. Geneva: United Nations Committee on the Rights of the Child.

CRITICAL CRIMINOLOGY

In applying contextual analysis to the study of 'crime', 'deviance' and 'conflict', critical criminology refutes simplistic notions of causation and individual and social pathology and emphasizes instead the complex relationships between individual actions, social interaction, institutional interventions and structural inequalities. It broadens analysis in its consideration of *harm* rather than crime, *social justice* rather than criminal justice, *treatment* rather than punishment and discourses of *rights* and *resistance* rather than discipline and compliance.

Critical criminology evolved from the challenge to established, mainstream social science disciplines and their domain assumptions regarding 'crime', 'deviance' and 'conflict'. It contested the portrayal of democratic societies as pluralist, participatory and consensual, in which the local and national democratic state, on behalf of its people, intervened through elected government to resolve conflict between competing interests.

Initially informed by neo-Marxist analyses of class, poverty and economic marginalization, it focused on the use of state power to discipline the masses, control the crimes of the poor and regulate political opposition and industrial conflict. Social scientists (including criminologists) were perceived as supporting the political management of the consequences of endemic structural inequalities. They were 'soft' interventionists working alongside coercive agencies to maintain the status quo, to guarantee continuity, manage conflict and reproduce the established social order. Mainstream social science research was identified as providing the knowledge base on which state power and influential corporate interests relied.

Predictably, critical analysis was challenged for economic reductionism and oversimplification verging on absolute determinism. Critics proclaimed the relative freedoms of democratic societies, the educational and work opportunities available for material advancement and the protection of the weak and vulnerable through freely available health and welfare services. They also considered law enforcement, due process of the courts and the use of sanctions, including imprisonment, as vital elements in securing a safe and stable social order. Self-styled 'left realists' argued persuasively that most 'victims' of crime in everyday life were those people made most vulnerable by structural inequalities: the poor, women and children and black communities. They proposed that crime had to be 'taken seriously' and dealt with through an alliance of researchers, politicians, community activists and state agencies working within a multi-agency framework. Being responsive to the manifestation of the 'crime problem' and its resolution, they shared some of the defining characteristics of administrative criminology while differing significantly in their concern for researching the broader contexts within which predatory behaviours arose.

Partly responding to these debates and also to the proposition that conceptually 'critical' criminology is inherently contradictory, the key theoretical principles were refined, developed and progressed. The initial objective of locating the experiential world of everyday life within the structural relations of power, authority and legitimacy provided a defining framework. Critical criminology accepts that people are agents in their own destinies, make choices, think differently, act, interact and react. As 'agents' they also resist the imposition of controls and regulations, and they organize, campaign and collectivize their actions in social movements. Yet structural relations and the interventions of state and private institutions set boundaries to social interaction and personal opportunity.

Rather than accepting 'crime' and 'anti-social behaviour' as outcomes of weak socialization or social dysfunction in a fair, equal and just meritocracy, critical analysis proposes that the overarching structural relations of advanced capitalism, patriarchy, neocolonialism and age are inherently conflictual and subjugating. The ownership and control of the means of production and distribution, the politics and economics of reproduction and normative heterosexuality, the colonial legacies of racism and xenophobia and the exclusion of children and young people from active participation, in both private and public spheres, reveal determining contexts that have consequences for all people in society. Power and authority are not limited to material (economic) or physical (force) interventions but are supported by deep-rooted ideologies – a social force of compliance and conformity. The populist appeal of authoritarianism, often connected to folk devils, demonization and moral panics, is a tangible manifestation of social forces.

The processes of marginalization and criminalization, particularly regarding the exclusion of children and young people, are central in explaining and analysing the relationships between definitions of crime and anti-social behaviour, discretionary law enforcement, the administration of law through the courts and linked restorative practices, and the presumed utility of punishment, especially imprisonment. Critical theorists argue that the regulation and criminalization of children and young people have achieved popular consent through mobilizing negative reputations, stereotypical images and collectivized, violent identities in popular discourse.

Critical analysis argues for a positive children's rights-based welfare approach challenging constructions of children as innocent, vulnerable or weak (to be protected) or as devious, ill-disciplined and anti-social (to be regulated). It is committed to 'promoting their right to information, expression of views and participation in decision-making', thus prioritizing their 'accounts and experiences, the meaning they invest in their acts and their active participation in the process' (Scraton and Haydon 2002: 325). Further it also 'expects full transparency of formal procedures and practices … effective political and professional accountability … decriminalisation, decarceration and diversion into welfare-based programmes sensitive to the contexts in which individuals live', alongside a significant rise in the age of criminal responsibility.

The significance of critical research and analysis is that it considers children's offending and anti-social behaviour, like other life experiences and personal opportunities, within the powerful determining contexts of their lives: poverty and class, 'race' and ethnicity, sectarianism, gender and sexuality. While accepting that 'each individual's experiences are distinctively mediated, these are powerful ideological as well as material determinants' (Scraton and Haydon 2002: 326).

Phil Scraton

Related entries

Abolitionism; Children's human rights; Criminalization; Demonization; Discrimination; Gender and justice; 'Race' and justice; Punitiveness; Social Exclusion; Social harm; Social justice.

Key texts and sources

Goldson, B. and Muncie, J. (eds) (2006c) *Youth Crime and Justice: Critical Issues.* London: Sage.
Muncie, J. (2004) *Youth and Crime* (2nd ed) London: Sage.
Scraton, P. (2007) *Power, Conflict and Criminalisation.* London: Routledge.
Scraton, P. and Haydon, D. (2002) 'Challenging the criminalization of children and young people: securing a rights-based agenda', in J. Muncie *et al.* (eds) *Youth Justice: Critical Readings.* London: Sage/Open University.

CROWN COURTS

> The Crown court is the higher court of first instance in criminal cases. Crown courts deal with the most serious criminal matters in respect of children/young people and adults. Because of the seriousness of offences *tried* in the Crown court, trials take place before a judge and jury.

The Crown court attends to the following:

- *Indictable-only offences*, such as murder, manslaughter, rape and robbery. Such cases can only be tried in Crown courts.
- *Either-way offences* transferred from the youth court or magistrates' court.
- *Appeals* from the youth court or magistrates' court.
- *Sentencing decisions* transferred from the youth court or magistrates' court. This occurs when magistrates decide – once they have heard the details of a case – that it might warrant a more severe sentence than they are legally empowered to impose.

The judges who normally sit in the Crown court are high court judges, circuit judges and recorders (part-time circuit judges who are otherwise barristers or solicitors in private practice). The most serious cases are allocated to high court judges and senior circuit judges. The remainder are dealt with by circuit judges and recorders, although recorders will normally preside over less serious work than circuit judges. The allocation of cases is conducted in accordance with directions issued by the Lord Chief Justice of England and Wales.

The Crown court is very formal, with judges and barristers wearing robes and wigs. It comprises an imposing and formidable setting, and many children and young people find it intimidating. When trying children, the Crown court should make special arrangements in accordance with a practice direction issued by the Lord Chief Justice in 2000. In turn, this was in response to a European Court of Human Rights judgment that the trial of the children convicted of the murder of James Bulger was not just. The

Lord Chief Justice's direction explicitly states that Crown courts must take into account the 'age, maturity and development (intellectual and emotional) of the young defendant on trial'. It emphasizes that the child/young person should not be exposed to avoidable intimidation, humiliation or distress, and specifies that appropriate action should be taken to assist children and young people to understand and participate in the proceedings.

Barry Goldson

Related entries

Bulger; Children's human rights; Grave offences; Magistrates; Sentencing framework; Sentencing guidelines; Tariff; Youth courts.

Key texts and sources

Nacro (2006c) *Nacro Guide to the Youth Justice System in England and Wales.* London: Nacro.

See also the Youth Justice Board's *Youth Justice System: Crown Court* (available online at http://www.yjb.gov.uk/en-gb/yjs/Courts/Crown Court.htm).

CROWN PROSECUTION SERVICE (CPS)

The Crown Prosecution Service (CPS) is the government department responsible for prosecuting criminal cases investigated by the police in England and Wales.

As the principal prosecuting authority in England and Wales, the Crown Prosecution Service (CPS) is responsible for:

- Advising the police on cases for possible prosecution;
- Reviewing cases submitted by the police;
- Where the decision is to prosecute, determining the charge in all but minor cases;
- Preparing cases for court;
- Presenting cases at court.

Primarily, the CPS was set up to establish an independent prosecution service previously undertaken by the Police Prosecuting Solicitor's Department. In order for a prosecution to take place, two major principles need to be followed in sequence: first, the evidential test (which is essentially about the 'realistic prospect of a conviction') and, secondly, the principle of the 'public interest'. Only if these two 'tests' are met will a prosecution proceed.

In the initial years of operation, the CPS was hampered by a poor reputation and was blamed for the failure to prosecute in some notable trials and, indeed, in a number of more routine cases. This was attributed, by some, to inadequate resources. More recently, however, the negative reputation no longer appears to apply.

Pivotal to the establishment and development of the CPS was the Home Office white paper, *An Independent Prosecution Service for England and Wales*, published in 1983. The Prosecution of Offences Act 1985 created the CPS. It established the Director of Public Prosecutions as the head of a department that incorporated the Police Prosecuting Solicitor's Department.

The CPS started operating in 1986 and, in the same year, Sir Allan Green was appointed Director of Public Prosecutions. Following the publication of the *Review of the Crown Prosecution Service* in 1998, in April 1999 the CPS changed from 14 to 42 geographical areas. Each area is co-terminus with existing police force boundaries, apart from CPS London, which covers the forces of the City of London Police and the Metropolitan Police. A chief Crown prosecutor is responsible for prosecutions within each area.

Richard Hester

Related entries

Criminal responsibility: Crown courts; Due process; Gravity factors (prosecution and sentencing); Youth courts.

Key texts and sources

The review of the CPS (1998) (summary of the main report with the conclusions and recommendations) is available online at http://www.archive.official-documents.co.uk/document/cm39/3972/3972.htm.

See also the CPS's website (http://www.cps.gov.uk/about/index.html).

CULTURAL CRIMINOLOGY

Cultural criminology is a theoretical, methodological and interventionist approach to the study of crime that places criminality and its control in the context of culture – that is, it views crime and the agencies and institutions of crime control as cultural products – as creative constructs.

Cultural criminology seeks to highlight the interaction between two key elements: the relationship between constructions upwards and constructions downwards. Its focus is always on the continuous generation of meaning around interaction: rules created, rules broken and a constant interplay of moral entrepreneurship, political innovation and transgression.

Although cultural criminology is a fairly recent development (dating from the mid-1990s; see Ferrell and Sanders 1995), it actually draws heavily on a rich tradition of sociologically inspired criminological work. This extends from the early subcultural and naturalistic ideas of the Chicago School, to the more politically charged theoretical analyses associated with critical criminology in the 1970s. However, while it is undoubtedly the case that many of the key themes and ideas associated with cultural criminology have been voiced elsewhere, it is clear that this dynamic body of work offers something new – primarily in the way it seeks to reflect the peculiarities and particularities of the late-modern sociocultural milieu.

With its focus on situated meaning, youth culture, identity, space, style and media culture – along with its commitment to understand and account for the ongoing transformations and fluctuations associated with hyper-capitalism – cultural criminology is an attempt to create a 'post' or 'late' modern theory of crime. Here criminal behaviour is reinterpreted as a technique for resolving certain psychic and emotional conflicts that are in turn viewed as being indelibly linked to various features of contemporary life (for example, see Hayward 2004 on the relationship between consumerism and certain forms of 'expressive criminality'). In other words, cultural criminology seeks to fuse a 'phenomenology of transgression' with a sociological analysis of late-modern culture. It is an approach, therefore, that is increasingly seen by many as extremely useful in helping us to understand various forms of youth criminality, including vandalism, the theft and destruction of cars, fire-starting, 'mugging', hoax emergency-service call-outs, peer group violence and other forms of street delinquency. Such behaviours have much to do with self-expression and the exertion of control in neighbourhoods where, frequently, traditional avenues for youthful stimulation and endeavour have long since evaporated.

Such complex foci require the utilization of a wide-ranging set of analytical tools. It is no surprise, then, that cultural criminology is stridently interdisciplinary, interfacing not just with criminology, sociology and criminal/youth justice studies but with perspectives and methodologies drawn from, *inter alia*, cultural, media and urban studies, philosophy, postmodern critical theory, cultural geography, anthropology, social movement studies and other 'action' research approaches. To quote Jeff Ferrell (1999: 396), a goal of cultural criminology is to be 'less a definitive paradigm' than an 'array of diverse perspectives'. The strength of the 'cultural approach', then, is the way it tackles the subject of crime and criminalization from a variety of new perspectives and academic disciplines. In effect, its remit is to keep 'turning the kaleidoscope' on the way we think about crime and, importantly, the legal and societal responses to it.

Keith Hayward

Related entries

Criminalization; Critical criminology; Labelling theory; Subcultural theory; Subculture..

Key texts and sources

Ferrell, J. (1999) 'Cultural criminology', *Annual Review of Sociology*, 25: 395–418.
Ferrell, J., Hayward, K., Morrison, W. and Presdee, M. (2004) *Cultural Criminology Unleashed*. London: Glasshouse.
Ferrell, J. and Sanders, C. (1995) *Cultural Criminology*. Boston, MA: Northeastern University Press.

Hayward, K.J. (2004) *City Limits: Crime, Consumer Culture and the Urban Experience*. London: Glasshouse.

Hayward, K.J. and Young, J. (eds) (2004) *Theoretical Criminology*, 8(3) (special edition on cultural criminology).

CURFEW ORDERS

Curfew orders are disposals imposed by the courts in response to offending by children and young people aged between 10 and 15. They are often enforced through electronic monitoring. Curfew orders require their subjects to remain at a specified place between set hours. The overall sentence can extend for up to 6 months.

Curfew orders are thought to be particularly useful in breaking up 'pattern offending', particularly in relation to young offenders who offend at night and/or in groups. They are most commonly imposed in response to breach of another order, theft and handling, and/or violence. It is a legislative requirement that curfew orders should not interfere with either education or employment: in practice, curfew hours tend to be fixed at night-time.

While curfew orders *can* be passed in conjunction with another community order, the system in England and Wales is unusual in that this is not a requirement. Approximately 25 per cent of young offenders are subject to another order while subject to a curfew order. The value of 'stand-alone' curfew orders is questionable. Taking a comparative approach, research in Canada has revealed that, without concurrent rehabilitative requirements, curfews have little effect on recidivism rates. When imposed alongside another community order, curfew orders may help support that order, potentially bringing routine and stability to disorganized lives. In practice, curfew orders are complied with in approximately two thirds of cases. Where breach does occur, this is normally either through failure to abide by curfew hours or by tampering with electronic monitoring equipment. Breach may result in revocation, resentencing and, ultimately, custody.

Whether or not curfew orders are a useful sentence for young offenders depends largely on how they are utilized in practice. If they are used as a high-tariff penalty – genuinely to keep those who are on the threshold of custody in the community – they may well serve a positive function. Conversely, if they target young people who would otherwise have received far less demanding and 'lower tariff' orders, then their legitimacy is open to question. The latter scenario raises the spectre of curfew orders – enforced by electronic monitoring – being used to 'widen the net' of social control through the creation of virtual prisons in young offenders' homes. In effect, human contact is replaced with surveillance technology. It must be remembered that curfew orders are a restrictive and demanding penalty: if the maximum term is imposed, they can lead to over 2,000 hours of curfew. However, the evidence suggests that curfew orders are not, in fact, normally used as a direct alternative to youth custody but, rather, replace other community sentences. Annual statistics on youth justice show that, although crime rates have remained stable, there has been a rise in the number of curfew orders passed and, moreover, custody levels have remained stubbornly high (Youth Justice Board 2007g).

If the relevant provisions of the Criminal Justice and Immigration Bill 2006–7 to 2007–8 are implemented, the curfew order will be replaced – along with the action plan order, the attendance centre order, the exclusion order and the supervision order – with the single 'menu-based' youth rehabilitation order.

Charlotte Walsh

Related entries

Community punishment and rehabilitation orders (CPROs); Crime (Sentences) Act 1997; Criminal Justice and Immigration Bill 2006–7 to 2007–8; Electronic monitoring; Powers of Criminal Courts (Sentencing) Act 2000; Sentencing framework.

Key texts and sources

Elliot, R., Airs, J., Easton, C. and Lewis, R. (2000) *Electronically Monitored Curfew for 10- to 15-year-olds – Report of the Pilot*. London: Home Office (available online at **http://www.homeoffice.gov.uk/rds/pdfs/occ-tagging.pdf**).

Walter, I. (2002) *Evaluation of the National Roll-out of Curfew Orders*. London: Home Office (available online at **http://www.homeoffice.gov.uk/rds/pdfs2/rdsolr1502.pdf**).

Youth Justice Board (2007g) *Youth Justice Annual Statistics*, 2005/06. London: Youth Justice Board (available online at **http://www.yjb.gov.uk/publications/Resources/Downloads/Youth%20Justice%20Annual%20Statistics%202005-06.pdf**).

See the Office of Public Sector Information's website (**http://www.opsi.gov.uk/acts/acts2000/20000006.htm**) for the text of the Powers of Criminal Courts (Sentencing) Act 2000, s. 37 (as amended by s. 88 of the Anti-social Behaviour Act 2003).

CUSTODY-FREE ZONES

The term 'custody-free zone' referred to local authority areas within which the courts had not imposed custodial sentences on children and young people for a period of time. The area was, therefore, 'custody free'. The term was in no sense a description of any formal arrangement but, rather, an aspiration of 'juvenile' justice practitioners and, in some cases, sentencers too. The term has been attributed to Andrew Rutherford (1992) as a description of the decarcerative impulses that developed in Hampshire in the late 1980s.

To understand the concept of a 'custody-free zone', it needs to be set in the context of juvenile justice debates in the mid-to-late 1980s and the impact of a group of researchers working out of Lancaster University (see Rutherford 1992). At the time there had been a major shift in the delivery of juvenile justice, from what some commentators claimed to be a more disorganized 'welfare'-based approach, to a new, 'justice'-based orthodoxy. The characteristics of the 'justice' approach centred around 'managing the system'. While this was seen by some as a 'managerialist' response underpinned by 'nothing works' imperatives and 'minimum intervention' principles, at the heart of the change was an organized body of practitioners passionate about reducing custody.

One of the many influences on the new practice was the publication of the Local Authority Circular 83(3) initiative by the Department of Health and Social Security, which encouraged the voluntary sector to set up 'alternative to custody' projects. In addition to this, the rise in use of police cautioning had the effect of reducing juvenile prosecution, and thus incarceration. In some areas the momentum was taken forward by both practitioners and sentencers to such an extent that it was reported that they had become 'custody-free zones'. It is true that the expression also owes some provenance to the 'Massachusetts experiment' led by Jerome Miller. In 1971 Miller was the head of the Department of Youth Services in Massachusetts, where he succeeded in removing most of the young people detained in state 'reform schools', setting up, instead, community alternatives (Miller 1998). The impact of this experiment on the volume of youth crime was negligible, thus questioning the need to incarcerate children. More recently, commentators have made the case for the abolition of penal custody for children in England and Wales, where the population of child prisoners has almost doubled since the early 1990s (Goldson 2005b).

Richard Hester

Related entries

Abolitionism; Alternatives to custody; Decarceration; Justice; Supervision orders; Systems management.

Key texts and sources

Goldson, B. (2005b) 'Child imprisonment: a case for abolition', *Youth Justice*, 5: 77–90.

Miller, J. (1998) *Last One Over the Wall: The Massachusetts Experiment in Closing Reform Schools* (2nd edn). Columbus, OH: Ohio State University Press.

Rutherford, A. (1992) *Growing Out of Crime: The New Era*. Winchester: Waterside Press.

CUSTODY RATE

Custody rates comprise statistical indicators that show the relative level of custody. Custody rates are frequently expressed as the percentage of total court disposals that lead to imprisonment. They may also be presented as the proportion of the offending population sent to prison (including those who are dealt with through pre-court measures) or, more broadly still, as the ratio of people imprisoned relative to the entire population.

The contemporary use of custody in the UK is extremely high, both by international and historical standards. Data published by the Council of Europe, for instance, show that, in England and Wales in September 2005, there were 142.7 persons (adults and children) in penal institutions per 100,000 of the general population. The corresponding figures for other countries include 102 in Italy, 95.7 in Germany and 67.2 in the Netherlands. The figure for England and Wales represents a considerable rise from 2002 when the rate of custody expressed in equivalent terms stood at 124.

The use of custody for children, more specifically, has drawn sharp criticism from the United Nations Committee on the Rights of the Child. The committee has contended that the number of children in penal institutions in England and Wales represents a breach of the United Nations Convention on the Rights of the Child. The committee's concluding observations on the UK government's record of compliance with the convention, published in October 2002, noted that it was:

deeply concerned at the high increasing number of children in custody generally, at earlier ages for less offences and for longer custodial sentences imposed by the recent increased court powers ... [D]eprivation of liberty is not being used only as a last resort for the shortest appropriate period of time, in violation of Article 37b of the Convention

(United Nations Committee on the Rights of the Child 2002).

Nacro (2005a, 2006b), while acknowledging some genuine difficulties of comparison, has estimated that, expressed as a proportion of the population aged below 18 years, the rate of custody in England and Wales is four times that in France, ten times that in Spain and 100 times that in Finland (see also Muncie and Goldson 2006).

Yet custody rates are not always the best measure of child imprisonment. It is widely accepted that the incarceration of children in England and Wales rose at an unprecedented rate during the 1990s, with the number sentenced to custody growing by almost 90 per cent between 1992 and 2000, despite a fall in youth crime of more than one quarter. Custodial *rates* for the same period, however, imply a less dramatic increase than the actual *absolute numbers*. The rate of custody for 15–17-year-old boys over the same period, for instance, expressed as a proportion of all those sentenced, increased from 11 to 15 per cent.

The explanation for the apparent tension between the two sets of figures is that the decision to prosecute, as opposed to imposing some form of pre-court disposal, is extremely sensitive to changes in policy, legislation and police practice. So in the eight years from 1992, the proportion of children whose offending resulted in a pre-court measure (caution, reprimand or final warning) *fell* from almost three quarters to just over half of all cases, leading to a corresponding *rise* in the number of children convicted despite the *fall* in the overall volume of offending. As a result, the custody rate has tended to understate the scale of the rise in *actual* custodial disposals.

Conversely, custody rates provide a better indicator of geographic variation in the extent to which young people are deprived of their liberty in criminal proceedings. For that purpose, absolute numbers are inevitably misleading, given significantly different populations and recorded levels of youth crime from one locality to another. Custody *rates*, by contrast, allow comparison of like with like and reveal significant regional differences. Thus figures published by the Sentencing Guidelines Council show that, expressed as a proportion of all disposals (bar financial penalties and discharges), the rate of custody in youth offending team areas varied, between April 2005 and March 2006, from 1 in every 100 cases resulting in a court conviction in Pembrokeshire, to more than 1 in 4 in Merthyr Tydfil.

Research has identified a range of factors that influence regional variations in custodial sentencing or, to put it another way, 'justice by geography'. Explanatory variables include the quality of pre-sentence reports; magistrates' perceptions of the quality of local youth justice services; and the confidence of the court that the local youth offending team will deliver, and enforce, community-based programmes in the manner described in court reports. Perhaps more significantly for current purposes, the rate of diversion – that is, the proportion of all cases that result in a caution, reprimand or final warning – appears to be strongly inversely correlated with the rate of custodial sentencing. In other words, as the proportion of cases resulting in a conviction rises, so too does the rate of custody. During 2004–5, for instance, London had the highest rate of custody of any region and the lowest proportionate use of diversion. At the other end of the scale, the South West region registered the highest proportionate use of diversionary disposals and enjoyed the second lowest rate of custody.

Such findings are perhaps counter-intuitive. One might anticipate, for instance, that a rise in the rate of prosecution, leading to a influx of less serious offending into the court arena, would generate a fall in the *rate* of custodial outcomes, as sentencing decisions compensate for the downward shift in the prosecution threshold. The statistical record, however, suggests the opposite. While the relationship between court throughput and the custody rate is no doubt complex, it would appear that early entry into the court system generates a longer 'criminal career' for an *equivalent* history of offending, leading to consequent escalation up the sentencing 'tariff' and a greater likelihood of custodial disposal.

Tim Bateman

Related entries

Alternatives to custody; Comparative youth justice; Decarceration; Diversion; Intensive Supervision and Surveillance Programme (ISSP); Justice by geography; Punitiveness; Supervision orders; Systems management.

Key texts and sources

Bateman, T. (2005c) 'Reducing child imprisonment: a systemic challenge', *Youth Justice*, 5:91–105.

Bateman, T. and Stanley, C. (2002) *Patterns of Sentencing: Differential Sentencing across England and Wales.* London: Youth Justice Board.

Muncie, J. and Goldson, B. (eds) (2006) *Comparative Youth Justice: Critical Issues.* London: Sage.

Nacro (2005a) *A Better Alternative: Reducing Child Imprisonment.* London: Nacro.

Nacro (2006b) *Reducing Custody: A Systematic Approach. Youth Crime Briefing.* London: Nacro.

United Nations Committee on the Rights of the Child (2002) *Concluding Observations of the Committee on the Rights of the Child: United Kingdom of Great Britain and Northern Ireland.* Geneva: Committee on the Rights of the Child. Available online at **http://www.unhchr.ch/tbs/doc.nsf/(Symbol)/CRC.C.15.Add.188.En?Open Document**.

Youth Justice Board (2000) *Factors Associated with Differential Custodial Sentencing.* London: Youth Justice Board.

D

DANGEROUSNESS

'Dangerousness' was introduced into sentencing by the Criminal Justice Act 2003. It concerns 153 sexual and violent offences 'specified' in Schedule 15 of the Act. The Act makes it mandatory for the Crown court to impose lengthy sentences where it has determined the case is one in which 'dangerousness' applies. Implemented on 5 April 2005, the provisions apply to offences committed after that time.

In determining whether 'dangerousness' applies, the court must be of the opinion that there is a significant risk to members of the public of serious harm occasioned by the likely commission of further *specified* offences. 'Serious harm' is defined by the Criminal Justice Act 2003 as 'death or serious personal injury whether physical or psychological'. 'Significant risk' has been defined by case law as 'noteworthy, of considerable amount or importance'. Case law has also established that assessing 'risk' should involve a 'two stage' test and that 'significant risk of further offence' should not be taken necessarily to imply 'significant risk of serious harm', nor vice versa.

Schedule 15 of the Criminal Justice Act 2003 sets out *specified* offences and *serious specified* offences. The latter are those that carry a maximum sentence – in the case of an adult – of imprisonment for 10 years or more. Whether a specified offence is serious or not is key to the sentences available to the court in cases where it has determined that 'dangerousness' exists.

If the offence is a specified offence, then a court must pass an 'extended sentence' of detention. If the offence is a serious specified offence, but the offence does not justify a life sentence, the court must choose between:

- an *extended sentence of detention*, if the court is of the opinion that this is adequate to protect the public from serious harm; or
- a *sentence of detention for public protection*, if the court considers an extended sentence will not be sufficient to protect the public from serious harm.

There is a separate process for those offences – which are also serious specified offences – that meet the criteria for sentence under s. 91 of the Powers of the Criminal Courts (Sentencing) Act 2000 with a maximum sentence of life. Here the court must impose a life sentence if it determines 'dangerousness' exists.

An 'extended sentence' consists of an appropriate custodial term, plus the extension period. The appropriate custodial term must be at least 12 months, with eligibility for early release at the discretion of the Parole Board after the midpoint. The possible length of the extension period depends on the type of offence. It can extend to 5 years for a violent offence or up to 8 years for a sexual offence. A sentence for public protection is an indeterminate sentence, with a specified minimum custodial term, but the individual may be detained indefinitely. There is no eligibility for release at the midpoint of the custodial term, which must be served in full.

Although the sentences are only available to the Crown court, and the definitive determination is at point of sentence, the youth court must take a view to decide whether or not to commit the case to the Crown court. The Criminal Justice Act 2003 allows the youth court to send a case to the Crown court at any time in the proceedings. This initially led to inapßpropriate requests to court officers to provide and/or undertake 'dangerousness assessments'. Case law has since clarified what is seen as proper procedure for the youth court, as follows:

consider whether the offence before the court is a grave offence; if so, consider whether the defendant is dangerous; if so, commit the case to the Crown court; if not, consider whether the grave crime test is satisfied; if it is, send the case to the Crown court; if it is not a grave offence, 'dangerousness' should not be considered at this stage; trials will be heard in the youth court and only on conviction should 'dangerousness' be considered; if the view of the court is that the defendant is 'dangerous', then the case should be committed for sentence in the Crown court.

When considering any specified offence in respect of a child/young person the court must commence any 'dangerousness' assessment from a 'neutral' position. Even if there is a previous specified offence in which 'dangerousness' was determined, there is no presumption in favour of 'dangerousness' with regard to the current matter before the court. This is different from cases involving adults. However, offences with a 'dangerousness determination' committed 'under 18' create a presumption of dangerousness if a further specified offence is due for sentence after the young person becomes an adult.

In assessing dangerousness a court must take account of all the information available about the nature and circumstances of the offence. It may take account of any information about any pattern of behaviour of which the offence forms part and any information about the offender that is before the court.

Case law indicates that, for a very young offender, an indeterminate sentence may be inappropriate, even where a serious specified offence has been committed and there is a significant risk of serious harm from further offences. Case law has reaffirmed the legislature's established policy that under-18s should, wherever possible, be tried in the youth court. The youth court should retain jurisdiction for trials for 'specified offences' that are not grave crimes or serious specified and only address dangerousness post-trial.

The sentencing court needs to be particularly rigorous before concluding there is a significant risk of serious harm, the determination for which is likely to require a pre-sentence report following assessment by a youth offending team. Although the decision ultimately lies with the court, there is an obvious role for the report author in informing that decision. Any case in which dangerousness is determined will require referral to the local multi-agency public protection arrangements.

Spike Cadman

Related entries

Assessment framework; Criminal Justice Act 2003; Detention for public protection (DPP); Grave offences; Hospital orders; Long term detention; Mandatory sentences; Offender management; Proportionality; Risk management.

Key texts and sources

Nacro (2005c) *Dangerousness in the Youth Justice System.* Youth Crime Briefing. London: Nacro.

Nacro (2006g) *The Dangerousness Provisions of the Criminal Justice Act 2003 and Subsequent Case-law.* Youth Crime Briefing. London: Nacro.

Youth Justice Board (2006a) *Criminal Justice Act 2003, 'Dangerousness' and the New Sentences for Public Protection: Guidance for Youth Offending Teams.* London: Youth Justice Board (available online at http://www.yjb.gov.uk/Publications/scripts/prodView.asp?idproduct=209&eP=).

Youth Justice Board (2006b) *Multi-agency Public Protection Arrangements: Guidance for Youth Offending Teams.* London: Youth Justice Board (available online at http://www.yjb.gov.uk/publications/scripts/prodView.asp?idProduct=283&eP).

See the Office of Public Sector Information's website (http://www.opsi.gov.uk/acts/acts2003/20030044.htm) for the text of the Criminal Justice Act 2003.

DEATHS IN CUSTODY

In youth justice, the term 'deaths in custody' normally refers to child deaths in custodial institutions, usually – although not exclusively – self-inflicted deaths.

Three key facts are important by way of introduction to deaths in custody. First, greater use of penal custody for children is made in England and Wales than in most other industrialized democratic countries in the world. Second, the juvenile inmates of state prisons (including young offender institutions and juvenile justice centres) and private jails (including secure training centres) routinely comprise some of society's most disadvantaged, distressed and damaged children. Third, 30 children died in penal custody (28 in state prisons and 2 in private jails) in England and Wales between July 1990 and November 2007, and literally thousands more were physically, emotionally and/or psychologically harmed (Goldson and Coles 2005). Similar 'abuses' of child prisoners have been reported in Northern Ireland (Scraton and Moore 2005) and Scotland (Scraton and Chadwick 1987).

The facts are clear enough but the means by which they are presented and interpreted are less clear cut. When required to account for the damage and harm experienced by many child prisoners in general, or child deaths in penal custody in particular, official discourse tends to privilege constructions of individual pathology, referring to 'imported' or 'innate' vulnerability, 'failure to cope', 'weakness' and 'inadequacy'. Such rationales necessarily *individualize* damage, harm and ultimately death, often by emphasizing the fragile mental health of specific child prisoners. In this way explanations are confined to an individual child in a given penal institution at a particular moment in time. Furthermore, with regard to child deaths in penal custody, such individualization is institutionalized through the case-specific nature of post-death investigations and coroners' inquests (Goldson and Coles 2005: 67–94). On one level this appears to be reasonable. On another level it is deeply problematic.

As stated, child prisoners are typically drawn from some of the most disadvantaged families, neighbourhoods and communities. It is also well known that the physical and mental health needs of child 'offenders' are often neglected. Lader *et al.* (2000), for example, in their wide-ranging study of 'psychiatric morbidity' among child prisoners, found high levels of 'personality disorder', 'psychotic disorder', 'sleep problems', 'hazardous drinking habits', 'drug use' and 'stressful life events'. In this context it is entirely legitimate to be concerned with the vulnerabili-

ties and, in some cases, the fragile mental health of individual child prisoners. The almost *exclusive* emphasis on mental ill-health and individualized constructions of pathology is inadequate, however. Such an approach serves not only to divert attention from state responsibility and accountability (the excessive reliance on incarceration and the inappropriate nature of penal regimes for children) but it also fragments an understanding of the commonalities of circumstance that give rise to the harm, damage and deaths of children in penal institutions. It follows that this limited 'way of seeing' is necessarily abstracted from analyses of youth justice policy and/or any consideration of the wider social, structural, material and institutional arrangements that typically define the circumstances of child prisoners.

Surprisingly little is known about child deaths in penal custody. There are at least five reasons why this is so. First, the scope and depth of post-death investigations and inquests are significantly circumscribed. Second, the findings and recommendations of the same post-death investigative and inquest processes are not published. Third, given the non-publication of findings and recommendations, there is no mechanism by which they can be systematically and collectively analysed, monitored or followed up. Fourth, up until very recently there was little detailed research available. Fifth, state agencies are consistently reluctant to allow thorough independent inquiry. So, in England and Wales for example, despite the deaths of 30 children since mid-1990, there has been no attempt by the authorities to undertake a comprehensive *aggregated* analysis of the circumstances that led to their deaths; to ascertain the *commonalities* that feature across such cases; and/or to make the findings of such inquiry available in the public domain.

Despite this, recent research has helped to define a range of features that consistently emerge with regard to child deaths in penal custody, including the following:

- The multiple and intersecting modes of disadvantage that beset child prisoners.
- A relational 'pathway' between public care and penal custody for significant numbers of child prisoners.

- System strain as a result of hardening policy responses to child offenders and penal expansion (for example, overcrowding, hastily implemented and thus incomplete 'assessments' and competing operational pressures that fundamentally compromise the 'duty of care').
- 'Placements' in penal custody that are not only unsuitable in nature but are also inappropriate by location (exposing children to danger and rendering family visits near impossible).
- Inadequate intra-agency and inter-agency communication and information exchange.
- Hostile institutional cultures predicated upon bullying and intimidation.
- The institutional (mis)conceptualization of 'need' as 'manipulation'.
- The corrosive impact of penal custody, on child prisoners.
- Persistent problems associated with the physical infrastructure of penal custody including cell design and access to ligature points.
- Poor medical care and limited access to specialist 'therapeutic' services.
- A failure to implement suicide prevention guidelines.
- The intrinsic degradation imposed by institutional responses to 'vulnerable' child prisoners, including the use of strip searches and restraint alongside solitary confinement and surveillance (as distinct from watchful care).
- Continuing deficits in terms of openness, transparency, rigour and independence with regard to investigative processes following child deaths in penal custody (Goldson and Coles 2005).

When the collective features and commonalities that characterize child deaths in penal custody are presented and interpreted in this way, the conventional emphasis on individual pathology is wholly inadequate: it is no longer possible to conceive such deaths as isolated and unconnected aberrations. Indeed, the consistent features and intersecting similarities of such cases illustrate the systemic failings that continue to be produced and reproduced through the practices and processes of child incarceration. It is here that questions of legitimacy, efficiency and integrity with regard to penal custody and youth justice policy become more contested.

There is a pressing need for a comprehensive and thorough review of the deaths of 30 child prisoners in England and Wales between July 1990 and November 2007. It is evident to many that only an independent body, possibly a 'Standing Commission on Custodial Deaths', can satisfactorily undertake such a review. A commission of this nature might collect, collate, analyse and publish findings in respect of child deaths; identify common issues; develop programmes of research; and assist in the development and delivery of 'best practice' in safeguarding children, promoting the 'duty of care' and, in the final analysis, sustaining the child's right to life.

Barry Goldson

Related entries

Abolitionism; Alternatives to custody; Children in custody; Mental health and young offenders; Restraint; Social harm; Vulnerability.

Key texts and sources

Goldson, B. (2006b) 'Fatal injustice: rampant punitiveness, child-prisoner deaths and institutionalised denial – a case for comprehensive independent inquiry in England and Wales', *Social Justice: A Journal of Crime, Conflict and World Order*, 33: 52–68.

Goldson, B. and Coles, D. (2005) *In the Care of the State? Child Deaths in Penal Custody in England and Wales*. London: Inquest.

Lader, D., Singleton, N. and Meltzer, H. (2000) *Psychiatric Morbidity among Young Offenders in England and Wales*. London: Office for National Statistics.

Scraton, P. and Chadwick, K. (1987) *In the Arms of the Law: Coroners' Inquests and Deaths in Custody*. London: Pluto.

Scraton, P. and Moore, L. (2005) *The Hurt Inside: The Imprisonment of Women and Girls in Northern Ireland* (rev. edn). Belfast: Northern Ireland Human Rights Commission.

See also Inquest's website (**http://inquest.gn.apc.org/main.html**).

DECARCERATION

Decarceration is the deliberate drive towards reducing, or even eliminating, the number of children and young people (and adults) held in custodial institutions. Also known as dein-stitutionalization, it is related to reductionism and abolitionism.

During the 1980s and into the early 1990s decarceration was an important feature of youth justice policy and practice in England and Wales. Policymakers and the courts showed a clear preference for community penalties over imprisonment for young people, and the numbers of children detained in custody fell accordingly. However, a political shift in the early 1990s, reinforced by moral panics over persistent young offenders and the murder of James Bulger, brought a sudden end to policies promoting decarceration. Since that time, the number of young people sentenced to custody has almost doubled in England and Wales.

These higher custody rates have prompted pressure groups to campaign for policies that will cut the number of young people in penal institutions (held both on remand and sentence). Decarceration would be completely in line with the UK's commitment to relevant international agreements. In particular, Article 37(b) of the United Nations Convention on the Rights of the Child provides that custodial detention should only be used as 'a measure of last resort and for the shortest appropriate period of time'. This principle of last resort is more evident in a number of countries (with notably lower custody rates than England and Wales), including Germany, Finland, Greece and Canada (Goldson and Muncie 2006a).

It is more common for supporters of decarceration to adopt a position of limited custodial use (reductionism) rather than to argue for no custodial provision at all (aboli-tionism). Supporters of decarceration usually concede that there are some young people for whom restriction of liberty is necessary, albeit not necessarily in prison custody.

There are a number of key arguments used by those advocating decarceration. The first is that prison does not work in preventing offending. Studies have consistently shown that approxi-mately four in every five (male) young offenders released from custody are reconvicted within two years – a higher recidivism rate than most com-munity sentences. Second, even if it did 'work', custody is a very expensive way to deal with youth offending. It costs more than £50,000 a year to keep a young person in a young offender institu-tion, and even more in other types of custodial institutions. This is much more than any type of community-based disposal. Consequently, the Youth Justice Board typically spends more than 70 per cent of its total budget on custodial places, for what amounts to only 7 per cent of young offend-ers. Third, prison is a dehumanizing environment, incompatible with developing young people as individuals within society. Instead of strengthen-ing protective relationships and activities for young people, incarceration damages links with family, school and the community and denies them any chance of a 'normal' childhood. Fourth, prison is a brutalizing and dangerous environ-ment that has consistently produced suicides, high rates of self-harm and endemic bullying among inmates. Fifth, prisons have consistently been dubbed 'colleges of crime', where child prisoners are more likely to learn how to become more effective and more serious offenders (for a detailed critique, see Goldson 2006c).

Although decarceration is a relatively mod-ern term, it is important to realize that these arguments have been used by juvenile prison reformers for the past two centuries – first, to argue for separate juvenile prisons and, then, for alternative provision, such as reformatory schools (in the mid nineteenth-Century).

Theoretically, decarceration is most closely associated with the rise of labelling theory since the 1960s. Advocates of this perspective argue that imprisonment (and other forms of process-ing in the formal youth justice process) reinforces the child's identity as 'criminal'. Decarceration has also developed, to some extent at least, in tandem with restorative justice, whereby locking children away is counter to the central principle of the social (re)inclusion of offenders.

The Youth Justice Board's (2007e) official line on custody for young people is clearly reductionist and echoes some of the above concerns. The board's strategy on sentencing young people to custody states that it should only be used as a last resort. Its primary tactic in trying to lower custody rates has been to offer courts alternative 'high tariff' community sanctions that incorporate strict social control. These include intensive supervision and surveillance programmes and electronic monitoring (tagging) in the community. However, it has proved difficult to translate this strategy into a real reduction in the use of custody without an equal commitment from government and the courts.

Northern Ireland has been more successful than England and Wales with decarceration in recent years. Like New Zealand, this has been achieved largely by introducing more diversion in youth justice processes, with particular emphasis on restorative conferences. Other ways to reduce custody have included making all prison sentences suspended (as a final chance) (Finland) and only permitting courts to remand a child in custody if a prison sentence on conviction is likely (Canada).

Neal Hazel

Related entries

Abolitionism; Alternatives to custody; Comparative youth justice; Custody rates; Politicization; United Nations Convention on the Rights of the Child (UNCRC).

Key texts and sources

Bateman, T. (2005c) 'Reducing child imprisonment: a systemic challenge', *Youth Justice*, 5: 91–105.

Goldson, B. (2006c) 'Penal custody: intolerance, irrationality and indifference', in B. Goldson and J. Muncie (eds) *Youth Crime and Justice*. London: Sage.

Goldson, B. and Muncie, J. (2006a) 'Rethinking youth justice: comparative analysis, international human rights and research evidence', *Youth Justice*, 6: 91–106.

Nacro (2006b) *Reducing Custody: A Systematic Approach. Youth Crime Briefing*. London: Nacro.

Youth Justice Board (2007e) *Position Statement on Sentencing Young People to Custody*. London: Youth Justice Board (available online at http://www.yjb.gov.uk/engb/yjb/MediaCentre/PositionStatements/sentencingchildrenandyoungpeopletocustody.htm).

DECRIMINALIZATION

> Decriminalization is a process that results in the removal of official 'criminal' status from certain acts and deviant behaviours. *De facto*, decriminalization involves 'criminal' acts no longer being prosecuted, despite formally remaining illegal.

The principle of decriminalization emerged from two main theoretical perspectives: abolitionism and labelling. Abolitionists argue that the existing penal system, including its current laws, offers an overly punitive, repressive and expensive way of reacting to crime. Indeed, de Haan (1990) recommends abandoning the category of 'crime' altogether and replacing it with conceptions of 'problematic events' and 'social harms'. Nils Christie (2004) goes further by suggesting that there is no such thing as 'crime'. Instead, certain acts are simply labelled as criminal by powerful social groups, so 'crime' exists as a social construction. Abolitionists maintain that a reflexive, welfare-orientated and socially just (non-penal) system would be a more appropriate, humanistic and sustainable response to actions deemed criminal. Integral to this reorientated criminal justice system is the decriminalization and, *de facto*, decriminalization of particular acts that can be, for example, victimless (minor drug use, prostitution), relatively minor offences (petty theft, vandalism, anti-social behaviour) or 'juvenile-status offences' (acts that would not be considered illegal if committed by an adult). However, these acts would still be addressed as 'social problems', thus distinguishing decriminalization from 'legalization'.

Labelling theorists argue that individuals who offend, particularly young people, are labelled 'offender' or 'juvenile delinquent'. They subsequently find this negative label extremely difficult to escape, such that it limits their opportunities and life chances, which can induce them to resort to more crime (the classic 'self-fulfilling prophecy') (Lemert 1972). Consequently, labelling theorists consolidate the abolitionist call for decriminalizing certain offences, particularly juvenile-status offences; for diverting young people from the youth justice system to avoid a stigmatizing label; and for encouraging them to lead productive, pro-social lives.

Decriminalization has been employed as a means of modifying youth justice systems to use non-criminal justice measures to differing degrees and with differing levels of success across the industrialized western world. For example, in Holland in the 1970s and in France in the 1980s, education, vocational opportunities, rehabilitation, democratic participation and penal welfarism heavily influenced the youth justice systems – a situation that can still be seen in Belgium. However, the notion of decriminalization has been criticized for its potential to send an inappropriate message to young people and to lead to a greater frequency of certain 'offences' because such behaviour is no longer subject to official censure, regardless of the associated physical and social harm associated with it.

Stephen Case

Related entries

Abolitionism; Critical criminology; Diversion; Informal action; Informalism; Justice; Labelling theory; Minimum necessary intervention; Normalization; Social harm.

Key texts and sources

Christie, N. (2004) *A Suitable Amount of Crime.* London: Routledge.
de Haan, W. (1990) *The Politics of Redress: Crime, Punishment and Penal Abolition.* London: Unwin Hyman.
Lemert, E. (1972) *Human Deviance, Social Problems and Social Control.* Englewood Cliffs, NJ: Prentice Hall.

DEFERRED SENTENCES

A deferred sentence is the procedure whereby a court delays sentence for a period of time following conviction.

The Criminal Justice Act 2003 (s. 278 and Schedule 23) inserts ss. 1–1D into the Powers of Criminal Courts (Sentencing) Act 2000, which give power to a criminal court to defer sentence for up to 6 months in order to have regard to the conduct after conviction, and any change in circumstances, of the offender. The offender must agree to the deferment. If the offender complies with the court's requirements, a non-custodial sentence will usually follow. The power to defer sentence cannot be exercised where the conditions in ss. 16 and 17 of the Powers of Criminal Courts (Sentencing) Act 2000 are met, thus requiring a referral order to be imposed.

In Scotland, sentence may be deferred as the court may determine under s. 202 of the Criminal Procedure (Scotland) Act 1995 (subject to s. 205A, which is not yet in force). The Social Work (Scotland) Act 1968 requires a local authority, if and to such extent as directed by the Scottish ministers, to provide advice, guidance and assistance to any person on whom sentence is deferred under s. 202(1) of the Criminal Procedure (Scotland) Act 1995 during the period of deferment while that person is in its area.

Sally Ireland

Related entries

Criminal Justice Act 2003; Powers of Criminal Courts (Sentencing) Act 2000; Social Work (Scotland) Act 1968.

Key texts and sources

See the Office of Public Sector Information's website for the texts of the Criminal Justice Act 2003 (http://www.opsi.gov.uk/acts/acts2003/20030044. htm) and the Criminal Procedure (Scotland) Act 1995 (http://www.opsi.gov.uk/acts/acts1995/ Ukpga_19950046_en_1.htm).

DELINQUENCY

Delinquency is a term that is used loosely to refer to any kind of youthful misbehaviour.

Criminologists frequently use the concepts of 'crime' and 'delinquency' interchangeably, especially when their object of study is young people. However, there are crucial differences. While a legal definition of crime refers to behaviour prohibited by criminal law, delinquency is also applied to all manner of behaviours that are deemed to be undesirable. It is capable of capturing the legally proscribed but also waywardness, misbehaviour, incorrigibility, the 'anti-social' and that believed to constitute the 'pre-criminal'. Much of this ambiguity derives from the establishment of separate systems of juvenile justice designed to punish and treat offenders but also to protect the vulnerable and neglected.

In the USA – under the statutes of various states – delinquency is in part defined, but it also retains a series of vague and imprecise standards that rest on the need to intervene early to prevent future offending or to tackle assumed family or psychological problems. These are often referred to as *status offences* – that is, the violation of formal or informal rules that are applied only to certain sections of society. The focus is less on the offence itself and more on who commits it. Status offences often apply only to children and include being 'incorrigible', truanting from school or behaving in a sexually 'precocious' manner.

Most historians agree that delinquency was first identified as a major social problem in the early nineteenth century. Social surveys and empirical investigations apparently served to 'discover' delinquency, but they also presupposed existing conceptions of how youths should behave, what relation should exist between different age groups and what should be the appropriate role of the family. In the early nineteenth century, with the rapid growth of industrial capitalism, factory production and high-density urban populations, the condition of the labouring classes became the object of considerable middle-class concern – whether this was fear of their revolutionary potential, disgust at their (im)morality or alarm at their impoverishment and criminal tendencies. In England these fears galvanized around images of 'naked, filthy, roaming, lawless and deserted children' moving around in 'gangs'. Accurate estimations of the extent of 'delinquency' were impossible,

not least because of its ill-defined nature but also because the received wisdom was that it was expanding and becoming more commonplace. Susan Magarey (1978) contends that expansion, such as it was, is explicable less with reference to 'increased lawlessness' and more with changes in the position of children in relation to the criminal law and the criminalization of behaviour for which previously there may have been no official action. In particular, the Vagrancy Act 1824 and the Malicious Trespass Act 1827 considerably broadened legal conceptions of 'criminality' to include, for example, suspicion of being a thief, gambling on the street and scrumping apples from orchards and gardens. Previous nuisances were transformed into criminal offences. This made many more street children liable to arrest. In these ways juvenile delinquency was 'legislated into existence'.

Such historical analysis is instructive when reflecting on more 'modern' developments in youth justice policy and practice, particularly the emphasis on targeting 'delinquent' children thought to be 'at risk' of offending; early intervention; and the inclusion of 'anti-social behaviour' and 'disorder' within the purview of formal youth justice systems.

John Muncie

Related entries

Anti-social behaviour (ASB); Criminalization; Early intervention; Gangs; Net-widening; Status offences.

Key texts and sources

Magarey, S. (1978) 'The invention of juvenile delinquency in early nineteenth century England', *Labour History*, 34: 11–25.
May, M. (1973) 'Innocence and experience: the evolution of the concept of juvenile delinquency in the mid-nineteenth century', *Victorian Studies*, 17: 7–29.
Tappan, P. (1949) *Juvenile Delinquency*. New York, NY: McGraw-Hill.
West, D. and Farrington, D. (1973) *Who Becomes Delinquent?* London: Heinemann.
West, D. and Farrington, D. (1977) *The Delinquent Way of Life*. London: Heinemann.

DEMONIZATION

> Demonization is a process through which individuals, groups or communities are ascribed a public, negative reputation associated with pathological malevolence often popularly represented as 'evil'. While ideological in construction and transmission, demonization has tangible consequences in social and societal reactions.

Stan Cohen described media and political reaction to regular clashes between 'mods' and 'rockers' as a *moral panic*, within which young people were characterized as *folk devils*. Folk devils were individuals or groups identified in popular discourse whose 'bad', 'anti-social' and/or 'criminal' behaviour was so serious it threatened the established social and political order. They symbolized a breakdown in shared moral values undermining the stability of otherwise coherent and consensual communities. The 'threat' was 'presented in a stylised and stereotypical fashion by the mass media', calling 'right-thinking people' to the 'moral barricades' (Cohen 1972: 9). Moral panics had 'serious and long-lasting repercussions', particularly in 'legal and social policy or even in the way society conceives itself' (see also Goldson 2001).

Cohen (2000: 40) comments that his initial 'folk devil' appears 'benign' in the contemporary context of 'public monsters': 'essentialist offenders: their actions are not the product of fashion, situation, setting, opportunity or chance, but express the essence of the type of person they are and always will be.' Central to the process of demonization is the apparent 'ease with which the moral discourse of evil, sin, monstrosity and perversion is coupled with the medical model of sickness, pathology and untreatability' (2000: 41–2).

In 1993 the killing of 2-year-old James Bulger by two 10-year-old boys resulted in their prosecution for murder in an adult court. Found guilty, the judge labelled the crime an act of 'unparalleled evil' and released their identities and photographs. 'Born to murder', 'Freaks of nature' were newspaper headlines accompanying publication of their photographs. The subsequent moral panic was profound and long lasting (Scraton 1997b). Media coverage of the 'crisis' in childhood was reminiscent of William Golding's *Lord of the Flies*. Children were possessed by the 'satan bug', 'devoid of innocence' or carrying within the 'mark of Cain'. They were 'rat boys', 'beasts' or 'animals'; a 'nation of vipers' had been spawned. The demonization of two boys presented an atypical case as typical of the criminal and anti-social behaviour of contemporary childhood. The atypical was transformed into the stereotypical, childhood was in 'crisis' and the social order was collapsing from within.

Phil Scraton

Related entries

'Adulteration'; Authoritarianism; Bulger; Critical criminology; Media reporting; Moral panic; Public attitudes to youth crime and justice; Punitiveness.

Key texts and sources

Cohen, S. (1972) *Folk Devils and Moral Panics.* London: MacGibbon & Kee.

Cohen, S. (2000) 'Some thoroughly modern monsters', *Index on Censorship*, 29: 36–43.

Goldson, B. (2001) 'The demonisation of children: from the symbolic to the institutional', in P. Foley *et al.* (eds) *Children in Society: Contemporary Theory, Policy and Practice.* Basingstoke: Palgrave.

Scraton, P. (ed.) (1997b) *'Childhood' in 'Crisis'?* London: UCL Press/Routledge.

Scraton, P. (2007) *Power, Conflict and Criminalisation.* London: Routledge.

DESISTANCE

> Desistance is the processes by which people come to cease, and to sustain cessation of, offending, with or without formal intervention.

Desistance research is concerned with when, why and how criminal careers come to their end. However, rather than focusing on the end points of criminal careers, most researchers now prefer to explore the *processes* by which this state is reached. Maruna and Farrall (2004) distinguish two phases in the desistance process: primary desistance refers to any lull or crime-free gap in the course of a criminal career; secondary desistance is the assumption of the identity of a non-offender or 'changed person'. While sharing some commonalities, theories of desistance may be broadly categorized as individual, structural and interactionist.

'*Individual' theories* have the longest history and locate explanations of desistance with age and maturation. The aggregate age–crime curve indicates a sharp increase in the arrest rate in the early teen years; a peak in the late teen or early adult years; and a decrease over the remaining age distribution. Explanations of this age–crime relationship can be located within 'ontogenic' theories which contend that, over time and with age, young people tend naturally to grow out of crime, attributing desistance to the physical, mental and biological changes that accompany maturation. The effect of age on crime is seen as natural, direct and invariant across social, temporal and economic conditions. However, critics of this approach argue that age indexes a range of different variables, including biological changes; life experiences and transitions; the impact of social or institutional processes; and internal factors, such as motivation or attitudinal change. Age in itself is not, therefore, a singular explanation.

'*Structural' theories* include social bond theories which postulate an association between desistance and circumstances external to the individual, stressing the significance of family ties, employment or education, for example, in explaining changes in criminal behaviour across the life course. These ties create a stake in conformity. However, most commentators agree that desistance cannot be attributed solely to social attachments acting as external forces. What matters, rather, is what these ties *mean* to 'offenders'; the perceived strength, quality and interdependence of these ties; and their impact in buttressing informal social controls that reduce both opportunities and motivations to offend. Structural theories also raise questions relating to gender. While there are similarities for young men and women in the process of

desistance, there is also evidence of interesting differences. Young women tend to desist abruptly as they leave home, form partnerships and have children; they also appear to be more sensitive to shame and stigma. The process of desistance for young men is typically more protracted. In general, young men seem to take longer to respond to the opportunities that life transitions provide.

'*Interactionist' theories* combine individual and structural explanations. These investigations of the dynamics of desistance often draw on offenders' accounts of their own experiences of desistance processes (Maruna 2001) and stress the significance of subjective changes in personal narratives and identity, reflected in changing motivations, greater concern for others and more consideration of the future.

Two important studies on young people and desistance have been published recently. Barry (2006) argues that offending and desistance are best understood as an age-related process of transition in which age and stage-related differences in the ability to accumulate and expend capital play a key role. The status of young people is structurally constructed so that they (at least in particular social contexts) are denied the means to accumulate legitimate capital. They are, therefore, particularly vulnerable in this period to being drawn into offending in order to acquire some sort of status and respect within their peer groups.

In similar vein, Webster *et al.* (2006) note that young people living in disadvantaged communities typically have very limited access to new networks and new opportunities. Moreover, for those involved in offending and drug use, family and community support is often increasingly limited, forcing them back into restrictive and destructive networks forged around their offending and/or drug use, frustrating any fledgling attempts to desist. In turn this produced an 'embedding' of the deeper disadvantage rooted in the area's long-term socio-economic decline.

Desistance is not simply a source of theoretical intrigue, however. Rather, it provides insights for youth justice practice. First and foremost, a desistance-focused approach to practice requires recognition of diversity in people's pathways to desistance. Interventions that aim to promote desistance need to be carefully individualized, for example, in terms of age and stage; gender and ethnicity; attitudes and motivations; and social bonds and life transitions. Though it is, therefore, difficult to generalize, some authors have tried to suggest how these diverse pathways may be best supported (McNeill 2006).

The relational aspects of supervision processes are frequently highlighted in such discussions as being key supportive factors in desistance processes. The role of relationships in youthful desistance is likely to be particularly significant because the relational experiences of most young people involved in offending are often characterized by disconnection and violation. If desistance from persistent offending is prompted and reinforced by someone believing in the young person and enabling the development of new identities, then the necessary focus on risks and needs will need to be explicitly balanced with an emphasis on strengths and possibilities, so as to avoid the reinforcement of negative messages about dangerousness and/or helplessness.

Indeed, findings in studies of 'assisted desistance' resonate with other research about young people's views of interventions, suggesting that the character of professional attitudes and approaches towards young people is vitally important. These studies highlight the need for individualized, active and participatory approaches that encourage and respect individual agency and self-determination.

Desistance research also suggests that interventions should be focused less on individuals and their supposed 'deficits' and more on their personal and social contexts. In particular, the relationships between offending, desistance and social capital suggest a critical focus for practice around accessing and developing social capital. This implies, among other things, a reassertion of the centrality of social advocacy as a core task for youth justice practitioners.

At a more personal level, desistance is often about discovering new purposes, achievements and forms of recognition that may be facilitated through involvement in diversionary and generative activities. Practitioners should therefore support young people to access opportunities to make a constructive contribution to local communities – for example, through voluntary work. This highlights the need to work *with* communities to build opportunities *for* young people to reconstruct themselves, as well as *with* young people in constructing safer communities.

Beth Weaver and Fergus McNeill

Related entries

Developmental criminology; Growing out of crime; Normalization; Recidivism; Resettlement; Social justice; Sport-based crime prevention; Supervision orders; What Works; Youth Lifestyles Survey (YLS).

Key texts and sources

Barry, M. (2006) *Youth Offending in Transition: The Search for Social Recognition.* London: Routledge.

Farrall, S. and Calverley, A. (2006) *Understanding Desistance from Crime.* Maidenhead: Open University Press.

Maruna, S. (2001) *Making Good: How Ex-convicts Reform and Rebuild their Lives.* Washington, DC: American Psychological Association.

Maruna, S. and Farrall, S. (2004) 'Desistance-focused criminal justice policy research' (introduction to a special issue on 'Desistance from crime and public policy'), *Howard Journal of Criminal Justice,* 43: 358–67.

McNeill, F. (2006) 'Community supervision: contexts and relationships matter', in B. Goldson and J. Muncie (eds) *Youth Crime and Justice: Critical Issues.* London: Sage.

Webster, C., MacDonald, R. and Simpson, M. (2006) 'Predicting criminality? Risk factors, neighbourhood influence and desistance', *Youth Justice,* 6: 7–22.

DETENTION AND TRAINING ORDERS (DTOs)

> The detention and training order (DTO) is the standard custodial sentence for children in England and Wales. The DTO consists of two elements: the first is served in a custodial establishment; the second is under statutory supervision in the community.

Introduced by the Crime and Disorder Act 1998, the detention and training order (DTO) replaced secure training orders and detention in a young offender institution to form a single custodial sentence available in the youth court from April 2000 for young people aged 12–17. The order is also available in the Crown court as one of a number of custodial options for children and young people.

DTOs are subject to the general statutory restriction on the use of custody and can be imposed only where sentencers consider that the offence is 'so serious that neither a fine alone nor a community sentence can be justified'. For defendants aged 12–14, there is an additional requirement that the court considers the child to be a 'persistent offender'. There is provision in the legislation – not yet implemented – to extend the DTO to children aged 10–11 years should the government consider it necessary.

The DTO is a determinate sentence, imposed for a specified duration of 4, 6, 8, 12, 18 or 24 months. By default, transfer to the community occurs at the halfway point but can be brought forward or delayed depending on progress during the custodial phase. Since 2002, there has been a presumption of release, subject to electronically monitored curfew, at the earliest permissible date unless the young person's behaviour 'demonstrates unsuitability' or the order was imposed for a sexual offence or serious violent offence.

The DTO undoubtedly contributed to a rise in the use of child custody. Between April 2000 (when the measure was introduced) and August of the same year, the population of the juvenile secure estate increased by 14 per cent. In part, this was explained by the fact that the order repre-sented a loosening of custodial criteria for children aged 12–14 and a doubling of the maximum sentence for those aged over 15. At the same time, the apparent focus on 'training' led some courts to consider that the new order might be more effective than those it had replaced.

Indeed, the government had welcomed the DTO as 'a more constructive and flexible custodial sentence'. Sentence planning, involving the youth offending team (YOT) responsible for supervising the second phase of the order, was intended to guarantee a seamless transition from custody to the community. The national evaluation of the first two years of operation of the order, however, found that YOTs consistently complained of an inadequate range of programmes to meet the needs of the young people in custodial institutions and that, where programmes existed, they were overly rigid and inflexible. Nor does the DTO appear to perform any better than the disposals it replaced in terms of rehabilitation: 78 per cent of young people released from custody in 2004 (the large majority of whom were subject to DTOs) were reconvicted within a year.

Tim Bateman

Related entries

Children in custody; Crime and Disorder Act 1998; Electronic monitoring; Juvenile secure estate; Persistant young offenders; 'Race' and justice; Resettlement.

Key texts and sources

Bateman, T. (2005b) 'Custody and policy', in T. Bateman and J. Pitts (eds) *The RHP Companion to Youth Justice.* Lyme Regis: Russell House.

Goldson, B. (2006c) 'Penal custody: intolerance, irrationality and indifference', in B. Goldson and J. Muncie (eds) *Youth Crime and Justice.* London: Sage.

Hazel, N., Hagell, A., Liddle, M., Archer, D., Grimshaw, R. and King, D. (2002) *Detention and Training: Assessment of the Detention and Training Order and its Impact on the Secure Estate across England and Wales.* London: Youth Justice Board.

Nacro (2000b) T*he Detention and Training Order. Youth Crime Briefing.* London: Nacro.

Nacro (2003a) *A Failure of Justice: Reducing Child Imprisonment.* London: Nacro.

DETENTION CENTRES

Detention centres were introduced by the Criminal Justice Act 1948 to allow the courts to sentence offenders aged 14–21 to periods of an explicitly punitive – 'short, sharp, shock' – regime. They were abolished in 1988.

Detention centres were established as an 'experiment' in deterrence but lasted 40 years. Their exact purpose in a juvenile penal sector – which also included Borstals and approved schools – was never precisely defined. There is strong evidence that their introduction was a result of a political quid pro quo for the abolition of corporal punishment (Land 1975). While they always promised the delivery of shock discipline, in the 1950s and 1960s their regime was not far removed from that of Borstals.

In the 1970s, in an effort to appease those who viewed the entire juvenile justice system as 'too soft', the Home Secretary announced the establishment of two 'experimental' regimes, emphasizing hard and constructive activities, severe discipline and tidiness, military drill and unquestioning respect for those in authority. It was famously declared that these would no longer be 'holiday camps' (Holt 1985). Their regimes were subsequently evaluated by the Home Office's Young Offender Psychology Unit. This research concluded that they had 'no discernible effect on the rate at which trainees were reconvicted'. At one centre (Send, for 14–17-year-olds), reconviction rates were 57 per cent both before and after the experiment; at the other (New Hall, for 17–21-year-olds), the rate rose from 46 to 48 per cent. Doubt was also expressed as to whether the new tougher regimes were actually experienced as more demanding. Indeed, some of the activities, such as drill and physical education, were comparatively popular – more so than the continuous chore of the humdrum work party they replaced (Thornton 1984).

Despite these limitations the tougher regimes were not abandoned but, in 1985, were *extended* to all detention centres. The rhetoric and political expediency of 'short, sharp, shock' appeared to take precedence over research evaluation or practical experience. Ironically, the subsequent demise of the detention centre appears to have been driven by the unintended consequences of further criminal justice legislation. The Criminal Justice Act 1982 provided sentencers for the first time with the power to sentence directly to youth custody centres (previously known as Borstals). This allowed the courts to give longer sentences than were available for detention centres. The ethos of a *short*, sharp shock began to unravel. Occupancy levels in detention centres dropped dramatically. By the mid-1980s detention centres also became subject to police investigation following allegations of brutality revealed anonymously by probation officers (Muncie 1990). The experiments in 'short, sharp shock' were formally abolished in 1988 when detention centres were merged with the wider network of young offender institutions.

John Muncie

Related entries

Boot camps; Borstals; Children in custody; Politicization; Punitiveness.

Key texts and sources

Holt, J. (1985) *No Holiday Camps: Custody, Juvenile Justice and the Politics of Law and Order.* Leicester: Association for Juvenile Justice.

Land, H. (1975) 'Detention centres: the experiment which could not fail', in P. Hall (ed.) *Change, Choice and Conflict in Social Policy.* London: Heinemann.

Muncie, J. (1990) 'Failure never matters: detention centres and the politics of deterrence', *Critical Social Policy*, 28: 53–66.

Thornton, D. (1984) *Tougher Regimes in Detention Centres.* London: Home Office.

DETENTION FOR PUBLIC PROTECTION (DPP)

Detention for public protection (DPP) is a form of custodial sentence introduced by the Criminal Justice Act 2003. It is available for 'serious specified' violent and sexual offences where the court is concerned about risk to the public arising from future offending. It is defined as a preventive sentence. Where the criteria are met, the sentence is mandatory and the length is indeterminate. It is available for children aged 10–17, with a similar sentence for adults.

The provisions relating to detention for public protection (DPP) are known as the 'dangerousness' provisions. The Criminal Justice Act (CJA) 2003 introduced the DPP together with another new related custodial sentence, the 'extended sentence'. The sentences are both defined in statute as preventive sentences in that they are only made in the context of future risk. They are only applicable to violent and sexual offences that are 'specified' by the CJA 2003. Over 150 specified offences are set out in Schedule 15 to the CJA 2003 and each carries a maximum adult custodial sentence of two years or more. Of these, a further sub-category is 'serious specified' offences carrying adult sentences of 10 years or more (or an indeterminate length).

The extended sentence is available on conviction for specified offences, and DPP applies for serious specified offences where a future risk of danger to the public is determined. A youth or other magistrates' court dealing with a person charged with a specified offence must form an opinion regarding future dangerousness and, where the criteria are met, must commit the case to the Crown court. In detail, the court must form an opinion as to whether there is a significant risk of the child or young person committing a further specified offence and, where that is the case, that the commission of that offence will cause serious harm to members of the public.

The sentences are only available in the Crown court. Therefore, the procedure in the youth or other magistrates' court is to form an opinion for the purposes of deciding to commit the case to the Crown court. This opinion is provisional in nature, and the Crown court will make the final decision. The lower court may decide to commit to the Crown court either before or after trial/conviction, although subsequent judgment has favoured the latter. In either court, if the perceived future risk is not sufficiently severe, the normal full range of sentencing options is available.

A feature of DPP that gives rise to particular concern is that it is available for offences that are less serious than those for which long-term detention is normally available. Furthermore, and crucially, the level of offence to which the future risk assessment applies need only be specified offences (that is, not necessarily serious specified offences) which might, for example, include affray or assault occasioning actual bodily harm. It should also be noted that, where the criteria are met for an extended sentence (for a less serious 'specified' offence), the court may make a DPP if it is of the opinion that an extended sentence would not be adequate to protect the public. In at least one such case, the court made a DPP in the light of the pre-sentence report assessment of future risk.

The matter of risk assessment is, therefore, of critical importance, and practitioners reporting to the court must bear in mind that it is the court that must form the relevant opinion. The dangerousness determination is set out to an extent in the CJA 2003. The court must take account of all information available about the nature and circumstances of the offence and may take into account patterns of behaviour of which the offence forms a part and any information about the child or young person that is before the court. In the case of children and young people, previous assessments for specified offences must be discounted and a fresh determination made. There have been a number of judgments since the CJA 2003 came into force that assist with risk assessment, and practitioners would benefit from keeping up to date with these and further cases. Since the introduction of DPP, the Youth Justice Board has revised the assessment tool (Asset) and the guidance on pre-sentence reports.

Locking up children from the age of 10 for an indeterminate, potentially lifelong sentence is an extremely serious matter, and the question arises as to whether this complies with international instruments that have been ratified in the UK. The United Nations Convention on the Rights of the Child (UNCRC), for example, is clear that detention should be used only as a matter of last resort and for the shortest appropriate period. It also categorically forbids life imprisonment without the possibility of parole or release. DPP does allow for release but the United Nations Committee on the Rights of the Child has added commentary about indeterminate sentences to help interpret the convention. The committee clearly recommends that sentences akin to DPP should be abolished:

> The use of deprivation of liberty has (very) negative consequences for the child's harmonious development and seriously hampers his/her reintegration in society... In cases of severe offences by children, dispositions proportional to the circumstances of the offender and (the gravity) the offence may be considered, including considerations of the needs of public safety and sanctions, but in cases of children such considerations must always be outweighed by the need to safeguard the well-being and the best interests of and to promote the reintegration of the young person... Given the likelihood that life imprisonment of a child will make it very difficult, if not impossible, to achieve the aims of juvenile justice despite the possibility of release, the Committee strongly recommends the States Parties to abolish all forms of life imprisonment for offences committed by persons under the age of 18 (United Nations Committee on the Rights of the Child 2007).

It is likely that DPP will be subject to adverse comment when the United Nations committee next scrutinizes the UK's compliance with the UNCRC. Furthermore, with the juvenile and adult secure and prison estates suffering persistently from overcrowding, the DPP and extended sentence will add pressure as the effect on the numbers detained is cumulative.

Geoff Monaghan

Related entries

Assessment framework; Criminal Justice Act 2003; Crown court; Dangerousness; Grave offences; Long-term detention; Risk management; Sentencing framework; United Nations Committee on the Rights of the Child; United Nations Convention on the Rights of the Child (UNCRC).

Key texts and sources

Nacro (2006g) *The Dangerousness Provisions of the Criminal Justice Act 2003 and Subsequent Case-law. Youth Crime Briefing.* London: Nacro.

United Nations Committee on the Rights of the Child (2007) *General Comment No. 10: Children's Rights in Juvenile Justice.* Geneva: Committee on the Rights of the Child (available online at **http://www.ohchr.org/english/bodies/crc/docs/AdvanceVersions/GeneralComment10-02feb07.pdf**).

Youth Justice Board (2006a) *Criminal Justice Act 2003: Dangerousness and the New Sentences for Public Protection.* London: Youth Justice Board.

Youth Justice Board (2006b) *Multi-agency Public Protection Arrangements: Guidance for Youth Offending Teams.* London: Youth Justice Board.

See the Office of Public Sector Information's website for the texts of the Criminal Justice Act 2003 (**http://www.opsi.gov.uk/acts/acts2003/20030044.htm**) and the Criminal Justice Act 2003 (Explanatory Notes) (**http://www.opsi.gov.uk/acts/en2003/2003en44.htm**).

DETERRENCE

Deterrence relates to the rationale that people can be 'frightened off' from committing crime by the prospect of receiving punishment. In relation to youth justice, the philosophy of deterrence presents punishment of the young offender as a way of deterring others from committing crimes for fear of the certainty of punishment. Deterence can be general (deterring the wider population) or individual (deterring an individual from reoffending).

Deterrence plays a key role in informing criminal justice policy and has often been used as the rationale behind a drive for harsher and more public punishments. Deterrence is also clearly linked into the concept of popular punitiveness, and the language of deterrence can be identified in contemporary governmental and policy discourses relating to youth justice. For example, this can be clearly identified in punitive rhetoric around sentencing that currently dominates governmental discourses about youth and crime.

Theoretically, deterrence can be rooted in the early classicist school of criminology, which argued that crime was the result of free will and individual decisions to commit an offence. Following this logic, therefore, the solution to crime was more effective punishment, which would deter others from deciding to offend. A more recent incarnation of this early classicist tradition can be seen in rational choice theory and, to an extent, in the emergence of 'right realism' in the 1970s. Again these theories move away from attempting to locate the structural conditions that can give rise to crime and/or identifying 'treatment', to focus on individual choice and the effectiveness of punishment in relation to its deterrent effect (Wilson 1975).

Community-based penalties – irrespective of their intensity or evidence of their efficacy – are rarely conceptualized in terms of their deterrent effect. Conversely, custodial penalties, served in austere conditions, are commonly associated with deterrence. However, it must be noted that a number of theorists go further. For example, Van Den Haag (1975) identifies a continuum of punishments – ranging from fines, through banishment and on to the death penalty – as effective deterrence. However, despite claims by conservative theorists such as Wilson and Van Den Haag regarding the efficacy of deterrence-based punishment, it is generally accepted that the deterrent effect is extremely difficult to measure.

Furthermore, a number of theorists, together with a range of evidence, suggest that utilizing austere 'shock incarceration' has little (if any) positive effect. McGuire and Priestley (1995) go further in arguing that harsh punishments have a negative effect on recidivism, increasing the likelihood of reoffending. In a similar vein, Hood (1989) has observed there is little evidence that the ultimate criminal sanction, the death penalty, acts as a deterrent.

Joe Yates

Related entries

Administrative criminology; Detention centres; Punitiveness; Remoralization; Retribution; Sentencing framework.

Key texts and sources

Cavadino, M. and Dignan, J. (eds) (2002) *The Penal System: An Introduction* (3rd edn). London: Sage.

Hood, R. (1989) *The Death Penalty: A World-wide Perspective*. Oxford: Oxford University Press.

McGuire, J. and Priestley, P. (1995) 'Reviewing "what works": past, present and future', in J. McGuire and P. Priestley (eds) *What Works: Reducing Offending Guidelines from Research and Practice*. Chichester: Wiley.

Van Den Haag, E. (1975) *Punishing Criminals*. New York, NY: Basic Books.

Wilson, J.Q. (1975) *Thinking About Crime*. New York, NY: Vintage.

DEVELOPMENTAL CRIMINOLOGY

The defining feature of developmental criminology is its focus on offending in relation to changes over time in individuals and their life circumstances, with most research being focused in practice on childhood and youth. Developmental criminologists are concerned with questions of continuity and change in behaviour, including the onset of, and desistance from, offending and patterns of offending over time.

Developmental criminology has its roots in mainstream criminology and positivist social science, and it studies the relationship between biological, psychological and social factors and offending across the life course, from conception to death. A foundational assumption is that the 'baggage' people carry from the past – the continuing effects of earlier experiences such as a happy childhood or sexual abuse – affects the ways they behave in the present. Thus developmental criminologists reject traditional approaches that emphasize between-group differences in favour of a study of within-individual changes in offending in relation to changes in many other factors. The field has been dominated by quantitative methods that aim to measure relationships between developmental processes and offending. A strong emphasis has been on the use of longitudinal research, with repeated measurements to determine correlations between risk factors, such as abuse or poverty, and subsequent offending. Famous studies include the Pittsburgh Youth Study in the USA and the Cambridge Study in Delinquent Development in the UK.

An early influence in developmental criminology was Cyril Burt and his study of adolescent offending in the 1920s. Since then, interest in developmental processes in offending has expanded. A major question in the 1980s was the relationship between age and offending. The claim that age simply matures people out of crime appeared to be supported by the general tendency for offenders to reduce their rate of offending as they get older. It was argued that some people are more prone to commit crime than others, particularly because their family socialization in the first few years of life had failed to build in them a sufficiently strong capacity for self-control. This propensity to offend, it was claimed, does not change over the life course, with crime-prone individuals committing more crime at all ages. Developmental critics of this view argued that crime trajectories or pathways, known as criminal careers, are far more varied than this simple model suggests, and that it is necessary to have separate models for exploring such processes as age of crime onset, participation levels, frequency, duration and desistance from crime, recognizing the different influences at various life phases and stages of criminal careers. Social and psychological factors after the early years, including peer influences and parenting practices, exert strong effects, with a failure to exercise self-control being only one risk factor.

In the 1990s developmental criminology took the idea of risk factors further and developed the risk and protective factors paradigm. While risk factors are associated with an increased probability of a negative outcome, protective factors are thought to buffer the effects of risk factors, helping to make people more resilient in the face of adversity. This approach was imported from public health, which had shown (for example) that smoking, fatty diets and a lack of exercise increased the risk of heart disease. Developmental criminologists have used this paradigm to explore many problems, including the relationship between the early onset of problem behaviour and future offending. Longitudinal research has identified relationships between a large number of risk factors and future offending. While causal pathways are complex and prediction at the individual level problematic, there is strong evidence that, as a group, those children and young people with multiple risk factors are more likely than others to be offenders in the future.

Until recently, most developmental criminologists in the USA and the UK have had little engagement with, or influence on, policy and practice. For example, the Pittsburgh Youth Study produced significant new knowledge on youth crime, yet its implications for policy and practice were not discussed. Recently, developmental criminologists have initiated a closer working relationship with policy and practice, however. First, they have been active in promoting and developing early intervention and prevention programmes. For example, in the 1990s programmes that aim to address levels of risk and protection in local communities, such as Communities that Care, were introduced in a number of countries. These use randomized controlled trials and quasi-experimental evidence of 'what works' to help policymakers and practitioners tackle local social problems. Second, the risk and protection model has had a significant influence on youth justice policy, especially in the UK. Not only has it influenced the development of the youth crime prevention strategy but it has also shaped the way offenders are assessed in terms of risk. Third, it has influenced the development of 'Every Child Matters' – a major UK government initiative to enhance the well-being of children and young people from birth to the age of 19.

Developmental criminology has made a major contribution to our understanding of the relationship between offending and a wide range of factors that vary across the life course. In the 1980s and 1990s the research and policy agenda in the UK emphasized offending as a rational choice, suggesting that punitive measures or measures that reduced the opportunities to commit crime offered the most promising prevention approaches. Situational techniques, such as target hardening and the increased policing of public and private spaces, together with new technologies such as closed-circuit television, were promoted as solutions to the crime problem. Developmental criminology, even in its most technical and quantitative forms, provided an alternative perspective and succeeded in placing psychological and social factors back on to the research and policy agenda. While there is much debate over the relationship between the psychological and the social, developmental criminology provided a timely reminder that offending must be located in its social context. For example, whatever their limitations in contributing to an understanding of underlying processes, risk factors direct attention to the importance of poverty and family adversity in explaining offending. Developmental criminology, therefore, provides strong support for the argument that a non-punitive response that strengthens families and communities is fundamental to the prevention of crime.

Developmental criminology, at least as it is understood in the UK, could make a more constructive policy contribution if several problems were addressed. First, policymakers have taken the research finding that, at the aggregate level, there is a strong degree of continuity in anti-social behaviour from childhood to youth to mean that risk factors can be used to identify and to intervene at an early age in the lives of 'risky individuals or families'. For example, a chart by Stephen Scott of the Institute of Psychiatry in the UK, reproduced in the British government's (2003) consultation paper, *Every Child Matters*, shows how half the children who are viewed as anti-social at the age of 8 can still be diagnosed as anti-social at the age of 17. While this indicates a strong statistical relationship between early anti-social behaviour and future problems, it also shows that a large number of false positives exist, with half the children *not* going on to have problems.

Second, developmental criminologists tend to see the relationship between offending and non-offending as unproblematic, having little to say about the role of the state in defining what is

'criminal'. This lacuna is exacerbated by the misunderstanding by policymakers of the evidence about the continuities in anti-social behaviour produced by developmental criminologists, leading in practice to the stigmatization and labelling of children and families identified through new batteries of tests and assessments.

Third, while developmental criminology does recognize social context, its focus tends to be limited to the influences of friends and family within a community. Consequently, developmental criminology has had little to say about wider influences on life-course outcomes, such as the global impact of restructured labour markets on national and local employment opportunities.

Finally, it has been too uncritical of government policies, failing to recognize that major risk factors for offending can be embedded unintentionally in new programmes when these fail to comprehend the complex realities of the lives of children and young people growing up in disadvantaged communities.

Alan France and Ross Homel

Related entries

Actuarialism; Assessment frameworks; Crime prevention; Criminalization; Desistance; Early intervention; Every Child Matters (ECM); Informalism; Labelling theory; Protective factors; Risk factors.

Key texts and sources

Farrington, D. (2002) 'Developmental criminology and risk focused prevention', in M. Maguire *et al.* (eds) *The Oxford Handbook of Criminology* (3rd edn). Oxford: Oxford University Press.

France, A. and Homel, R. (eds) (2007) *Pathways and Crime Prevention: Theory, Policy and Practice.* Cullompton: Willan Publishing.

France, A. and Utting, D. (2005) 'The paradigm of "risk and protection focused prevention" and its impact on services for children and families', *Children and Society*, 19: 77–90.

Homel, R. (2005) 'Developmental crime prevention', in N. Tilley (ed.) *Handbook of Crime Prevention and Community Safety.* Cullompton: Willan Publishing.

Sampson, R.J. and Laub, J. (2005) 'A life-course view of the development of crime', *Annals of the American Academy of Political and Social Science*, 602: 12–45.

DEVIANCE AMPLIFICATION

> Deviance amplification is the outcome of actions taken to prevent or reduce deviance that result in an increase in deviance, often accompanied by a wider moral panic.

Rooted in the sociology of deviance, the term 'deviance amplification' was first used by Leslie Wilkins (1964). According to Wilkins, deviants are relatively uncommon in society and there is a tendency for them to be isolated from the mainstream – thus comprising a phenomenon essentially hidden or little understood. Wilkins argues that, when information about particular deviants or types of deviance comes to light, it is transmitted to the wider public through mediating social mechanisms (primarily the media), and that this transmission creates the possibility, even the tendency, for distortion. Thus an extreme picture of the deviants and/or their deviance is presented which exacerbates the deviant characteristics and creates the image of the 'other' – someone or something outside the 'normal'. The effect of this distortion is deviancy amplification.

The amplificatory process is further exacerbated by the reaction to this image of the wider majority and state agencies, such as the police. Thus the reaction of society is not to the 'real' behaviour but to the distorted and amplified image of the behaviour. This amplified image then begins to take on a life of its own, clearly identifying and demarcating a deviant identity to which others are drawn – thus creating more deviants and an increasingly repressive response from control agencies. Inevitably, information about the resulting amplified deviance is transmitted to the wider public and this information is, in turn, distorted and amplified further still.

Several key research studies have demonstrated the consequences of deviance amplification, notably Young (1971a) in respect of marijuana smokers in west London and Cohen (1980) concerning the 'Mods and Rockers' phenomenon of the 1960s. Both studies clearly demonstrate how media interest in these groups rapidly expanded into a moral panic within the media itself, forming and then feeding off the wider moral panic in civil society. Both studies chart the amplificatory effects of the moral panic, including the encapsulation of larger numbers of (young) people as deviants and the escalation of repressive social control. The catalytic role and power of the media in defining and amplifying new types of deviants and new forms of deviance cannot be underestimated. One only has to think about the moral panic and subsequent responses to youth anti-social behaviour to appreciate the power of these social mechanisms.

Deviance amplification is a term that has also been used to signify the potential amplificatory effect of being labelled a delinquent. It can also be applied to signal the potential for criminal justice interventions to amplify rather than reduce delinquency. Thus the detention centre 'experiment' of the 1970s and 1980s, based on the purported deterrent effect of a 'short, sharp, shock', rather than reducing offending had the unintended consequence of increasing delinquency.

Kevin Haines

Related entries

Criminalization; Delinquency; Demonization; Detention Centre; Gender and justice; Labelling theory; Media reporting; Moral panic.

Key texts and sources

Cohen, S. (1980) *Folk Devils and Moral Panics*. London: Routledge.

Jewkes, Y. and Letherby, G. (2002) *Criminology: A Reader*. London: Sage.

Muncie, J., Hughes, G. and McLaughlin, E. (2002) *Youth Justice: Critical Readings*. London: Sage.

Wilkins, L. (1964) *Social Deviance*. London: Tavistock.

Young, J. (1971a) 'The role of the police as amplifiers of deviancy', in S. Cohen (ed.) *Images of Deviance*. Harmondsworth: Penguin Books.

DIFFERENTIAL ASSOCIATION

> Differential association concerns the processes by which contacts or associations with people and/or social groups disposed towards crime increase the likelihood of an individual becoming an offender him or herself. The claim is that, through early, intense and frequent associations with such individuals and/or groups, a young person can develop definitions (meanings), attitudes, morals and skills that are supportive of criminal activity.

The concept of differential association was introduced by Edwin Sutherland (following his groundbreaking ethnographic study, *The Professional Thief* (1937)). Sutherland discovered that groups of 'thieves' developed their own subculture of techniques, status, organization and traditions. He concluded that thieves restricted their physical and social contacts to like-minded others. Sutherland's research elaborated upon the social explanations of offending that were emerging from the University of Chicago, which challenged individual genetic, biological and psychological explanations for crime by citing the influence of social disorganization and the cultural transmission of delinquent values in disadvantaged neighbourhoods, thus shifting pathology from the individual to social structures. Sutherland's study of thieves, therefore, identified links between social cohesion/organization and crime, particularly where frequent and consistent association seemed to produce criminal behaviour. The resultant 'differential association theory' suggested that association did not need to be with criminals but, rather, with individuals who encouraged crime or failed to censure criminal acts.

The early version of differential association theory was considered overly narrow and deterministic in its prescriptions of how offending was learnt through contact with others more/less disposed to delinquency. It also neglected to explore how 'contamination through exposure' could be resisted, and it ignored the influence of psychological factors (including conscience and moral understanding). Sutherland (1947) and, later, Sutherland and Cressey (1960), revised differential association theory, explaining that offending occurs when sentiments favourable to law-breaking *outweigh* non-criminal tendencies. It was not considered necessary to explain why people develop associations, simply that differential social organization exposed people to different associations.

Differential association theory has been revised by Akers (1985), who produced a four-stage differential association theory that included the following:

- *Differential association*: the most important source of social learning, but now acknowledging the indirect influence of more distant reference groups (including the media).
- *Definitions*: meanings that the individual and group apply to their behaviour (for example, not viewing drug use as deviant).
- *Differential reinforcement*: the actual or anticipated consequences of a behaviour (including rewards and punishments).
- *Imitation*: observing others and imitating them if they and their behaviour have attractive characteristics and consequences.

Differential association theory was arguably the first integrated social psychological account of crime, with its focus on the influence of social forces in defining crime combined with psychological (social) learning through associations and interactions. It is popular for its rejection of individual pathology in favour of the normality of the learning that can produce offending. However, differential association theory has been criticized for the amount of questions it leaves unanswered, including the following:

- Exactly how does learning occur?
- What exactly are the social conditions that facilitate the learning of criminal skills and attitudes?
- Why do individuals who are not in contact with criminogenic dispositions become criminals?
- What is the role of personality traits or differential opportunities to offend?

Despite these limitations, the concept of differential association sets a research agenda for future generations, particularly those theorists interested in the development of delinquent subcultures.

Kevin Haines

Related entries

Delinquency; Subculture; Subcultural theory.

Key texts and sources

Akers, R.L. (1985) *Deviant Behaviour: A Social Learning Approach.* Belmont, CA: Wadsworth.
Sutherland, E.H. (1937) *The Professional Thief: By a Professional Thief.* Chicago, IL: University of Chicago Press.
Sutherland, E.H. (1947) *Principles of Criminology* (5th edn). Philadelphia, PA: Lippincott.
Sutherland, E.H. and Cressey, D.R. (1960) *Criminology.* Philadelphia, PA: Lippincott.

DISCRIMINATION

Discrimination occurs when an individual, group or community is treated less than fairly or equally than is the established norm by those who have discretionary power and authority. Usually it relates to grounds of perceived age, class, culture, disability, ethnicity, gender, sexuality or religion.

The definition of, and responses to, discrimination are highly controversial and contested. In communities and societies diverse in material circumstances, culture, ethnicity and belief systems, the existence of prejudice solely on the basis of perceptions of others is well established. In most, if not all, societies there are deep-seated prejudices regarding gender, sexuality, disability and age. Such prejudice is manifested in popular discourse, jokes, graffiti and other forms of representation demonstrating certain key assumptions about the identities of those targeted. The terms used to portray such attitudes include racism, sectarianism, sexism, disablism and ageism. Negative and offensive,

the consequences are most appropriately represented as a continuum from insults and other verbal abuse through to harassment and violence, including death. When negative attitudes and responses cease to be reactive and become proactive, embodying a hatred of identifiable individuals, groups or communities, they become mobilized as xenophobia, misogyny or homophobia, yet there is no equivalent representation of 'child-hate'.

Much of the contemporary debate has centred on the relationship between personal, negative attitudes and institutional, negative responses. While individuals in everyday life can be discriminatory in the way they treat others with whom they have contact, *discrimination* assumes a relationship based on power and the authority underpinning its use. Housing officers, social workers, teachers, doctors, police officers, youth justice workers, prison guards and so on possess institutional powers and the lawful discretion to regulate and control as well as facilitate and care for their 'clients'. Should they discriminate in the context of their work, the issue is whether the discrimination is a personal and attitudinal response or collective and institutional phenomena embedded in established custom and practice.

Following a protracted debate regarding racism within the police, the Macpherson Report into the police response to the racist murder of Stephen Lawrence concluded that there had been 'fundamental errors' in an investigation 'marred by a combination of professional incompetence, institutional racism and a failure of leadership by senior officers' (1999: 317). Macpherson defined 'institutional racism' as a 'collective failure of an organisation to provide an appropriate and professional service to people because of their colour, culture or ethnic origin'. Its presence 'can be seen or detected in processes, attitudes and behaviour which amount to discrimination through unwitting prejudice, ignorance, thoughtlessness, and racist stereotyping which disadvantage minority ethnic people' (1999: 321).

Acclaimed as far sighted and radical, Macpherson defended police policies, placing responsibility on institutionally accepted racist practices and individual, personally held racist attitudes. He confirmed the existence of institutional racism within and across institutions. Institutionalized racism, however, is more profound. This is racism as a prevalent ideology underpinning policies, priorities and practices within institutions rather than an expression of an institution's policies, priorities and practices. Extending the scope of institutionalized discrimination to children and young people, it is clear that, for all the rhetoric of inclusion and stakeholding, they are peripheral, rarely consulted and regularly vilified.

Risk, protection and prevention are promoted as interventionist priorities specific to children and young people. The reality is regulation, criminalization and punishment derived in a form of authoritarianism specific to children and young people. The problems faced by children and young people are exacerbated by the stigma, rumour and reprisals fed by the public process of naming and shaming.

Phil Scraton

Related entries

Gender and justice; Institutionalized intolerance; Naming and shaming; 'Race' and justice; Victimization; Youth and policing.

Key texts and sources

Cole, M. (ed.) (2006) *Education, Equality and Human Rights* (2nd edn). London: Routledge.

Franklin, B. (2002) *The New Handbook of Children's Rights: Comparative Policy and Practice*. London: Routledge.

Macpherson, Sir W. (1999) *The Stephen Lawrence Inquiry: Report on an Inquiry by Sir William Macpherson of Cluny* (Cm 4262-I). London: HMSO.

Rubenstein, M. (2006) *Discrimination*. London: Lexis Nexis Butterworths.

Thompson, N. (2006) *Anti-discriminatory Practice*. London: Palgrave Macmillan.

DISPERSAL ORDERS

The Anti-social Behaviour Act 2003 (ss. 30–36) gives the police in England and Wales powers to *disperse* groups of two or more people from areas where there is believed to be persistent anti-social behaviour and a problem with groups causing intimidation.

With local authority agreement, a police superintendent can designate an area as a 'dispersal order' zone. This decision must be published in a local newspaper or by notices in the area. Designation can be for a period of up to six months and may be renewed. The designated area must be clearly defined. Within a designated zone, a police constable or community support officer may disperse groups where their presence or behaviour has resulted, or is likely to result, in a member of the public being harassed, intimidated, alarmed or distressed. Individuals who do not reside in the designated area can then be directed to leave the locality and may be excluded from it for up to 24 hours. A person does not commit an offence because an officer has chosen to use the power to disperse, but if individuals refuse to follow the officer's directions, they will be committing an offence.

In Scotland a similar power was introduced by the Anti-social Behaviour (Scotland) Act 2004. In Scotland, however, orders may last only three months (renewable), and there is no discretionary power to exclude those dispersed from the area for up to 24 hours.

The Anti-social Behaviour Act 2003 (s. 30(6)) also creates a power to remove to their home any young person under 16 who is out on the streets in a dispersal zone between 9 p.m. and 6 a.m. and not under the control of an adult. In an early judgment in July 2005, the High Court ruled that this power did not allow the use of reasonable force (see *R* (W) v. *Metropolitan Police and the London Borough of Richmond*). Consequently, police forces around the country suspended the use of what colloquially became known as the 'curfew' element of dispersal orders.

In May 2006 the Court of Appeal overturned the earlier judgment but laid down two conditions for the exercise of reasonable force in relation to the original power (see *R. (on the application of W)* v. *Commissioner of Police of the Metropolis*). Young people can only be removed to their home from a dispersal zone if they are either at risk or vulnerable from anti-social behaviour and crime or are causing (or at risk of causing) anti-social behaviour. Subsequently, new guidance was published (Home Office 2006e), and the Home Office minister, Tony McNulty, challenged the police and practitioners 'to take a more robust and unremitting approach to tackling anti-social behaviour by making maximum use of the dispersal powers available to them'. The power to escort home is not available in Scotland, partly because of concerns raised about its coercive nature and potential conflict with wider child welfare policies.

Since coming into effect in January 2004, dispersal orders have been used in diverse localities, ranging from areas as small as a single street or shopping arcade to a large city centre. They have been used to address issues including prostitution, begging and illegal street vending but are most commonly used in relation to groups of young people. The Home Office (2005h) estimated that, by 30 June 2005, over 800 zones were designated for the purpose of dispersal order powers. Three forces accounted for a quarter of all areas designated, whereas four forces had designated no areas and five had designated only one area. Over a quarter of designations (27 per cent) were renewed, suggesting a failure to resolve the underlying issues that triggered the application within the time frame allotted. More recently, a survey of crime and disorder reduction partnerships across England and Wales (Home Office 2007) shows a reduction in the use of dispersal powers in 2005–6, as compared with 2004–5 (355 and 610, respectively). Interestingly, dispersal orders were the only anti-social behaviour-related power to have substantially declined in use over the period.

Controversially, the dispersal order only requires that the group's *presence* is sufficient to be *likely* to offend a member of the public. While groups gathering in dispersal zones are not *per se* in violation of the law, they can fall foul of the legislation where their demeanour or dress may be sufficient to frighten others. Appearance, as much as specific behaviour, may be caught by the power. In relying on the perceptions of others as a trigger for intervention, dispersal orders potentially criminalize youthful behaviour dependent on the anxieties that young people congregating in groups may generate. The power is potentially less concerned with the *actual behaviour* of the individuals who are the subjects of regulation than with the assumptions that are made about what they *might do*.

The discretionary nature of the powers places pressures of professional judgement on individual police officers in situations that may precipitate rather than reduce conflict, leaving scope for inconsistent implementation in ways that can impact negatively on perceptions of procedural fairness. The powers raise concerns about displacement from designated zones, the impact on police resources to implement, the raised expectations that designation can generate and what strategies need to be in place beyond the end of the designated period. Nevertheless, experiences of implementation suggest that, where used creatively, the powers may precipitate more extensive problem-solving and preventive work through local partnerships.

Against the background of rising concerns about young people 'hanging about' (as evidenced by the British Crime Survey), it is easy to grasp the manner in which dispersal orders tap subjective and context-specific inter-generational fears about 'youth' and may serve to stigmatize and criminalize youthful behaviour. Where implemented, the powers convey powerful messages about appropriate conduct, control over space, ownership and belonging. It may be that the Victorian adage 'children should be seen and not heard' is being rewritten. Now, apparently, 'children should be not seen and not heard'.

Adam Crawford

Related entries

Actuarialism; Anti-social behaviour (ASB); Anti-social Behaviour Act 2003; Anti-social Behaviour (Scotland) Act 2004; Authoritarianism; Crime and disorder reduction (CDR); Criminalization; Fear of Crime; Local child curfew schemes (LCCSs); Respect (government action plan); Youth and policing.

Key texts and sources

Home Office (2005h) *Use of Dispersal Powers.* London: Home Office.

Home Office (2006e) *Respect and Dispersal Powers.* London: Home Office.

Home Office (2007) *Tools and Powers to Tackle Anti-social Behaviour.* London: Home Office.

See the Office of Public Sector Information's website for the texts of the Anti-social Behaviour Act 2003 (**http://www.opsi.gov.uk/acts/acts2003/20030038. htm**) and the Anti-social Behaviour (Scotland) Act 2004 (**http://www.opsi.gov.uk/legislation/scotland/ acts2004/20040008.htm**).

DISTRICT JUDGES

District judges sit in the youth court and the adult magistrates' court. They were formerly known as stipendiary magistrates. Since August 2000 – as a consequence of the Access to Justice Act 1999 – they were renamed in order to recognize them as members of the professional judiciary. They are formally known as 'district judges (magistrates' courts)'.

A district judge will sit *alone* in the youth court or adult magistrates' court. They are legally qualified and are empowered to decide whether a child/young person is guilty or not and to determine the nature of the sentence. There are full-time district judges and part-time district judges known as deputy district judges. District judges are normally required to have at least seven years' experience as a barrister or solicitor and two years' experience as a deputy district judge.

Barry Goldson

Related entries

Magistrates; Sheriff courts; Summary justice; Youth courts.

Key texts and sources

Her Majesty's Court Services' document, *Magistrates and Magistrates' Courts*, is available online at **http://www.hmcourts-service.gov.uk/infoabout/ magistrates/index.htm**.

DIVERSION

Diversion is convenient shorthand for a wide range of decisions designed to divert people from crime, from court and from custody.

Diversion is usually used to refer to alternatives to prosecution for children and young people. The most common mechanisms for achieving diversion are informal warnings and police cautions, now replaced by reprimands and warnings for young people. The theory behind diversion is that young people habitually commit minor crimes or behave in ways that can be categorized as 'criminal', but left to their own devices they will grow out of it. Labelling theory suggests that official reactions to youthful deviant behaviour, particularly prosecution, trial and sentence, are likely to confirm deviant identities and, therefore, create 'career' criminals. The best policy, therefore, is not to intervene.

In addition to theoretical arguments there are pragmatic grounds for pursuing a policy of diversion. Diversion is cost effective, proportionate and works in the sense that young people who are cautioned are less likely to be reconvicted than those who are prosecuted. It also has a basis in practitioner research. Thorpe *et al.* (1980) found that early intervention with 'at risk' children had the effect of accelerating them 'up tariff' and into custody if they had received 'intermediate treatment' prior to a first prosecution. This realization created a 'new orthodoxy' among juvenile justice workers in the 1980s' of 'non-intervention' and 'systems management' aimed at keeping young people out of the criminal justice system whenever possible. More recently the 'what works' literature has also concluded that early intervention increases the likelihood of reconviction.

The policy of diversion became official Home Office policy in the 1980s and early 1990s. In a series of Home Office circulars on cautioning (14/85, 59/90, 18/94), chief constables were advised that prosecution should be used as a last resort for juveniles. Indeed, even an official caution was conceived as a 'serious intervention', so the police were encouraged to make use of informal warnings and were advised that, because a child had already received a caution, this should not necessarily prevent him or her receiving further cautions. In addition, the police were encouraged to consult with other relevant agencies when making their decisions, giving rise to interagency juvenile liaison panels and bureaux. By the early 1990's the majority of juveniles were cautioned rather than prosecuted. Evans and Wilkinson (1990) document the complex array of 'diversionary' mechanisms that were developed in this period, including unrecorded and recorded informal warnings; instant cautions made at the police station; deferred cautions referred for interagency consultation; and 'caution plus'. They also document the differential use of this range of options within and between police forces and how these differences in policy and practice had a direct impact on differences in rates of 'diversion'. By the mid-1990s government enthusiasm for 'diversion' had waned, to be replaced by a more punitive approach and demands for cautions to be accompanied by interventions. As a result, reprimands and final warnings were introduced by the Crime and Disorder Act 1998 and implemented in England and Wales in 2000. The rate of diversion fell from 74 per cent in 1992 to 56 per cent in 2003, and the pattern since the implementation of the final warning scheme continues the trend towards greater intervention (Nacro 2005e).

The policy of diversion for young people is not just a question of domestic law and policy (Gillespie 2005). In the landmark judgment in *R v. Durham Police*, the Law Lords considered the issue of parental consent in relation to the final warning scheme. Whereas the consent of a parent or guardian was a condition of juvenile cautioning, they determined that consent is no longer required for reprimands and warnings. This finding is highly significant as it means that a child or his or her parent has no effective way of legally challenging a reprimand or warning or the evidence on which either may rest. In her opinion, Baroness Hale noted that diversion from court was in accordance with international law and, in particular with the United Nations Convention on the Rights of the Child and the United Nations Standard Minimum Rules for the Administration of Juvenile Justice (the 'Beijing Rules'). While she had grave doubts that the statutory final warning scheme is consistent with international instruments dealing with children's rights, she ultimately concurred with the judgment on consent. Evans and Puech (2001) have questioned whether the scheme is compliant with the incorporation of the European Convention on Human Rights and Fundamental Freedoms as incorporated into the Human Rights Act 1998. For example, if young people accept a reprimand or warning in preference to a trial, then this could be construed as an inducement to admit an offence contrary to Article 6.

The police may also use diversion from court with adults, although the opposite presumption to that for juveniles applies. Adults will normally be prosecuted unless they are in an 'at risk' group, such as the elderly or the mentally disordered, when they may be cautioned. Systems for diverting mentally disordered offenders may be police station or court based. More recently, the Criminal Justice Act 2003 has introduced the 'conditional caution' for adults, modelled on the final warning and requiring participation in a rehabilitation programme or reparation. The decision to give a conditional caution lies with the Crown Prosecution Service (CPS) rather than the police. Some critics have argued that one of the curiosities of the prosecution process in England and Wales is that, while prosecution decisions are subject to review by the CPS – to see whether they meet the 'evidential sufficiency' and 'public interest' tests – diversion decisions are not, except that is for the adult 'conditional caution'.

Other forms of diversion include diversion from crime – using, for example, situational and social crime prevention techniques – and diversion from custody. For example, arrest referral schemes for drug users attempt to intervene to reduce use or harm during the period between arrest and a court appearance. The compliance and success or failure of participants in such programmes may then be taken into account in sentencing, particularly if they are at risk of custody.

Roger Evans

Related entries

Alternatives to custody; Caution; Criminal Justice Act 2003; Crown Prosecution Service (CPS); Decriminalization; Early intervention; Growing out of crime; Informalism; Labelling theory; Minimum necessary intervention; Normalization; Reprimands and final warnings; Systems management.

Key texts and sources

Evans, R. and Puech, K. (2001) 'Warnings and reprimands: popular punitiveness or restorative justice?', *Criminal Law Review*, 794–805.

Evans, R. and Wilkinson, C. (1990) 'Variations in police cautioning policy and practice in England and Wales', *Howard Journal of Criminal Justice*, 29: 155–76.

Gillespie, A. (2005) 'Reprimanding juveniles and the right to due process', *Modern Law Review*, 61: 1006–15.

McAra, L. and McVie, S. (2007) 'Youth justice? The impact of system contact on patterns of desistance from offending', *European Journal of Criminology*, 4: 315–45.

Nacro (2005e) *Out of Court: Making the Most of Diversion for Young People. Youth Crime Briefing.* London: Nacro.

Thorpe, D.H., Smith, D., Green, C.J. and Paley, J.H. (1980) *Out of Care: The Community Support of Juvenile Offenders.* London: George Allen & Unwin.

DRUG TREATMENT AND TESTING ORDERS (DTTOs)

The drug treatment and testing order (DTTO) was introduced by the Crime and Disorder Act 1998 as a new community sentence for those aged 16 and over. It superseded the underused s. 1A(6) requirement of the Criminal Justice Act 1991 that stipulated that offenders attend drug treatment as a condition of a probation order.

Over the past two decades a wide range of different strategies have been employed to tackle the 'drugs problem'. In recent years the criminal justice system has taken centre stage to coerce problem drug users to become drug free. The drug treatment and testing order (DTTO) is an intensive court order that can last between six months and three years. It involves the offender having to: undertake regular drug tests throughout each week; engage in drug treatment; report to a probation officer/youth offending team officer; and to attend regular court reviews to monitor progress. By 2000, after an 18 month-trial period in Croydon, Gloucestershire and Liverpool, results were, at best, mixed. Some 67 per cent of offenders had their order revoked and, overall, two-year reconviction rates stood at 80 per cent (Hough *et al.* 2003). However, the minority who did successfully complete their order did make some significant progress in terms of reconviction.

The introduction of the DTTO marked a major step towards a more intensive and intrusive criminal justice strategy to tackle the UK drug problem. It aligned the UK more closely to the US drug strategy and it risks driving more drug users into prison through the back door of 'failed treatment'. The reasons for this USA/UK alliance must be more political than evidence based, given that the USA sends proportionately more people to prison than any other country in the world *and* has one of the worst drug problems. Perhaps not surprisingly in Europe, the UK is rapidly acquiring similar notoriety.

The DTTO also marked a shift away from voluntary treatment (accessed via the National Health Service) towards more coercive treatment (accessed via the criminal justice system). The long-term success of compulsory or coercive treatment such as the DTTO has yet to be proven (in the USA or the UK), but the momentum of a 'tough' approach criminalizing drug policy has been established (Stevens 2007) and further reinforced by powers to drug test people on charge (introduced under the Drugs Act 2005).

The justification for a tough approach tied into the criminal justice system is based on a belief that the underlying cause of much persistent acquisitive offending is problem drug use. While there are undoubtedly associations between these two factors, a simplistic causal connection is unlikely (Seddon 2006). For many individuals problem drug use is the presenting problem, masking the underlying and pre-existing social and psychological problems of a damaged and disadvantaged childhood/adolescence exacerbated by structural inequalities

(Buchanan 2004; Melrose 2004). Until these underlying problems are addressed, progress in tackling problematic drug use will flounder.

The Criminal Justice Act 2003 introduced a major overhaul of community sentencing in the UK and, for offences committed after April 2005, the DTTO was replaced with the drug rehabilitation requirement. Interestingly, there is a separate requirement available for people who have alcohol-related problems – the alcohol and alcohol treatment requirement.

Julian Buchanan

Related entries

Crime and Disorder Act 1998; Menu-based sentencing; Probation Service; Rehabilitation.

Key texts and sources

Buchanan, J. (2004) 'Missing links: problem drug use and social exclusion', *Probation Journal* (special issue on 'Rethinking drugs and crime'), 51: 387–97.

Buchanan, J. (2007) 'Understanding and engaging with problematic substance use', in S. Green *et al.* (eds) *Addressing Offending Behaviour: Context, Practice, Values.* Cullompton: Willan Publishing.

Hough, M., Clancy, A., McSweeney, T. and Turnbull, P.J. (2003) *The Impact of Drug Treatment and Testing Orders on Offending: Two-year Reconviction Results. Home Office Research Findings* 184. London: Home Office.

Melrose, M. (2004) 'Fractured transitions: disadvantaged young people, drug taking and risk', *Probation Journal* (special issue on 'Rethinking drugs and crime'), 51: 327–42.

Seddon, T. (2006) 'Drugs, crime and social exclusion: social context and social theory in British drugs-crime research', *British Journal of Criminology*, 46: 680–703.

Stevens, A. (2007) 'When two dark figures collide: evidence and discourse on drug-related crime', *Critical Social Policy*, 27: 77–99.

DUE PROCESS

Due process is a core legal principle dating from the Magna Carta of 1215. Due process is also enshrined in the Fifth and Fourteenth Amendments to the US Constitution: 'that no person shall be deprived of life, liberty, or property without due process of law.'

The concept of due process is found in the debate between 'welfare' and 'justice' approaches to youth justice. While there is a need to consider the welfare of the child (Children and Young Persons Act 1933), there is an equal need to ensure that 'justice is done'. In the fierce debates on this issue, those who advocate 'justice' appeal to 'due process' in supporting their call for 'just deserts'.

Throughout the more recent history of youth justice policy and practice, due process has been compromised. For example, the use of s. 7(7) care orders (introduced by the Children and Young Persons Act 1969) essentially bypassed due process. As a result of such orders, the institutionalization and incarceration of Children in England and Wales increased dramatically. While such children were initially prosecuted for committing criminal offences, they were often sentenced with reference to their ostensible 'welfare' needs (Thorpe *et al.* 1980).

More recently still, the development of 'formal cautions' and, later, reprimands and final warnings, can also be seen as potentially circumventing due process, not least because an admission of guilt is required before these options may be considered. Consequently, by opting for a citable 'formal caution' or, as it is now, a reprimand or final warning, it could be argued that due process is negated as guilt does not need to be proven in a court of law (see Goldson 2000d: 43).

Of most concern perhaps, in the contemporary youth justice system, is the use of anti-social behaviour orders (ASBOs), introduced by the Crime and Disorder Act 1998. When ASBOs were first introduced, many argued that they would lead to 'net-widening'. The processes of civil prosecution required in

ASBO proceedings evade the need for the more rigorous 'burden of proof' required in criminal proceedings. Thus 'due process' is again compromised. Moreover, this is compounded because failure to comply with an ASBO can lead to a criminal prosecution.

Finally, attempts to speed up the youth justice process and to 'avoid delay' – under the rubric of 'the swift administration of justice', for example – further risk circumventing 'due process'.

Richard Hester

Related entries

Anti-social behaviour (ASB); Anti-social behaviour orders (ASBOs); Critical criminology; Just deserts; Justice; Justice by geography; Police and Criminal Evidence Act 1984 (PACE); Referral orders; Reprimands and final warnings; Retribution; Social justice.

Key texts and sources

Goldson, B. (2000d) 'Wither diversion? Interventionism and the new youth justice', in B. Goldson (ed.) *The New Youth Justice*. Lyme Regis: Russell House.

Thorpe, D.H., Smith, D., Green, C.J. and Paley, J.H. (1980) *Out of Care: The Community Support of Juvenile Offenders*. London: Allen & Unwin.

Youth Justice Board (2006) *Swift Administration of Justice*. London: Youth Justice Board (available online at **http://www.yjb.gov.uk/Publications/Scripts/prodView.asp?idProduct=47&eP=**).

E

EARLY INTERVENTION

Early intervention is underpinned by an assumption that youth crime can be anticipated and that measures can put in place to prevent young people becoming offenders.

Early intervention rests on a belief that children and young people are not 'fully formed' individuals. As such they are more susceptible to influences – both positive and negative – that will impact on their behaviour. Early intervention can also be based on a holistic approach to need. Addressing problems of social disadvantage such as poverty and family disruption can help to provide a wide range of benefits, including crime prevention, given what is known about the precursors of subsequent offending behaviour (Farrington 1996). Therefore, investment in appropriate interventions is expected to offer positive returns by 'nipping offending in the bud'. There has been some evidence to support this argument – for example, the HighScope/Perry Pre-school programme in the USA appeared to lead to long-term social benefits, including reduced levels of subsequent criminality.

In the UK, interest in early intervention to prevent youth offending dates back to the 1960s and was supported by 'prevention theory' (Thorpe *et al.* 1980: 104). Policy initiatives of the time (for example, the white paper, *Children in Trouble*) provided the basis for new forms of practice, such as intermediate treatment (IT). At first, this was intended to be a court-based intervention that would prevent the need to remove a child from home on the grounds of offending. In practice, IT became associated with the identification of children 'at risk' of offending and the expansion of intervention into a whole new area of activity, leading to 'system creep' and problems associated with 'net-widening', ultimately resulting in the recruitment of a new population of young people into institutional systems of care and justice.

Subsequent attempts to reframe early intervention and to minimize some of these negative consequences led to strategies based on the principle of 'diversion', which concentrated on avoiding the use of official sanctions, wherever possible, and developing various forms of informal activity to address the problems associated with offending.

Subsequent developments influenced by principles of risk management have led to a reassertion of the belief that, with proper targeting, young people 'at risk' of offending can be identified and provided with services that will reduce or eliminate potential criminality. Thus a range of programmes has been developed – including youth inclusion panels; youth inclusion and support panels, Positive Action for Young People and Summer Splash – with the aim of reducing the likelihood of offending. Youth inclusion projects, for example, were targeted on neighbourhoods considered to be most susceptible to crime and, more specifically, on young people within the targeted areas deemed to be most prone to offend. The kind of activities undertaken represent a fairly well established 'curriculum', including 'constructive use of leisure', community work, mentoring, parent support and educational and training opportunities.

Parallel policy developments across wider children's services (for example, 'Every Child Matters') also share a commitment to early identification and preventive programmes, across the range of potential problems children might experience. Extensive government programmes,

152

such as Sure Start and the Children's Fund, have also been informed by this philosophy.

Evaluation research commissioned by the Youth Justice Board revealed that offending declined where youth inclusion panels were established, but such 'successes' did not appear to be sustained over time (Morgan Harris Burrows 2003). Not only does this improve the life chances of young people, it is claimed, but additionally it is said to promote community safety and save money (Audit Commission 2004).

Belief in the efficacy of early intervention has led to an intensification of activity in this area, incorporating the emerging concern with anti-social behaviour. New measures have been put in place to provide parenting programmes, as well as specific requirements such as individual support orders, that can be linked to anti-social behaviour orders in order to address problematic behaviour.

Despite the apparent attractions of early intervention, there are a number of problems associated with it. First, the evidence is not always as convincing as it might appear and is often based on limited and unrepresentative samples. Second, there is a clear risk of 'unintended consequences', with the problem of young people being 'labelled' and subjected to targeted and sometimes compulsory interventions on the basis of minor infractions or rather unspecific risk factors, such as 'parenting difficulties' or 'non-constructive spare time/easily bored'. Third, targeted approaches run the risk of stigmatizing communities, neighbourhoods or specific ethnic groups on the basis of generalized assumptions. The problem of stigmatization and labelling has been substantiated through evaluations of crime prevention projects sponsored by the Youth Justice Board (Powell 2004). Fourth, predictions of future behaviour are known to be unreliable, and the identification and selection of young people for special forms of intervention on this basis potentially compound divisions and social exclusion. Fifth, the narrow emphasis on offence-related targets – such as reduced arrest rates – means that wider needs can be overlooked as programmes are skewed to narrowly defined and very specific outcomes. Sixth, intervention programmes are likely to prioritize 'behaviour management' and control over the quality of the experience for young people, and 'failure to comply' – even with informal interventions – can have negative 'up-tariffing' consequences.

Early intervention in youth justice is thus questionable on at least two counts. It relies on overconfident claims of a direct link between antecedent 'risk factors' and 'offending behaviour', and it is compromised by an excessive focus on a narrow range of outcomes that limit its capacity to engage in meaningful ways with the broader needs of young people.

Roger Smith

Related entries

Actuarialism; Anti-social behaviour (ASB); Crime prevention; Diversion; Every Child Matters (ECM); Intermediate treatment (IT); Labelling theory; Positive Activities for Young People (PAYP); Protective factors; Risk factors; Risk management; Sure Start; Youth inclusion and support panels (YISPs); Youth inclusion programmes (YIPs).

Key texts and sources

Audit Commission (2004) *Youth Justice 2004: A Review of the Reformed Youth Justice System.* London: Audit Commission.

Farrington, D. (1996) *Understanding and Preventing Youth Crime.* York: Joseph Rowntree Foundation.

Goldson, B. (2000d) 'Wither diversion? Interventionism and the new youth justice', in B. Goldson (ed.) *The New Youth Justice.* Lyme Regis: Russell House.

Morgan Harris Burrows (2003) *Evaluation of the Youth Inclusion Programme.* London: Youth Justice Board.

Powell, H. (2004) *Crime Prevention Projects: The National Evaluation of the Youth Justice Board Crime Prevention Projects.* London: Youth Justice Board.

Smith, R. (2006) 'Actuarialism and early intervention in contemporary youth justice', in B. Goldson and J. Muncie (eds) *Youth Crime and Justice: Critical Issues.* London: Sage.

Thorpe, D.H., Smith, D., Green, C.J. and Paley, J. H. (1980) *Out of Care: The Community Support of Juvenile Offenders.* London: George Allen & Unwin.

EDUCATION ACTION ZONES (EAZs)

> Education action zones (EAZs) were introduced in 1997 with the aim of encouraging innovative approaches to raising educational standards in socially disadvantaged areas. An EAZ was typically based around a cluster of secondary schools and their feeder primaries. The aim was to create new public/private partnerships between schools, parents, communities, local authorities and local businesses.

The performance of education action zones (EAZs) against their aim of addressing educational underachievement and school exclusion was limited and inconsistent. While there was some evidence of innovative practice, this was not supported by evidence of improved pupil performance or sustained improvement in teaching practices. Pressure to meet short-term exam, exclusion and non-attendance targets was seen to be a significant barrier to the development of innovative practice and success. There was no evidence of zone schools performing better than non-zone schools in the sample of local education authorities examined. Few zones had representation of the wider community, with little involvement of parents, students, local businesses or staff from public services outside education. The EAZs have since been disbanded.

Martin Stephenson

Related entries

School non-attendance; School exclusion.

Key texts and sources

National Audit Office (2001) *Education Action Zones: Meeting the Challenge – the Lessons Identified from Auditing the First 25 Zones. Report by the Comptroller and Auditor General* (HC 130 Session 2000–2001). London: HMSO.

Office for Standards in Education (2003) *Excellence in Cities and Education Action Zones: Management and Impact* (HMI 1399). London: Ofsted.

EFFECTIVENESS

> Effectiveness is the extent to which a youth justice intervention has its desired effect – usually the extent to which it can be shown to reduce the rate of reoffending.

Official demands that the youth justice system should be able to demonstrate its effectiveness have grown since the early 1990s, along with the expectation that practice should be, where possible, evidence based. The most obvious and apparently straightforward sense of effectiveness relates to the reduction of offending by the young people who come into contact with the system, and this has been the focus of much evaluative research. It is, however, very difficult to establish the impact on reoffending of any intervention because, for example, it is hard to demonstrate cause and effect; to obtain a convincing control or comparison group; and even to be sure that an apparent change in the rate of offending – normally measured by reconvictions – has actually occurred (since reoffending and reconviction are obviously not the same thing). The problems increase when, as is now generally the case, evaluations attempt to measure not only effectiveness but also cost effectiveness. This requires a calculation not only of the costs of the intervention but also of the costs of different types of crime and the savings that may result if crimes are prevented.

The effectiveness of the system as a whole can be conceived more broadly than the effectiveness of a particular programme and, while some of the dimensions on which the system could be judged may be easier to measure than reoffending, others are beyond practical measurement. The Youth Justice Board (YJB), for example, claims that it has a 'vision of an effective youth justice system'. According to the board, this is one in which more offenders are caught, held to account and stop offending; children and young people get the support they need to live without offending; victims are better supported; and public confidence in the system increases. It is easy to think of other possible elements of effectiveness – for example, that the system should deal with alleged offenders as quickly as possible; that it should avoid doing further harm; and that it should produce outcomes that relevant parties see as fair, appropriate and helpful. In fact, some of these appear in the YJB's 15 specified 'Key Elements of Effective Practice', including restorative justice; 'the swift administration of justice'; and local youth crime prevention programmes.

While it would not be sensible to defend ineffective practice, the preoccupation with effectiveness has been criticized for focusing too narrowly on questions of technical performance and for ignoring ethical and political issues. Targets, key performance indicators and measures of system efficiency are prioritized over more fundamental questions about values and purposes. The concern with effectiveness and its measurement can be seen as part of a wider managerial preoccupation with reducing risk and uncertainty and increasing predictability and control.

David Smith

Related entries

Audit Commission; Evaluative research; Evidence-based policy and practice (EBPP); Key Elements of Effective Practice (KEEPs); Managerialism; Positivism; What works.

Key texts and sources

Burnett, R. and Roberts, C. (eds) (2004) *What Works in Probation and Youth Justice: Developing Evidence-based Practice.* Cullompton: Willan Publishing.

Lobley, D. and Smith, D. (2007) *Persistent Young Offenders: An Evaluation of Two Projects.* Aldershot: Ashgate.

Mair, G. (ed.) (1997b) *Evaluating the Effectiveness of Community Penalties.* Aldershot: Avebury.

Smith, D. (2006a) 'Youth crime and justice: research, evaluation and "evidence"', in B. Goldson and J. Muncie (eds) *Youth Crime and Justice: Critical Issues.* London: Sage.

Smith, R. (2006a) 'Actuarialism and early intervention in contemporary youth justice', in B. Goldson and J. Muncie (eds) *Youth Crime and Justice: Critical Issues.* London: Sage.

ELECTRONIC MONITORING

Electronic monitoring is a general term that applies to the process by which offenders' movements or locations may be checked, for the purpose of regulating and enforcing curfews or other forms of court orders. Various technologies are available, the most common being a small electronic device, or 'tag', fitted to the young person's ankle or wrist with compliance being checked through a monitoring unit at his or her home.

Although the electronic monitoring of offenders has been in use in the USA for over 20 years, it was not until 1995 that it became available for sentencers in Britain, and a further two years before a pilot scheme for young offenders began. However, children and young people now represent about 13 per cent of all electronically monitored offenders, of whom around 14,000 are being supervised on any one day.

For children and young people, electronic monitoring can be applied to a range of court disposals. A curfew order can be imposed by the court as a stand-alone penalty, or it can be combined with other orders such as a supervision order, or as part of an intensive supervision and surveillance programme. It can be used as a condition of bail – either on its own or in conjunction with a bail supervision and support programme – and in conjunction with a detention and training order as part of early-release arrangements or at the normal release date. Finally, it can be part of release arrangements in very serious or 'life licence' cases (in accordance with ss. 90–91 of the Powers of Criminal Courts (Sentencing) Act 2000).

The stated aims of the Youth Justice Board in using electronic monitoring are to reduce offending; to reduce the use of custody; to support compliance with community penalties; and to provide reassurance to courts and the public that penalties are being rigorously enforced. Electronic monitoring may be used for a maximum of three months with regard to any of the above disposals.

The extension of the use of electronic monitoring from adults to children and young people was not without controversy. There could hardly be a more obvious element of labelling than the 'tag' – concealment during a normal school day is not possible and it makes nonsense of the anonymity supposedly offered by the youth court. Conversely, there were concerns that many young offenders would use it as a status symbol with their peers and attempt to live up to the image it projected. Above all, there were fears that, because of its capacity to record all breaches, the 'tag' would accelerate the path to custody because of the inevitable return to court any breach would involve.

Experience suggests some fairly mixed results so far. Electronic monitoring may have some potential when used with young people who have difficulties with 'authority'. It offers a completely impersonal set of boundaries and can also be the perfect 'opt-out' for those who need help to resist peer pressure to join risky or criminal activities. But the level of breaches is high, especially for time violations, and although successful completion rates seem good, the very short-term nature of the orders (which often results in orders finishing before breach proceedings are completed) means that such compliance should not be confused with effectiveness.

One area that needs further study is the impact on families, for whom the tag may seem equally intrusive and an additional pressure in an already troubled situation. Two UK studies have highlighted specific relationship problems arising from electronic monitoring and, in Scotland, parents spoke of being 'unpaid warders' and said they had no idea of the impact it would have on their lives.

Despite such reservations, growth in the use of electronic monitoring with children and young people has been significant, and the Youth Justice Board oversees the largest 'tagging' anywhere in the world. Since England and Wales now jails eight times as many children under 15 years of age as it did ten years ago, there are those who argue that anything that might offer a credible community alternative should be explored. Electronic monitoring also has the 'virtue' of being relatively cheap: a 90-day order with 'tagging' costs about £1,300, which is substantially less costly than any custodial disposal.

There are, however, real difficulties in evaluating the effectiveness of electronic monitoring and, consequently, judging whether its use has long-term benefits for the youth justice system. The original rationale was that curfews with electronic monitoring would become a real alternative to custody, but 'tagging' is now promoted more generally as a relatively 'cheap' option at all sentencing levels, and the danger of 'net widening' is apparent. Reoffending/reconviction research has so far been very limited and inconclusive – the Home Office judgment is that it is 'offence neutral' – but there are some signs that monitored curfews may help in two ways. First, by 'buying time' to enable planned interventions; a curfew can disrupt patterns of behaviour effectively and, while the effect may be short term, it can provide opportunities for longer-term strategies to begin and, perhaps, to 'work'. Second, it may help improve compliance and completion rates on programmes. This support role – for which some evidence is emerging – may be particularly useful with volatile young offenders, but effectiveness research is extremely difficult.

The expansion of electronic monitoring generally, and not just with young offenders (which has involved over 300,000 offenders since 1999), is remarkable given the paucity of any real effectiveness research, particularly in view of the danger of 'net-widening'. If tagging is used for 'low risk' young people who do not warrant this level of surveillance, it will not only increase costs unnecessarily but it may also accelerate the path to custody owing to increased breaches, however minor.

Electronic monitoring can take various forms, including 'radio frequency tagging' (the most commonly used method, normally referred to as the 'first generation' system); 'voice recognition' systems; and 'satellite tracking' (which provides monitoring of movement and the ability to enforce exclusion zones and curfew compliance). A Home Office pilot project during 2004–5 tested it on over 300 offenders, of whom 91 were young offenders on intensive supervision programmes.

Electronic monitoring of adults has established itself as a sentence of the court, a condition of bail and a device to enable early release from prison. These have been mirrored in youth justice, but the short-term nature of tagging and indeed the limited nature of what it can offer suggest that selective, well targeted use offers the best way forward. The tag needs to 'add value' if it is to have a longer-term future in youth justice.

Dick Whitfield

Related entries

Alternatives to custody; Anti-social Behaviour (Scotland) Act 2004; Bail; Bail supervision and support (BSS); Criminal Justice and Immigration Bill 2006–7 to 2007–8; Curfew orders; Decarceration; Detention and training orders (DTOs); Enforcement; Exclusion orders; Intensive Supervision and Surveillance Programme (ISSP); Menu-based sentencing; Net-widening; Probation Service; Remand; Surveillance.

Key texts and sources

Mayer, M., Haverkamp, R. and Levy, R. (eds) (2003) *Will Electronic Monitoring Have a Future in Europe?* Freiburg: Max Planck Institute.

Moore, R. (2005) 'The use of electronic and human surveillance in a multi-modal programme', *Youth Justice*, 5: 17–32.

Nellis, M. (2004) 'The "tracking" controversy: the roots of mentoring and electronic monitoring', *Youth Justice*, 4: 77–99.

Whitfield, D. (2001) *The Magic Bracelet: Technology and Offender Supervision*. Winchester: Waterside Press.

ENFORCEMENT

Enforcement is action taken by youth offending teams to ensure that the requirements of court orders are fulfilled in accordance with the National Standards for Youth Justice Services.

The credibility of community penalties as 'punishment' rests on their content – they must be seen to be sufficiently demanding – and on the manner of their enforcement. This challenge of enforcement is peculiar to community penalties given that the subjects of orders are required to 'do things' – to keep appointments as instructed; to participate in activities; to refrain from specified company and places; to attend school and/or work – and this admits a possibility of default. The more demands are made, the greater the potential for default. Indeed, the combination of more requirements with their more rigorous enforcement is likely to lead to an increase in the incidence of breach.

None of the objectives of a community penalty – 'punishment', 'rehabilitation', 'reparation' – can be achieved without sufficient levels of contact. During the late 1990s, however, there was an emerging suspicion – substantially borne out by audits of probation services – that practice in relation to missed appointments and other expressions of non-compliance was variable and inconsistent. The consequences of non-compliance for young offenders and the standardized expectations on youth offending team (YOT) staff have accordingly been clarified and strengthened in law and policy. Under the National Standards for Youth Justice Services, persistent non-compliance must now lead to a return to court for breach proceedings.

This aspiration to raise standards of enforcement, then, was seen by policymakers as uncontroversial. Anthony Bottoms et al (2002), however, have suggested that the focus of policy and practice should move from 'enforcement' to (voluntary) compliance. The term enforcement may have a satisfyingly 'tough' sound to it, but the real challenge is to ensure that a 'treatment' or 'reparative' programme is actually completed constructively. Bottoms has drawn attention to the 'normative' dimensions of compliance, suggesting that it at least partly depends on the young person's perception of the fairness of the demands made on him or her and on his or her relationship with his or her supervising YOT officer.

Many young offenders are substantially inured to the threat of punishment, and the prospect of a return to court is not always sufficient to ensure compliance. Moreover, a reliance on 'threat' can undermine positive relationships. In short, there are many reasons why people may fail to comply with the requirements of an order, and the response to non-compliance must try to engage with those reasons. There is an important place for encouragement and positive incentives, for motivation through normative claims and for assistance to overcome practical difficulties.

It should also be recognized that, in matters of enforcement no less than in other aspects of practice, justice requires not only that like cases be treated alike but also that relevant differences be acknowledged and respected. These considerations complicate judgements about consistency – which is not ensured by treating everyone in the 'same' way.

Rob Canton and Kaushika Patel

Related entries

Authoritarianism; Desistance; Electronic monitoring; National Objectives and Standards for Scotland's Youth Justice Service; National Standards for Youth Justice Services; Punishment in the community.

Key texts and sources

Bottoms, A. (2001) 'Compliance and community penalties', in A. Bottoms *et al.* (eds) *Community Penalties: Changes and Challenges.* Cullompton: Willan Publishing.

Canton, R. and Eadie, T. (2005) 'Enforcement', in T. Bateman and J. Pitts (eds) *The RHP Companion to Youth Justice.* Lyme Regis: Russell House.

Eadie, T. and Canton, R. (2002) 'Practising in a context of ambivalence: the challenge for youth justice workers', *Youth Justice*, 2: 14–26.

Hearnden, I. and Millie, A. (2004) 'Does tougher enforcement lead to lower conviction?', *Probation Journal*, 51: 48–59.

Hedderman, C. and Hough, M. (2004) 'Getting tough or being effective: what matters?', in G. Mair (ed.) *What Matters in Probation.* Cullompton: Willan Publishing.

McNeill, F. (2006) 'Community supervision: contexts and relationships matter', in B. Goldson and J. Muncie (eds) *Youth Crime and Justice: Critical Issues.* London: Sage.

EUROPEAN CONVENTION ON HUMAN RIGHTS (ECHR)

The European Convention on Human Rights (ECHR) was drafted following the atrocities of the Second World War. The UK government ratified it in 1951 and, 15 years later, accepted the right of UK citizens (including children) to petition the European Court of Human Rights.

The European Convention on Human Rights (ECHR) guarantees fundamental rights and freedoms to all those living in the 46 Council of Europe member states. British lawyers played a major role in drafting the ECHR, and the UK was the first member state to sign it. Unlike the United Nations Convention on the Rights of the Child, the ECHR is justiciable: this means individuals can seek to enforce their rights legally through the European Court of Human Rights in Strasbourg. The UK has allowed its citizens to bring cases to the European Court since 1966. The decisions of the court are legally binding, supervised by the Council of Ministers, and individuals can be awarded damages.

The ECHR contains 59 articles and several protocols. The first 12 articles give every individual a set of legally enforceable rights. The articles most relevant to youth justice are as follows:

- *Article 2*: the right to life.
- *Article 3*: protection from torture and inhuman or degrading treatment or punishment.
- *Article 4*: protection from forced labour.
- *Article 5*: the right to liberty and security.
- *Article 6*: the right to a fair trial.
- *Article 7*: no punishment without law.
- *Article 8*: the right to respect for private and family life.
- *Article 9*: freedom of thought, conscience and religion.
- *Article 12*: the right to an effective remedy.

Article 14 (the right to all the rights in the ECHR without discrimination) must always be read in conjunction with one or more of the other convention rights, though the connection with a substantive article (Articles 2–12) can be fairly loose.

Two significant judgments are *T* v. *UK* and *V* v. *UK*, and *SC* v. *UK*. *T* v. *UK* and *V* v. *UK* concern two children who, at the age of 11 were convicted of the murder of 2-year-old James Bulger at Preston Crown Court in November 1993. The trial judge sentenced the boys to an indefinite period of detention, with a minimum tariff of eight years. The Lord Chief Justice increased this sentence to 10 years in 1994. Following intense public outcry and a petition organized by the *Sun* newspaper, the Home Secretary Michael Howard increased the minimum tariff to 15 years. In December 1999, the European Court of Human Rights found the UK to have breached the convention in three main ways. First, there was an Article 6(1) violation due to the absence of any review of the continuing lawfulness of the boys' detention. Second, there was an Article 6(1) breach in the way in which the boys' trial was conducted. Third, there was a breach under Article 6(1) of the convention on account of the Home Secretary intervening to fix the minimum period of detention. The judgment led to a practice direction in February 2000 from the Lord Chief Justice in relation to the trial of children in Crown courts.

SC v. *UK* concerned an 11-year-old tried in an adult Crown court. A consultant clinical psychologist had advised the judge that the boy had significant learning impairments, with a developmental age of between 6 and 8 years. Yet the judge continued with the proceedings, and an application to the Court of Appeal failed. The Strasbourg court agreed in 2004 that the boy's Article 6 right to a fair trial had been breached.

The Human Rights Act 1998 – which came into force in 2000 – incorporated the ECHR into UK law.

Carolyne Willow

Related entries

Bulger; Children's human rights; Council of Europe; Human Rights Act 1998.

Key texts and sources

Kilkelly, U. (1999) *The Child and the European Convention on Human Rights.* Aldershot: Ashgate.

See the Office of Public Sector Information's website (**http://www.opsi.gov.uk/ACTS/acts1998/19980042.htm**) for the text of the Human Rights Act 1998. The European Convention on Human Rights is available online at **http://conventions.coe.int/treaty/en/Treaties/Html/005.htm**.

See also the websites of the Howard League for Penal Reform (**http://www.howardleague.org**) and the Children's Rights Alliance for England (**http://www.crae.org.uk**).

EVALUATIVE RESEARCH

Evaluative research is intended to assess the value and effectiveness of any form of intervention, generally concerned with the identification of outcomes but also often with process (how the intervention was implemented).

Evaluative research on youth justice received considerable impetus in the mid-1990s with the revival of faith that something might 'work' in interventions with young offenders and, after 1997, from the government's insistence that practice should be 'evidence based'. For the previous 20 years or so, most evaluative work on youth (and adult) justice had been concerned with the impact of interventions on the youth justice system, not on young people who had offended. Youth justice in the 1980s, for example, was mainly evaluated (when it was evaluated at all) in terms of the extent to which it achieved its aims of diversion from the formal system and from custody, and of working only with young people who would be at risk of relatively severe penalties if they reoffended. In making such judgements, evaluative research typically concentrated on issues of process – how effectively agencies worked together, how quickly cases were dealt with, what effect youth justice workers had on local sentencing patterns, whether projects avoided net-widening and worked only with their intended target groups and so on – rather than on outcomes. It was widely assumed that there was little point in looking at the effectiveness of interventions on subsequent offending because research had supposedly shown that 'nothing worked'. Indeed, it was sometimes argued that the best way of reducing the reoffending rate was to do as little as possible, since intervention risked drawing young people further into a system whose effects were guaranteed to be negative. Evaluative research, therefore, often amounted to little more than the routine monitoring of practice in relation to its influence on the local youth justice system.

With the revival of optimism about the possibility of making a worthwhile difference to young people's propensity to offend came a renewal of interest in using scientific methods to assess the results of interventions. A few commentators on social work in Britain, notably Brian Sheldon (2001), had long argued that social work needed to become far more evidence based, and that the only way of achieving this was through the application of scientific methods of measurement to social work activity. The ideal – according to Sheldon and fellow advocates of a positivist approach to social research – is a controlled experimental design in which the relevant population (say, of persistent young offenders) is randomly divided into 'experimental' and 'control' groups, in the hope that these will be matched as far as possible on variables such as age, sex, class, ethnicity and so on, as well as on the seriousness and extent of their offending. Relevant data are collected on both groups, after which one (the 'experimental group') receives the 'treatment' or intervention, whatever it may be, while the other (the 'control group') ideally receives no 'treatment'. At the end of the 'treatment' period data are collected on both groups, and differences between the groups, as well as differences between the way they are now and the way they were when the experiment began, are identified and analysed. If differences are found in the 'experimental group' that are not found in the 'control group', and no other factor seems to explain this, then they can be attributed with reasonable confidence to the intervention, thus demonstrating a 'treatment effect'. This classic experimental design is sometimes called the OXO model, in which the first O represents the condition of each group before the treatment (pre-test), X represents the treatment and the second O represents the condition of the groups after the treatment (post-test).

This model, which is widely used in medicine – for example, in testing the efficacy of a new drug – is still often regarded as the ideal to which evaluative research on social programmes ought to aspire. Other methods, it is argued, lack scientific rigour and reliability and tend to produce unclear, ambiguous results. There are, however, problems in implementing the model. For example, it is difficult to be sure that the 'experimental' and 'control' groups are perfectly matched: there may be non-obvious variations that, in fact, explain any differences in results. It is also rarely possible (unlike in medicine) to withhold 'treatment' altogether from the 'control group' so that the comparison is usually between two different kinds of 'treatment' rather than between 'treatment' and nothing. It is also impossible to control everything that happens to the members of the groups during the experiment, and any pre-test and post-test differences could result from experiences unconnected with the experiment. Perhaps most crucially, designs of this kind, even when they do identify clear outcomes that can confidently be attributed to the 'treatment' (which in practice they rarely do), make it difficult to say just what it was about the 'treatment' that made the difference. That is, they are so focused on the identification and analysis of *outcomes* that they tend to have little to say about *processes* – what went on in the 'black box' of 'treatment' that may have made the difference. For instance, a Freudian therapist may consistently achieve better results than a Jungian one, but this may not be because Freudian theory is true and Jungian theory false but because the Freudian therapist is able to convey warmth, acceptance and empathy in a way that the Jungian therapist cannot.

Recognizing these limitations, researchers have developed alternatives to the experimental model that are better adapted to the evaluation of social programmes. An important example is the tradition of 'realistic evaluation' which, as presented by Ray Pawson and Nick Tilley (1997), stresses the importance of understanding the mechanisms involved in any process of change and the context in which these operate. Realistic evaluation will use experimental controls if there is an opportunity to do so, but does not regard them as essential for the identification of effective practice or the development of theory. It sees any intervention as having a causal effect only if its outcome is triggered by a mechanism acting in a context. For example, an offer to help someone reduce his or her drug use may motivate this person to see this as a problem that he or she can do something about and, in the right context – one that provides relevant sources of support – he or she may be able to achieve the desired outcome. Here the relevant mechanism is the motivation to change, and it can work effectively because of the helpful context. This means that, in a different context, it would not work, and one of the implications of 'realistic evaluation' is that it is never possible fully to replicate a successful programme because the context will always be different (in terms of resources, staff, opportunities for alternative activities and so on). This helps to explain the tendency for results to be disappointing when an approach that was successful on a small, local scale is 'rolled out' nationally. Realistic evaluation is more conceptually complex than the experimental model but it is also more practical to put into effect, and most evaluations of social programmes probably use, knowingly or not, elements of the realist approach. Evaluations of this kind will rarely produce results of the unambiguous, clear-cut kind that politicians and bureaucrats long for, but they can produce results that suggest what is likely to work, for whom and in what contexts.

Like all evaluations, however, they will only be influential if they can gain an attentive, relevant audience. The literature on evaluative research is full of complaints that nobody with the power to make a difference pays any attention to it, suggesting that Brian Sheldon's complaint that social work is insufficiently evidence based applies to other professions as well. The solution, according to many writers in the field, is for evaluative researchers to become political actors and to argue in the public arena for the relevance of their findings for policy. The spread of offending-focused cognitive-behavioural programmes is an example where this was done successfully. More generally, the lesson is that evaluative research is inherently as much a *political* as a *scientific* enterprise. In youth justice research, different groups and agencies, not necessarily with the same interests, are likely to have a stake in the results and are liable to interpret them in ways that accord with their preconceptions. For example, if referral orders were shown to be associated with a reduced rate of reoffending, the finding might be interpreted as giving support to the principle of early intervention or as showing the efficacy of restorative justice. A negative finding (say, that a 'scared straight' programme made things worse rather than better) is politically still more sensitive – just as agencies may compete to get the credit for a good result, so they are likely to try to avoid the blame for a bad one. In either case, the values of scientific rationality are unlikely to be of much use to the evaluator.

David Smith

Related entries

Audit Commission; Cognitive-behaviour programmes; Desistance; Effectiveness; Evidence-based policy and practice (EBPP); Managerialism; Politicization; Positivism; Recidivism; What works.

Key texts and sources

Lobley, D. and Smith, D. (2007) *Persistent Young Offenders: An Evaluation of Two Projects.* Aldershot: Ashgate.

Mair, G. (ed.) (1997b) *Evaluating the Effectiveness of Community Penalties.* Aldershot: Avebury.

Pawson, R. and Tilley, N. (1997) *Realistic Evaluation.* London: Sage.

Sheldon, B. and Chilvers, R. (2001) *Evidence-based Social Care: A Study of Prospects and Problems.* Lyme Regis: Russell House.

Smith, D. (2006a) 'Youth crime and justice: research, evaluation and "evidence"', in B. Goldson and J. Muncie (eds) *Youth Crime and Justice: Critical Issues.* London: Sage.

Wilcox, A. (2003) 'Evidence-based youth justice? Some valuable lessons from an evaluation for the Youth Justice Board', *Youth Justice*, 3: 19–33.

EVERY CHILD MATTERS (ECM)

'Every Child Matters' (ECM) is the government action plan for a system-wide reconfiguration of children's services at local government level in England.

The *Every Child Matters* (ECM) green paper, published in September 2003, brought together various policy strands, including a Treasury review of children at risk; the government's response to the inquiry into the death of Victoria Climbié; and a cross-government overarching strategy for children and young people. The paper identified a number of policy challenges – better prevention, a stronger focus on parents and families, and earlier intervention – then went on to discuss how best to achieve these while improving accountability for, and integration of, services at all levels and raising the status of and reforming the children's workforce. A series of policy and practice documents published under the ECM banner developed these themes and led to the passage of the legislative framework for ECM – the Children Act 2004.

Five key outcomes for children and young people lie at the heart of ECM, and the performance of all relevant services will be measured against these outcomes. The outcomes provide that *all* children should have the opportunity to be healthy; to stay safe; to enjoy and achieve; to make a positive contribution; and to achieve economic well-being. ECM is not rights based – the outcomes framework will be used to measure the availability or quality of service provision rather than a child's individual need for, or entitlement to, a service.

The elements of ECM encompass broad structural change as well as attempts to clarify lines of accountability across a diverse local partnership and the introduction of a set of tools to encourage joint working. In addition and perhaps at the centre of the initiative lie extensive and radical plans for workforce reform. ECM is based on strategic-level changes that are intended to break through existing professional barriers and service silos and to introduce common working practices and shared objectives. In the longer term, the government expects that they will lead to the integration of services around the needs of children.

Children's trusts are the preferred model in the ECM reforms and are underpinned by s. 10 of the Children Act 2004. Local authority children's services, health, police, probation, youth offending teams (YOTs) and other partners are under a reciprocal duty to co-operate in order to improve the well-being of children in their area, as defined by the five key outcomes. All the partners must contribute to a statutory 'Children and young people's plan' (CYPP) that should also align with the area's youth justice plan, among other things. CYPPs are meant to be drawn up in consultation with local children and young people, their parents and carers, and practitioners, and should arrange proposed actions based on an audit of need under each of the five outcomes. The first CYPPs were in place in April 2006.

In 2006, the National Foundation for Educational Research surveyed a sample of 75 CYPPs in which the involvement of YOTs and other criminal justice agencies was best represented by a variety of targets to reduce negative behaviour under the 'Making a positive contribution' outcome.

A director of children's services (DCS) and lead member (elected councillor) with responsibility for children's services must be appointed in each local authority. The DCS is responsible for overseeing the delivery of the CYPP and, with the children's trust partners, commissions the services that will help them meet their service objectives. It is too early to judge how readily YOTs are engaging with local authority children's services through the children's trust partnership. In an interim report on the YOT/children's trust interface (National Children's Bureau 2006), researchers found 'There is a sense of uncertainty among many of the 49 YOT managers who responded to the survey concerning the implications of local structural arrangements for their alignment with children's services and criminal justice partners, and for service delivery'.

The Children Act 2004 also introduced joint inspections led by the Office for Standards in

Education (Ofsted). The first began in September 2005, and early indications are that support for children and young people who offend or reoffend is an area needing improvement. As they evolve, these joint area reviews will investigate how well the local children's trust partnership delivers against national and local targets, using indicators developed under each of the five key outcomes.

Improved joint working (partnership working) is supposed to lead to better protection for children at risk of harm and neglect. Section 11 of the Children Act 2004 places a duty to safeguard and promote the welfare of children on the children's trust partners, as well as on the governors of young offender institutions (YOIs) and secure training centres (STCs). In addition, the Act introduces statutory local safeguarding children boards (LSCBs) to replace area child protection committees. Local authorities that have a YOI or STC in their area should ensure they are represented on the LSCB.

The continuing theme of intra- and inter-agency working is also underpinned by the introduction of 'tools' designed to assist front-line practitioners. The Act establishes an information-sharing database – described by government as an electronic telephone directory – that will contain a basic record on every child between 0 and 18, as well as contact details for their education and primary health providers and other service providers, including (where relevant) YOT workers. However, a national database – 'ContactPoint' – will be maintained by local authorities and should be in operation by the end of 2008.

In order to reduce the numbers of times a child or parent might be asked to undergo similar and often intrusive assessments, ECM has developed a common assessment framework (CAF). The CAF is an initial assessment form that is designed to be used by any practitioner who may have a concern about a child and wishes to explore it further. This initial assessment can lead to a referral to another service or may be retained by the original assessor whose contact details will be recorded on the child's information record. The Youth Justice Board

has published a poster that maps the CAF to Asset, though it is clear that Asset continues to be the preferred assessment framework for the youth justice system.

When a child needs a package of services, a lead professional may be appointed to help that child and his or her family to negotiate their way through the system. For example, a YOT worker may be asked to take on the lead professional role in the case of a child released from custody who might need help to find accommodation, an education place and/or counselling services.

Lisa Payne

Related entries

Actuarialism; Assessment framework; Children Act 2004; Children's commissioners; Children's trusts; Developmental criminology; Early intervention; Partnership working; Safeguarding; Youth Justice Board (YJB); Youth justice plans; Youth Matters; Youth offending teams (YOTs).

Key texts and sources

Department for Education and Skills (2003) *Every Child Matters*. London: DFES (available online at http://www.everychildmatters.gov.uk/_files/EBE7EEAC90382663E0D5BBF24C99A7AC.pdf).

Department for Education and Skills (2004a) *Every Child Matters: Change for Children in the Criminal Justice System*. London: DFES (available online at http://www.everychildmatters.gov.uk/_files/2F732FAF176ADC74EC67A78251B69328.pdf).

Lord, P., Wilkin, A., Kinder, K., Murfield, J., Jones, M., Chamberlain, T., Easton, C., Martin, K., Gulliver, C., Paterson, C., Ries, J., Moor, H., Stott, A., Wilkin, C. and Stoney, S. (2006) *Analysis of Children and Young People's Plans, 2006*. Slough: National Foundation for Educational Research (available online at http://www.nfer.ac.uk/research-areas/pims-data/summaries/analysis-of-cypp-2006.cfm).

National Children's Bureau (2006) *Interim Findings from the Research Study into the Developing Relationship between Youth Offending Teams and Children's Trusts* (available online at http://www.everychildmatters.gov.uk/resources-and-practice/search/rs00012/).

See the Office of Public Sector Information's website (http://www.opsi.gov.uk/acts/acts2004/20040031.htm) for the text of the Children Act 2004.

EVIDENCE-BASED POLICY AND PRACTICE (EBPP)

Evidence-based policy and practice (EBPP) is the deliberate and explicit use of evidence derived from methodologically robust research to improve decision-making and to inform the development of public policy.

Although the origins of evidence-based policy and practice (EBPP) lie in the natural sciences – in particular, the growth of evidence-based medicine – it has now become a central feature of government and policy discourse across a wide range of disciplines. It is essentially a pragmatic rather than an ideological approach to decision-making that perhaps goes part way to explaining why it has assumed such prominence in the New Labour era of 'what matters is what works'.

The rise of EBPP prompts a fundamental question about what should count as reliable and usable evidence. While government policy papers may have embraced a relatively broad definition of 'evidence', the focus in the youth justice context has been primarily on using research to find out 'what works' in reducing offending. In trying to measure the effectiveness of interventions, much emphasis has been given by both the Home Office and the Youth Justice Board (YJB) to the idea of a 'hierarchy of evidence' in which experimental random control trials are seen as the 'gold standard' of primary research. Other favoured approaches include attempts to make better use of existing secondary data through systematic reviews and meta-analyses.

The move towards a more strategic approach to obtaining evidence is also seen in the setting up of such bodies as the Social Care Institute for Excellence – which has a responsibility to collect and disseminate up-to-date knowledge – and in the fact that one of the statutory functions of the YJB is to 'commission research and publish information'. Another example would be the way in which evaluation is now routinely built into new programme implementation.

While there is much to be welcomed in such developments, they also raise concerns and questions. Is there a danger of over-control if the research agenda and research questions are so frequently set by government? Does it matter if academic research is viewed primarily as a means to economic and social development rather than a worthwhile end in its own right? Should more attention be given to the role that evidence could play in answering other critical policy questions, such as why does this work? Who should do it? Is it cost effective? In addition, there is a significant and ongoing debate within the social policy arena about what constitutes 'good evidence'.

One reason why the impact of 'evidence' on policy and practice has, in reality, often been disappointing may be that practitioners do not have the time or resources to find and digest relevant (but sometimes complex) research findings. Dissemination of evidence is critical if it is to have an impact, and one way in which the YJB has attempted to achieve this is by publishing a series of 'key elements of effective practice' to distil research evidence for youth justice practitioners. However, while much of the emphasis so far has been on communicating information from the centre, it is also important to consider ways of increasing the 'demand' for evidence from those who implement new policy and practice on the ground.

The link between research and policy is complex. Evidence may contribute directly to problem-solving or may sometimes have a more indirect role in developing conceptual thinking. It is, however, only one of many influences on the formation of policy, and there will be times when political or financial imperatives take precedence. There is also a tension between the importance of the ongoing collection of evidence and the pressure to take action. Examples of this in youth justice include the referral order and the Intensive Supervision and Surveillance Programme, in which the decision to roll out the schemes nationally was taken long *before* the evaluations of the 'pilots' could be completed. While this may be understandable politically, there is a danger that it contributes to a culture in which people become cynical about how knowledge is being used.

Similarly, the link between evidence and practice is multifaceted rather than simply linear. The front-line delivery of services will be influenced by a range of factors, including practitioners' values, resource constraints and the responses of clients. Research can inform but not replace professional expertise – in fact, the latter will always be needed in order to determine how evidence can best be applied when working with individual young people who offend.

Interestingly, there is little evidence to show that EBPP works in terms of producing more effective outcomes. However, since few would seriously argue that we should ignore research altogether, the critical issues are about what types of research are needed and how the findings can best be used. Can evidence be relevant at all stages of the policy cycle – in shaping the questions, informing choices, implementing new initiatives and then monitoring their impact? Achieving this may require a more imaginative research strategy than has so far been seen from the YJB and Home Office – one that values descriptive, analytical and theoretical research alongside the more typical programme evaluations.

And, given the complexities of the research–policy–practice chain, is it more appropriate to speak of 'evidence influenced' or 'evidence aware' rather than evidence based? Despite the government-led emphasis on the importance of evidence, the political and practical realities of policymaking mean that its impact on practice in youth justice is more likely to be measured and gradual than dramatic and obvious.

Kerry Baker

Related entries

Audit Commission; Effectiveness; Evaluative research; Key Elements of Effective Practice (KEEPs); Managerialism; Politicization; Positivism; What works.

Key texts and sources

Davies, T., Nutley, S. and Smith, P. (2000) *What Works? Evidence-based Policy and Practice in Public Services.* Bristol: Policy Press.
Goldson, B. and Muncie, J. (eds) (2006c) *Youth Crime and Justice: Critical Issues.* London: Sage.
Nutley, S., Walter, I. and Davies, T. (2007) *Using Evidence: How Research can Inform Public Services.* Bristol: Policy Press.
See also the websites of ESRC UK – Centre for Evidence Based Policy and Practice (**http://www.evidencenetwork.org/**) and The Policy Hub (**http://www.policyhub.gov.uk**).

EXCLUSION ORDERS

The exclusion order was introduced by the Criminal Justice and Court Services Act 2000 to prohibit a person from entering designated areas for a maximum of two years, or three months in the case of a child below the age of 16. It is a community penalty and can only be made if the court considers that the offending was 'serious enough' to warrant such a sentence. The prohibition is monitored electronically.

The exclusion order imposes restrictions on a person's freedom of movement alongside an increasing number of measures in the youth justice system that focus primarily on containment and surveillance. Although available as a stand-alone disposal, Home Office guidance suggests that the order will usually be part of a broader programme of interventions.

The order was implemented, using satellite-tracking technology, on a pilot basis in three sites – the Greater Manchester, West Midlands and Hampshire/Wessex youth offending team areas – from September 2004 (Home Office 2004c). However, for adults committing offences after April 2005, the order is replaced by an exclusion requirement that can be attached to the new community order. As a consequence, exclusion orders are only available for those below the age of 18 years, sentenced in the pilot areas. The pilot was to be evaluated over a 12-month period but, at the time of writing, no evaluation has been published. The number of exclusion orders imposed on young people is not recorded as a distinct category in the Home Office Sentencing Statistics or the Youth Justice Board's Youth Justice Annual Statistics.

If the relevant provisions of the Criminal Justice and Immigration Bill 2006–7 to 2007–8 are implemented, the exclusion order will be replaced – along with the curfew order, action plan order, attendance centre order and supervision order – with the single 'menu-based' youth rehabilitation order.

Tim Bateman

Related entries

Criminal Justice and Court Services Act 2000; Criminal Justice and Immigration Bill 2006–7 to 2007–8; Electronic monitoring; Surveillance.

Key texts and sources

Home Office (2004c) *Piloting Exclusion Orders and Satellite Tracking Technology under Provision of the Criminal Justice and Court Services Act 2000* (Circular 61/04). London: Home Office.

EXTENDING ENTITLEMENT (NATIONAL ASSEMBLY FOR WALES)

'Extending Entitlement' is both the title of a landmark report produced by the post-devolution Welsh Assembly Government and a summary of a far wider approach to the provision of public services in Wales.

The report, *Extending Entitlement: Supporting Young People in Wales*, was published in 2000 as a statement of policy intent in relation to *all* young people but especially those young people whose needs are least well met by mainstream services. In that sense, it is of direct and continuing relevance to those who provide youth justice services in Wales. As the title suggests, *Extending Entitlement* begins from a belief that young people are citizens possessed of rights rather than simply dependants owed and owing responsibilities. The path it sets out to securing a better future for marginalized and disadvantaged young people is one that strengthens those rights, both by extending the range of services on which they can draw and by securing access to such services for those who most need them.

In designing a comprehensive system of advice and support, available to *all* young people in Wales, the *Extending Entitlement* report takes as its basis that 'we should do more to strengthen the fences that prevent people from falling over the cliff – rather than providing more ambulances and police vans when they do' (Welsh Assembly Government Policy Unit 2000: 5). In providing this extra support, 'the ethos should be one of guiding and encouraging all young people to take up their entitlement – not on policing their participation' (2000: 7).

The approach set out in *Extending Entitlement* has been developed further in a number of core Welsh Assembly Government policy documents, most significantly *Making the Connections*, the overarching statement of the Welsh Assembly Government's approach to public service provision (Welsh Assembly Government 2006). From a youth justice perspective, three key themes emerge that are of particular relevance.

First, at the heart of Assembly Government policymaking lies a preference for *co-operation* rather than *competition* as the defining relationship between public service providers and as the primary means of improving performance. In Wales, 'policy competitiveness' has been rejected as inimical to equality and destructive of the trust relationships on which effective public services rely. In criminal justice this means, for example, that the Assembly Government has been openly hostile to the policy of contestability in probation services. In youth justice, the preference for co-operation is plainly to be seen in the *All Wales Youth Offending Strategy* (Welsh Assembly Government/ Youth Justice Board 2004).

Second, *progressive universalism* has been adopted as a guiding principle in the broader effort to extend the range of services available to the population. Thus, wherever possible, the Assembly Government has a preference for universal measures – for example, abolishing charges to museums and galleries for everyone; making prescriptions free for every patient; providing free breakfasts for children in every participating primary school; and providing free swimming for children in school holidays. While at a UK level behavioural conditionality has become the hallmark of restricted social entitlement, the Welsh Assembly's approach has been to make services available to *all*. In addition to universality, however, policies in Wales also draw on a form of targeting to provide additional help, over and above the universal measure, to those whose needs are greatest. A single example will be provided here in relation to children and young people. In the 2006 budget, the Chancellor of the Exchequer provided substantial new funding for schools which, in England, he directed to be distributed directly to head teachers on a simple formula based on school size. In Wales, the Assembly Cabinet decided to concentrate the same funding exclusively on those schools serving most disadvantaged areas and on the education of looked-after children. In doing so, it acted entirely within the spirit of the original *Extending Entitlement* document, looking to widen the range of services available to those young people most in need and to strengthen access to services for the most disadvantaged communities.

Progressive universalism matters in the field of youth justice because it identifies young people in trouble as having a *greater* not *lesser* call on public services. This call is not, of course, as that most shallow of criticisms suggests, a reward for bad behaviour but a recognition both that offending is often the product of deficits earlier in a child's life and that additional investment in remedying these difficulties is the best means of preventing crime in the future.

Third, the wider *Extending Entitlement* approach is based on a particular model of the relationship between users and providers of services which regards both parties as jointly engaged in a set of common tasks, based on trust and reciprocity. Users are not passive objects of providers' expertise; neither are providers intent on knavishly exploiting their position in order to extract maximum personal benefit as monopoly suppliers to a powerless public. Rather, the Welsh model advocates a citizen-centred approach in which the different, but equally important, contribution of both parties is recognized and valued.

Young people in trouble are among the groups most vulnerable to having their human rights eroded and/or neglected, on the basis that their behaviour has disqualified them from services. The entitlement approach, however, provides for the rights of young people, even those who have offended, to having their voice heard and their views respected. The single most important and practical step to have been

taken in this area came with the appointment of the UK's first ever Children's Commissioner in Wales in 2001. While the devolution settlement means that youth justice services themselves do not fall directly within the commissioner's remit, this did not prevent the first holder of that office from commenting directly on the way in which children's lives are affected when getting into trouble with the law (Children's Commissioner for Wales 2003).

To summarize, *Extending Entitlement* is both a specific policy and a general approach to service provision in Wales. It seeks to reinforce a set of citizenship rights for all while improving the access to services of those most in need. It positively extends this approach to young people and provides a platform from which work in the youth justice system can be carried out.

Mark Drakeford

Related entries

All Wales Youth Offending Strategy; Child Poverty; Children First; Children's Commissioners; Children's Human Rights; Social exclusion; Social inclusion; Vulnerability; Welsh Assembly Government.

Key texts and sources

Children's Commissioner for Wales (2003) *Annual Report*. Swansea: Children's Commissioner for Wales.

Haines, K., Case, S., Isles, E., Rees, I. and Hancock, A. (2004) *Extending Entitlement: Making it Real*. Cardiff: Welsh Assembly Government.

Welsh Assembly Government (2006) *Making the Connections – Delivering beyond Boundaries: Transforming Public Services in Wales*. Cardiff: Welsh Assembly Government.

Welsh Assembly Government Policy Unit (2000) *Extending Entitlement: Supporting Young People in Wales*. Cardiff: Welsh Assembly Government (available online at http://www.ecoliinquirywales.org.uk/topics/educationandskills/policy_strategy_and_planning/extending_entitlement/eepublications/ supportyoungpeople?lang=en).

Welsh Assembly Government/Youth Justice Board (2004) *All Wales Youth Offending Strategy*. Cardiff: Welsh Assembly Government and Youth Justice Board.

FAMILY GROUP CONFERENCING

Family group conferencing is a process that aims to promote decision-making by the family. The role of professionals is to provide the space in order to facilitate the family (and their supporters) to develop a plan to address their child's needs, and to provide services to support such plans.

Family group conferences (FGCs) developed in New Zealand in the early 1980s, becoming formalized through legislation (Children, Young Persons and their Families Act 1989) as the primary decision-making mechanism for children and young people in *both* civil and criminal matters.

A FGC is a meeting involving the young person, his or her extended family, close friends and victims (with support if they wish). The meeting is arranged by an independent co-ordinator and is also attended by professional workers. The meeting provides an opportunity for frank discussion of offences committed by the young person, the effects of such offences and any problems or issues that are leading the young person to offend. The purpose of the meeting is for the young person and his or her family – having received information from the victims and professional workers present – to create a plan that will make some amends for the harm done to the victims, and also to avoid further trouble.

In England and Wales – following recognition in the early 1990s of the potential for FGCs to encourage participation and to 'empower' families in key decision-making processes – the use of FGCs has become quite widespread in child welfare and child protection work. As yet, the application of FGCs in the youth justice sphere has been quite limited, however, even though research reveals that the clusters of 'risk' relating to young people in the justice system are strikingly similar to those that apply to children in welfare/child-care systems.

Typically, the FGC has four distinct stages:

1. Discussion of the offence and righting the wrong to the victim.
2. Addressing individual needs and the risk of reoffending.
3. Private family-planning time.
4. Sharing and finalizing the plan with professionals.

Evaluation has consistently demonstrated that FGCs can encourage the production of effective plans for young people and significantly reduce reoffending among those who take part. Furthermore, experience suggests that victims who attend benefit from the opportunity to be heard in a safe environment; to receive answers to lingering questions and explanations for behaviour; and to receive an apology or reparation for harm done.

It has been suggested that the relative neglect of family group conferencing in the youth justice system has been a consequence of restorative approaches focusing on 'responsibilizing' young people and placing reparation above reintegration.

Peter Gill

Related entries

Mediation; Reparation; Restorative justice; Restorative youth conferencing; Victims.

Key texts and sources

Family Group Conference Service (2002) *Research Outcomes and Lessons Learned.* Essex: Essex County Council Family Group Conference Service.

Jackson, S. (1999) 'Family group conferences and youth justice: the new panacea?', in B. Goldson (ed.) *Youth Justice: Contemporary Policy and Practice*. Aldershot: Ashgate.

Sherman, L.W. and Strang, H. (2007) *Restorative Justice: The Evidence*. London: Smith Institute. (available online at **www.smith–institute.org.uk/publications.htm**)

See also the Family Rights Group's website (**http://www.frg.org.uk**).

FAMILY PROCEEDINGS COURT

The family proceedings court is the name given to the magistrates' court when members of the family panel sit. It is a court of first instance in England and Wales that deals with family matters.

The Children Act 1989 provides the statutory basis for matters that are heard in the family proceedings court. Other statutes that have a direct bearing on the family proceedings court include the Adoption and Children Act 2002, the Child Support Act 1991, the Domestic Proceedings and Magistrates' Courts Act 1978, the Magistrates' Courts Act 1980 and the Family Law Act 1996.

The family proceedings court fulfils major statutory functions with regard to child care/welfare in two key forms:

- *Public law* cases, including applications – usually from local authorities – for secure accommodation orders and care and/or supervision orders in respect of children who are 'at risk of significant harm'.
- *Private law* cases – for example, disputes between parents/carers concerning the upbringing of children.

Many children and young people in the youth justice system are known to social services departments as a result of welfare issues and/or care proceedings. In this respect the purpose and function of the family proceedings court are significant in the youth justice context.

Barry Goldson

Related entries

Care orders; Children Act 1908; Children Act 1989; Juvenile courts; Looked after children (LAC); Secure accommodation; Supervision orders; Welfare.

Key texts and sources

See the Office of Public Sector Information's website for the texts of the Children Act 1989 (**http://www.opsi.gov.uk/acts/acts1989/ukpga_19890041_en_1.htm**) and the Family Proceedings Courts (Children Act 1989) Rules 1991 (**http://www.opsi.gov.uk/si/si1991/uksi_19911395_en_1.htm**).

See also the website of the Children and Family Court Advisory and Support Service (**http://www.cafcass.gov.uk/**). The Judicial Studies Board's document, *Family Court Bench Book*, is available online at **http://www.jsboard.co.uk/magistrates/family_court/index.htm**.

FAMILY TIES OF YOUNG PRISONERS

The family ties of young prisoners can, in some cases, contribute to their offending behaviour and, in others, contribute to the way out of it. The term is used here in the context of a pathway to resettlement.

It is well documented that young offenders are a group likely to have experienced disruptive family relationships. In the community this may manifest itself in homelessness. In custody, which unavoidably produces family separation, the potential for intensifying family problems is obvious. The maintenance and strengthening of family ties, therefore, except where this has been shown to be damaging to the young person, are key elements in both prevention and rehabilitation.

In the adult justice system, the importance attached to the family ties of offenders is reflected in the fact that 'Children and families of offenders' is the title of one of the seven pathways to reducing reoffending identified in the *Reducing Re-offending Delivery Plan* (Home Office 2005g). In respect of the youth justice system, a range of reports from the Youth Justice Board (YJB), the Social Exclusion Unit and the Department for

Education and Skills have also emphasized the centrality of family support and accompanying services in reducing further offending by young people. Even where it is not feasible for young offenders to live at home, it is suggested that their independent living arrangements will prove more stable if they can maintain the support of significant family members.

Young offenders are not only 'children' but they may also be parents. There is some evidence to suggest that family and parenting variables may be predictive of offending behaviour throughout the life course. In other words, this implies an inter-generational connection. Murray and Farrington (2005), for example, have argued that having a parent imprisoned during childhood comprises a 'risk factor' for a child's future anti-social behaviour and/or delinquency. The need for intervention to mediate this potential cycle is, therefore, desirable.

Currently, there is a gap in long-term outcome research into family-based interventions for young offenders. In respect of those living in the community, mentoring, family mediation, parenting skills and SureStart programmes (some of which involve young offenders' families) have been shown to provide beneficial results, particularly where participation is voluntary. Research has also revealed the importance of respecting parents' wishes to operate within their own informal support systems, while complementing this with access to fully integrated multi-agency provision from healthcare, education, social services and youth justice services.

In respect of young people in custody, continuing contact with their parents, siblings and other key family members via visits, telephone and letter is usually high on their agenda. Further (in the absence of routinely collected data by prisons about parental status), estimates of the proportion of young prisoners who are themselves parents range from 25 to 42 per cent. Some girls/young women may give birth in prison and look after their babies there for a limited period. Thereafter, if they are serving anything other than a short sentence, the baby will be removed from them, with all the associated distress of parent–child separation. For boys/young men, preserving a relationship with their (inevitably young) children can be particularly difficult – especially if relations

with the child's mother are fractured – but is none the less important, both in itself and for future successful resettlement. Furthermore, for the children of young prisoners themselves, regular contact matters in terms of their developing identity and their human right 'to maintain contact with a parent from whom they are separated' – unless this contact is known to be damaging – as provided by Article 9 of the United Nations Convention on the Rights of the Child. It follows that supporting the young parent–child relationship during imprisonment is important.

The YJB states – on the young people in custody section of its website – that 'to help maintain and strengthen family ties for children and young people in custody, we always try, where possible, to locate young people as close to home as possible, both in distance, and in terms of transport links and accessibility'. The YJB also has an Assisted Visits Scheme, which contributes to the travel, certain subsistence and unavoidable overnight costs (of one visit per week by up to two visitors aged over 16 +) and the needs of any children under 16 who must accompany the adults. If a family has young children they are unable to bring with them, the YJB will also help with registered childminder costs. However, Boswell and Wedge's national study of imprisoned fathers and their children (2002) and Pugh's study of a young offender institution (2005) showed that distance from home (on average in excess of 100 miles) was one of the biggest barriers to maintaining family contact. The rigidity of the visits process, children sometimes being distressed by search procedures and cost constituted further disincentives to visit.

The reasons for the maintenance of good family ties for young offenders, together with some of the difficulties associated with this process, are fairly clear. Youth justice workers may be able to mediate the difficulties, however. Family ties services are typically being led by the voluntary sector, in partnership with key criminal justice agencies, health, education, youth justice and children's services, in order to provide a 'joined up' approach to resolving family difficulties. Families themselves may often be best placed to suggest positive solutions to the young offender's difficulties and should, where appropriate, be afforded the opportunity to contribute to pre-sentence reports and sentence plans with the aim of improving the accuracy of information and the efficacy of interventions. The locus of 'failure' or 'success' for the still-developing young offender can lie in his or her functioning as a child, partner or parent.

Gwyneth Boswell

Related entries

Children in custody; Children's human rights; Developmental criminology; Juvenile secure estate; Parenting orders; Protective factors; Rehabilitation; Resettlement; Risk factors.

Key texts and sources

Boswell, G. and Wedge, P. (2002) *Imprisoned Fathers and their Children*. London and Philadelphia, PA: Jessica Kingsley.

Home Office (2005g) *Reducing Re-offending Delivery Plan*. London: Home Office Communication Directorate.

Murray, J. and Farrington, D. (2005) 'Parental imprisonment: effect on boys' anti-social behaviour and delinquency through the life course', *Journal of Child Psychology and Psychiatry*, 46: 1269–78.

Pugh, G. (2005) H*MP/YOI Warren Hill: Visits and Family Ties Survey, 2004/5*. Ipswich: Ormiston Children and Families Trust.

See also the websites of the Youth Justice Board (http://www.yjb.gov.uk/en-gb/) and Action for Prisoners' Families (www.prisonersfamilies.org.uk).

FAST-TRACKING

Fast-tracking refers to the speeding up of the time taken in processing the cases of 'persistent' young offenders between arrest and sentence.

There has been some concern for many years about 'delay' in dealing with young people who offend, especially those typically described as 'persistent' young offenders. Before the election of the first New Labour government in 1997, Jack Straw, who was to become Home Secretary, expressed dismay at what he called the 'adjournment culture' in the youth justice system. As a result, one of the Labour Party's five manifesto pledges prior to the 1997 election was to 'fast track' persistent young offenders. Specifically, it promised to halve the time for this group – defined as someone aged 10–17 who has been sentenced for one or more recordable offences on three or more separate occasions and is arrested again within three years of last being sentenced – to be dealt with. Research in 1996 showed that the time it took from arrest to sentence for this group averaged 142 days (Audit Commission 1996). The government committed itself to reducing this average time to 71 days or less. It achieved this target by August 2001, though the national average conceals some significant regional disparities.

There appear to be *some* good, though diverse, reasons for seeking to achieve this goal. Justice delayed is considered by some to be justice denied, and there was some evidence of 'bail bandits' who regarded the law with impunity. Victims of youth crime can become frustrated at the delays in dealing with those who have offended against them, and there is tentative evidence that 'speedier' youth justice does bring about a reduction in reoffending rates.

On the other hand, there are concerns about simply focusing on speed. Some cases demand careful attention to the complexities of some young people's lives – both their offending profiles and their broader life circumstances. This requires, sometimes, a number of adjournments. Over-speedy administration may impede the possibility for victims to consider their involvement in more restorative alternatives. There is always the risk of further net-widening and the acceleration of young people towards custodial options that are proven to be ineffective at preventing reoffending.

Of most significance, however, in relation to the fast-tracking agenda, is the definition of 'persistent' youth offending. Beyond the formal definition advanced by the government, 'fast-tracking' allowed for alternative definitions based on local factors, especially to do with 'spree' offending. Academic research suggests that the criteria invoked to define 'persistency' tend to produce quite different populations of young offender (Hagell and Newburn 1994). Moreover, robust sentences imposed speedily on any group of 'persistent' young offenders often come too late to address either their offending behaviour or their wider needs.

Perhaps the greatest lesson of 'fast-tracking' is that high-level political commitment can effect swift change in youth justice practice, irrespective of the evidence base on which it has been developed.

Howard Williamson

Related entries

Audit Commission; Due process; No More Excuses; Persistent young offenders; Youth courts.

Key texts and sources

Audit Commission (1996) *Misspent Youth*. London: Audit Commission.

Audit Commission (2004) *Youth Justice 2004: A Review of the Reformed Youth Justice System*. London: Audit Commission.

Hagell, A. and Newburn, T. (1994) *Persistent Young Offenders*. London: Policy Studies Institute.

Hill, M., Walker, M., Moodie, K., Wallace, B., Bannister, J., Khan, F., McIvor, G. and Kendrick, A. (2007) 'More haste, less speed? An evaluation of fast track policies to tackle persistent youth offending in Scotland', *Youth Justice*, 7: 121–37.

Home Office (1997b) *Tackling Delays in the Youth Justice System: A Consultation Paper*. London: Home Office.

FEAR OF CRIME

> Fear of crime is a sense of worry, dread or anxiety occasioned by the subjective assessment, whether rational or otherwise, of one's risk of, and vulnerability to, criminal victimization.

Fear of crime is a complex phenomenon influenced by a range of interconnected social and demographic variables, including perceptions of risk and vulnerability; age; social class; geographical location; ethnicity; personal experience of criminal victimization; media reporting; and popular wisdom (Hale 1996). It can have a variety of effects on individuals' 'quality of life', ranging from not walking home alone at night to withdrawing from society altogether and living in isolation. Felt or expressed fear of crime bears no necessary relationship to the objective risk of victimization and, paradoxically, those who tend to demonstrate the greatest fear – older people and women – are often those who are least at risk (Ferraro 1995). For this reason, some have questioned just how 'rational' fear of crime really is.

In the 1980s, for example, 'left idealists' suggested that much fear of crime was unduly amplified by media-induced moral panics orchestrated to legitimate the authoritarian state and fuel a law-and-order agenda. By contrast, 'left realists' highlighted the disproportionate concentration of crime in socially deprived, inner-city areas and, on behalf of those whose fears appeared entirely rational, they determined to 'take crime seriously' (Lea and Young 1984). Fear of crime became a serious policy issue around the same time, when the British Crime Survey claimed that it was becoming as big a problem as crime itself (Hough and Mayhew 1983). Since then, a massive private security industry has mushroomed out of the crime–risk–fear complex, and politicians and criminal justice professionals – recognizing its political currency – routinely discuss tackling both crime *and* the fear of crime.

Attempts to tackle fear of crime are often targeted at young people, since 'youth' remains closely associated with the visible street crimes that generate such intense public anxiety and worry. Frequently accompanied by populist rhetoric and sensationalist headlines, youth crime initiatives are often punitive and situational rather than socially reforming because it is believed such measures will produce more immediately visible results, and thus be more popular with the voting public. However, high-profile, short-term government initiatives targeting 'visible' youth deviance and offending do much to ensure the continued presence of youth offending in the headlines and in the public imagination. This, in turn, may help explain why a fall in recorded crime rates is not necessarily accompanied by a corresponding fall in public fear of crime (Collier *et al.* 2005).

Chris Greer

Related entries

Authoritarianism; British Crime Survey (BCS); Community safety; Crime and disorder reduction (CDR); Deviance amplification; Dispersal orders; Local child curfew schemes (LCCSs); Media reporting; Moral panic; Politicization; Prolific and other priority offenders (PPOs) strategy; Public attitudes to youth crime and justice; Punitiveness; Responsibilization; Street crime; Victimization; Victims.

Key texts and sources

Collier P. (2005) *Managing Police Performance: Accountabilities, Performance Measurement and Control.* Swindon: Economic and Social Research Council (ESRC).

Ferraro, K. (1995) *Fear of Crime: Interpreting Victimisation Risk.* Albany, NY: State University of New York Press.

Hale, C. (1996) 'Fear of crime: a review of the literature', *International Review of Victimology*, 4: 79–150.

Hough, M. and Mayhew, P. (1983) *The British Crime Survey.* Home Office Research Study 76. London: HMSO.

Lea, J. and Young, J. (1984) *What is to be Done about Law and Order – Crisis in the Eighties.* Harmondsworth: Penguin Books.

FINES

A fine is a financial penalty that forms part of the lowest level of sentences a court has available to it. Fines are suitable for cases that do not merit the restriction of liberty involved in either a community or a custodial sentence.

Ideally, fines for similar offences should have an equal impact on individuals irrespective of wealth. In setting the level of fine, account should be taken of the offender's (or his or her parent's/guardian's) ability to pay. A fine should, therefore, be proportionate to the seriousness of the offence and the offender's capacity to pay.

In the case of children aged 10–15, the responsibility for payment of the fine must be made on a parent or guardian. In the case of 16 and 17-year-olds, the court has discretion

against whom the order is made. If the responsibility is on the parent/guardian, it is his or her financial circumstances that are assessed. In setting the level of the fine the court must have regard to the maximum amount available for the offence and the individual's 'means'. In calculating 'means', account must be taken of income, outgoings, savings or disposable assets and other liabilities to pay fines. There are separate maxima for 10–17-year-olds from those for adults. At the time of writing these are £250 for 10–13-year-olds (unless the maximum for the offence is lower) and £1,000 for both 14–15 and 16–17-year-olds.

Fines are payable on the day of imposition, although time may be allowed for payment, usually within a year. Before leaving the court, the person responsible for paying the fine should be given details of the total payment, the place of payment and, if time has been granted for payment, the rate and date of the first payment. Fines fall between 'compensation' and 'costs' in order of priority for payment.

Courts may set a date to review the payment of the fine. In the event of doing so then the court can undertake a new financial assessment. The court has a number of options available to it should there be failure to pay. Such options apply particularly to 16-17 year-olds and include the following:

- An attendance centre order.
- A money payment supervision order: an adult supports and encourages payment.
- A deduction from benefit – part of the individual's benefit is paid directly to the court.
- An attachment of earnings order: an employer pays part of earnings directly to the court.
- A distress warrant: bailiffs can seize goods for sale to pay the fine and to cover their costs.

Spike Cadman

Related entries

Crime (Sentences) Act 1997; Criminal Justice Act 1991; Deterrence; Magistrates; Menu-based sentencing; Parental bind overs; Parental compensation orders (PCOs); Penalty notices for disorder (PNDs); Proportionality; Sentencing framework; Sheriff courts; Summary justice; Tariff.

Key texts and sources

Magistrates' Association (2004) *Magistrates' Court Sentencing Guidelines*. London: Magistrates' Association (available online at **http://www.js board.co.uk/downloads/acbb/section2a.pdf**).

See the Office of Public Sector Information's website (**http://www.opsi.gov.uk/acts/acts2000/20000006. htm**) for the text of the Powers of the Criminal Courts (Sentencing) Act 2000. The Judicial Studies Board's document, *Youth Court Bench Book*, is available online at **http://www.jsboard.co.uk/ magistrates/ycbb/index.htm**.

FIRST-TIME ENTRANTS

First-time entrants are children and young people engaged in their first formal process or proceedings in the youth justice system. Prosecution and associated court proceedings most clearly define 'entrance' to the system, but reprimands and final warnings have a formal statutory basis and are also recorded for the purpose of monitoring the numbers of first-time entrants.

The term 'first-time entrant' has no statutory footing and no historical basis. Rather, it emerged by way of a recent 'key performance indicator' established by the Youth Justice Board (YJB) as a driver for targeted prevention initiatives. Thus it relates primarily to the youth justice system in England and Wales.

'First-time entrant' is an imprecise term as it does not include all the ways in which a child or young person can be dealt with in the youth justice system in its broadest sense. For example, it takes no account of informal actions, fixed-penalty notices or anti-social behaviour orders. It can also include children who are prosecuted but later acquitted. It derives from 'performance management' arrangements, particularly in response to a rising concern about increasing numbers of children and young people entering the youth justice system for minor offences that might previously have been dealt with informally or by way of diversion.

The numbers of children and young people entering the youth (or juvenile) justice system had been falling from the 1980s. The number who were convicted or cautioned (reprimanded or warned from 1998) fell by over a quarter between 1992 and 2002, for example. However, numbers increased significantly thereafter. The YJB annual Youth Justice Statistics show that the total number of disposals (court and pre-court) rose by over a quarter between 2002–3 and 2005–6.

This trend was noted by the Audit Commission in 2004 and it recommended actions to reduce the number of first-time entrants. The commission suggested that youth offending team (YOT) resources should be targeted at more serious offending and that too many children and young people were being brought into the formal system. Moreover, the increased numbers being formally dealt with was not a result of increased offending by children and young people but, rather, because a greater proportion of minor offences were being met with a formal response. This trend has been exacerbated as a consequence of government-imposed targets, including bringing offences to justice and the related crime recording standards, which have the effect of reducing police discretion and increasing formal responses to minor offending. From a children's human rights perspective, this is indicative of the unnecessary criminalization of children and a youth justice system that fails to deal informally with offending and to reserve formal proceedings as a 'last resort'.

In response to such trends, the YJB introduced a 'performance measure' related to reducing, year on year, the number of first-time entrants to the youth justice system. Significant government funding, administered by the YJB, has been provided for services targeted at preventing children and young people considered to be 'at risk' (of offending or involvement in anti-social behaviour) from entering the youth justice system. An example of such a service develoment is the Youth Inclusion and Support Panel (YISP). Although YOTs have been required to comply with new counting rules to monitor this new performance measure, data have only been collected since April 2005 and it is too early to discern any substantive trends. Some YOTs continue to report increased numbers of first-time entrants. In other areas, however, local youth justice plans indicate a modest reduction. The YJB target for reducing the numbers of first-time entrants has been mirrored in other local authority measures and in targets contained in local children's planning and area agreements in many parts of the country. In addition, the 'prevent and deter' strand of the government's prolific and other priority offenders strategy supports the target of reducing first-time entrants (by identifying those most at risk of becoming first-time entrants and providing enhanced prevention services).

In the context of formal criminal process, the inclusion of reprimands and final warnings in the definition of first-time entry is incongruent with the notion of diversion. Such arrangements tend to draw younger children to the attention of youth justice agencies and compound the effects of the low age of criminal responsibility in the UK.

The current definition of first-time entrants is destined to require modification. Apart from reprimands and final warnings, children may be subject to anti-social behaviour measures as well as financial penalties in the form of penalty notices for disorderly behaviour and fixed-penalty notices. New legislation is progressing through Parliament, and it is likely to provide a version of the (adult) 'conditional caution' for children and young people. Furthermore, an informal police-administered restorative justice option is also being introduced (not in statute). This array of 'pre-court' options clouds the current definition of first-time entry, particularly as YOTs are devoting a significant proportion of their budgets to 'targeted prevention', such as youth inclusion programmes.

Detailed monitoring of those entering the formal criminal justice system is important from many perspectives, including cost, planning and children's human rights. But the current definition of first-time entrants is flawed. Prevention and pre-court measures have become increasingly complex, with an uncomfortable interplay between diversion, formal youth justice and the burgeoning anti-social behaviour agenda.

Geoff Monaghan

Related entries

Audit Commission; Caution; Criminalization; Early intervention; Informalism; Labelling theory; *Politicization; Net-widening; Reprimands and final warnings; Restorative youth conferencing; Youth inclusion and support panels (YISPs); Youth inclusion programmes (YIPs); Youth Justice and Criminal Evidence Act 1999; Youth justice plans.*

Key texts and sources

Audit Commission (2004) *Youth Justice 2004: A Review of the Reformed Youth Justice System.* London: Audit Commission.

Goldson, B. (2005a) 'Beyond formalism: towards "informal" approaches to youth crime and youth justice', in T. Bateman and J. Pitts (eds) *The RHP Companion to Youth Justice.* Lyme Regis: Russell House.

Home Office, Department for Constitutional Affairs and the Attorney General's Office (2006) *Delivering Simple, Speedy, Summary Justice.* London: Department for Constitutional Affairs.

Nacro (2005e) *Out of Court: Making the Most of Diversion for Young People. Youth Crime Briefing.* London: Nacro.

United Nations (1985) *United Nations Standard Minimum Rules for the Administration of Juvenile Justice.* New York, NY: United Nations.

Youth Justice Board (2006) *Corporate and Business Plan, 2006/07–2008/09.* London: YJB (available online at **http://www.yjb.gov.uk/Publications/ Scripts/prodDownload.asp?idproduct=301&eP**).

FIXED-PENALTY NOTICES (FPNs)

A fixed-penalty notice (FPN) is notice of a financial penalty following the commission of specific offences often called 'environmental crimes'. A FPN can be issued by 'authorized officers' of a local authority and/or community support officers for specific offences.

Originating from anti-dog-fouling and anti-littering powers, the Anti-social Behaviour Act 2003 extended the range of 'offences' within the reach of a fixed-penalty notice (FPN) to include nuisance parking, vehicle abandonment, waste disposal, noise, graffiti, littering, fly-posting and flyer distribution.

FPNs are distinct from penalty notices for disorderly behaviour. For certain offences, 'local authority' can mean parish councils. Issuing a FPN allows 14 days for the payment of the penalty to the local authority. Payment discharges liability from prosecution. The FPN states the amount of the penalty and may offer a 'discount' for quick payment (normally within the first seven days). Failure to pay results in prosecution, the outcome of which will be at least a fine greater than the amount of the original penalty.

The FPN provisions apply to children and young persons aged 10 upwards, with no requirement to involve a parent/guardian at any point, although guidance suggests that parents/guardians should be present at the point of issue. It also suggests that parish councils should not issue FPNs to 10–15-year-olds. Records of the issue of FPNs will be needed to keep track of payments and are required by the Secretary of State.

There is no provision for formally making a parent liable for payment of an FPN issued to a child/young person, other than by prosecution. Guidance has been issued by the Department for the Environment, Food and Rural Affairs (Defra) for FPNs overall. Supplementary guidance applies specifically to under 18-year-olds.

FPNs will bring children/young people into contact with 'justice' officials other than uniformed constables. Those issuing FPNs have the power to take a photograph of the subject. It is unclear what happens to the photographs after payment is made. The possible extension of FPNs may form part of the expansion of summary justice under the 'Respect' agenda.

Spike Cadman

Related entries

Anti-social Behaviour Act 2003; Fines; First-time entrants; Respect (government action plan).

Key texts and sources

Defra (2004) *Guidance for Part 6, Anti-social Behaviour Act 2003*. London: Defra (available online at http://www.defra.gov.uk/environment/localenv/pdf/asbact-guidance).

Defra (2006a) *Fixed Penalty Notices: Guidance on the Fixed Penalty Notice Provisions of the Environmental Protection Act 1990, the Clean Neighbourhoods and Environment Act 2005, and Other Legislation*. London: Defra (available online at http://www.defra.gov.uk/environment/localenv/legislation/cnea/fixedpenaltynotices).

Defra (2006b) *Issuing Fixed Penalty Notices to Juveniles: Guidance on Issuing Fixed Penalty Notices Contained within the Clean Neighbourhoods and Environment Act 2005*. London: Defra (available online at http://www.defra.gov.uk/environment/localenv/legislation/cnea/juveniles).

Nacro (2004a) *Anti-social Behaviour Orders and Associated Measures. Part 2. Youth Crime Briefing*. London: Nacro.

See the Office of Public Sector Information's website (http://www.opsi.gov.uk/acts/acts2003/20030038.htm) for the text of the Anti-social Behaviour Act 2003.

The Home Office's document, *Fixed Penalty Notices*, is available online at http://www.homeoffice.gov.uk/anti-social-behaviour/penalties/penalty-notices/. The Respect Agenda's document, Fixed Penalty Notices, is available online at http://www.respect.gov.uk/members/article.aspx?id=7990.

FOSTERING

Fostering refers to out-of-home placements for children and young people aged under 18 (in some instances, under 21). The term includes emergency, respite, therapeutic, specialist, treatment, remand, post-custody and intensive fostering. Placements may be short, medium or long term and can be provided by social services, independent fostering agencies, extended family (kinship care) or through private agreements with non-relatives. In the USA, the term 'foster care' also includes placement in residential units.

Foster care is the main form of care for children who cannot be looked after at home. There are approximately 42,000 children in foster care in England alone (70 per cent of the total 'looked after' population). It is often used to provide temporary care for children who are, or whose parents are, experiencing severe difficulties, including illness, bereavement, neglect or abuse.

Since the 1970s, the use of foster care has been extended to new populations of children who were previously thought to present too many difficulties to be placed with foster carers. Evidence now demonstrates that, given sufficient support, remuneration and recognition, foster carers can be recruited and retained to look after these children successfully, enabling children who would otherwise be placed in institutions to be looked after in the community. Children in foster care now include those with physical disabilities and/or mental health difficulties, those with complex psychological and social needs and those involved in offending and/or anti-social behaviour. This has resulted in the development of a number of fostering initiatives, including multi-dimensional treatment foster care and therapeutic foster care that aim to help the child change his or her behaviour. Children involved in the youth justice system may be provided with a foster care placement while they are on remand ('remand fostering'), as part of a supervision order ('intensive fostering') or post-custody (for example, while on licence from a detention and training order).

Foster care was traditionally provided by two-parent families, but carers can now be sole carers (male or female), gay or lesbian and/or disabled. Only 5 per cent of mainstream foster carers in England and Wales are from black or minority ethnic backgrounds, despite increasing recognition that the needs of black and minority ethnic children and young people are best met within foster families of the same ethnic or cultural background. Foster carers are typically paid an allowance. From April 2007, the government has introduced national minimum fostering allowances of between £100 and £175 per child per week, depending on the age of the child, but rates can be as high as £700 per child per week.

Despite a stated commitment to increase placement stability, many children who are fostered long term experience frequent moves between foster placements, residential units and/or home, often with negative consequences for the children themselves. Placement planning and regular review are key to good outcomes for children, but many placements are made hurriedly. Placements are known to be disrupted more often when social workers are not open with foster carers about the extent of the young people's difficulties. Foster carers are often able to manage some very difficult behaviour – including violence, aggression and sexualized behaviour – provided they are fully informed and supported by social services authorities. Furthermore, fostered children also need information about the foster carers before they move in with them, and many currently feel insufficiently involved in pre-placement decisions and placement planning. However, placements made in the youth justice context are often, of necessity, expedited.

It is widely accepted that it is more problematic to provide foster care for adolescents than for younger children, and there is a high rate of disruption in adolescent placements. Disruption rates appear to decrease where the levels of support for carers and for children are highest, and this raises important issues for youth offending teams. Evidence suggests that children and young people who have spent time in the 'care system' are significantly more likely to experience unemployment, drug use, mental health problems, debt and imprisonment, with about a third facing serious long-term difficulties. Research from the USA indicates that a service that provides a highly supported environment for children has more successful outcomes post-placement.

Jo Lipscombe and Barbara Russell

Related entries

Alternatives to custody; Children Act 1989; Children Act 2004; Criminal Justice Act 1991; Criminal Justice and Immigration Bill 2006–7 to 2007–8; Looked-after children (LAC); Menu-based sentencing; Remand; Remand fostering; Remand management; Safeguarding; Supervision orders.

Key texts and sources

Chamberlain, P. (1994) *Family Connections: A Treatment Foster Care Model for Adolescents with Delinquency.* Eugene, Oregon: Castalia Publishing.
Farmer, E., Moyers, S. and Lipscombe, J. (2004) *Fostering Adolescents.* London: Jessica Kingsley.

Sellick, C. and Howell, D. (2003) *Innovative, Tried and Tested: A Review of Good Practice in Fostering.* London: Social Care Institute for Excellence.

Wilson, K., Sinclair, I., Taylor, C., Pithouse, A. and Sellick, C. (2004) *Fostering Success: An Exploration of the Research Literature in Foster Care. Knowledge Review 5.* London: Social Care Institute for Excellence.

See also the websites of the British Association for Adoption and Fostering (**www.baaf.org.uk**) and the Fostering Network (**www.fostering.net**).

G

GANGS

In early usage, the term 'gang' tended to refer to groups of adolescent boys residing in a particular neighbourhood who had developed shared bonds based around loyalty to the group and territorial boundaries. In later manifestations it is used to denote more organized groups that are engaged in illegal activities. In this sense 'gangs' are hierarchically organized, often adopt identifying insignia and engage in behaviours that may be particularly prone to the use of violence. Since the 1980s the phenomenon of the 'girl gang' has also emerged.

Much of the research that has been conducted around 'gangs' and 'gang cultures' has taken place in the USA. The first significant academic research into gangs was conducted by Frederic Thrasher (1927) in 1920s Chicago. He saw gangs as resulting from boys' attempts to provide meaning, structure and excitement to their chaotic but often mundane lives. By the 1950s, however, discussion of gangs was much more likely to be associated with delinquent behaviour. Albert Cohen (1955) famously theorized that delinquent subcultures develop in working-class areas wherever young people are denied the status available in middle-class society. Young people then adjust to their circumstances by constructing alternative social norms and values in their peer groups. Subcultural theories of the gang have flourished in the USA and elsewhere, but the gang 'problem' itself has ebbed and flowed. This has highlighted the tendency for gangs to emerge in times of economic stress where legitimate opportunities for social and economic advancement are severely curtailed.

After a period of relative prosperity in the 1960s, gangs appeared to be a dwindling phenomenon across the USA. They re-emerged in the 1980s recession, however, in many towns and cities and were closely associated with the production and sale of illegal drugs. It has been argued that these newly 'organized gangs' are run along business lines and that their members are more likely to use guns and violence to protect lucrative drug markets.

There is a particular stereotype of US gangs: predominantly male, adopting gang insignia and 'colours', and recruiting younger 'members' to ensure their longevity. They are highly organized, territorial and in open conflict with other rival gangs. However, research appears to show that there are as many different types of gang as there are urban neighbourhoods, and each adapts to local circumstances which change over time and from city to city. Not all 'gangs' or 'gang members' are involved in breaking the law or are associated with violence and guns. Some appear to offer more in the vein of practical and emotional support to their members and associates and wither away as local conditions change. The inherent 'maleness' of gangs has also been questioned. Anne Campbell (1984) has explored the position of girls in contemporary US gangs, and there is some evidence to show that 'girl gangs' are beginning to organize in some US cities. Many have argued that gangs are negativistic and malicious but others contend that the activities of gangs are highly organized, have evolved as an adaptive response to structural conditions such as unemployment, poverty and racism and are deeply entrenched in the normative values of American society.

In the UK the 'gang problem' is more difficult still to locate. Many researchers have looked for gangs over successive decades and simply not found them. They appear to be few and far between, and those that have been identified do not conform to the US stereotypes. The typical gang in Britain has hitherto been made up of older, established 'career criminals', although there is some concern that groups of young people may be adopting US gang styles in cities such as Birmingham, Manchester and London. A recent spate of high-profile gun-related fatalities has given rise to a new wave of concern about young people and gangs in the UK. It is important to retain a measured response to such phenomena, however, and to avoid moral panic. Although the issues require serious attention, many groups of young people identified as 'gangs' may actually be little more than peer groups and friends who have become involved in typical adolescent behaviour in the public realm.

Karen Evans

Related entries

Delinquency; Gender and justice; Media reporting; Moral panic; Street crime; Subculture; Subcultural theory; Youth and policing.

Key texts and sources

Batchelor, S. (2002) 'The myth of girl gangs', in Y. Jewkes and G. Letherby (eds) *Criminology: A Reader*. London: Sage.

Campbell, A. (1984) *The Girls in the Gang: A Report from New York City*. Oxford: Blackwell.

Cohen, A.K. (1955) *Delinquent Boys: The Culture of the Gang*. Glencoe, IL: Free Press.

Mares, D. (2000) 'Globalization and gangs: the Manchester case', *Focaal*, 35: 151–69.

Patrick, J. (1973) *A Glasgow Gang Observed*. London: Eyre Methuen.

Pitts, J. (2007) 'Violent youth gangs in the UK', *Safer Society: The Journal of Crime Reduction and Community Safety*, 32: 14–17.

Thrasher, F.M. (1927) *The Gang: A Study of 1,313 Gangs in Chicago*. Chicago, IL: University of Chicago Press.

GATEKEEPING

Gatekeeping is concerned with monitoring young offenders' entry to, and progression through, the youth justice system with a view to diversion and proportionality.

The police are often the primary gatekeepers at the entry point of the youth justice system because of their discretionary powers to divert or prosecute/charge. However, gatekeeping applies equally to the youth justice system where it might refer to attempts by youth offending teams to divert persistent and/or serious young offenders from custody through the development of alternative community-based programmes.

Gatekeeping reflects a concerted effort to avoid the pitfalls of net-widening, up-tariffing and, ultimately, the overuse of custody. In the 1980s, influenced by a justice as opposed to a welfare model, youth justice practitioners (including police officers, social workers and probation officers) worked collaboratively to monitor and manage the processing of young offenders to ensure that interventions were proportionate to their offending and avoided unneccesary levels of penetration into the youth justice system. The 'new orthodoxy' in youth justice became one of systems management, maximum diversion from court and custody and minimum intervention in young offenders' personal lives commensurate with the seriousness of offending.

In practice this meant that police cautioning decisions were carefully scrutinized and 'gatekept' to ensure that they were used as alternatives to prosecution. Similarly, sentencing recommendations in court reports were monitored to ensure maximum diversion from custody and the deployment of intensive community-based programmes solely as direct alternatives. The systems management ethos underlying gatekeeping in the 1980s was backed up by criminal justice legislation and Home Office policy. This served officially to sanction the expansion of police cautioning and placed tight restrictions on the power of the courts to confer custodial sentences on young offenders.

By effectively monitoring and managing the processing of young offenders through the youth justice system, the gatekeeping policies and practices of the 1980s were successful in substantially reducing the number of prosecutions brought against children and the rate of custody without incurring any significant increase in the level of youth crime. The politicization of youth crime and youth justice since the early 1990s, however, has meant that gatekeeping initiatives have tended to fall out of favour. Indeed, the Crime and Disorder Act 1998 prioritized robust early intervention in order to 'nip offending in the bud'. A new statutory system of police reprimands and final warnings – often accompanied by 'rehabilitation programmes' – has been set in place which undermines the notion of diverting young people from the damaging consequences of criminalization. The number of young people officially prosecuted has escalated dramatically, despite a drop in known offending, and early entry to the youth justice system has again accelerated young offenders' progress through the sentencing tariff, leading to a sharp rise in the rate of custody.

Patricia Gray

Related entries

Caution; Crime and Disorder Act 1998; Diversion; Early intervention; Net-widening; Pre-sentence reports (PSRs); Politicization; Proportionality; Systems management; Youth Diversion Scheme.

Key texts and sources

Bateman, T. (2006a) 'Youth crime and justice: research, evaluation and "evidence"', in B. Goldson and J. Muncie (eds) *Youth Crime and Justice: Critical Issues.* London: Sage.

Goldson, B. (2000d) 'Wither diversion? Interventionism and the new youth justice', in B. Goldson (ed.) *The New Youth Justice.* Lyme Regis: Russell House.

Morris, A. and Giller, H. (1987) *Understanding Juvenile Justice.* London: Croom Helm.

Pitts, J. (1992) 'The end of an era', *Howard Journal of Criminal Justice*, 31: 133–49.

Rutherford, A. (1992) *Growing Out of Crime: The New Era.* Winchester: Waterside Press.

GENDER AND JUSTICE

Gender in the context of youth justice is often taken to relate to the differences in patterns of crime, sentencing and treatment responses to boys/young men and girls/young women. But there is also a deeper meaning that relates to 'social constructions' and expectations of young people's behaviour. In other words, societal expectations of, and assumptions about, gender-appropriate behaviour can shape both criminal actions and formal responses to them.

There are volumes of research about young people and delinquency. Most of this research reflects studies and understandings of boys' delinquent behaviour, whether from a psychological or sociological perspective. But it is only recently that searching questions have been asked as to whether theories generated to describe boys' or men's offending can apply to girls and women (what is commonly called the 'generalizability problem'). The implication is that general theories of crime must be able to take account of both boys' and girls' (criminal) behaviour, and must be able to highlight factors that operate differently on them. Beyond this, there has been recent recognition of gender relations in which gender is seen not as a natural fact but as a complex, historical and cultural product – a 'social construction'. Thus complex gender codes are internalized in a myriad of ways to regulate behaviour.

Although the 'maleness of crime' has traditionally been acknowledged in mainstream criminology, it has not often been viewed as a socially constructed concept. But a sociology of masculinity has now emerged and, given the fact criminal statistics – as well as self-report studies – reflect that more boys than girls are involved in crime, a key question is perhaps: what is it in the social construction of maleness that is so criminogenic? Notions of power, toughness, authority and competition all spring to mind. Equally, we might ask what it is about the way in which femaleness is constructed that seemingly leads to lower levels of involvement in youth crime.

The treatment of boys should not be taken to be either the norm or acceptable, of course. There have been, and there continue to be, major concerns about the number of boys in custody, for example. But policies and practices that particularly affect *girls* are deserving of particular attention: first, because girls have tended to be overlooked in youth justice discourse; and, second, due to the symbolic import of changes – in society in general and the youth justice system in particular – that have affected youth justice system responses to girls in recent years.

The key points to note here are that girls have always been treated differently from boys in the youth justice system, and the response has been 'welfare dominated' in the main. This differentiation has arguably been based on myths, muddles and misconceptions about girls' delinquent behaviour that reflect societal attitudes and expectations of behaviour as much as *actual* behaviour. Indeed, research has consistently shown that decisions about girls have often been motivated by concerns about their sexuality and their independence as much as their criminal behaviour. Thus welfare concerns, shaped by social expectations about what might be appropriate for boys and girls, have been reflected in their treatment, with girls commonly being brought into allied agencies (such as social service departments and children's homes) as well as the youth justice system. Related to concerns about girls' behaviour is the fact that they have often been seen as a 'difficult group' with whom to work, but this belief sometimes masks a double standard applied to girls who do not manifest 'gender-appropriate' behaviour.

Changes in girls' offending behaviour have been noted in recent times but, while there are justifiable concerns by an evident upturn in girls' involvement in crime, such changes arguably reflect broader trends in society. The late twentieth century witnessed something of a moral panic about girls and crime. They were seen to be committing more crime, becoming more violent and becoming more likely to form or join a gang, as well as engaging in illegal drug taking alongside boys. There has been some statistical support for such claims, but much media exaggeration and deviance amplification as well.

Nevertheless, perceptions of change have fuelled concerns about the abandonment of traditional welfare-oriented approaches to offending by girls, and there has been an increasingly interventionist and punitive response to them, in spite of limited evidence of their overall increased criminality in recent years. We have seen a sharp rise in the use of community penalties and increases in the number of girls in custody.

In part this may reflect the increasing visibility of girls, with the 'culture of the bedroom' (as a place for girls to meet, listen to music and so on) having been replaced by a construction of adolescence that revolves around out-of-home leisure activities. Thus moral panics about girls and their changing behaviour have been influenced by conspicuous consumption among the young and the leisure pursuits of 'pubbing' and 'clubbing', which involve a conspicuous street presence.

Contemporary challenges for gender and youth justice revolve around the need to make national provision for young people 'gender sensitive'. There is need to find a way of responding to girls' *real* needs without fuelling stereotypical ideas about their behaviour.

Loraine Gelsthorpe

Related entries

Adolescence; Critical criminology; Delinquency; Deviance amplification; Gangs; Media reporting; Moral panic; Punitiveness; Welfare.

Key texts and sources

Alder, C. and Worrall, A. (2004) 'A contemporary crisis?', in C. Alder and A. Worrall (eds) *Girls' Violence: Myths and Realities*. Albany, NY: State University of New York Press.

Batchelor, S. and Burman, M. (2004) 'Working with girls and young women', in G. McIvor (ed.) *Women Who Offend*. London: Jessica Kingsley.

Chesney-Lind, M. and Sheldon, R. (2004) *Girls, Delinquency and Juvenile Justice* (3rd edn). Belmont, CA: Wadsworth/Thomson.

Gelsthorpe, L. and Sharpe, G. (2006) 'Gender, youth crime and justice', in B. Goldson and J. Muncie (eds) *Youth Crime and Justice: Critical Issues*. London: Sage.

Heidensohn, F. and Gelsthorpe, L. (2007) 'Gender and crime', in M. Maguire *et al.* (eds) *The Oxford Handbook of Criminology*. Oxford: Oxford University Press.

GOVERNANCE

> The concept of 'governance', though often used in an eclectic and loose fashion, refers to any act, means or tactic of governing – whether that involves how to be governed, how to govern others or how to govern oneself. Crucially, it draws attention to processes of governing 'beyond government'.

The key feature of governance theory is its break with state-centred thinking about the exercise of political power. Typically it directs our attention to changes in the meaning of government: *new* processes of governing, *changing* conditions of ordered rule and *new* methods by which society is governed (Rhodes 1997). The concept has been employed by criminologists in a number of ways to explore changes in the control of crime, shifts in the salience of crime as a political/public issue and competing ways of constructing and controlling 'problem' populations.

In one interpretation of 'governance', Simon (1997) has argued that the salience of law and order in the USA is such that its citizens are continually governing themselves through their reaction to crime. The continual reworking and expansion of justice systems; a never-ending stream of legislation apparently dominating all other government concerns; the political use of crime as a means to secure electoral gain; the excessive media fascination with all things 'criminal'; and the obsession with regulation, whether through families, schools or training programmes, all contrive to reduce tolerance and encourage negative attitudes to the 'diverse' and the 'different'. Crime (and increasingly youth disorder) has become prioritized in the allocation of public resources. Reaction to crime has become a driving force in (changing) lifestyles.

Crawford (1997) argues that attempts to control crime through partnerships of statutory, commercial and voluntary organizations also imply a new process of governing through negotiation and bargaining, rather than command and coercion. The devolution and privatization of functions previously undertaken by statutory agencies suggest a fragmentation of power into a plurality of competing agencies with none being able to exercise overall control. The idea of 'joined-up' government to tackle multifaceted and complex problems (such as youth offending) through multi-agency partnerships – employing a broad spectrum of social policy interventions – represents a significant break with some forms of centralized power.

A further conception identifies the omnipresent plurality and hybridity of 'modes of youth governance' rather than any neat correspondence between policy discourse, policy formation and practical implementation. Muncie (2006), for example, notes that, while contemporary youth justice is embroiled in neoliberal processes of responsibilization and risk management coupled with neoconservative authoritarian strategies, it also works alongside (or within) 'new' conceptions of social inclusion and restoration. These contradictory strategies reinforce multiple localized translations of policy and practice rather than any form of international or national uniformity.

John Muncie

Related entries

Anti-social behaviour (ASB); Crime and disorder reduction (CDR); Crime prevention; Criminalization; Criminalization of social policy; Governmentality; Net-widening; Surveillance.

Key texts and sources

Crawford, A. (1997) *The Local Governance of Crime: Appeals to Community and Partnerships*. Oxford: Clarendon Press.

Muncie, J. (2006) 'Governing young people: coherence and contradiction in contemporary youth justice', *Critical Social Policy*, 26: 770–93.

Newman, J. (2001) *Modernising Governance*. London: Sage.

Rhodes, R.A.W. (1997) *Understanding Governance: Policy Networks, Governance, Reflexivity and Accountability*. Buckingham: Open University Press.

Simon, J. (1997) 'Governing through crime', in G. Fisher and L. Friedman (eds) *The Crime Conundrum: Essays on Criminal Justice*. Boulder, CO: Westview Press.

GOVERNMENTALITY

> Govermentality is a theoretical approach,
> derived from the French philosopher, Michel
> Foucault, that draws attention to the numerous
> means through which power is exercised and
> how particular 'mentalities' of governing are
> constructed, both within *and* beyond the state.

Foucault (1991) uses the term 'governmentality' to refer to a range of techniques and processes concerned with the regulation of conduct – that is, any activity aimed at shaping, guiding or affecting the conduct of individuals and populations. Such activities might include, for example, state-sponsored techniques of domination but also techniques for self-government. Foucault suggested that, rather than framing investigations of regulation and control in terms of the state or politics, it would be more productive to investigate the formation and transformation of rationalities, discourses, proposals, strategies and technologies in order to explore, in his terms, 'the conduct of conduct' (Dean 1999).

Governmentality theory challenges reductionist analyses by focusing on how particular modes of power depend on specific ways of thinking (rationalities of power) and of acting (technologies of power) (Garland 1997). It is less concerned, for example, with how law is *imposed* and more with the *tactic* of using particular knowledges to arrange things in such a way that populations accept being governed and begin to govern themselves. It implies that power is not simply achieved through sovereign state dominance but through myriad institutions, procedures, reflections and calculations in which citizens are 'made up' and come to realize themselves. Governing is viewed as heterogeneous in thought and action – captured to a certain extent in the various words available to describe and enact it: education, control, influence, regulation, administration, management, therapy, reformation, guidance (Rose 1999).

In criminology in general, and in youth justice studies in particular, governmentality theory has typically been employed in the context of exploring forms of neoliberal governance. It draws attention, for example, to the 'ways of thinking' that underpin processes of new managerialism; to where governance is achieved 'at a distance'; to where a language of risks and rewards has transformed that of care and control; and to where partnerships, communities and families have been 'responsibilized' to take an active role in their own self-government. Recognition of this dispersal of governance has opened a door to examining how youth crime is 'governed', not simply by the police and formal control agents in the youth justice apparatus but also by the 'rationalities' employed by the likes of the insurance industry, employers, potential victims, head teachers, shopping-centre managers, cognitive psychologists, parenting counsellors and so on.

This raises fundamental questions for youth justice research, such as how has the nature of young offenders been re-imagined in shifts from welfare to neoliberal forms of governance? How can multiple, overlapping and sometimes contradictory discourses of youth justice coexist? What new constructions of youth offending emerge, and what are the practical outcomes of managing 'mixes' of the protective, the preventive and the punitive (Muncie and Hughes 2002)?

John Muncie

Related entries

Governance; Managerialism; Responsibilization.

Key texts and sources

Dean, M. (1999) *Governmentality: Power and Rule in Modern Society*. London: Sage.

Foucault, M. (1991) 'Governmentality', in G. Burchell *et al.* (eds) *The Foucault Effect: Studies in Governmentality*. Hemel Hempstead: Harvester.

Garland, D. (1997) '"Governmentality" and the problem of crime', *Theoretical Criminology*, 1: 173–214.

Muncie, J. and Hughes, G. (2002) 'Modes of youth governance: political rationalities, criminalisation and resistance', in J. Muncie *et al.* (eds) *Youth Justice: Critical Readings*. London: Sage.

Rose, N. (1999) *Powers of Freedom*. Cambridge: Cambridge University Press.

GRAVE OFFENCES

> A grave offence is an offence committed by a child or young person considered sufficiently serious to justify the imposition of long-term detention.

There is no legal definition of a grave crime. Rather, the statutory framework delineates a large category of offences that may, at the discretion of the court, be considered a grave crime in a particular case. Where the youth court takes the view that a sentence of more than two years – the standard maximum custodial penalty available for those below the age of 18 – is a 'real possibility', jurisdiction will be refused. The case will instead be tried at the Crown court, and the young person will be liable to a sentence of long-term detention.

Originally, such arrangements were limited to the offences of homicide and wounding with intent. Recent case law has confirmed that the use of custody outside the mainstream penalties available in the youth court should be viewed as 'very much a long stop, reserved for very serious offences'. Nonetheless, the scope of the sentencing provisions has been widened significantly over time, leading to a corresponding expansion in the range of offences that can be deemed 'grave crimes' and a rapid growth in the use of long-term detention.

The Criminal Justice Act 1961 provided for the application of the grave crime procedures for any offence for which an adult could receive a custodial sentence of 14 years or more. Prior to 1994, long-term detention for children aged 10–13 was restricted to cases of murder, attempted murder and manslaughter. The Criminal Justice and Public Order Act 1994 lowered – from 14 to 10 – the age at which the grave crime provisions apply. Moreover, subsequent legislation has added a number of further offences that can be tried and sentenced as grave crimes even though the adult maximum penalty is below 14 years. Consequently, any of the following can now be deemed a grave crime:

- An offence punishable in the case of an adult with 14 years or more imprisonment including rape, robbery, residential burglary, supplying drugs, aggravated vehicle taking, and handling stolen goods.
- A range of sexual offences including sexual assault, child sex offences committed by a child or young person, sexual activity with a family member and inciting a child family member to engage in sexual activity.
- Particular firearms offences (if committed by young people aged 16 or 17), which must be tried and sentenced in the Crown court and which carry a statutory *minimum* penalty of three years detention.

The youth justice system in England and Wales has attracted substantial criticism for being insufficiently distinct in its treatment of children and young people and adult offenders ('adulteration'). The grave crime provisions, by linking the treatment of children and young people to maximum *adult* penalties, exemplify some of the problems inherent in this approach. Legislation primarily directed at adults can, by default, expand the pool of offences that can be considered a grave crime in the case of a child or young person. Thus the Theft Act 1968 – that increased the maximum sentence for burglary to 14 years' detention – produced the immediate (and perhaps unintended consequence) that children charged with burglary became liable to long-term detention.

Tim Bateman

Related entries

'Adulteration'; Criminal Justice and Public Order Act 1994; Crown court; Dangerousness; Detention for public protection (DPP); Gravity factors (prosecution and sentencing); Long-term detention; Youth courts.

Key texts and sources

Bateman, T. (2005b) 'Custody and policy', in T. Bateman and J. Pitts (eds) *The RHP Companion to Youth Justice*. Lyme Regis: Russell House.

Nacro (2002a) *Children who Commit Grave Crimes*. London: Nacro.

Nacro (2004c) *The Grave Crimes Provisions and Long Term Detention. Youth Crime Briefing*. London: Nacro.

Stone, N. (2002) 'Shorter terms of Section 91 detention', *Youth Justice*, 2: 47–9.

GRAVITY FACTORS (PROSECUTION AND SENTENCING)

> Gravity factors relate to the key criteria relevant in deciding whether to charge, warn or reprimand a young person for an offence. They include the young person's offending history; the seriousness of the offence; the nature of the offence and the circumstances that surround the offence and the context within which it was committed. Gravity factors also impact on court sentencing.

The conditions that can make the assessment of an offence 'more serious' are known as aggravating factors, while mitigating factors lead to a 'less serious' assessment. Some factors apply to all offences (known as 'general factors'), while others (known as 'offence-specific gravity factors') apply to specific offences only. Gravity factors impact on decisions at the level of charge and prosecution and at the level of sentence. Gravity factors were provided by the Crime and Disorder Act 1998 and were illuminated via Home Office guidance. They are not a new phenomenon, however, and existed before the 1998 Act.

Holdaway (2003) notes: 'in 1995 the Association of Chief Police Officers issued a list of gravity factors that was intended to promote greater consistency in cautioning decisions.' Holdaway's research into the introduction of final warning schemes, however, suggested that many police officers were not accustomed to using formal assessment instruments and that there was little evidence of gravity scores being systematically applied.

In 2006, Annex D of Home Office Circular 14/06 served to:

- incorporate the offences in the new legislation into the existing gravity factor matrix;
- discourage the use of reprimands/warning in inappropriate cases – that is, for offences for which offenders should be charged;
- seek greater consistency between police force areas; and
- promote the better recording of reprimands and warnings.

The gravity factor score matrix can be seen as part of a general 'managerialist' approach to youth justice whereby there is a reliance on pre-determined tables and numbers on which to base decisions to prosecute. Their introduction was designed to seek greater consistency although, as a result of the application of this standardized system, young people are being 'processed' by the youth justice system who might have previously been diverted away from it.

Gravity factors, in the more general sense, have been applied to the process of sentencing for some considerable time – both mitigating and aggravating circumstances have long been considered by sentencers when determining the nature and length of a sentence.

Richard Hester

Related entries

Assessment framework; Crime and Disorder Act 1998; Managerialism; Proportionality; Reprimands and final warnings; Risk management.

Key texts and sources

Holdaway, S. (2003) 'The final warning: appearance and reality', *Criminology and Criminal Justice*, 3: 351–67.

Home Office (2006g) *The Final Warning Scheme* (Circular 14/06). London: Home Office.

Pragnell, S. (2005) 'Reprimands and final warnings', in T. Bateman and J. Pitts (eds) *The RHP Companion to Youth Justice*. Lyme Regis: Russell House.

Stanley, C. (2005) 'The role of the courts', in T. Bateman and J. Pitts (eds) *The RHP Companion to Youth Justice*. Lyme Regis: Russell House.

GROUPWORK

> Groupwork is a form of intervention designed to explore collectively the different experiences and perspectives of a number of young people in order for them to work together to address particular challenges in their lives.

At its simplest, groupwork can be contrasted with individual work with young offenders. It is, however, a very complex task, characterized by numerous layers and levels that have to be linked together purposefully if the practice of groupwork is to have the desired effect. Groupwork has a long history in work with young people, although it only became a staple of work with young offenders following the inception of 'intermediate treatment' during the late 1960s and 1970s. It can take many forms but, as a concept, it is now established and accepted as an important method of intervention in the field of youth justice.

The rationale for groupwork is quite self-evident: most people live their lives in groups of one kind or another. Indeed, young offenders often tend to operate in groups. It seems logical, therefore, to address concerns about their attitudes and behaviour in a group context, using groupwork skills to encourage reflection on the past and to engender change in the future. However, although the objective of such groupwork is the purposeful and positive reinforcement of new law-abiding directions, there is always the risk of negative peer reinforcement unless the group process is managed very carefully. There are also difficulties relating to attrition and poor attendance, which can jeopardize the sustenance of effective group dynamics.

This raises a host of questions about *who* and *how many* should be in such groups, *when* such groups should be formed, *what* they should address (and *why*), *how* they should be organized and *where* they should take place. The fundamental challenge lies in the dual task of both managing the group and maintaining focus on the issues in question. This demands balancing the needs of the individuals within the group and adhering to specified group objectives. It requires attention to numerous levels of communication, participation and interaction – between group members and between members of the group and the staff involved. It calls for careful observation of roles and status in the group – roles can be allocated or chosen; status can be ascribed or achieved. All these issues, and more, will affect the effective functioning of the group and determine the extent to which it will remain 'on track'.

Engaging with all eventualities, and turning them into resources for group development in the direction of the group's objectives, is the essential skill of the groupworker. This is easier said than done, especially with often very challenging young people who are usually not voluntary participants.

Howard Williamson

Related entries

Cognitive-behaviour programmes; Intermediate treatment (IT).

Key texts and sources

Chapman, T. (2005) 'Group work with young people who offend', in T. Bateman and J. Pitts (eds) *The RHP Companion to Youth Justice*. Lyme Regis: Russell House.

Doel, M. and Sawdon, C. (1999) *The Essential Groupworker*. London: Jessica Kingsley.

Tuckman, B. (1965) 'Developmental sequence in small groups', *Psychological Bulletin*, 63: 384–99.

The Youth Justice Board's document, *Key Elements of Effective Practice: Offending Behaviour Programmes*, is available online at **http://www.yjb.gov.uk/Publications/Scripts/prodView.asp?idproduct=43&eP=PP**.

GROWING OUT OF CRIME

The peak years for offending are from the mid-teens to the mid-20s. Beyond that age prevalence declines sharply, to a low by the late 20s, and gradually becomes even lower as people get older. This process is known as 'growing out of crime', a term normally attributed to Andrew Rutherford.

While most child offenders do not go on to be adult offenders, most adult offenders were offenders as children. Because a child commits an offence, there is no reason to suppose that the world will have to wait until he or she becomes 23 before offending begins to slow down and stop. For children, offending can often be short-lived and can cease early, and there is plenty of research that portrays it as low level and opportunistic. It should come as no surprise that cautioning schemes, without any 'plus' elements, have been shown to be successful in terms of low rates of processed reoffending.

Growing out of crime normally refers to the generality of offences relating to property, certain crimes against the person and disorder. Other crimes – including fraud, theft from the workplace and sex offending – do not necessarily conform to the 'growing out of' thesis. There is a difference between male and female desistance, with girls/young women tending to leave criminal behaviour behind them earlier than boys/young men. Offending, as is well known, is overwhelmingly a male activity.

Growing out of crime is not just about growing out of offending; it is also about becoming less likely to be a victim of crime. There is evidence that being a victim by the age of 12 is one of the most significant indicators that a child will offend by the age of 15. Offenders and victims are often the same people, and the respective age-range distribution is similar.

Most of the interest shown by politicians, academics and professionals has been in why people offend rather than why they stop. This is changing, however, now that more interest, knowledge and information about desistance are emerging, but much work remains to be done. Relatively little is known about the characteristics that distinguish persistence from desistance in a life of crime. Of the possible explanations for desistance (coming mainly from North America), one posits age itself as the determining factor – that desistance just happens according to chronological ageing, irrespective of external considerations. Another makes a distinction between 'age' and 'maturity', with the argument that the latter is the key consideration and is about the development of personal 'social efficacy' such that desistance is normative and expected.

A further account based on development identifies two distinct delinquency categories. The first is the 'adolescence limited' group who typically will have no history of delinquency in earlier childhood, but this develops as normative and ends in the same way. The second group are the 'life-course persistent offenders' who typically started in early childhood and continue during adulthood and without desistance, irrespective, for example, of work and relationships.

A life-course explanation advances the argument that criminal activity is stable and persistent for only a small number of people who exhibit marked behaviour problems over many years and who, typically, do not desist. On the other hand, most young people will experience and ultimately cope with change and, for those who commit offences, they will desist. This account points out the significance of life events on behaviour. Factors such as work, relationships, social bonds and informal social control have an impact on desistance.

Desistance researchers who accept that there is more to stopping offending than just growing older have talked about the importance of both 'personal capital' and 'social capital'. In other words, while they need personal attributes and skills, offenders who want to stop committing crimes also need social resources, such as jobs, accommodation and relationships, to work in their favour to support successful transitions. Studies based in the UK show that people who offend and who are processed by the criminal justice system typically have higher levels of difficulties and exclusion than the general population. These include problems with accommodation, education, training and employment, health (particularly mental health), income, substance misuse, relationships, attitudes and behaviour.

Transitions from childhood to adulthood can be described as either 'slow track' or 'fast track'. Those who are slow track tend to stay longer in education and remain financially dependent on their parents and, generally speaking, experience a more successful transition. On the other hand, fast-trackers (those who are out in the world early, have few educational achievements, a disrupted background – perhaps including local authority care – and limited prospects) are much more likely to have a difficult time of it.

Stopping offending during young adult years generally takes place over time and tends not to be a single, sudden break from old behaviours. In other words, it is a *process* as distinct from an *event*. One of few longitudinal studies (the Cambridge Study in Delinquent Development) found, for those male offenders who did desist, that breaking ties with male companions from adolescence, seems to be significant. There is other (but not necessarily conclusive) evidence that employment and training prove most promising as turning points around the mid-20s. Similarly, relationships (cohabitation and/or marriage) have been shown to make more of a difference around this age, rather than earlier.

The Barrow Cadbury Trust report, published in 2006, argued that criminal justice policies in England and Wales do unnecessary damage to the life chances of young offenders and often make them more, not less, likely to reoffend. They make it harder to lead crime-free lives and exacerbate the widespread problems of social exclusion that other government policies aspire to ameliorate.

Transition from the youth to the adult criminal justice system in England and Wales is typically fragmented and can bring to an end programmes that give opportunities and diversions. In British courts there is no age flexibility that can take account of differing levels of maturity, unlike in some European jurisdictions. The Probation Service heralded a major strategic imperative for working with young adult offenders in 2001. That sense of a coherent, co-ordinated approach quickly disappeared, however, and to date it has not reappeared. Nor has desistance theory yet had much visible impact on how services are organized and delivered.

Paul Kelly

Related entries

Delinquency; Desistance; Developmental criminology; Diversion; Gender and justice; Informalism; Labelling theory; Normalization; Persistent young offenders; Victimization; Victims.

Key texts and sources

Barrow Cadbury Commission on Young Adults in the Criminal Justice System (2006) *Lost in Transition: Report.* London: Barrow Cadbury Trust.

McAra, L. and McVie, S. (2007) 'Youth justice? The impact of system contact on patterns of desistance from offending', *European Journal of Criminology*, 4: 315–45.

Rutherford, A. (2002b) *Growing Out of Crime: The New Era* (2nd edn). Winchester: Waterside Press.

The Edinburgh Study of Youth Transitions and Crime is available online at **www.law.ed.ac.uk/cls/esytc**.

H

HOSPITAL ORDERS

> Hospital orders provide a sentence for young offenders diagnosed with mental disorder and, as such, comprise an alternative to penal custody.

Hospital orders are available to youth and Crown courts in England and Wales in cases where mental health criteria are met that justify 'detention' in hospital and where the offence is punishable by a custodial sentence. A hospital order results in 'detention' for up to six months. Decisions to release or further detain are made under mental health legislation and procedures. A Crown court making a hospital order can add a restriction order requiring detention for a specified or indeterminate period. Hospital orders are also available where a formal conviction has not been possible due to certain categories of mental disorder or where the young person is 'unfit to plead'. Further, the order can provide an alternative to 'preventive custodial sentences' relating to 'dangerousness'.

Mental health problems are disproportionately identified among children in the criminal justice system, yet statutory mental health provisions are rarely used. Despite concern that the youth justice system provides the primary response to those whose needs are best met in health or other systems, there remains a lack of consensus regarding the relationship between mental health and criminal and welfare responses.

Similar provision is made in Northern Ireland under the Mental Health (Northern Ireland) Order 1986 (recently amended after legal challenge regarding human rights). In Scotland, 'compulsion orders' are provided by the Mental Health (Care and Treatment) Act 2003. The law in Northern Ireland and in England and Wales is under review as per the Mental Health Bill 2004.

Geoff Monaghan

Related entries

Children in custody; Dangerousness; Mental health and young offenders; Mental health legislation; Vulnerability.

Key texts and sources

Ashford, M., Chard, A. and Redhouse, N. (2006) *Defending Young People in the Criminal Justice System* (2nd edn). London: Legal Action Group.

Crown Prosecution Service (2004) *The Code for Crown Prosecutors.* London: Crown Prosecution Service (available online at http://www.cps.gov.uk/publications/docs/code2004english.pdf).

Jones, R. (2006) *Mental Health Act Manual* (10th edn). London: Sweet & Maxwell.

Nacro (2005d) *Mental Health Legislation and the Youth Justice System. Youth Crime Briefing.* London: Nacro.

HUMAN RIGHTS ACT 1998

> The Human Rights Act 1998 incorporates into UK law the rights and freedoms of the European Convention on Human Rights. It came into force in Scotland in 1999 and in England and Wales in 2000.

At the Labour Party conference in 1997, Jack Straw – the Home Secretary at the time – referred to the incorporation of the European Convention on Human Rights (ECHR) into UK law as 'bringing rights home'. Many of the rights in the ECHR – the right to a fair trial, freedom of expression, protection from torture and the right to privacy – date back to the Magna Carta. The Human Rights Act 1998 allows individuals to bring a human rights case to a British court rather than having to make a claim to the European Court of Human Rights in Strasbourg (which can take several years). The Act thus makes it easier for both children and adults – who believe their human rights have been violated – to bring a case to court.

Far more significant is the duty that the Act imposes on government to ensure that any new law that is introduced is compatible with the rights and freedoms in the ECHR. This duty is overseen by the Parliamentary Joint Committee on Human Rights, which scrutinizes each piece of legislation passing through Parliament.

There are mixed views about the impact of the Human Rights Act 1998. There is widespread disappointment among children's rights advocates that the Act is not being sufficiently used to enforce the rights and freedoms of children. Indeed, of almost 430 Human Rights Act cases analysed by the Human Rights Research Project, children initiated less than 20 (O'Brien and Arkinstall 2002). Many children do not know about their rights, and those in the most difficult circumstances – including children in custody or those subject to 'naming and shaming'– are, by definition, the least likely to have high expectations of adults generally or the courts in particular.

However, the core value of the Human Rights Act in moderating policy and practice cannot be overstated, particularly in the contested area of criminal justice. As the Lord Chancellor and Secretary of State for Constitutional Affairs (Falconer 2007) explained recently:

> The knowledge that infringements can be enforced so much more quickly has had an effect much more profound than the effect on the comparatively small number of litigants who have been saved the air-fare to the European Court of Human Rights in Strasbourg ... The fact you might be breaking English law is a profound pressure on the way policy-makers frame legislation.

In addition to legal obligations to uphold the rights and freedoms in the ECHR, 'public authorities' – including schools, hospitals, social services establishments and prisons – must work in a way that upholds human rights principles: treating everyone with respect and dignity; being fair and open when making decisions; working towards equality while valuing difference; and ensuring everyone can reach his or her full potential. This has far-reaching potential for youth justice policy and practice.

Two significant Human Rights Act cases that relate explicitly to youth justice include the following:

- *The Munby judgment:* the Howard League for Penal Reform brought a successful judicial review on the applicability of the Children Act 1989 to prison (*The Howard League for Penal Reform* v. *The Secretary of State for the Home Department and the Department of Health*).
- *Lifetime privacy injunctions:* the High Court stopped three powerful news organizations from publishing the details of two 18-year-olds who had served custodial sentences for a murder they committed when they were 10 years old (*Venables and Thompson* v. *News Group Newspapers Ltd*).

While the Human Rights Act 1998 is extremely important for children, it is the United Nations Convention on the Rights of the Child that provides the most authoritative and comprehensive framework for ensuring every child can reach his or her potential.

Carolyne Willow

Related entries

Children's human rights; European Convention on Human Rights (ECHR); Human Rights Act 1998; Munby judgment; Naming and shaming; United Nations Convention on the Rights of the Child (UNCRC).

Key texts and sources

Department for Constitutional Affairs (2006) *Making Sense of Human Rights: A Short Introduction.* London: Department for Constitutional Affairs.

Falconer, C. (2007) 'Human rights are majority rights.' The Lord Morris of Borth-y-Gest Memorial Lecture, 23 March, Bangor University.

Kilkelly, U. (1999) *The Child and the European Convention on Human Rights.* Aldershot: Ashgate.

O'Brien, C. and Arkinstall, J. (2002) *Human Rights Act Project Database of Cases under the Human Rights Act 1998.* London: Doughty Street Chambers (available online at **http://www.doughtystreet.co.uk/hrarp/summary/index.cfm**).

Sceats, S. (2007) *The Human Rights Act – Changing Lives.* London: British Institute of Human Rights.

See the Office of Public Sector Information's website (**http://www.opsi.gov.uk/ACTS/acts1998/1998004 2.htm**) for the text of the Human Rights Act 1998.

I

INDIVIDUAL SUPPORT ORDERS (ISOs)

The individual support order (ISO) is an order introduced by the Criminal Justice Act 2003 that can be attached to an anti-social behaviour order (ASBO) made in civil proceedings in respect of a child below the age of 18. While an ASBO consists of negative prohibitions, the ISO imposes 'positive obligations'. An ISO is not available in cases where the ASBO is imposed in criminal proceedings.

Individual support orders (ISOs) have been available since May 2004. The court is obliged to impose an order if it considers it desirable to prevent a repetition of the behaviour leading to the application for the anti-social behaviour order (ASBO). The order places the young person under the supervision of a youth offending team (YOT) for up to six months and requires the young person to attend a maximum of two sessions a week. Breach is a criminal offence punishable by a fine.

Although the ISO was introduced, in part, to counter criticism of the ASBO as a negative measure, take-up of the new power in the courts has been slow. Only seven orders were made between May and December 2004 and, despite dedicated funding to YOTs in the following year, only 42 ISOs were imposed throughout 2005. A lack of awareness by the courts perhaps goes some way to explain the muted response. At the same time, many young people made subject to ASBOs are already receiving more intensive YOT supervision than that which could be provided through the ISO.

Tim Bateman

Related entries

Anti-social behaviour orders (ASBOs); Criminal Justice Act 2003; Criminal Justice and Immigration Bill 2006–7 to 2007–8; Early intervention.

Key texts and sources

National Audit Office (2006) *Tackling Anti-social Behaviour: Report by the Comptroller and Auditor General* (HC 99 Session 2006–2007). London: Home Office.
Solanki, A.-R., Bateman, T., Boswell, G. and Hill, E. (2006) *Anti-social Behaviour Orders*. London: Youth Justice Board.
Youth Justice Board (2006g) *Individual Support Orders (ISO) Procedure: A Protocol to be Used and Adapted by YOTs when Managing ISOs*. London: Youth Justice Board.

INFORMAL ACTION

Informal action represents measures taken (normally by the police) that fall short of formal charging. It rests on the principle that formal intervention is problematic, counterproductive, stigmatizing and criminogenic. No criminal record is opened on the child/young person following informal action.

Informal action derives from the idea that young people in trouble should be diverted away from formal criminal justice. While rooted philosophically in the 1960s and 1970s, informal action is a term associated with youth justice policy and practice during the 1980s. During this period the principles of diversion, decriminalization and decarceration were pivotal. The period was identified as a 'successful revolution in youth justice' because there was a reduction in young people formally processed through the criminal justice system, reduced numbers of young people in custody and a reduction in the number of offences committed by young people (Goldson 1997; Smith 2007).

Goldson (2005a) argues that informalism is rooted in at least seven intersecting theoretical and practice traditions. However, one of the main drivers for informal action is labelling theory. This identified that formal criminal justice responses could serve to stigmatize young people, confirming them in criminal pathways rather than diverting them away from criminality. This led, in turn, to a belief that 'radical non-intervention' is an appropriate way of minimizing the adverse effects of involvement with the justice system.

During the 1980s, diversion from formal processes towards more informal means of dealing with offences was widely accepted as 'good practice' and was promoted by theorists, policy-makers and practitioners alike. Indeed, the Home Office (1985) recognized that 'both in theory and practice . . . delaying the entry of a young person into the formal criminal justice system may help to prevent his entry into that system altogether'. Despite considerable evidence supporting the effectiveness of informal action (Kemp *et al.* 2002), it came under attack in the mid-1990s. With the implementation of the Crime and Disorder Act 1998 – which introduced the reprimand and final warning – informal alternatives were marginalized. Although police officers retain strictly limited discretion to take informal action in exceptional circumstances, the presumption favours the reprimand or final warning. Interestingly, more recently there has been a renewed call to explore various forms of diversion. This is probably related to concerns regarding the extent to which the youth justice system is becoming overburdened with low-level young offenders.

Joe Yates

Related entries

Arrest and decision-making process; Caution; Diversion; First-time entrants; Informalism; Labelling theory; Minimum necessary intervention; Reprimands and final warnings; Youth Diversion Scheme.

Key texts and sources

Goldson, B. (1997) 'Children in trouble: state responses to juvenile crime', in P. Scraton (ed.) *'Childhood' in 'Crisis'?* London: UCL Press.

Goldson, B. (2005a) 'Beyond formalism: towards "informal" approaches to youth crime and youth justice', in T. Bateman and J. Pitts (eds) *The RHP Companion to Youth Justice.* Lyme Regis: Russell House.

Home Office (1985) *The Cautioning of Offenders* (Circular 14/85). London: Home Office.

Kemp, V., Sorsby, A., Liddle, M. and Merrington, S. (2002) *Assessing Responses to Youth Offending in Northamptonshire.* Research Briefing 2. London: Nacro.

Newburn, T. and Souhami, A. (2005) 'Youth diversion', in N. Tilley (ed.) *Handbook of Crime Prevention and Community Safety.* Cullompton: Willan Publishing.

Pragnell, S. (2005) 'Reprimands and final warnings', in T. Bateman and J. Pitts (eds) *The RHP Companion to Youth Justice.* Lyme Regis: Russell House.

Smith, R. (2007) *Youth Justice: Ideas, Policy, Practice* (2nd edn). Cullompton: Willan Publishing.

INFORMALISM

Youth justice systems typically draw children and young people into *formal* mechanisms of control and regulation. Informalism challenges conventional orthodoxies and is underpinned by a range of radical alternative principles and perspectives. It rests on a robust evidence base and offers the prospect of more imaginative, humane, responsive, effective and cost-efficient approaches to children and young people in trouble.

Since the early part of the nineteenth century, policymakers, child welfare agencies, penal reformers and 'experts' from a range of 'professions' and 'disciplines' have been largely preoccupied with developing *formal* mechanisms of intervention and control – designed to hold 'delinquents' and 'young offenders' to account – while, in most cases, also seeking to protect them from the full rigours of adult criminal justice processes. Informalist approaches deviate from this dominant tradition and derive from a range of sociological, penological and political perspectives within which conventional youth justice systems are essentially conceived as being ethically problematic, counterproductive (when measured in terms of preventing youth offending and providing community safety), extraordinarily costly, frequently harmful and often unnecessary.

While there is no unitary 'model' of formal youth justice, 'formalism' (in its most generic sense) might be taken to refer to systems that:

- routinely prosecute children and young people;
- require children and young people to attend tribunals and/or criminal courts of law where they are exposed to prescribed rituals and adversarial processes;
- involve a range of formal 'actors', including any combination of police officers, prosecutors, defence advocates, court officials, magistrates, judges, social workers, psychologists, psychiatrists, teachers, counsellors and institutional personnel;
- pass sentences and open official criminal records on children and young people;
- impose court orders, conditions and/or statutory interventions with which children and young people are legally obliged to comply, and reserve additional (often more intrusive/punitive) sanctions for those who fail to do so; and
- ultimately retain powers to remove children and young people from their families and communities and to place them in correctional institutions (including children's homes, secure facilities and/or prisons).

Informalism, on the other hand, comprises an amalgam of theoretical perspectives and practical propositions that combine to challenge the legitimacy of formal youth justice systems. The conceptual foundations of informalism emerged in the 1960s and 1970s, alongside a burgeoning scepticism regarding the efficacy and legitimacy of 'closed' or 'total' institutions. As they have developed, informalist approaches have broadened their focus, contending that the range and depth of state intervention should be minimized across the entire youth justice system. The 'destructuring impulse' has thus been applied to 'all parts of the machine' (Cohen 1985: 36).

Central to informalist perspectives is the contention that the formal interventions of youth justice processes essentially stigmatize children and young people by applying criminogenic 'labels'. Such 'labelling' is not evenly applied by state agencies, and working-class, black and minoritized children and young people and, in certain circumstances, girls and young women, are particularly susceptible. Furthermore, labelling triggers negative 'social reaction' that, in turn, has enduring and spiralling consequences. In this way it is argued that formal intervention and labelling 'create' (or at least consolidate and confirm) criminogenic 'identities' for specific constituencies of structurally disadvantaged children that, once established, tend to produce further offending. This led Edwin Lemert (1967) to conclude that 'social control leads to deviance', and David Matza (1969: 80) to comment on the 'irony' and self-defeating nature of certain professional interventions: 'the very effort to prevent, intervene, arrest and "cure" persons ... precipitate or seriously aggravate the tendency society wishes to guard against.'

In short, informalism shifts the conceptual emphasis by problematizing the formal legal and disciplinary apparatus of youth justice, as distinct from the 'young offender'. But advocating informalism should not be taken to imply either that nothing should be done in relation to youth crime or that children and young people who transgress the law should be left to fend for themselves without the care, guidance, support and supervision they may need. The central argument, however, is that, at the policy level, the solutions to such complex problems, conflicts and harms are to be found in the broad corpus of social and economic policy rather than the narrower confines of youth justice policy. Criminalization, and formal exposure to youth justice systems, is more likely to compound the very problems it aims to prevent.

Informalist approaches seek to *replace*, as distinct from *coexist with*, formal youth justice interventions. If diversionary and informalist initiatives simply become an adjunct to the youth justice system, rather than a direct alternative to it, then they will merely serve to draw more children and young people into its reach ('net-widening'), to intensify the *level* of intervention ('net-strengthening') and, ultimately, serve to provide new *forms* of intervention ('different nets') (Austin and Krisberg 1981). Equally, informal initiatives must be available to *all* 'young offenders' rather than being limited to those who are deemed to be most compliant. Otherwise, 'bifurcated' responses are created whereby the 'undeserving' are routinely exposed to formal criminalization (and often custodial detention), while the 'alternatives' are reserved for a select constituency of 'deserving' children and young people.

Informal practices, therefore, might rest on the following applied principles:

- State policy should comprehensively address the social and economic conditions that are known to give rise to conflict, harm, social distress, 'crime' and criminalization, particularly poverty, inequality and social polarization.
- The 'normal' institutions of society – including families (however they are configured), schools and other forms of educational/training provision, 'communities', youth services, health provision, leisure and recreational services and youth labour markets – should be required, and adequately resourced, to provide the widest range of opportunities for *all* children and young people.
- Children and young people should be routinely *diverted* away from formal youth justice interventions, and such systems should be replaced by universal services providing support, guidance, advice, opportunities, holistic care and welfare.
- Interventions that are known to aggravate the very problems that they seek to reduce (perhaps most notably child imprisonment) should be abolished.
- In the minority of cases where *only* formal intervention is deemed appropriate, it should be provided outside the youth justice system, its intensity and duration should be limited to what is absolutely necessary, and its rationale should be explicit, evidence based

and likely to provide positive outcomes for the 'young offender' and any injured party.

- All forms of intervention should be consistent with the provisions of the Human Rights Act 1998, together with the full range of international standards, treaties, conventions and rules that have been formally adopted by the UK government – especially the United Nations Convention on the Rights of the Child.
- Systematic efforts should be made to increase public knowledge, tolerance and understanding of 'youth crime'.

Such principles may seem little more than naive ideals, but they are actually grounded in robust research evidence and substantial practice experience (Goldson and Muncie 2006a; 2006b).

Barry Goldson

Related entries

Abolitionism; Bifurcation; Children's human rights; Diversion; Extending Entitlement (National Assembly for Wales); Gender and justice; Informal action; Labelling theory; Minimum necessary intervention; Normalization; 'Race' and justice; Social harm.

Key texts and sources

Austin, J. and Krisberg, B. (1981) 'Wider, stronger and different nets: the dialectics of criminal justice reform', *Journal of Research in Crime and Delinquency*, 18: 165–96.

Cohen, S. (1985) *Visions of Social Control: Crime, Punishment and Classification.* Cambridge: Polity Press.

Goldson, B. and Muncie, J. (2006a) 'Rethinking youth justice: comparative analysis, international human rights and research evidence', *Youth Justice*, 6: 91–106.

Goldson, B. and Muncie, J. (2006b) 'Critical anatomy: towards a principled youth justice', in B. Goldson and J. Muncie (eds) *Youth Crime and Justice: Critical Issues.* London: Sage.

Lemert, E. (1967) *Human Deviance, Social Problems and Social Control.* Englewood Cliffs, NJ: Prentice Hall.

Matza, D. (1969) *Becoming Deviant.* Englewood Cliffs, NJ: Prentice Hall.

INSTITUTIONALIZED INTOLERANCE

'Institutionalized intolerance' is a term coined to capture the mood of youth justice reform in England and Wales in the late 1990s when policy provided that youth 'incivility' and 'anti-social behaviour' would 'no longer' be tolerated and would be made as much a target for formal intervention as criminal behaviour.

The term 'institutionalized intolerance' was first used in Muncie's (1999) critical analysis of the Crime and Disorder Act 1998. This observed that the rationale for this major reforming project was based on the notion that previous youth justice policy had 'failed'. The white paper preceding the 1998 Act heralded a crackdown on disorder by famously declaring that there would be 'no more excuses' (Home Office 1997a). Such intolerance to the 'troubled and troublesome' has subsequently been realized in the targeting of the 'pre-criminal'; increases in child prosecutions; and in the continuance of the highest rate of juvenile custody in western Europe (Goldson 2006c).

John Muncie

Related entries

Authoritarianism; Crime and Disorder Act 1998; Criminalization; Net-widening; No More Excuses; Punitiveness; Respect (Government Action Plan); Zero tolerance.

Key texts and sources

Goldson, B. (2006c) 'Penal custody: intolerance, irrationality and indifference', in B. Goldson and J. Muncie (eds) *Youth Crime and Justice: Critical Issues.* London: Sage.
Home Office (1997a) *No More Excuses: A New Approach to Tackling Youth Crime in England and Wales* (Cm 3809). London: HMSO.
Muncie, J. (1999) 'Institutionalized intolerance: youth justice and the 1998 Crime and Disorder Act', *Critical Social Policy*, 19: 147–75.

INTENSIVE SUPERVISION AND SURVEILLANCE PROGRAMME (ISSP)

The Intensive Supervision and Surveillance Programme (ISSP) is a robust multi-modal community programme designed for persistent and serious young offenders in England and Wales.

Intensive community programmes are firmly established in the USA and are becoming an increasingly integral part of penal policy in other jurisdictions. In England and Wales, persistent and serious young offenders can now be placed on the Intensive Supervision and Surveillance Programme (ISSP). This is much more intensive than many of its predecessors and it is a key element of the multifaceted framework of the 'new youth justice', particularly through its combination of supervision and surveillance. Its primary goal is to reduce reoffending, but the further desire to reduce custody rates has become more apparent over time, particularly with the widening of the target group to include offenders committing one-off serious offences as well as persistent offenders.

ISSP targets persistent and serious offenders both pre- and post-sentence and pre- and post-custody. However, the intention of the Youth Justice Board, in adherence to its desire for ISSP to reduce custody rates, has been for the majority of young people to spend six months on the programme as part of a supervision order. In such cases, the first three months should entail a structured supervision programme of at least five hours every weekday (that is, 25 hours per week), following which there must be provision for day-to-day contact for at least one hour each weekday (that is, a minimum of five hours contact per week).

All programmes should contain the following five core 'supervision modules':

- education and training;
- changing offending behaviour;
- interpersonal skills;
- family support; and
- restorative justice.

Other 'modules' should be provided according to the needs of the individual, encompassing work to address 'risk factors', such as mental health, drug or alcohol misuse and accommodation problems, as well as provision for counselling or mentoring and some form of constructive recreation.

ISSP is not, however, merely another project with more help, more care and more resources, but is based on the strict enforcement of rules and requirements and consistent monitoring involving electronic and human tracking, whenever possible. ISSP teams should carry out surveillance checks at least twice daily and should have the facility for around-the-clock surveillance for those cases in which it is deemed necessary. One of the following four forms of surveillance has to be provided in every case: tagging, voice verification, human tracking or 'intelligence-led policing'.

The political impetus behind the introduction of ISSP and other intensive community programmes is thus clear, demonstrating a desire to tackle prison overcrowding while, at the same time, strengthening provision in the community and still appearing 'tough on crime'. The programmes have also benefited from their ability to combine elements from the welfare, justice and actuarial 'risk management' models of youth justice, and from their multifaceted theoretical foundations.

An evaluation of the initial ISSP schemes found that, while a range of implementation difficulties were encountered, most schemes were able to establish viable programmes relatively quickly. There was, however, considerable variation in the style and quantity of intervention provided, and practitioners reported particular difficulties in accessing education, accommodation, mental health and drugs services in some locations. The electronic tag was the most commonly utilized form of ISSP surveillance, and combining human tracking with the tag was perceived to be a particularly stringent form of surveillance. Maintaining engagement with young people while also imposing rigorous enforcement was far from straightforward, and many of those cases that completed 'successfully' had been breached at some stage.

In terms of outcomes, the ISSP evaluation found that clear inroads were being made into tackling the underlying problems of the young people, especially with those who completed the programme successfully. While large reductions in offending frequency were achieved, the 'comparison groups' performed at least as well. Furthermore, while the vast majority of sentencers believed ISSP provided a useful option for the youth courts, the introduction of the programme had little direct impact, at a national level, on the use of custody. Sentencers were keen to emphasize that custody remained the only option in certain instances.

A review of the more general evidence base for intensive community programmes indicates varying degrees of success. In terms of reducing reoffending, those programmes targeting 'high risk' offenders and including a strong rehabilitative component have proven most effective. As for reducing custody rates, the twin dangers of 'net-widening' and increased levels of breach have become increasingly apparent. Careful thought has to be given, therefore, to both the theoretical model and the targeting of the programmes. Any tensions between the caring and controlling aims need to be resolved, and establishing close liaisons with a range of departments and organizations appears critical, ideally resulting in 'interagency' working. Maintaining programme integrity would also appear essential, with strong leadership an important ingredient. There are arguments in favour of graduated responses to non-compliance and a less stringent approach towards enforcement, with incentives needed to encourage and reward compliance. Finally, attention has to be paid to maintaining the confidence of the practitioners themselves, the local police, sentencers and the local communities.

While the evidence base for intensive community programmes such as ISSP is clearly growing, there are a number of unresolved concerns. Difficulties remain in defining persistence and in identifying 'high risk' offenders, with the potential danger of labelling a subgroup of offenders as 'innately criminal'. Applying Cohen's (1985) 'dispersal of control' thesis, the programmes can be seen as resulting in wider, denser and different nets, and there are arguments in favour of less punitive approaches and lower levels of intervention. Finally, while politicians and policymakers have promoted the surveillant aspects of intensive community programmes, particularly electronic monitoring, the benefits of such monitoring within an intensive multi-modal programme remain unclear.

Robin Moore

Related entries

Desistance; Electronic monitoring; Enforcement; Mentoring; Net-widening; Persistent young offenders; Rehabilitation; Risk management; Supervision orders; Surveillance.

Key texts and sources

Armstrong, T.L. (ed.) (1991) *Intensive Interventions with High-risk Youths: Promising Approaches in Juvenile Probation and Parole*. Monsey, NY: Willow Tree Press.

Bottoms, A., Brown, P., McWilliams, B., McWilliams, W. and Nellis, M. with Pratt, J. (1990) *Intermediate Treatment and Juvenile Justice*. London: HMSO.

Cohen, S. (1985) *Visions of Social Control: Crime, Punishment and Classification*. Cambridge: Polity Press.

Moore, R., Gray, E., Roberts, C., Merrington, S., Waters, I., Fernandez, R., Hayward, G. and Rogers, R.D. (2004) *National Evaluation of the Intensive Supervision and Surveillance Programme: Interim Report to the Youth Justice Board*. London: Youth Justice Board for England and Wales.

Moore, R., Gray, E., Roberts, C., Taylor, E. and Merrington, S. (2006) *Managing Persistent and Serious Offenders in the Community: Intensive Community Programmes in Theory and Practice*. Cullompton: Willan Publishing.

INTERMEDIATE TREATMENT (IT)

Intermediate treatment (IT) is a form of generic intervention with children and young people 'in trouble' or 'in need' that is *intermediate* between family work and the removal of the child/young person from his or her family.

Intermediate treatment (IT) was a service provided for children and young people 'in trouble', 'at risk' or 'in need' although, in practice, these terms were never very clearly defined. IT was never a stand-alone sentence of the court and it is not mentioned in any Act of Parliament, although many young people were referred to IT projects as a condition of a supervision order following an appearance in a juvenile court – for criminal or civil (care/welfare) matters. Additionally, many young people, loosely defined as in trouble, at risk or in need, attended IT projects on a 'voluntary' basis – that is, not following any court appearance but as a result of a recommendation of a social worker who deemed IT to be an appropriate or useful intervention.

Just as diverse as the young people engaged in IT – and their routes on to IT projects – were the range of services provided under the IT rubric. The provision of IT ranged from meeting one evening per week for a couple of hours, to full-time projects five days a week and sometimes even weekend contact. The content of IT programmes varied too (certainly between projects but also within projects), including activities (including games), structured (and unstructured) discussion, social skills, outings and visits, sports, education (as an alternative to full-time schooling) and 'outward bound' or adventure training. IT became a catch-all term for a wide range of direct interventions with young people and almost anything that social workers did directly with young people was called IT. Notwithstanding this diversity, groupwork was common across all projects. Groups involved both girls and boys, often of mixed ages, and included young people 'in trouble' and young people 'in need'.

The term 'intermediate treatment' was first used in the Home Office white paper, *Children in Trouble* (1968), which preceded the Children and Young Persons Act 1969. The thinking expressed in the white paper was that child neglect and juvenile delinquency should not be treated separately, as both were products of deprivation. The 1969 Act transferred responsibility for child-care services from the Home Office to the Department for Health and Social Security (DHSS), which, henceforth, became responsible for the newly unified social services departments and their generic responsibilities, including children. However, the Home Office retained responsibility for all custodial provision for juveniles and the Probation Service retained a role in working with juvenile offenders aged 14 years or more. IT was initially slow to develop, perhaps because the 1970s was a time of complex organizational change and there was a lack of clarity surrounding its nature and purpose.

Concerned by the lack of development of IT in the 1970s and its lack of impact on how the system was dealing with young people, the DHSS established the National Fund for Intermediate Treatment in England and Wales in 1978 – providing central government financial support for the development of IT projects. Known as the 'IT Fund' and administered by the Rainer Foundation, it adopted the following definition of IT:

Intermediate Treatment, within the context of community care, seeks to provide a wide range of educational, recreational and work-training opportunities designed to meet the identified needs of young people who are in trouble or at risk of being so. The purpose is to enable them to fulfil their potential and reach a standard of achievement which will give them confidence to face the realities of the world they live in and compete on equal terms with children from more secure backgrounds. This entails creating projects and opportunities where none exist, or modifying existing resources within the conventional social work and youth education system. Intermediate Treatment, therefore, stands between traditional social work methods, to which an increasing number of delinquents are failing to respond, and removal to institutional care which IT tries to avoid.

A major wave of government funding followed in 1983, promulgated in DHSS Local Authority Circular (LAC) (83)3. This initiative provided £15 million central government funding for local authorities to develop, in partnership with voluntary agencies, intensive IT programmes expressly targeted as direct community-based alternatives to custody (a Borstal or detention centre sentence). However, at this time, 'old-style' preventative IT was not ruled out and persisted for much of the 1980s – as a service to both young people in need and in trouble. From the early

1980s, IT did indeed develop as an alternative to custody across England and Wales, although many areas also retained more generic provision (Bottoms *et al.* 1990).

Other forces were at work in the 1980s. Many academics and, indeed, practitioners were becoming increasingly critical of the consequences, for young people, of importing welfare concerns into juvenile justice – giving rise to a justice or back-to-justice movement. New ideas about juvenile delinquency were gaining ground. The ability of social workers to 'diagnose' the causes of delinquency and to provide effective 'treatment' was being increasingly questioned at the same time as ideas about the minor and transient nature of juvenile offending garnered widespread support. As a result, cautioning and diversion from prosecution became official government policy and a practice imperative, championed by juvenile justice teams who wrested IT from generic social work practice. By the end of the 1980s and into the early 1990s, pro-diversion and alternatives to custody strategies formed the 'new orthodoxy' of juvenile justice in England and Wales, and IT as a concept and a practice waned.

Stephen Case

Related entries

Alternatives to custody; Children and Young Persons Act 1969; Cognitive-behaviour programmes; Diversion; Early intervention; Groupwork; Rehabilitation; Supervision orders; Systems management; Welfare.

Key texts and sources

Bottoms, A., Brown, P., McWilliams, B., McWilliams, W., Nellis, M. with Pratt, J. (1990) *Intermediate Treatment and Juvenile Justice*. London: HMSO.
Curtis, S. (1989) *Juvenile Offending: Prevention through Intermediate Treatment*. London: Batsford.
Haines, K. and Drakeford, M. (1998) *Young People and Youth Justice*. Basingstoke: Macmillan.
Pratt, J. (1987) 'A revisionist history of intermediate treatment', *British Journal of Social Work*, 17: 417–36.
Stevens, M. and Crook, J. (1986) 'What the devil is intermediate treatment?', *Social Work Today*, 8 September: 10–11.

J

JUST DESERTS

'Just deserts' is a concept derived from a justice-based model that maintains that punishment should be determinate and reflect the seriousness of the offence. It is the emphasis on proportionality that is the distinguishing characteristic of just deserts. Justice-based models also emphasize that the legal rights of young people must be adequately protected during judicial proceedings. This is generally referred to as due process or procedural justice.

The principle of just deserts gained ascendancy in the 1980s as part of the 'back to justice' critique of welfare-based youth justice. Advocates of 'back to justice' challenged notions of assessment and treatment, arguing that they centred on unjustifiable discretion. Welfare considerations, they argued, allowed the court not only to scrutinize the offence but also to examine the entire social and family circumstances of young offenders. Morris and McIsaac (1978) argued that a tariff 'based on needs' was grafted on to a 'tariff based on deeds', with the result that young people were ultimately treated more harshly and were exposed to disproportionate levels of intervention – not because of the severity of their offences but because of perceived problems in their social and family background that required 'treatment'. The 'back to justice' movement demanded a return to natural justice, proportionality and/or just deserts in order to safeguard the legal rights of young people and to put an end to discretionary, indeterminate and disparate sentencing practices.

The 'back to justice' critique and the concept of just deserts were influential in the development of youth justice legislation in the 1980s and early 1990s. The Criminal Justice Act 1991, in particular, placed considerable emphasis on separating offending and 'welfare' matters in youth justice proceedings. However, since the early 1990s the concept of just deserts has been railroaded by advocates of deterrent and retributive models of youth justice, underpinned by a return to punitive principles in the sentencing of young offenders. This has led to the concept of just deserts mistakenly being linked with deterrent retribution rather than the broader objective of proportional justice.

Patricia Gray

Related entries

Criminal Justice Act 1991; Deterrence; Due process; Justice; Proportionality; Retribution.

Key texts and sources

Clarke, J. (1985) 'Whose justice? The politics of juvenile control', *International Journal of the Sociology of Law*, 13: 407–21.

Hudson, B. (1987) *Justice through Punishment: A Critique of the 'Justice' Model of Corrections.* London: Macmillan.

Morris, A. and McIsaac, M. (1978) *Juvenile Justice? The Practice of Social Welfare.* London: Heinemann.

von Hirsch, A. (1976) *Doing Justice: The Choice of Punishments.* New York, NY: Hill & Wang.

JUSTICE

Central to the concept of justice (in respect of youth justice) is the proposal that the intensity of formal intervention should be proportionate to the severity/gravity of the offence, rather than the level of perceived 'need'. This principle derives from a classical formula comprising due process and proportionality.

The practical application of the justice principle has three primary implications. First, the legal rights of children and young people must be secured and safeguarded through due legal process, by professional representation and the engagement of lawyers. Second, formal intervention is conceived in terms of 'restrictions of liberty' that must be limited to the minimum necessary, in accordance with principles of proportionality. Third, custodial sentencing should be used strictly as a 'last resort' for the most serious offences/offenders and, when imposed, it should be for the shortest appropriate time. Such justice-based priorities essentially prevailed in England and Wales from the early 1980s to the early 1990s, and they were incrementally bolstered by the provisions of successive statute, particularly the Criminal Justice Acts of 1982, 1988 and 1991 and the Children Act 1989.

By the late 1970s, the concepts of 'welfare' and 'treatment' in respect of youth justice had become almost synonymous with excessive intervention and intensified control. Informed by academic research (Thorpe *et al.* 1980), many practitioners came to realize that the road to residential care and/or penal custody had too often been paved by misguided 'good intentions'. It was in this context that support developed for an approach derived from a classical 'justice' model:

- The intensity of intervention/punishment should be proportionate to the seriousness of the child's offending (as distinct from responding to his or her perceived 'needs').
- The same intervention/punishment should be determinate in accordance with sentences

fixed by the court (as distinct from the relatively indeterminate nature of 'welfare' interventions).
- Administrative/professional discretion based on spurious 'assessments' and perceived 'needs' should be curtailed.
- Equality of treatment should prevail in the youth justice process.
- Children's legal rights should be protected by proper representation and due process.

The 'justice' approach consolidated around three fundamental principles (diversion, decriminalization and decarceration) and, in turn, formed the cornerstones of an innovatory and unified practice accompanied, in the words of Rutherford (1995: 57), by 'one of the most remarkably progressive periods of juvenile justice policy'.

For a number of paradoxical and complex reasons, the approach found favour with government ministers and policymakers and was supported by the provisions of statute (Goldson 1997). The Criminal Justice Act 1982 imposed some tighter criteria for custodial sentencing and introduced the 'specified activities order', whereby a programme of community-based activities could be specified in court as an alternative to custodial detention. In 1983 the Department for Health and Social Security released £15 million for voluntary agencies, working in partnership with local authorities, to establish and develop community-based 'alternative to custody' projects for juveniles. The Criminal Justice Act 1988 tightened the criteria for custodial sentencing further, and the Children Act 1989 abolished the 'criminal care order' and finally removed all civil care proceedings from the juvenile court, thus formally separating 'welfare' and 'justice' jurisdictions. Finally, the Criminal Justice Act 1991 consolidated the diversionary, decriminalizing and decarcerative priorities by establishing the youth court and providing for the extension of such practices to include 17-year-olds; by abolishing prison custody for 14-year-old boys; by providing for the similar abolition of penal remands for 15–17-year-olds (although this provision was never implemented); and by placing a duty on all those engaged in the criminal justice system to 'avoid discriminating against people on the grounds of race or sex or any other improper reason'. The combined effect of this produced a very dramatic increase in diversionary practices, and an equally impressive reduction in the numbers of children and young people being sent to custodial institutions.

The progressive and effective justice-based policy and practice that developed through the 1980s and into the 1990s were brought to an abrupt end in the post-1993 period, however. The combination of political imperative and 'moral panic' served to reintroduce 'tough' approaches favouring intensive intervention, system expansion and, ultimately, custodial detention (Goldson 2002a).

Barry Goldson

Related entries

Children Act 1989; Criminal Justice Act 1982; Criminal Justice Act 1988; Criminal Justice Act 1991; Decarceration; Decriminalization; Diversion; Due process; Minimum necessary intervention; Politicization; Proportionality; Youth court.

Key texts and sources

Goldson, B. (1997) 'Children in trouble: state responses to juvenile crime', in P. Scraton (ed.) *'Childhood' in 'Crisis'?* London: UCL Press.

Goldson, B. (2002a) 'New punitiveness: the politics of child incarceration', in J. Muncie *et al.* (eds) *Youth Justice: Critical Readings.* London: Sage.

Rutherford, A. (1995) 'Signposting the future of juvenile justice policy in England and Wales', in Howard League for Penal Reform (ed.) *Child Offenders UK and International Practice.* London: Howard League for Penal Reform.

Thorpe, D.H., Smith, D., Green, C.J. and Paley, J.H. (1980) *Out of Care: The Community Support of Juvenile Offenders.* London: Allen & Unwin.

JUSTICE BY GEOGRAPHY

Justice by geography refers to the potential for young people who offend to receive differential treatment from the youth justice system, depending on the geographic area in which they live and/or are processed.

The contention that sentencing practices (and particularly the use of custody) for young people are contingent upon local area was advanced in the 1980s. A report published by Social Information Systems highlighted large variations in the sentencing of young people in six local authority areas, with custodial sentencing – as a percentage of all sentences imposed – ranging from 2.9 to 7.9 per cent (Richardson 1991).

A study of youth custodial sentencing in magistrates' courts during 1998 found further evidence of differential 'justice' outcomes for young people based on their geographic location. Nearly one third of petty sessional areas (geographical areas over which magistrates have authority) avoided the use of custodial sentences, yet one sixth of the areas studied contained a custody rate of 10 per cent or over (Youth Justice Board 2000a). Most recently, the Sentencing Guidelines Council (2006) identified extensive geographic differentials in custody for young people in England and Wales (January–June 2005), with average rates ranging from 11 per cent in the North West to 6 per cent in the North East and South West.

It has been argued that variations in the procedural characteristics and the sentencing practices of youth courts are a result of differences in the social structure and context of urban, suburban and rural areas. Feld (1991) asserts that the heterogeneity, density and diversity of youth populations in urban areas weaken social cohesion and mechanisms for informal social control (for example, family and community), producing an increased reliance on methods of formal control in the youth justice system. This formal control includes bureaucracy (for example, the presence of solicitors), a due process orientation and greater severity in pre-trial detention and sentencing practice. In contrast, rural areas are allegedly more homogeneous and stable in their demographic composition and prevailing belief systems, fostering greater informal social control and encouraging less formal, more lenient sentencing of young people (Feld 1991).

Some might argue that differential sentencing patterns do not in themselves indicate that the system is unjust. In order to test for injustice, therefore, it is necessary to examine the relation between the seriousness of offences and the nature of sentences that courts impose. For example, a study conducted by Nacro for the Youth Justice Board (2000b) investigated whether differential custody rates for young people could be related to differential patterns of youth offending in local areas (for example, frequency and seriousness). However, the research revealed evidence of inconsistent sentencing and exposed high rates of custody in areas with relatively low levels of youth offending. Furthermore, the nature of offending was no more serious than that which characterized low-custody areas. Nacro suggested that a mutually reinforcing culture can emerge among local practitioners, whereby 'Previous court decisions influence subsequent pre-sentence report (PSR) proposals; these, in turn, substantiate the court's view of appropriate levels of sentence. A circular mechanism of the sort described makes it difficult for those working within the framework to see beyond it' (Youth Justice Board 2000b: 44). This prompted the then Chairman of the Youth Justice Board, Norman Warner, to pronounce in 2001: 'justice by geography discredits our system; it makes justice a lottery dependent upon postcode.'

In response to data pointing to justice by geography, the Youth Justice Board has implemented a system of monitoring local rates of custodial sentencing to enable local areas to compare their sentencing practices with the national average; to evaluate the reasons for any differential sentencing; and to assess whether more could be done to make better use of high-tariff community sentences, such as the Intensive Supervision and Surveillance Programme.

Stephen Case

Related entries

Anti-social behaviour orders (ASBOs); Caution; Custody rate; First-time entrants; Menu-based sentencing.

Key texts and sources

Feld, B. (1991) 'Justice by geography: urban, suburban and rural variations in juvenile justice administration', *Journal of Criminal Law and Criminology*, 82: 156–210.

Richardson, N. (1991) *Justice by Geography II*. Knutsford: Social Information Systems.

Sentencing Guidelines Council (2006) *The Sentence. Newsletter Issue 4*. London: Sentencing Guidelines Council (available online at **http://www.sentencing-guidelines.gov.uk/docs/the_sentence_four.pdf**).

Youth Justice Board (2000a) *Analysis of the First Quarterly Returns Provided by the Youth Offending Teams in England and Wales*. London: Youth Justice Board.

Youth Justice Board (2000b) *Factors Associated with Differential Rates of Youth Custodial Sentencing: Report to the Youth Justice Board*. London: Youth Justice Board.

JUSTICE (NORTHERN IRELAND) ACT 2002

The Justice (Northern Ireland) Act 2002 substantially reformed the youth justice system in Northern Ireland following the publication of the *Review of the Criminal Justice System* (Criminal Justice Review Group 2000), which itself followed the 'Good Friday Agreement' of 1998.

The 'Good Friday Agreement' of 1998 had, among a range of other commitments, set up a comprehensive review of criminal justice that was subsequently given effect through the Justice (Northern Ireland) Act 2002. The Act made provisions for the appointment of the judiciary and the appointment of law officers. It replaced the office of the Director of Public Prosecution with a Public Prosecution Service and established the office of Chief Inspector of Criminal Justice. It also introduced significant reforms in respect of access to information for victims, community safety and the legal aid system.

The Act – in fulfilling the Criminal Justice Review Group recommendation that the aims of a youth justice system should be laid out – specifies that the principal aim of the youth justice system is to protect the public through the prevention of offending by children. This is perceived by some as being in conflict with the child's 'best interest' principle as provided by the Children (Northern Ireland) Order 1995. The Justice (Northern Ireland) Act 2002 specifies that those working in the youth justice system must encourage children to recognize the effects of their offending and to take responsibility for their actions. It further specifies that those working in the system must have regard to the welfare of the child – particularly in relation to his or her personal, social and educational needs – and remain aware that delay in the justice process is prejudicial to the child's welfare. The Act extends the definition of 'children' to include all those under the age of 18 (previously 17 under the Criminal Justice (Children) (Northern Ireland) Order 1998).

The Act introduced reparation orders, community responsibility orders and the, as yet unimplemented, custody care order. The reparation order and community responsibility order were introduced to meet the Criminal Justice Review Group recommendations that reparation and a form of community service should be available to the court as disposals. The reparation order was designed to allow the child to make reparation either to the victim of his or her offence or to the community at large for up to 24 hours. The order specifically requires the involvement of the victim in agreeing the reparative activity and, if the court is minded to impose a reparation order, it must seek a report on the proposed activity and the victim's attitude to it. Responsibility for the delivery of the reparation order is vested in the Youth Justice Agency, but it has been little used by the court.

Much greater use has been made of the community responsibility order, however. This order, of between 20 and 40 hours' duration, requires the child to participate in instruction in citizenship (which the Act defines as the responsibility

the individual owes the community); to explore the impact of crime on victims; and to address 'any factors … which may cause him to commit offences'. The Act requires that, during this period of instruction in citizenship, the child be assessed for suitable practical activities that might be carried out as part of the order and allows that the practical activity may be reparative. Evaluation of the community responsibility order has shown that it is effective in addressing offending behaviour and attitudes.

The Criminal Justice Review Group was particularly explicit that the accommodation needs of children under 14 involved in offending behaviour should be met by the child-care rather than the youth justice system – in effect, children under 14 should not be admitted to the Juvenile Justice Centre. The custody care order was an attempt to respond to this recommendation and stated that a child, subject to a custody care order, should be placed in secure accommodation provided by the child-care authority. In Northern Ireland such accommodation is heavily oversubscribed and no agreement has been reached between the relevant bodies in respect of applying this provision. Consequently, the order has never been implemented. The number of children between 10 and 13 entering custody is very small, however, and it has been suggested that making secure accommodation available might well serve to increase that number.

The most significant impact on youth justice imposed by the Justice (Northern Ireland) Act 2002 was the introduction of the youth conference and the youth conference plan. The youth conference is a meeting – convened by a conference co-ordinator – to consider how a child might be dealt with for an offence. The conference aims to devise a plan specifying how the child will make reparation for the offence and will address his or her offending behaviour and/or meet the needs of the victim. The Act gives a range of options that may be included in a plan, including making an apology, making reparation or participating in activities to address offending. A conference must include a co-ordinator, the child, an appropriate adult and a police officer. The victim of the offence has the right to attend, and the co-ordinator may invite others whose presence might add value. However, a key aspect of the youth conference is that neither the child, the child's parents or guardian nor the victim can be compelled to participate.

The youth conference may be offered to the child by the Public Prosecution Service (PPS) – in cases where the child has admitted guilt – as an alternative to prosecution in the youth court. These are referred to as diversionary youth conferences. The co-ordinator may recommend a conference plan, prosecution or no further action. If, however, the case proceeds to court, the youth conference must be offered to the child by the court following a finding of guilt, except in limited circumstances of seriousness or where the court is considering discharge. With court-ordered youth conferences, the conference co-ordinator can recommend a plan, or that the court exercise its other options or that a plan be combined with a period of custody.

The conference model is the focus of considerable interest from other jurisdictions, both for its applicability to children and for its applicability to adults.

David Weir

Related entries

Criminal Justice (Children) (Northern Ireland) Order 1998; Diversion; Justice (Northern Ireland) Act 2004; Juvenile Justice Centre; Mediation; Reparation; Restorative justice; Restorative youth conferencing; Secure accommodation; Victims; Youth Justice Agency.

Key texts and sources

Criminal Justice Review Group (2000) *Review of the Criminal Justice System in Northern Ireland.* Belfast: HMSO (available online at http://www.nio.gov.uk/review_of_the_criminal_j ustice_system_in_northern_ireland.pdf).
See the Office of Public Sector Information's website for the texts of the Children (Northern Ireland) Order 1995 (http://www.opsi.gov.uk/si/si1995/ Uksi_19950755_en_1.htm), the Criminal Justice (Children) (Northern Ireland) Order 1998 (http://www.opsi.gov.uk/si/si1998/19981504.htm) and the Justice (Northern Ireland) Act 2002 (http://www.opsi.gov.uk/acts/acts2002/20020026. htm).

JUSTICE (NORTHERN IRELAND) ACT 2004

The Justice (Northern Ireland) Act 2004 made some amendments to the Justice (Northern Ireland) Act 2002.

The significance of the Justice (Northern Ireland) Act 2004 to youth justice lies solely in the fact that it confirmed the dissolution of the Juvenile Justice Board and the establishment of the Youth Justice Agency.

David Weir

Related entries

Justice (Northern Ireland) Act 2002; Youth Justice Agency.

Key texts and sources

See the Office of Public Sector Information's website (http://www.opsi.gov.uk/acts/acts2004/20040004. htm) for the text of the Justice (Northern Ireland) Act 2004.

JUVENILE COURTS

The juvenile court is a specialist court for children – normally up to the age of 16 – that usually addresses both civil (child care/ welfare) and criminal (juvenile justice/ punishment) matters. Juvenile courts first emerged in the late nineteenth and early twentieth centuries.

At the beginning of the nineteenth century the construction of 'childhood' as a separate and independent social category from 'adulthood' had yet to be fully institutionalized. Accordingly, the practices of the criminal justice and penal systems did not discern between children and adults: there was no distinct legal category of 'juvenile delinquent' or 'child offender'. The age of criminal responsibility was set at 7 in many jurisdictions. As such, once a child reached his or her seventh birthday he or she was held to be equally accountable before the law, and exposed to precisely the same penalties, as an adult.

A combination of philanthropy, social reform and 'child saving' emerged and developed throughout the nineteenth century, however, bolstered by prevailing moral anxieties and political concerns. By the end of the nineteenth century, therefore, 'juvenile delinquency' had not only been 'discovered' but also a recognizably 'modern' construct of the juvenile 'offender' had been institutionalized through consolidating strands of law and policy. It followed that, in the USA and many European countries, the need for a special jurisdiction for children was increasingly recognized.

The first separate court for children charged with committing criminal offences was established in Illinois in 1899. The Illinois Juvenile Court Act 1899 created a special court in Chicago for neglected, dependent and/or delinquent children under the age of 16. In Britain, it was not until the election of a reformist Liberal government in 1906 that state action was taken to place juvenile courts on a statutory footing and, in so doing, to complete the administrative separation of the child and adult jurisdictions. In introducing the Children Bill the Home Secretary, Herbert Samuel, proposed that the 'courts should be agencies for the *rescue* as well as the *punishment* of juveniles' (cited in Gelsthorpe and Morris 1994: 950), and the subsequent Children Act 1908 attempted to reconcile welfare and justice imperatives. The Act provided the new juvenile courts with both civil jurisdiction (welfare) over the 'needy' child *and* criminal jurisdiction (justice) over the child 'offender'. This made the court itself a 'locus for conflict and confusion, a vehicle for the simultaneous welfarization of delinquency and the juridicization of need' (Harris and Webb 1987: 9). Indeed, the awkward coexistence of welfare and justice within the juvenile court represented a 'penal-welfare complex' (Garland 1985) within which policies and practices could no longer simply be seen as either singularly humanitarian or exclusively repressive.

In England and Wales the juvenile court survived more or less in its original form until the Children Act 1989 formally removed its civil functions by creating family proceedings courts. Furthermore, the Criminal Justice Act 1991 extended the jurisdiction of the juvenile courts to include 17-year-olds and, as such, they were formally renamed youth courts. Despite such developments, the deep-rooted tensions between welfare and justice – that are intrinsic to law, policy and practice in respect of children in trouble and that have characterized the history of youth justice in many jurisdictions – continue to comprise the source of contestation and complexity.

Barry Goldson

Related entries

Children Act 1908; Children Act 1989; Children and Young Persons Act 1933; Criminal Justice Act 1991; Criminal Justice (Children) (Northern Ireland) Order 1998; Delinquency; Family proceedings court; Justice; Penal welfarism; Welfare; Youth court.

Key texts and sources

Garland, D. (1985) *Punishment and Welfare: A History of Penal Strategies*. Aldershot: Gower.
Gelsthorpe, L. and Morris, A. (1994) 'Juvenile justice, 1945–1992', in M. Maguire *et al.* (eds) *The Oxford Handbook of Criminology*. Oxford: Clarendon Press.
Harris, R. and Webb, D. (1987) *Welfare, Power and Juvenile Justice*. London: Tavistock.

JUVENILE JUSTICE CENTRE

The Juvenile Justice Centre is a custodial centre in Northern Ireland for children aged 10–17. The Woodlands Juvenile Justice Centre, near Bangor, Co. Down, is currently the single custodial centre for children in Northern Ireland, accommodating up to 48 boys and girls.

The Juvenile Justice Centre was created by the Criminal Justice (Children) (Northern Ireland) Order 1998 through the renaming of four existing training schools. St Joseph's for girls in Middletown, Armagh, closed in 2000. St Patrick's in West Belfast originally held only Catholic boys, although a small number of Protestant boys were detained there prior to its closure. Rathgael, near Bangor, accommodated boys and girls. Established for the accommodation of 'non-Roman Catholic' children, it was latterly used for girls and a small number of younger or more vulnerable boys. Lisnevin, in Millisle, was a highly secure centre built on the model of a Category C prison and accommodating boys of any religion. A review of the criminal justice system in Northern Ireland, carried out following the 'Good Friday'/Belfast Agreement (1998) and reporting in 2000, recommended the closure of Lisnevin, the inclusion of 17-year-olds in the youth justice system and the creation of custody-care orders for 10–13-year-olds (although these have not yet been implemented) (Criminal Justice Review Group 2000).

In November 2000 St Patrick's was closed as part of a government rationalization of the juvenile justice estate, and plans were also announced for the closure of Lisnevin and the creation of a single Juvenile Justice Centre. Lisnevin was eventually closed in October 2003 and the boys there moved to Rathgael, which had been refurbished and renamed the Juvenile Justice Centre for Northern Ireland. The changes following the introduction of the Criminal Justice (Children) (Northern Ireland) Order 1998 resulted in a decrease in capacity from 110 places to 40 custodial places (since increased to 48).

The current Woodlands Juvenile Justice Centre opened on the Rathgael site in 2007, accommodating up to 48 boys and girls aged 10–17 remanded or sentenced to criminal justice centre orders, or remanded under the Police and Criminal Evidence (Northern Ireland) Order 1989. Criminal justice centre orders are determinate sentences of between six months and two years whereby the child serves half the sentence in custody and half in the community under the supervision of the Probation Board. Although some 17-year-olds are accommodated in the Juvenile Justice Centre, children as young as 15 can, in theory, still be detained in adult prison custody in Northern Ireland (although in practice this has been restricted in recent years to 17-year-olds).

Recent research commissioned by the Northern Ireland Human Rights Commission found progress in caring for children in custody, but concluded that rights are still breached, especially in relation to the low age of criminal responsibility; the over-representation of children from care backgrounds entering custody; and the imprisonment of 17-year-old children in adult prisons.

Linda Moore

Related entries

Children in custody; Criminal Justice (Children) (Northern Ireland) Order 1998; Deaths in custody; Justice (Northern Ireland) Act 2002; Remand; Training schools; Youth Justice Agency.

Key texts and sources

Convery, U. and Moore, L. (2006) *Still in Our Care: Protecting Children's Rights in Custody in Northern Ireland.* Belfast: Northern Ireland Human Rights Commission.

Criminal Justice Review Group (2000) *Review of the Criminal Justice System in Northern Ireland.* Belfast: HMSO (available online at http://www. nio.gov.uk/review_of_the_criminal_justice_system_in_northern_ireland.pdf).

Kilkelly, U., Kilpatrick, R., Lundy, L., Moore, L., Scraton, P., Davey, C., Dwyer, C. and McAlister, S. (2004) *Children's Rights in Northern Ireland.* Belfast: Northern Ireland Commissioner for Children and Young People.

Kilkelly, U., Moore, L. and Convery, U. (2002) *In Our Care: Promoting the Rights of Children in Custody.* Belfast: Northern Ireland Human Rights Commission.

McKeaveney, P. (2005) *Review of 10–13 Year Olds Entering Custody.* Belfast: Youth Justice Agency.

See the Office of Public Sector Information's website (http://www.opsi.gov.uk/si/si1998/19981504.htm) for the text of the Criminal Justice (Children) (Northern Ireland) Order 1998.

See also the Youth Justice Agency for Northern Ireland's website (www.youthjusticeagencyni.gov.uk).

JUVENILE SECURE ESTATE

The 'juvenile secure estate' is the generic term used to describe the system of penal custody for children and young people in England and Wales.

The 'juvenile secure estate' comprises three different types of institution each managed within a separate but interrelated 'penal domain'. Secure children's homes (SCHs) – often referred to as 'secure accommodation' – are normally managed by social services departments (local government agencies) under the national aegis of the Department of Health and the Department for Education and Skills. They are primarily defined by a 'welfare' ethos, are comparatively small and have a high ratio of staff to children. Secure training centres (STCs) are private jails owned and managed by global security corporations under contract to the Home Office. They hold children aged 12–17 who have been remanded and/or sentenced to penal custody. Young offender institutions (YOIs) are prisons normally managed by the Prison Service within the Home Office. YOIs are significantly larger than SCHs and STCs and they hold approximately 85 per cent of the total population of child prisoners in England and Wales.

In recent years concerns have been expressed from numerous authoritative sources relating to the conditions and treatment of child prisoners in England and Wales. When the Council of Europe's Commissioner for Human Rights reviewed the circumstances of children in prison in England and Wales in 2005, he could only conclude that 'the prison service is failing in its duty of care towards juvenile inmates' (Office for the Commissioner for Human Rights 2005: para. 93). Recent intensification of pressure on the juvenile secure estate (especially YOIs) – necessitating 'compulsory cell sharing' and 'bring[ing] back into service as quickly as possible cells that are currently out of commission' (Youth Justice Board 2006c) – will only compound such problems.

The very term 'juvenile secure estate' is itself problematic. It implies a 'secure' environment within which children are nurtured, cared for and looked after. In this sense, it recalls Cohen's (1985: 276) observation with regard to the way in which 'special vocabularies' are mobilized to 'soften and disguise the essential (and defining) feature of punishment systems – the planned infliction of pain'. Furthermore, Stern (1998: 157) notes that 'prisons for children and young people are given a variety of names ... the names are intended to show that these are not prisons, but places of good intent, where the previous bad influences of the young people's lives will be corrected by caring people'. Thus, the juvenile secure estate is the preferred euphemism for describing the child prison system in England and Wales. Such euphemism is employed, to borrow the words of Orwell (1954: 245), 'not so much to express meanings as to destroy them'. In this way the very term 'juvenile secure estate' obfuscates the harms, abuses and violations that routinely occur in penal institutions – particularly prisons – holding children (Carlile 2006; Goldson 2006a).

Barry Goldson

Related entries

Assessment framework; Children in custody; Children's human rights; Deaths in custody; Detention and training orders (DTOs); Looked-after children (LAC); Remand management; Restraint; Secure accommodation; Secure training centres (STCs); Sentencing framework; Youth Justice Board (YJB).

Key texts and sources

Carlile, A. (2006) *The Lord Carlile of Berriew QC: An Independent Inquiry into the Use of Physical Restraint, Solitary Confinement and Forcible Strip Searching of Children in Prisons, Secure Training Centres and Local Authority Secure Children's Homes.* London: Howard League for Penal Reform.

Cohen, S. (1985) *Visions of Social Control: Crime, Punishment and Classification.* Cambridge: Polity Press.

Goldson, B. (2006a) 'Damage, harm and death in child prisons in England and Wales: questions of abuse and accountability', *Howard Journal of Criminal Justice,* 45: 449–67.

Office for the Commissioner for Human Rights (2005) *Report by Mr Alvaro Gil-Robles, Commissioner for Human Rights, on his Visit to the United Kingdom, 4–12 November 2004.* Strasbourg: Council of Europe.

Orwell, G. (1954) *Nineteen Eighty-four.* London: Penguin Books.

Stern, V. (1998) *A Sin against the Future: Imprisonment in the World.* London: Penguin Books.

Youth Justice Board (2006c) 'The secure estate for children and young people is nearing operational capacity.' News release, 8 August (available online at **http://www.yjb.gov.uk/en-gb/News/Secure+EstatePressures.htm?area=Corporate**).

KEY ELEMENTS OF EFFECTIVE PRACTICE (KEEPs)

The Key Elements of Effective Practice (KEEPs) are a set of guidance documents published by the Youth Justice Board intended to provide a research-informed overview of the factors that contribute to the effective delivery of youth justice services.

The Key Elements of Effective Practice documents (known as KEEPs) are part of the Youth Justice Board's (YJB's) effective practice strategy designed to reflect the principles of evidence-based policy and practice. Effective practice is described by the YJB as a term referring to those programmes, processes and ways of working that have the highest level of validation from research and evaluation. The KEEPs are seen as central to developing a 'culture of evaluation' in youth justice services.

In contrast to the adult criminal justice agencies, the YJB has decided not to focus attention on 'accredited programmes' but, rather, to promote a wider range of multi-modal methods of working. As a result, the KEEPs are intended to identify the features an effective service should contain rather than providing a prescribed formula for working with young offenders.

The set of 15 KEEPs is currently being revised, and the new set of documents – due for publication in 2008 – will cover the following 10 areas:

- Engaging young people.
- Assessment, planning interventions, supervision and risk management.
- Accommodation.
- Education, training and employment.
- Mental health.
- Substance misuse.
- Offending behaviour interventions.
- Young people who sexually abuse.
- Parenting.
- Restorative justice, reparation and victims.

In stipulating that the revised KEEPs should be based on systematic reviews of research literature, the YJB intended to demonstrate that these guidance documents capture all the recent, relevant evidence. While the comprehensive nature of these reviews is to be welcomed, questions remain about the types of evidence included. For example, has the emphasis on quantitative studies led to a neglect of research exploring how young people perceive and respond to different interventions?

One way in which the YJB has tried to ensure that the KEEPs have a real impact on practice is by linking them closely to training materials and staff development opportunities. The various 'learning pathways' that make up the National Qualifications Framework are designed to provide staff with the skills required to deliver the services described in the KEEPs. In addition, the KEEPs provide a foundation for the quality assurance framework used by youth offending teams and secure children's homes through which managers monitor the performance of their services. However, given that the KEEPs are not used across the majority of the juvenile secure estate, their impact on the end-to-end case management of young people across the youth justice system is perhaps limited.

Kerry Baker

Related entries

Effectiveness; Evaluative research; Evidence-based policy and practice (EBPP); Managerialism; Positivism; Risk management; What works; Youth Justice Board (YJB); Youth justice plans.

Key texts and sources

Fullwood, C. and Powell, H. (2004) 'Towards effective practice in the youth justice system', in R. Burnett and C. Roberts (eds) *What Works in Probation and Youth Justice: Developing Evidence Based Practice.* Cullompton: Willan Publishing.

The Youth Justice Board's document, *Key Elements of Effective Practice*, is available online at **http://www.yjb.gov.uk/Publications/Scripts/prod List.asp?idCategory=16&menu=item&eP.**

L

LABELLING THEORY

In its most general sense, labelling theory refers to a sociological approach to the study of crime and deviance that focuses on the meanings (or labels) given to criminal and/or deviant acts and actors and their consequences. More narrowly it refers to the proposition that methods of social control can actually exacerbate deviance or crime as a result of stigmatization and exclusion.

Labelling theory (also sometimes referred to as social, or societal, reaction theory) is a convenient shorthand, referring to a sociological approach that was very influential in criminology and the sociology of deviance in the late 1960s and early 1970s, particularly in the USA and the UK. In contrast to conventional approaches – that were only concerned with the offender or deviant actor and the causes of their behaviour – labelling theory focuses attention on the way in which formal agencies respond to such behaviour, including both formal and informal social control processes. In particular, the focus is on the way in which formal labels become attached and the consequences of this. In its broadest sense, Plummer (1979: 88) suggests that labelling theory is concerned with exploring the characteristics of deviant or criminal labels, their sources, the ways in which they are applied and their consequences.

The more narrow focus of labelling theory is implied in the title of Howard Becker's (1963) seminal book, *Outsiders*. This conceives the labelling process as stigmatizing, casting deviants and/or offenders as outsiders and resulting in their behaviour becoming more problematic – a process sometimes termed deviance amplifica-

tion. This is likely for a number of reasons, such as the incorporation of the label into self and social identity, the resultant exclusion from what Becker called 'conventional routines' (such as jobs and education) and the adoption of unconventional routines, including deviant or criminal subcultures. The policy implication is to avoid social control measures, if at all possible. This became formalized in Schur's (1973) notion of 'radical non-intervention'. This pessimistic view of social control was later tempered by Braithwaite's (1989) contention that 'reintegrative shaming' without stigmatization is possible and effective in certain circumstances.

At the beginning of the 1970s, labelling theory was displaced by the growing influence of radical or critical criminology. Labelling theory was regarded as not so much wrong as incomplete: it had been right to point to issues of power in the creation and enforcement of laws but it did not incorporate a sufficiently radical view of the state from which this could be analysed. Issues of labelling continued to be a focus within critical criminology, though the process was cast more as one of criminalization and the emphasis was on the ways in which this operated in the interests of the state and the powerful.

Dave King

Related entries

Criminalization; Critical criminology; Decriminalization; Deviance amplification; Diversion; Minimum necessary intervention; Normalization; Radical non-intervention; Reintegrative shaming; Subculture.

Key texts and sources

Becker, H.S. (1963) *Outsiders: Studies in the Sociology of Deviance*. New York, NY: Free Press.

Braithwaite, J. (1989) *Crime, Shame and Reintegration.* Cambridge: Cambridge University Press.

Goffman, E. (1963) *Stigma: Notes on the Management of Spoiled Identity.* Englewood Cliffs, NJ: Prentice Hall.

Plummer, K. (1979) 'Misunderstanding labelling perspectives', in D. Downes and P. Rock (eds) *Deviant Interpretations.* Oxford: Martin Robertson.

Schur, E.M. (1973) *Radical Non-intervention: Rethinking the Delinquency Problem.* Englewood Cliffs, NJ: Prentice Hall.

LEFT REALISM

Left realism (sometimes referred to as 'radical realism') is a theoretical perspective on crime and crime control that emerged out of radical or critical criminology. Its proponents have presented it as correcting perceived flaws both in the right-wing perspectives (that dominated public policy in the 1980s) and in what Jock Young called 'left idealism'.

In the early 1980s, a number of criminologists began to articulate a range of criticisms of the two main approaches in the field of criminology at that time. On the one hand, it was argued that left idealism – a descendant of labelling theory filled out with Marxist analyses – failed to conceive crime as a 'problem'. Either it dismissed the 'crime problem' as largely an illusion constructed by the state via the mass media for ideological purposes, or it romanticized crime as one way in which the 'oppressed' were resisting their 'oppressors'. Thus, it was argued that left idealism had little interest in the traditional criminological project of explaining criminal behaviour or in devising ways of dealing with it.

On the other hand, policies towards crime in the UK during the 1980s were dominated by what Jock Young called 'administrative criminology'. Although this saw crime as a real problem, it was criticized for assuming that criminal behaviour was simply a feature of human nature. The policy emphasis then was, first, on crime prevention (which was construed as defensive measures to be taken by potential victims, such as the fitting of security devices to houses and cars and neighbourhood watch schemes); and, secondly, on developing measures to increase the likelihood and the cost of being caught in order to deter potential offenders.

In response to left idealism, left realism began by accepting that crime really is a problem. This chimed with an increasing focus on the victims of crime, aided partly by the development of national and, particularly, local victim surveys and partly by the development of a feminist critique of criminology. Left realists argued that it was people living in working-class communities and particularly disadvantaged neighbourhoods who suffer most from crime, disorder and anti-social behaviour, and local surveys revealed a demand for more to be done to deal with such problems.

In contrast to both 'left idealism' and 'administrative criminology', left realism resurrected a concern with the causes of crime. The main cause of criminal behaviour, according to left realism, is relative deprivation. Although relative deprivation can occur at any level of society, left realists argue (in a way that echoes anomie theory) that it is people who are excluded from conventional opportunities for success who experience the greatest pressure towards crime.

While being critical of capitalist societies with high levels of inequality, left realism's concern for the victims of crime has meant that, unlike its radical predecessors, it has focused on exploring practical ways of intervention to deal with the crime problem. Some of these do not look markedly different from those emanating from other approaches – for example, better policing, support and protection for victims, community involvement and addressing the causes of criminal behaviour.

Dave King

Related entries

Administrative criminology; Anomie theory; Community safety; Crime and disorder reduction (CDR); Crime prevention; Critical criminology; Fear of crime; Social exclusion; Victims.

Key texts and sources

Lea, J. and Young, J. (1993) *What's to be Done about Law and Order?* (2nd edn). London: Pluto Press.

Matthews, R. and Young, J. (eds) (1986) *Confronting Crime*. London: Sage.

Matthews, R. and Young, J. (1992) *Rethinking Criminology: The Realist Debate*. London: Sage.

Young, J. (1994) 'Incessant chatter: recent paradigms in criminology', in M. Maguire *et al.* (eds) *The Oxford Handbook of Criminology*. Oxford: Oxford University Press.

Young, J. and Matthews, R. (eds) (1992) *Issues in Realist Criminology*. London: Sage.

LEGAL AID

Legal aid is a government-funded scheme that enables people to receive legal advice, assistance or representation for free or on a subsidized basis, provided that they either do not have sufficient means to pay for it themselves or there is some other good reason that the legal work should be funded by the government.

Legal aid was first introduced following the Rushcliffe Committee report in 1945. Since then it has grown in scope and cost and is widely acclaimed as one of the best systems in the world for ensuring access to justice. Legal aid was originally administered by the Law Society and then by the Legal Aid Board. However, following the Access to Justice Act 1999, the Legal Services Commission, a quasi-non-governmental organization, became directly responsible to government for operating the scheme. Unlike other national services, publicly funded legal advice has traditionally been provided by private law firms (solicitors and barristers) who may do a mixture of public and private work. Part of the reason for this is to retain a level of independence – especially where lawyers are challenging the actions of the state.

The criteria for funding different types of legal work change frequently and are often complex. The Legal Services Commission's website provides up-to-date information about how legal aid is administered. A rise in the spend on legal aid – partly attributed to the need to comply with human rights obligations, such as the right to a fair trial – has resulted in many changes to legal aid, including the abandoning and then reintroduction of means testing in the magistrates' courts.

Civil work and criminal work are subject to different funding criteria. In general, the criteria combine financial eligibility with a 'sufficient benefit' test. An applicant will, therefore, need to prove his or her limited means and the benefit to be gained from legal advice or representation. In certain instances, those who are entitled to particular state benefits will be 'passported' through the financial eligibility test.

Recent years have seen a raft of proposed changes to the legal aid system, the most recent of which was Lord Carter's review (2006). These changes envisage a move to a market-based model where law firms bid for government contracts to do legal aid work, following an interim period where lawyers represent clients on a fixed-fee basis. This has been heavily criticized and there is mounting concern that such a system would compound injustices and inequalities.

Laura Janes

Related entries

Children's human rights; Due process; Human Rights Act 1998; Justice; United Nations Committee on the Rights of the Child.

Key texts and sources

Carter, Lord (2006) *Legal Aid: A Market-based Approach to Reform* (available online at http://www.legalaidprocurementreview.gov.uk/publications.htm).

See the Office of Public Sector Information's website (http://www.opsi.gov.uk/ACTS/acts1999/19990022.htm) for the text of the Access to Justice Act 1999.

See also the websites of the Department for Constitutional Affairs (http://www.dca.gov.uk/), the Legal Aid Practitioners' Group (http://www.lapg.co.uk/) and the Legal Services Commission (http://www.legalservices.gov.uk/).

LOCAL CHILD CURFEW SCHEMES (LCCSs)

> If implemented – in accordance with s. 14 of the Crime and Disorder Act 1998 – local child curfew schemes (LCCSs) ban children under the age of 16 from being present in a designated public place during specified hours (falling between 9.00 p.m. and 6.00 a.m.), unless under the supervision of a 'responsible adult'.

The government describes local child curfew Schemes (LCCSs) as having a dual purpose: to protect the local community from anti-social behaviour and to protect young people from the risks of being unaccompanied on the streets at night. Tellingly, perhaps, only the first of these claimed objectives is enshrined within the legislation.

While s. 14 of the Crime and Disorder Act 1998 provides for a blanket curfew, accompanying guidance specifies that children out during curfew hours who are perceived to be going about 'legitimate' business will be spared being returned home by a police officer – and the ensuing house call from social services – as provided for in other circumstances by s. 15 (ss. 14–15 are amended by ss. 48 and 49 of the Criminal Justice and Police Act 2001). All encounters will necessitate self-justification and potentially damage relations between the police and young people. Further, the issue of which activities are 'legitimate' is highly subjective and, arguably, should be of no concern to the police unless they fall within the realm of the 'criminal'.

The potential for LCCSs to conflict with the European Convention on Human Rights (ECHR) and the Human Rights Act 1998 is very substantial, specifically in relation to Articles 5, 8 and 11: the rights to liberty, privacy and assembly, respectively. LCCSs also threaten to breach Article 14, which requires that convention rights should be accorded in a non-discriminatory manner, regardless of age. The fact that curfews are *local* as opposed to national also raises the danger of racial / class-based targeting when identifying so-called 'hotspots'.

Whether legitimacy and proportionality can ever be guaranteed within the parameters of a 'blanket' curfew is obviously questionable. Conventionally reserved for times of war or other social crises, the fact that the law now provides for curfews to be routinely directed at children speaks volumes about prevalent attitudes towards young people. LCCSs are the product of a politics of fear though, ironically, their existence is actually likely to legitimize and feed public fears. The lack of proportionality in a curfew-based response becomes more problematic given that research into similar schemes in the USA has consistently found little or no preventative effect in terms of crime rates.

In practice to date, no LCCSs have been implemented. Thus, their compatibility with the ECHR and the Human Rights Act 1998 remains untested in the courts. The caution that has characterized the approaches of local authorities and the police with regard to implementing LCCSs seems to stem from the perceived practical difficulties inherent in enforcement. Accordingly, in 2003 the government introduced dispersal orders. These have a similar effect to LCCSs, but legislation anticipates their use on a discretionary case-by-case basis. They have proved far more popular, thus appearing to have usurped LCCSs.

Charlotte Walsh

Related entries

Anti-social behaviour; Children's human rights; Crime and Disorder Act 1998; Criminalization; Curfew orders; Discrimination; Dispersal orders; European Convention on Human Rights (ECHR); Fear of crime; Human Rights Act 1998; 'Race' and justice; Youth and policing.

Key texts and sources

Home Office (2001c) *Local Child Curfews Guidance Document: Working Draft*. London: Home Office (available online at **http://www.homeoffice.gov.uk/documents/guidance-child-curfew?view=Binary**).

Jeffs, T. and Smith, M. (1996) 'Getting the dirtbags off the streets: curfews and other solutions to juvenile crime', *Youth and Policy*, 53: 1–14.

Walsh, C. (1999) 'Imposing order: child safety orders and local child curfew schemes', *Journal of Social Welfare and Family Law*, 21: 135–49.

Walsh, C. (2002) 'Curfews: no more hanging around', *Youth Justice*, 2: 70–81.

See the Office of Public Sector Information's website for the texts of the Crime and Disorder Act 1998 (http://www.opsi.gov.uk/acts/acts1998/1998 0037.htm) and the Criminal Justice and Police Act 2001 (http://www.opsi.gov.uk/acts/acts2001/2001 0016.htm).

LONG-TERM DETENTION

Long-term detention is any custodial sentence imposed on a child or young person for longer than two years. Long-term detention is only available in the Crown court for offences of murder, for other 'grave crimes' (or grave offences) and in cases where the court deems the young person to be 'dangerous'.

The maximum custodial sentence available in the youth court is a two-year detention and training order. In certain, exceptional, circumstances, however, the Crown court may impose longer periods of detention up to the maximum available in the case of an adult. Young people convicted of murder must be sentenced to be detained 'during her Majesty's pleasure' – the functional equivalent of an adult mandatory life sentence. The young person serves a minimum period of detention, specified by the court in the 'tariff', following which he or she will remain in custody until the Parole Board considers it safe to release him or her into the community under statutory supervision for life.

Young people convicted of other 'grave crimes' – such as rape, robbery and domestic burglary – may be liable to a term of detention up to the maximum available for an adult. The first part of the sentence is served in custody, with release at the halfway stage subject to community supervision until the end of the order.

The Criminal Justice Act 2003 introduced two new custodial sentences for young people who commit sexual or violent offences specified in the legislation and who are considered by the court to be 'dangerous' – defined as posing a *significant* risk to the public of *serious* harm. Young people dealt with under these provisions will receive:

- *detention for public protection* – similar in most respects to a life custodial sentence; or
- an *extended sentence* – a term of detention of at least one year, followed by an extended licence period of up to five years for a violent offence or eight years for a sexual offence.

The growth in the use of long-term detention is a cause for concern. In 1970 only 6 orders were made for 'grave crimes', rising to 65 in 1980, 154 in 1985 and 706 in 2002. This rapid escalation is largely a consequence of legislative change that has expanded the category of offences that can be considered 'grave crimes' and that has reduced the age at which the grave crime provisions are activated, combined with a punitive turn that has characterized youth justice policy since the early 1990s. A reduction in such sentences since 2002 is, in part, a consequence of the increased terms available in the youth court with the introduction of the detention and training order.

Use of the new provisions for 'dangerous' young people, while lower, is not insignificant and is well above the level anticipated by the government prior to implementation. Some 99 such orders were imposed in the eight months from April 2005, when the measures were introduced. Criticism of these powers has tended to focus on their actuarial nature: they are imposed in relation to future 'risk' – what the child *might* do – rather than in relation to the seriousness of what the child *has* done.

Tim Bateman

Related entries

Crown court; Dangerousness; Detention for public protection (DPP); Detention and training orders (DTOs); Grave offences; Risk management; Tariff.

Key texts and sources

Bateman, T. (2005b) 'Custody and policy', in T. Bateman and J. Pitts (eds) *The RHP Companion to Youth Justice*. Lyme Regis: Russell House.

Nacro (2002a) *Children who Commit Grave Crimes*. London: Nacro.

Nacro (2006g) *The Dangerous Provisions of the Criminal Justice Act 2003 and Subsequent Case Law. Youth Crime Briefing*. London: Nacro.

Stone, N. (2002) 'Shorter terms of Section 91 detention', *Youth Justice*, 2: 47–9.

LOOKED-AFTER CHILDREN (LAC)

Looked-after children (LAC) are those to whom the state, through local authority structures, has statutory responsibilities and duties: to safeguard their welfare; to provide services for their care and accommodation; and/or to support them while living with a parent or guardian.

The legal obligation to 'look after' a child arises where he or she has no parent, is lost or abandoned, or is prevented from living with a 'parent' (a person with legal 'parental responsibility'), for whatever reason. In addition, a child may become looked after subject to a court order where that is necessary to protect him or her from 'serious harm' (and in some circumstances in order to provide immediate protection while carrying out child protection investigations).

Children in the youth justice system may also become 'looked after' subject to other court orders, such as remand to local authority accommodation or being subject to certain community sentences (for example, supervision orders with residence requirements that may be replaced by youth rehabilitation orders with residence/fostering requirements subject to the Criminal Justice and Immigration Bill 2006–7 to 2007–8). Where it is necessary to protect the child or others, a court may order that he or she is looked after in secure accommodation. A number of principles are embodied in law giving primacy to the child's welfare – for example, looking after children in partnership with par-

ents where possible and taking account of the views of children and other relevant people. With regard to youth justice, the local authority is permitted to override such duties and responsibilities in order to protect the public from serious injury.

The law governing looked-after children (LAC) is largely provided by the Children Act 1989 in England and Wales, which introduced the terminology of being 'looked after' rather than being 'in care' (although the latter term remains valid in some circumstances and law). Subsequently, legislation with similar provisions and principles was introduced in Northern Ireland and Scotland through the Children (Northern Ireland) Order 1995 the Children (Scotland) Act 1995. The differences between these are of limited significance, apart from the way in which authorities gain parental responsibility in Scotland and in responsibilities and duties to those who have left, or are leaving, 'care' (statutory provision is weaker in Scotland). In addition, in Scotland children can become compulsorily looked after through either the court or the children's hearing system. Across all jurisdictions there is concern about poor outcomes and experiences for LAC, including not only those relating to education and health but also those relating to juvenile or youth justice.

There are many children who live away from their parents or guardians in formal settings that include residential (group) homes, family placement (fostering), hospitals, educational boarding schools and penal institutions. Others may be living in hostels, bed-and-breakfast accommodation, informally with friends, in independent accommodation or are homeless. Some may be unaccompanied child refugees or asylum seekers. To varying degrees, local authorities and other agencies have responsibilites towards such children in the context of their welfare and other needs, but, in some cases, this goes so far as to be statutorily responsible for their care, welfare and accommodation – to look after the child in the manner of a good parent. Nevertheless, where the child is subject to a court order – such as a care order or remand to local authority accommodation – he or she may be placed with a parent or guardian while retaining 'looked after' status. A child may also be looked after as a result of a children's hearing (in Scotland) or on the basis of a voluntary arrangement subject to statutorily defined criteria.

In all cases, statutory agencies (primarily local authorities) have duties, responsibilities or powers to make assessments, to plan and review and to provide for the various needs of the LAC. The specific functions of particular agencies may differ, but the concept of corporate parenting demands joint approaches where appropriate. In England and Wales, the Children Act 2004 placed duties and responsibilities on a range of agencies – including youth offending teams and custodial institutions. The principles that the welfare of the child is paramount and that the views of the child should be sought and taken into account apply to *all* jurisdictions in the UK, although these principles are sometimes in tension with the provisions of youth justice legislation.

Collectively, LAC have tended to suffer a degree of stigma, often being perceived as troublesome or even criminal. It is the case that recorded offending rates are disproportionately high among LAC compared with the general population. Nevertheless, the large majority of LAC do not come to the attention of the youth justice system, and it is their experience of abuse and neglect that is the principal reason for their looked-after status. Research indicates a number of factors that are associated with the 'risk' of youth offending as well as those that are 'protective' in nature. Most of these factors are also associated with other social problems, such as poor mental health and, indeed, being looked after. Thus, many LAC are disadvantaged in numerous respects and may have faced, for example, loss (bereavement), abuse and violation, a disrupted education, welfare neglect, poverty and low self-esteem. Being looked after should not be a factor leading to an increased risk of offending in itself, although in practice many of the experiences of LAC compound 'risk factors', including multiple changes of relationships and accommodation and interrupted schooling. There is a corresponding absence of stable relationships and other 'protective factors'. It is also apparent that LAC, when they do offend or in some cases simply 'misbehave', are brought to police attention and criminalized more readily than children living in their own families. This has been found to be the case in residential (group) homes in particular.

LAC can also face additional disadvantage if and when they do come to the attention of the youth justice system. For example, those already looked after may be less likely to be remanded to local authority accommodation as opposed to custody, and those who are out late or running away may be labelled as having a history of 'absconding' where other children may not have this brought to the attention of a court. Furthermore, those who have been in foster care may not be thought suitable for a community order requiring such care as an alternative to custody – on the grounds that it has been tried and 'failed'.

The law governing looked-after status in the youth justice system is notoriously complex and fraught with anomaly. Research by the National Children's Bureau (Hart 2006) has highlighted that many managers and practitioners in the youth justice system do not easily or accurately identify looked-after status. Assessment tools employed by youth offending teams often fail to record properly looked-after status, as is also often the case in the juvenile secure estate.

The most serious anomalies concern those who lose their liberty as a result of custodial remands and sentences. In England and Wales, for example, a 15-year-old girl detained on remand will assume looked-after status and will be accommodated in secure accommodation or in a privately run secure training centre. A boy of the same age is more often than not detained in a young offender institution without gaining looked after status. Furthermore, a child – female or male – who has been looked-after on remand will lose that status if he or she receives a subsequent custodial sentence, even in cases where his or her actual 'placement' remains unchanged.

The position for young people aged 17 conflicts with the provisions of the United Nations Convention on the Rights of the Child because they are treated as 'adults'. Thus, a child who is looked after on remand at the age of 16 loses that status on reaching 17 during the proceedings and may be transferred from local authority 'care' to a young offender institution. Although the government has stated its intention to review this position, it currently considers the resolution of such problems to be too complex.

For LAC in general, the level of support through adolescence, and beyond the age of 18, on 'leaving-care' has been improved by the Children (Leaving Care) Act 2000. The Act introduced criteria under which LAC may become eligible for leaving-care services. Children who are detained in penal institutions, however, with minor exception, do not have their time living compulsorily away from home counted in the context of leaving-care criteria. This is particularly stark for children and young people serving long-term detention or indeterminate sentences who are not eligible for leaving-care services if they are released either before or after attaining 18 and who are required to live independently.

There is a considerable history of government initiatives to improve the circumstances of LAC, including the 'Quality Protects' programme of the late 1990s and early 2000s. Most recently, the 2006 green paper, *Care Matters*, and the white paper, *Care Matters: Time for Change* (DfES 2007), set out proposals for improving outcomes for LAC. The agenda contained in the white paper promises much for LAC in general, but there are no specific proposals to clarify looked-after status or to improve the experiences of children and young people in the youth justice system. Moreover, it is those who are compulsorily 'in the care of the state' but who do not receive the full benefits of being looked after who continue to be the most neglected.

It is incumbent on those working in the youth justice system to ensure that LAC are not discriminated against; that there is clarity of roles between agencies; that systems are in place to identify properly 'looked after' and 'leaving care' status; that good-quality planning and reviewing processes are implemented; that local authorities carry out their legal (and moral) duties; and that the needs of children in and leaving custody are fully addressed and met.

Geoff Monaghan

Related entries

Assessment framework; Care orders; Child abuse; Children Act 1989; Children Act 2004; Children in custody; Children (Leaving Care) Act 2000; Children (Scotland) Act 1995; Children's human rights; Children's trusts; Every Child Matters (ECM); Extending Entitlement (National Assembly for Wales); Munby judgment; Protective factors; Remand; Risk factors; Secure accommodation; Social exclusion; Supervision orders.

Key texts and sources

Department for Education and Skills (2007a) *Care Matters: Time for Change.* London: DfES.

Hart, D. (2006) *Tell Them Not to Forget about Us: A Guide to Practice with Looked After Children in Custody.* London: National Children's Bureau.

Nacro (2005h) *A Handbook on Reducing Offending by Looked After Children.* London: Nacro.

Nacro (2006f) *The Children (Leaving Care) Act 2000 – Implications for the Youth Justice System. Youth Crime Briefing.* London: Nacro.

MAGISTRATES

In youth courts in England and Wales, magistrates (also known as justices of the peace – JPs) hear prosecutions and dispose of 'summary offences' and 'triable either way' offences. The actual term 'magistrate' is derived from the Middle English term 'magistrat', meaning a person who administers the law.

Magistrates who sit in the youth court receive additional specialist training. They are selected by the Lord Chancellor for Inner London and are elected by their peers outside London. A common system of selection will be introduced when, and if, s. 50 of the Courts Act 2003 comes into force.

There are two types of magistrate in England and Wales: lay magistrates (those without professional legal education and training) and legal professionals permanently employed by the Department for Constitutional Affairs. The first group – of about 30,000 people, half of whom are women – are known as lay justices of the peace (JPs). They sit voluntarily although they receive allowances to cover travel and subsistence expenses. They are appointed to their local bench and are provided with specialist guidance and/or advice in court – especially with regard to sentencing powers – by a professionally qualified court legal adviser (clerk to the justices). A youth court 'bench' normally comprises three magistrates, one of whom acts as the chairperson. The second group – professional magistrates – were previously known as stipendiary magistrates but are now known as district judges (magistrates' courts) (DJMC). A DJMC must be a barrister or solicitor of at least ten years' standing, and she or he sits alone – usually dealing with the longer or more complicated summary cases.

The sentencing powers of youth courts (and adult magistrates' courts) include fines and financial penalties, and community orders – which can include curfews, electronic tagging and/or supervision – and custodial detention. Magistrates hear committal proceedings for certain offences and establish whether sufficient evidence exists to refer the case to a higher court for trial and sentencing. Magistrates have the power to pass summary offenders to higher courts for sentencing when, in the opinion of the bench, a penalty greater than that which can be imposed by the youth court/magistrates' court is warranted.

Richard Hester

Related entries

District judges; Family proceedings court; Sentencing framework; Sentencing guidelines; Youth courts.

Key texts and sources

See the following websites: Courts in Northern Ireland (http://www.direct.gov.uk/en/Gtgl1/GuideToGovernment/Judiciary/DG_4003300); the Department for Constitutional Affairs (http://www.dca.gov.uk/); Her Majesty's Courts Service (http://www.hmcourts-service.gov.uk/); the Criminal Justice System for England and Wales (http://www.cjsonline.gov.uk/); the Judicial System in Scotland (http://www.direct.gov.uk/en/Gtgl1/GuideToGovernment/Judiciary/DG_40 03292); the Magistrates' Association (http://www.magistrates-association.org.uk/); and the Magistrates' Association 'Youth site' (http://www.magistrates-association.org.uk/youth_site/youth_index.html).

MANAGERIALISM

> Managerialism comprises a set of techniques and practices – driven by notions of efficiency, effectiveness and economy – that aim to transform the structures and to reorganize the processes for both the funding and delivery of youth and criminal justice.

Managerialism stresses the need to develop a connected, coherent, efficient and, above all, *cost-effective* series of policies and practices. It is ostensibly governed by pragmatism rather than any fundamental penal philosophy. Managerialism provides a means by which philosophical dispute can be sidestepped. Its concern is not necessarily one of individual reform, training or punishment but of implementing policies that 'work', whether pragmatically or politically (Clarke and Newman 1997). Under the guise of 'modernization', New Labour, in particular, has initiated a 'new wave' of 'joined up' managerialization to entrench 'performance management' across the public sector. This has involved the following:

- The establishment of consistent and mutually reinforcing aims and objectives.
- The installation of a 'what works'/'best practice' culture.
- The development of an evidence-based approach to the allocation of resources.
- The institutionalization of performance management to improve productivity.
- The setting of explicit targets and performance indicators to enable the auditing of efficiency and effectiveness.
- The costing and market testing of all activities to ensure value for money.
- The privatization and deregulation of designated responsibilities.
- The establishment of multi-agency co-operation on a statutory basis (McLaughlin *et al.* 2001).

In the field of youth justice, the Audit Commission's (1996) 'value for money' report on waste and inefficiency was pivotal. New Labour embraced its agenda and identified new public management as the route through which an economical and accountable youth justice system could be created. The past was declared a 'failure' in order to clear the ground (despite the 'successes' of the late 1980s in reducing youth crime and custody rates). Policy has become dominated by concerns for identifying the risk conditions rather than the causes of youth crime; for setting statutory time limits from arrest to sentence; for introducing performance targets for youth offending teams (YOTs); for discovering 'what works' via evaluative research; for establishing YOTs to 'join up' local agencies; and for constructing means of standardizing risk conditions (through uniform Asset and other standardized assessment tools). It is an environment in which the multi-agency co-operation of 1980s corporatism and the risk assessment strategies of actuarialism are fused into an overarching 'task environment' based on audit, market testing, performance targets, productivity remits, cost effectiveness and the quantifiable ethos of 'what works' (Feeley and Simon 1992). It is capable of shifting the core purpose of youth justice to the meeting of SMART (Specific, Measurable, Achievable, Realistic and Timetabled) targets.

Certainly, the idea of 'joined-up' government to tackle multifaceted and complex problems (such as youth offending), through multi-agency partnerships employing a broad spectrum of social policy interventions, represents a definitive break with traditional means of responding to young offenders. Significantly it creates new objects of governance (Newman 2001). Youth offending, for example, ceases to be defined only in terms of 'criminality' and subject to the expertise of youth justice professionals. It also becomes a problem of education, health, employment and housing management. Its core business becomes not just that of crime control but also of assessing the risks of 'social exclusion', disorder and 'anti-social behaviour'.

John Muncie

Related entries

Audit Commission; Contestability; Evaluative research; Governmentality; Risk management; What works; Youth justice plans.

Key texts and sources

Audit Commission (1996) *Misspent Youth*. London: Audit Commission.

Clarke, J. and Newman, J. (1997) *The Managerial State*. London: Sage.

Feeley, M. and Simon, J. (1992) 'The new penology: notes on the emerging strategy of corrections and its implications', *Criminology*, 30: 449–74.

McLaughlin, E., Muncie, J. and Hughes, G. (2001) 'The permanent revolution: New Labour, new public management and the modernization of criminal justice', *Criminal Justice*, 1: 301–18.

Newman, J. (2001) *Modernising Governance*. London: Sage.

MANDATORY SENTENCES

A mantatory sentence is a sentence that *must* be imposed following conviction for a specified offence(s).

Mandatory sentences for children and young people include those for murder: in England and Wales, the defendant must be sentenced to detention at Her Majesty's Pleasure under s. 90 of the Powers of Criminal Courts (Sentencing) Act 2000; in Scotland to detention without limit of time under s. 205(2) of the Criminal Procedure (Scotland) Act 1995; and in Northern Ireland to detention at the Secretary of State's Pleasure under Article 45 of the Criminal Justice (Children) (Northern Ireland) Order 1998.

However, there are also a number of firearms offences where a minimum sentence must be imposed in the absence of 'exceptional circumstances' on offenders aged 16 or over, under s. 51A of the Firearms Act 1968, the Firearms (Northern Ireland) Order 2004 and the Violent Crime Reduction Act 2006 (the 1968 Act phrase was defined in *R* v. *Rehman*; *R* v. *Wood*. Further, the 'dangerous offenders' provisions of the Criminal Justice Act 2003 require the court to impose certain types of sentence where a child or young person has committed one of a scheduled list of violent or sexual offences, following a finding of 'dangerousness'.

Disqualification from driving is also mandatory on conviction for certain offences, and some commentators have argued that the referral order – in England and Wales – is, in practice, essentially mandatory.

Sally Ireland

Related entries

Dangerousness; Grave offences; Referral order; Tariff.

Key texts and sources

See the Office of Public Sector Information's website for the texts of the Criminal Justice (Children) (Northern Ireland) Order 1998 (http://www.opsi.gov.uk/si/si1998/19981504.htm); the Criminal Justice Act 2003 (http://www.opsi.gov.uk/acts/acts2003/20030044.htm); the Firearms (Northern Ireland) Order 2004 (http://www.opsi.gov.uk/si/si2004/20040702.htm); the Powers of Criminal Courts (Sentencing) Act 2000 (http://www.opsi.gov.uk/acts/acts2000/20000006.htm); the Violent Crime Reduction Act 2006 (http://www.opsi.gov.uk/acts/acts2006/20060038.htm); and the Youth Justice and Criminal Evidence Act 1999 (http://www.opsi.gov.uk/acts/acts1999/19990023.htm).

MEDIA REPORTING

Media reporting concerns the news media representation of children and young people as victims and offenders.

The most striking thing about the media reporting of young people with respect to crime and criminal justice is their overwhelming representation as offenders rather than victims. Research consistently finds that well over half of young people surveyed have suffered some form of criminal victimization within the past 12 months (Muncie 2004). Yet their experiences as victims of all but the most serious offences would appear to be of little interest to journalists.

Even as victims of serious crime, not all young people are deemed equally newsworthy. The gender, age, ethnicity and social class of the victim interact with the dynamics of news production and the wider socio-political environment to produce a 'hierarchy of victimhood' that can dramatically influence levels of media attention and public interest. The right 'type' of young victim may dominate the headlines, generate significant changes to youth justice policy and practice and, in murder cases, invoke public mourning on a global scale. Alternatively, children and young people who never achieve legitimate victim status may pass virtually unnoticed in the wider social world (Greer 2007).

While the everyday criminal victimization of young people is under-represented in the news, their everyday criminality remains a topic of perennial media interest. In line with the key determinants of newsworthiness – including drama, novelty and personalization – crimes of interpersonal violence, such as 'muggings' and assaults, feature prominently. Reporting is often racialized, and black youths – whether as 'muggers', rioters or gun-toting gang members – are routinely portrayed as the dangerous 'criminal other' (Webster 2007). Following demonstrations against the first and second Gulf Wars, and the culture of fear and suspicion that characterizes the post-9/11 'war on terror', the association between ethnicity and crime has more recently extended to Asian youth (Alexander 2000). Equally, the visibility of female youth offending has also increased in recent years, with British girls reported in 2006 to be 'among the most violent in world' (*Guardian* 2006).

At times, sensationalist reporting of particular forms of youth 'deviance' – from children who kill, to drug taking, to subcultural affiliations – may form the basis of 'moral panics' (Cohen 2002), typified by exaggerated public concern and heavy-handed methods of control or exclusion. The high-profile reporting of individual incidents or 'crime waves', against a mediatized backdrop of everyday offending, reinforces the image of 'youth' as a problem to be solved. Since media explanations of youth crime tend to be individualistic (portraying feckless, hedonistic juveniles, 'out of control' in a 'permissive society') rather than social-structural – and related, for example, to relative deprivation in a ruthlessly exclusive consumer culture – proposed solutions tend to involve more punishment and control rather than wider social change.

Young people may respond to their distorted representation in a variety of ways, from passively accepting or cynically rejecting media images, to embracing and defiantly flaunting precisely those characteristics that are being demonized. Whatever the response, much media reporting merges the 'problem of youth' and the 'problem of crime' into one conceptual category and presents youth offending as a visible index for society's ills.

Chris Greer

Related entries

Bulger; Demonization; Deviance amplification; Fear of crime; Gender and justice; Moral panic; Public attitudes to youth crime and justice; 'Race' and justice; Victimization; Victims.

Key texts and sources

Alexander, C. (2000) *The Asian Gang: Ethnicity, Identity, Masculinity*. Oxford: Berg.

Cohen, S. (2002) *Folk Devils and Moral Panics: The Creation of Mods and Rockers*. London: Routledge.

Greer, C. (2007) 'News media, victims and crime', in P. Davies *et al.* (eds) *Victims, Crime and Society*. London: Sage.

Guardian (2006) 'British girls among most violent in world', 23 January.

Muncie, J. (2004) *Youth and Crime* (2nd ed). London: Sage.

Spalek, B. (2002) *Islam, Crime and Criminal Justice*. Cullompton: Willan Publishing.

Webster, C. (2007) *Understanding Race and Crime*. Cullompton: Willan Publishing.

MEDIATION

Conflict mediation is a process by which an impartial third party helps two (or more) disputants work out how to resolve a conflict. The disputants, not the mediators, decide the terms of any agreement reached. Mediation usually focuses on future rather than past behaviour. More specifically, victim–offender mediation is a process in which an impartial third party helps the victim(s) and offender(s) to communicate, either directly or indirectly.

Mediation is one of the key processes in restorative justice. It can lead to greater understanding for both parties and sometimes to tangible reparation. It is used in two main ways:

- In a general way to resolve any conflicts in a young person's life. Mediation starts with a 'level playing-field', apart from any power issues involved.
- To help victims and offenders to communicate after a crime. Victim–offender mediation starts with an acknowledgement that the offender takes responsibility for the crime before mediation is contemplated (not always the same as pleading guilty). Victim–offender mediation starts with an acknowledgement that one of the parties has harmed the other.

Sometimes the two overlap – for example, where a young offender has committed criminal damage in the home or stolen from members of his or her family. Then mediation has elements of both – acknowledgement of the harm done and resolution of any conflicts lying behind it.

The benefits of mediation are as follows:

- It encourages people to focus on the *problem* rather than on each other.
- It gives both parties an opportunity to tell their version of events fully and to listen to the other party.
- People are more likely to change if they hear how their behaviour is affecting the other person(s).

- Mediation helps people think about how they want the situation to be from now on (important in a continuing relationship).
- Mediation is confidential.

The mediation process follows a three-tier structure. First, *separate meetings* involve the mediator visiting both parties (or offender(s) and victim(s)) separately, to assess suitability and to discuss all options. Second if appropriate, *preparation for direct mediation* is undertaken. Third, a *joint meeting* is arranged that comprises a process as follows:

- *Opening statement*: introductions and ground rules.
- *Uninterrupted time*: each person tells his or her story.
- *Exchange*: opportunity for questions.
- *Building agreement*: (if appropriate).
- *Writing agreement*: (if appropriate).
- *Closing*: arranging follow-up.
- *Mediator's debrief.*

However, within this structure, there is no prescribed 'script' as there is usually in restorative conferencing. The mediator(s) help the parties to develop their own dialogue. The process can be carried out with two parties or with several (in which case it is more like conferencing).

Conflict mediation and victim-offender mediation started in the UK in the early 1980s, mostly with adults. After the Crime and Disorder Act 1998, several youth offending teams developed victim–offender mediation in their restorative justice work. Others set up partnerships with local (independent) mediation services to undertake mediation in suitable cases. In some areas, cases of anti-social behaviour by young people are addressed by community mediation services.

Marian Liebmann

Related entries

Family group conferencing; Referral orders; Reparation; Restorative cautioning; Restorative justice; Social harm; Victims.

Key texts and sources

Beer, J. with Stief, E. (1997) *The Mediator's Handbook*. Philadelphia, PA: Friends Conflict Resolution Programs.

European Forum for Restorative Justice (ed.) (2000) *Victim–Offender Mediation in Europe: Making Restorative Justice Work*. Leuven: Leuven University Press.

Liebmann, M. (ed.) (2000) *Mediation in Context*. London: Jessica Kingsley.

Liebmann, M. (2007) *Restorative Justice: How it Works*. London: Jessica Kingsley.

Quill, D. and Wynne, J. (1993) *Victim and Offender Mediation Handbook*. Leeds: Save the Children/West Yorkshire Probation Service.

MENTAL HEALTH AND YOUNG OFFENDERS

Mental health should be thought of as a spectrum, with mental health at one end and serious mental illness at the other. Various terms are used to describe mental health (for example, 'emotional well-being' and 'positive mental health') and mental health difficulties (for example, 'mental health problems', 'mental disorders' and 'mental illness'). Some of these terms are quite generic and are used interchangeably, but other terms – such as 'mental disorder' or 'illness' – tend to refer to the severity of the problem.

It is well known that young offenders have a wide range of needs, including mental health needs. Mental disorders are very prevalent among young offenders, with some estimates suggesting that up to 95 per cent of children and young people in trouble might have one or more disorder.

It is generally agreed that there are factors that impact on mental health. These can be 'risk factors': problems within ourselves (for example, learning disabilities, genetic predisposition); problems in the family (for example, divorce, child abuse); and/or environmental/structural problems (for example, poverty, deprivation). It is known that not everyone who experiences risk factors goes on to develop mental health problems. This may be because there are also protective factors that have a positive impact on mental health (for example, family support, individual self-esteem, individual capacity to resolve and/or resist problems, resilience).

Various studies illustrate the factors that put young offenders at a higher risk of developing mental disorders. A report from the Youth Justice Board (2005a) looks at the multiple needs of young offenders, which include peer and family problems, problems of being in care, problems at school (including academic performance), and substance and alcohol misuse, as well as mental health problems. Other studies have found similar problems, including that many young offenders had experienced at least one stressful event and some had experienced many more.

The problems for young offenders are multi-dimensional, and tackling them is not easy or simple. For the population generally, there is a lot of stigma surrounding mental health, and mental health services are often considered inappropriate or inaccessible to young people. So young people may not want to access mental health services, and potentially either do not or cannot access services until they become so ill that they need more specialist treatment, are 'sectioned' under the mental health legislation or, in some cases, end up in the youth justice system.

Young offenders, like all other children and young people, should have access to a comprehensive range of mental health services that meet their needs, but this is not always the case. For instance, in England some of the problems are connected to partnership arrangements between Child and Adolescent Mental Health Services (CAMHS) and youth offending teams, as well as the general lack of capacity within CAMHS. However, current policy drivers in all four countries of the UK include improving mental health services for young offenders, but all are slightly different and are at varying stages of development. However, if implemented, there should be some improvement in mental health services.

Paula Lavis

Related entries

Assessment framework; Child abuse; Child and Adolescent Mental Health Services (CAMHS); Children in custody; Deaths in custody; Fostering; Hospital orders; Intensive Supervision and Surveillance Programme (ISSP); Looked-after children (LAC); Mental health legislation; Resettlement; Risk factors; Protective factors; Secure accommodation; Vulnerability; Young offender institutions (YOIs); Youth justice plans; Youth Matters.

Key texts and sources

Bailey, S. and Williams, R. (2005) 'Forensic mental health services for children and adolescents', in R. Williams and M. Kerfoot (eds) *Child and Adolescent Mental Health Services.* Oxford: Oxford University Press.

Department of Health (2007) *Promoting Mental Health for Children Held in Secure Settings: A Framework for Commissioning Services.* London: Department of Health.

Healthcare Commission (2006) *Let's Talk About It: A Review of Healthcare in the Community for Young People who Offend.* London: Healthcare Commission.

Lader, D., Singelton, N. and Meltzer, H. (2000) *Psychiatric Morbidity among Young Offenders in England and Wales.* London: Office for National Statistics.

Youth Justice Board (2005a) *Mental Health Needs and Provision.* London: Youth Justice Board.

MENTAL HEALTH LEGISLATION

There are different laws in Scotland, Northern Ireland, and England and Wales that provide the legal framework under which a child or adult can be deprived of liberty in order to receive compulsory mental health treatment. In England and Wales, the Mental Health Act 2007 recently amended the Mental Health Act 1983. In Scotland, the Mental Health (Care and Treatment) (Scotland) Act 2003 is the principal statute and, in Northern Ireland, it is the Mental Health (Northern Ireland) Order (1986).

In 2006 the government in England and Wales abandoned its attempt to introduce a new Mental Health Act and introduced, instead, minimal amendments to the Mental Health Act 1983. The proposed amendments were challenged by service users and professionals – in particular, the introduction of supervised community treatment orders and the replacement of the 'treatability test' with an 'appropriate treatment test' which, according to some practitioners, was designed to close a loophole that allowed service users with dangerous personality disorders to go untreated. Professionals and service users were especially concerned that there is no equivalent right to receive services to prevent mental health deterioration and compulsion and pointed to the Scottish Act as an example of good practice.

Campaigners won a key concession from the government to ensure that under 18-year-olds – whether detained or voluntary patients – will be accommodated in environments that meet their particular needs, and this is enshrined in the Mental Health Act 2007. This Act is modelled on the Mental Health (Care and Treatment) (Scotland) Act 2003, with the aim of ending inappropriate placement of under 18s on adult mental health wards.

Young people in the youth justice system who are, or who become, so unwell that they need to be treated under compulsion will need to be transferred to an appropriate secure hospital for treatment. Young people who have treatment under compulsion will need considerable support and aftercare and should be transferred with a fully negotiated care plan when they leave a secure psychiatric setting.

Kathryn Pugh

Related entries

Assessment framework; Dangerousness; Hospital orders; Mental health and young offenders.

Key texts and sources

The text of the Mental Health Act 2007 is available online at **http://www.publications.parliament.uk/pa/pabills/200607/mental_health.htm**. See the Office of Public Sector Information's website (**http://www.opsi.gov.uk/legislation/scotland/acts 2003/20030013.htm**) for the text of the Mental Health (Care and Treatment) (Scotland) Act 2003.

The Department of Health's document, *Reforming the Mental Health Act 1983*, is available online at http://www.dh.gov.uk/en/Policyandguidance/Healthandsocialcaretopics/Mentalhealth/DH_077352. The World Health Organization's document, *Use of the Mental Health (Northern Ireland) Order 1986*, is available online at http://www.mentalneurologicalprimarycare.org/content_show.asp?c=16&fc=006003&fid=1272.

See also the websites of YoungMinds (http://www.youngminds.org.uk) and the Mental Health Alliance (http://www.mentalhealthalliance.org.uk/).

MENTORING

Mentoring provides a popular means of working with 'disaffected' young people that typically involves a relationship between an older, more experienced mentor and an unrelated young protégé (mentee). The mentor provides guidance, instruction and encouragement with the aim of developing the competence and character of his or her protégé. Such relationships have a long history, which can be traced back to the ancient Greeks. According to Homer's epic poem *The Odyssey*, Odysseus entrusted Mentor to act as guardian and tutor to his only son, Telemachus.

Mentoring may take place in the context of naturally occurring relationships, but the term itself has generally come to be used to describe formalized versions of this type of relationship. Formal or 'artificial' mentoring is generally thought of as a relationship between two strangers, instigated by a third party, who intentionally matches the mentor with the mentee according to the needs of the latter as a part of a planned intervention or programme. Formal mentoring typically concentrates on young people who, for varying reasons, are considered to be 'at risk' – whether this be because of disruptive behaviour, non-attendance at school or contact with the youth justice system.

As a means of working with young people, formal mentoring was largely pioneered in the USA. Big Brothers Big Sisters of America (BBBSA), as it has come to be known, played a particularly important role in this regard. Established in 1904 by Ernest Coulter, a court clerk from New York City, BBBSA claims to be one of the biggest mentoring programmes in the world and targets young people with 'associated risk factors', including residence in a single-parent home or a history of abuse or neglect. The young people are then paired with an unrelated adult volunteer, whom they meet between two and four times a month for at least a year, with an average meeting lasting approximately four hours. The programme is not aimed at specific 'problems' but, rather, focuses on developing the 'whole person' (Tierney *et al.* 1995).

Although of much more recent origin, formal mentoring has quickly become very popular in the UK. The Dalston Youth Project (DYP) was one of the first mentoring programmes to be established in England and was set up in 1994 by Crime Concern in the London Borough of Hackney. DYP targets 'disaffected' young people and seeks to build their skills and confidence through one-to-one mentoring relationships with adult volunteers, alongside a structured education and careers programme. Its stated aims are to reduce youth crime and other at-risk behaviour; to help 'at-risk' young people back into education, training and employment; and to enable community members to become involved in solving community problems through volunteering.

DYP is widely considered to have been a successful project and, within two years of being set up, was cited as an example of good practice in the Audit Commission's (1996) *Misspent Youth – review of youth justice*. Mentoring was given a further boost by the election of the first New Labour government in 1997 as it fitted comfortably with the new government's emphasis on social inclusion, civic renewal and community responsibility. By 2000, the Youth Justice Board had funded almost 100 mentoring schemes, and the Home Office had also become a significant funder of local mentoring programmes.

Despite this, mentoring has been subject to several criticisms. One of the main difficulties with this approach is pinning down precisely what it is. Developing a clear definition is complicated by the fact that mentoring practices vary and may include one or more of the following: facilitation, coaching, buddying, befriending, counselling, tutoring, teaching, lifestyling and role modelling. Added to this definitional difficulty, mentoring lacks a strong theoretical base. What Kate Philip (2000) describes as 'the classical model of mentoring' is said to rest on an uncritical acceptance of traditional developmental theories of youth. It is also said to make gender-bound assumptions about family and organization and tends to neglect structural conditions, including poverty and social exclusion. Reflecting these criticisms, Philip concludes that the classical model of mentoring is highly individualistic (having at its heart a relationship that is essentially private and isolated from young people's social environments) and highly gendered (privileging white male experience), paying relatively little regard to the young person's stated needs. Other commentators have noted that the way in which mentoring may be expected to bring about changes in young people's attitudes, behaviours or lifestyles is far from clear. As such, it has been suggested that mentoring has been under-theorized (Newburn and Shiner 2005).

The popularity of mentoring has been based largely on its 'commonsense' appeal rather than convincing evidence of its effectiveness. This approach has been subject to surprisingly little empirical research, and that which has been conducted has generally failed to meet even the most basic criteria of evaluative rigour. Only a handful of independent evaluations have been published and, though some have been reasonably rigorous, others have been limited by their scale and design.

This is not to say that mentoring is without merit. Many young people talk positively about having had a mentor, and some of the evaluations that have been conducted have yielded some positive results. An evaluation of BBBSA reported substantial benefits for participants in relation to drug and alcohol use, violent episodes and school attendance (Sherman et al. 1997). In addition, the largest and most robust evaluation of mentoring in Britain to date also pointed to some positive outcomes – specifically in relation to engagement in education, training and work, though *not* offending (Newburn and Shiner 2005). Under these circumstances, mentoring can best be described as a 'promising' approach to crime prevention (Sherman et al. 1997).

Tim Newburn and Michael Shiner

Related entries

Bail supervision and support (BSS); Connexions; Desistance; Developmental criminology; Early intervention; Intensive Supervision and Surveillance Programme (ISSP); Protective factors; Rehabilitation; Risk factors; Risk management; Social exclusion; Social inclusion; Surveillance; Youth inclusion programmes (YIPs).

Key texts and sources

Newburn, T. and Shiner, M. (2005) *Dealing with Disaffection: Young People, Mentoring and Social Inclusion.* Cullompton: Willan Publishing.

Philip, K. (2000) 'Mentoring: pitfalls and potential for young people', *Youth and Policy*, 67: 1–15.

Sherman, L., Gottfredson, D., MacKenzie, D., Eck, J., Reuter, P. and Bushway, S. (1997) *Preventing Crime: What Works, What Doesn't, and What's Promising: A Report to the United States Congress.* Washington, DC: National Institute of Justice.

Skinner, A. and Fleming, J. (1999) *Mentoring Socially Excluding Young People: Lessons from Practice.* Manchester: National Mentoring Network.

Tierney, J.P., Grossman, J.B. and Resch, N.L. (1995) *Making a Difference: An Impact Study of Big Brothers Big Sisters.* Philadelphia, PA: Public/Private Ventures.

MENU-BASED SENTENCING

The term 'menu-based sentencing' is often used to describe a core community order with a significant number of specific requirements that can be attached either alone or in combination. The court can select any number of requirements from a 'menu' if the relevant criteria are met. Such disposals are also referred to as generic community sentences in that they can contain treatment, support, punishment and/or surveillance. A menu-based youth rehabilitation order is contained in the Criminal Justice and Immigration Bill 2006–7 to 2007–8.

Menu-based sentencing is not an entirely new concept and it might be argued that the supervision order, with a range of possible requirements, is a long-established form of 'menu based' sentence (albeit not entirely 'generic' in that some elements, such as drug treatment and testing, are provided by an entirely different order). The referral order might be viewed similarly, although the 'ingredients' are negotiated between the youth offender panel and the child or young person rather than being selected from a 'menu' by a court. For 17-years-olds, the probation order (community rehabilitation order) has a considerable array of different requirements available. However, recent government policy and new legislation have developed generic menu-based sentencing more fully.

The development of menu-based sentencing originates in the Home Office (2001a) publication, *Criminal Justice: The Way Ahead*, and was developed further in the Halliday Review of sentencing (Home Office 2001b). The white paper, *Justice for All* (Home Office 2002b), formed the statutory basis of sentencing reform that was implemented by the Criminal Justice Act 2003. Specifically, this introduced the generic menu-based (adult) community order with a range of 12 requirements (the 'menu') from which the court can construct a sentence that is tailored to the seriousness and nature of the offending, and the needs of the offender.

The intention is to provide a more flexible sentence that is more clearly understood by both courts and offenders. Increased geographic consistency and parity were a further aim.

This order has been in place in England and Wales since 2005 and has been supported by guidance from the Sentencing Guidelines Council and the National Probation Service. These have introduced some principles for how courts should use the community order and, for example, how pre-sentence report authors should prepare their reports. In line with Halliday's recommendations, the guidance adopts a three-tier concept within the community order based on seriousness: low, medium and high. Thus, for a case of low seriousness, guidance suggests that normally no more than a single requirement is appropriate. Complex models have been developed to assist the selection of proportionate levels of intervention (requirements) according to the seriousness ranking of the offence(s) and the circumstances of the offender. Elements of the sentence can include 'restriction', 'practical support', 'personal change', 'treatment' and 'control' (including public protection arrangements). To illustrate further, the guidance on proportionality suggests that unpaid work (community service/reparation) should be limited to between 40 and 80 hours in the lower 'seriousness' tier, between 80–150 and in the middle tier and between 150 and 300 in the upper tier.

With more specific regard to the youth justice system, similar provisions are included in the Criminal Justice and Immigration Bill 2006–7 to 2007–8 by way of the youth rehabilitation order. The bill provides for the abolition of five existing orders: the curfew order, the attendance centre order, the exclusion order, the action plan order and the supervision order. In addition, the remaining 'adult' orders that can be applied to older children in the youth justice system – the 'community rehabilitation order', the 'community punishment order' and the 'community rehabilitation and punishment order' – are also removed.

Thus the lower sentencing band is left unchanged in the bill – with fines, discharges and the reparation order remaining as the main options in cases where a referral order is not made. However, the community sentencing band might consist solely of the youth rehabilitation order. If the new order is implemented, the court will be able to select requirements from a menu consisting of:

- an activity
- supervision
- unpaid work (for those aged 16 or 17)
- a programme
- attendance centre
- prohibited activity
- curfew
- exclusion
- residence
- local authority residence
- mental health treatment
- drug treatment
- drug testing.

The Criminal Justice and Immigration Bill 2006–7 to 2007–8 also provides for electronic monitoring requirements (that the court will be bound to consider with curfew and exclusion requirements). The bill contains considerable detail regarding each of the above requirements (including criteria, age ranges, issues of consent, information requirements, limitations and exceptions) and it contains provisions for enforcement that are tighter than existing arrangements and that reduce the discretion of the supervising officer.

More controversially, the bill allows for a requirement for intensive supervision and surveillance and for fostering (but not both at the same time). These options are only made available in more serious cases where the court would otherwise have made a custodial sentence. It had earlier been proposed that a separate intensive supervision and surveillance order – which would be a direct alternative to custody – would better serve to reduce custodial sentencing rates.

The question arises as to whether generic menu-based sentences will prove to be effective and achieve the desired aims. The main concerns are that, in practice, courts might use an excessive number of requirements (sometimes to meet perceived needs) that are disproportionate to the seriousness of the offending and aggravating factors. This would risk driving the individual child or young person up a notional tariff towards cus-

todial sentencing in the event of a further conviction. Furthermore, excessive requirements may be complex and unduly demanding for children and young people who might struggle to comply with, and understand, the youth rehabilitation order, possibly due to inadequate adult support systems. Despite the order being generic in nature, the actual operation of a set of requirements could prove to be quite fragmented for the child or young person, who may well be expected to attend different agencies and to see a range of professional personnel. In such cases, the child could be 'set up to fail', resulting in a further increase in breach proceedings. In such cases, adverse and punitive public opinion and media coverage might undermine confidence in repeated use of the order. With regard to parity and consistency, there is a history of new provisions that have failed to reduce what is known as 'justice by geography', including the final warning scheme and the use of anti-social behaviour orders. A youth justice system with a single community sentence and no high-tariff separate order (as a pre-custody buffer) lays a considerable weight of responsibility on courts and youth offending teams to avoid the premature use of custody and to *manage* the youth justice system accordingly.

The lessons from the adult, generic menu-based community order are only beginning to emerge and may not all be directly transferable to the youth justice context. The Centre for Crime and Justice Studies published a report in 2007, having analysed data and practitioner experience over a period of under two years (Cross *et al.* 2007). Although the authors note that it may well be too early to draw full conclusions, preliminary findings that might also be relevant to youth justice include the following:

- There was not yet evidence of serious over-use of requirements.
- There had been little innovation, with a mirroring of previously available orders.
- Unpaid work had become more popular, to the concern of many probation officers.
- Half the menu requirements had been used only rarely or not at all.
- There was wide variation geographically regarding the number and type of requirements used.

- There was no evidence that menu-based sentencing had had an impact either on reducing custody or up-tariffing.
- Breach had become a serious issue.

Geoff Monaghan

Related entries

Community rehabilitation orders; Criminal Justice Act 2003; Criminal Justice and Immigration Bill 2006–7 to 2007–8; Gravity factors (prosecution and sentencing); Net-widening; Proportionality; Referral orders; Rehabilitation; Sentencing framework; Sentencing guidelines; Supervision orders.

Key texts and sources

Cross, N., Mair, G. and Taylor, S. (2007) *The Use and Impact of the Community Order and the Suspended Sentence Order.* London: Centre for Crime and Justice Studies.

Home Office (2001a) *Criminal Justice: The Way Ahead.* London: Home Office.

Home Office (2001b) *Making Punishments Work: Report of a Review of the Sentencing Framework for England and Wales.* London: Home Office (available online at **http://www.homeoffice.gov.uk/documents/halliday-report-sppu/**).

Home Office (2002b) *Justice for All.* London: HMSO.

Home Office (2005c) *Criminal Justice Act 2003: Implementation on 4 April* (PC 25/2005). London: Home Office.

MINIMUM NECESSARY INTERVENTION

Minimum necessary intervention concerns limiting the extent of intervention from formal criminal/youth justice agencies with children and young people to the absolute minimum necessary.

Once an act defined as 'criminal' has occurred, formal processing by the criminal/youth justice system normally follows, typically resulting in an official intervention. Proponents of minimum necessary intervention claim that such processes are often unduly invasive and threaten to stigmatize and label children and young people. This can serve to exacerbate an already problematic situation. Thus, it is argued that, in order to offset such negative (sometimes unintended) consequences, youth justice intervention should be avoided, or certainly limited, wherever possible.

Minimum necessary intervention is a variant of progressive minimalism and radical non-intervention. The sociologist, Edwin Lemert (1972), argued for progressive minimalism. This includes diversion from court and dealing with young people who have committed minor offences by informal and/or 'normalized' means (Goldson 2005a). More serious offenders should be diverted into non-stigmatizing and non-criminalizing community programmes that address the problems underpinning their behaviour or, if absolutely necessary, into secure educational and therapeutic establishments as a last resort and for the shortest possible time. Proponents of minimum necessary intervention do *not* deny that youth offending can be problematic or reject the utility of intervention *per se*. Rather, they argue that intervention should not be excessive or superfluous; nor should it contravene a young person's human rights and/or legal safeguards.

Edwin Schur (1973) argued for the diversion of young people from the formal court system and the decriminalization of juvenile status offences. Progressive policymakers and practitioners have advocated that the youth justice system should leave young people alone to grow out of crime, especially in the light of 'Evidence that it [the youth justice system]…contributes to juvenile crime or inaugurates delinquent careers by the imposition of the stigma of wardship, unwise detention or incarceration of children in institutions which don't reform and often corrupt' (Lemert 1970: 120).

Minimum necessary intervention was at the height of its popularity in the 1980s in the UK. It is viewed by some as having the potential to weaken both direct and indirect control over young people by agents of the state. It has also been accused of underestimating the deleterious consequences of youth crime while idealizing young people and negating individual 'pathology' and 'dysfunction'. Progressive minimalism, in particular, has been criticized by the UK government as ideological, pre-scientific and impractical. However, it has received support from advocates of the maturation thesis (young people grow out of crime), labelling theorists and campaigners for the decriminalization of status offences and other delinquent acts.

Stephen Case

Related entries

Diversion; Decriminalization; Growing out of crime; Informalism; Justice; Labelling theory; Normalization; Radical non-intervention.

Key texts and sources

Becker, H. (1963) *Outsiders: Studies in the Sociology of Deviance*. New York, NY: Free Press.

Goldson, B. (2005a) 'Beyond formalism: towards "informal" approaches to youth crime and youth justice', in T. Bateman and J. Pitts (eds) *The RHP Companion to Youth Justice*. Lyme Regis: Russell House.

Lemert, E. (1970) *Social Action and Legal Change: Revolution within the Juvenile Court*. Chicago, IL: Aldine Press.

Lemert, E. (1972) *Human Deviance, Social Problems and Social Control*. Englewood Cliffs, NJ: Prentice Hall.

Rutherford, A. (2002a) 'Youth justice and social inclusion', *Youth Justice*, 2: 100–7.

Schur, E. (1973) *Radical Non-intervention: Rethinking the Delinquency Problem*. Englewood Cliffs, NJ: Prentice Hall.

MORAL PANIC

A moral panic occurs when an event or sequence of events (often unrelated and exaggerated) is labelled, portrayed and amplified through media and political discourse as posing a threat to social stability and societal values so serious that urgent regulatory measures are necessary.

In the early 1970s, Jock Young's (1971) research with 'drug takers' and Stan Cohen's (1972) research into 'mods' and 'rockers' showed how issues of social and political concern were subject to disproportionate social reaction, amplified through often exaggerated media coverage. Through actions defined as 'criminal' or 'deviant', identifiable individuals or groups were represented publicly and graphically as posing demonstrable and serious threats to the established social and political order. Stan Cohen (1972: 9) noted that moral panics occur when:

A condition, episode, person or group of persons emerges as a threat to societal values and interests; its nature is presented in a stylised and stereotypical fashion by the mass media; the moral barricades are manned by editors, bishops, politicians and other right-thinking people; socially accredited experts pronounce their diagnoses and solutions; ways of coping are evolved or resorted to … [sometimes] it has serious and long-lasting repercussions that might produce such changes as those in legal and social policy or even in the way society conceives itself.

In the early 1970s the label 'mugging' was imported from the USA, 'entramelled in the whole American panic about race, crime, riot and lawlessness … in the *anti*-crime, *anti*-black, *anti*-riot, *anti*-liberal, "law-and-order" backlash' (Hall *et al.* 1978: 28). The representation of 'mugging' in Britain and its perceived and symbolic threat had serious and longlasting consequences, especially for young black males. The mugging moral panic established 'discrepancies … between threat and reaction, between what is perceived and what that is a perception of', amounting to 'ideological displacement' (Hall *et al.* 1978: 29).

Further classic moral panics of recent times include immigration, asylum seekers, homosexuality, football hooliganism, militant trades unionism, welfare fraud and paedophilia. Their successful transmission into popular discourse exploits existing fears that have strong historical roots nurtured by ideological myths and assumptions. They appeal to 'common sense' and provoke righteous indignation. The exaggerated representation of the 'folk devil' feeds a 'deviancy amplification spiral' in which fact and fiction, actual events and apocryphal commentaries become impossible to disentangle.

Within a relatively short period, 'folk devils' and 'moral panics' enter popular vernacular. Critiques note their relativism and ubiquity, arguing that, conceptually, they are ideological constructions not grounded in material conditions. Yet in creation, and the social and societal reactions they induce, folk devils are tangible. Far from being inventions of arbitrary social reaction, moral panics are orchestrated, hostile and disproportionate responses emanating from state institutions that mobilize surveillance, containment and regulation. Strident interventionism gains legitimacy from 'heightened emotion, fear, dread, anxiety, hostility and a strong sense of righteousness' (Goode and Ben-Yehuda 1994: 31). Further, in the midst of a moral panic:

> the behaviour of some of the members of a society is thought to be so problematic to others, the evil they do, or are thought to do, is felt to be so wounding to the body social, that serious steps must be taken to control the behaviour, punish the perpetrators, and repair the damage ... typically [it] entails strengthening the social control apparatus of society – tougher or renewed rules, more intense public hostility and condemnation, more laws, longer sentences, more police, more arrests and more prison cells ... a crackdown on offenders. (ibid)

Far from being ideologically reductionist, political and material consequences are directly related to structural inequalities: 'the more power a group or social category has, the greater the likelihood it will be successful in influencing legislation ... consistent with the views, sentiments and interests of its members' (Goode and Ben-Yehuda 1994: 31). The moral outrage around a particular act or sequence of events is accompanied by a widely and immediately disseminated rush to judgement, invariably feeding highly publicized calls for increasingly regulatory interventions. More broadly, moral panics 'form part of a sensitizing and legitimizing process for solidifying moral boundaries, identifying "enemies within", strengthening the powers of state control and enabling law and order to be promoted without cognisance of the social divisions and conflicts which produce deviance and political dissent' (Muncie 1996:

55). The 'public anxiety and uncertainty' triggered and sustained by moral panics have the capacity not only to stigmatize but also to criminalize and ostracize.

Research into social and societal reactions to children and young people provides a body of evidence demonstrating the regularity with which moral panics occur. The post-1950s litany is familiar: Teddy boys, mods, rockers, skinheads, punks and so on. Much of the portrayal loosely connects style, subculture, music and language and, occasionally, politics. During the early 1990s, however, attention turned to the proliferation of 'dismembered' or 'dysfunctional' families and the growth of 'barbarism' and 'lawlessness' among children and young people. Britain's streets were portrayed as inhabited by drug users, runaways, joyriders and persistent young offenders; schools suffered the excesses of bullies, truants and disruptive pupils; and families had been replaced by lone mothers, characterized by absent fathers. This was presented as the direct consequence of the 'nihilistic 1960s' and its associated 'moral degeneracy'.

In the wake of 'youth riots' in Burnley, Oxford and Cardiff, James Bulger was abducted and killed by two children in Bootle, Merseyside. The case and the reaction that followed were projected by the media and by opportunist politicians as illustrative of a profound 'crisis' in childhood, itself connected to 'crises' in the family and in adult authority (Scraton 1997a). It assumed a 'loss of decency', 'corrupted innocence', 'barbarism' and 'moral malaise' only resolvable by reaffirming childhood as a period of innocence, protection and evolving capacity and by reconstituting adult authority through prevention, discipline and correction. It is ironic that the renewal of authoritarianism occurred at the moment institutionalized abuse of children in local authority homes, church schools and young offender institutions was disclosed, as 'reasonable chastisement' was adopted as a euphemism for formalized assaults on children and as bullying, taxing and the suicide of children, young men and young women in custody reached unprecedented levels.

Phil Scraton

Related entries

Adolescence; Authoritarianism; Bulger; Critical criminology; Decarceration; Demonization; Deviance amplification; Fear of crime; Gangs; Gender and justice; Justice; Media reporting; Politicization; Public attitudes to youth crime and justice; Punitiveness; 'Race' and justice; Remoralization; Social harm; Street crime; Subcultural theory.

Key texts and sources

Cohen, S. (1972) *Folk Devils and Moral Panics.* London: MacGibbon & Kee.

Goode, E. and Ben-Yehuda, N. (1994) *Moral Panics: The Social Construction of Deviance.* Cambridge, MA: Blackwell.

Hall, S., Critcher, C., Jefferson, T., Clarke, J. and Roberts, B. (1978) *Policing the Crisis: Mugging, the State and Law and Order.* Basingstoke: Macmillan.

Muncie, J. (1996) 'The construction and reconstruction of crime', in J. Muncie and E. McLaughlin (eds) *The Problem of Crime.* London: Sage.

Scraton, P. (1997a) 'Whose "childhood"? What "crisis"?', in P. Scraton (ed.) *'Childhood' in 'Crisis'?* London: UCL Press/Routledge.

Young, J. (1971) *The Drugtakers.* London: Paladin.

MULTI-AGENCY PUBLIC PROTECTION ARRANGEMENTS (MAPPAs)

Multi-agency public protection arrangements (MAPPAs) are systems and processes involving a range of agencies, but most notably the police, the Prison and Probation Services, focused on the assessment and management of 'high risk' violent and sexual offenders.

Multi-agency public protection arrangements (MAPPAs) were given legislative force by ss. 67–68 of the Criminal Justice and Courts Services Act 2000. The Act formalized already existing arrangements between police, prisons, probation and social services to assess jointly the level of risk posed by sexual and violent offenders and to formulate risk management packages. These arrangements had evolved inconsistently, and the Act, followed by subsequent guidance, has imposed a legislative requirement and clear guidelines for best practice.

Sections 325–327 of the Criminal Justice Act 2003 further defined the duties of MAPPAs and made an important distinction between agencies who are 'responsible authorities' and those who have a 'duty to co-operate'. The responsible authorities – police, probation and prisons – have the clear lead in the assessment and management of offenders under MAPPAs. Other agencies – such as social services and housing departments and youth offending teams – have a duty to co-operate by providing information to assess risk and in assisting with the delivery and monitoring of management plans.

Assessments usually take place in a case conference where management plans are determined. A lead agency and worker are agreed, and cases are regularly reviewed. The accountability and management of MAPPAs are delivered by the strategic management board, and daily operations are the responsibility of a MAPPA co-ordinator.

MAPPAs are concerned with three 'categories' of offender (including young offenders):

- *Category 1*: registered sex offenders who have been convicted or cautioned since September 1997 of certain sexual offences and who are required to register personal and other relevant details with the police in order to be effectively monitored. The police have primary responsibility for identifying Category 1 offenders.
- *Category 2*: violent and other sexual offenders receiving a custodial sentence of 12 months or more (since April 2001), a hospital or guardianship order, or are subject to disqualification from working with children. All these offenders are subject to statutory supervision by the National Probation Service, which is responsible for the identification of Category 2 offenders.
- *Category 3*: other offenders considered by the 'responsible authority' to pose a 'risk of serious harm to the public'. Identification is largely determined by the judgement of the responsible authority, based upon two main considerations: the offender must have a

conviction that indicates he or she is capable of causing serious harm to the public; and the responsible authority must reasonably consider that the offender may cause harm to the public. The responsibility of identification lies with the agency that initially deals with the offender (Home Office 2004b).

MAPPAs also have a three-tiered pyramid structure, aimed at targeting resources at the highest level of risk or the 'critical few'. Level 1, or 'Ordinary risk management' is targeted at low to medium-risk offenders where the agency responsible for the offender can manage the risk without the significant involvement of other agencies. Level 2, or 'local interagency risk management', applies where there is 'active involvement' of more than one agency in risk management plans, either because of a higher level of risk or because of the complexity of managing the offender. Level 3 covers those offenders defined as the 'critical few' who pose a high or very high risk and are subject to a management plan drawing together key partners who will take joint responsibility for the community-based management of the offender. Level 3 cases can be 'referred down' to Level 2 when risk of harm reduces (Home Office 2004b).

MAPPAs comprise a 'community protection model' characterized by the use of restriction, surveillance, monitoring and control, and compulsory treatment; and by the prioritization of victim/community rights over those of offenders. Special measures such as licence conditions, tagging, exclusions, registers, selective incarceration and, more recently, satellite tracking, are all extensively used. While impact measures for the work of MAPPAs are embryonic, nationally, 2005–6 saw a reduction in the number of serious further offences in the MAPPA caseload from 79 (0.6 per cent) to 61 (0.44 per cent) (Home Office 2006a).

While MAPPAs have made a significant contribution to the management of high-risk offenders, a number of issues have proved problematic. Risk levels have been prone to inflation, with both those referring to MAPPAs and panel meetings over-assessing risk, particularly in the light of high-profile risk management 'failures'.

Decisions tend towards the precautionary principle, and defining precisely those offenders who constitute the 'critical few' has been difficult. Information exchange has also been an area fraught with difficulty, not least in ensuring that all agencies with a duty to co-operate actually do so. This can be particularly acute for the very few young offenders who are actually referred to a MAPPA. Lack of familiarity with the process and lack of trust among the key agencies can impact on the frankness of information exchange. The disclosure of information to third parties (for example, to protect potential victims) has also proved a challenge to MAPPAs. Currently, this is facilitated by a process of 'controlled disclosure', limiting both the content of what is passed on and the agencies/personnel to whom it is disclosed.

Hazel Kemshall

Related entries

Assessment framework; Criminal Justice Act 2003; Criminal Justice and Immigration Bill 2006–7 to 2007–8; Dangerousness; Offender management; Partnership working, Probation Service; Risk management, Sex Offender Register; Surveillance.

Key texts and sources

Connelly, C. and Williamson, S. (2000) *Review of the Research Literature on Serious Violent and Sexual Offenders. Crime and Criminal Justice Research Findings* 46. Edinburgh: Scottish Executive Central Research Unit.

Home Office (2004b) *MAPPA Guidance*. London: Home Office.

Home Office (2006a) *MAPPA – the First Five Years: A National Overview of the Multi-agency Public Protection Arrangements, 2001–2006*. London: Home Office.

Kemshall, H., Mackenzie, G., Wood, J., Bailey, R. and Yates, J. (2005) *Strengthening Multi-agency Public Protection Arrangements*. Practice Development Report 45. London: Home Office.

See the Office of Public Sector Information's website for the texts of the Criminal Justice and Court Services Act 2000 (http://www.opsi.gov.uk/acts/acts2000/20000043.htm) and the Criminal Justice Act 2003 (http://www.opsi.gov.uk/acts/acts2003/20030044.htm).

MUNBY JUDGMENT

> The Munby judgment is a leading High Court judgment issued in 2002 by Mr Justice Munby. The judgment confirms that duties owed to children under the Children Act 1989 do not cease to apply to children placed in young offender institutions.

The Munby judgment, formally known as *The Queen (on the Application of the Howard League) v. Secretary of State for the Home Department and the Department of Health* [2003] 1 FLR 484, resulted from an application by the Howard League for Penal Reform.

The Children Act 1989 contains a raft of safeguards and duties that are designed to protect the welfare of persons under 18, including specific procedures where a child/young person may be 'at risk' of serious harm or 'in need'. However, prior to this judgment, government policy guidance contained in Prison Service Order 4950 (PSO 4950) had stated that the Children Act 1989 did not apply to persons under 18 years of age in prison establishments.

The judgment states that children in custody 'are, on any view, vulnerable and needy children ... Over half of the children in YOIs [young offender institutions] have been in care'. Many children previously in the care system were not receiving the additional support they were entitled to because they had been placed in YOIs, and children who were vulnerable as a result of being incarcerated were not receiving protection under the Children Act 1989.

The judgment held that the Children Act continued to apply to children in prison, subject to the necessary requirements of imprisonment. Therefore, where appropriate, children in custody should be assessed under the Children Act either to determine current needs or needs on release. In addition, child protection procedures can be initiated under the provisions of the Act while a child is in custody.

As a result of this case, the duties towards children in custody under the Children Act 1989 have been recognized and incorporated into PSO 4950. Although the PSO already contained detailed child protection procedures, the crucial development as a result of the judgment is the clear confirmation that local authorities continue to owe duties to children while they are in prison.

Local Authority Circular 2004/26 provides detailed guidance as to who should be responsible for carrying out functions under the Children Act 1989 and creates a rather complex referral mechanism whereby the social services authority covering the area within which the YOI is located has a duty to make referrals – in appropriate cases – to the social services authority covering the area in which the child normally resides. In addition, on the basis of compelling evidence, the Munby judgment paints a damning picture of the state of YOIs in England and Wales and formally recognizes the vulnerabilities of children in custody. Although the Munby judgment has resulted in significant progress in safeguarding children in custody, there is still much to be done, as revealed by the report of the Carlile Inquiry published in 2006.

Laura Janes

Related entries

Children Act 1989; Children in custody; Looked-after children (LAC); Safeguarding; Vulnerability; Young offender institutions (YOIs).

Key texts and sources

Carlile, A. (2006) *The Lord Carlile of Berriew QC: An Independent Inquiry into the Use of Physical Restraint, Solitary Confinement and Forcible Strip Searching of Children in Prisons, Secure Training Centres and Local Authority Secure Children's Homes.* London: Howard League for Penal Reform.

Howard League for Penal Reform (2006a) *Chaos, Neglect and Abuse: The Duties of Local Authorities to Provide Children with Suitable Accommodation and Support Services.* London: Howard League for Penal Reform.

See the Office of Public Sector Information's website (**http://www.opsi.gov.uk/acts/acts1989/Ukpga_19890 041_en_1.htm**) for the text of the Children Act 1989.

Local Authority Circular (2004) 26 (*Safeguarding and Promoting the Welfare of Children and Young People in Custody*) is available online at http://www.dh.gov.uk/en/Publicationsandstatistics/ Lettersandcirculars/LocalAuthorityCirculars/AllLoc alAuthority/DH_4089979. The Munby judgment *(The Queen (on the Application of the Howard League) v. Secretary of State for the Home Department and the Department of Health* [2003] 1 FLR 484) is available online at http://www.howardleague. org/index.php?id=legalachievements00. Prison Service Order 4950 (*Regimes for Juveniles*) is available online at http://www.hmprisonservice.gov. uk/resourcecentre/psispsos/listpsos/.

NAMING AND SHAMING

'Naming and shaming' relates to publicizing the details of young offenders. This has included posting pictures of young people on local authority websites, leafleting local areas and releasing photographs and details of children and young people to the press.

The naming and shaming of children and young people involved in the youth justice system was, until relatively recently, deemed to be largely unacceptable. Under the provisions of the Children and Young Person Act 1933, the presumption of privacy in reporting on court proceedings for children in trouble was clearly established. The United Nations Convention on the Rights of the Child (Article 40(2)(vii)) also provides for the privacy of children and young people in the justice system 'at all stages of the proceedings'.

Naming and shaming is now routinely applied in England and Wales, however. This has been most prominent in the drive to tackle 'anti-social behaviour'. It is here that naming and shaming has become a central plank in the approach of local authorities. This has been possible because anti-social behaviour orders (ASBOs) are *civil* orders and, therefore, have circumvented the presumption of child privacy during *criminal* proceedings. This has been compounded by the Serious and Organized Crime Act 2005 and a number of court rulings that have upheld the right to name and shame children as young as 10.

The government has argued that naming and shaming can reassure the public by providing evidence that something is being done; increase confidence in the youth justice system; assist in the enforcement of ASBOs (by publicizing conditions); and act as a general deterrent to others.

There are a number of concerns regarding naming and shaming, however, including its stigmatizing potential and, conversely, the prospect of it being seen as a 'badge of honour'. Research reveals that shaming individuals without subsequent reintegration can increase the risk of reoffending (Braithwaite 1989). There is also a large body of evidence that indicates that children in trouble are some of the most vulnerable young people in society. There are clearly ethical issues involved in publicizing the details of such vulnerable young people that could place them at risk of reprisals. Furthermore, it is also apparent that current practice in respect of naming and shaming breaches the United Nations Convention on the Rights of the Child (Liberty 2006) and, it could be argued, the European Convention on Human Rights (Article 8) and the Human Rights Act 1998, each of which upholds the right to private and family life.

Joe Yates

Related entries

Anti-social behaviour; Children and Young Persons Act 1933; Demonization; Discrimination; Fear of crime; Human Rights Act 1998; Media reporting; Penal welfarism; Punitiveness; Reintegrative shaming; Summary justice; Vulnerability.

Key texts and sources

Braithwaite, J. (1989) *Crime, Shame and Reintegration.* Cambridge: Cambridge University Press.

Hibbert, P. (2005) 'The proposed extension of "naming and shaming" to the criminal youth court for breaches of ASBO's', *The Barrister*, 24 (available online at **http://www.barristermagazine.com/articles/issue24/pamhibbert.htm**).

Liberty (2006) 'Senior government advisors question policies on ASBOs and "naming and shaming"' (press release). London: Liberty.

NATIONAL OBJECTIVES AND STANDARDS FOR SCOTLAND'S YOUTH JUSTICE SERVICES

The National Objectives and Standards for Scotland's Youth Justice Services are a strategic framework produced by the Improving the Effectiveness of the Youth Justice System Working Group (Scottish Executive 2002a). This framework accompanied an 'action programme to reduce youth crime' (Scottish Executive 2002b).

The National Objectives and Standards for Scotland's Youth Justice Services are intended to operate in the context of integrated children's services at a national and local level as part of local authority corporate responsibility under the Children (Scotland) Act 1995. The strategy sets out a number of requirements at both the local and national level to direct the consistency and effectiveness of approaches in dealing with young people who offend. These include the following:

- A *national youth justice strategy group* to provide advice to ministers and support to local strategy groups.
- An *inter-agency youth justice strategy group* in every local authority to ensure progress towards meeting national objectives and standards. Membership should include senior local authority staff responsible for relevant services, including social work; education; housing/development and leisure; the police; health; the local children's reporter and children's panel members; voluntary sector representatives; the local fiscal service; the Economic Development Agency; community representatives; and representatives of the youth justice teams.
- A specialist operational *youth justice service team* in each local authority with specific operational responsibilities for: liaison with appropriate agencies (if they are not co-located in the youth justice team); the co-ordination of youth justice-related work to support young people who receive behaviour support at school, who are truanting or

who are excluded from school, who are homeless or misusing drugs or alcohol; improving links with diversionary initiatives and employment and training schemes; implementing measures aimed at youth crime prevention; and reducing the number of persistent young offenders by 10 per cent by 2006 and a further 5 per cent by 2008.

There are six core objectives.

Objective 1 ('Improving the quality of the youth justice process') stresses the overarching aim of reducing reoffending and the need to reduce variability in the quality of assessment and decision-making. Specific service standards include requirements for the following:

- Initial and comprehensive assessment for offending behaviour using Asset or YLS-CMI assessment tools.
- An 'action plan' stating intervention options, who will deliver, case management arrangements; and the intensity of contact required.
- Initial reviews within two months then at a further three months and thereafter as agreed.

Objective 2 ('To improve the range and availability of programmes to stop youth offending') stresses the importance of having an appropriate range of programmes available to tackle and reduce offending informed by data from crime audits in each local authority area. A core repertoire for community-based programmes is provided and includes:

- intensive community-based support and supervision;
- restorative justice approaches;
- family/parent support;
- cognitive skills;
- anger management;
- alcohol, drugs and mental health programmes; and
- diversionary projects.

Specific standards require that:

- individual programmes are based on a comprehensive assessment of offending behaviour and personal circumstances;
- programmes recommended in 'action plans' are made available; and
- supervision requirements are implemented.

Objective 3 ('To reduce the time taken to reach and implement hearing decisions') stresses the importance of avoiding unnecessary delay between charge, children's reporter decisions and implementing hearings' decisions. Specific standards set out the time requirements.

Objective 4 ('To improve information on youth justice services to victims and local communities') provides a renewed focus on information for victims of crime and communication with local communities. Specific standards include the following:

- Information for every victim on the process for dealing with the young person and the outcome.
- The opportunity to engage in a mediation or reparation scheme for every victim, where appropriate.
- Annually published performance information about the area's youth justice system, patterns of youth offending and information on the nature of offences committed.

Objective 5 ('To target the use of secure accommodation appropriately and ensure it is effective in reducing offending behaviour') stresses the importance of sound principles of assessment, planned and appropriate throughcare and aftercare arrangements for all young people in secure accommodation. Detailed requirements are outlined for the following:

- A named caseworker.
- Concerns about the young person's risk of harm either to self or to others to be communicated immediately.
- Detailed background information passed by the caseworker to the secure unit within two working days of admission.
- An 'action plan' to be formed within 10 days and to be reviewed at least monthly.

- Secure authorization reviews within three months.
- An agreed aftercare plan reviewed after three months.
- Contact between the young person and the caseworker within one working day of release and at least weekly meetings thereafter.

Objective 6 ('To improve the strategic direction and co-ordination of youth justice services by local youth justice strategy teams') stresses the importance of effective strategic planning and co-ordinated action. Specific standards include requirements to:

- produce an annual report on the area's youth justice services, including detailed performance data;
- commission and update an annual audit of youth crime;
- identify, allocate and pool resources;
- provide financial monitoring information to the Scottish Executive; and
- produce an annual area communications strategy.

Bill Whyte

Related entries

Children (Scotland) Act 1995; Crime and disorder reduction (CDR); Crime prevention; Effectiveness; Enforcement; Partnership working; What Works.

Key texts and sources

Scottish Executive (2002a) *A Report by the Improving the Effectiveness of the Youth Justice System Working Group* (available online at **http://www.scotland. gov.uk/Publications/2002/12/16030/15870**).

Scottish Executive (2002b) *Scotland's Action Programme to Reduce Youth Crime* (available online at **http://www.scotland.gov.uk/Publications/ 2002/01/10601/File-1**).

NATIONAL OFFENDER MANAGEMENT SERVICE (NOMS)

> The National Offender Management Service (NOMS) emerged from the government Review of Correctional Services – led by Patrick Carter – published in December 2003 and endorsed by the Home Secretary at that time, David Blunkett, in the companion document, *Reducing Crime – Changing Lives* (Home Office 2003c). The aim was to bring the Prison and Probation Services into a single administrative entity in order to overcome the perceived 'silos' of service provision.

Lord Carter's Review of Correctional Services outlined three priorities for the National Offender Management Service (NOMS) and the criminal justice system: the introduction of contestability; the deployment of end-to-end offender management; and the 'rebalancing' of sentencing to reduce the burden on prison and probation resources. Under the new structure, the Chief Executive of NOMS reports directly to the Permanent Secretary of the Home Office and is, in turn, supported by the NOMS board, which includes the Director General of HM Prison Service and the Director of Probation.

The concept of commissioning – 'contestability' – is central to the NOMS vision. Service-level agreements and contracts are established between the nine regional offender managers and a wide range of offender management and intervention services from the public, private and voluntary and community sectors. In Wales, this role is undertaken by the Director of Offender Management. *The National Reducing Re-offending Delivery Plan* (Home Office 2004e) sets out NOMS' key commitments to reduce reoffending and to better protect the public. This is delivered via regional 'reducing reoffending' plans.

NOMS has been viewed as both a necessary conduit to ensuring 'end-to-end' offender management and/or as a means of introducing contestability into another public sector service. It was introduced just three years after the creation of the National Probation Service – under the provisions of the Criminal Justice and Court Services Act 2000 – with little time for the new organization to 'bed in'.

There would seem to be three core challenges facing NOMS. First, there is the impact of record levels of imprisonment in undermining its ability to provide targeted programmes and to achieve the aims of the National Offender Management Model. Second, in the wake of the creation of NOMS, there has been a forceful restatement of the need to retain a strong local element to service delivery. A criticism of the National Probation Directorate was that it attempted to impose generic solutions on local probation areas and failed to recognize the diverse nature of communities. Third, is the challenge intrinsic to bringing together two complex organizations, each with its own distinctive cultures and traditions.

While there remains a degree of uncertainty regarding the future structural shape of NOMS, a number of key appointments at national and regional levels have been made and a Voluntary Sector Unit established. The recent creation of a Ministry of Justice raises concerns about distancing the increasingly close and effective relationship between probation and the police at the local level.

Lol Burke and Steve Collett

Related entries

Contestability; Offender management; Probation Service; Youth offending teams (YOTs).

Key texts and sources

Burke, L. (2005) *From Probation to the National Offender Management Service: Issues of Contestability, Culture and Community Involvement*. London: National Association of Probation Officers.

Home Office (2003c) *Reducing Crime – Changing Lives: The Government's Plans for Transforming the Management of Offenders*. London: HMSO.

Home Office (2004e) *The National Reducing Re-offending Delivery Plan*. London: HMSO.

Hough, M., Allen, R. and Padel, U. (eds) (2006) *Reshaping Probation and Prisons: The New Offender Management Framework*. Bristol: Policy Press.

NATIONAL STANDARDS FOR YOUTH JUSTICE SERVICES

> The National Standards for Youth Justice Services are ultimately set by the Home secretary, who receives advice from the Youth Justice Board. The standards prescribe the minimum level of service required from agencies delivering youth justice services – principally youth offending teams – to help fulfil the principal statutory aim of the youth justice system: to prevent offending by children and young people.

National standards are still a relatively new concept to youth justice practitioners. First introduced into the Probation Service in 1989 for adult and young offenders – aged 17 and over – in relation to community service (now unpaid work), the standards were expanded to reinforce the statutory provisions contained in the Criminal Justice Act 1991. It was not until the mid-1990s that a *Statement of Principles and Practice Standards* was produced for youth justice services. This became the precursor to a set of specific National Standards for Youth introduced alongside the establishment of youth offending teams (YOTs) in April 2000.

The first National Standards for Youth Justice stated that they were designed to provide a basis for promoting 'high quality effective work with children, young people, their families, and victims' (Youth Justice Board 2000c: 1). It was further intended that they would comprise a benchmark against which quality and effectiveness could be inspected.

The standards were revised and expanded in 2004 to include the following (Youth Justice Board 2004a):

- *National Standard 1*: preventive work.
- *National Standard 2*: remand management.
- *National Standard 3*: work in courts.
- *National Standard 4*: assessment.
- *National Standard 5*: restorative justice, work with victims of crime and community payback.
- *National Standard 6*: final warnings.

- *National Standard 7*: reports for courts and youth offender panels.
- *National Standard 8*: court-ordered interventions.
- *National Standard 9*: intensive supervision and surveillance programmes.
- *National Standard 10*: secure accommodation.
- *National Standard 11*: integrated work with young offenders sentenced to a detention and training order.
- *National Standard 12*: Section 90/91 (formerly Section 53) pre- and post-release supervision.

The standards apply to the full range of court-ordered interventions for children and young people, apart from those orders designed for adult offenders and imposed on 16–17-year-olds. These are enforced by Probation National Standards, a key difference being that breach action is required after one unacceptable absence whereas, for the Youth Justice Standards, it is two. The standards state:

General principles must be agreed in the YOT about what constitutes an acceptable and unacceptable reason for non-attendance. These must be defensible to the general public. Sickness or work commitments should be evidenced where possible. If an absence is deemed unacceptable, a warning must be issued to the young offender in writing (Youth Justice Board 2004a: 46–7).

The intention is that a more transparent breach policy helps to reassure sentencers and the public that orders of the court for young offenders are being strictly enforced and adhered to. A factor making this more complex for youth justice practitioners is the need to balance the welfare of the child with the strict enforcement requirements set out in the standards.

YOT staff are required to ensure that the children and young people subject to court orders understand both what is required of them *and* the consequences of failing to comply. Practitioners must also keep in mind diversity and acknowledge individual needs and differences in circumstances with regard to compliance with the sentence of the court. For example, it is (usually) reasonable to expect an adult offender to take responsibility for ensuring he or she has sufficient money for bus fare to the reporting centre or probation office, but what should a YOT worker's response be to a 13-year-old who says she could not catch the bus because her mother did not have the money for the fare?

National standards seek to promote confidence in community penalties, encouraging compliance and making practitioner decision-making more transparent and accountable. Given the prescriptive nature of the standards, concerns have been raised about the threat to professional discretion (Eadie and Canton 2002). Accountability is not necessarily incompatible with discretion, and standards that are too rigid will constrain a practitioner's authority to make a professional judgement about what (or what not) to do in a given situation. Policymakers must remember that YOT staff work with some of society's most disadvantaged and distressed young people. and they are in the best position to make judgements about the appropriateness or otherwise of breach action at certain points in an order. National standards offer useful guidelines for best practice but should not be used as a straitjacket that forces practitioners to treat each young offender in precisely the same way.

National standards have never been evidenced based, and conformity with such standards, while plausibly a measure of efficiency, is not necessarily synonymous with effectiveness. Youth justice services should ideally avoid a mechanistic and rigid application of standards that contributes towards the meeting of performance management targets at the expense of a fair and individualized service to young offenders in which staff are properly held to account for their practice.

Tina Eadie and Rob Canton

Related entries

Criminal Justice Act 1991; Crime and disorder reduction (CDR); Crime prevention; Effectiveness; Enforcement; Managerialism; Partnership working; What Works; Youth justice plans.

Key texts and sources

Eadie, T. and Canton, R. (2002) 'Practising in a context of ambivalence: the challenge for youth justice workers', *Youth Justice*, 2: 14–26.

Youth Justice Board (2000c) *National Standards for Youth Justice*. London: Youth Justice Board.

Youth Justice Board (2004a) *National Standards for Youth Justice Services*. London: Youth Justice Board (available online at **http://www.yjb.gov.uk/Publications/Scripts/prodView.asp?idproduct=155&eP=PP**).

NET-WIDENING

Net-widening refers to the counterproductive tendencies of the criminal/youth justice system that serve to draw people deemed to be 'offenders', or 'at risk' of becoming offenders, into the system often at higher points up the tariff than is proportionate to their behaviour and typically in ways that are not necessary, just or effective.

Stan Cohen's (1979, 1985) challenge to any taken-for-granted faith in the benefits of corrections proved to be influential and enduring. He warned of the detrimental effects of 'wider nets', 'denser nets' and 'different nets' in the way in which the criminal justice system draws people in. According to Cohen, social control is a self-perpetuating enterprise that is expansionist by nature. He argued that the community-penalties 'movement' was in effect spreading the correctional network beyond the confines of the prison system and fixing the apparatus of social control more deeply into society. For Cohen, a 'major result of the new networks of social control has been to increase rather than decrease, the amount of offenders who get into the system in the first place', which in turn means that 'diversion becomes not a movement out of the system but movement into a programme in another part of the system'.

It is not difficult to find evidence that supports Cohen's thesis. 'Alternatives to custody' have too often been up-tariffing alternatives to lesser sentences (for example, intensive super-vision and surveillance programmes). The Children and Young Persons Act 1969 allowed care orders to be imposed in respect of children convicted of crimes. Perceived 'treatment needs' meant that significant numbers of children were deprived of their liberty for long, indeterminate periods far beyond the seriousness of their offences and typically to no good effect. The dangers and injustice of the 'treatment model' were eventually recognized, and the 1969 Act 'criminal care order' provisions were repealed by the Children Act 1989. Nevertheless the impulse to intervene and to 'spread the net' remains strong. A broader range of 'tough' community sentences is likely to feed that process rather than reduce the number of children going into custody.

Youth offending teams can find that around half their caseload comprises children unnecessarily on final warnings and referral orders. Many such children could have been dealt with informally to no detriment. Moreover, there is evidence that labelling and processing children through formal proceedings increase rather than decrease the likelihood of further criminal behaviour. Targets are quite likely to be part of the net-widening process. Currently there is a police target for 'crimes brought to justice' that creates a powerful incentive to respond formally (prosecution) rather than informally (caution). There are examples of children already 'looked after' by local authorities being reported to the police for trivial matters. They find themselves being formally charged and prosecuted (criminalized) rather than receiving a precautionary 'word in the ear' (diverted).

Net-widening can be part of the unequal and discriminatory application of the law. For example, even though young black people are no more likely to commit offences than young white people, they are six times more likely to be stopped and searched by the police. Furthermore, black children and young people are more likely to receive higher tariff disposals (including custody) and less likely to receive reprimands and final warnings.

Paul Kelly

Related entries

Criminalization; Criminal Justice and Immigration Bill 2006–7 to 2007–8; Diversion; Early intervention; First-time entrants; Gender and justice; Intensive Supervision and Surveillance Programme (ISSP); Intermediate treatment (IT); Labelling theory; Looked-after children (LAC); 'Race' and justice; Risk management; Tariff; Welfare.

Key texts and sources

Cohen, S. (1979) 'The punitive city: notes on the dispersal of social control', *Contemporary Crisis*, 3: 339–63.

Cohen, S. (1985) *Visions of Social Control: Crime, Punishment and Classification*. Cambridge: Polity Press.

Goldson, B., Lavelette, M. and McKechnie, J. (eds) (2002) *Children, Welfare and the State*. London: Sage.

Nacro (2005b) *A Handbook on Reducing Offending by Looked After Children*. London: Nacro.

Webster, C. (2006) '"Race", youth crime and justice', in B. Goldson and J. Muncie (eds) *Youth Crime and Justice: Critical Issues*. London: Sage.

NEW DEAL FOR YOUNG PEOPLE

The New Deal for Young People was launched nationwide in 1998. The target group are unemployed 18–24-year-olds and the aim is to transfer them from welfare to work.

Eligible young people who have been unemployed for at least six months must enter the New Deal for Young People programme or face loss of benefit. After an initial 'gateway' period of assessment, if participants have not found employment, they progress to one of four types of placement:

- employment with a subsidy to the employer from the programme budget (usually £60 a week);
- a 'job' in the voluntary sector;
- an environmental task force;
- full-time education or training.

Young people who are placed in the voluntary sector or on the environmental task force receive benefits plus an allowance. Those who are placed in full-time education or training receive benefits plus expenses. An expectation has been that less unemployment in the age group will mean less offending and reoffending.

During the first three and a half years of the New Deal over 600,000 18–24-year-olds entered the programme. In different UK regions, between 47 and 57 per cent exited for sustained (for at least 13 weeks) employment. Unemployment among 18–24-year-olds declined by 130,000, and there remained just 34,000 in the target age group (who would shortly enter the New Deal) who had been unemployed for six months or more. These figures suggest that the New Deal has proved an outstanding 'success'. However, the New Deal's apparent achievements include 'deadweight'. Some of the participants would have moved into jobs even if there had been no New Deal. When allowances are made for 'deadweight', the number of 18–24-year-olds estimated to have been removed from unemployment by the programme – at 18 months after entry – falls to just 15,000.

Critics claim that, in the UK regions with the highest unemployment, there are simply insufficient jobs to accommodate everyone who passes through the 'gateway'; that the jobs the young people enter are generally poor quality; and that the apparent 'success' of the programme is largely due to 'churning' – keeping the unemployed circulating between benefits, the programme, short-lived jobs, then unemployment again. However, it can be counter-argued that poor jobs are better than no jobs and that being 'churned' is preferable to becoming long-term unemployed.

The achievements of the New Deal for Young People have led to the birth of a suite of similar new deals – for the 25-plus age group, for the over-50s, for lone parents, for disabled people, for partners (of the unemployed) and for musicians.

Ken Roberts

Related entries

Connexions; Desistance; Probation Service; Social exclusion; Social inclusion.

Key texts and sources

Mizen, P. (2006) 'Work and social order: the "new deal" for the young unemployed', in B. Goldson and J. Muncie (eds) *Youth Crime and Justice: Critical Issues.* London: Sage.

Percy-Smith, B. and Weil, S. (2002) 'New deal or raw deal? Dilemmas and paradoxes of state interventions into youth labour markets', in M. Cieslik and G. Pollock (eds) *Young People in Risk Society.* Aldershot: Ashgate.

Worth, S. (2005) 'Beating the "churning" trap in the youth labour market', *Work, Employment and Society,* 19: 403–14.

See also the New Deal programme's website (www.newdeal.gov.uk).

NO MORE EXCUSES

No More Excuses: A New Approach to Tackling Youth Crime in England and Wales was a white paper that proposed 'root and branch' reforms to the youth justice system in England and Wales. It was published in 1997 and many of the proposals were subsequently implemented in the Crime and Disorder Act 1998 and the Youth Justice and Criminal Evidence Act 1999.

The first New Labour government, elected in May 1997, introduced far-reaching reforms to the youth justice process. Soon after its election, the administration published four consultation papers, each proposing reforms to aspects of the process. The 1997 white paper draws on each of the consultation papers and offers final proposals for implementation by statute. Rather unusually for a white paper, the government offered a consultation period during which views on the proposals could be received.

No More Excuses sets out the government's view of the nature and extent of youth crime, before proposing a series of measures aimed at preventing youth crime and reoffending by known offenders. In broad terms, the government proposed a youth justice system with a clear strategy to provide mechanisms for young people to 'take responsibility' for their offending behaviour; to provide effective intervention where the 'causes' of youth crime can be identified and alleviated; and to introduce a 'fast-track' trial process that reduces delays between the arrest and sentencing of young offenders. The 'new youth justice' (Goldson 2000b) was to be implemented by agencies working in partnership, principally through youth offending teams monitored and guided by a new national Youth Justice Board, and all working under a principal statutory aim to 'prevent offending'. In addition, the government wished to see these agencies 'nipping crime in the bud' by providing intervention for young people where their troublesome behaviour at an early age may indicate future offending.

The overriding 'statutory aim' seeks to implement the pledge made by New Labour in 1996 to 'end confusion over punishment and welfare'. This, it is claimed, gives practitioners a clearer focus in terms of the policy ideals that underpin the legislation and removes the historical and political 'see-sawing' between hard-line punishment approaches and more constructive, rehabilitative responses based on welfare concerns for young people who offend. The detailed proposals, however, draw from both welfare and punishment models, ranging from the parenting order and the quasi-welfare early intervention and community penalties, on the one hand, to expanded custodial sentences on the other. An indication of the respective priority to be given to each can be found both in the 'tough' title of the white paper and in the Preface by the then Home Secretary, Jack Straw, in which it is clearly stated that youth justice practitioners should abandon notions that young people may 'grow out of crime' and should bring an end to 'excuse culture'. Practitioners were urged instead to focus on confronting young people with the consequences of their behaviour and to encourage them to take responsibility for it.

Julia Fionda

Related entries

Authoritarianism; Bulger; Crime and Disorder Act 1998; Criminal responsibility; Institutionalized intolerance; Politicization; Responsibilization.

Key texts and sources

Goldson, B. (ed.) (2000b) *The New Youth Justice*. Lyme Regis: Russell House.
Home Office (1997a) *No More Excuses: A New Approach to Tackling Youth Crime in England and Wales*. London: HMSO (available online at http://www.homeoffice.gov.uk/documents/jou-no-more-excuses?view=html).

NORMALIZATION

Normalization is a concept that – in the context of youth justice – normally applies to understanding the relative normality of adolescent transgression and low-level youth offending.

Many self-report studies reveal that it is relatively normal for children and young people to transgress conventional behavioural boundaries and to commit low-level offences. Furthermore, the same reports also serve to demystify and 'normalize' offences that otherwise appear to be serious. The Offending, Crime and Justice Survey (Budd *et al*. 2005: 1), for example, based on interviews with 5,000 children and young people, revealed that most self-reported youth 'crime' is 'dominated by the less serious behaviours'. Moreover, many 'incidents' officially recorded as 'violent' were, in actual fact, 'non-injury incidents often committed on the "spur of the moment" against someone the perpetrator knew and involving relatively low levels of force ... attributed to being annoyed or upset with someone'. Indeed, 68 per cent of the 'violent incidents' reported by 10–17-year-olds were 'non-injury assaults ... a grab or a push [or] a punch, slap or hit' (Budd *et al*. 2005: ii). Similarly, the majority of 'property offences' reported by children were low level, involving 'miscellaneous thefts from school of items of relatively low value' (2005: ii).

Evidence also reveals that most children and young people 'grow out of crime' as part of the normal maturational process (Rutherford 2002b). Advocates of the normalization thesis, therefore, argue that 'labelling' children and young people – by way of formal youth justice intervention – is not only unnecessary in many cases but it is also counterproductive. 'Criminalizing' 'normal' behaviour invokes negative social reaction and can serve to confirm 'delinquent' and 'offender' identities. Diversion, informalism and/or minimum necessary intervention are the preferred approaches (McAra and McVie 2007).

Barry Goldson

Related entries

Criminalization; Diversion; Growing out of crime; Informalism; Labelling theory; Minimum necessary intervention; Radical non-intervention; Self-reported offending; Youth Lifestyles Survey (YLS).

Key texts and sources

Budd, T., Sharp, C., Weir, G., Wilson, D. and Owen, N. (2005) *Young People and Crime: Findings from the 2004 Offending, Crime and Justice Survey. Home Office Statistical Bulletin* 20/05. London: Home Office.

McAra, L. and McVie, S. (2007) 'Youth justice? The impact of system contact on patterns of desistance from offending', *European Journal of Criminology*, 4: 315–45.

Rutherford, A. (2002b) *Growing Out Of Crime – the New Era* (2nd edn). Winchester: Waterside Press.

O

OFFENDER MANAGEMENT

> The term 'offender management' has been used in different ways to describe the network of staff responsibilities, structures and processes through which offenders are managed. The government has piloted a National Offender Management Model that is intended to be the normal operating model for all sentenced prisoners by April 2009.

Essentially, the offender management approach rests on the pivotal role and authority of a single offender manager to 'manage' an offender. This is based on a tiering that determines the allocation and type of supervision to the level of risk of reoffending posed by the offender (Home Office 2006h). The model involves the development of a single plan, drawn up by the offender manager, which spans the whole sentence and which describes what is to be done by whom and when in order to achieve all the objectives of the sentence passed, and any other objectives associated with the implementation of the sentence. The model also identifies the key roles of offender supervisor and case administrator that, along with the offender manager, constitute the offender management team.

Offender management was introduced into England and Wales by the Correctional Services Review – the Carter Review – in 2003. Its origins can be traced back to case management models developed in health and social care settings, which were subsequently applied to probation practice (Holt 2000; Home Office 2006h). The development of a 'National Offender Management Model' that can be applied to both young and adult offenders has been one of the key strands of the emerging National Offender Management Service (NOMS).

The model refers to a single, universal approach in which one person, the offender manager, determines the overall shape and direction of the sentence while others deliver specific elements of it, within the framework of a single plan. The notion of 'one offender, one manager' draws on research into case management that stressed the importance of continuity in the supervision process and the failures associated with frequent changes in personnel, fragmentation of processes and poor information flows in those cases where offenders under supervision have gone on to commit further serious offences. The model emphasizes a teamwork approach, including offender supervisors (who are responsible for implementing the plan set by the offender manager on a day-to-day basis), case administrators (who are responsible for ensuring that the sentence is administered in line with specific timescales, procedures, deadlines and standards) and service providers (who provide a range of interventions to ensure that specific objectives of the sentence plan are met).

The language and terminology used in the model are intended to be neutral so that the model can be applied across different agencies and organizations and, on one level, can be seen as a practical manifestation of current polices to align the work of the 'correctional services'. A key element of the model is the development of a 'communication system' to support a single case record (C-NOMIS). The level of intervention directed towards each offender is based on a four-tiered framework (punish, help, change, control) in line with the level of risk of reoffending or dangerousness posed. The offender manager role is not defined by grade or agency but, in reality, initially most have been probation officers for tier 3 and 4 cases, while probation service officers (previously probation assistants) undertake the management of tier 1 and 2 cases.

The findings of the evaluation into the first phase of the Pathfinder Project in the North West of England were published in July 2005. Part of the evaluation considered the management of young adult offenders through custodial sentences and post-release supervision. It found that the model was viewed positively by the young offenders interviewed, who saw it as an improvement on their previous experience of sentence planning in custody. Although many of the young prisoners interviewed did not fully understand the terminology or formal structures of the model, subsequent unpublished research also found support for the model among adult prisoners and staff. However, there remained a lack of clarity over the respective roles and responsibilities and a duplication of information.

In many respects staff support for the model is unsurprising as, in many ways, it restates good practice principles, especially in relation to continuity of contact throughout the custodial element of the sentence, which have all too often been undermined by resource constraints in the past. However, the real test will be with the planned national roll-out of the model and, ultimately, its 'success' will be determined by the political will to keep the prison population at a manageable level. Regional offender managers – appointed within the NOMS structure – will also have an important role to play in ensuring that appropriate services are commissioned that are responsive to the diverse needs, risks and circumstances of individual offenders.

Lol Burke and Steve Collett

Related entries

Corporatism; Dangerousness; Enforcement; Multiagency public protection arrangements (MAPPAs); National Offender Management Service (NOMS); Partnership Working; Probation Service; Risk management; Youth offending teams (YOTs).

Key texts and sources

Holt, P. (2000) *Case Management: Context for Supervision. Community and Criminal Justice Monograph 2.* Leicester: De Montfort University.
Home Office (2006h) *The NOMS Offender Management Model.* London: HMSO.

PA Consultancy Group and MORI (2005) *Action Research Study of the Implementation of the National Offender Management Model in the North West Pathfinder.* London: Home Office.
Partridge, S. (2004) *Examining Case Management Models for Community Sentences.* London: Home Office.
Robinson, G. (2005) 'What works in offender management?', *Howard Journal of Criminal Justice,* 44: 307–17.

ON TRACK

On Track is a preventive programme aimed at developing multi-agency partnerships and delivering a range of services to children aged 4–12 and their families. It is a long-term initiative aimed at children 'at risk' of getting involved in crime.

On Track was launched in December 1999 and, from April 2001, it was incorporated into the government's £966 million Children's Fund programme. On Track services will possibly be transferred into the new children's trusts along with other Children's Fund initiatives.

There are 24 On Track projects in areas of high deprivation in England, each covering around 2,000 children. In each area an enhanced range of 'preventive services' (including parent training, home–school partnerships, structured pre-school education, home visiting and family therapy) is being developed for children aged between 4–12 and their families. Interagency co-operation is being developed so that children 'at risk' of offending are identified early. The projects are sensitive to concerns about stigmatization and seek to impact positively on educational and health outcomes.

Each On Track project is managed by a local partnership, including health, educational and social service providers, youth offending teams, the police and relevant voluntary sector organizations. The projects aim to link together existing services for children and families. The key aim is to foster approaches that deliver real reductions in delinquency in 'high-crime communities' and provide answers to pressing questions about 'what works' best in terms of early intervention/prevention.

The effectiveness and value for money of the arrangements are being evaluated. The interim research – published in 2004 and involving 12,700 children from 26 schools – reported some positive findings. Some 14 'risk factors' were measured over three years. At the same time, seven 'protective factors' were also measured. With regard to a number of risk factors, positive change/improvement was reported, including school exclusion; truancy; sibling anti-social behaviour (ASB); challenging attitudes; attitudes to ASB; alcohol misuse; offending; and association with 'anti-social' peers. The one risk factor that was compounded was 'neighbourhood perception'. Some four of the 'protective factors' showed statistically significant improvement. The On Track school surveys have provided evidence that, despite the gloomy picture often painted in the media about declining standards of behaviour among children and young people and deteriorating standards of parenting, the story is not wholly negative.

In April 2007, a Department for Education and Skills Parliamentary Under-secretary of State for Children and Young People wrote to local authority directors of children's services indicating that lasting benefit should be seen from the government's investment in the Children's Fund. This followed government plans set out in *Aiming High for Children: Supporting Families* (Department for Education and Skills and HM Treasury 2007).

Peter Ashplant

Related entries

Actuarialism; Children's trusts; Early intervention; Labelling theory; Partnership working; Protective factors, Risk factors; Risk management.

Key texts and sources

Department for Education and Skills and HM Treasury (2007) *Aiming High for Children: Supporting Families*. London: DfES and HM Treasury (available online at **http://www.policyhub. gov.uk/news_item/families_policy07.asp**).

The Department for Children, Schools and Families and the Department for Innovation, Universities and Skills' document, *The National Evaluation of On Track, Phase Two: Interim Findings from the First Wave of the Longitudinal Cohort Study*, is available online at **http://www.dfes.gov.uk/rsgateway/DB/ RRP/u014889/index.shtml**; the document, *The National Evaluation of On Track, Phase Two: Qualitative Study of Service Providers' Perspectives*, is available online at **http://www.dfes. gov.uk/rsgateway/DB/RRP/u014888/index.shtml**.

See also the National Evaluation of the Children's Fund's website (**http://www.ne-cf.org/**).

P

PARENTAL BIND OVERS

> Section 58(2) of the Criminal Justice Act 1991 lays a duty on magistrates to bind over parents – of convicted children under 16 – to make them 'take proper care ... and exercise proper control' over the child, so as to prevent further offending. The recognizance may be any sum up to £1,000, potentially forfeited if the child reoffends. A parent who refuses to be bound over may be fined.

The bind over is a historic power traditionally requiring someone to 'keep the peace'. An agreed sum of money is payable if conditions are broken. It is not a sentence and the Law Commission, in 1994, said that it was an anomaly and should be abolished. However, more recently it has found favour with the government as an instrument to control anti-social behaviour, provided specific conditions are made.

The use of the bind over as a means of enforcing parental responsibility was first proposed as long ago as 1891, in a government bill that was never enacted. Precisely a century later it was introduced by a Conservative government in a wave of political indignation against the parents of recalcitrant children. The measure was controversial and the Magistrates' Association's Juvenile Courts Committee opposed it on the grounds that it would not work and would harm family relationships. When parenting orders were introduced in the Crime and Disorder Act 1998 it was mooted that bind overs on parents should be dropped. However, the power continues in occasional use by the courts.

Elizabeth Burney

Related entries

Anti-social behaviour (ASB); Criminal Justice Act 1991; Fines; Parenting orders.

Key texts and sources

Drakeford, M. (1996) 'Parents of young people in trouble', *Howard Journal of Criminal Justice*, 35: 242–55.

Drakeford, M. and McCarthy, K. (2000) 'Parents, responsibility and the new youth justice', in B. Goldson (ed.) *The New Youth Justice*. Lyme Regis: Russell House.

Gelsthorpe, L. (1999) 'Youth crime and parental responsibility', in A. Bainham *et al.* (eds) *What is a Parent? A Socio-legal Analysis*. Oxford: Hart Publishing.

See the Office of Public Sector Information's website (**http://www.opsi.gov.uk/acts/acts1991/Ukpga_19 910053_en_1.htm**) for the text of the Criminal Justice Act 1991.

PARENTAL COMPENSATION ORDERS (PCOs)

> The parental compensation order (PCO) is a civil order that applies to parents of children under the age of criminal responsibility (10 years in England and Wales) who take or damage property by way of acts that would be criminal if the child was aged over 10. The local authority applies to a magistrate for an order to pay the owner compensation not exceeding £5,000. From July 2006 the order was being piloted in 12 areas.

The parental compensation order (PCO) is an example of 'early intervention' – a measure targeting 'offences' and anti-social behaviour by children too young to be 'offenders'. It is intended to reinforce parental responsibility but, by introducing parental liability, it breaks new ground, since parents are not normally liable in law for property loss or damage by their children. This now applies uniquely to children under 10 and it raises a number of concerns and questions. What will happen, for example, if two brothers, one aged 8 and the other 10, together cause damage worth £2,000? It would be hard to prove that the responsibility lay with the 8-year-old, but the aggrieved party might stand more chance of compensation if it did.

Schools may seek compensation under this law, but an anomaly is caused when 'looked after' children are responsible, since local authorities cannot be subject to a PCO – but the children's birth parents still may be. The government's guidance advises that mediation and voluntary reparation should be encouraged before a PCO is considered. An assessment will look at family circumstances and may trigger further interventions, such as a parenting order.

Elizabeth Burney

Related entries

Anti-social behaviour (ASB); Compensation; Early intervention; Looked-after children (LAC); Mediation; Parenting orders; Reparation.

Key texts and sources

Department for Education and Skills and the Home Office (2006) *Parental Compensation Order Guidance (October 2006)*. London: DfES and the Home Office (available online at **www.homeoffice. gov.uk/documents/parental-compensation-guid**).

PARENTING CONTRACTS

A parenting contact is a voluntary but formal agreement between a parent and a youth offending team or a school. It has no binding force but, if broken, may lead to a parenting order. The parent undertakes requirements intended to help prevent criminal or anti-social behaviour by a child of any age or, in the case of a school, to prevent truancy or exclusion. The authorities agree to provide guidance or counselling to help the parent comply.

The parenting contract has been widely used to address perceived 'parenting deficit'. It received statutory recognition in the Anti-social Behaviour Act 2003. Its use was extended to local authorities and registered social landlords in the Police and Justice Act 2006. Contracts are used regularly for truancy (along with other methods), but only a handful of education authorities use them for exclusions. There is no reliable total of the thousands of contracts agreed from all sources and no information about the number of failed contracts that lead to parenting orders.

Home Office *et al.* (2004a) guidance makes no bones about the coercion implicit in the parenting contract. It states (para. 2.14) that 'Refusing to enter into a contract can support an application for an order and may persuade a reluctant parent to engage'. The contract is seen as the next step after purely voluntary working. It 'should normally' (para. 3.15) include a parenting programme and may thus be almost indistinguishable in content from a parenting order. Contracts typically list supervision requirements or action on school attendance.

Elizabeth Burney

Related entries

Anti-social behaviour (ASB); Anti-social Behaviour Act 2003; Parenting orders; School exclusion; School non-attendance.

Key texts and sources

Department for Education and Skills (2004b) *Guidance on Education-related Parenting Contracts, Parenting Orders and Penalty Notices.* London: DfES.

Home Office, Department for Constitutional Affairs and the Youth Justice Board (2004a) *Circular: Parenting Orders and Contracts for Criminal Conduct or Anti-social Behaviour.* London: Home Office, Department for Constitutional Affairs and Youth Justice Board.

See the Office of Public Sector Information's website for the texts of the Anti-social Behaviour Act 2003 (http://www.opsi.gov.uk/acts/acts2003/20030038. htm) and the Police and Justice Act 2006 (http://www.opsi.gov.uk/acts/acts2006/20060048. htm).

PARENTING ORDER

The parenting order is a civil order, introduced in s. 8 of the Crime and Disorder Act 1998, that compels parents of convicted children aged under 16 to attend parenting programmes lasting up to three months and to obey any other requirements for a maximum of 12 months, with a view to preventing further offending by the child.

Parenting orders should always be made after a child's conviction (except after a referral order), unless the court considers it unnecessary. The court may also make a parenting order after a child safety order, an anti-social behaviour order or sex offender order on the child, or for school non-attendance. Breach of an order is a crime, with a maximum penalty of £1,000. Under the Anti-social Behaviour Act 2003, (ASBA), stand-alone orders can be made – not dependent on a conviction and with no lower age limit – if the youth offending team (YOT) considers it necessary. Appeals against parenting orders can be made to the Crown court.

Prior to its election in 1997, the Labour Party declared that enforcing parental responsibility would be an important plank of its drive against youth crime. This idea had taken various forms

in the past, from forcing parents to pay upkeep in Victorian reformatory schools to making them responsible for paying children's fines and imposing parental bind overs. The parenting order introduced a new element – enforced training. The growth of parental interventions sits oddly with the abolition of *doli incapax*, whereby children are now deemed fully responsible for their crimes.

Many models of parental training exist, and a large body of research shows how voluntary classes for parents of very young children are beneficial in terms of later behaviour and school performance. Few models apply to the parents of adolescents, and the consensus is that, by this stage, a parent has diminishing influence on a child's activities and associations, although improved relationships can help.

There is no doubt that parents, especially single mothers, are often desperate for advice and support in dealing with teenagers. It has been possible for many YOTs to obtain voluntary attendance at classes, where parents can share concerns and learn techniques for setting boundaries and obtaining greater compliance. Some practitioners do not believe in forced training – one reason why parenting orders are very unevenly spread around the country. Also, training programmes are sometimes in short supply although, in the early 2000s, following the introduction of the 'Respect' agenda, 77 areas in England and Wales received funding for extra parenting courses under so-called 'super-nannies' aimed at 'malfunctioning' families.

The only evaluation of the effectiveness of parenting orders, carried out for the Youth Justice Board (Ghate and Ramella 2002), was positive, but the research was weak in a number of ways. For example, there was no control group and although the young people involved did show reduced rates of reoffending, this may have been because they had mostly been subject themselves to YOT interventions, or they had grown out of offending. Parents expressed high satisfaction with the courses – those on orders as much as the majority who attended voluntarily – but parents who did not respond to the questionnaire may have been more disaffected. The authors admitted that the effect of these short courses may not last, and they believed a wholly voluntary system would be preferable.

The ASBA 2003 extended the scope of parenting orders. It permitted a residential element to be included (provided interference in family life is 'proportionate') and it gave education authorities the power to seek parenting orders where pupils have been excluded from school on disciplinary grounds. They were also given the option of fixed penalties as an alternative to prosecuting parents for allowing their children to truant. Teachers expressed strong opposition to the idea of disciplinary parenting orders and, to date, there is no record of any orders imposed on account of excluded children. Parenting orders are used by some education authorities for non-attendance, but there are a number of less severe options available in this context.

Comprehensive data on parenting orders are not very reliable and usage is patchy. In 2005–6, crime and disorder reduction partnerships reported 2,268 orders, nearly three- and-a-half times more than two years earlier – possibly due to an increase in the availability of training schemes. There is no information on breached parenting orders, which are likely to be rare on account of the complex procedure. Surprisingly, no use was made of parenting orders in conjunction with child anti-social behaviour orders (ASBOs) until this became a presumption under ASBA 2003 and, even by 2005, under 2 per cent of ASBOs on under 16-year-olds were accompanied by a parenting order. Legislation is one thing; its application another.

Yet, as more agencies are able to apply for parenting orders on the grounds of belief that a child has behaved anti-socially, net-widening is predictable. The Police and Justice Act 2006 gave this power to local authorities and a similar one to registered social landlords. Since 2003, YOTs have been able to apply for parenting orders without a conviction if children, even those under the age of 10, are thought to display 'anti-social' or 'criminal' tendencies.

The parenting order represents a new degree of state intervention into family life but has not been found incompatible with the European Convention on Human Rights. In *R (M)* v. *Inner London Crown Court*, it was ruled that, although an infringement of family life (Article 8), it was justified as necessary but must be proportionate. It was also ruled that a parenting order does not breach Article 6 (right to a fair trial) since it is based on evaluation rather than a particular standard of proof.

Like all such interventions, the parenting order falls most heavily on the poor who, for nearly two centuries, have been blamed for lax supervision of children and therefore responsibility for their crimes (Goldson and Jamieson 2002b). The ambivalence of government family policy is shown in the way parenting orders are presented as both supportive and punitive, linking parent training with the drive against anti-social behaviour. The focus on the failings of individual parents does not acknowledge that poverty, social exclusion, lack of welfare support and environmental factors are, in most cases, the real issues.

Elizabeth Burney

Related entries

Anti-social Behaviour Act 2003; Crime and Disorder Act 1998; Parental bind overs; Parenting contracts; Respect (government action plan); School exclusion; School non-attendance.

Key texts and sources

Department for Education and Skills (2004) *Guidance on Education-related Parenting Contracts, Parenting Orders and Penalty Notices.* London: DfES.

Ghate, D. and Ramella, M. (2002) *Positive Parenting: The National Evaluation of the Youth Justice Board's Parenting Programme.* London: Policy Research Bureau for the Youth Justice Board.

Goldson, B. and Jamieson, J. (2002b) 'Youth crime, the "parenting deficit" and state intervention: a contextual critique', *Youth Justice*, 2: 82–99.

Home Office, Department for Constitutional Affairs and the Youth Justice Board (2004a) *Circular: Parenting Orders and Contracts for Criminal Conduct or Anti-social Behaviour.* London: Home Office, Department for Constitutional Affairs and Youth Justice Board.

See the Office of Public Sector Information's website for the texts of the Anti-Social Behaviour Act 2003 (http://www.opsi.gov.uk/acts/acts2003/20030038.htm) and the Crime and Disorder Act 1998 (http://www.opsi.gov.uk/acts/acts1998/19980037.htm).

PARTNERSHIP WORKING

> Partnership working involves collaboration between agencies in the funding, management and/or delivery of services. Also described as 'multi-agency' or 'interagency' working, partnerships may include representatives of relevant agencies or organizations across the statutory, voluntary and commercial sectors as well as members of local communities.

Over the last two decades the advantages of a partnership approach to crime prevention have been espoused by both policymakers and practitioners. Since the mid-1980s, multi-agency strategies have been strongly advocated in numerous Home Office circulars and reports and, in 1991, the Home Office Standing Conference on Crime Prevention (the 'Morgan Report') was set up to explore the ways in which a partnership approach to crime prevention could become a normal part of practice and policy (Home Office 1991). At the same time, influential multi-agency initiatives (of which the Northamptonshire juvenile liaison bureaux are the best known) were developed by practitioners and agencies as part of a 'systems management' approach to divert young people from the formal criminal justice system.

The emerging consensus about the advantages of multi-agency strategies was consolidated in the Crime and Disorder Act 1998, which made partnership work in the youth justice system a statutory duty. The Act required local authorities with responsibility for education and social services, together with their statutory partners (the police, probation services and health authorities), to form interagency youth offending teams (YOTs) for the delivery of youth justice services. The agencies were required to commit resources to the YOT – whether in the form of cash, staff or services – and to participate in their governance through multi-agency management boards. In this way, the management, funding and delivery of youth justice services became a multi-agency responsibility. As well as being interagency teams in themselves, YOTs also work in partnership with a range of services across the statutory, voluntary and corporate sectors. They therefore exemplify both 'ideal' types of partnership work identified by Crawford (1997): 'multiagency' working, where agencies come together to address a particular problem, and 'interagency' working, where there is a degree of 'melding' of relations between agencies, usually resulting in new structures and forms of working.

The benefits of partnership working are premised on the understanding that crime has multiple causes and effects. Young people who offend are likely to experience a range of problems connected to, for example, their family and social, economic, health or education needs. It is therefore not possible for any sole agency to address all aspects of offending behaviour. Instead, an effective approach requires the input of a variety of agencies. In this context, partnership working has three key advantages.

First, because they can pool information and expertise, multi-agency teams can identify the range of service user needs and provide a 'holistic' service to address them. This allows partnerships to identify children and young people thought to be at most 'risk' of offending and to intervene to attempt to prevent them from doing so. In the context of the current emphasis on pre-emptive, preventative strategies in addressing offending behaviour, this is considered a particularly important benefit of partnership arrangements in YOTs.

Second, by consolidating the diverse expertise and resources of staff from different agencies into a single structure, partnerships allow for a more co-ordinated and more efficient use of resources, whether funding, expertise, effort or information. In particular, it can remove obstructions to co-operation between agencies, allowing practitioners to make faster and more efficient referrals and providing quicker and easier access to information held by different agencies. Further, by co-opting various professional and interest groups into a collective whole with consistent aims and objectives, the capacity for conflict and disruption between these agencies is reduced. In other words, partnership work attempts to 'design out' conflict between the different parts of the youth justice system to allow for its smooth running.

Third, partnership work can encourage creativity and innovation. It enables staff to work outside their traditional structures and practices and allows for the development of new ways of working. Further, partnership structures can raise the status of the services delivered. The multi-agency governance structure of YOTs, for example, was explicitly intended to encourage the local authority and all statutory partners to participate in their operation and to see youth offending as their corporate responsibility.

However, the blurring of boundaries between agencies that partnership work represents can also be problematic in at least two ways. First, it can lead to unaccountable working practices, in particular in relation to information sharing. While the ability to bypass the formal and often bureaucratic systems of communication between agencies is considered a central strength of partnership work, the ease and informality with which information can be exchanged within partnerships can lead to unacceptable practices, including breaches of confidentiality.

Second, partnership working raises some important challenges for practitioners. The relationships between participating agencies are a particular source of difficulty. Power differentials between agencies make conflict a central feature of multi-agency work. More powerful agencies can dominate decision-making and are able to define the objectives of the partnership, the problems to be addressed and the actions considered legitimate. Differences in the cultures of participating agencies, whether real or perceived, can be a particularly potent focus of conflict. Tensions are often expected to be especially acute between the police and social services staff as they appear to represent opposing interests in the youth justice system.

Yet, while it is recognized that interagency conflict is inevitable in partnership work, it is not necessarily destructive and/or fatal in terms of collaboration. However, it can also be seen as an important and productive part of interagency relations that allows the tensions between the diverse claims and interests of the various parts of the youth justice system to be recognized and negotiated.

Anna Souhami

Related entries

Assessment framework; Children's trusts; Corporatism; Crime and Disorder Act 1998; Crime and disorder reduction (CDR); Crime prevention; Every Child Matters (ECM); Managerialism; Multi-agency public protection arrangements (MAPPAs); Responsibilization; Risk management; Safeguarding; Surveillance; Systems management; Youth justice plan; Youth offending teams (YOTs).

Key texts and sources

Audit Commission (1996) *Misspent Youth: Young People and Crime.* London: Audit Commission.

Crawford, A. (1997) *The Local Governance of Crime: Appeals to Community and Partnership.* Oxford: Clarendon Press.

Home Office (1991) *Safer Communities: The Local Delivery of Crime Prevention through the Partnership Approach* (the Morgan Report). London: Home Office.

Souhami, A. (2007) *Transforming Youth Justice: Occupational Identity and Cultural Change.* Cullompton: Willan Publishing.

PENALTY NOTICES FOR DISORDER (PNDs)

A penalty notice for disorder (PND) is a financial penalty issued following the commission of a 'penalty' offence. Payment of the penalty within 21 days discharges liability for conviction of the offence. Notices can be issued by police officers and community support officers to 16–17-year-olds and by police officers only to 10–15-year-olds.

The use of penalty notices for disorder (PNDs) was extended by the Anti-social Behaviour Act 2003 to children and young people (under the age of 18). PNDs were implemented nationally on 20 January 2004 for 16–17-year-olds and, seven 'pilots' for 10–15-year-olds commenced in mid-2005. Non-payment of the PND results in enforcement proceedings of the penalty sum as a fine. Currently there are two rates of penalty, with lower rates for 10–15-year-olds. The Home Secretary can vary the PND by order.

For 16–17-year-olds the parent/guardian cannot be made liable for payment of the penalty without a court appearance. They are, however, made liable for PNDs in respect of 10–15-year-olds. In the latter case, parents/guardians must be notified that a PND has been issued to their child/young person, albeit not until after the event. This lack of parent/carer involvement means that the guidance that applies in the case of adults (setting out interviews/questioning before PND issue consistent with Police and Criminal Evidence Act 1984 procedures) cannot be followed in the case of the youngest children.

The child/young person can elect for trial within the payment period. Identity disputes in enforcement proceedings result in a 28-day adjournment for investigation. Identity is then reconsidered, with the court applying the 'balance of probabilities' to the child's/young person's claim he or she was not the person involved. If the claim is rejected, the court imposes a fine. There is guidance for PNDs in respect of 10–15-year-olds, and supplementary guidance to that for adults for 16–17-year-olds.

Spike Cadman

Related entries

First-time entrants; Fines; Fixed-penalty notices (FPNs); Respect (government action plan).

Key texts and sources

Ashford, M., Chard, A. and Redhouse, N. (2006) *Defending Young People in the Criminal Justice System* (3rd edn). London: Legal Action Group.

Home Office (2002a) *Criminal Justice and Police Act 2001: Penalty Notices for Disorder – Police Operational Guidance.* London: Home Office.

Home Office (2005a) *The Use of Penalty Notices for Disorder for Offences Committed by Young People Aged 16 and 17: Supplementary Operational Guidance for Police Officers.* London: Home Office.

Home Office (2005b) *Criminal Justice and Police Act 2001 (ss. 1–11) – Penalty Notices for Disorder for Offences Committed by Young People Aged 10 to 15: Police Operational Guidance.* London: Home Office.

Nacro (2004a) *Anti-social Behaviour Orders and Associated Measures. Part 2. Youth Crime Briefing.* London: Nacro.

The Home Office's document, *Operational Policing: General Information on Penalty Notices*, is available online at **http://police.homeoffice.gov.uk/operational-policing/crimedisorder/index.html/penalty-notice-introduction11**.

See the Office of Public Sector Information's website (**http://www.opsi.gov.uk/acts/acts2003/20030038.htm**) for the text of the Anti-social Behaviour Act 2003.

PENAL WELFARISM

'Penal welfarism' is a concept closely associated with the work of David Garland (1985, 2001). It is characterized by a complex of institutional arrangements driven by positive rehabilitative rather than negative retributive imperatives. The tensions intrinsic to the welfare *and* justice objectives of the juvenile court epitomize the penal welfare complex and, in many respects, this applies more generally to the history of youth justice policy reform.

Penal welfarism is underpinned by the rehabilitative ideal. In this sense rehabilitation is:

> *the hegemonic organising principle, the intellectual framework and value system that [binds] together the whole structure and [makes] sense of it for practitioners. It [provides] an all-embracing conceptual net that [can] be cast over each and every activity in the penal field allowing practitioners to render their world coherent and meaningful* (Garland 2001: 35).

Welfare principles in youth justice encapsulate penal welfarism. It centres on such practices as expert 'assessment'; individual 'treatment' programmes; aetiological research and the evaluation of treatment effectiveness; social work with children in trouble and their families; and, where institutionalization is thought to be necessary, an emphasis on education, reintegration and resettlement. Penal welfare principles reject the concept of prison as punishment, viewing it as counterproductive when measured in terms of reform, rehabilitation and individual correction. Community-based 'treatment' interventions are favoured and, when secure detention is used, 'constructive regimes' rather than punishments are emphasized.

Penal welfare generally, and the youth justice system more particularly, is pitted with tensions and contradictions. As Morris and Giller (1987: 32) have observed: 'humanitarianism and coercion are essentially two sides of the same coin.' In this way, the 'normalizing', 'correcting' and 'segregating' (Garland 1985) dimensions of the penal welfare complex are neither exclusively humanitarian nor simply repressive.

At a macro level, penal welfarism seeks to balance individual freedom with responsibility and collective security. Social insurance, social security and social welfare are pivotal in terms of their inclusionary impulses, on the one hand, and their capacity to inculcate and regulate 'correct' behaviour on the other. In this sense penal welfarism rests on a social contract whereby security, welfare and protection are provided in return for social obligation and social responsibility.

In youth justice policy and practice, penal welfarism has, in many respects, disintegrated since the late 1960s. This is partly due to the problematics of free-ranging discretionary welfare and unbridled net-widening (Thorpe *et al.* 1980). Moreover, there is less emphasis on social structural contexts, child welfare and rehabilitation and, instead, a consolidating concentration on constructions of individual responsibility, 'risk' and regulation. In recent times policy and practice have taken new directions, and phenomena such as 'risk'; electronic monitoring; surveillance; 'naming and shaming'; centrally imposed 'national standards' and prescribed models of 'effective practice'; victim impact statements; punishment in the community; private jails; and high rates of child imprisonment are anathema to penal welfarism.

Indeed, Garland (2001) argues that, in contrast to 'penal welfarism,' contemporary policy can be distinguished by the (re)emergence of punitive sanctions and expressive justice, the return of the victim and the politicization of policy responses. Ultimately, perhaps, this is most clearly expressed by high rates of child imprisonment. In the penal welfare complex

prisons are essentially conceived as 'schools for crime', as counterproductive and very much a last resort. Significant effort is expended on the task of creating alternatives to incarceration and encouraging sentencers to use them. For most of the post-war period a secular shift away from carceral punishment was evident but – particularly in England and Wales – this trend is no longer observable in contemporary youth justice policy. Garland (2001: 4) argues that:

[Previously] those involved in the business of [youth] crime control shared a common set of assumptions about the frameworks that shaped criminal justice and penal practice ... Today, for better or for worse, we lack any such agreement, any settled culture, or any clear sense of the big picture. Policy development appears highly volatile, with an unprecedented amount of legislative activity, much dissension in the ranks of practitioner groups, and a good deal of conflict between experts and politicians ... [This] leads us into unfamiliar territory where the ideological lines are far from clear and where the old assumptions are an unreliable guide.

Barry Goldson

Related entries

Alternatives to custody; Decarceration; Governance; Governmentality; Intermediate treatment (IT); Justice; Juvenile court; Net-widening; Rehabilitation; Politicisation; Punitiveness; Welfare.

Key texts and sources

Garland, D. (1985) *Punishment and Welfare: A History of Penal Strategies.* Aldershot: Gower.
Garland, D. (2001) *The Culture of Control: Crime and Social Order in Contemporary Society.* Oxford: Oxford University Press.
Morris, A. and Giller, H. (1987) *Understanding Juvenile Justice.* London: Croom Helm.
Muncie, J. (2004) *Youth and Crime* (2nd edn). London: Sage.
Thorpe, D.H., Smith, D., Green, C.J. and Paley, J.H. (1980) *Out of Care: The Community Support of Juvenile Offenders.* London: Allen & Unwin.

PERSISTENT YOUNG OFFENDERS

There is no straightforward definition of a persistent young offender. UK jurisdictions apply a wide range of definitions, but usually three or more offences or episodes within a specified period, ranging from three months to three years.

Persistent offending by young people is a prominent concern attracting the attention of the media, politicians and public alike. Most young offenders will not persist, and those who do represent only a very small proportion of all known offenders. Studies have suggested the rate may vary from between 3 per cent (Graham and Bowling 1995) and 8 per cent (Audit Scotland 2001), depending on the definition applied. There is, however, consistent evidence that a small group of young people are responsible for a disproportionate number of offences and who present significant challenges in all jurisdictions. Self-reported data also suggest that the same young people also tend to be involved in a significant amount of undetected or unreported crime.

The first major British study of persistent young offenders applied three definitions of 'persistence' to a sample of 10–16-years-olds, all of whom had a minimum of three offences in a 12-month period (Hagell and Newburn 1994). The definitions employed were: the top 10 per cent of the most frequently arrested young people; those with 10 offences in a three-month period; and 12–14-year-olds with three or more imprisonable or serious offences. Only three young people, aged 12–14, were common to each defined group. Those identified as committing offences most frequently were not those who committed many offences over a short period ('spree offenders') and were not the most serious offenders. The researchers concluded that 'no two definitions of persistence will lead to the identification of the same individuals' (Hagell and Newburn 1994: 121).

Studies provide little evidence of criminal specialism in persistent young offenders, and patterns of offending are seldom continuous but tend to involve bursts of activity over short periods. The most commonly admitted or recorded offences tend to be of a minor nature relating to dishonesty for both males and females – for example, theft, handling stolen goods and vandalism. Few offend entirely on their own and those who persist are not disproportionately engaged in the most serious and violent crimes (Graham and Bowling 1995).

Young people who get into trouble persistently often have an interrelated set of difficulties that differentiates them from those who get into trouble once or twice. Their shared characteristics are less often to do with their offending and more to do with their adverse personal and social circumstances. Studies provide a fairly consistent picture of persistent young offenders, however defined. Typical 'biographies' include poverty and disadvantage; contact with social services for welfare reasons, often including periods in public care; family disruption and irregular parental supervision; criminality in the family; mental health problems; alcohol and drug-related difficulties; and schooling difficulties, including truancy, exclusion, poor school attachment and poor educational achievement.

Some commentators have distinguished between 'adolescence-limited' and 'life-course' persistent offenders. Adolescence-limited offending increases rapidly in early adolescence before declining at around the age of 18 and beyond. Life-course persistent offending starts very early and persists across the life course. The contention is not that early offending locks some young people into a cycle of reoffending; rather, early onset is indicative of a range of other characteristics that adversely influence personal and social development and behaviour. Other commentators would argue that the distinction between the two categories is less clear-cut (Smith 2002), and adolescence-limited offenders may experience many of the same sorts of difficulties that account for persistent offending but to a lesser degree. Nonetheless, the risk of becoming a persistent offender has been found to be two to three times higher for children who commence offending under 12 years of age than for young people whose onset of offending comes later.

While children exposed to multiple 'risk factors' are disproportionately more likely to become persistent offenders, this cannot be predicted with accuracy (Graham 1998). Not all children and young people exposed to multiple risk factors become offenders, nor do all children and young people who offend grow up in socio-economic difficulty. There are important aspects of the lives of young people that can protect them against risk in the same way that some personal and social factors are strongly associated with the likelihood of offending. Many children appear to survive even serious risky experiences with no major developmental disruptions (Kirby and Fraser 1998). In this sense 'protective factors' that might serve to offset 'risk' include: having a resilient temperament or a positive social orientation; close friendships with peers; positive and warm relationships that promote close bonds with family members and other adults who encourage and recognize a young person's competence; and features of schooling, including positive relationships with teachers, rewards, sanctions and systems of pupil support.

In general terms, 'vulnerable' and 'risky' young people who become 'persistent young offenders' can often be described as 'children in need' as defined by UK legislation and the standards set by international instruments, including the United Nations Convention on the Rights of the Child. Research findings indicate the need for well resourced, holistic responses, if young people with multiple difficulties (including persistent offending) are to be dealt with effectively.

Bill Whyte

Related entries

Audit Commission; Child poverty; Children in custody; Desistance; Developmental criminology; Extending Entitlement (National Assembly for Wales); Growing out of crime; Prolific and other priority offenders (PPOs) strategy; Protective factors; Risk factors; Self-reported offending; Social exclusion; Youth and policing; Youth courts.

Key texts and sources

Audit Scotland (2001) *Youth Justice in Scotland: A Baseline Report.* Edinburgh: Audit Scotland.

Graham, J. (1998) *Schools, Disruptive Behaviour and Delinquency: A Review of Research.* London: Home Office.

Graham, J. and Bowling, B. (1995) *Young People and Crime. Home Office Research Study* 145. London: Home Office.

Hagell, A. and Newburn, T. (1994) *Persistent Young Offenders.* London: Policy Studies Institute.

Kirby, M. and Fraser, M. (1998) *Risk and Resilience in Childhood: An Ecological Perspective.* Washington, DC: NASW Press.

Smith, D. (2002) 'Crime and the life course', in M. Maguire *et al.* (eds) *The Oxford Handbook of Criminology* (3rd edn). Oxford: Oxford University Press.

Whyte, B. (2003) 'Young and persistent: recent developments in youth justice policy and practice in Scotland', *Youth Justice,* 3: 74–85.

POLICE AND CRIMINAL EVIDENCE ACT 1984 (PACE)

The Police and Criminal Evidence Act 1984 (PACE) is the most comprehensive and significant statute defining police powers and safeguards for suspects. It is accompanied by detailed procedures in the codes of practice, and, together, these regulate the stop and search, search and seizure, arrest, detention, questioning and identification of detainees. There are some special provisions for children.

The Police and Criminal Evidence Act 1984 (PACE) rationalized police powers and suspects' rights in response to demands to strike a balance between crime control and due process by the Royal Commission on Criminal Procedure (1981). It also improved police accountability by instituting, first, a new system for dealing with complaints against the police and, secondly, arrangements for obtaining the views of the community on policing. The Act followed concerns about the misuse of police powers, particularly in relation to children and young people and mentally vulnerable suspects, and the somewhat contradictory public concern that the police lacked the necessary powers to halt the rise in crime. Since then, various sections of the Act have been amended and the codes have been regularly revised. A new Code H, concerning the detention of terrorism suspects, came into effect in July 2006. In March 2007, the Home Office announced a public consultation exercise regarding possible reforms to PACE. New codes are expected in 2008.

The main safeguards are as follows:

- The various recording requirements for each exercise of a police power, most notably in the form of the custody record to be maintained by a custody officer (a police officer with the duty of overseeing suspects' detention).
- The rights to have someone informed of the arrest and to legal advice.
- The tape (or video) recording of interviews.
- The court's power to exclude improperly obtained evidence.

Most of the provisions of PACE and the codes apply equally to adults and juveniles, but there are some additional requirements for juveniles (those appearing to be under 17 years of age), including the following:

- The person responsible for the juvenile's welfare must be informed of the juvenile's arrest.
- An 'appropriate adult', who may be someone different, should be present during a juvenile's questioning and detention.
- A parent's consent is normally required for an identification procedure.

There has been some division among commentators on the impact of PACE and the codes on detention and questioning. However, they have established a clear statutory framework for police powers and suspects' rights in an area where there was previously little clarity. Several other countries have modelled their police procedures on the provisions laid down by PACE. Moreover, the procedures have largely been incorporated into routine practice in England and Wales. For example, empirical evidence suggests that suspects are generally informed of their rights and are legally represented more often than before PACE. However, it has also been suggested that compliance has assumed little more than symbolic value at times. Researchers have questioned the independence of custody officers, who have often been found to inform suspects of their rights in a vague or discouraging way, especially where juveniles are concerned. At the same time, concerns remain about the discriminatory use of police powers, with research frequently suggesting that young, ethnic minority men are stopped and searched and arrested at higher rates than other groups.

Harriet Pierpoint

Related entries

Appropriate adult; Arrest and decision-making process; Bail; Criminal Justice Act 2003; Penalty notices for disorder (PNDs); 'Race' and justice; Remand management; Youth and policing.

Key texts and sources

Brookman, F. and Pierpoint, H. (2003) 'Access to legal advice for young suspects and remand prisoners', *Howard Journal of Criminal Justice*, 42: 452–70.

Home Office (2005e) *Police and Criminal Evidence Act 1984 (s. 60(1)(a), s. 60A(1) and s. 66(1)): Codes of Practice A–G*. London: HMSO (available online at http://police.homeoffice.gov.uk/operational-policing/powers-pace-codes/pace-code-intro/).

Home Office (2006c) *Police and Criminal Evidence Act 1984 (s. 66(1)): Codes of Practice C and H*. London: HMSO (available online at http://police.home office.gov.uk/operational-policing/powers-pace-codes/pace-code-intro/).

Newburn, T. and Reiner, R. (2004) 'From PC Dixon to Dixon PLC: policing and policing powers since 1954', *Criminal Law Review*, 601–18.

Pierpoint, H. (2004) 'A survey of volunteer appropriate adult services in England and Wales', *Youth Justice*, 4: 32–45.

POLITICIZATION

> Politicization is the process whereby politicians are inclined to respond to issues on the basis of perceived public opinion and whereby policy is determined more in accordance with political imperative than evidence and rationality.

In the early 1990s, media coverage of car crime, of outbreaks of civil unrest in which children and young people appeared to be prominent players and the construction of the 'bail bandit' and 'persistent young offender' (children apparently beyond the reach of the law) fuelled moral panic and the 'folk devilling' of children and young people. There was little, if any, considered and dispassionate analysis during this period and no attempt was made to provide separate accounts for the different strands of 'youth deviance'. Rather, a reductionist assimilation of disparate behaviours was presented. Moreover, Bottoms and Stevenson (1992: 23–4) observe that:

> *It is a fact well known to students of social policy that reforms of the system often take place not so much because of careful routine analysis by ministers and civil servants in the relevant Department of State ... but because one or more individual incident(s) occurs, drawing public attention to ... policy in a dramatic way which seems to demand change ... the reforms would not have taken place without the public attention created by the original incident.*

The tragic death of James Bulger in February 1993 and the subsequent conviction of two 10-year-old boys for his murder became one such 'individual incident' and, as a consequence, youth crime in general became highly politicized.

Days after the toddler's death, the Prime Minister at the time, John Major, proclaimed that 'society needs to condemn a little more and understand a little less', and the Home Secretary, Kenneth Clarke, referred to 'really persistent nasty little juveniles' (*Daily Mail* 22 February 1993). Three months later and after a Cabinet reshuffle, Michael Howard made his first public pronouncement as the new Home Secretary,

referring to a 'self centred arrogant group of young hoodlums ... who are adult in everything except years [and who] will no longer be able to use age as an excuse for immunity from effective punishment ... they will find themselves behind bars' (*Daily Mail* 3 June 1993). In October 1993, to rapturous applause at the Conservative Party conference, Howard declared that he was speaking for the nation: 'we are all sick and tired of young hooligans who terrorise communities.' He promised a 'clamp down' and offered assurances that 'prison works'.

Although the 'clamp down' that Michael Howard promised belied evidence and rationality, the rhetoric was nonetheless institutionalized through law and policy. Tonry (1996: 179) has observed that:

> *Crime is an emotional subject and visceral appeals by politicians to people's fears and resentments are difficult to counter. It is easy to seize the low ground in political debates about crime policy. When one candidate campaigns with pictures of clanging prison gates ... and disingenuous promises that newer, tougher policies will work, it is difficult for an opponent to explain that crime is a complicated problem, that real solutions must be long term, and that simplistic toughness does not reduce crime rates. This is why, as a result, candidates often compete to establish which is tougher in his views about crime. It is also why less conservative candidates often try to pre-empt their more conservative opponents by adopting a tough stance early in the campaign.*

On the one hand, Michael Howard, as Conservative Home Secretary, argued that, to take account of children's disadvantaged backgrounds in analyses of juvenile crime was to 'take the criminals' side' and to succumb to 'excuses' from 'bleeding heart' social workers and probation officers who are a 'relic from the 1970s' (*Independent on Sunday* 4 August 1996; *Guardian* 16 October 1997). On the other hand, the principal 'opposition' party, New Labour, claimed that:

> *punishment is important as a means of expressing society's condemnation of misbehaviour ... all this is common sense ... The*

government seems to have lost sight of this guiding principle. We intend to restore it, changing the law if necessary ... Labour is not going to stand by watching things get even worse (Straw and Michael 1996: passim).

The politicization of youth crime and youth justice became concretized. Notions of family support and relief were reframed as questions of parental irresponsibility and family failure, and the wealth of research evidence and practice experience confirming that child 'offenders' are almost exclusively drawn from the most disadvantaged, neglected, damaged and distressed families, neighbourhoods and communities was dismissed as an 'excusing' distraction in a context in which there could be 'no more excuses'. On coming to power in 1997, New Labour's political calculations were such that being 'tough on crime', and hard on the children who commit it, was crucial, despite all the manifest contradictions. The consequences included a 'blizzard of initiatives, crackdowns and targets' (Neather 2004: 11) and a 'toughening up [of] every aspect of the criminal justice system' (Blair 2004: 6).

'Tough on crime' policies bear little, if any, relation to actual patterns of crime. Instead, they derive from political machinations as distinct from genuine crime-and-disorder reduction and/or community safety imperatives:

[it] is very much a political process. It is governed not by any criminological logic but instead by ... political actors and the exigencies, political calculations and short-term interests that provide their motivations. In its detailed configuration, with all its incoherence and contradictions, [it] is thus a product of the decidedly aleatory history of political manoeuvres and calculations (Garland 2001: 191 emphasis in original).

Thus political priorities and 'electoral anxieties' (Pitts 2000) come to exercise greater influence over youth justice policy formation than measured criminological rationality.

Barry Goldson

Related entries

Authoritarianism; Bulger; Media reporting; Moral panic; Penal welfarism; Public attitudes to youth crime and justice; Punitiveness.

Key texts and sources

Blair, T. (2004) 'Foreword', in *Confident Communities in a Secure Britain: The Home Office Strategic Plan, 2004–08*. London: HMSO.

Bottoms, A. and Stevenson, S. (1992) 'What went wrong? Criminal justice policy in England and Wales, 1945–70', in D. Downes (ed.) *Unravelling Criminal Justice*. London: Macmillan.

Garland, D. (2001) *The Culture of Control: Crime and Social Order in Contemporary Society*. Oxford: Oxford University Press.

Neather, A. (2004) 'Fears haunting New Labour', *Evening Standard*, 5 April.

Pitts, J. (2000) 'The new youth justice and the politics of electoral anxiety', in B. Goldson (ed.) *The New Youth Justice*. Lyme Regis: Russell House.

Straw, J. and Michael, A. (1996) *Tackling Youth Crime: Reforming Youth Justice – a Consultation Paper on an Agenda for Change*. London: Labour Party.

Tonry, M. (1996) 'Racial politics, racial disparities and the war on crime', in B. Hudson (ed.) *Race, Crime and Justice*. Aldershot: Dartmouth.

POSITIVE ACTIVITIES FOR YOUNG PEOPLE (PAYP)

Positive Activities for Young People (PAYP) was funded from April 2003 to March 2006 as a national, targeted, cross-departmental government programme providing diversionary and developmental activities for young people aged 8–19. From 1 April 2007, following a transitional period, the funding for these activities passed to local authorities.

Launched in 2003, Positive Activities for Young People (PAYP) targeted young people aged 8–19 identified as 'at risk' of social exclusion, committing crime or being a victim of crime. The programme was based in areas of deprivation and encouraged participants to take part in a range of voluntary activities out of school hours and during school holidays. Young people identified as most 'at risk' were allocated a 'key worker' to provide one-on-one support and to encourage (re)engagement with education, training and employment.

The programme aimed to achieve seven key objectives. To:

- reduce crime and anti-social behaviour in the short and long term;
- support young people back into education or training and to help them stay there, by working with those at risk of truancy;
- ensure that young people are supported as they move from primary to secondary school;
- provide access to arts, sports and cultural activities and to make provision for those with an interest and/or talent in any area to continue after the programme has ended;
- bring together young people from different geographical and ethnic communities to help break down prejudice and misunderstanding;
- give young people opportunities for personal development, including the development of self-discipline, self-respect and self-confidence, enabling them to communicate more effectively with a range of people and to work effectively in a team; and
- encourage young people to contribute to their communities through volunteering and active citizenship.

The national evaluation of PAYP described it as a 'success', although it also suggested that too little consideration was given to how some outcomes (including crime reduction) could be evidenced. Between 2003 and 2006, approximately 290,000 young people participated in PAYP activities, of which 85 per cent were judged to meet the 'at risk' criteria and 39 per cent received key worker support (Department for Education and Skills 2006a: 103, 102, 12).

PAYP consolidated several existing funding streams for summer activities and was supported by various government departments, the Youth Justice Board and the Big Lottery Fund. The total budget allocated over three years was £124.5 million (Department for Education and Skills 2006a: 2). PAYP was co-ordinated at a regional level by the government offices, which identified local agencies to deliver the programme, including Connexions partnerships, the Youth Service and

youth offending teams. From 1 April 2007, following a transitional period, funding passed to local authorities and was incorporated into local area agreements. Provision is now locally planned, in line with the wider reforms proposed in the green paper, *Youth Matters* (Department for Education and Skills 2006b).

Laura Kelly

Related entries

Connexions; Crime prevention; Early intervention; Positive Futures; Risk factors; Sport-based crime prevention; Youth Matters.

Key texts and sources

Department for Education and Skills (2005c) *Youth Matters.* London: DfES.
Department for Education and Skills (2006a) *Positive Activities for Young People: National Evaluation.* London: DfES.
Department for Education and Skills (2006b) *Youth Matters: Next Steps.* Norwich: HMSO.
Home Office (2004) *Prolific and Other Priority Offender Strategy: Prevent and Deter.* London: Home Office.

POSITIVE FUTURES

Positive Futures is a 'national sports and activity-based social inclusion programme' that works with young people aged 10–19 in England and Wales. On 1 April 2006, the charity Crime Concern took over responsibility for managing the programme on behalf of the Home Office Crime and Drug Strategy Directorate.

Launched in 2000, Positive Futures is funded by the Home Office Crime and Drug Strategy Directorate until March 2008, with additional funding from the Football Foundation. The programme is delivered through approximately 120 projects, focusing on areas of deprivation and young people thought to be 'marginalized within the community'. Two national strategies have emphasized central priorities, such as building relationships between project staff and participants, but projects are locally developed by lead agencies and partnerships:

> Positive Futures is not a conventional 'diversionary' or sports development project. It is a relationship strategy. Key to its approach is engaging with young people through an ability to teach them or help them learn something they think is worthwhile: starting from 'where they are' in a non-judgemental way. Central to its success is the commitment to a flexible, organic local development strategy and the role of community coaches (Home Office 2003a: 8, see also Crime Concern 2006: 12).

The first national strategy suggested that 'Positive Futures' overall aim is to have a positive influence on individual participants' substance misuse, physical activity and offending behaviour by widening horizons and access to lifestyle, educational and employment opportunities within a supportive and culturally familiar environment' (Home Office 2003a: 6). This aim was reproduced in the second strategy (Crime Concern 2006: 10), which re-emphasized many existing objectives, advocated the expansion of non-sports activities and highlighted the programme's relevance to current policy priorities, including 'building a culture of respect, increasing youth volunteering, responding to the issues in Youth Matters, and supporting the achievement of all the key outcomes identified as vital for children and young people' (Crime Concern 2006: 6).

Positive Futures has been subject to extensive monitoring and evaluation since 2002. Key findings from the Positive Futures evaluation include the following:

- Some 109,546 young people were involved in regular project activity from 2002 to September 2005.
- Between March and September 2005, almost 600 participants began to seek, and a similar number obtained, employment; 509 began volunteering; and over 4,000 signed up for, or completed, awards or training.
- Some 76 per cent of partners believe Positive Futures makes a positive difference to reducing anti-social behaviour and 68 per cent believe it reduces local crime rates.

- Some 90 per cent of partners believe Positive Futures makes a positive difference to the availability of sports activities (Home Office 2006d: 4–5).

'Substance', an agency involved with the Positive Futures Case Study Research (Crabbe 2006), has developed a comprehensive new monitoring, evaluation and reporting system, collecting quantitative and increased levels of qualitative data. This system has been implemented by Positive Futures and the Football Foundation initiative, 'Kickz'.

Laura Kelly

Related entries

Desistance: Every Child Matters (ECM), Positive Activities for Young People (PAYP); Sport-based crime prevention; Youth Matters.

Key texts and sources

Crabbe, T. (2006) Knowing the Score – Positive Futures Case Study Research: Final Report. London: Home Office.

Crime Concern (2006) Be Part of Something. London: Crime Concern.

Home Office (2003a) 'Cul-de-sacs and Gateways': Understanding the Positive Futures Approach. London: Home Office.

Home Office (2006d) Positive Futures Impact Report: End of Season Review. London: Home Office.

See also the Positive Futures website (**http://www.drugs.gov.uk/young-people/positive-futures/**).

POSITIVISM

Positivism is the view that the social sciences can and should follow the procedures of the natural sciences – particularly the use of experimental methods – in testing theories and that, in doing so, they can produce knowledge that is comparable in terms of reliability with the discoveries of the natural sciences.

Positivist approaches to the study of crime and offending were dominant for much of the twentieth century. Whether from biological, psychological or sociological perspectives, they sought to identify scientifically what it was that differentiated people who broke the law from those who obeyed it (the latter group being assumed to be 'normal' and in the great majority).

The assumptions of the positivist approach began to be seriously questioned with the growing influence from the early 1960s of the labelling perspective, which argued that deviance (including criminality) was the product of a process of social interaction and that all that was different about deviants was that a 'label' had been successfully applied to them. It was argued that the positivist attempt to answer the question 'Why do some people offend?' overlooked the political and ethical processes involved in the construction of deviance. It followed that positivism was conceived as politically conservative as well as methodologically naïve in its belief in the feasibility of identifying the causes of crime and delinquency and, therefore, the means of preventing or treating it.

Since then, arguments about positivism in criminology and social work have sometimes become very polarized. At one extreme are commentators influenced by postmodern ideas who argue that the social world is inherently unknowable. At the other extreme are those who argue that all that is needed in order to acquire exact knowledge about crime and how to deal with it is the rigorous application of scientific methods. In between are those who argue, for example, that the scientific emphasis of positivist approaches leaves a great deal of human reality unaccounted for, or that the positivist preoccupation with 'outcomes' tends to ignore the processes involved in producing them, as well as overestimating the accuracy with which such outcomes can be measured.

There is no doubt that the positivist promise of delivering scientific certainty makes the approach attractive to managers and politicians anxious to believe that crime and deviance can be brought under control. There is equally no doubt that research has so far failed to realize

that promise. Positivism has brought to the social sciences the virtues of accuracy, rationality and the careful analysis of data. But it has also tended to make exaggerated claims for itself, and the social world remains more messy and unpredictable than positivists or their bureaucratic sponsors would like it to be.

So, while it is important to acknowledge the real achievements of positivist methods in identifying nonsense (explanations of delinquency based on supposed racial characteristics, for example), it would not be sensible to embrace positivism to the exclusion of other methods and perspectives. An important lesson of much recent research in youth justice and related fields is that knowledge is harder to reach, and more ambiguous, than positivists have hoped, and that researchers should be modest, cautious and provisional in the claims they make about their results.

David Smith

Related entries

Actuarialism; Critical criminology; Effectiveness; Evaluative research; Evidence-based policy and practice (EBPP); Labelling theory; Managerialism; Risk management; What Works.

Key texts and sources

Braithwaite, J. (1993) 'Beyond positivism: learning from contextual integrated strategies', *Journal of Research in Crime and Delinquency*, 30: 383–99.

Pawson, R. and Tilley, N. (1997) *Realistic Evaluation*. London: Sage.

Smith, D. (1987) 'The limits of positivism in social work research', *British Journal of Social Work*, 17: 401–16.

Smith, D. (ed.) (2004) *Social Work and Evidence-based Practice*. London: Jessica Kingsley.

Smith, D. (2006a) 'Youth crime and justice: research, evaluation and "evidence"', in B. Goldson and J. Muncie (eds) *Youth Crime and Justice: Critical Issues*. London: Sage.

POWERS OF CRIMINAL COURTS (SENTENCING) ACT 2000

The Powers of Criminal Courts (Sentencing) Act 2000 introduced special measures for young people who commit 'grave crimes' and amended and detailed rules regarding various sentences available to young offenders. The Act also introduced exclusion orders and consolidated parental responsibility for young offenders, and it updated sentencing guidelines regarding proportionality by listing the 'sentencing bands' and defining the threshold criteria.

The Powers of Criminal Courts (Sentencing Act 2000) introduced special measures (under ss. 90 and 91) for young people who commit 'grave crimes' including murder (replacing procedures that previously existed under s. 53 of the Children and Young Persons Act 1933). It also amended and detailed rules regarding various sentences available to young offenders, particularly the referral order (ss. 16–32), but also other community orders including the supervision order, the attendance centre order, the action plan order, the reparation order and the curfew order. The Act further introduced exclusion orders and consolidated parental responsibility for young offenders. Lastly, it updated sentencing guidelines regarding proportionality by listing the 'sentencing bands' (custodial, community and 'lower level' disposals, including financial penalties, discharges and reparation) and by defining the threshold criteria.

A generous view of this statute is that it represented a consolidation and clarification of sentences and their detailed application. However, Fionda (2005: 155) asserts that, similar to the Criminal Justice and Court Services Act 2000, this attempt at clarification was predicated on a 'very muddled set of provisions' whereby seemingly endless youth justice reform had increased the range of sentences 'into a menu of options providing every conceivable intervention to prevent offending'.

It is useful to focus on the provisions for serious young offenders. Section 90 of the Act deals with young people convicted of murder and requires them to be detained 'during Her Majesty's pleasure' – an indeterminate sentence that is equivalent to the mandatory 'life' sentence for adults. A mandatory minimum (tariff) period is fixed by the court and only then can release be granted with the permission of the Parole Board. Children and young people sentenced in this way remain on 'licence' for life. Section 91 covers other 'grave crimes' – primarily crimes for which an adult can be sentenced to at least 14 years in custody. Generally, the court is given the same maxima sentencing limits for children and young people as those relating to adults. Bateman (2005b: 160) has commented that, following this Act, 'a succession of legislative changes has brought an even greater number of offences within the ambit of section 91', leading to a dramatic increase in long-term custodial sentences for young offenders.

In relation to the update of 'sentencing bands' contained in the Act, the threshold criterion for reaching the community sentence level is that the offending was 'serious enough to warrant such a sentence'. The threshold for a custodial disposal is that the offending was 'so serious that only such a sentence can be justified'.

Jane Pickford

Related entries

Exclusion orders; Grave offences; Long-term detention; Menu-based sentencing; Proportionality; Tariff.

Key texts and sources

Bateman, T. (2005b) 'Custody and policy', in T. Bateman and J. Pitts (eds) *The RHP Companion to Youth Justice.* Lyme Regis: Russell House.

Dugmore, P. and Pickford, J. (2006) *Youth Justice and Social Work.* Exeter: Learning Matters.

Fionda, J. (2005) *Devils and Angels: Youth Policy and Crime.* Oxford: Hart Publishing.

Nacro (2003d) *The Sentencing Framework for Children and Young People. Youth Crime Briefing.* London: Nacro.

See the Office of Public Sector Information's website (**http://www.opsi.gov.uk/acts/acts2000/20000006. htm**) for the text of the Powers of Criminal Courts (Sentencing) Act 2000.

PRE-SENTENCE REPORTS (PSRs)

A pre-sentence report (PSR) is a report pre-pared for the court to inform the sentencing process. A PSR is defined by the Criminal Justice Act 2003 as a 'report which, with a view to assisting the court in determining the most suitable method of dealing with an offender, is made or submitted by an appro-priate officer'. The 'appropriate officer' is, in the case of an adult, a probation officer. Where the defendant is below the age of 18 years, the PSR is normally prepared by a member of a youth offending team.

The report of the Streatfield Committee in 1961 (Williams 1961) marked the first official recognition that it was good practice, in appropriate cases, for sentencers to have access to written information as to the defendant's personal and social circumstances, and what forms of intervention might be most effective in addressing his or her offending behaviour. Social inquiry reports (SIRs) (as court reports were then known) continued, however, to have no statutory basis. This led to considerable inconsistency, both in terms of the frequency with which reports were requested and in the format and content of reports when they were requested.

Pre-sentence reports (PSRs) were introduced by the Criminal Justice Act 1991 as part of a package of measures designed to enhance the courts' confidence in non-custodial measures. The Act required that the court obtain a written report before imposing a custodial penalty or any of the more intensive community sentences available to it. In turn, the report author was required to conclude with a proposal for sentence, although ultimate responsibility for determining sentence lay with the court. The new requirements laid down by the 1991 Act were much needed. Research published in 1989 had revealed that 59 per cent of those subject to immediate custody in the Crown court were sentenced in the absence of any report. The new legislation produced a marked increase in the use of reports. By 1998, for instance, the Audit Commission found that PSRs were requested in 41 per cent of all cases sentenced in the youth court. In that year, the Crime and Disorder Act 1998 defined youth justice services for the first time and included the provision of reports to the court as one such service.

The most recent legislative provisions, contained in the Criminal Justice Act 2003, require that the court obtains, and considers the contents of, a PSR before imposing any custodial sentence or community penalty. While the court may, in the case of an adult, dispense with a report if it considers it unnecessary, there is no equivalent provision where the defendant is below the age of 18 years. In such cases, a PSR *must be obtained* unless the court has access to a previous report. The National Standards for Youth Justice Services (2004) contain – what is by comparison with earlier editions of national standards rather limited – guidance on the preparation of PSRs. Reports should be:

- based on information from all relevant sources, including an Asset assessment;
- balanced, impartial, timely, focused, free from discriminatory language, verified and accurate, and written in a manner that the young person can understand;
- produced within 10 working days where the young person meets the definition of a 'persistent young offender' or is eligible for an intensive supervision and surveillance programme, and within 15 working days in all other cases; and
- produced to a consistent format using the following headings: 'sources of information'; 'assessment of young person'; 'assessment of risk of harm to the community'; and 'conclusion'.

The clear purpose of placing court reports on a statutory footing was to oblige sentencers to consider what community-based options were available before imposing a custodial disposal, so that such alternatives might be fully explored. It might, accordingly, have been anticipated that the introduction of PSRs would, in conjunction with other measures intended to promote the use of community sentences, lead to a reduction in child incarceration. In the event, however, the number of custodial sentences imposed on children and young people rose by almost 90 per cent in the ten years from

1992. The reasons for the rapid escalation in the detention of children are no doubt complex, but it should not be concluded that there is no potential for PSRs to influence sentencing in a decarcerative direction.

The sentencing framework permits the imposition of a lesser penalty on the basis of mitigation unrelated to the seriousness of the offence, and in particular on the basis of the child's welfare. Sentencers are also required to have regard to the principal aim of preventing offending. The PSR is the primary mechanism by which issues of welfare might be brought to the court's attention and the vehicle through which arguments for the rehabilitative potential of non-custodial interventions – relative to the 'criminogenic' effects of custody – might, in the case of the child before the court, be most effectively put. Indeed, research confirms that the rate of detention in a particular area is inversely related to the quality of court reports: lower custody areas are, in other words, characterized by better PSRs. Well formulated reports can thus have a significant impact on sentencing outcomes, particularly by promoting the use of community alternatives in 'borderline cases' close to the custody threshold.

There is, however, evidence to suggest that the potential of PSRs to reduce child imprisonment is not being fully exploited. In 2004, the National Audit Office noted that more than two thirds of youth offending teams (YOTs) did not have a policy precluding custodial proposals. Figures published by the Youth Justice Board show that, in 17 YOT areas, more than half of all custodial penalties – imposed between October 2000 and March 2004 – were actively proposed by the PSR author. Such findings suggest a fundamental shift in practice since 1995 when guidance produced for youth justice staff routinely required that PSRs should always propose a community-based alternative. Custody should not be proposed as it is for the court to decide on total removal of liberty.

Tim Bateman

Related entries

Alternatives to custody; Assessment framework; Court officers; Criminal Justice Act 1991; Criminal *Justice Act 2003; Custody rate; Dangerousness; Detention for public protection (DPP); Family ties of young prisoners; Gravity factors (prosecution and sentencing); Justice by geography; Menu-based sentencing; National Objectives and Standards for Scotland's Youth Justice Service; National Standards for Youth Justice Services; Sentencing framework; Specific sentence reports (SSRs); Youth Justice Agency; Youth offending teams (YOTs).*

Key texts and sources

Bateman, T. (2005a) 'Court reports', in T. Bateman and J. Pitts (eds) *The RHP Companion to Youth Justice*. Lyme Regis: Russell House.

Bateman, T. and Stanley, C. (2002) *Patterns of Sentencing: Differential Sentencing across England and Wales*. London: Youth Justice Board.

Nacro (2003c) *Pre-sentence Reports for Young People: A Good Practice Guide* (2nd edn). London: Nacro.

Nacro (2005f) *Pre-sentence Reports and Custody. Youth Crime Briefing*. London: Nacro.

Williams, J.E. (1961) 'Report of the Interdepartmental Committee on the Business of the Criminal Courts', *Modern Law Review*, 24: 360–5.

Youth Justice Board (2000b) *Factors Associated with Differential Custodial Sentencing*. London: Youth Justice Board.

PROBATION SERVICE

The National Probation Service was formed from the 54 existing probation areas in England and Wales in 2001. It employs around 21,000 staff. There are currently in excess of 200,000 offenders under the community supervision of the National Probation Service, of which over a quarter are under the age of 21. The modern Probation Service derives from nineteenth-century philanthropic effort.

The origins of the Probation Service can be traced to the pioneering activities of philanthropists and a number of uncoordinated voluntary experiments conducted during the nineteenth century, intended to aid the rehabilitation of offenders instead of simply punishing them.

The Church of England Temperance Society employed the first 'police court missionaries' to supervise conditionally, individuals who, in the main, had been charged with either drunkenness or drink-related offences. Some commentators have suggested that such initiatives reflected wider concerns about the perceived moral degeneration of the working class (Raynor and Vanstone 2002).

The Probation of Offenders Act 1887 was the first piece of legislation in this field, but it contained no provisions with regard to statutory supervision. It was the Probation of Offenders Act 1907, therefore, that placed probation work on a statutory footing by empowering the courts to appoint and pay probation officers whose role was to 'advise, assist and befriend' offenders under their supervision. The standard conditions of probation imposed an undertaking on the offender to report to his or her probation officer as directed; to lead an honest and industrious life; to be of good behaviour; and to keep the peace. In 1925 the appointment of at least one probation officer to each court became a mandatory requirement (although this responsibility was sometimes discharged by part-time officers). The work of the Probation Service was expanded during the first half of the twentieth century to include juveniles and families, as well as adult offenders. Probation officers also dealt with matrimonial problems and it was through this work that the role of the divorce court welfare officer emerged.

The early ethos of rehabilitation through religion gave way to a more secular form of professionalism, whereby probation officers conducted treatment based on a social scientific evaluation of offenders on a one-to-one 'casework' basis. The Probation Service subsequently became a more bureaucratic and professional organization. The Criminal Justice Act 1948 repealed all earlier enactments relating to the Probation Service and resulted in improved training and strengthened links with the courts through new probation committees.

The development of the welfare state ensured that rehabilitation in the form of social casework, was an established part of probation practice throughout the 1950s and 1960s, and this corre-

sponded with a significant expansion of the Probation Service into new areas of work, such as the aftercare of released prisoners. In 1964, probation officers were given responsibility for the aftercare of detention centre trainees, and some three years later this was extended to Borstal trainees and young prisoners. However, the responsibility for juvenile offenders and their families was in the main transferred to the local authority social services departments under the Children and Young Persons Act 1969.

By the end of the 1970s rehabilitation was being criticized on both empirical and ethical grounds. This period is often simplistically characterized with reference to 'nothing works'. However, some commentators have argued that this perceived penological pessimism had in reality little impact on the everyday work of probation officers (Mair 1997a). Nonetheless, by the 1980s it had ushered in a move away from 'doing good' through treatment to reducing the use of imprisonment through the provision of alternatives to custody. Community service had become an essential part of the Probation Service and was extended to all areas in England and Wales in 1974.

The 1980s witnessed a further policy shift in relation to probation, based on the notion of punishment in the community as a mechanism for reducing prison overcrowding. The desire to gain judicial and public acceptance of community punishments was accompanied by a range of measures aimed at 'toughening up' the delivery of community sentences. As Newburn (2003: 140) notes: 'Community-based sanctions were to be thought of as punishments which restricted liberty, but which enabled offenders to face up to the effects of their crimes, thus potentially being of benefit to the victim, and economical for the taxpayer.'

The Criminal Justice Act 1991 advocated a key role for probation and introduced a new sentencing framework based on the notion of just deserts. Probation orders became a sentence in their own right, and the purpose of probation was defined as the protection of the public, the reduction of offending and the rehabilitation of the offender. The Act brought together elements of the juvenile and adult court systems through the introduction of the youth court, which dealt with offenders aged 10–17 (as opposed to 10-16 in the juvenile court which it replaced). The Act was accompanied by new national standards for the Probation Service that sought to limit the traditional discretion of the probation officer and thereby bring about greater consistency of service delivery. The Criminal Justice Act 1991 was successful for a short time in reducing the prison population.

In the early 1990s, however, the law-and-order discourse took a more punitive turn, exemplified by the 'prison works' mantra of the then Home Secretary, Michael Howard. Ironically, at the same time research findings, predominantly from North America, were reigniting interest in rehabilitation. As the 'what works' approach of the 1990s developed, examples of community-based programmes which seemed to have a positive impact in reducing reoffending came to the fore. Although the strength of the evidence base on which 'accredited programmes' have been based has been questioned, community sanctions have continued to be shaped around the multi-dimensional features of programmes directed at the most serious and prolific offenders (Davies *et al.* 2005: 409). In relation to young offenders, this led to the development of intensive supervision and surveillance programmes (for 10–17-year-olds) and the Intensive Control and Change Programme, introduced in 2003 (for 18–20-year-olds).

Under successive New Labour administrations since 1997 the pace of fundamental change in the Probation Service has continued unabated and has been directed towards 'a stronger focus in probation practice on the delivery of punishment, on cost-effective and outcome-monitored management, on working in partnership, and on actuarial risk' (Easton and Piper 2005: 282). Electronic monitoring, reparation and drug treatment and testing have been added to key probation functions. In 2001, the National Probation Service was created under the leadership of a National Director appointed by the Home Secretary. Structurally, the number of probation areas was reduced from 54 to 42, and family court welfare work was transferred to a new Children and Family Court Advisory and Support Service.

In the mid-1990s the requirement that probation officers be qualified social workers had been abolished, which, for many, symbolized the changing function of probation – from a social work service providing welfare and rehabilitation to offenders to a law-enforcement 'correctional' agency (Davies *et al.* 2005: 402). This corresponded with moves to align further the work of the Probation Service with the Prison Service and the Youth Justice Board, under the guise of a more streamlined and co-ordinated criminal justice system (Chui and Nellis 2003). This ultimately became expressed through the establishment of the National Offender Management Service – and the imposition of contestability – just three years after the creation of the National Probation Service.

The Probation Service has demonstrated throughout its history an ability to adapt to social changes, new ideas, new work and new opportunities. The introduction of the Management of Offenders Bill 2007 brings with it a new set of challenges linked to a very different philosophy and sense of values. The bill proposes to end the statutory monopoly of the 42 local probation boards to provide probation services. Instead the Secretary of State will assume direct responsibility in a system centred on nine regional offender managers who will commission probation work from a multiplicity of providers through contractual arrangements. The challenge according to Wargent (2006: 168) is whether or not probation will 'survive the labyrinthine structures necessary to support effective service delivery' and continue to make its unique contribution to the criminal justice system. In the meantime the Probation Service continues to make an important contribution to the delivery of youth justice services, and probation officers have a significant presence in youth offending teams.

Lol Burke and Steve Collett

Related entries

Alternatives to custody; Children and Family Court Advisory and Support Service (CAFCASS); Contestability; Electronic monitoring; Intensive Supervision and Surveillance Programme (ISSP); National Offender Management Service (NOMS); Punishment in the community; Rehabilitation; Reparation; Youth offending teams (YOTs).

Key texts and sources

Chui, W.H. and Nellis, M. (2003) *Moving Probation Forward: Evidence, Arguments and Practice.* Harlow: Pearson.

Davies, M., Croall, H. and Tyrer, J. (2005) *Criminal Justice: An Introduction to the Criminal Justice System in England and Wales.* Harlow: Pearson.

Easton, S. and Piper, C. (2005) *Sentencing and Punishment: The Quest for Justice.* Oxford: Oxford University Press.

Mair, G. (1997a) 'Community penalties and the Probation Service', in M. Maguire *et al.* (eds) *The Oxford Handbook of Criminology.* Oxford: Oxford University Press.

Newburn, T. (2003) *Crime and Criminal Justice Policy.* Harlow: Longman.

Raynor, P. and Vanstone, M. (2002) *Understanding Community Penalties: Probation, Policy and Social Change.* Buckingham: Open University Press.

Wargent, M. (2006) 'Contestability: is the model for NOMS "fit for purpose"?', *Vista*, 9: 162–8.

PROLIFIC AND OTHER PRIORITY OFFENDERS (PPOs) STRATEGY

The prolific and other priority offenders (PPOs) strategy is a national strategy launched in 2004 to target the most active 5,000 offenders (of all ages) thought to be responsible for 1 in 10 offences. Of the three strands of the programme, activities to 'prevent and deter' aim specifically to stop young people engaging in offending behaviour and graduating into prolific offenders. The other two strands (which aim to 'catch and convict' and 'rehabilitate and resettle') are also relevant to youth justice.

On 30 March 2004, the Prime Minister announced a new strategy to reduce the harm that prolific and other priority offenders (PPOs) cause to communities and to themselves. The PPO strategy focuses on the relatively small number of people who are thought to cause a disproportionate amount of crime, damaging people's confidence in the youth/criminal justice system and increasing fear of crime. Implemented nationally from September 2004, the programme has three complementary parts. A 'prevent and deter' strand aims to stop young people engaging in offending behaviours and graduating into prolific offenders. A 'catch and convict' strand aims actively to tackle those who are already prolific offenders. A 'rehabilitate and resettle' strand works with identified prolific offenders to stop their offending by offering a range of supportive interventions backed by a threatened return to court. The programme builds on previous initiatives with persistent offenders, including the youth justice system's work on the swift administration of justice and reducing delays for persistent young offenders.

Locally, PPO work is led by crime and disorder reduction partnerships (CDRPs) in England and Community Safety Partnerships in Wales. The emphasis is on multi-agency approaches, with local criminal justice boards also playing a co-ordination role. An early evaluation of the 'catch and convict' and 'rehabilitate and resettle' strands found that fewer than a third of CDRPs had dedicated staff and that much of the PPO work is undertaken alongside other tasks. This PPO work includes a premium criminal justice service to expedite PPO cases through the courts; the provision of intensive packages of intervention with more frequent contacts; fluent information exchange between agencies; and the tracking of offenders and regular home visits.

Interdepartmental guidance has been produced on each of the three strands, and the Youth Justice Board produced specific guidance for youth offending teams in September 2004. The guidance stresses that a 'prevent and deter' multi-agency panel should be set up in each local authority area to oversee high-risk cases, to share information and to allocate resources. The guidance expects CDRPs on average to target between 20 and 50 named individuals in this way, with the very largest CDRPs extending beyond this range. The programme is intended to make use of other youth justice programmes, including youth inclusion and support panels and youth inclusion programmes.

Evaluative research has revealed reduced rates of offending by people joining the 'catch and convict' and 'rehabilitate and resettle' strands, but it is not possible to say how much this is due solely to the PPO intervention. There has been no evaluation of the 'prevent and deter' strand.

Rob Allen

Related entries

Crime and disorder reduction (CDR); Fear of crime; First-time entrants; Partnership working; Persistent young offenders; Risk management; Surveillance; Youth inclusion and support panels (YISPs); Youth inclusion programmes (YIPs).

Key texts and sources

Dawson, P. (2005) *Early Findings from the Prolific and Other Priority Offenders Evaluation. Home Office Development and Practice Report* 46. London: Home Office.

Dawson, P. and Cuppleditch, L. (2007) *An Impact Assessment of the Prolific and Other Priority Offender Programme. Home Office Online Report* 08/07. London: Home Office.

Home Office, Youth Justice Board and Department for Educations and Skills (2004b) *Prolific and Other Priority Offenders Strategy. Guidance Note 3: Prevent and Deter.* London: Home Office.

Youth Justice Board (2004c) *Prolific and Other Priority Offenders Strategy Guidance for Youth Offending Teams.* London: Youth Justice Board (available online at **http://www.yjb.gov.uk/en-gb/practitioners/ ImprovingPractice/PPO/**).

The Home Office's Prolific and Other Priority Offenders Strategy is available online at **http:// www.crimereduction.gov.uk/ppo/ppominisite 01.htm.**

PROPORTIONALITY

> The Criminal Justice Act 1991 applied the principle of proportionality to sentencing. Based on 'just deserts', the sentence of the court – and any restriction of liberty – should be proportionate to, or commensurate with, the seriousness of the offence. Not a new concept, proportionality underpinned measures in the Criminal Justice Acts of 1982 and 1988 in restricting the use of custody for those under 21 years of age. The adoption of proportionality as the basis for all sentencing, however, was intended to ensure consistent, fair, most effective and suitable responses to offending.

The Criminal Justice Act 1991 provided a sentencing structure with three 'bands' of sentence and two 'thresholds'. The three bands are:

- custodial sentences;
- community penalties; and
- 'lower level' sentences – discharges and financial penalties.

The thresholds that have to met before a particular sentence might be imposed are as follows:

- *For a custodial sentence*, the offence is 'so serous that only such a sentence can be justified'.
- *For a community sentence*, the offence is 'serious enough' to warrant such a restriction of liberty.

Assessing seriousness is not an exact science, of course. The core components are as follows:

- The *inherent nature* of the offence: thus robbery is seen as more serious than theft from a store.
- Any *aggravating* or *mitigating* factors: thus burglary that involves a night-time forced entry of an occupied house with actual or threatened violence is conceived as being more serious than taking a £5 note off a window ledge via an open kitchen window of an unoccupied dwelling in daylight, for example.
- Any *individual mitigation* unrelated to the offence.

Some features are statutorily aggravating – for example, offending while on bail and offending based on discrimination (racial, religious, disability or sexual orientation) – and some features are routinely mitigating – for example, a 'timely' guilty plea that results in a 'discount' of sentence of up to a third. Personal mitigation can take the sentence into a lower sentencing band.

There has been significant erosion of proportionality since 1991. Unit fines, disregard of previous convictions and the practice of only considering the most serious offence and possibly one associated with it were soon abandoned. Additionally, statutory sentences under the 'three strikes' legislation, the recently introduced sentences related to 'dangerousness' and the imposition of community penalties on persistent petty offenders or fine defaulters all run counter to proportionaility. Furthermore, the imperatives of 'nipping offending in the bud' and early intervention can lead to disproportionate responses (particularly if there is a perceived welfare need), and the formulaic nature of pre-court disposals (reprimands and final warnings) linked to the mandatory referral order means a compulsory minimum three-month intervention no matter how minor the offence. More problematic still is the burgeoning prevention agenda – with interventions focused on those 'most likely' to offend and, in some cases, targeted at those below the age of criminal responsibility.

The effect of proportionality on young people's responses to disposals and the 'outcomes' of intervention is also important. A sentence not perceived as proportionate or a 'fair response' to a young person's behaviour will be seen as excessive and may well undermine any motivation to respond positively to a resultant programme.

Spike Cadman

Related entries

Criminal Justice Act 1991; Criminal Justice Act 1993; Criminal Justice Act 2003; Dangerousness; Due process; Gatekeeping; Gravity factors (prosecution and sentencing); Just deserts; Justice; Menu-based sentencing; Referral orders; Reprimands and final warnings; Retribution; Sentencing framework; Supervision orders; Welfare; Youth Justice and Criminal Evidence Act 1999.

Key texts and sources

Cadman, S. (2005) 'Proportionality in the youth justice system', in T. Bateman and J. Pitts (eds) *The RHP Companion to Youth Justice*. Lyme Regis: Russell House.

Nacro (2000a) *Proportionality in the Youth Justice System. Youth Crime Briefing*. London: Nacro.

Nacro (2003d) *The Sentencing Framework for Children and Young People. Youth Crime Briefing*. London: Nacro.

See http://www.legislation.gov.uk/acts/acts1991/Ukpga_19910053_en_1.htm for the text of the Criminal Justice Act 1991.

PROTECTIVE FACTORS

> Protective factors are factors associated with resilience to 'risk', particularly the risk of reoffending.

Protective factors are those factors in the social circumstances, immediate family and locale of a young person that literally provide protection from risk. These can include involvement with pro-social networks and peers, a positive family environment and a constructive school/educational experience. Protective factors are often included in 'risk assessment' tools to enable youth justice practitioners to identify and build on them and, in some instances, to promote them through mentoring schemes that link young people with pro-social mentors, for example. The risk prevention approach that underpins early intervention emphasizes the maintenance and strengthening of protective factors.

However, protective factors cannot simply be understood as the inverse of 'risk factors'. The means by which protective factors mitigate risk factors are complex and are not particularly well understood. Why does protective factor A inhibit risk factor B? What is the 'tipping point' for any individual child or young person whereby protection outweighs risk, or vice versa? Such questions have resulted in more recent attention – in research and policy – focusing on the concept of resilience. This approach recognizes the interactive nature of 'protective factors' that may combine over time to enhance the protection of an individual child or young person.

Resilience has been described as a rich mixture of factors inherent to the individual child, factors in his or her immediate environment and sources of support available to the child (Garmezy 1993). In essence, risk protection is seen as a process, and resilience as a range of personal attributes generated and supported by positive networks, such as parenting programmes and school inclusion. However, how these factors actually interact has proved difficult to discern (Kemshall *et al.* 2006) and, hence, this makes translation into effective programmes more difficult. Some children prove to be remarkably resilient and respond well. Others do not, although their risk markers may be very similar. This makes a 'one size fits all' approach to programmes to promote resilience difficult, and highly individualized approaches are likely to have more impact.

Hazel Kemshall

Related entries

Assessment framework; Desistance; Developmental criminology; Early intervention; Looked-after children (LAC); Mental health and young offenders; Mentoring; On Track; Persistent young offenders; Risk factors; Risk management; Sport-based crime prevention; Youth inclusion and support panels (YISPs); Youth Lifestyles Survey (YLS).

Key texts and sources

Garmezy, N. (1993) 'Vulnerability and resilience', in D. Funder and R. Parke (eds) *Studying Lives through Time: Personality and Development.* Washington, DC: American Psychological Association.

Kemshall, H., Marsland, L., Boeck, T. and Dunkerton, L. (2006) 'Young people, pathways and crime: beyond risk factors', *Australian and New Zealand Journal of Criminology*, 39: 339–53.

Schoon, I. and Bynner, J. (2003) 'Risk and resilience in the life course: implications for interventions and social policies', *Journal of Youth Studies*, 6: 21–31.

Youth Justice Board (2001) *Risk and Protective Factors Associated with Youth Crime and Effective Interventions.* London: Youth Justice Board.

Youth Justice Board (2005b) *Risk and Protective Factors.* London: Youth Justice Board.

PUBLIC ATTITUDES TO YOUTH CRIME AND JUSTICE

On the surface, people express a great deal of dissatisfaction with youth justice, but they tend to be poorly informed. Closer analysis reveals that public attitudes are more nuanced and less punitive than is often supposed.

Although there has been extensive survey research into public attitudes to crime and justice, work on opinion about youth justice is limited. Only one study has set out systematically to explore public opinion, youth crime and justice (Hough and Roberts 2004). The survey examined the following:

- Levels of public confidence in youth justice.
- Levels of public knowledge and understanding about the youth justice system.
- The relationship between knowledge about, and confidence in, youth justice.
- Whether people find current youth sentencing practice broadly acceptable.

This study has brought us closer to understanding the nature of contemporary public opinion about youth crime and youth justice in England and Wales. Opinion on the topic is multi-layered and sometimes contradictory in nature. There is considerable pessimism about trends in youth crime but, in part, this reflects systematic misperceptions.

Most people think that young people are less respectful now than previous generations. Most also believe that the number of young offenders has increased since 2001, although statistical trends suggest that this is only true for a limited range of offences. Similarly, people tend to overestimate the proportion of all crime for which young offenders are responsible, the proportion of youth crime involving violence and the proportion of young offenders who will be reconvicted of a criminal offence.

People tend to be poorly informed about youth justice. Over three quarters of the sample acknowledged that they had not heard anything about youth offending teams. Most respondents rated youth courts as doing a 'poor job'; only 10 per cent rated youth courts as doing a 'good job'. Consistent with survey data in other countries, most people believe that sentences imposed on young offenders are too lenient.

Coexisting with this public pessimism and scepticism is a different and somewhat contradictory set of attitudes, however. The public is not as concerned about youth crime as some commentators have suggested. Youth crime is an important issue for the public, but it is not perceived to be the most important or the most serious crime problem today. People also distinguish clearly between crimes committed by adults and those committed by young offenders in thinking about effective responses. For example, while people tended to see tougher sentencing as the best way of reducing adult crime, more discipline in schools was the most popular choice for reducing youth crime.

Nor do people favour locking up young offenders as much as one might infer from their responses to general questions about the adequacy of youth court sentencing. When asked to 'pass sentence' in specific cases, there was a wide spread of preferences, even for quite serious offences committed by young offenders with previous convictions, which typically would attract custodial sentences. There was strong support for non-custodial options, and the more detail that respondents had about the child/young person they were 'sentencing', the less likely they were to favour the imposition of a term of custody. There was support for responses to youth offending involving restorative justice. Moreover, many of those people who selected custody regarded community penalties as acceptable substitutes to custody when these involve supervision and reparation.

The main conclusions of the survey are as follows. The public have a more pessimistic view of youth crime than is justified by the official crime statistics; people also know little about the structure of youth justice in Britain. The public gives poor ratings to the youth courts in Britain, in large measure because they believe that the sentences imposed on young offenders are too lenient.

The dissatisfaction that people express with youth justice is 'real', whether or not it is grounded in the realities of current sentencing practice. There has to be *some* response to these public views. There is a pressing need to improve the quality of information available to the public about youth crime and youth justice.

While people generally thought that the youth courts were too soft, the study also found strong support for alternatives to imprisonment – especially when the scope for community penalties was drawn to respondents' attention. When public opinion is complex and multi-layered in this way, there can be no policy justification for privileging people's unconsidered desire for tougher punishment and ignoring other dimensions to their views.

Finally, there is clearly potential for building on public support for new approaches to sentencing young offenders, including reparation. People want offenders to apologize, to express remorse, to feel remorse and to translate this emotion into some form of practical reparation for the crime victim.

Mike Hough

Related entries

Anti-social behaviour (ASB); British Crime Survey; Demonization; Fear of crime; Media reporting; Moral panic; Politicization; Punitiveness.

Key texts and sources

Hough, M. and Roberts, J. (2004) *Youth Crime and Youth Justice: Public Opinion in England and Wales.* Bristol: Policy Press.
Roberts, J. and Hough, M. (2005a) *Understanding Public Attitudes to Criminal Justice.* Maidenhead: Open University Press.
Roberts, J. and Hough, M. (2005b) 'Sentencing young offenders: public opinion in England and Wales', *Criminal Justice*, 5: 211–32.

PUNISHMENT IN THE COMMUNITY

> Punishment in the community expresses the idea that demanding punishment can take place in the community, so avoiding some of the damaging consequences of custody or institutional care. Less constructively, the expression can be taken to imply that punishment is the most appropriate response to offending.

The idea of punishment in the community first came to prominence in the late 1980s. Punishment was affirmed as a proper response to offending but, at the same time, it was emphasized that this need not involve custodial detention. Could a sceptical public be persuaded that community penalties might afford the same punitive weight or public protection as custody? To allay misgivings, the punitive character of community-based disposals – their demanding content and rigorous enforcement – was increasingly emphasized. One of the hazards of framing policy in these terms was that other legitimate responses to offending – notably rehabilitation and reparation – were peripheralized. Even as the Children Act 1989 was reaffirming the paramountcy of the child's welfare in *all* court proceedings, the priority of punishment was being asserted as the focus of 'justice' policy.

Originally, punishment in the community was advanced for adult offenders, but the emphasis on punishment also had consequences for policy in relation to young people. Although there were successful practice-led attempts to limit the numbers of young offenders in custodial establishments during the 1980s – at a time when the Conservative government was 'talking tough' about young offenders – it is ironic and instructive that the affirmation of punishment in the community presaged the steep increases in levels of youth incarceration during the 1990s.

The concept of punishment in the community occupies a hazardous political place. It is vulnerable to attack from those who advocate higher levels of punishment and equate this with custodial detention. Conversely, it is sometimes regarded warily by liberals who see punishment *in* the community as an extension of projects of 'discipline' and surveillance into the community – or even, when these disciplinary devices are more widely extended, punishment *of* the community.

Although the actual term 'punishment in the community' is less commonly deployed in contemporary youth justice discourse, the concept of 'tough' community penalties is a persistent motif. The relationship between the intensity and severity of community sentences and the size of the prison population is far from straightforward, however, and it is not at all clear that a reliance on extending the use of community punishment can in itself reduce the number of children and young people in penal custody.

Rob Canton and Kaushika Patel

Related entries

Alternatives to custody; Penal welfarism; Politicization; Probation Service; Punitiveness.

Key texts and sources

Bottoms, A., Gelsthorpe, L. and Rex, S. (eds) (2001) *Community Penalties: Changes and Challenges.* Cullompton: Willan Publishing.

Goldson, B. (2002a) 'New punitiveness: the politics of child incarceration', in J. Muncie *et al.* (eds) *Youth Justice: Critical Readings.* London: Sage.

Worrall, A. and Hoy, C. (2005) *Punishment in the Community: Managing Offenders, Making Choices* (2nd edn). Cullompton: Willan Publishing.

PUNITIVENESS

> Punitiveness is an extension of means of punishment that rely on an emotive and vindictive infliction of pain and harm in order to humiliate and dehumanize offenders.

Throughout the twentieth century, penal welfarism underlined an optimism for offender reformation and improvement. Yet numerous developments since the 1980s, particularly, but not always, originating in the USA, have led some analysts to consider whether penal policy and practice – both nationally and internationally – are now reverting back to that which prevailed 200 years ago. In particular, mass imprisonment, chain gangs, boot camps, supermax prisons, naming and shaming, the public humiliation of offenders, 'three strikes' laws, mandatory minimum sentencing, austere prison regimes and zero tolerance policing all signify a (re)emergence of repressive and draconian responses to offending. This punitiveness appears to abandon not only welfare and rehabilitation but also retributive just deserts and deterrence in favour of incapacitation. Penal punishment has become tainted with vengeance and cruelty; its purpose driven by the humiliation, pain and suffering of others (Simon 2001; Pratt et al. 2005).

Explanations of contemporary punitiveness are many and varied, but reference is usually made to 'cultures of control' characterized by the rise of neoliberalism alongside traditional conservatism; the politicization of law and order; the decline of the welfare consensus; the proliferation of existential fears and insecurities; and the advent of the 'risk society' (Pratt *et al.* 2005). Some or all of these factors are seen to have created a more punitive climate in which intolerance and threats to civil liberties and human rights have flourished.

Paradoxically, contemporary punitiveness has *not* developed in the context of rising crime rates – in fact, the reverse. The term 'populist punitiveness' was coined by Bottoms (1995) to refer to an assumed broad public appeal and approval for punitive sentencing and increased resort to prison. From here come widespread assumptions about a 'punitive public', governments merely acting to satisfy such public opinion and prevailing public attitudes in respect of youth crime and other offending.

Pratt (2003) has acknowledged that these new forms of punishment are both 'ostentatious' and 'emotive', heralding more extreme forms of shaming, humiliation and brutalization. However their ubiquity, even in the USA, may be called into question. 'Dramatic denunciation' is located alongside contra pressures for cost-effective, efficient and effective penal measures. Further, the shift towards emotive expression in punishment is also present in restorative justice initiatives whose ultimate aim is one of reconciliation, not further pain and exclusion. For Pratt, such contradictions are likely to produce a combination of 'civilizing and decivilizing' forces, pushing and pulling state punishment in different directions. Critical commentaries on the concept have also queried its ill-defined nature; its inability to capture contradictions in criminal and youth justice reform; and the extent of its general applicability. Certainly, a significant number of neoliberal democracies (such as Japan, Italy and Finland) do not seem to have experienced a post-1980 'punitive turn' at all. A key question is how far such punitiveness does indeed have an international character, or whether it is a function of American (and UK) exceptionalism (Matthews 2005).

John Muncie

Related entries

Authoritarianism; Comparative youth justice; Fear of crime; Institutionalized intolerance; Penal welfarism; Politicization; Public attitudes to youth crime and justice; Restorative justice; Zero tolerance.

Key texts and sources

Bottoms, A. (1995) 'The philosophy and politics of punishment and sentencing', in C. Clarkson and R. Morgan (eds) *The Politics of Sentencing Reform*. Oxford: Clarendon Press.

Matthews, R. (2005) 'The myth of the new punitiveness', *Theoretical Criminology*, 9: 175–201.

Pratt, J. (2003) 'Emotive and ostentatious punishment', *Punishment and Society*, 2: 417–39.

Pratt, J., Brown, D., Brown, M., Hallsworth, S. and Morrison, W. (eds) (2005) *The New Punitiveness*. Cullompton: Willan Publishing.

Simon, J. (2001) 'Entitlement to cruelty: neo-liberalism and the punitive mentality in the United States', in K. Stenson and R. Sullivan (eds) *Crime, Risk and Justice*. Cullompton: Willan Publishing.

R

'RACE' AND JUSTICE

> Black and some minority ethnic groups are over-represented at various stages of the youth justice process, from stop and search to youth custody, compared with their numbers in the general population. It is argued either that this reflects their elevated offending compared with other groups or that they are discriminated against because of their racial or ethnic background.

Nationally, black children and young people are three times more likely to be arrested, twice as likely to be cautioned and five times more likely to be serving a custodial sentence than would be expected from their numbers in the general population. In contrast, Asian children and young people aged 10–17 are substantially under-represented in arrests, cautions and youth custody. Black and mixed-parentage young males and females are very considerably over-represented in penal remands and detention and training orders compared with other groups. Local studies of youth justice have found that over-representation and different or discriminatory treatment vary by youth offending team area. The over-representation of black males and females in the youth justice system is long-standing, however. For example, during the 1970s and 1980s, black children and young people constituted over a third of detention centre and Borstal populations in the south of England.

A great deal of caution is needed in inferring different offending rates between 'minority' and 'majority' groups from their representation in the youth justice system. Known suspects and offenders in the youth justice system may be unrepresentative of the actual offender popula-

tion. When self-report surveys ask young people of different ethnic backgrounds whether they have offended or not, the findings consistently show that white and black young people offend at similar rates and Asian young people offend less than white and black. This discrepancy between self-reported offending and the over-representation of some groups in the youth justice system suggests that black children and young people are more likely to be drawn into the system (criminalization) and, once there, to be treated differently and less favourably than their white counterparts (discrimination). A corresponding explanation is that they are more likely to be targeted by the police for certain types of offence, such as drug use or street robbery. For example, black (mostly male) children and young people aged 10–17 comprise 3 per cent of the general population for this age range, yet over a quarter of the 'offender' population in respect of robbery offences dealt with by youth offending teams. Again, this disproportionate relation is *not* reflected in self-report studies.

When studies collect information on a wide range of relevant legal and social variables – such as prior offending, seriousness of the offence, education, school exclusion, employment status, family structure and other 'risk factors' – which might singularly or together influence youth justice decision-makers, they find different and less favourable treatment of black and mixed-parentage children and young people compared with other groups. Once the characteristics of their cases have been taken into account, discriminatory treatment occurs in a number of ways. Youth court magistrates seem more ready to commit marginal cases involving black young people to the Crown court. Asians and mixed-parentage – but not black – young males are more likely to be sentenced to a more restrictive community sentence than whites. Overall, studies would appear to show that there are different outcomes that are consistent with the discriminatory treatment of Asian and black males, and especially mixed-parentage males and females, in respect of prosecution, remand, conviction, the use of more restrictive community penalties and more and longer custodial sentences.

Youth justice processes (in respect of 'race' and ethnicity) cannot be understood in isolation or divorced from their wider context found in other institutional processes of social and economic change. These wider processes can have a direct impact on who ends up in the youth justice system and in youth custody. They also influence the ways in which individuals are treated and judged once having arrived there. Children and young people's experiences of family, schooling, policing, being 'looked after' (in care), neighbourhoods, children and young people's services, drugs, housing, training opportunities and labour markets will influence their transitions. Any experience of discrimination in these different dimensions of their lives is as important and may be linked to any discrimination in the youth justice system.

Changes in these dimensions over 30 years – including eligibility and entitlement to welfare and other benefits – have worsened the social conditions of successive groups of working-class white, black and minority ethnic children and young people, often marginalizing and polarizing their experiences. Black and minority ethnic children and young people's contact and conflict with the police have been such as to construct them as a 'suspect population'. These groups disproportionately live in neighbourhoods destabilized by deindustrialization and they experience growing poverty, crime and family dissolution. Black and minority ethnic children and young people are likely to attend the 'worst' schools, to suffer low school expectations of their abilities and performance and are more likely to be disaffected, bored and failing, and to be excluded from school. Known offender populations are disproportionately drawn from young people not engaged in education, employment or training (NEET), and from those who have lived in the care system. For minority ethnic young people the disadvantages of care interact with

their experience of racism in care. Black and minority ethnic young people aged 16–17 are over-represented in the NEET population.

'Race' and justice is perhaps best understood as black and minority ethnic children and young people being disproportionately marginalized and discriminated against across different domains and intersecting social processes.

Colin Webster

Related entries

Criminalization; Discrimination; Self reported offending; Social exclusion; Youth and policing.

Key texts and sources

Bowling, B and Phillips, C. (2002) *Racism, Crime and Justice.* London: Longman.

Feilzer, M. and Hood, R. (2004) *Difference or Discrimination? Minority Ethnic People in the Youth Justice System.* London: Youth Justice Board.

Goldson, B. and Chigwada-Bailey, R. (1999) '(What) justice for black children and young people?', in B. Goldson (ed.) *Youth Justice: Contemporary Policy and Practice.* Aldershot: Ashgate.

Mhlanga, B. (1997) *The Colour of English Justice: A Multivariate Analysis.* Aldershot: Avebury.

Webster, C. (2006) '"Race", youth crime and justice', in B. Goldson and J. Muncie (eds) *Youth Crime and Justice: Critical Issues.* London: Sage.

RADICAL NON-INTERVENTION

Constructed by Edwin Schur, radical non-intervention emerged during the 1970s and – concluding that the criminal justice system was blunt, ineffective and overreaching – it argued that the least detrimental means of dealing with delinquency was to avoid all intervention unless it was absolutely necessary. Delinquency was seen as normal, generally non-serious and self-correcting. In essence the best response was 'to leave the kids alone wherever possible'.

Radical non-intervention connected with labelling theory and focused on how criminal behaviour becomes defined rather than on individual causation. In this tradition, ascribing what is criminal and deploying methods of control lie with the powerful. It follows that the activities of the marginalized, excluded and dispossessed receive far more attention than the activities of the powerful. This is particularly so under 'get tough' regimes. That the youth justice system itself serves to perpetuate criminal behaviour is at the heart of the radical non-intervention critique. The system is conceived as part of the problem rather than the solution. For example, attempts to identify 'pre-delinquents' routinely get it wrong, and too much effort is put into working with children who only commit occasional, non-serious offences and who would not become 'hardened offenders' and would cease without intervention.

Based on 'leaving the kids alone wherever possible', radical non-intervention represented a dramatically different approach from traditional thinking. It did not deny that delinquency existed or that interventions were sometimes required. Examples advocated by Schur include prevention schemes having a 'collective or community focus' and voluntary programmes that are non-institutional in nature and not dominated by 'professionals'. Better, then, for the youth justice system to step out of the picture and allow informal and non-criminal social justice processes – including universal social and youth policies – to deal with delinquency most of the time.

But there are problems with the approach when the politics of non-intervention underplay the high levels of crime victimization experienced in low-income districts where people are likely to want more official intervention to deal with harmful and anti-social behaviour. On the other hand, there is substantial justification for thinking the youth justice system intrudes too extensively and that there would be benefits in more closely defined and limited boundaries.

Non-interventionist 'benign neglect' found its best expression in England and Wales during the 1980s when a 'quiet consensus' among professionals, academics and politicians meant that diversion was central to the agenda of juvenile justice, and over-intervention, particularly custody, was frowned upon. The short-lived but influential 'non-treatment paradigm' gave a

congruent framework for practice under the argument that, while surveillance, particularly of high-risk offenders, was legitimate, generally 'help is better than treatment'.

Paul Kelly

Related entries

Delinquency; Diversion; Informal action; Informalism; Labelling theory; Left realism; Minimum necessary intervention; Normalization.

Key texts and sources

Bottoms, A. and McWilliams, W. (1979) 'A non-treatment paradigm for probation practice', *British Journal of Social Work*, 9: 159–202.

Goldson, B. (2005a) 'Beyond formalism: towards "informal" approaches to youth crime and youth justice', in T. Bateman and J. Pitts (eds) *The RHP Companion to Youth Justice.* Lyme Regis: Russell House.

Matthews, R. and Young, J. (eds) (2003) *The New Politics of Crime.* Cullompton: Willan Publishing.

Schur, E.M. (1973) *Radical Non-intervention: Rethinking the Delinquency Problem.* Englewood Cliffs, NJ: Prentice Hall.

RECIDIVISM

Recidivism refers to the reconviction rates of young offenders who have completed specific pre-court, community-based and/or custodial programmes or sentences. Recidivism is often used as a key measure to assess the effectiveness of such programmes and/or sentences in reducing further offending.

Recidivism rates are generally measured as the proportion of young offenders who have been reconvicted within a two-year follow-up period after sentence or the completion of a programme. Such a measure is problematic, however, as it relates to patterns of reconviction as distinct from reoffending and thus only captures those 'offenders' brought to justice.

Reconviction data appear to show a fall in reconviction rates for most community interventions following the implementation of the Crime and Disorder Act 1998. However, the reliability of this data has been questioned because it relies on 'adjusted predicted' rates of reoffending, and the most significant drop in reconvictions relate to pre-court and 'low tariff' interventions where a low rate of reconviction might be expected anyway (Bateman and Pitts 2005). Community-based interventions aimed at more persistent and/or serious young offenders show little change. The two-year reconviction rates for young offenders released from custody have remained consistently high – ranging in recent years from 60 per cent to almost 90 per cent in different research studies (Goldson 2006c).

The evidence-based 'what works' paradigm currently dominates evaluative research on the effectiveness of correctional programmes in reducing recidivism or the likelihood of further offending. Proponents of this paradigm argue that 'offending behaviour programmes' – whether run in the community or in prisons – that adopt cognitive-behavioural techniques are the most effective in reducing offending. However, this approach has been challenged because of its over-simplification of research evidence and because of its belief that young offenders' individual 'deficits' are the most salient 'risk factors' associated with recidivism. Critics question whether cognitive-behavioural interventions alone can have any significant effect on recidivism when research on desistance shows that young people are most likely to cease offending following combinations of changes in their relationships, their ways of thinking, their maturity and, most importantly, the social context in which they live (Farrall 2002; McNeill 2006). The current preoccupation with correcting individual 'deficits' through cognitive-behavioural programmes tends to disassociate recidivism from broader social contexts, particularly those relating to inadequate educational and employment opportunities.

Patricia Gray

Related entries

Desistance; Effectiveness; Evaluative research; What Works.

Key texts and sources

Bateman, T. and Pitts, J. (2005) 'Conclusion: what evidence tells us', in T. Bateman and J. Pitts (eds) *The RHP Companion to Youth Justice*. Lyme Regis: Russell House.

Farrall, S. (2002) *Rethinking What Works with Offenders: Probation, Social Context and Desistance from Crime*. Cullompton: Willan Publishing.

Goldson, B. (2006c) 'Penal custody: intolerance, irrationality and indifference', in B. Goldson and J. Munchie (eds) *Youth Crime and Justice: Critical Issues*. London: Sage.

McNeill, F. (2006) 'Community supervision: context and relationships matter', in B. Goldson and J. Muncie (eds) *Youth Crime and Justice: Critical Issues*. London: Sage.

Muncie, J. (2002) 'A new deal for youth? Early interventino and correctionalism', in G. Hughes *et al.* (eds) *Crime Prevention and Community Safety: New Directions*. London: Sage.

REFERRAL ORDERS

Referral orders are the standard sentence in England and Wales for children and young people pleading guilty to a first conviction unless the court decides to pass an immediate custodial sentence; an absolute discharge (for some very minor offences); or a hospital order (under mental health legislation). Perhaps the most distinctive feature of the order – other than it being almost mandatory – is that it devolves decisions regarding the content of the order to a panel of community volunteers.

Referral orders were introduced into the youth justice system in England and Wales by the Youth Justice and Criminal Evidence Act 1999 (subsequently consolidated in the Powers of Criminal Courts (Sentencing) Act 2000). They have become the standard disposal for children and young people at first conviction.

Within 20 days of a referral order being made in court, the young person, accompanied by a parent/carer if he or she under 16, must attend a youth offender panel (YOP). The panel is intended to provide a less formal forum than the youth court in which to consider the circumstances of the offence, the offender and the victim. Principles of restorative justice underpin the official guidance to the legislation (Home Office *et al.* 2002). In addition to at least two local volunteers and the youth offending team (YOT) representative, victims may be encouraged to attend and/or contribute to the panel in other ways. Other members of the young offender's family and/or people who may be able to contribute can also be included.

While the court sets the duration of the sentence – between 3 and 12 months – it is only activated by agreement of a 'contract' at the YOP meeting. Further panel meetings may be convened through the duration of the order to monitor compliance, progress and achievement. In the event of a contract not being agreed and/or fulfilled, the YOP may opt to vary the contract or refer the young person back to court for resentencing. A satisfactorily completed referral order is immediately considered 'spent' under the terms set out in the Rehabilitation of Offenders Act 1974.

Referral orders represent the most systematic attempt to integrate principles of restorative justice into the youth justice in England and Wales. Referral orders now constitute almost one third of all sentences made in youth courts (Youth Justice Board 2003). Since full implementation in 2001, over 5,000 volunteer panel members have been recruited and trained to sit on YOPs. Tens of thousands of panel meetings are conducted each year in community centres, village halls and YOT offices. Each involves the young person and, to varying degrees, victims, family members, carers, teachers and other members of local communities.

The operation of referral orders is complex and challenging. Heavily structured by legislation and formal guidance, they nevertheless offer the potential for inventive and creative interaction between youth justice professionals, community volunteers, victims, young people and their families (Crawford and Newburn 2003). They can be seen as part of New Labour's attempt to knit together a new consensus on youth crime built largely on communitarian principles and to synthesize 'partnership', 'responsibility' and 'community'.

The referral order is, at least in part, derived from, and influenced by, practice found north of the English border in the Scottish children's hearings and south of the equator in the Aotearoa/New Zealand policy of family group conferences. Both are distinguished by allowing the state's welfare agencies to lead provision for children and young people in trouble.

Despite the potential for effective and creative practice, the referral order has also been subjected to critique. Some have argued that it might be seen as the epitome of disproportionate early intervention and as compromising principles of proportionality and due process and, in so doing, negating children's human rights (Goldson 2000a, 2000b; Haines 2000).

Rod Earle

Related entries

Children's hearing system; Early intervention; Family group conferencing; First-time entrants; Mandatory sentences; Powers of Criminal Courts (Sentencing) Act 2000; Proportionality; Restorative justice; Youth Justice and Criminal Evidence Act 1999.

Key texts and sources

Crawford, A. and Newburn, T. (2003) *Youth Offending and Restorative Justice: Implementing Reform in Youth Justice.* Cullompton: Willan Publishing.

Earle, R. and Newburn, T. (2002) 'Creative tensions? Young offenders, restorative justice and the introduction of refferal orders', *Youth Justice*, 1: 3–13.

Earle, R., Newburn, T. and Crawford, A. (2003) 'Refferal orders: some reflections on policy transfer and what works', *Youth Justice*, 2: 141–50.

Goldson, B. (2000a) 'Youth Justice and Criminal Evidence Bill. Part 1. Referrals to youth offender panels', in L. Payne (ed.) *Child Impact Statements, 1998/99.* London: National Children's Bureau and Unicef.

Goldson, B. (2000b) 'Wither diversion? Interventionism and the new youth justice', in B. Goldson (ed.) *The New Youth Justice.* Lyme Regis: Russell House.

Haines, K. (2000) 'Referral orders and youth offender panels: restorative approaches and the new youth justice', in B. Goldson (ed.) *The New Youth Justice.* Lyme Regis: Russell House.

Home Office (2002c) *The Introduction of Refferal Orders into the Youth Justice System: Final Report. Home Office Research Study* 242. London: Home Office.

Home Office, Lord Chancellor's Department and Youth Justice Board (2002) *Referral Orders and Youth Offender Panels: Guidance for Courts, Youth Offending Teams and Youth Offender Panels.* London: Home Office (available online at http://www.yjb.gov.uk/NR?rdonlyres/7A25AD98-8515-427F-8976-A6625789B54C/0/referral_order_and_YOPs.pdf).

Nacro (2004) *The Referral Order: A Good Practice Guide* (2nd edn). London: Nacro.

Youth Justice Board (2003) *Referral Orders: Research into Issues Raised in 'The Introduction of the Referral Order into the Youth Justice System'.* London: Youth Justice Board.

REHABILITATION

Rehabilitation involves changing an offender's circumstances, attitudes or behaviour in order to prevent further offending.

In contrast to retributive models, in which punishment is seen as an intrinsically 'just' response to crime, the rehabilitative approach is built on the premise that intervention and/or punishment should lead to benefits for the individual concerned and for wider society by reducing offending. Arguments in favour of rehabilitation reflect an assumption that people can change their behaviour. The rehabilitative ethos is a powerful force in shaping the values and structures of youth justice systems as it fits well with the widespread perception that the behaviour of children and young people is more amenable to change than that of adults.

In practice, rehabilitative interventions can take many forms, including mentoring, education or skills training, treatment for addiction and/or substance misuse, and the provision of practical help. The recent growth of interest in effectiveness has led to greater confidence among both researchers and practitioners that at least some interventions succeed in changing offenders' thought patterns and behaviours and, consequently, can have an impact on reducing offending.

The youth justice system needs to strike a balance between addressing the needs of children and young people who offend and protecting the public from the harm they might cause. In comparison with other jurisdictions internationally – and other 'models' operating in the UK, such as the children's hearing system in Scotland and youth conferencing in Northern Ireland – the youth justice system in England and Wales places more emphasis on 'risk management' and less on rehabilitation. However, it is interesting to note the proposal in the Criminal Justice and Immigration Bill 2006–7 to 2007–8 for a new generic community sentence known as the youth rehabilitation order (YRO). While the title of the proposed order will not guarantee the nature of intervention, it is perhaps encouraging that 'rehabilitation' is profiled.

The introduction of a YRO might also highlight some interesting questions. First, one feature of the proposed order is that it provides a menu-based approach to sentencing, ostensibly aimed at matching interventions with individual risks and/or needs. But who will decide exactly how much 'rehabilitation' a child or young person should recieve, and how equitable will this be? Second, to what extent is it acceptable to coerce children and young people to participate in rehabilitation and/or to breach them for 'failing to co-operate' with the rehabilititave requirements of an order? Such questions might signal the significant challenges involved in implementing the intuitively appealing concept of rehabilitation in youth justice.

Kerry Baker

Related entries

Children's hearing system; Cognitive behaviour programmes; Criminal Justice and Immigration Bill 2006–7 to 2007–8; Desistance; Effectiveness; Mentoring; Menu-based sentencing; Penal welfarism; Probation Service; Restorative youth conferencing.

Key texts and sources

von Hirsch, A. and Maher, L. (1998) 'Should penal rehabilitation be revived?', in A. von Hirsch and A. Ashworth (eds) *Principled Sentencing: Readings on Theory and Policy.* Oxford: Hart Publishing.

Zedner, L. (2004) *Criminal Justice.* Oxford: Oxford University Press.

See http://www.lawontheweb.co.uk/rehabact.htm for the text of the Rehabilitation of Offenders Act 1974.

REINTEGRATIVE SHAMING

> The theory of reintegrative shaming is based on the belief that it can be productive to subject offenders to expressions of community disapproval of what they have done, as long as this is followed by some kind of gesture symbolizing their reacceptance into the law-abiding community.

Initially formulated by John Braithwaite (1989), 'reintegrative shaming' has been very influential among both supporters of restorative justice and more widely. It encapsulates the old Christian idea that those working with offenders should 'love the sinner, hate the sin' (in secular terms), and it builds on it by suggesting that shaming and reintegration can be aspects of the same event (such as a family group conference) where these occur in a logical sequence. First the offender is confronted with what he or she did, and shaming 'labels the act as evil while striving to preserve the dignity of the offender as essentially good' (Braithwaite 1989: 101). Immediately afterwards, it is made clear that the offence is in the past, and the offender is encouraged to make amends and to look to the future with the support of those who took part in (and often shared) the shaming. The event is often concluded with a symbolic act of reintegration (such as a handshake or sharing refreshments).

Reintegrative shaming is commonly contrasted with disintegrative shaming, which labels the offender and typically makes no attempt at reintegration; prison is the classic example of this. Critics have pointed out that, for reintegrative shaming to be effective, the offender has to be susceptible to feelings of shame and there has to be someone who cares enough to reintegrate him or her. Braithwaite counters that almost all offenders can call on the help of a 'community of care' or 'micro-community', although communities are increasingly fragmented in many countries and it may take some effort to assemble an offender's community of care. However, 'when supporters are invited to attend these [family group] conferences, they generally come' (Braithwaite 2002: 215).

Notwithstanding this, the concept of reintegrative shaming has been criticized for sentimentalizing the reality of life in contemporary urban societies and for 'exaggerating the potential for community involvement in the rehabilitation of individual offenders' (Williams 2005: 63). In some jurisdictions where restorative justice conferences are chaired by police officers, concerns have also been raised about their neutrality and their capacity to deliver reintegrative shaming based on respect for all the parties involved (Maxwell and Morris 2002: 277).

Brian Williams

Related entires

Family group conferencing; Restorative justice.

Key texts and sources

Braithwaite, J. (1989) *Crime, Shame and Reintegration.* Cambridge: Cambridge University Press.
Braithwaite, J. (2002) *Restorative Justice and Responsive Regulation.* Oxford: Oxford University Press.
Maxwell, G. and Morris, A. (2002) 'The role of shame, guilt, and remorse in restorative processes for young people', in E.G.M. Weitekamp and H.-J. Kerner (eds) *Restorative Justice: Theoretical Regualtion.* Cullompton: Willan Publishing.
Williams, B. (2005) *Victims of Crime and Community Justice.* London: Jessica Kingsley.

REMAND

> Remand is a legal term meaning that a child/young person accused of an offence can be refused bail and placed in a non-secure or secure setting while awaiting trial or sentence. It is the converse of bail, which allows for a child/young person to be temporarily released from the custody of the court into the community pending trial or sentence.

When a young person appears in court and the hearing is adjourned for any reason, he or she will be required to return at a future date and time specified by the court. A consideration for the court is whether the young person remains at liberty during this period or not. This will be determined by the likelihood of the young person committing further offences; failing to appear at a future date; or interfering with witnesses or otherwise impeding the course of justice. When bail is denied, a young person can be remanded into local authority non-secure or secure accommodation or custody. This will be for up to eight days after his or her first appearance in court and thereafter for periods of up to a maximum of 28 days.

The remand status of the young person is largely determined by his or her age and gender. All those aged 10 and 11, 12–16 year-old girls and 12–14-year-old boys can be remanded to local authority non-secure accommodation. However, the latter two groups can also be remanded to local authority secure accommodation if a court imposes a court-ordered secure remand. Boys aged 15 and 16 should be remanded to local authority accommodation but can be placed in secure accommodation if assessed as vulnerable, or in Prison Service custody if not. Boys aged 17 can only be remanded to Prison Service custody and, as such, are treated as adults.

A primary principle in respect of decisions relating to bail and remand is that consideration is always given to imposing the least level of restriction necessary. A remand to local authority accommodation (non-secure and secure) and custody represent more restrictive requirements than either conditional or unconditional bail. Even a non-secure remand is intended to provide a degree of containment. This form of remand can also be subject to any conditions that may be attached to bail and can include those that curtail freedom of movement and association (for example, curfews and electronic monitoring).

The type of placement that can be used for a non-secure remand is determined by s. 23(2) of the Children and Young Persons Act 1969. This allows local authorities discretion, and placements can be with the child's family, with another relative or with another suitable person; in a registered children's home; or in other 'appropriate accommodation', such as a remand foster placement. Courts can also impose a condition that the young person is *not* placed with a named individual, which may be relevant if the circumstances in which he or she had been living contributed to his or her offending behaviour.

There is evidence to suggest that remands to local authority non-secure accommodation have declined in use in recent years, which means that young people may be exposed to more restrictive forms of remand than was previously the case. Children and young people who are remanded in 'secure' settings (particularly young offender institutions) often comprise especially vulnerable prisoners. Many such children self-harm in prison and several have died in penal custody. In almost all cases, best practice in youth offending teams is to avoid remands by rigorously implementing remand management strategies and providing bail support services.

Sue Thomas

Related entries

Bail; Bail information schemes (BISs); Bail supervision and support (BSS); Children in custody; Electronic monitoring; Looked-after children (LAC); Remand fostering; Remand management; Secure accomodation; Vulnerability.

Key texts and sources

Ashford, M., Chard, A. and Redhouse, N. (2006) *Defending Young People in the Criminal Justice System* (3rd edn). London: Legal Action Group.

Goldson, B. (2002b) *Vulnerable Inside: Children in Secure and Penal Settings*, London: Children's Society.

Goldson, B. and Jamieson, J. (2002a) 'Community bail or penal remand? A critical analysis of recent policy developments in relation to unconvicted and/or unsentenced juveniles', *British Journal of Comminity Justice*, 1: 63–76.

Nacro (2004b) *Remands to Local Authority Accomodation. Youth Crime Briefing,* London: Nacro.

Nacro (2005b) *A Handbook on Reducing Offending by Looked After Children.* London: Nacro.

Thomas, S. and Hucklesby, A. (2002) *Key Elements of Effective Practice for Remand Management.* London: Youth Justice Board

REMAND FOSTERING

Remand fostering comprises care for children and young people, aged 10–16, remanded to local authority accommodation, or for those aged 17 bailed to reside as directed by magistrates while awaiting trial or sentence.

The use of foster placements for children remanded to local authority accommodation comprises an essential part of youth offending teams' (YOTs) remand management strategies. Schemes may be managed by YOTs, social services departments or independent fostering agencies.

The effectiveness of remand fostering builds on the premise that adults who take a supportive interest, supervise closely, reinforce positively and use consistent sanctions can exert a positive and lasting influence on the behaviour of children and young people in trouble. Carers' intensive contact with a child gives them a unique opportunity to engage with the child, but the carers must be appropriately recruited, assessed, approved, trained and supported. Carers have training in more traditional areas of foster care – such as child and adolescent development – and in aspects of youth justice. Carers who are both financially and emotionally supported can serve as role models and advocates, encouraging a child's emotional and behavioural development, and can play a key role in multi-agency preventative work, can provide support with education, training or employment and can work with the birth family.

Research (Lipscombe 2006) has shown that remand foster care can be more effective in preventing offending during the remand period than placements in local authority residential units. The majority of young people appreciated the individual attention and the chance to 'sort themselves out' away from negative pressures. Although tempered by a lack of appropriate accommodation and support post-placement, the benefits of remand foster care extend beyond the remand period itself, with a third of the group of children and young people studied by Lipscombe avoiding crime for several months after the placement and more than half saying that the experience had helped them change for the better.

YOTs and sentencers need to be given guidance about those for whom remand foster care is most appropriate. For example, although not prohibitive, there may be particular difficulties in finding placements for children who are accused of violent or sexual offences. Many children remanded in custody have not been considered for a remand foster placement.

Jo Lipscombe and Barbara Russell

Related entries

Fostering; Looked-after children (LAC); Remand; Remand management.

Key texts and sources

Fry, E. (1994) *On Remand – Foster Care and the Youth Justice Service.* London: National Foster Care Association.

Lipscombe, J. (2006) *Care or Control? Foster Care for Children and Young People on Remand.* London: British Association for Adoption and Fostering.

Nacro (2006e) *Remand Fostering: Establishing a Service.* London: Nacro.

Russell, B. and Fry, E. (2005) 'In care and in trouble? The contribution family placement can make to effective work with young offenders', in A. Wheal (ed.) *The RHP Companion to Foster Care* (2nd edn). Lyme Regis: Russell House.

Sinclair, I. (2005) *Fostering Now – Messages from Research.* London: Jessica Kingsley.

REMAND MANAGEMENT

Remand management is a strategic 'systems management' approach that includes the provision of services for children and young people who are at risk of having their liberty denied due to an appearance in either a police station or a court. It also incorporates reviewing the situation and circumstances of those who have been remanded in custody. The primary aim is to provide community-based alternatives to remands in local authority accommodation and/or secure and penal settings.

Remand management is based on evidence that custodial remands are undesirable for children and young people and that the loss of liberty should only occur as a matter of absolute last resort. It provides a systematic mechanism for proactively – whenever possible – identifying children and young people 'at risk' of local authority, secure and/or penal remands and for presenting alternative community-based packages of bail support when their cases are under deliberation at the police station and/or court. In circumstances where children and young people are remanded into local authority accommodation or custody, remand management involves retrospectively reviewing their circumstances and/or providing new information in order to intervene positively to effect change in their remand status.

Thomas and Hucklesby (2002) describe remand management as a systematic process that begins at the point of arrest and incorporates decisions made at each discrete stage of the youth justice process that impact on whether or not the young person is bailed or remanded. Effective remand management includes the identification and targeting of young people at greatest risk of losing their liberty; consideration of, and accessing, the most appropriate community-based options that might be made available to them; advocacy on their behalf (at the police station and/or court); and the provision of support and assistance in the community to help them comply with any conditions of bail.

The principal components of remand management include the provision of appropriate adults when children and young people are being inter-viewed in the police station; access to accommodation for young people in respect of s. 38(6) of the Police and Criminal Evidence Act 1984 (PACE); bail information schemes; bail supervision and support services; the availability of appropriate accommodation – including remand fostering; and systematic mechanisms for reviewing children and young people. Remand management strategies tend to be most effective when they are underpinned by established interagency systems between youth offending teams (YOTs), social services departments, the police, the courts and the juvenile secure estate.

The origins of remand management go back to the early 1980s and to the introduction of legislation governing pre-trail proceedings, such as PACE. More specifically, it derives from concerns about the increasing numbers of children and young people remanded in institutional settings and the need to take proactive action to address this. Bail supervision and support can be traced back to 1983 and bail information to 1986.

Some areas of remand management have been strengthened over the years. For example, it has become a statutory duty for YOTs to provide bail supervision and support under the provisions of the Crime and Disorder Act 1998, and bail intensive supervision and surveillance programmes were introduced in 2001. However, other elements of effective remand management have declined in use, notably the transfer of young people from the police station to local authority accommodation and the use of local authority accommodation to offset penal remands. Additionally, pioneering 'remand review' initiatives have not always been sustained. Despite this, remand management remains as important as ever, not least because the impact of appearing in court from custody continues to influence final sentencing decisions regarding the deprivation of liberty.

Sue Thomas

Related entries

Appropriate adult; Bail; Bail information schemes (BISs); Bail supervision and support (BSS); Intensive Supervision and Surveillance Programme (ISSP); National Standards for Youth Justice Services; Police and Criminal Evidence Act 1984 (PACE); Remand; Remand fostering; Systems management.

Key texts and sources

Ashton, J. and Grindrod, M. (1999) 'Institutional troubleshooting: lessons for policy and practice', in B. Goldson (ed.) *Youth Justice: Contemporary Policy and Practice.* Aldershot: Ashgate.

Davies, H. (1999) 'Managing juvenile remands and developing community-based alternatives to secure accomodation in Wales: towards a strategic approach'. in B.Goldson (ed.) *Youth Justice: Contemporary Policy and Practice.* Aldershot: Ashgate.

Drakeford, M., Haines, K., Cotton, B. and Octigan, M. (2001) *Pre-trial Services and the Future of Probation.* Cardiff: University of Wales.

Goldson, B. and Jamieson, J. (2002a) 'Community bail or penal remand? A critical anaylsis of recent policy developments in relation to unconvicted and/or unsentenced juveniles', *British Journal of Community Justice,* 1: 63–76.

Thomas, S. (2003) *Remand Management.* London: Youth Justice Board.

Thomas, S. (2005a) 'Remand management', in T. Bateman and J. Pitts (eds) *The RHP Companion Guide to Youth Justice.* Lyme Regis: Russel House.

Thomas, S. and Hucklesby, A. (2002) *Key Elements of Effective Practice for Remand Management.* London: Youth Justice Board.

REMORALIZATION

Remoralization is a strategy of social intervention that is based on the assumption that crime and disorder results from a break-up of the moral fabric of communities, families and individuals.

Against a backcloth of increasing recorded crime rates, industrial unrest and urban disorder, Conservative politicians in the 1980s depicted crime as the outcome of a broader decline in moral values. The new and reinvigorated themes of neoconservative criminology – emphasizing individual responsibility, self-control and deterrence – found a ready market in a vigorous moral campaign against various forms of deviance. The Prime Minister in waiting, Margaret Thatcher, made crime a primary election issue in 1979 in promising to re-establish 'Victorian values' and to overturn the suppos-edly permissive culture of the 1960s. Left-wing theory and progressive policy were denounced not only for a failure to respond to public concerns but also for creating conditions of 'demoralization' rooted largely in their indifference to 'family disintegration' (Dennis 1993). In political terms, such ideology has been translated into critiques of welfare dependency, illegitimacy, teenage pregnancy and single parenting and to the formation of a criminogenic 'underclass'. These themes have proved just as appealing to New Labour as they did to Conservative politicians (Muncie 2000).

The chief protagonist on the political right is the American social scientist, Charles Murray (1990, 1994). He claims that increasing rates of illegitimacy, violent crime and drop-out from the labour force are clear signs of the presence of a demoralized underclass. In this view the restoration of the two-parent family, through marriage, is the only way to ensure the survival of 'free institutions and a civil society'. This is to be encouraged by reducing welfare benefit levels for single, unmarried mothers. In Britain this analysis was largely shared by such 'ethical socialists' as Norman Dennis and George Erdos (1992). They argued that children from 'fatherless families' would grow up without appropriate role models and supervision, which would undermine their own chances of becoming competent parents. For these authors it is 'common sense' that family breakdown and rising crime will go hand in hand.

Such a vision first percolated through to Conservative policymakers in the UK. Single parenting has often been cited as a chief cause of moral decline and rising lawlessness. In 1995 it was suggested that single mothers should be ineligible for state support unless they had first tried and failed to have their children adopted. The notion of a 'parenting deficit' has also informed Labour Party policy (Goldson and Jamieson 2002b). In 1998, parenting orders were introduced to give courts powers to force parents to take responsibility for their children's care and control. In 2001 the concept of 'aggravated truancy' was introduced, carrying a three-month prison sentence for those parents who fail to ensure their children attend school regularly. In

2006 plans were laid to force teenage mothers and 'problem families' back to work and/or accept compulsory guidance. Once again the root cause of youth crime is viewed in terms of a breakdown of morality associated with 'dysfunctional families' and a 'feckless underclass'.

The techniques of remoralization, then, typically involve a strengthening and deepening of family policy. Rather than implying state withdrawal, remoralization – as a mode of governing – is based on overt regulation, surveillance and monitoring of entire families and communities. It rests crucially on the identification of an 'at risk' underclass who, through a combination of refusal to work, teenage parenthood and single parenting, are believed to threaten the entire moral fabric of society.

John Muncie

Related entries

Authoritarianism; Criminalization of Social Policy; Demonization; Governance; Institutionalized intolerance; Parenting orders; Reparation; Respect (Government Action Plan); Responsibilization.

Key texts and sources

Dennis, N. (1993) *Rising Crime and the Dismembered Family*. London: Institutes of Economic Affairs.

Dennis, N. and Erdos, G. (1992) *Families without Fatherhood*. London: Institute of Economic Affairs.

Goldson, B. and Jamieson, J. (2002b) 'Youth crime, the "parenting deficit" and state intervention: a contextual critique', *Youth Justice*, 2: 82–99.

Muncie, J. (2000) 'Pragmatic realism? Searching for criminology in the new youth justice', in B. Goldson (ed.) *The New Youth Justice*. Lyme Regis: Russell House.

Murray, C. (1990) *The Emerging Underclass*. London: Institute of Economic Affairs.

Murray, C. (1994) *Underclass: The Crisis Deepens*. London Institute of Economic Affairs.

REPARATION

Reparation is the idea that justice involves the compensation by offenders to victims of their crime for loss, harm or damage. Typical forms include financial payment to the victim or, more commonly in the youth justice system, the undertaking of unpaid work, either to the victim or to society as a whole through community service.

Reparation plays an important part in many youth justice systems. It is a component of restorative justice, referring particularly to the actions undertaken by an offender to make amends for his or her wrongdoing. Reparation is seen as meeting a number of aims. It can provide compensation to the victim and allow him or her to gain a greater insight into the reasons for the offence, thereby helping the victim to come to terms with it and to put it behind him or her. It can also provide benefits to society in the case of community reparation. For young offenders, the aim is to enable them to understand the harm done to victims and communities by their behaviour. It is also seen as providing a visible but useful sanction, easily understood by all concerned and capable of increasing confidence on the part of the public in community-based sentences. The principle of reparation dates back to Anglo-Saxon courts in England and has roots in many legal cultures. Courts must consider making compensation part of the sentence in every case, and they should explain their reasons if they do not.

Encouraging reparation to victims by young offenders has been a particular objective of the reformed youth justice system in England and Wales since 2000. As well as a specific reparation order, reparation can form part of a range of other interventions at different stages of the process. Final warnings, the referral order and community penalties, including intensive supervision and surveillance schemes, can, and do, all provide the opportunity for offenders to undertake reparation. England and Wales is, in this respect, similar to other jurisdictions such as the Netherlands, where the HALT programme comprises reparative work and compensation to victims from petty offenders; Germany, where community service and victim compensation are among the disciplinary measures that can be imposed by the youth court; and New Zealand, where most cases dealt with by the police involve apologies and one third community work, and where community work and reparation are the most commonly agreed recommendation from family group conferences. Reparation does not play a role in more overtly welfare-based systems, such as the children's hearing system in Scotland.

The practice of reparation in England varies across the country, but it appears that community reparation is rather more widespread than direct reparation to victims. An evaluation of projects funded by the Youth Justice Board found that the most common form of 'restorative' intervention was community reparation (35 per cent), followed by victim awareness (21 per cent). The proportion of cases involving direct meetings between offenders and victims was 13.5 per cent, which is low in comparison with other jurisdictions (Wilcox and Hoyle 2004). The evaluation of the intensive supervision and surveillance programme also found considerable variation in the types of 'restorative' practices being delivered. Reparation work was popular, but victim mediation was rarely used because it was considered too complicated and challenging to arrange. The majority of activity described was indirect reparation rather than victim mediation. Young people expressed negative views with regard to such activities as litter collection and leafleting and were unable to relate to them, describing them as 'pointless' and a 'waste of time'. Young people preferred being involved in constructive activities where they learnt new skills, such as gardening, charity work and working with other people.

Three issues stand out in relation to the use and practice of reparation in youth justice in England and Wales. First is the continuing over-reliance on community reparation rather than reparation to individual victims. While it is clearly more complex and time-consuming to involve victims and to arrange suitable placements, the evidence suggests the investment could be worthwhile in terms of outcomes in respect of reoffending and victim satisfaction. Moreover, public opinion surveys show that almost 40 per cent of people say that they would be likely to want to take part in a meeting with the offender if they were the victim of a burglary – a much higher proportion than actually do so.

Second, there is a need to ensure that community reparation is meaningful rather than simply punitive. Evaluation has found such reparation to be more effective when it is clearly offence related, matches the young person's skills or interests (or develops new ones) and encourages the young person to consider the victim's perspective. Third, there is a need to consider the interaction between, on the one hand, reparation agreed directly with victims or arranged by a youth offending team as part of a referral order and, on the other, court-ordered compensation. It has been suggested that this provides a kind of double jeopardy.

Rob Allen

Related entries

Comparative youth justice; Compensation; Family group conferencing; Mediation; Reintegrative shaming; Reparation orders; Restorative justice; Social harm; Victims.

Key texts and sources

Moore, R., Gray, E., Roberts, C., Taylor, E. and Merrington, S. (2006) *Managing Persistent and Serious Offenders in the Community: Intensive Community Programmes in Theory and Practice.* Cullompton: Willan Publishing.

Walgrave, L. (2004) 'Restoration in youth justice', in M, Tonry and A. Doob (eds) *Youth Crime and Youth Justice: Comparative and Cross National Perspectives.* Chicago, IL: University of Chicago Press.

Wilcox, A. and Hoyle, C. (2004) *The National Evaluation of the Youth Justice Board's Restorative Justice Projects.* London: Youth Justice Board.

REPARATION ORDERS

A reparation order is available for any 10–17-year-old who has been convicted of an offence. It requires the young offender to make specific reparation either to the individual victim of his or her crime – where the victim desires this – or to the community. Any reparation required under this order may last for a maximum of 24 hours and must be carried out over a maximum period of three months from the date that the order is made by the court.

Introduced in the Crime and Disorder Act 1998, the reparation order was intended substantially to displace the conditional discharge. The order is overseen by a youth offending team. Reparation carried out under a reparation order should be reparation in kind rather than financial reparation. The courts are already able to make a compensation order if they believe that financial reparation is appropriate.

It is a primary requirement of a reparation order that the victim of the crime in question agrees to reparation being made. Before a young offender can receive a reparation order, the victim's views will be sought. If the victim wants no further contact with the offender, then no such contact will take place and reparation may instead be made to the community at large. If the victim is prepared to receive direct reparation from the young person, consultation will continue to establish the kind of reparation the victim would consider to be suitable and would be prepared to accept. The guidance makes it clear that reparation under the order is intended to challenge the young offender's behaviour and attitudes. It should not be a mechanistic process based upon an 'eye for an eye' approach – any reparation should be tailored both to meet the needs of the victim(s) (if they wish to be involved) or benefit the wider community, and to address the young person's offending. Examples of possible reparation include writing a letter of apology or meeting the victim in person to apologize, repairing damage to property for which the young person has been responsible, cleaning graffiti or collecting litter.

If the young person fails to co-operate with the reparation order, he or she will be breached and returned to court. The court may continue the order and/or replace it with a fine of up to £1,000, or impose an attendance centre order. If the reparation order was made in the Crown court, the young offender may be committed back to the Crown court for re-sentence.

In 2005–6, just over 4,000 reparation orders were imposed. Theft and handling stolen goods, criminal damage and public-order offences accounted for more than half the orders, although it was also imposed for offences of violence against the person more than 700 times.

Rob Allen

Related entries

Community payback; Compensation; Crime and Disorder Act 1998; Justice (Northern Ireland) Act 2002; Menu-based sentencing; Powers of Criminal Courts (Sentencing) Act 2000; Remoralization; Reparation; Responsibilization; Restorative justice; Sentencing framework; Specific sentence reports (SSRs); Supervision orders; Victims; Youth Justice Agency.

Key texts and sources

Youth Justice Board (2004a) *National Standards for Youth Justice Services*. London: Youth Justice Board (available online at **http://www.yjb.gov.uk/Publications/Scripts/prodView.asp?1dproduct=155&eP=PP**).

The Home Office's document, *The Crime and Disorder Act Guidance Document: Reparation Order*, is available online at **http://police.homeoffice.gov.uk/news-and-publications/publication/operational-policing/reparation_order.pdf?view= Binary**. The Youth Justice Board's document, *Reparation order*, is available online at: **http://www.yjb.gov.uk/en-gb/practitioners/CourtsAndOrders/Disposals/ReparationOrder/**.

REPRIMANDS AND FINAL WARNINGS

> The Final Warning Scheme (FWS) is a system of reprimands and warnings that replaced the juvenile caution in 2000. Its stated aim is to divert young people from their offending behaviour before they enter the court system. Depending on the seriousness of the offence, a reprimand is normally given for a first offence and a final warning for a second offence. A final warning triggers a risk assessment by the youth offending team, using the Asset assessment tool, and, in the majority of cases, a rehabilitation and change programme.

The Final Warning Scheme (FWS) was introduced by the Crime and Disorder Act 1998 as part of New Labour's reform of the youth justice system. New Labour were influenced by the Audit Commission's (1996) report, *Misspent Youth*, which argued that repeat cautions were ineffective; that young people needed to take responsibility for their actions; and that cautions were not accompanied by any interventions aimed at preventing further offending.

The FWS process provides that if a young person is arrested for committing an offence and the police are considering a reprimand or warning, then the seriousness of the offence is assessed using gravity factors approved by the Association of Police Officers (ACPO). If the seriousness of the offence warrants a reprimand or final warning, this is issued by a police officer, usually an inspector, and a referral is made to the youth offending team (YOT). A member of the YOT then uses the Asset assessment tool in order to assess whether the young person requires a 'rehabilitation and change' programme to address his or her offending behaviour. The FWS guidance for the police and YOTs issued in 2004 set a target that an intervention programme should support 80 per cent of final warnings. Although it seems a contradiction in terms, a young person may receive two 'final warnings' depending on the length of time between offences and their seriousness.

The conditions for a reprimand or warning are similar to those for cautioning, in four respects: the young person must have no previous convictions; there must be sufficient evidence for a realistic prospect of conviction; the young person must admit the offence; and it is not thought to be in the public interest to prosecute. There is, however, an absolutely critical difference in that the police can give reprimands and warnings without the consent of the young person or his or her parents or carers as determined by the decision of the House of Lords in *R* v. *Durham Police*. In essence this means that the FWS is a system of administrative punishment without there being any process to challenge it. So, for example, as in *R* v. *Durham Police*, if a young person is warned for an alleged sexual assault, without realizing that this would lead to him or her being placed on the sex offenders' register, the young person has no way of challenging the legality of the warning or contesting the evidence, short of seeking a judicial review. The significance of this landmark judgment is that it assumes that the police will comply with due process whereas, in fact, many of the criticisms of cautioning in this respect apply equally to the FWS.

One of the main criticisms of cautioning was that it was inconsistent between and within police force areas. The architects of the FWS assumed that the scheme would lead to a more uniform approach because it was based in statute, used the ACPO gravity factors and was supported by detailed guidance about its operation. In fact there is little evidence to say whether the FWS is any more or less consistent than cautioning. There is certainly evidence to suggest that net-widening may be taking place because the police no longer have the option of using informal warnings, although the possibility of their reintroduction has been canvassed recently. There is also evidence to suggest that the police do not place any greater value on due process than they did with cautioning. For example, Holdaway (2003) comments that there is not always evidence of a clear and reliable admission to the offence or even that an offence has been committed at all. Police officers use the criterion of 'sufficient evidence' to charge rather than a full admission. They also tend to use their own judgements about the seriousness of offences and use the gravity factors in order to justify their decisions rather than to arrive at them. In addition, in contrast to the police, young people often see their behaviour as personal and private – for example, in disputes between peers – rather than illegal, and this is reflected in the blurring of the 'official' boundaries between crime and anti-social behaviour.

The use of the Asset assessment tool in the FWS has also attracted criticism because of its intrusiveness and lack of proportionality in relation to the seriousness of the offences considered appropriate for a reprimand or warning. In its original version, the Asset contained over 200 items in 13 sections and took on average two hours to complete. This has now been replaced by a shorter version, but it is still considered to be overly intrusive. The Youth Justice Board (YJB) target that 80 per cent of final warnings should be supported by intervention has never been met. Evans and Puech (2001) note that intervention would be disproportionate to the seriousness of the offence in the majority of cases. Although participation in any 'change programme' is 'voluntary', non-participation can be cited in court proceedings. It is of particular concern that young people may feel compelled to participate in a 'change programme' without a judicial finding of guilt and that this may be contrary to the Human Rights Act 1998. Although it was originally intended that intervention should incorporate some form of reparation involving victims, there is very little evidence of 'restorative justice' in the actual administration of warnings by individual police officers, in interventions, or in the overall design of the schemes. In Evans and Puech's (2001) study, the lack of due process, the lack of proportionality and the intrusiveness of assessments led young people and their parents to view their experience of the FWS as 'arbitrary, unfair and disproportionate'.

Although the primary aim of the reformed youth justice system is to prevent offending, the evidence on whether the FWS is more effective than cautioning in achieving this is mixed. Evans and Puech (2001) found that the FWS was no more or less effective in terms of re-offence rates but at a considerably higher cost because of the resources required to support assessments and interventions. Hine and Celnick (2001) found that the FWS had a statistically better outcome by 6 per cent than a comparison caution group but that there was no difference in convictions rates between those who received a 'change programme' and those who did not. Indeed, there is evidence from the 'what works' research that too early intervention with low-risk offenders is likely to increase the risk of reconviction.

The FWS was supposed to ensure that there was a more uniform and structured approach to diversion from court within the context of the reformed youth justice system. The YJB set the parameters for the FWS, established national standards and monitored outcomes, while the YOTs were charged with delivering the service in compliance with these. The YJB 'steers' while individual YOTs 'row', and the relationship between the two is best conceived as a franchise arrangement – yet Holdaway's (2003) study documents in detail the gap between policy and practice, as has most of the subsequent research.

In part the gap between policy and practice can be explained in terms of the difficulties of delivering the scheme with limited resources. Common examples from the research are the difficulties in securing appropriate and stable staffing, resourcing 'change programmes' and any elements of restorative justice. The reformed youth justice system was intended to be at the cutting edge of multi-agency working but, again, the research documents the gap between rhetoric and reality and the tensions that exist between different occupational groups – for example, the police and youth justice staff – because of their different philosophies, training, targets, conditions of employments, occupational cultures and so on. Rather than being joined up, the police are responsible for deciding whether a reprimand or final warning is appropriate and for imposing them, and the YOT is responsible for assessment and intervention.

Roger Evans

Related entries

Audit Commission; Assessment framework; Caution; Children's human rights; Crime and Disorder Act 1998; Due process; Early intervention; Gravity factors (prosecution and sentencing); Labelling theory; Net-widening; Proportionality; Reparation.

Key texts and sources

Evans, R. and Puech, K. (2001) 'Warnings and reprimands: popular puntiveness or restorative justice?', *Criminal Law Review*, 794–805.

Hine, J. and Celnick, A. (2001) *A One-year Conviction Study of Final Warnings*. London: Home Office.

Holdaway, S. (2003) 'The final warning: appearance and reality', *Criminal Justice*, 3: 351–67

Keightley-Smith, L. and Francis, P. (2007) 'Final warning, youth justice and early intervention: reflections on the findings of a research study carried out in northern England', *Web Journal of Current Legal Issues* (available online at http://webjcli.ncl.ac.uk/2007/contents2.html).

See the Office of Public Sector Information's website (www.opsi.gov.uk/acts/acts1998/0037.htm) for the text of the Crime and Disorder Act 1998.

RESETTLEMENT

Resettlement is the effective reintegration of a young person back into the community following a custodial sentence. The concept is, however, regarded as problematic, given that many young people are not settled or integrated into the community prior to custody.

Each year, around 6,500 children and young people pass through young offender institutions, secure training centres and secure children's homes, with about 3,000 in custody at any one time. The vast majority are serving detention and training orders, where half the sentence is served in custody and half in the community. Given the nature of this sentence, resettlement planning is expected to begin at the pre-court stage, to continue through custody and to extend into the community and beyond the end of the young person's licence. Nonetheless, approximately 80 per cent of young people are reconvicted within two years of their release from custody.

Many young people in custody come from highly disadvantaged backgrounds. A significant proportion have been in local authority care, have experienced violence and abuse, have educational difficulties and have high levels of substance misuse and mental health problems (Goldson 2002b). This lack of previous family, school and community integration can make successful resettlement and desistance from crime difficult to achieve. Moreover, the custodial experience further compounds these problems by dislocating the young person from his or her family and community and from mainstream services.

In 2006, the Youth Justice Board (YJB) published its national youth resettlement action framework, which aims to reduce reoffending through greater strategic direction and co-ordination across government and statutory and non-statutory agencies. The framework focuses on case management and transitions; accommodation; education, training and employment; health; substance misuse; families; finance; and benefits and debt.

At a local level, youth offending teams (YOTs), alongside custodial establishments, have responsibility for ensuring delivery of resettlement services. YOTs provide a supervising officer for a young person who receives a custodial sentence. The officer should attend regular meetings with the young offender in the juvenile secure estate to arrange suitable offending behaviour work and to ensure any other resettlement services – such as appropriate accommodation, education or employment – are available on release.

The YJB's National Standards for Youth Justice Services set out guidelines regarding the crucial transitional stage in transferring from custody to the community. For example, on returning to the community, the 'training plan' must be reviewed within 10 days; a member of the custodial facility must attend the first review; parents or primary carers must be encouraged to attend; the YOT supervising officer must see the offender on the day of release; and a home visit must be made within five working days of transfer. Contact must be at least twice weekly for the first 12 weeks after transfer, and then at least once every 10 working days. Despite these clear guidelines, post-transfer supervision is not always a smooth process for the young person (National Audit Office 2004).

Meeting the practical, emotional, health and other needs a young person may have and providing him or her with a level of stability are key factors in successful resettlement. In addition, meeting these needs is more likely to bring about desistance from crime.

Finola Farrant

Related entries

Children in custody; Desistance: Detention and training orders (DTOs); Family ties of young prisoners; National Objectives and Standards for Scotland's Youth Justice Services; National Standards for Youth Justice Services; Penal welfarism; Social exclusion; What Works; Youth justice plans.

Key texts and sources

Farrant, F. (2006) *Out for Good: The Resettlement Needs of Young Men in Prison*. London: Howard League for Penal Reform.

Goldson, B. (2002b) *Vulnerable Inside: Children in Secure and Penal Settings*. London: Children's Society.

Hagell, A. (2004) *Key Elements of Effective Practice – Resettlement*. London: Youth Justice Board.

National Audit Office (2004) *Youth Justice 2004: A Review of the Reformed Youth Justice System*. London: National Audit Office.

Youth Justice Board (2006l) *Youth Resettlement: A Framework for Action*. London: Youth Justice Board.

RESPECT (GOVERNMENT ACTION PLAN)

For the New Labour government, 'respect' is embodied in the shared cultural values of a respectable society, which, they argue, include a 'consideration for others, a recognition that we all have responsibilities as well as rights, civility and good manners' (Blair in Respect Taskforce 2006: 1). Worklessness, drug and alcohol misuse, disorder, anti-social behaviour and criminal activity are attributed to a lack of respect for societal values and, for the government, constitute a legitimate focus for intervention. The 'Respect' action plan centres on strategies to address neighbourhood renewal; anti-social behaviour; alcohol and violent crime; the promotion of parental/guardian responsibility; and the encouragement of respect for public servants and services.

New Labour has been committed to forge a new political ideology: the 'third way'. In contrast to the traditional (Old) Labour concerns with social democracy, New Labour rejects the belief that the 'big state' can solve every problem. Rather, it conceptualizes the 'enabling state' whereby the emphasis is firmly placed on the responsibilities of citizens. A strong civic society is a place where rights come with responsibilities, and the government's broad social policy agenda has sought to emphasize individual duty in the belief that balancing social obligation and civic behaviour is necessary for a 'respectful' society. As such, the 'Respect' action plan comprises a central component of the government's pursuit of a 'responsive inclusive citizenship' (Squires and Stephen 2005: 78).

The 'Respect action plan' draws variously on Wilson and Kellings' (1982) 'Broken windows' thesis, which advocates zero-tolerance approaches to minor incivilities; on Putnam's (2000) ideas with regard to 'social capital' and its legacy of reciprocal social relations; and – arguably most significantly – on a conservative variant of Etzioni's (1995) communitarianism, which calls for a renewal and revitalization of community values and institutions alongside the prioritization of the needs and rights of victims and 'law-abiding' citizens. Accordingly, the action plan incorporates the state's disciplinary powers to define, legislate and sanction in relation to the duties and obligations it views as fundamental to the membership rights of the 'respectful' society.

The government's commitment to 'respect' was heralded in the publication of the white paper: *Respect and Responsibility: Taking a Stand against Anti-social Behaviour* (Home Office 2003d), and was formally launched with the establishment of a new cross-governmental 'Respect Taskforce' on 2 September 2005. Initially based within the Home Office and more recently transferred to the Department for Children, Schools and Families, the taskforce has been given a budget of £420 million (Respect Taskforce 2006: 3). The taskforce is responsible for the co-ordination and delivery of the action plan which seeks to 'tackle bad behaviour and nurture good'. Ostensibly a continuation of the government's drive to tackle 'anti-social behaviour', the action plan encompasses a range of strategies to 'support' parents; to target intervention on the 'most challenging families'; to provide activities for children and young people; and to strengthen communities.

Notwithstanding an emphasis on problematic or 'disrespectful' behaviour some positive strategies are included under the auspices of the action plan – for example, investment in a new Youth Opportunities Fund; youth opportunity cards; mentoring and befriending projects; opportunities for children and young people to engage in sport, the arts and environmental and community volunteer schemes; improved provision for children and young people suspended or excluded from school; improved national parenting services; and a commitment to providing support and services to those parents in need of most help. However, the ostensibly inclusionary potential of these measures is significantly undermined by a range of more punitive and authoritarian strategies that include new legislation to tackle poor behaviour in schools; legislation to expand the use of parenting orders; the introduction of intensive family support schemes – with the potential for residential requirements – for the most 'challenging' families; and the strengthening of summary and civil powers in relation to anti-social behav-

iour. Indeed, the government's commitment to effective enforcement and community justice in order 'to ensure effective, swift and proportionate responses and sanctions' is demonstrated through its promotion of the use of anti-social behaviour injunctions, anti-social behaviour orders, demotion orders, dispersal orders, family intervention projects, fixed penalty notices and parenting orders. Furthermore, the flirtation with such sanctions as housing benefit withdrawal and eviction from the social housing sector clearly signals that those families living in the most challenging material circumstances comprise the prime targets of the government's action plan.

The punitive emphasis of the action plan provides an expressive means by which to demonstrate intolerance and to reassure the public that firm measures are in place to deal with 'disrespectful' behaviour. Such measures may well provide some respite from disrespectful behaviour in the short term and may even serve to deter involvement in such activities, but the legitimacy, justification and desirability of the action plan are questionable. The vilification inherent in the pejorative rhetoric of the action plan and its emphasis on enforcement and sanctions promote profoundly negative portrayals of the children, young people and parents primarily targeted. The danger of this strategy is not only that it encourages hostility and intolerance but also that it is likely to prove alienating, damaging and ultimately counterproductive. Moreover, the emphasis on individualized blame serves to mask the often complex and diverse needs underlying 'parenting deficits' and 'anti-social' and 'criminal' behaviour and obscures the fact that the government and 'respectful' society also have responsibilities, not least the responsibility for ensuring that social justice extends to all members of society, particularly those children and young people living in the most disadvantaged families, neighbourhoods and communities.

Janet Jamieson

Related entries

Anti-social behaviour (ASB); Anti-social Behaviour Act 2003; Anti-social behaviour orders (ASBOs); Authoritarianism; Criminalization of social policy;

Dispersal orders; Fixed-penalty notices (FPNs); Institutionalized intolerance; Parenting orders; Positive Activities for Young People (PAYP); Remoralization; Responsibilization; Social justice; Zero tolerance.

Key texts and sources

Etzioni, A. (1995) *The Spirit of the Community.* London: Fontana.

Home Office (2003d) *Respect and Responsibility: Taking a Stand against Anti-social Behaviour.* London: Home Office.

Jamieson, J. (2006) 'New Labour, youth justice and the question of "respect"', *Youth Justice*, 5: 180–93.

Putnam, R. (2000) *Bowling Alone – the Collapse and Revival of American Community.* New York, NY: Simon & Schuster.

Respect Taskforce (2006) *Respect Action Plan.* London: Home Office (avaliable online at **http://www.homeoffice.gov.uk/documents/respect-action-plan**).

Squires, P. and Stephen, D.E. (2005) *Rougher Justice: Anti-social Behaviour and Young People.* Cullompton: Willan Publishing.

Wilson, J.Q, and Kelling, G. (1982) 'The Police and neighbourhood safety: broken windows', *Atlantic Monthly*, March: 29–38.

See also the website of the Respect Taskforce (**http://www.respect.gov.uk/**).

RESPONSIBILIZATION

Responsibilization concerns a shift of primary responsibility for crime prevention and public security away from the state and towards businesses, organizations, individuals, families and communities. It is generally expressed in practical and discursive terms, including 'crime and disorder reduction partnerships'; 'interagency co-operation'; 'partnership working'; and 'joined-up government'.

At its most basic, the concept of 'responsibilization' draws attention to any crime control strategy that aims to make 'offenders' (of any age) take full responsibility for their actions. But theoretically it derives from the analysis of those processes (most strongly associated with neoliberalism) that encourage the private sector and communities to take a more active role in reducing criminal opportunities. The term itself was probably first used in Rose's (1996) analysis of 'advanced liberal' modes of governance. Garland (1996) develops the notion in the context of crime control and refers to a community responsibilization strategy, involving central government seeking to act upon crime by directly involving non-state agencies and organizations. For example, he notes how, from the mid-1980s onwards, numerous campaigns (such as Neighbourhood Watch), organizations (such as Crime Concern) and projects (such as Safer Cities) were established in the UK to encourage interagency co-operation and local initiative. The key message was (and remains) that property owners and manufacturers, as well as school authorities, families and individuals, all have a responsibility to reduce criminal opportunities and to increase informal social controls. No longer can the state be expected to control youth crime and disorder on its own.

Significantly, this responsiblization of citizens has developed alongside the government's critique of state dependency and its withdrawal from universal measures of state protection and welfare support. It coalesces with a number of related developments whereby aspects of youth justice have come to reflect market-like conditions and processes, the welfarist core has been eroded, elements of the system have become privatized and access to resources made dependent on acting 'responsibly' (Muncie and Hughes 2002).

The concept has helped to open up a series of important debates about the relationship between the public and the private spheres; about the extent to which the state is prepared (or is preparing) to 'govern at a distance'; about what constitutes 'acceptable' and 'responsible' citizenship; and how communities and families can be 'empowered' in their self-governance (Rose 2000). Certainly, the notion captures the essence of many aspects of contemporary youth justice reform, such as the statutory requirement for local authorities to co-ordinate services to tackle youth offending and for youth offending teams to form partnerships between social services, police, probation, education, health and housing authorities.

It is important to remember, though, that responsibilization forms only one of various simultaneous youth justice strategies. For example, techniques of remoralization typically involve a strengthening and deepening of state intervention-ist programmes, as do authoritarian modes of governance whereby the state routinely reasserts its sovereign power as expressed most obviously through the institution of the prison. Processes of responsibilization (which suggest active citizenship and empowerment) sit alongside parallel initia-tives that do more to demonize children and to promote hostility towards young people through the pursuance of a politics of fear and vengeance (Goldson 2002a; Muncie and Hughes 2002).

John Muncie

Related entries

Authoritarianism; Crime and disorder reduction (CDR); Crime prevention; Demonization; Governance; Partnership working; Remoralization; Respect (Government Action Plan).

Key texts and sources

Garland, D. (1996) 'The limits of the sovereign state: strategies of crime control in contemporary soci-ety', *British Journal of Criminology*, 36: 445–71.

Goldson, B. (2002a) 'New punitiveness: the politics of child incarceration', in J. Muncie *et al.* (eds) *Youth Justice: Critical Readings.* London: Sage.

Muncie, J. and Hughes, G. (2002) 'Modes of youth governance: political rationalities, criminalisation and resistance', in J. Muncie *et al.* (eds) *Youth Justice: Critical Readings.* London: Sage.

Rose, N. (1996) 'Governing "advanced" liberal democracies', in A. Barry *et al.* (eds) *Foucault and Political Reason.* London: UCL Press.

Rose, N. (2000) 'Government and control', *British Journal of Criminology*, 40: 321–39.

RESTORATIVE CAUTIONING

Restorative cautioning brings the traditional practice of police cautioning within a restorative framework. Such cautions (or final warnings) emphasize the impact of the offence on the vic-tim while attempting to reintegrate the young person back into his or her community.

The traditional caution focused on the police being able to deliver a stern warning to young offenders, especially if it was their first offence.

Though not a conviction, it is kept on record and can influence future prosecution and court decisions. Young offenders are required to have an appropriate adult with them when being cautioned, but victims and others affected by the offence are not invited. Previous research had shown that cautioning sessions were some-times used to humiliate and stigmatize children and young people and that often there was little training in how to administer a caution, no supervision of practice and no expectation of consistency (Lee 1998; Wilcox *et al.* 2004).

The development of a restorative framework in the delivery of cautioning (final warning) has been encouraged by the Youth Justice Board, and practice has been led by police forces, including the Thames Valley and Northern Ireland Police. In essence, this approach seeks to deal with crime and its aftermath by attempting to make offenders 'ashamed' of their behaviour, but in a way that promotes their reintegration into the community and that is delivered by trained officers (Hoyle *et al.* 2002).

Hoyle *et al.* (2002), researching the Thames Valley scheme (which included children and adults), described the restorative approach as a significant improvement on the 'old style' and rather idiosyncratic approach to police caution-ing. They found high levels of satisfaction with the process, both in terms of how conferences were facilitated and how fairly the participants were treated. Nearly all the victims who attended the restorative cautions expressed sat-isfaction with how their conference was handled and felt that it was a good idea, and some 71 per cent said they felt better following the confer-ence. Most of the victims who attended meetings said they felt differently about the offender as a result of the conference, and just under 60 per cent said the conference helped them to put the offence behind them. While subsequent research has shown restorative cau-tions to be no more effective in reducing reoffending rates than traditional cautioning, the high levels of satisfaction with the process and outcome for both victims and offenders remain (Wilcox *et al.* 2004).

Similarly research in Northern Ireland, on the police-led restorative cautioning scheme for juve-niles, found it to be a significant improvement on previous cautioning practice (O'Mahony *et al.* 2002). The researchers noted that the schemes were successful in securing some of the traditional aims of restorative practice. Reintegration was achieved through the avoidance of prosecution and through a process that emphasized that the young person was not 'bad' while highlighting the impact of the young person's offending on the victim (O'Mahony and Doak 2004).

However, both the Thames Valley and Northern Ireland schemes had fairly low levels of victim participation. Only 14 per cent of the cautioning sessions for the Thames Valley research and 20 per cent of the cases in the Northern Ireland research were attended by an actual victim. This limited the restorative potential of such work. A further concern from the research conducted in Northern Ireland was some evidence of net-widening, whereby some young people who had committed petty offences were unnecessarily drawn into the process (O'Mahony and Doak 2004).

Despite these concerns, research has found the police to be generally enthusiastic and sincerely committed to the restorative process. The schemes have resulted in officers being well trained and better able to deliver cautions, and it was clear from the interviews with the young people, their parents and the victims involved that they had a high degree of confidence in and support for such schemes.

David O'Mahony

Related entries

Appropriate adult; Caution; Mediation; Net-widening; Reintegrative shaming; Restorative justice; Victims.

Key texts and sources

Hoyle, C., Young, R. and Hill, R. (2002) *Proceed with Caution: An Evaluation of the Thames Valley Police Initiative in Restorative Cautioning.* York: Joseph Rowntree Foundation.
Lee, M. (1998) *Youth, Crime and Police Work.* Basingstoke: Macmillan.

O'Mahoney, D., Chapman, T. and Doak, J. (2002) *Restorative Cautioning: A Study of Police Based Restorative Cautioning in Northern Ireland. Northern Ireland Office, Research and Statistical Series.* Belfast: Northern Ireland Office.
O'Mahony, D. and Doak, J. (2004) 'Restorative justice – is more better? The experience of police-led restorative cautioning pilots in Northern Ireland', *Howard Journal of Criminal Justice,* 43: 484–505.
Wilcox, A., Young, R. and Hoyle, C, (2004) *An Evaluation of the Impact of Restorative Cautioning: Findings from a Reconviction Study. Home Office Findings 255.* London: Home Office (avaliable online at **http://www.homeoffice.gov.uk/rds/pdfs 04/r255.pdf**).

RESTORATIVE JUSTICE

Restorative justice aims to resolve conflict and to repair harm. It encourages those who have caused harm to acknowledge the impact of what they have done and gives them an opportunity to make reparation. It offers those who have suffered harm the opportunity to have their harm or loss acknowledged and amends made.

Restorative justice covers a range of activities all aimed at repairing the harm done by crime and involving victims as well as offenders in the process. It includes such practices as victim–offender mediation, restorative conferencing, family group conferencing, victim–offender groups, victim awareness work and reparation to the victim. Restorative justice can also be used in non-criminal settings, such as schools and communities. Similar processes are used to repair harm that has been done without using the labels 'victim' and 'offender'.

The hallmarks of restorative justice are as follows:

- Victim support and healing is a priority.
- Offenders take responsibility for what they have done.
- There is dialogue to achieve understanding.
- There is an attempt to put right the harm done.

- Offenders look at how to avoid future offending.
- The community helps to reintegrate both victim and offender

(Liebmann 2007: 26–7).

Restorative justice offers potential benefits for victims, offenders and communities. *Victims* have the opportunity to:

- learn about the offender and to put a face to the crime;
- ask questions of the offender;
- express their feelings and needs after the crime;
- receive an apology and/or appropriate reparation;
- educate offenders about the effects of their offences;
- sort out any existing conflict;
- be part of the criminal justice process; and
- put the crime behind them.

Offenders have the opportunity to:

- own the responsibility for their crime;
- find out the effect of their crime;
- apologize and/or offer appropriate reparation; and
- reassess their future behaviour in the light of this knowledge.

Communities have the opportunity to:

- accept apologies and reparation from offenders; and
- help reintegrate victims and offenders.

Restorative justice is not new – it is the most ancient and prevalent approach in the world to resolve harm and conflict. Many of the recent attempts to provide a more victim-centred form of justice have drawn on customs of Aboriginal, Maori and First Nations (Native American) people. Many African and Asian countries also have restorative traditions.

The first recorded victim–offender mediation and reparation service in recent times in the western hemisphere took place in Canada in Kitchener, Ontario, in May 1974. A Mennonite probation officer, Mark Yantzi, took two young men to apologize to 22 victims whose houses they had vandalized. The idea was taken up more generally in Canada and the USA, then in the UK, where many victim–offender mediation projects started in the 1980s, mostly with adult offenders. In 1985 there were 31 victim–offender schemes in the UK.

In 1989 New Zealand's radical Children, Young Persons and their Families Act established family group conferences as the method of responding to offending behaviour in children and young people. This resulted in far fewer young people going to court or custody. The conferencing idea spread to Australia in the early 1990s, where police in Wagga Wagga developed the restorative conferencing model based on a carefully worked-out script. This model then travelled to the UK and was adopted by Thames Valley Police, who pioneered it in police work with cautions in the mid-1990s. The term 'restorative justice' came into general use in youth justice as a consequence.

The Crime and Disorder Act 1998 provided for reparation to be included in final warnings, reparation orders, action plan orders, supervision orders and detention and training orders. The Youth Justice Board provided funding for 46 youth offending teams (YOTs) to set up restorative justice schemes. The Youth Justice and Criminal Evidence Act 1999 introduced referral orders for 10–17-year-olds and consolidated restorative approaches in youth justice in England and Wales.

While some YOTs really do have restorative work with victims as their focus, many tend to ignore victims and to conceptualize reparation as conventional 'community service' – a number of hours of work on a community project. The reasons for this include a shortage of resources (time) to include victims in a meaningful way; too many other targets to fulfil; the pressure to achieve 'swift justice'; and a lack of training (only 46 YOTs received funding out of 156).

In England and Wales the Youth Justice Board adjusted restorative justice targets from April 2007, to encourage YOTs to do more restorative work and to ensure that victims participate in restorative processes in 25 per cent of relevant disposals. The target also requires that 85 per cent of victims participating in such processes should be satisfied with the service. In Scotland, cases can be referred to local restorative justice services by children's reporters. This can take place at any stage: as diversion from a children's hearing; prior to a children's hearing; and as the basis of referral from a children's hearing. The reporter can request a report from restorative justice services, to be taken into account at the children's hearing. In Northern Ireland the Youth Conference Service was established by the Justice (Northern Ireland) Act 2002, based on the New Zealand model, to be the main disposal. By 2006, youth conferencing was available in Belfast and three other areas, with the aim of complete 'roll-out' in 2007. It gives an opportunity for young people who offend to make right the harm caused to victims, and gives victims an opportunity to have a say in what the young person should do to show remorse and commitment towards redressing the harm. The victim participation rate is very high – 69 per cent, much higher than that for most of England and Wales.

Research on restorative justice outcomes has generally been positive. There have been many studies and also some meta-analyses. Most studies show high degrees of victim and offender satisfaction and many reveal a reduction in recidivism (Sherman and Strang 2007). 'Best practice' factors that make for effective restorative processes include:

- preparation;
- providing victims and offenders with realistic options;
- consulting all parties;
- safe procedures and safeguarded rights for all;
- confidentiality;
- allowing as much time as is needed;
- developing processes that encourage empathy and understanding;
- working towards agreed outcomes that make amends to victims to the extent that this is possible;
- following up agreements and monitoring outcomes;
- providing feedback to victims and professionals about the completion of agreed tasks;
- providing ongoing support for both offenders and victims; and
- secure and adequate funding.

Marian Liebmann

Related entries

Children's hearing system; Comparative youth justice; Diversion; Family group conferencing; Mediation; Reintegrative shaming; Reparation; Responsibilization; Restorative youth conferencing; Social harm; Victims; Youth Justice and Criminal Evidence Act 1999.

Key texts and sources

Home Office (2004a) *Best Practice Guidance for Restorative Practitioners*. London: Home Office (available online at **http://www.homeoffice.gov. uk/documents/rj_bestpractice.pdf?version=1**).
Johnstone, G. and Van Ness, D. (2006) *Handbook of Restorative Justice*. Cullompton: Willan Publishing.
Liebmann, M. (2007) *Restorative Justice: How It Works*. London: Jessica Kingsley.
Sherman, L. W. and Strang, H. (2007) *Restorative Justice: The Evidence*. London: Smith Institute (avaliable online at **www.smith-institute.org.uk/ publications.htm**).
Youth Justice Board (in association with Mediation UK) (2003) *Restorative Justice*. London: Youth Justice Board.
Zehr, H. (2002) *The Little Book of Restorative Justice*. Intercourse, Pennsylvania: Good Books.
See also the Restorative Justice Consortium's website (**www.restorativejustice.org.uk**).

RESTORATIVE YOUTH CONFERENCING

Restorative youth conferencing is a process that gives young offenders the opportunity to understand and make amends to their victims and community for the consequences of their offending. It holds offenders accountable for their actions and also provides victims with an opportunity to be heard and to be directly involved in how the harm they have experienced is addressed.

Restorative youth conferencing is based on the principles of restorative justice, which is about healing the harm done to victims and communities as a result of criminal acts while making offenders accountable for their actions. The process typically involves a meeting comprising the young offender, his or her parent/guardian, the victim, the police, a conference co-ordinator and, if appropriate, community representatives and supporters. Restorative conferencing processes can take place in different forms and at differing stages of the youth justice system, including 'mainstreamed' schemes where it is used as the principal method of delivering justice.

Perhaps the best-known restorative youth conferencing scheme is the family group conferencing model developed in New Zealand under the Children, Young Persons and their Families Act 1989. The legislation made conferencing the main youth justice disposal for all but the most serious offences, such as murder and manslaughter. Young people can only be prosecuted if they have been arrested and referred by the police through a family group conference. The courts are also required to send offenders for family group conferences – following an admission or finding of guilt – and are required to consider the recommendations of the conference, and generally do not deal with cases until they have had a conference recommendation (Morris and Maxwell 1998).

The main aim of the conference is to agree a plan that should involve a process of dialogue between the offender (and his or her family) and the victim (and community representatives, where appropriate). In the conference the victim and offender participate in the decision about how best to deal with, and make amends for, the offending (Morris and Maxwell 1998). Restorative conferencing has also been developed in other jurisdictions, though many of these schemes have been targeted towards less serious offending and are often used as an alternative to prosecution.

Research examining the New Zealand family group conferencing model has found it to be successful in meeting many of its objectives, and satisfaction levels are considerably higher than they are in traditional court process. Research conducted by Morris and Maxwell (1998) showed that about 85–90 per cent of conferences resulted in an agreed outcome and that 80 per cent of young people completed their agreements. They found that participants were generally satisfied with the process and out-comes and that around 85 per cent of offenders and their parents were satisfied with the conferencing process. However, about a third of victims said they were dissatisfied with conferencing. Feelings of dissatisfaction were often linked to being unhappy with the conference outcome, such as judging it to be too lenient or harsh, but more often it was simply because they were not informed of the outcome. Reconviction data show that conferencing is at least as effective as court-based sanctions in reducing reoffending. However, in conferences where the restorative elements were achieved – such as meeting the victim and the offender, apologizing and showing remorse – they were more likely to result in reduced reoffending rates (compared with court disposals). International research in respect of youth conferencing also reveals generally high levels of satisfaction among victims and offenders in relation to the process and outcomes (Dignan 2007). Conferencing can have positive effects on reducing victims' anger and their fear of offenders.

Currently the only part of the UK to adopt mainstreamed statutory-based restorative conferencing for young offenders is Northern Ireland. The new youth conferencing system was introduced in 2003. The youth conferencing arrangements have statutory footing in the Justice (Northern Ireland) Act 2002. The new measures provide for two types of disposal: diversionary and court-ordered conferences. Both types of conference take place to allow a youth conference co-ordinator to provide a plan to the prosecutor or court on how the young person should be dealt with for his or her offence.

Diversionary conferences are referred by the Public Prosecution Service and are not intended for minor first-time offenders, who are normally dealt with by the police by way of a warning or police caution. For the prosecutor to make use of the diversionary restorative conference, the young person must admit to the offence and consent to the process (O'Mahony and Campbell 2006).

Court-ordered conferences, on the other hand, are referred for conferencing by the court and, like diversionary conferences, the young person must agree to the process and must either admit guilt or have been found guilty in court. An important feature of the legislation is that the courts *must* refer all young persons for youth conferences, except for offences carrying a mandatory life sentence. The court *may* refer cases that are triable by indictment only or scheduled offences under the Terrorism Act 2000. In effect, the legislation makes conferencing mandatory, except for a small number of very serious offences.

The format of the youth conference normally involves a meeting, chaired by an independent and trained youth conference facilitator, with the offender (and his or her guardian), the victim (who is encouraged to attend) and a police officer. Following a dialogue, a 'youth conference plan' or 'action plan' will be devised that should take into consideration the offence, the needs of the victim, the needs of the young person and, where appropriate, the needs of the wider community. The young person must consent to the plan, which can run for a period of not more than one year and which usually involves some form of reparation or apology to the victim (O'Mahony and Campbell 2006).

Research on the youth conferencing system in Northern Ireland has found it to be successful (Campbell *et al.* 2005). It achieved relatively high levels of victim participation (62 per cent of conferences had some form of victim participation) and engagement in the process. Nearly all conferences observed, where a victim was present, resulted in the offender apologizing directly to the victim as part of his or her plan, and most contained elements of reparation or restitution. The process achieved high levels of satisfaction from both victims and offenders in terms of fairness, and 71 per cent of offenders and 79 per cent of victims were 'satisfied' or 'very satisfied' with the agreed plan. The vast majority of participants expressed predominately positive feedback on their experience of conferencing, with most offenders (91 per cent) and victims (81 per cent) saying they preferred it to court. Indeed, the vast majority of offend-

ers (86 per cent) and victims (88 per cent) said they would recommend a conference to a person in a similar situation.

The success of conferencing in terms of holding young people to account and in getting them to face the consequences of their offending, as well as satisfying victims' interests, is bound up in the quality and 'restorativeness' of the process. Youth conferencing provides an alternative and promising method of dealing with young offenders, when it is properly implemented and resourced.

David O'Mahony

Related entries

Comparative youth justice; Diversion; Family group conferencing; Justice (Northern Ireland) Act 2002; Mandatory sentence; Reparation; Restorative justice; Social harm; Victims.

Key texts and sources

Campbell, C., Devlin, R., O'Mahony, D., Doak, J., Jackson, J. and Corrigan, T.; and McEvoy, K. (2005) *Evaluation of the Northern Ireland Youth Conferencing Scheme. Northern Ireland Office, Research and Statistics Series.* Belfast: Northern Ireland Office.

Dignan, J. (2007) 'Juvenile justice, criminal courts and restorative justice', in J. Johnstone and D. Van Ness (eds) *Handbook of Restorative Justice.* Cullompton: Willan Publishing.

Haines, K. and O'Mahony, D. (2006) 'Restorative approaches: young people and youth justice', in B. Goldson and J. Muncie (eds) *Youth Crime and Justice: Criminal Issues.* London: Sage.

Morris, A. and Maxwell, G. (1998) 'Restorative justice in New Zeland: family group conferences as a case study', *Western Criminology Review*, 1 (available online at http://wcr.sonoma.edu/v1n1/morris.html).

O'Mahony, D. and Campbell, C. (2006) 'Mainstreaming restorative justice for young offenders through youth conferencing: the experience of Northern Ireland', in J. Junger-Tas and S. Decker (eds) *International Handbook of Youth Justice.* Amsterdam: Springer Academic Press.

RESTRAINT

The term 'restraint' is used to describe situations where physical means are used to prevent an individual's free movement. Distinctions may be drawn between 'restraint' (implying the use of force), 'holding' (seen as more benign), and 'physical intervention' (employing measures such as blocking a person's path). The preferred term currently used by the Youth Justice Board is 'restrictive physical intervention', defined as those situations when 'force is used to overpower a young person'.

The practice of physically restraining children is not limited to youth justice settings: children in residential care, schools and hospitals – and, of course, in families – may all be subjected to physical means of control. In an era that emphasizes the importance of empowering children, the fact that adults are authorized to overpower them is a source of unease. This is compounded by the lack of a legal framework providing for when and how restraint can be used. Different policies apply across the range of children's services and consist mainly of statements of principle rather than detailed guidance. For example, statements refer to restraint being a 'last resort', justifiable only to 'prevent harm not to punish or secure compliance', and the degree of force should be 'minimal', 'reasonable' or 'proportionate'. These are subjective judgements, of course, and, in the absence of clear direction about what they can/should or cannot/should not do, some staff have expressed a reluctance to touch children in their 'care' at all. Interestingly, consultation with children does not support this stance. They expect staff to care enough about them to keep them safe and accept that this sometimes requires physical means of control. Their request is that it should be 'done properly', meaning only when the circumstances genuinely warrant it and without the use of excessive force.

There have been consistent calls for a review of the use of restraint. In 2002, the United Nations Committee on the Rights of the Child suggested that the UK may be in breach of the United Nations Convention on the Rights of the Child through its frequent use of restraint in residential institutions and in penal custody. This concern was echoed in the Joint Chief Inspectors' report on safeguarding in 2005, which called on the relevant government departments to 'issue one agreed set of principles for the use of control methods in all settings where children are cared for, including secure settings' (Commission for Social Care Inspectorate *et al.* 2005). At the time of writing, this recommendation has not been acted upon.

In 2003 the Youth Justice Board (YJB) undertook a review of policies and methods of restraint in different types of custodial establishment (Hart and Howell 2003). Significant differences were found as to when staff in the institutions across the juvenile secure estate physically restrained the young people in their 'care'. Young offender institutions could use restraint if behaviour was 'violent', 'recalcitrant' or 'disruptive', whereas the other establishments could only use it when the child's behaviour was posing a risk, whether that risk was to self, others or property or the risk of escape. In terms of techniques, young offender institutions use 'control and restraint' (C and R), which involves restraining children and young people through 'pain compliant' means, such as an arm lock. This method was initially developed for use with adult prisoners. Secure training centres use 'physical control in care' (PCC), based on a series of escalating 'holds' depending on the seriousness of the situation. PCC is said not to cause pain (although there are three additional 'distraction' techniques for use in 'violent situations' which do deliver a short episode of pain) and had been approved by a panel of experts as being 'safe' for use on children. For secure children's homes, there is no single recommended system and a variety of methods are used.

Following the 2003 review, the YJB decided that it was not feasible to impose a single method of restraint across the juvenile secure estate settings but that it would develop a common 'code of conduct'. This placed physical restraint within a wider context of behaviour management and only sanctioned its use if there was a 'risk of harm'. The Prison Service also agreed to pilot a non-pain-compliant method of restraint. A more recent initiative has been to introduce a national reporting and monitoring system for incidents of 'restrictive physical intervention' across the juvenile secure estate. This might enable a picture to be built up about its overall use (and/or misuse), to identify trends and to establish if particular 'techniques' are proving to be harmful.

In April 2004, Gareth Myatt died at the age of 15 after being physically restrained in Rainsbrook Secure Training Centre. A number of internal inquiries and a police investigation took place, and the circumstances that led to his death have been considered by an inquest. Gareth choked on his own vomit and asphyxiated while being subjected to an 'approved' PCC hold. Following Gareth's death, the Howard League for Penal Reform commissioned a review of the treatment of children in custody, led by Lord Carlile. He – and a team of expert advisers appointed to support the independent inquiry – visited a wide range of custodial establishments and talked directly to children about their experience of physical restraint, forcible strip searching and solitary confinement. Concern was raised that restraint could be used in an abusive way, compounded by the lack of monitoring and external scrutiny.

Gareth Myatt's death and the Carlile Report have focused attention on the juvenile secure estate. On 12 July 2007, Justice Minister, David Hanson, announced a joint review of restraint issues in juvenile secure settings to be carried out by the Ministry of Justice and the Department for Children, Schools and Families. Furthermore, on 26 July 2007, the Parliamentary Joint Committtee on Human Rights – which has previously expressed the view that the extent of physical restraint experienced by children in secure training centres contravened the United Nations Convention on the Rights of the Child – announced its own inquiry into the use of restraint in secure training centres. Despite this, there is no room for complacency in other children's services where the use of restraint remains a largely 'hidden' problem. Aside from the complex ethical questions, there is a worrying lack of robust evidence about the safety and effectiveness of restraint techniques, combined with a failure to provide clear and consistent guidance to staff or to establish effective monitoring systems.

Diane Hart

Related entries

Child abuse; Children in custody; Children's human rights; Deaths in custody; Juvenile Secure Estate; Looked after children (LAC); Safeguarding; Secure accommodation; Secure training centres (STCs); United Nations Committee on the Rights of the Child; United Nations Convention on the Rights of the Child (UNCRC); Young offender institutions (YOIs).

Key texts and sources

Carlile, A. (2006) *The Lord Carlile of Berriew QC: An Independent Inquiry into the Use of Physical Restraint. Solitary Confinement and Forcible Strip Searching of Children in Prisons, Secure Training Centres and Local Authority Secure Children's Homes.* London: Howard League fo Penal Reform.

Commission for Social Care Inspectorate, Healthcare Commission, Her Majesty's Inspectorate of Constabulary, Her Majesty's Inspectorate of Probation, Her Majesty's Inspectorate of Prisons, Her Majesty's Crown Prosecution Service Inspectorate, Her Majesty's Inspectorate of Courts Administration and Office of Standards in Education (2005) *Safeguarding Children: The Sencond Joint Chief Inspectors' Report on Arrangements to Safeguard Children.* London: Department of Health Publications. *www.safe guardingchildren.org.uk.*

Goldson, B. (1995) *A Sense of Security.* London: National Children's Bureau.

Goldson, B. (2006a) 'Damage, harm and death in child prisons in England and Wales: questions of abuse and accountability', *Howard Journal of Criminal Justice*, 45: 449–67.

Hart, D. and Howell, S. (2003) *Report to the Youth Justice Board on the Use of Physical Intervention within the Juvenile Secure Estate.* London: Youth Justice Board (available online at **www.yjb.gov.uk/ engb/practitioners/Custody/BehaviourManagem ent/RestrictivePhysicalInterventions/**).

Morgan, R. (2004) *Children's Views on Restraint.* Newcastle: Office of the Children's Rights Director (available online at **www.ofsted.gov.uk/assets/ Internet_Content/Shared_Content/Migration/crd/ Restraint_crd.pdf**).

Youth Justice Board (2006h) *Managing the Behaviour of Children and Young People in the Secure Estate: A Code of Conduct.* London: Youth Justice Board (available online at **ww.yjb.gov.uk/en-gb/practitioners/ custody/behaviourmanagement**).

RETRIBUTION

> Retribution is punishment inflicted on offenders in consequence of their wrongdoing.

The dominant philosophical justifications for punishment are typically to be found either in retributive theory, which advocates retribution and just deserts, and/or in utilitarian theory, which advocates incapacitation, deterrence and rehabilitation. While the latter is designed to prevent *future* offending, the former is most concerned to respond to *past* offences (Lacey 1988).

Retribution features prominently in western notions of criminal justice because it is often accepted as the most fundamental human response to crime and deviance. It is 'natural' to resent and to retaliate against any harm done. Such ideas are deeply ingrained in many theological texts such as the *lex talionis*, the Mosaic doctrine expressed in Exodus 21: 23–25: 'and if any mischief follows, then thou shalt give life for life, eye for eye, tooth for tooth, hand for hand, foot for foot, burning for burning, wound for wound, stripe for stripe.' Punishing the sinner is conceived as a positive moral duty. The moral order can only be restored by inflicting pain on the guilty. This philosophical school of thought dates back at least to the late eighteenth century and is associated most strongly with the work of Immanuel Kant.

Retribution concentrates on the detection and sanctioning of the criminal act that has already occurred. It is not interested in the future conduct of offenders or in crime prevention. It holds that an individual who deliberately violates the rights of others should and must be punished. The act of punishment restores the moral order that was breached by the wrongdoing. If an individual has been found guilty of a crime, it is not only possible to punish him or her but it is also necessary to do so. This focus disentangles criminal and youth justice systems from the world of welfare and social problems. Rather, the system is rationalized by concentrating on its core task – identifying young offenders and inflicting punishment.

Retribution has gone through something of a revival since the 1970s, particularly in the USA and the UK. Partly in critique of rehabilitation/correctional strategies, it was argued that any wrongdoing should be met with a sanction proportionate to the severity of the offence. Justice is served when the guilty are given their 'just deserts' – that is, they are punished according to the gravity of their offence within a system of commensurate penalties. The leading proponent of this 'modern retributivism' was Andrew von Hirsch (1976). He argued for a reinstatement of retributive principles but tempered by an acknowledgement of the individual's right to have his or her case dealt with 'fairly' and 'equitably' through procedures of due process. He advocated that the following (neoclassical) concepts be at the centre of contemporary penal philosophy:

- Proportionality of punishment to crime, or the offender is handed a sentence that is in accordance with what the offence deserves.
- Determinacy of sentencing and thus an end to indeterminate, treatment-oriented sentences.
- An end to judicial, professional and administrative discretion.
- An end to disparity in sentencing.
- Equity and protection of rights through due process.
- The predication of penal philosophy on justice and not on control or public condemnation.

In theory, 'retributive just deserts' seems to set limits to punishment (whether in custodial or treatment settings) in some coherent fashion, but the approach has also been subject to critique from all shades of the political spectrum:

- There is a recurring difficulty in achieving any consensus on calculations of seriousness, the ranking of offences and, therefore, what would comprise proportionate and 'acceptable' retribution.
- By denying the social and political contexts in which crime and criminal justice operate, it can readily be appropriated to legitimize punitive penal policies.
- Punitiveness can be tempered by other means – for example, a commitment to rights agendas rather than relying on judicial parsimony (Hudson 1996).

John Muncie

Related entries

'Adulteration'; Community punishment and rehabilitation orders (CPROs); Criminal Justice Act 1991; Due process; Just deserts; Justice; Proportionality; Punitiveness; Sentencing framework; Tariff.

Key texts and sources

Hudson, B. (1996) *Understanding Justice*. Buckingham: Open University Press.

Lacey, M. (1988) *State Punishment: Political Principles and Community Values*. London: Routledge & Kegan Paul.

von Hirsch, A. (1976) *Doing Justice: The Choice of Punishment*. New York, NY: Hill & Wang.

RISK FACTORS

Risk factors are used to predict reoffending and to identify areas for intervention and management.

Risk factors are used to identify and categorize offenders for levels of intervention, to determine sentences and to decide whether offenders are 'safe' enough for release from custodial institutions. Risk factors are derived from meta-analytic studies of offenders in order to identify and define those factors most correlated with offending behaviour. Often referred to as 'criminogenic needs' or risks, these factors can be used in structured assessment tools (such as Asset) to assist practitioners in assessing risk. These tools produce a categorization of risk that might help youth justice practitioners to formulate a risk management plan. Risk factors, particularly for young offenders, are associated with the risk prevention paradigm aimed at identifying 'problem' youngsters and their families for early intervention. Risk factors are used to identify children and young people likely to develop a 'delinquent pathway', with interventions aimed at interrupting these risk trajectories. This approach has gained popularity and momentum in youth justice policy and practice, not least because it appears to be more resource effective.

However, risk prediction remains complex, with the linkage of risk factor(s) to criminal pathway(s) proving to be particularly problematic (Farrington 2000). This is due in large part to the difficulty in establishing the relationship between risk factor(s) and subsequent offending – in essence, demonstrating causal relationships and establishing the relative causal weight of differing risk factors. For example, causal relationships may only be correlations, and it is difficult to attribute weight to different factors when actual causes may be multifactorial and extremely complex (Farrington 2000: 7). For a young person it may be the range and interaction of risk factors that are important, and not just their presence or absence. Furthermore, risk factors can have a differential impact; what impacts on one young person does not necessarily impact on another.

Risk assessment tools usually comprise inventories of risk factors, such as school absence, delinquent peer association, previous convictions and behavioural problems. These inventories can be very wide ranging, covering home and family, immediate networks and locale, attitudes and behaviour, and past convictions. Some assessment tools score risk factors and subsequently assign a risk of reconviction score to the offender. Others are used to identify the problems requiring attention under a risk management plan. Risk factors fall into two broad categories: static and dynamic. Static factors are those that are fixed or are least amenable to change (for example, previous convictions, age and gender). Derived from large-scale studies of offenders, static factors are used to calculate probabilistic reconviction scores. Dynamic factors are those most likely to change over time (for example, employment or housing) and the most open to intervention and change by practitioners (for example, through behavioural programmes, support and/or advocacy). Most assessment tools seek to combine both types of factors and to produce both a reoffence/reconviction probability score and an inventory of dynamic factors amenable to intervention.

While risk factors have increased the consistency and rigour of risk assessment and have enabled practitioners to adopt a more focused approach on 'criminogenic needs', they have also been critiqued on a number of grounds, most notably for producing a 'risk factorology' that reduces offenders (and particularly young offenders) to a mere repository of risks. Concerns have been expressed about the negative consequences of this, particularly for children and young people and for the potential for labelling and net-widening as children who meet a particular 'risk profile' are pulled into the prevention paradigm. Such factors also tend to produce a focus on individual offenders and their families, and less attention on structural factors, such as poverty or social exclusion.

Risk factors are not necessarily universal. Those produced from large cohorts of white young males, for example, may not readily transfer across 'race' and gender. Equally, risk factors associated with specific offences (such as serious sexual crime) might not apply to other offences (such as theft). Recent research and policy attention has turned towards protective factors (those factors that literally provide protection or a barrier to a delinquent career path) and to why some children have resilience to risk factors and how such resilience operates in practice. Within this approach youth justice practitioners and other professionals might seek to strengthen protective factors and to enhance the resilience of the young people in their care.

Risk trajectories for delinquency are also extremely complex and are not necessarily easily predictable on the basis of risk factors. This may require the recognition that delinquent pathways are social processes that have multiple causes; that such causes are not necessarily 'additive' or routinely cumulative (Farrington 2000: 7); and that subtle differences in initial conditions may, over time, produce large differences in outcomes (Byrne 1998: 2–28). This might help to explain why children initially similarly 'risked marked' go on to have quite different pathways and why a proportion of children assessed as 'high risk' at a young age do not actually offend as they grow up.

Hazel Kemshall

Related entries

Actuarialism; Child poverty; Dangerousness; Delinquency; Desistance; Developmental crimin-

ology; Gender and justice; Labelling theory; Multi-agency public protection arrangements (MAPPAs); Net-widening; Protective factors; 'Race' and justice; Social exclusion.

Key texts and sources

Byrne, D. (1998) *Complexity Theory and the Social Sciences.* London: Routledge.
Farrington, D. P. (1995) 'The development of offending and antisocial behaviour from childhood: key findings from the Cambridge Study in Delinquent Development', *Journal of Child Psychology and Psychiatry,* 36: 929–64.
Farrington, D. P. (2000) 'Explaining and preventing crime: the globalization of knowledge – the American Society of Criminology 1999 Presidential Address', *Criminology,* 38: 1–24.
Kemshall, H. (2003) *Understanding Risk in Criminal Justice.* Buckingham: Open University Press.
Sampson, R. J. and Laub, J. H. (1993) *Crime in the Making: Pathways and Turning Points through Life.* Cambridge, MA: Harvard Univerity Press.

RISK MANAGEMENT

Risk management is the reduction of the likelihood that a risky offence, behaviour or event will occur, and/or the reduction of the impact or harm occasioned by the offence, behaviour or event.

Risk management has gained substantial momentum in both youth justice policy and practice as part of the risk prevention paradigm. This is concerned with identifying problematic youths and their families for early intervention. Risk management techniques take many forms but concentrate on alleviating the risk factors that are identified by the use of structured assessment tools. Management interventions range from early preventative programmes (concentrating on parenting, 'correcting' anti-social attitudes and behaviours, and assisting families to lead more socially responsible lives) to intensive cognitive behavioural programmes (delivered either in the community or in custodial settings).

For prolific and serious offenders, risk management may require a multi-modal package provided by a range of agencies and comprising intensive therapy or programmes, educational provision and community support for children and families. Risk management is largely delivered to young offenders through youth offending teams that have the range of agency staff to provide multi-modal interventions. Risk management packages can also contain restrictive conditions – that is, conditions attached to licences or supervision orders (such as curfews and exclusion zones) intended to limit the opportunities to offend or to protect potential victims. Serious sexual and violent offenders can be referred to the multi-agency public protection arrangements for additional resources and closer agency involvement, although the numbers of such offenders are very small (Kemshall *et al.* 2005).

The key elements of effective risk management include expeditious response/intervention to escalating risk and deteriorating behaviour; consistency of worker(s); a close adherence to agency policies; and clearly defined contingency plans in case of breakdown or significant changes in circumstances. Risk management in custodial settings requires a combination of effective programmes, pro-social modelling by staff, pastoral care and positive regimes. Harm reduction, rather than the elimination of all risk, is a key principle of risk management and 'zero risk' is rarely a possibility. Risk management interventions should be well matched to the risk factors identified, proportionate, justified, fair, equitable and delivered as intended. Plans that have included the young offender, that have estab-lished a degree of motivation to comply and that are well balanced between restrictive conditions, support and treatment tend to work best.

The current approach to risk management has been critiqued for overemphasizing restrictive conditions and risk prevention at the expense of rehabilitation and reintegration. The balance between the rights of young offenders and the rights of the wider community – although complex – needs to be carefully considered, as does the appropriate balance between rights, justice and risks (Kemshall forthcoming).

Hazel Kemshall

Related entries

Actuarialism; Administrative criminology; Children's human rights; Cognitive-behaviour programmes; Crime and disorder reduction (CDR); Early intervention; Governance; Intensive Supervision and Surveillance Programme (ISSP); Key Elements of Effective Practice (KEEPs); Multi-agency public protection arrangements (MAPPAs); Protective factors; Rehabilitation; Risk factors; 'Schedule one' offenders.

Key texts and sources

Kemshall, H. (forthcoming) 'Risks, rights and justice: understanding and responding to youth risk', *Youth Justice*.

Kemshall, H., Mackenzie, G., Wood, J., Bailey, R. and Yates, J. (2005) *Strengthening the Multi-agency Public Protection Arrangements. Practice and Development Report* 45. London: Home Office.

Lipsey, M. W. and Wilson, D. B. (1999) 'Effective interventions with serious juvenile offenders', in R. E. Loeber and E. P. Farrington (eds) *Serious and Violent Juvenile Offenders*. London: Sage.

S

SAFEGUARDING

> Safeguarding is the responsibility upon individuals and agencies (through statute and/or guidance) to protect children from maltreatment and to promote their welfare.

The move towards the concept of 'safeguarding' in social policy – signalling a wider agenda than just the protection of children from harm – has reflected core concerns that have been raised through many public inquiries, official reports and guidance and published research, including inquiries led by Sir William Utting (1991, 1997); the Laming Report into the death of Victoria Climbié (2003); both joint chief inspectors' reports entitled *Safeguarding Children* (2002, 2005); the Department of Health publications entitled *Working Together to Safeguard Children* (1991, 1999, 2006); and the Department of Health guidance entitled *Framework for the Assessment of Children and their Families* (2000).

Key themes to have emerged from such publications include the importance of partnership working between agencies and with families; information sharing; multidisciplinary working; integrated services; the accountability and transparency of the delivery of services; and the recognition that all children – irrespective of the 'labels' attached to them – have similar developmental needs.

The Children Act 2004 placed a statutory 'duty' on specified individuals and agencies to ensure the delivery of services to children to promote their welfare. Local safeguarding children boards comprise the key statutory organizational mechanism to safeguard and promote the welfare of children in each local area. Furthermore, the establishment of children's trusts in all local authority areas by 2008 is intended to enable agencies to communicate and work together in fulfilling their duties to safeguard and protect vulnerable children.

The official document that focuses most explicitly on the youth justice system – *Every Child Matters: Change for Children in the Criminal Justice System* (Department for Education and Skills 2004a) – emphasizes two of the five key Every Child Matters outcomes: 'making a positive contribution' (by 'encouraging' children to make 'law-abiding' choices); and 'staying safe' (by 'ensuring' children are safe from 'crime, exploitation, bullying, discrimination and violence'). The document also refers to the importance of 'narrowing the gap' between the outcomes for disadvantaged young people and other children. This passing reference to disadvantage among children in the youth justice system perhaps understates both the level and complexity of adversity typically experienced by such children *and* the need to 'safeguard' them from, and within, the youth justice system itself. There are also tensions between the 'inclusionary' imperatives of Every Child Matters and the 'exclusionary' consequences of much youth justice legislation, policy and practice. The latter includes the 'tough' political and media rhetoric towards children in conflict with the law; the rise in the numbers of children incarcerated; and the use of anti-social behaviour orders for children who are often 'vulnerable' and who might just as readily be conceptualized as 'children in need'.

Sue Howarth

Related entries

Assessment framework; Child abuse; Children in custody; Children's human rights; Child prostitution; Children Act 2004; Children's trusts; Every Child Matters (ECM); Looked-after children (LAC); Munby judgment; Partnership working; Restraint; Vulnerability.

Key texts and sources

Commission for Social Care Inspectorate, Healthcare Commission, Her Majesty's Inspectorate of Constabulary, Her Majesty's Inspectorate of Probation, Her Majesty's Inspectorate of Prisons, Her Majesty's Crown Prosecution Service Inspectorate, Her Majesty's Inspectorate of Courts Administration and Office of Standards in Education (2005) *Safeguarding Children: The Second Joint Chief Inspectors' Report on Arrangements to Safeguard Children*. London: Department of Health Publications (available online at **www.safeguardingchildren.org.uk**).

Department of Health (2006b) *Working Together to Safeguard Children: A Guide to Inter-agency Working to Safeguard and Promote the Welfare of Children*. London: HMSO.

Parton, N. (2006) *Safeguarding Childhood: Early Intervention and Surveillance in a Late Modern Society*. Basingstoke: Palgrave Macmillan.

See the Office of Public Sector Information's website (**http://www.opsi.gov.uk/acts/acts2004**) for the text of the Children Act 2004.

SAFER SCHOOLS PARTNERSHIP (SSP)

The Safer Schools Partnership (SSP) programme aims to promote safety in schools. Programmes vary considerably in structure but, generally, have active police involvement in schools, often in collaboration with other support staff. The role of the police is to work in partnership with children and young people, and school staff in a selected secondary school and its feeder primaries, to identify those most at risk of victimization, offending and social exclusion. The objectives are to improve key behavioural issues in schools, including non-attendance, bullying, anti-social behaviour and offending.

Despite the ostensibly benign objectives of the Safer Schools Partnership (SSP), concerns have been expressed that it represents the expansionary social control tendencies of the youth justice system and might serve to amplify rather than allay anxieties about the delinquent behaviour of some children and young people.

Evaluation of the programme has found a significant reduction in rates of absence (both authorized and unauthorized) in the SSP schools relative to those in comparison schools. GCSE performance also improved relative to the comparison schools. Difficulties with the data prevented much examination of changes in levels of bullying and anti-social behaviour in schools, however. Similarly, the data were unable to support school-level analyses of convictions or arrest, making it impossible to present any robust findings of the impact of the SSP on offending.

Martin Stephenson

Related entries

Anti-social behaviour (ASB); Early intervention; Labelling theory; Net-widening; School non-attendance; Social exclusion; Victimization.

Key texts and sources

Bhabra, S., Hill, E. and Ghate, D. (2004) *Safer School Partnerships: National Evaluation of the Safer School Partnerships Programme*. London: Youth Justice Board and Department for Education and Skills.

Bowles, R., Garcia Reyes, M. and Pradiptyo, R. (2005) *Safer Schools Partnerships*. London: Youth Justice Board (available online at **http://www.yjb.gov.uk/Publications/Scripts/prodView.asp?idProduct=269&eP=**).

'SCHEDULE ONE' OFFENDERS

A 'Schedule One' offender is a convenient but unsatisfactory – and now formally discouraged – shorthand term for a person convicted of an offence against a child under the age of 18 years, with enduring statutory and non-statutory implications for child protection and risk management.

'Schedule One' offences are listed in the first schedule of the Children and Young Persons Act 1933, substantially augmented by ensuing legislation, particularly in respect of sexual offending, such as the Sexual Offences Act 2003. It is often assumed incorrectly that Schedule

One offending pertains exclusively to the sexual abuse of children or to offending by adults. The schedule, however, extends further than this and includes, first, physical assault, cruelty and the neglect of a child under the age of 16; and, secondly, child-on-child offending.

The 1933 Act deals specifically with the implications for convicted persons in respect of fostering, being a registered childminder or working in children's homes, but identification as a Schedule One offender has had much wider non-statutory implications. Prominently, the Prison Service has exercised responsibility (under Instruction to Governors 54/94) to notify the police, probation and local authorities prior to his or her release of anyone identified as such. Notification has enabled local authorities to maintain registers of individuals so identified. Where a Schedule One offender is known to be living with children, a child protection investigation is likely to be activated.

The use of Schedule One as a benchmark in protecting children has proved problematic. The term has proved ill-defined and a source of uncertainty and inconsistent application. It defines persons on a lifelong basis by their offending history rather than the ongoing risks they may pose. It has proved particularly problematic in respect of young offenders who have committed a Schedule One offence against another young person, but who do not necessarily pose a continuing risk towards children.

During 2004 a multi-agency working group undertook a review of Schedule One and its associated procedures. Though Schedule One of the Young Persons Act 1933 remains unrepealed, the review team agreed that the term should be discontinued. In its place a non-statutory list of offences has been identified and circulated, including the major offences that may be committed against children. The use of the term 'Schedule One offender' has been discouraged and new terminology has been adopted: 'an offender who has been identified as presenting a risk or potential risk to children.' Prison notification procedures have been modified accordingly.

It has long been recognized that there should be a measure of local authority discretion, enabling persons with Schedule One status to be approved for fostering or adoption purposes.

There remains a case for a clear, consistent approach to young persons who have committed Schedule One offences to ensure that their status reflects assessed risk rather than a default response to a conviction.

Nigel Stone

Related entries

Child abuse; Children and Young Persons Act 1933; Multi-agency public protection arrangements (MAPPAs); Risk management; Safeguarding; Sex Offender Register; Sexual Offences Act 2003.

Key texts and sources
HM Prison Service (2005) *Change to Procedures set out in IG 54/1994* (Prison Service Instruction 22/05). London: HM Prison Service.
Home Office (2005d) *Guidance on Offences against Children. Home Office Circular* 16/05. London: Home Office.
Nacro (2003b) *Children and Young People who Commit Schedule One Offences.* London: Nacro.
Youth Justice Board (2006i) *Offences against Children.* London: Youth Justice Board.

SCHOOL EXCLUSION

In terms of current legislation, school exclusion is perceived as the consequence of an extreme breach of an authority relationship leading to a child or young person being formally debarred from school. There are three types of exclusion: fixed term, 'informal' and permanent. Rather than a one-off event, permanent exclusion is perhaps better understood as the culmination of a young person's increasing detachment and often follows lengthy periods of non-attendance or periodic fixed-term exclusions.

In 2004–5 there were 389,560 fixed-term exclusions in England. The average length of a fixed-term exclusion was just under four days, but periods of exclusion can extend up to 45 days. The second type of exclusions are those that are sometimes termed 'informal'. This is actually an illegal practice and is, therefore, impossible to quantify precisely, but it has been estimated that it affects up to 18,000 children and young people per annum.

With regard to trends in permanent exclusions, the evidence suggests that, from the mid-1980s, the national totals began to increase quite rapidly from a relatively low base, with a dramatic increase in the early 1990s, a fall at the end of the decade and the resumption of an upward trend by 2001 that has since stabilized at about 10,000 young people per annum. Just as the youth custody population rose substantially during the same period – despite no increase in youth crime – there is little hard evidence of worsening behaviour in schools, although contrary public and professional perceptions and lower tolerance may lie behind both trends.

Exclusion predominantly affects young white males but young black males, young people with special educational needs and 'looked-after children' are disproportionately represented. There is a clear link between the education and youth justice systems and a strong relationship between exclusion from school and offending. There is increasing evidence that this may even be a 'causal relationship'. This may occur through the creation of delinquent peer groups, both outside school and in segregated education; an increased opportunity for offending; the loss of the positive socialization effects of school; a weakening of supervision; and increased chances of later unemployment.

Magistrates often attach considerable importance to educational issues, and school exclusion can serve to ratchet children and young people up the sentencing 'tariff'. Excluded young people are up to twice as likely to receive a custodial sentence as their peers.

Martin Stephenson

Related entries

Children in custody; Connexions; On Track; 'Race' and justice; Risk factors; School non-attendance; Tariff; Youth Lifestyles Survey (YLS).

Key texts and sources

Blyth, E. and Milner, J. (eds) (1996) *Exclusion from School: Inter-professional Issues for Policy and Practice*. London: Routledge.

Parsons, C. (1999) *Education, Exclusion and Citizenship*. London: Routledge.

Stephenson, M. (2007) *Young People and Offending: Education, Youth Justice and Social Inclusion*. Cullompton: Willan Publishing.

SCHOOL NON-ATTENDANCE

School non-attendance covers a large number of children and young people who miss compulsory schooling for a variety of reasons. The overwhelming majority of absences are authorized by the school as a consequence of illness, religious observance, study leave, bereavements or family holidays during term times. A significant number of absences are unauthorized, however. Unauthorized absence includes truancy or parents keeping their children out of school without permission. Children and young people who are long-term non-attenders are often at highest risk of being involved in the youth justice system.

There are virtually no reliable data on long-term school absenteeism and no official definition of what constitutes it or the point when 'unauthorized absence' becomes 'long-term absence'. Some researchers have divided children who do not attend school into two categories: 'truants' and 'school refusers'. The difference is apparently that truants wilfully miss school without parental consent or knowledge whereas school refusers are too afraid to attend school and may stay at home, perhaps with parental consent. Several putative categories of truants have been identified: the traditional or typical truant; the psychological truant; the institutional truant; and the generic truant. These categories are arguably simplistic and too static and serve to obscure complex relations and realities. The actual word 'truant' originated as a term of abuse and is still used pejoratively, which adds little to the analysis of school non-attendance and only compounds the presumption that the fault lies with the child or young person.

Despite the high profile of school non-attendance under successive governments, it is impossible to be precise about its current scale, nature and trends. Methods of data collection and official government statistics do not enable a detailed analysis of the nuances of school non-attendance, which can vary considerably. For example, a child who does not attend school at all for one month makes a similar impact on the statistics as a child who misses one day a week for a complete school term. The causes of the respective non-attendance and the impact on the children – particularly in relation to risks of offending – could be very different in each instance. Furthermore, it is almost impossible to differentiate between non-attendance at particular lessons while at school; sporadic non-attendance at school; regular non-attendance but involving no more than one day a week; and those young people who rarely or never attend. There may be 100,000 long-term school non-attenders, many of whom are involved in the youth justice system.

The causes of school non-attendance have been analysed in terms of individual characteristics, family influences, deprivation, social class, school effectiveness and labour market conditions. In terms of the impact of individual personality/psychology, there is no substantial agreement in the literature. While some researchers have claimed to find an association between non-attendance and unhappiness and unsociability, others have argued that there is no significant correlation between non-attendance and concepts of 'maladjustment'. A much greater degree of consensus is reached over the impact of the family on school non-attendance. A whole range of family difficulties have been identified as contributing to non-attendance, including poverty, unemployment, overcrowded accommodation/housing, disrupted home lives and parents with a history of offending. Chronic non-attendance might be related to parental attitudes to school and parental levels of education.

The correlates of non-attendance for both males and females include delinquent friends, weak parental supervision and low attachment to family and siblings.

The quality of the school environment may also have a crucial role in explaining non-attendance. Furthermore, the withering of the youth labour market since the 1980s – exacerbated by the restrictions of the National Curriculum – has been seen as undermining the 'social contract' with children and young people and as increasing their alienation from school. While there are reported differences in school non-attendance between social groups – with much higher rates among young people from working-class backgrounds – there are also differential effects. High levels of absence have a disproportionate impact on young people from more socially and economically deprived backgrounds.

The unintended consequences of non-educational agency interventions have also been implicated as affecting school attendance. For children 'looked after', regular placement moves often necessitate changes of schools and multiple disruptions may be influential in causing chronic non-attendance. Similarly, the involvement of a child in the youth justice system may accelerate him or her out of the education system. The disruption, loss in school time and 'labelling' effect of (multiple) court appearances tend to disrupt education, and this can be exacerbated by the involvement of youth justice practitioners, which can lead to negative reactions from schools. There is a well established literature linking school non-attendance and offending, but the precise nature of the relationship is unclear.

Young people who are persistently absent from school are far more likely not to participate in education and training after compulsory school age. This may increase the likelihood of offending given that non-participation for 16–18-year-olds is the single most important predictor of unemployment at the age of 21, and there is a significant correlation between offending and unemployment. Achieving stability and quality of employment – which is likely to be affected by academic and vocational qualifications – also appears to be an important variable in respect of desistance and reducing reoffending.

The primary policy response to reduce school non-attendance has been to emphasize the responsibilties of parents to ensure attendance, with increasing sanctions (including imprisonment for those who 'fail' to do so). This has had little apparent effect on the numbers of children and young people out of school, however, and several commentators have argued that the consequences of this approach are likely to be counterproductive.

Martin Stephenson

Related entries

Child poverty; Connexions; Labelling theory; Looked-after children (LAC); New Deal for Young People; Parenting orders; Risk factors; School exclusion; Social exclusion.

Key texts and sources

Stephenson, M. (2007) *Young People and Offending: Education, Youth Justice and Social Inclusion.* Cullompton: Willan Publishing.

Youth Justice Board (2006d) *Barriers to Engagement in Education, Training and Employment for Young People in the Youth Justice System.* London: Youth Justice Board.

SECURE ACCOMMODATION

Secure accommodation refers to children's homes that provide accommodation for the purpose of restricting liberty, approved under Regulation 3 of the Children (Secure Accommodation) Regulation 1991 by the Secretary of State. Secure accommodation in this context means secure children's homes managed by local authorities, the voluntary sector and, more recently, the private sector, as distinct from young offender institutions or secure training centres.

Secure children's homes developed from the approved schools tradition and also have links to community homes with education. They provide accommodation for children and young people with a range of complex problems and behaviours who are thought to place themselves and/or others at significant risk of offending, substance and drug misuse, self-harm, sexual exploitation, running away and going missing, and mental health issues.

Children and young people can be 'placed' in secure accommodation under the provisions of civil (child care/welfare) and criminal (youth justice) statute. In civil cases children are placed as a result of social work planning and decision-making based on their need for protection and safety. For a local authority to place, and keep, a child in secure accommodation, it must apply for, and obtain, a 'secure accommodation order' in a family proceedings court by demonstrating that certain criteria are met as specified by s. 25 of the Children Act 1989. The criteria specified under s. 25 are as follows:

a. i. He/she has a history of absconding and is likely to abscond from any other description of accommodation;

and

ii. If he/she absconds, he/she is likely to suffer significant harm;

or

b. That if he/she is kept in any other description of accommodation, he/she is likely to injure him/herself or other persons.

However, meeting the criteria in itself does not justify restricting the liberty of a child. Only the determination of a court, in granting the secure accommodation order, can do this. These are measures designed to ensure that proper legal safeguards are applied. Additionally, s. 25 criteria only provide for a 'permissive' order. In other words, while it *allows* a local authority to restrict the liberty of a child, it does not *compel* it to do so and it may only do so for as long as the criteria continue to be met.

There are currently 23 secure children's homes in England and Wales. A number have closed in recent years as a result of the fall in the use of secure accommodation for civil/welfare cases and because of the impact of the Youth Justice Board 'block purchasing' contracted beds. The homes provide over 350 places, 230 of which are contracted to the Youth Justice Board, which is responsible for 'placing' children who are remanded or serving custodial sentences (the justice/control function of secure accommodation). Managing the 'mix' of children placed for 'welfare' purposes and those held under youth justice statute presents particular challenges. Although the needs of the two 'groups' of children are very similar, there are differences that arise from managing the reasons for their restriction of liberty; the criteria for the placements; and responding to children's own perceptions of why they are in secure accommodation. There are also key gender issues to consider, with some units being mixed and others being single sex. Owing to the location of the units, children may also be placed many miles from home. A small number of homes offer only welfare/care placements.

Secure children's homes range in size from 5 to 38-bed establishments. The larger homes are normally subdivided into small living units of six or eight children. There is a high staff-to-child ratio that reflects the diverse needs, experiences and behavioural difficulties of the children placed there. The primary task of the homes is to care for children while managing and challenging their often chaotic lives in an effort to promote positive change for a safer lifestyle. In doing so the homes have to tread a careful balance between 'care' and 'control', managing as they do the needs of a group of children who have been brought together through circumstances not of their own choosing.

Secure children's homes introduce a structure into the children's lives based on their social, emotional, health and educational needs. Individual 'plans' and 'packages' are developed to address the specific reasons for the placement and are often complemented by therapeutic interventions and groupwork, along with family work and planning for the child's return into the community.

The homes also aim to ensure that children's primary and specialist health needs are assessed and met. Meeting the mental health needs of children is a particular challenge, and some units have developed resources in partnership with local or regional Child and Adolescent Mental Health Services. However, given the range and depth of needs this is an area that needs to be developed further in order to ensure timely assessment, the identification of needs and intervention, both in the home and in the community, once the child has moved on.

Secure children's homes also offer educational provision, based on the National Curriculum, which often re-engages children who have either been rejected by schools or who have rejected education themselves. The work undertaken is often initially remedially based, allowing children, in some cases, to catch up on many years of school non-attendance and/or school exclusion. In other cases educational provision enables some children and young people to complete GCSE examinations they would otherwise have missed. Inventive and imaginative methods of engaging children in small group settings (that secure accommodation allows) often unearth hidden talents around art and writing, providing children with a means of expressing their life experiences in a constructive and often therapeutic way.

Staff in secure children's homes work in an often volatile and challenging environment on a shift-based system, seven days a week. The quality of the training and development offered to them is improving but, given their role and the scale of their task, more investment is needed.

Secure homes are licensed to operate by the Department for Education and Skills for a maximum of three years and are subject to rigorous 'announced annual' and 'triennial inspections', as well as 'unannounced inspections'. They have to meet the requirements of the Children Act 1989, the Care Standards Act 2000 and the Children's Homes Regulations 2001.

While the placement of children in secure accommodation on civil/welfare grounds has courted controversy for many years, there is at least some consensus that, in certain circumstances, this is necessary. On the other hand, there is overwhelming agreement that, for children whose liberty is restricted in the youth justice system, secure children's homes provide a far more effective and child-centred service than young offender institutions.

Roy Walker

Related entries

Child and Adolescent Mental Health Services (CAMHS); Child prostitution; Children Act 1989; Children in custody; Community homes with education (CHEs); Family proceedings court; Gender and justice; Groupwork; Juvenile secure estate; Looked-after children (LAC); Mental health and young offenders; Remand; Safeguarding; School exclusion; School non-attendance; Vulnerability.

Key texts and sources

Bind, J. and Gerlach, L. (2007) *Improving the Emotional Health and Wellbeing of Young People in Social Care*. London: National Children's Bureau.

Gabbidon, P. and Goldson, B. (1997) *Securing Best Practice*. London: National Children's Bureau.

Goldson, B. (1995) *A Sense of Security*. London: National Children's Bureau.

Goldson, B. (2002b) *Vulnerable Inside: Children in Secure and Penal Settings*. London: Children's Society.

Harris, R. and Timms, N. (1993) *Secure Accommodation in Child Care: Between Hospital or Prison or Thereabouts?* London: Routledge.

O'Neill, T. (2001) *Children in Secure Accommodation: A Gendered Exploration of Locked Institutional Care for Children in Trouble*. London: Jessica Kingsley.

Rose, J. (2002) *Working with Young People in Secure Accommodation*. Hove: Brunner-Routledge.

See also the Secure Accommodation Network's website (http://www.secureaccommodation.org.uk).

SECURE TRAINING CENTRES (STCs)

Secure training centres (STCs) form one part of the juvenile secure estate (alongside young offender institutions and local authority secure children's homes – secure accommodation) in England and Wales. They aim to provide education, vocational training and correction in a secure institutional environment for 12–17-year-olds. Such privately owned and managed centres currently only exist in England and are unique in the context of western European youth justice.

Secure training centres (STCs) are purpose-built centres for child offenders – male and female – up to the age of 17. In 2006 there were four centres, all in England, each run by private operators working under the terms of a private finance initiative with the Youth Justice Board and the Home Office. The four centres are Oakhill in Milton Keynes (opened 2004); Hassockfield in County Durham (opened 1999); Rainsbrook in Rugby (opened 1999); and Medway in Kent (opened 1998). Medway and Rainsbrook are run by Rebound, a subsidiary of Group 4; Oakhill is run by Securicor; and Hassockfield by Premier Custodial Group Ltd. Planning permission to build a fifth centre in Glynneath, Wales, was granted in 2003 but plans for a sixth at Brentwood, Essex, were abandoned in 2004.

STCs differ from young offender institutions in that they have a higher staff-to-young-offender ratio (a minimum of three staff members to eight 'trainees'), are smaller in size and admit children as young as 12. The regimes in STCs, it is claimed, are more constructive and education focused. 'Trainees' are supposedly provided with formal education 25 hours a week, 50 weeks of the year.

STCs were originally formally proposed in 1993, just days after the murder of James Bulger. The original plan was to build five centres for 12–14-year-olds to tackle an assumed 'epidemic' of persistent offending. A secure training order (STO) for 12–14-year-olds was first introduced by the Criminal Justice and Public Order Act 1994. The contract for the first centre at

Medway, however, was not signed until 1997, and the centre did not open until well into the first year of the first New Labour administration in April 1998. It then had places for 40 children. A further two centres of similar size at Rainsbrook and Hassockfield opened in 1999. In 2002 capacity at Medway and Rainsbrook was increased to 76 beds and at Hassockfield to 42. The fourth centre, Oakhill, opened in August 2004 with places for 80 children. In all, the four centres can now accommodate up to 274 children. In July 2006 their population was 234, at a cost of some £164,000 per place a year. The existence of STCs is widely assumed to be the root cause of an 800 per cent rise in under 15-year-olds being sent to custody in England and Wales between 1992 and 2001.

The detention and training order (DTO) replaced the STO in 2000, and the STCs began providing custody for a wider age range (12-17) of DTO 'trainees'. STCs also hold children and young people serving longer terms of detention under ss. 90 and 91 of the Powers of Criminal Courts (Sentencing) Act 2000. The Criminal Justice and Police Act 2001 also provided for young people who had been remanded with a security require-ment to be placed in an STC with the consent of the Secretary of State. In 2002 almost one third of 'trainees' were being held on remand; by 2003 that figure had risen to almost a half.

STCs have proved to be consistently contro-versial, in particular attracting criticism from the United Nations Committee on the Rights of the Child for enabling the incarceration of children at such a young age. An emphasis on security, and the fact that the children are referred to as 'trainees', defines the ethos. A third of all children in STCs are located over 50 miles away from their homes. Visiting hours are not open. Evaluation of the first two years of Medway found a reof-fending rate of 67 per cent. Institutional support following release was notably lacking. The turnover rate of staff in STCs is also extremely high. The adequacy of their training has also been consistently questioned in Commission for Social Care Inspection reports. At Medway, 101 of the 256 staff left in 2003.

Mounting concern about the suitability of such regimes for particularly young and vulnera-ble offenders has grown since two child deaths occurred at Rainsbrook and Hassockfield in 2004.

Gareth Myatt, aged 15, died after being restrained by staff at Rainsbrook STC. He was five feet tall, weighed less than eight stones and was just three days into a 12-month sentence. Adam Rickwood, aged 14, became the youngest person to die in penal custody in the UK at Hassockfield STC. The Carlile Inquiry was established soon after Gareth's death. Lord Carlile's terms of reference were to investigate the use of physical restraint, solitary confinement and forcible strip searching of chil-dren in young offender institutions, STCs and local authority secure children's homes and to make recommendations.

A system of 'restraint' known as 'physical control in care' (PCC) was developed in the late 1990s for use in STCs. In 2002, 'restraint' was used on 2,461 occasions; in 2003 it was used on 3,289 occasions. It has been estimated that, in each STC, restraint is used about twice a day, every day of the year. At Medway 1,818 injuries to children as a result of restraint were reported between January 2004 and June 2005; at Rainsbrook there were 118; Hassockfield reported 177; and Oakhill listed 48 from its opening in August 2004 to August 2005. This suggests the routine use of physical control, not a technique of last resort. Lord Carlile's report in 2006 observed that such treatment would be considered abusive in any other setting.

John Muncie and Barry Goldson

Related entries

Bulger; Child abuse; Children in custody; Criminal Justice and Public Order Act 1994; Deaths in cus-tody; Detention and training orders (DTOs); Every Child Matters (ECM); Family ties of young prison-ers; Juvenile secure estate; Long-term detention; Looked-after children (LAC); Remand; Restraint; Secure accommodation; United Nations Committee on the Rights of the Child; Young offender institu-tions (YOIs); Youth Justice Board (YJB).

Key texts and sources

Carlile, A. (2006) *The Lord Carlile of Berriew QC: An Independent Inquiry into the Use of Physical Restraint, Solitary Confinement and Forcible Strip Searching of Children in Prisons, Secure Training Centres and Local Authority Secure Children's Homes.* London: Howard League for Penal Reform.

Goldson, B. and Coles, D. (2005) *In the Care of the State? Child Deaths in Penal Custody in England and Wales.* London: Inquest.

Hagell, A., Hazel, N. and Shaw, C. (2000) *Evaluation of Medway Secure Training Centre.* London: Home Office.

SELF-REPORTED OFFENDING

Self-report offending surveys provide a supplementary measure of the extent and nature of youth offending alongside official records and victim surveys.

Self-report offending surveys ask people directly about their offending behaviour and can provide information on patterns of offending; the characteristics of offenders; the key correlates of offending; and, if undertaken periodically, trends over time. They provide a useful supplement to officially recorded crime data, which only provide a partial measure of offending as many offenders (and offences) are never formally processed. Moreover, most official data sources do not allow examination of the criminal careers of individual offenders and, for international comparative purposes, are severely hampered by different legal definitions of offences and what is and is not officially recorded as an offence. While victimization surveys are able to overcome some of these shortcomings, they cannot provide data on offenders; do not cover so-called 'victimless crimes' (such as drug misuse); and, as they are usually household surveys, they tend to omit information on offences such as shoplifting and employee theft.

During the 1990s there were two national self-report surveys of youth offending behaviour, one undertaken in 1993 (Graham and Bowling 1995), the other in 1999 (Flood-Page *et al.* 2000). The first survey found that a small minority of young people – no more than 3 per cent – were responsible for over a quarter of all offences attributable to children and young people. Perhaps more significantly, it cast serious doubt on the notion that young people (and young men in particular) tend to grow out of crime as they age. By measuring behaviour rather than official responses to behaviour

(convictions), the survey demonstrated for the first time how young men, as they get older (and presumably smarter), switch to offences with lower detection rates – such as fraud and theft from the workplace – which is not discernible from officially recorded crime data.

Since the end of the 1990s, the Youth Justice Board has published the results of an annual Mori survey, which shows that the overall self-reported offending rate for 11–16-years-olds has been stable over the last five years, with about one in four admitting to committing at least one offence in the previous 12 months. The stability of offending behaviour by young people based on self-report survey data is also confirmed by the Offending, Crime and Justice Survey, conducted by the Home Office between 2003 and 2006 (Wilson *et al.* 2006) and in other countries (Junger-Tas and Decker 2006).

Although self-report offending rates have been successfully validated against officially recorded crime rates, the findings from self-report offending surveys, like data from any survey, still have to be interpreted with care. Response rates tend to be around 70 per cent, and it is likely that the lifestyles of non-respondents are probably more chaotic than those of respondents and their behaviour more deviant. Furthermore, self-report surveys usually exclude young people not living at home – the homeless, for example, or those in prisons or living in residential care homes – and these young people are also more likely to be involved in offending behaviour. Self-report surveys, therefore, tend to underestimate the prevalence, incidence and, especially, the seriousness of offending by young people, although research has shown that, since the numbers of excluded groups are small, their omission does not unduly affect overall prevalence rates (for a more detailed examination of the weaknesses of self-report offending surveys, see Coleman and Moynihan 1996).

John Graham

Related entries

British Crime Survey (BCS); Comparative youth justice; Crime statistics; Gender and justice; Normalization; Persistent young offenders; 'Race' and justice; Victimization; Youth Lifestyles Survey (YLS).

Key texts and sources

Coleman, C. and Moynihan, J. (1996) *Understanding Crime Data*. Buckingham: Open University Press.

Flood-Page, C., Campbell, S., Harrington, V. and Miller, J. (2000) *Youth Crime: Findings from the 1998/99 Youth Lifestyles Survey. Home Office Research Study* 209. London: Home Office.

Graham, J. and Bowling, B. (1995) *Young People and Crime. Home Office Research Study* 145. London: Home Office.

Junger-Tas, J. and Decker, S.H. (eds) (2006) *International Handbook of Juvenile Justice*. Dordrecht: Springer.

Wilson, D., Sharp, C. and Patterson, A. (2006) *Young People and Crime: Findings from the 2005 Offending Crime and Justice Survey. Home Office Online Report* 17/06. London: Home Office (available online at **http://www.homeoffice.gov.uk/rds/offending_survey.html**).

SENTENCING FRAMEWORK

A court imposes a sentence within the bounds of a sentencing framework that is determined by statutory aims and principles, human rights obligations, common and case law, sentencing guidelines and statutory criteria and limitations. Thus, sentencing frameworks change or adapt over time.

In England and Wales, the proportionality principle has conventionally played a major part in defining the sentencing framework but, more recently, the emphasis has tended towards sentencing the *offender* rather than the *offence*. The human rights principle that the best interests of the child should have primacy is also undermined, placing youth justice sentencing at odds with international conventions, standards, treaties and rules. The youth justice system in Northern Ireland has been reviewed in recent years and there is a relatively new framework in place. A stronger welfare principle than exists in England and Wales and the introduction of youth conferences in statute have embodied a restorative approach. The Scottish system is also traditionally welfare oriented and all but the most serious offending is dealt with through children's hearings. The system in Scotland, however, is facing changes that are controversial, and a youth court has been piloted in recent years.

The emphasis here rests with England and Wales where, at the time of writing, there are around 20 substantive sentences available to either, or both, the youth and Crown courts, together with a number of ancillary orders. These include fines and discharges, the referral order, a range of community orders and a number of custodial sentences. Most orders have a minimum and maximum duration – or value – and some have a variety of requirements that can be attached. Some can be combined with others, as is commonly the case with curfew orders.

In the face of such a range of options – and to ensure some degree of proportionality, consistency, fairness, parity and justice – a sentencing framework has evolved that limits sentencing options according to the nature of the particular offence and the offender. On the other hand, justice demands that the court has some degree of discretion to allow for consideration of the individual characteristics and circumstances on a case-by-case basis. There is, therefore, a difficult balance to be struck between the mandatory and the discretional. In recent years, there has been something of a shift towards the mandatory, exemplified by the referral order and preventive custodial sentences (detention for public protection).

The statutory aim of the youth justice system, provided by s. 37 of the Crime and Disorder Act 1998, is to prevent offending by children and young persons, and this applies to the work of all of those involved in the system. The Youth Justice Board has overseen the development of policies and practices that seek to be congruent with that aim. The courts have, for centuries, sentenced in accordance with a set of, sometimes competing, aims and purposes that have included, for example, deterrence, retribution, prevention, the protection of the public and rehabilitation. The government is proposing to introduce statutory purposes of sentencing for the youth court that are contained in the Criminal Justice and Immigration Bill 2006–7 to 2007–8. These include rehabilitation and restoration but also introduce punishment. Perhaps the most contentious relationship in respect of sentencing falls between the imperatives of 'preventing offending' and 'punishment', on the one hand, and the 'best interests' and 'welfare of the child' principles on the other. The 'welfare of the child' (a paramount principle in family court proceedings) and the 'best interests of the child' (given primacy in the United Nations Convention on the Rights of the Child) are of limited applicability in the youth justice context. At present, criminal courts must 'have regard' to the welfare of the child or young person – under the terms of s. 44 of the Children and Young Persons Act 1933 – but this provision falls short of paramountcy. Equally, the United Nations Committee on the Rights of the Child has urged the government to give greater primacy to the 'best interests' of the child, but this has not been realized to date.

The most significant principle in the current youth justice system is arguably that of proportionality, an important human right in criminal proceedings. The current sentencing framework has proportionality at its centre, as provided by the Criminal Justice Act 1991 (CJA). In essence, the CJA 1991 required that the severity of the disposal should be commensurate with the seriousness of the offence, often referred to as 'just deserts'. The severity of the sentence is notionally measured by the degree of restriction of liberty involved. Thus, at the sharpest end of the spectrum is a custodial sentence (removing all liberty) and, at the less severe end, are restrictions brought about by financial penalties.

The CJA 1991 established thresholds that, in effect, created three sentencing bands within which most available sentences are now located in law, although there are exceptions. The higher band is where custodial sentences are located and the court must be of the opinion that the offence, or combination of offences, is 'so serious' that only such a sentence is justified. The middle band comprises the range of community sentences, including action plan orders, attendance centre orders and supervision orders. A new 'menu-based' youth rehabilitation order is proposed by the Criminal Justice and Immigration Bill 2006–7 to 2007–8 that is currently before Parliament and, if passed, it will replace all existing community orders. In sentencing in the community sentence band, the court must form an opinion that the offence, or combination of offences, is 'serious enough' to warrant such a sentence. The lower band consists of less severe disposals, including fines, discharges and the reparation order.

Some sentences do not fit neatly into the three bands, and this applies particularly to the referral order. Several commentators have argued that the referral order is, at least potentially, at odds with the principle of proportionality. Furthermore, and arguably more problematically, are the custodial orders that can be made not only according to the seriousness of the offence but also on the basis of 'assessments' of potential future 'risk' of harm to the public in the event of further offending. Thus, detention for public protection and the extended sentence were implemented in 2005 and are defined in statute as preventive sentences. A number of non-governmental organizations consider these to be contrary to children's human rights, and such actuarial measures have certainly led to increasing numbers of children and young people being detained in the juvenile secure estate.

In establishing the level of seriousness prior to passing sentence, the court should make an initial assessment. Courts may turn to sentencing guidelines and/or their own 'bench book', which provide a matrix of specific offences and corresponding 'gravity scores', and the possible effect of aggravating or mitigating factors. Some factors are considered to be aggravating by statute, including racially aggravated offending and offending whilst on bail. Nevertheless, the court should also take account of personal mitigation – factors relating to the child or young person – including welfare factors, age and maturity and positive attributes. It is also possible for the court to take account of 'good character' and/or to reduce the severity of the sentence in recognition of early guilty pleas.

In finally selecting a sentence, the court may take account of information that indicates what is most likely to prevent reoffending; to help to rehabilitate; to make reparation to a victim; and to promote the welfare of the child or young person. For example, the court should not make a sentence that removes a child from his or her family if avoidable (also a matter of children's human rights). Equally, the sentence – taking account of all factors – should be the one that is most suitable for the child or young person.

There is little doubt that proportionality is now under threat as policy dialogue and statute have moved from a focus on the *offence* to a focus on the *offender*. The former approach, which held sway under the CJA 1991, has been significantly eroded as courts are able, or are required, to take greater account, for example, of the child's offending history and/or the persistence of minor offending. In particular, the Criminal Justice Act 2003 provided for courts to regard previous convictions as aggravating factors. This allows for more severe sentencing than the offence(s) actually before the court would and, ultimately, a relatively minor offence can result in a custodial sentence where there are previous convictions. It is clear that changes in the sentencing framework can have a significant impact, most particularly on custodial sentencing rates.

Geoff Monaghan

Related entries

Children's human rights; Crime and Disorder Act 1998; Criminal Justice Act 1991; Criminal Justice Act 1993; Criminal Justice and Immigration Bill 2006–7 to 2007–8; Criminal Justice and Public Order Act 1994; Crown courts; Dangerousness; Detention for public protection (DPP); Gravity factors (Prosecution and sentencing); Mandatory sentences; Menu-based sentences; Pre-sentence reports (PSRs); Proportionality; Rehabilitation; Reparation; Sentencing guidelines; United Nations Convention on the Rights of the Child (UNCRC).

Key texts and sources

Cadman, S. (2005) 'Proportionality in the youth justice system', in T. Bateman and J. Pitts (eds) *The RHP Companion to Youth Justice.* Lyme Regis: Russell House.

Nacro (2003d) *The Sentencing Framework for Children and Young People. Youth Crime Briefing.* London: Nacro.

Nacro (2006c) *Nacro Guide to the Youth Justice System in England and Wales.* London: Nacro.

Piacentini, L. and Walters, R. (2006) 'The politicization of youth crime in Scotland and the rise of the "Burberry court"', *Youth Justice,* 6: 43–61.

Whyte, B. (2005) 'Youth justice in other UK jurisdictions: Scotland and Northern Ireland', in T. Bateman and J. Pitts (eds) *The RHP Companion to Youth Justice.* Lyme Regis: Russell House.

SENTENCING GUIDELINES

Sentencing guidelines are produced to assist sentencers in deciding on the appropriate disposals and to encourage consistency in sentencing.

In England and Wales, sentencing guidelines are now produced by the Sentencing Guidelines Council (SGC), an independent body established by the Criminal Justice Act 2003, which is chaired by the Lord Chief Justice and which also includes seven judicial and four non-judicial members. The SGC is advised by the Sentencing Advisory Panel (created by the Crime and Disorder Act 1998), and there is also extensive consultation on new guidelines. Previously, guidelines were developed by the Court of Appeal and the Magistrates' Association. The SGC has not yet produced a general guideline on the sentencing of children and young people but has made provision for youths. For example, its guidance on robbery gives a separate guideline and factors to be taken into consideration for young offenders. Further, in its guideline entitled *Overarching Principles: Seriousness*, it states (para. 1.25) that youth, where it affects the responsibility of the individual defendant, is a factor indicating significantly lower culpability.

Section 172 of the Criminal Justice Act 2003 imposes a duty on the court to have regard to sentencing guidelines issued by the SGC as definitive, as revised by subsequent guidelines so issued. For many offences, however, no SGC guidelines have yet been produced. In the youth court, therefore, for many offences the relevant guidelines remain those produced in the *Youth Court Bench Book* by the Judicial Studies Board.

Guidelines may also appear in statute. Schedule 21 to the Criminal Justice Act 2003 includes 'general principles' for the sentencing of murder, for example, with a number of starting points and aggravating/mitigating factors. While not formally termed 'guidelines', they are of the same character.

In Scotland, the Sentencing Commission for Scotland published a report in September 2006 recommending the setting up of an Advisory

Panel for Sentencing in Scotland to produce draft sentencing guidelines which could then be adopted, with any appropriate modifications, by the Appeal Court of the High Court of Justiciary.

Sally Ireland

Related entries

Criminal Justice Act 2003; Crown courts; Gravity factors (prosecution and sentencing); Menu-based sentencing; Sentencing framework; Youth courts.

Key texts and sources

Judicial Studies Board (2006) *Youth Court Bench Book* (2nd edn). London: Judicial Studies Board (available online at **http://www.jsboard.co.uk/ magistrates/ycbb/index.htm**).

Sentencing Commission for Scotland (2006) *The Scope to Improve Consistency in Sentencing.* Edinburgh: Sentencing Commission for Scotland (available online at **http://www.scottishsentencing commission.gov.uk/publications.asp**).

Tonry, M. (2004) *Punishment and Politics.* Cullompton: Willan Publishing.

See the Office of Public Sector Information's website (**http://www.opsi.gov.uk/acts/acts2003/20030044. htm**) for the text of the Criminal Justice Act 2003.

See also the Sentencing Guidelines Council's website (**http://www.sentencing-guidelines.gov.uk**).

SEX OFFENDER REGISTER

The 'Sex Offender Register' is the common expression for the records held by the police arising from the statutory requirement that sex offenders should notify the police of their address details and change of circumstances. The register is intended to provide greater knowledge of the whereabouts of such offenders in the interests of public protection.

The Sex Offenders Act 1997 provides that offenders convicted of – or cautioned, warned or reprimanded for – a 'relevant offence' are subject to 'notification requirements' (commonly known as registration requirements) in respect of specified personal details, recorded and retained by the police. The current statutory scheme falls within Part Two of the Sexual Offences Act 2003, 'relevant offences' being listed in Schedule Three of the Act and not restricted to offending against children. The obligation to notify does not depend on a court order and lasts for the duration of the 'notification period'. This varies on a sliding scale according to the outcome or disposal of the offender's case. Where the offender is sentenced to a custodial term of 30 months or longer, liability is indefinite, while a custodial term exceeding 6 months but less than 30 months attracts a period of 10 years. Failure to notify is a criminal offence punishable by up to five years' imprisonment.

Duration liability is modified for offenders aged under 18 in respect of periods of 10 years or less, running for a half of the period specified for adults. In respect of young offenders the court may make 'parental directions' requiring the adult with parental responsibility to comply with notification requirements, non-compliance being an offence. The Probation Service and youth offending teams are not under any statutory duty to inform the police about sex offenders known to them but may do so in accordance with good practice protocols.

The offender is required to provide initial notification within 72 hours of sentence/caution or his or her release from custody, supplying his or her date of birth, home address (and other addresses at which he or she regularly stays), name(s) used and National Insurance number. Thereafter, the offender must supply any changes in notification details within three days. Additionally, the offender must re-notify his or her details, even where these have not changed, within 12 months of the last time when he or she was required to notify. On notification the police can require the offender to be photographed and fingerprinted.

As Plotnikoff and Woolfson (2000) identified in their research on registration under the Sex Offenders Act 1997, the scheme is not fully comprehensive, given that the legislation has very limited retrospective effect and there can be slippage in the provision of information by relevant agencies to the police. There is also no national 'sex offender register' as such, local force information being relayed to the Police

National Computer. However, the Home Office estimates a notification compliance rate of 97 per cent, and recent developments in police intelligence (such as the ViSOR database – Violent and Sex Offenders Register) have enhanced access to pertinent information.

Nigel Stone

Related entries

Multi-agency public protection arrangements (MAPPAs); 'Schedule One' offenders; Sexual Offences Act 2003.

Key texts and sources

Plotnikoff, J. and Woolfson, R. (2000) *Where Are They Now? An Evaluation of Sex Offender Registration in England and Wales. Police Research Series Paper* 126. London: Home Office.

SEXUAL OFFENCES ACT 2003

The Sexual Offences Act 2003 aims to enhance public protection by reframing the ambit and punishment of sexual crime and by expanding the statutory regulation of sex offenders in the community.

The ambitious Sexual Offences Act 2003 – which came into force on 1 May 2004 (but without retrospective effect) – seeks to overhaul the spectrum of sexual crime to provide a code that more accurately encapsulates the range of exploitation and invasiveness. For example, 'rape' now encompasses the penile penetration of a victim's vagina, anus or mouth, while the former over-general crime of 'indecent assault' is replaced by new offences of 'assault by penetration' (penetration of the vagina or anus with any part of the perpetrator's body or by an object); 'sexual assault' (any kind of intentional sexual touching of the victim's body); and 'causing a person to engage in a sexual activity'. In each instance the absence of active consent is critical, 'consent' being defined as agreement by

choice where the individual has the freedom and capacity to make that choice. An honest but unreasonable belief that the complainant was consenting no longer affords a defence.

As regards the sexual abuse of children, the Act clarifies that sexual activity with a child aged under 13 is always unlawful and that children of that age cannot give valid consent. Penile penetration of a child under 13 thus counts as 'rape', and other forms of sexual exploitation of this age group attract heightened penalties. The legal age for young persons to consent to sexual activity remains 16, and the Act specifies a range of offences intended to afford extra protection for children aged 13–15. However, where the offender is aged under 18, the maximum penalties are lower.

The government and the Crown Prosecution Service have acknowledged that the letter of the new law encompasses sexual activity between adolescents of a consensual and non-exploitative nature – whether through experimentation or mutual affection – and have sought to offer guidance to ensure that criminal justice sanctions do not apply inappropriately to sexual activity involving young persons of similar age where there is no evidence of coercion or corruption.

To reflect the high incidence of sexual exploitation within families, the Sexual Offences Act 2003 creates offences such as 'sexual activity with a child family member', covering children up to age 18, while widening the definition of 'family' to include such persons as foster-siblings and lodgers in the household. As regards sexual misconduct of a non-contact nature – whether as a prelude to or in place of 'contact' offending – the Act introduces a raft of new offences, such as 'meeting a child following grooming' and 'voyeurism'.

In seeking to manage the risk of sexual reoffending, the Act revises, in strengthened form, provisions requiring offenders to notify their details to the police, also introducing the power to impose 'sexual offences prevention orders' prohibiting specified conduct and 'risk of sexual harm orders'.

Nigel Stone

Related entries

Child abuse; Child prostitution; Safeguarding; 'Schedule one' offenders; Sex Offender Register.

Key texts and sources

Stevenson, K., Davies, A. and Gunn, M. (2004) *Blackstone's Guide to the Sexual Offences Act 2003*. Oxford: Oxford University Press.

The Crown Prosecution Service's document, *Sexual Offences Act 2003*, is available online at http://www.cps.gov.uk/legal/section7/chapter_a.html; Sexual Offences and Child Abuse by Young Offenders is available online at http://www.cps.gov.uk/legal/section4/chapter_b.html#26.

See the Office of Public Sector Information's website (http://www.opsi.gov.uk/acts/acts2003/20030042.htm) for the text of the Sexual Offences Act 2003.

SHERIFF COURTS

The sheriff court is one of three types of criminal court in Scotland (the others are the district and high court). It deals with cases under two procedures: summary (less serious cases), where the sheriff adjudicates on questions of fact and on sentence; and solemn (more serious cases), where a jury of 15 makes decisions on questions of fact (a simple majority is sufficient to convict) and the sheriff determines the sentence. Appeals from the sheriff court on conviction and/or sentence are dealt with in the high court, which sits as an appeal court. The sheriff court also has a number of functions in respect of both the children's hearing system (dealing with matters of proof in disputed cases and also with appeals) and civil cases (relating, for example, to divorce, property disputes and debt).

The sheriff court is involved with child offenders in three main ways. First, children over the age of 8 (currently the age of criminal responsibility in Scotland) can be prosecuted in the criminal courts. Although such prosecutions are rare in the case of children under the age of 16 (with most being dealt with in the children's hearing system), the overwhelming majority of 16 and 17-year-old offenders are dealt with by the courts. However, the courts do have the power to remit cases (of all children under the age of 18) to the children's hearing system for advice and/or disposal and must remit for advice if the child is subject to a children's hearing supervision requirement.

Second, the sheriff court is involved in proof hearings where the grounds for referral to a hearing are disputed by the child or his or her parents. In the case of offence referrals, the sheriff must decide whether the grounds have been established beyond reasonable doubt (for non-offence cases, the standard of proof is on the balance of probabilities). Third, the sheriff court deals with appeals against hearing's decisions. In such cases the sheriff is empowered to substitute his or her decision for that of the panel.

Under summary procedure the sheriff can impose a fine of up to £5,000 in common law crimes and a maximum prison sentence of three months (although this can be increased to six months for those convicted of a second or subsequent offence of dishonesty or personal violence). The Criminal Proceedings (Reform) (Scotland) Act 2007, however, will increase these powers to fines of up to £10,000 and 12 months' imprisonment. Under solemn procedure the sheriff can impose unlimited fines in common law crimes and a maximum of three years' imprisonment (although cases can be remitted to the high court if a longer prison sentence is needed). For children under the age of 16, the most commonly used disposal is remit to the children's hearing system; for all other cases the most common disposal is a fine (around two thirds of cases each year).

Lesley McAra

Related entries

Anti-social Behaviour (Scotland) Act 2004; Appeal; Children (Scotland) Act 1995; Children's hearing system; Summary justice.

Key texts and sources

Scottish Executive (2007) *Criminal Proceedings in Scottish Courts, 2005/06. Statistical Bulletin, Criminal Justice Series*. Edinburgh: Scottish Executive (available online at http://www.scotland.gov.uk/Publications/2007/03/21083652/0).

See the Office of Public Sector Information's website for the texts of the Criminal Procedure (Scotland) Act 1995 (http://www.opsi.gov.uk/ACTS/acts1995/Ukpga_19950046_en_1.htm) and the Criminal Proceedings (Reform) (Scotland) Act 2007 (http://www.opsi.gov.uk/legislation/scotland/acts2007/20070006.htm).

SOCIAL EXCLUSION

The 'official' conceptualization of 'social exclusion' was provided in a speech by Tony Blair, the Prime Minister at the time, at the launch of the Social Exclusion Unit in 1997: 'Social exclusion is a shorthand term for what can happen when people or areas suffer from a combination of linked problems such as unemployment, poor skills, low incomes, poor housing, high crime environments, bad health and family breakdown.'

Throughout the 1980s and 1990s, the UK had witnessed startling increases in poverty: between 1979 and 1989, the numbers of those at or below the official 'poverty line' (in receipt of income support) increased from 7.7 million (14 per cent of the general population) to 11.3 million (20 per cent of the general population). The proportion of the population with incomes below 50 per cent of average income increased from 4.4 million to 10.4 million. By the late 1990s, the UK had one of the highest levels of child poverty of any industrialized country, as well as very substantial inequality. These, and other poverty measures, pointed to the fact that poor people did not just have less than others (that is, received unequal income) but had inadequate resources to meet their, and their families', needs. Poverty was about what people had or did not have (Alcock *et al.* 1995).

However, the experience of being poor was not just about cash income and expenditure. It was about lacking decent housing, health and education. The concept of 'deprivation', introduced in the 1970s, captured the wider ideas of having an inadequate lifestyle in contemporary society and the inability of people to gain access to services or to participate in what most would regard as normal activities – taking a holiday, having regular hot meals or going to the cinema. Deprivation was thus about what people were able to do, or not to do.

The term 'social exclusion' gained wide currency in political, policy and academic circles from the late 1990s, suggesting a process, rather than a state, of poverty (Howarth *et al.* 1988; Gordon *et al.* 2000). It initially focused not just, or even primarily, on poor people themselves in order to explain their poverty. People experienced social exclusion because of others' actions or inactions. For example, one study found that a quarter of a million young people had disappeared from education, employment and training. Disproportionate numbers of these were black and Asian and had dropped out because of the effects of racism in schools or the care system, because of crises at home and because of the failure of agencies to support them (Britton *et al.* 2002).

Social exclusion potentially affects a wider range of people than those who are just materially poor, for the actions of others can exclude people on the basis of their ethnicity, age, or disability, for example. These forms of exclusion can be both overlapping and cumulative over time and, in this way, can create or accentuate social divisions and isolate social groups. As a result, measuring social exclusion involves looking at a wide range of indicators. Social exclusion and the implications of this for those who are excluded were, it was initially argued, the results of social processes within the broader society and not due to the failings of those who are excluded. Social exclusion was thus a matter of what others do to us, or how we experience the structures, mechanisms and processes which shape our lives, although some commentators (such as the American theorist, Charles Murray) continued to regard social exclusion as self-inflicted. Institutional racism, as described in the Macpherson Report (1999), is another good example of the way in which social exclusion could operate to exclude people – here on the basis of their ethnicity.

Over the past ten years, the government's Social Exclusion Unit (SEU) has produced a substantial series of reports focusing on differing population groups, including young people, those who are excluded from school, those living in poor neighbourhoods and members of minority ethnic groups. These have provided often comprehensive analyses of the nature of social exclusion linked to a series of policy proposals that have found their way into major national social programmes. For example, the origins of the Children's Fund and Sure Start programmes can be traced to early SEU reports.

However, the term social exclusion is neither new nor unproblematic. It can be traced back to the 1950s within a French context where it was used in a perjorative way to talk about groups at the margins of society, but it became a more mainstream descriptor during the lives of the three European anti-poverty programmes of the 1980s and 1990s. As recently as 2000, the EU announced a programme 'of community action to encourage co-operation between member states to combat social exclusion'.

The contradictions in the use of the term are shown most clearly in the work of the SEU itself: its brief excludes it from examining such basic questions as the adequacy of benefits (which a huge volume of research shows to be quite insufficient to maintain decent standards of living) or of the causes of inequality. Further, it focuses not on the actions of those controlling the mechanisms and processes excluding the poor but, again, on the poor themselves, thus implicating them in their own exclusion. This narrows the focus of its work on to shaping the behaviour of organizations and individuals, particularly the poor themselves. Thus the term, while widely used in current policy debates, in reality obscures as much as it clarifies the nature and causes of poverty. From a radical perspective, a focus on social exclusion can be seen as an organized attempt by the state to incorporate people at the margins into flexible and increasingly global labour markets characterized by insecurity, low wages and poor conditions (Byrne 1999). Increasingly, this process of incorporation will require stigmatizing the poor – as recent policy on lone-parent and disability benefits has demonstrated – and the key question then is: exclusion from or inclusion into what? The answer is to a society characterized by huge structural inequalities.

Gary Craig

Related entries

Child poverty; Critical criminology; Looked-after children (LAC); 'Race' and justice; School exclusion; School non-attendance; Social inclusion; Social justice; Sure Start.

Key texts and sources

Alcock, P., Craig, G., Dalgliesh, K. and Pearson, S. (1995) *Combating Local Poverty*. London: Local Government Management Board.
Britton, L., Chatrik, B., Coles, B., Craig, G., Bivand, P., Mumtaz, S., Burrows, R., Convery, P. and Hylton, C. (2002) *Missing Connexions: The Career Dynamics and Welfare Needs of Black and Minority Ethnic Young People at the Margins*. Bristol: Policy Press.
Byrne, D. (1999) *Social Exclusion*. Buckingham: Open University Press.
Gordon, D., Adelman, L., Ashworth, K., Bradshaw, J., Levitas, R., Middleton, S., Pantazis, C., Patsios, D., Payne, S., Townsend, P. and Williams, J. (2000) *Poverty and Social Exclusion in Britain*. York: Joseph Rowntree Foundation.
Howarth, G. et al. (1998) *Monitoring Poverty and Social Exclusion*. York: Joseph Rowntree Foundation/New Policy Institute (and subsequent annual updates).
Macpherson, Sir W. (1999) *The Stephen Lawrence Inquiry: Report of an Inquiry by Sir William Macpherson of Cluny* (Cm 4262-1). London: HMSO.
Mathiesen, T. (1974) *The Politics of Abolition*. Oxford: Martin Robertson.

SOCIAL HARM

Social harm refers to social practices and discourses that occur *within* and *beyond* the criminal justice arena as a means to highlight how serious harm or injurious practices do not, of necessity, become recognized within legal and/or state-defined discourses.

A focus on social harm provides critical criminologists with a means of challenging narrow and fairly predictable state-legal definitions of 'crime' as the predominant lens through which advanced societies identify, process and sanction harmful acts. This points to an acknowledgement that criminology itself promotes a tapered approach in its overarching commitment to state-fostered definitions of crime. 'Crime', in other words, is a vehicle for talking about what are mostly petty events that create relatively modest physical, financial and social burdens. Utilizing the vehicle of 'crime' – with its peculiar focus on the street and 'troublesome' youth – deflects attention and debate from more pressing social harms (corporate crime, child poverty, sexual and domestic violence and injurious acts committed by state servants), while fuelling a criminalization process which 'foreclose[s] social policy or other responses to events' (Hillyard and Tombs 2005: 10).

Importantly, from a social harm perspective, criminalization is a form of social injury in itself that – in leading to punishment – neither rehabilitates nor deters but inflicts further penalization through social stigma, loss of work and instability in home life. Crime control practice is itself, therefore, ineffective (in terms, for example, of reconviction rates on release from prison), expensive and philosophically bankrupt. And yet 'crime' (its imagery and ideological thrust) remains a powerful, political organizing tool not least in relation to the work of criminologists but also in relation to expenditure on law and order in the UK outstripping other social policy interventions (Hillyard *et al.* 2004).

A social harm approach identifies and challenges political priorities in the social policy arena and requires a rethinking of victimization beyond the narrow remit of legal boundaries. This could include consideration of physical harms (including 'accidents', child abuse, illness, harms resulting from brutality and/or omissions by state or private officials); financial and economic harm resulting from fraud and the redistribution of wealth and income between rich and poor; emotional and psychological harm (for example, those inflicted by criminal justice practice itself); and cultural harms emanating from blocked access to educational and intellectual development. A social harm approach attempts to 'measure' harm in part by utilizing indicators (statistical *and* qualitative) often ignored in official crime control approaches and criminological research. This is done for two primary reasons: first, in order to reconfigure what is meant by 'harm'; and, second, to formulate possible responses organized in social and public policy arenas that rely less on merely criminal justice procedures.

The implications of developing a social harm perspective in relation to 'youth justice' are significant both in terms of what goes on *inside* the formal arena of youth justice, and in terms of extra-judicial factors that impact on the life chances of young people. As many critical voices recognize, these two arenas are interrelated and can reinforce and reflect harmful practice in each domain. First, in opposition to seeing young people as public demons or folk devils (Valentine 2006) – as the central symbolic and visualized harbingers of 'public harm' – a social harm perspective challenges long-standing moral panics around youth as a form of discursive violence which acts as a backdrop to the legitimation of other 'corrective' youth-orientated interventions. Second, this point is particularly salient when we consider that the children and young people who are typically drawn into youth corrective networks (in particular, child prisoners) are from poor and often violent backgrounds characteristic of multiple social deprivation (Goldson and Coles 2005). Third, youth justice policy has, in the last 20 years, come to reinforce social deprivation in being increasingly circumscribed through a crime, law and disorder agenda, with a more recent emphasis on 'toughness' and punitive intervention. Despite the stabilization of serious juvenile crime in this period, 'we have seen a renewed emphasis being placed on the need to detect the alleged criminal proclivities of the children of the unemployed and working poor' (Garrett 2004: 63). The increase in resources and effort that underpin this punitive policing and surveillance agenda can be contrasted to the paucity of resources made available for cultural and leisure activity for the young – which currently stands at 17 pence a day for each teenager in the UK. The politics of social disadvantage at work here is compounded for the children from relatively poor backgrounds – a group that has expanded by 200,000 to 3.8 million in 2005–6 (its highest point since 1961). Fourth, this can be contrasted with an intensification in the delivery of pain within crime-come-social policy responses to young people evident in the increase in 12–14-year-olds held in penal custody in England and Wales (up by 800 per cent between 1994 and 2004). In 2003–4 it cost £293.5 million to keep children in penal custody. The levels of death, self-injury and attempted suicide have become 'more commonplace' and 'given the increasing use of penal custody for children … more death, harm and damage is certain to follow' (Goldson and Coles 2005: xviii–xx).

Forcing a debate on social harm encourages us to confront the wider process of cultural and political disenfranchisement and economic disadvantage that underpins the criminalization of youth. The youth justice system is not in the best position to deal with the myriad of problems that young people can find themselves up against. Widening the focus and challenging the harm of official policy also mean reclaiming space for children as legitimate members of the polity (Valentine 2006). Therefore, in reversing the image of the youthful predatory stalker of public realms, critical academics are also engaged in supporting the voice and capacity of young people to shape and enrich the meaning of 'public space'.

Roy Coleman

Related entries

Abolitionism; Child poverty; Criminalization; Criminalization of social policy; Deaths in custody; Decriminalization; Demonization; Punitiveness; Social exclusion; Social inclusion; Social justice.

Key texts and sources

Garrett, P.M. (2004) 'The electronic eye: emerging surveillant practices in social work with children and families', *European Journal of Social Work*, 7: 57–71.

Goldson, B. and Coles, D. (2005) *In the Care of the State? Child Deaths in Penal Custody in England and Wales*. London: Inquest.

Hillyard, P., Sim, J., Tombs, S. and Whyte, D. (2004) 'Leaving a "stain upon the silence": contemporary criminology and the politics of dissent', *British Journal of Criminology*, 44: 369–90.

Hillyard, P. and Tombs, S. (2005) 'Beyond criminology', in P. Hillyard *et al.* (eds) *Criminal Obsessions: Why Harm Matters more than Crime*. London: Crime and Society Foundation.

Valentine, G. (2006) *Public Space and the Culture of Childhood*. Aldershot: Ashgate.

SOCIAL INCLUSION

Social *exclusion* largely refers to what some people (with power) do to others (without power), or how identifiable groups of people experience the structures, mechanisms and processes that shape and limit their lives. Social *inclusion* might be defined as policy directed at changing the same structures, mechanisms and processes in order to remove the barriers that hinder people's full participation in society.

While social *exclusion* is a widely used, if problematic, term, there has been comparatively little discussion of the concept of social *inclusion*. This is largely because most commentators tend to see social inclusion simply as the obverse of social exclusion, often using the terms interchangeably (although the Scottish Executive has consistently used the term social inclusion). In this way, social exclusion and social inclusion are conceived as antonyms, whereby 'exclusion' describes the condition or issue and 'inclusion' describes the aspiration or objective. Social exclusion – conceptualized by the Social Exclusion Unit as the loss of access to the most important life chances that a modern society offers; the condition of being detached from the very organizations and communities of which society is composed – has social, cultural, economic and political dimensions that comprise a complex process rather than a state of being. Social inclusion then becomes the policy objective to address it.

This objective has been taken up by a wide range of organizations and has formed the basis of numerous central and local government initiatives. The Local Government Association (LGA) (1999) – representing English and Welsh local authorities – published evidence of the ways in which local authorities aim to promote social inclusion. These accounts cover policy and service interventions in the areas of anti-poverty work, equal opportunities, regeneration, health, education, training and employment, community safety and transport. The LGA argues that local councils, which had historically developed anti-poverty strategies based on benefits take-up and debt counselling, widened these strategies to include these other interventions, thus 'broadening their anti-poverty strategies into social inclusion strategies'. The term social inclusion, however, is not defined in this report except, again, as a polar opposite to social exclusion. Local councils are, the LGA reports, engaged in many area-based initiatives to tackle social exclusion.

In Scotland, the language of social inclusion has been preferred at a political level with, (briefly), a Minister for Social Inclusion responsible for 'opening the door to a better Scotland', and research and action projects promoted within the overarching framework of the Scottish Social Inclusion Network. One report to this network described inclusive communities as ones where people 'are able to participate in community life, have influence over decisions affecting them, are able to take responsibility for their communities, have right of access to appropriate information and support, and equal access to services and facilities' (Scottish Executive 1999). This 'better' Scotland, however – as with the UK in general – remains deeply divided in terms of income and wealth.

Gary Craig

Related entries

Abolitionism; Child poverty; Community safety; Criminalization of social policy; Governance; Mentoring; Positive Futures; Social exclusion; Social justice; Sport-based crime prevention.

Key texts and sources

Local Government Association (1999) *Case Studies of the Local Government Role in Promoting Social Justice and Social Inclusion*. London: Local Government Association.
Scottish Executive (1999) *Inclusive Communities*. Edinburgh: Scottish Executive.

SOCIAL JUSTICE

Social justice is the process through which the key principles of fairness, equality, opportunity and needs within society are established, protected and realized to ensure that all people benefit from its productive capacity.

The contemporary debates around 'justice' tend to be dominated by criminal/youth justice priorities and resolutions. The phrases 'seeking' or 'demanding' justice invariably suggest holding children, young people and others to account through prosecution, conviction and punishment. Criminal justice establishes retributive measures through due process for law-breaking and its intended or unintended consequences. Punishment through criminal/youth justice inflicts 'pain' (imprisonment) on the offender in recognition of the 'pain' inflicted on the 'victim' or 'survivor'. It also 'protects society' while encouraging desistance from further offending behaviour. Finally, it serves as a deterrent. In administering criminal justice, particularly penal sanctions, the significance of social inequalities and social injustice as mitigating factors in offending behaviour remains controversial. While just desert theorists establish equivalence of crime and punishment, social justice theorists propose that a criminal/youth justice process without mitigation is inherently unfair.

Critical theorists argue that 'crime' is a partial category, restricted to established laws selectively enforced. It fails to address the breadth of social harm arising from structural inequalities. This is not simply a debate regarding under-policing the 'crimes of the powerful' and over-regulating the 'crimes of the powerless'. It extends to numerous 'safety' issues, such as pollution, transport, the workplace, poverty and disease. Further, Green and Ward (2004: 5) analyse state crime as 'one category of organisational deviance, along with corporate crime, organised crime, and the neglected area of crime by charities, churches and other non-profit bodies'. State institutions can also be 'deviant actors'. Proposing that criminology is limited in focusing on crime while perpetuating the 'myth of crime', Hillyard and Tombs (2004) consider it gives legitimacy to the expansion of crime control and the criminal/youth justice system. They conclude that a 'social harm' approach has a greater opportunity to secure 'social justice' by working outside the constraints of law and the frame of criminal justice. Reliance on a criminal/youth justice approach enables powerful interests, whether state institutions or private corporations, to 'do harm' with impunity.

Alternatives to criminal/youth justice, such as restorative approaches or youth conferencing, emphasize reparation from 'offender' to 'victim' supported by personal contact. Yet such processes often mirror criminal/youth justice imperatives in identifying and personalizing the 'act', in holding the 'offender' personally responsible and in seeking redress (not necessarily visibly punitive yet potentially more damaging and pathologizing than conventional punishment). It is not necessarily progressive to personalize restitution without addressing the social, political and material context. Potentially, social justice as a critical concept seeks to understand and interpret behaviour within the determining contexts of structural relations, thereby challenging injustices endured by children and young people while protecting and promoting their rights.

Phil Scraton

Related entries

Abolitionism; Children's human rights; Critical criminology; Radical non-intervention; Social harm; Social inclusion.

Key texts and sources

Green, P. and Ward, T. (2004) *State Crime: Governments, Violence and Corruption.* London: Pluto Press.
Hillyard, P. and Tombs, S. (2004) 'Beyond criminology', in P. Hillyard *et al.* (eds) *Beyond Criminology: Taking Harm Seriously.* London: Pluto Press.
Hudson, B. (2003) *Justice in the Risk Society.* London: Sage.

SOCIAL WORK (SCOTLAND) ACT 1968

The Social Work (Scotland) Act 1968 provided the original legislative basis for the Scottish children's hearing system and placed restrictions on the prosecution of children under the age of 16 (such prosecutions require the express permission of the Lord Advocate, the head of the Scottish prosecution service). It created new, local-authority social work departments whose duty was to promote social welfare. The functions of the formerly specialist Probation Service were subsumed within the new generic departments.

The passage of the Social Work (Scotland) Act 1968 marked a watershed in Scottish juvenile and adult criminal justice because of the primacy accorded to social welfare values. The ethos and institutional infrastructure of the children's hearing system, as set out in the Act, were based on the recommendations of the Kilbrandon Committee. This committee had been established in 1961 to consider the law of Scotland in relation to juvenile offenders, children in need of care and protection and those beyond parental control. The emergent 'Kilbrandon philosophy' advocated a holistic approach to troubled children based on a social educational model of care. It advocated the separation of adjudication on the facts of a case from decisions on disposal. The former was to be the responsibility of a new official, the reporter; the latter the responsibility of a lay panel. The impact of the Act was to remove the overwhelming majority of child offenders from the criminal courts and, where supervision was thought necessary, into the care of social work departments.

Although the Kilbrandon Committee had been set up to review the law relating to children, its influence also extended to adult criminal justice. Under the arrangements introduced by the Social Work (Scotland) Act 1968, the functions of the then Probation Service were transferred to the new, local-authority social work departments, and social workers became responsible for the supervision of offenders in the community and the provision of social inquiry and other reports to the criminal justice system.

Overall the Act helped shape a distinctively Scottish approach to crime and punishment and, for around a quarter of a century, set both the juvenile and adult justice systems on a different trajectory from a number of their European and US counterparts (which drifted towards more punitive and actuarial forms of justice during the 1970s and 1980s).

Lesley McAra

Related entries

Children (Scotland) Act 1995; Children's hearing system; Comparative youth justice; Welfare.

Key texts and sources

Kilbrandon Committee (1964) *Report on Children and Young Persons, Scotland.* Edinburgh: HMSO.

Lockyer, A. and Stone, F. (1998) *Juvenile Justice in Scotland: Twenty-five Years of the Welfare Approach.* Edinburgh: T. & T. Clark.

McAra, L. (2005) 'Modelling penal transformation', *Punishment and Society,* 7: 277–302.

McNeill, F. (2005) *Offender Management in Scotland: The First Hundred Years.* CJScotland (available online at **http://www.cjscotland.org.uk/pdfs/Offender%20management.pdf**).

The Social Work (Scotland) Act 1968. London: HMSO.

SPECIFIC SENTENCE REPORTS (SSRs)

Specific sentence reports (SSRs) were first introduced by Probation Service national standards in 2000. SSRs, unless there are exceptional circumstances, should be produced on the same day as the report is requested by the court. The reports can be presented orally or in written form. There are clear differences between how SSRs are framed for adults and young offenders.

Specific sentence reports (SSRs) first appeared in National Standards for the Probation Service issued in 2000. From 2000, therefore, youth courts could request SSRs for young offenders aged 16–17 who were being considered for community punishment of less than 100 hours. However, the SSR was not introduced fully into youth justice until the National Standards for Youth Justice Services were issued in 2004. The purpose of the SSR, in youth justice, is to provide timely information to determine the offender's suitability for a specific sentence (normally reparation orders and action plan orders) envisaged by the court. SSRs were primarily designed to reduce delays and to increase the capacity of courts to deliver and administer justice swiftly. Thus, while youth offending teams are allowed 15 days to produce a pre-sentence report (PSR) and 10 days to prepare a PSR on a persistent offender, the courts can require that an SSR is prepared on the day it is requested. However, the guidance identifies that, in exceptional circumstances, five days can be allowed for the production of an SSR.

Similar to PSRs, the National Standards for Youth Justice Services indicate that SSRs should be based on Asset and should assess the young person's suitability for the specific order envisaged by a court. The Asset on which the SSR is based should be 'recent'. When no 'recent' Asset is available, five days can be allowed for an Asset to be completed and the SSR produced. In addition, the 2000 version of national standards indicate that an SSR should be based on an interview with the young person; where appropriate, a discussion with the offender's parents or primary carer(s); and the inclusion of relevant and available information from other agencies.

While it is assumed that SSRs provide benefits as they speed up justice and make the link between actions and outcomes clearer for young people, there are clearly a number of potential problems. 'Risk' is dynamic and – due to the nature of adolescence – changes occur rapidly in young people's lives. However, with an SSR there is no guarantee that the report will be based on an up-to-date Asset assessment. This is an important point as an action plan order's 'menu' can be very complex, including groupwork programmes, drug rehabilitation work and parenting classes, all of which require careful and considered assessment. In addition, reparation orders can be direct to the victim or indirect to the community, but assessing whether or not it might be appropriate even to contact a victim needs to be carefully considered and should not be rushed in a crude attempt to 'speed up' the administration of justice.

Joe Yates

Related entries

Action plan orders (APOs); Assessment framework; Fast-tracking; Pre-sentence reports (PSRs); Punishment in the community; Reparation orders.

Key texts and sources

Nacro (2007b) *Working in the Courts: Essential Skills for Practitioners in the Youth Justice System. Youth Crime Section Good Practice Guide Series.* London: Nacro.
Youth Justice Board (2000c) *National Standards for Youth Justice.* London: Youth Justice Board.
Youth Justice Board (2004a) *National Standards for Youth Justice Services.* London: Youth Justice Board (available online at **http://www.yjb.gov.uk/ Publications/scripts/prodView.asp?idproduct=155 &eP=PP**).

SPORT-BASED CRIME PREVENTION

Sport-based crime prevention is a contemporary policy emphasis whereby the promotion of sporting activities forms a central feature of (usually targeted) programmes aimed at youth crime prevention or reduction. 'Sport' is often viewed as a 'hook' to engage young people into services. Historically, sport has also been seen to offer opportunities for ethical training and 'moral improvement', and these associations sometimes colour contemporary debates.

In contemporary UK policy, both sporting bodies and government departments contend that sport can make a valuable contribution to social policy objectives. Several targeted youth programmes in England and Wales, for example, provide sporting activities for engaging young people 'at risk' of crime, anti-social behaviour and social exclusion (for example, Positive Futures, Kickz and Splash Cymru).

The contribution that sport can make to broader 'regeneration' and 'social inclusion' strategies is also emphasized. The report from Policy Action Team 10 to the Social Exclusion Unit observed that 'Arts and sport, cultural and recreational activity, can contribute to neighbourhood renewal and make a real difference to health, crime, employment and education in deprived communities' (Department for Culture, Media and Sport 1999: 8).

Current initiatives can be situated in relation to a long tradition of sport-based youth provision, historically supported by an enduring association with the Victorian belief in the moral value of sport. However, providing conclusive empirical evidence of the impact of sport-based programmes on youth crime has proved problematic. Some programme evaluations have found that particular initiatives have reduced recorded crime and/or known offending among participants (Nichols 2007), but research often also points to the complexity of measuring the impact of sport-based programmes on youth crime prevention. The issues raised include the following:

- Even where it can be shown that offending among participants has been reduced, it may not be possible to disaggregate the effect of any individual programme in a context of multiple interventions or to evaluate the importance of the common sports component in otherwise diverse programmes.
- High numbers and/or the sporadic involvement of participants in some programmes may make individual follow-up unrealistic. Even where available, reconviction data may fail to reflect levels of offending among participants.
- Evaluations of prevention programmes often draw on official crime statistics, aiming to establish if there is any variation between levels of recorded crime where/when the programme operated and a control area or time period. However, such comparisons present methodological difficulties. Police-recorded crime statistics will inevitably provide an incomplete measure of crime, and the age of the perpetrators may not be available. Measures of 'youth nuisance' and 'anti-social behaviour' may present additional difficulties.

- Others have highlighted the politicized context in which research is often conducted. Robust evaluation may be challenged by limited resources and a need for swift results.
- Finally, some question the positivistic tendencies of much evaluation research and question whether programmes can ever produce easily measurable 'outcomes'. Case studies often feature in evaluation research, but their representativeness may not be made clear. A major qualitative evaluation of the Positive Futures programme has suggested that 'Attempts at proving such direct "outputs" are inevitably problematic' and has advanced a new approach to assessing the value of programmes that tries to combine quantitative and qualitative methods to gain a 'complete picture' of how projects influence participants' engagement and development (Crabbe 2006: 7).

Nevertheless, many have supported the suggestion that 'There are strong theoretical arguments for the potentially positive contribution which sport can make to reducing the propensity to commit crime' (Coalter *et al.* 2000: 44).

The debate about the relationship between sports participation and crime has sometimes been divided into theories of prevention/diversion and theories about the rehabilitation of offenders. However, this distinction is increasingly less helpful, in part due to the influence of developmental theories of crime and the consequent blurring of boundaries between 'young offenders' and those identified as 'at risk' of offending. A related division, often found in contemporary policy discourse, is between 'diversionary' and 'developmental' activities.

Theories of 'diversion' (which here implies diversion from crime or 'anti-social behaviour', not from the criminal justice system) propose that sports programmes offer 'diversionary activities' that prevent participants from committing offences for the duration of that session. Consequently, sessions are commonly scheduled at times when high levels of youth offending are predicted (such as weekends, evenings and during the school holidays). These activities are often open to all young people in a specified age range, although they are commonly targeted at geographical areas with high levels of recorded crime.

Theories concerning the rehabilitation of offenders have attempted to explore why participating in sports programmes could lead to desistance, often drawing on aetiological theories of crime (see Coalter *et al.* 2000 for a discussion). Some more recent perspectives have argued that participating in sports programmes could impact on crime through the development of 'pro-social' behaviour among participants. For example, Nichols (2007) and Nichols and Crow (2004: 270) combine dominant theories of risk and protective factors with a model of psycho-social 'self-development' directed by 'pro-social values'. They argue that participation in sport-based crime prevention programmes (and, particularly, intensive or long-term schemes) can increase 'self-esteem, locus of control and cognitive skills', while also exposing participants to the positive 'value systems' of 'significant others', who may include peers and programme leaders. In contemporary policy, sport is also presented as a catalyst for relationship building and a way of fostering the 'personal development' of participants (Crabbe 2006). Education, training or employment opportunities may also be described as 'developmental activities'.

Laura Kelly

Related entries

Crime prevention; Criminalization of social policy; Desistance; Early intervention; Evaluation research; Positive Activities for Young People (PAYP); Positive Futures; Rehabilitation; Remoralization.

Key texts and sources

Coalter, F., Allison, M. and Taylor, J. (2000) *The Role of Sport in Regenerating Deprived Areas.* Edinburgh: Scottish Executive.

Crabbe, T. (2006) *Knowing the Score – Positive Futures Case Study Research: Final Report.* London: Home Office.

Department for Culture, Media and Sport (1999) *Policy Action Team 10: Report to the Social Exclusion Unit – Arts and Sport.* London: HMSO.

Nichols, G. (2007) *Sport and Crime Reduction: The Role of Sports in Tackling Youth Crime.* London: Routledge.

Nichols, G. and Crow, I. (2004) 'Measuring the impact of crime reduction interventions involving sports activities for young people', *Howard Journal of Criminal Justice*, 43: 267–83.

STATUS OFFENCES

'Status offences' can only be committed by people of a certain status or with certain characteristics. In the youth justice context this most often refers to offences that can only be committed by those below a given age.

Globally, status offences often 'concern situations where the child has run away from home, is considered to be out of control and/or is indigent' (United Nations Children's Fund 1998). The United Nations Standard Minimum Rules for the Administration of Juvenile Justice (the Beijing Rules) are specifically applied to 'status offences' by virtue of rule 3.1. Furthermore, the United Nations Guidelines for the Prevention of Juvenile Delinquency (the Riyadh Guidelines) specifically mandate the repeal of status offences, stating, at Guideline 56, that: 'In order to prevent further stigmatization, victimization and criminalization of young persons, legislation should be enacted to ensure that any conduct not considered an offence or not penalized if committed by an adult is not considered an offence and not penalized if committed by a young person.'

Typical 'status offences' in youth justice jurisdictions include truancy, sexual immorality and violation of alcohol laws. Taking the last as an example, in England and Wales and Scotland 'offences' that can only be committed by children include the purchase and consumption of alcohol as provided by ss. 149–150 of the Licensing Act 2003 and ss. 105–106 of the Licensing (Scotland) Act 2005. Some status offences have a particularly gendered application (for example, 'official' concerns directed at girls because of their sexual behaviour, whereas few boys attract formal censure on these grounds).

Sally Ireland

Related entries

Children's human rights; Criminalization; Decriminalization; Delinquency; Gender and justice; Minimum necessary intervention; Net-widening; Normalization; United Nations Guidelines for the Prevention of Juvenile Delinquency; United Nations Standard Minimum Rules for the Administration of Juvenile Justice.

Key texts and sources

United Nations Children's Fund (1998) *Innocenti Digest 3: Juvenile Justice.* Florence: Unicef International Child Development Centre (available online at **http://www.unicef-icdc.org/ publications/pdf/digest3e.pdf**).

The United Nations' *Standard Minimum Rules for the Administration of Juvenile Justice* are available online at **http://www.unhchr.ch/html/menu3/b/ h_comp48.htm**; the *Guidelines for the Prevention of Juvenile Delinquency* are available online at **http://www.unhchr.ch/html/menu3/b/h_comp 47.htm**.

STREET CRIME

Street crime is a general term primarily used to refer to such offences as robbery, theft from the person, snatch theft, 'mugging', firearms offences, street-related wounding (knife attacks), car-jacking and, sometimes, prostitution. It is occasionally referred to as 'visible crime'.

Street crime is often associated (at least in populist and/or media discourse) with drug misuse and particular representations of 'youth'. From classic concerns about 'mugging' (Hall *et al.* 1978) to the more recent preoccupation with the youth-drugs-gangs-crime nexus, 'street crime' imposes a powerful totemic effect and places 'youth crime' into sharp focus (as distinct from less visible white-collar crime, for example). Interestingly, recent research has shown that links between drug misuse and street crime are more complex and less deterministic than might otherwise be thought (Allen 2005).

Street crime, like crime more generally, is also associated with economic cycles (Arvanites and Defina 2006). This appears to be primarily a characteristic of 'robbery' rather than other, violent, non-acquisitive street crime. Thus it is the case that, in times of relative prosperity, incidents of robbery tend to decrease. Conversely, higher levels of consumption can also serve to 'inflate' the incidence of street robbery by increasing opportunities – mobile phone theft being a classic example in the realms of youth justice.

Recently, both 'gun crime' and 'knife crime' have focused public concern on the problem of 'disengaged' and 'uncontrollable' youth (often with a racialized emphasis on black children and young people). This has served to add weight to the call for more surveillance, tougher penalties and additional police powers directed at young people, thus fuelling further 'moral panic'.

Richard Hester

Related entries

Demonization; Fear of crime; Gangs; Media reporting; Moral panic; 'Race' and justice; Substance misuse; Victimization.

Key texts and sources

Allen, C. (2005) 'The links between heroin, crack cocaine and crime: where does street crime fit in?', *British Journal of Criminology*, 45: 355–72.

Arvanites, T. and Defina, R. (2006) 'Business cycles and street crime', *Criminology*, 44: 139–64.

Hall, S., Critcher, C., Jefferson, T., Clarke, J. and Roberts, B. (1978) *Policing the Crisis: Mugging the State, and Law and Order*. Basingstoke: Macmillan.

SUBCULTURAL THEORY

Subcultural theory, in its broadest sense, can refer to any theory concerned with those circumstances in which crime or deviance becomes a part of the culture or way of life of a particular group or community. More narrowly it refers to a body of criminological work that was particularly influential in the late 1950s and early 1960s.

The awareness that crime can be part of the 'way of life' has a long history, but the emergence in criminology of 'subcultural theory' only arose in the 1950s when a number of writers focused on explaining the development and persistence of young male delinquent activity. The most notable of these were Cohen (1955) and Cloward and Ohlin (1960). Their work was heavily influenced by Merton's anomie theory, which they developed and embellished.

Cohen noted that, while many explanations of delinquent behaviour saw it as a consequence of contact with a delinquent subculture, there had been no attempt to explain the origins of such subculture. In attempting to fill this gap, Cohen argued that a delinquent subculture arose, like any other subculture, as a solution to a problem faced by a number of people in a similar structural position. In this case, working-class boys faced the problem of being denied status in conventional terms as they were unable to meet the criteria fostered in the education system and in society more widely. Cohen argued that the norms of the delinquent subculture turned the norms of the wider culture upside down and provided alternative criteria of status that could be met. Cohen's conception of subcultures as 'collective solutions' has been widely influential.

Cloward and Ohlin also focused on the issue of the availability of opportunities to achieve cultural goals. However, they criticized Merton's anomie theory for assuming that, if legitimate opportunities were not freely available, then illegitimate ones were. Instead, they argued that illegitimate opportunities were also limited and differentially available. Thus responses to denied or frustrated opportunities would depend on what was available locally. Here they explicitly attempted to link anomie with another tradition in studies of delinquency – that of cultural transmission and, particularly, Sutherland's theory of differential association: anomie provides the pressure, differential association influences the nature of the solution.

With the rise of labelling theory during the 1960s, subcultural theories were criticized for their determinism, most notably by Matza (1964). But labelling itself, in demonizing and stigmatizing certain groups of young people as 'folk devils' and creating 'moral panics', came to be seen as another factor in the creation and maintenance of subcultures. During the 1970s, particularly in the work of the Centre for Contemporary Cultural Studies at Birmingham University, attention shifted away from delinquency to youth cultures more generally, although the focus was still on working-class youth. Drawing on Marxism and semiotic analysis, the basic approach was to read youth styles as sites of resistance (albeit symbolic) to structural inequalities.

Dave King

Related entries

Anomie theory; Delinquency; Differential association; Labelling theory; Social exclusion; Subculture.

Key texts and sources

Cloward, R. and Ohlin, L. (1960) *Delinquency and Opportunity*. London: Routledge & Kegan Paul.
Cohen, A.K. (1955) *Delinquent Boys: The Culture of the Gang*. New York, NY: Free Press.
Gelder, K. and Thornton, S. (eds) (1997) *The Subcultures Reader*. London: Routledge.
Hall, S. and Jefferson, T. (eds) (1976) *Resistance through Rituals: Youth Subcultures in Post-war Britain*. London: Hutchinson.
Matza, D. (1964) *Delinquency and Drift*. London: Wiley.
Sutherland, E.H. (1947) *Principles of Criminology* (5th edn). Philadelphia, PA: Lippincott.

SUBCULTURE

Subculture as a sociological concept was first used by Albert Cohen (1955). Cohen explored how groups of working-class young people suffering from 'status frustration' reject and reverse the dominant values of society by creating their own subcultures. In this way subcultural theorists moved away from individually pathologizing young people towards a position that was more 'appreciative' of 'delinquent' subcultures in a context of class-based inequality.

One of the earliest studies of 'gangs' was undertaken by Thrasher (1927: 33), who argued that they provide a 'substitute for what society fails to give ... [they] fill a gap and afford an escape'. Early theorizing around gangs and the functions they fulfil for their members comprised the precursor for the concept of subculture and the development of subcultural theory.

Albert Cohen developed the concept of subculture to account for how young people negotiated the pressures they faced during adolescent transitions from their specific positions with reference to class and 'race'. Cohen argued that some youth subcultures had a different value system from 'mainstream' society. In Cohen's analysis, acts of delinquency were seen as *acceptable* within particular subcultures purely on the basis that they were seen as *unacceptable* by wider society.

Initially, subcultural theorists focused on delinquency as a defining feature of the groups they were seeking to understand. While the early work of Cohen (1955) identified the importance of particular styles of dress and vocabularies, the primary distinguishing feature of subcultures was presented as being delinquency. However, in the 1960s research began to move towards exploring the vocabulary, dress style and leisure activities of young people as defining features of subculture: 'pregnant with significance ... movements towards a speech which offends the "silent majority"' (Hebdige 1979: 18). The work of Downes (1966) and, later, the Birmingham Centre for Contemporary Cultural Studies (Hall and Jefferson 1976) developed subcultural theory in the British context.

The concept of subculture and the work of the early subcultural theorists have been criticized for focusing almost exclusively on working-class male youth and as uncritically accepting particular definitions of 'crime' and 'delinquency'.

Joe Yates

Related entries

Delinquency; Differential association; Gangs; Labelling theory; Social exclusion; Subcultural theory; Substance misuse.

Key texts and sources

Cohen, A. (1955) *Delinquent Boys: The Culture of the Gang*. New York, NY: Free Press.
Downes, D. (1966) *The Delinquent Solution*. London: Routledge & Kegan Paul.
Hall, S. and Jefferson, T. (eds) (1976) *Resistance through Rituals: Youth Subcultures in Post-war Britain*. London: Hutchinson.
Hebdige, D. (1979) *Subculture: The Meaning of Style*. London: Methuen.
Thrasher, F.M. (1927) *The Gang: A Study of 1,313 Gangs in Chicago*. Chicago, IL: Chicago University Press.

SUBSTANCE MISUSE

Substance misuse refers to the use of legal or illegal substances in a manner that is judged to be harmful, to the individual, to his or her family and/or to the wider community. The substance may be an illegal drug, such as heroin, cocaine, cannabis; a legal drug, such as alcohol, tobacco, caffeine; or a chemical that could be found in a range of products, such as polish, glue, aerosols.

People have used substances throughout history. Substance use is embedded in society and everyone has his or her favourite drug – the most common being caffeine, alcohol, tobacco and cannabis. Most people use substances on a recreational basis without posing any significant risk or harm to themselves or others. The term 'substance' includes legal and/or illegal drugs, although those who use legal drugs (alcohol, tobacco and caffeine) rarely consider themselves as 'substance users'. The term tends to be reserved for those who use illegal drugs. However, the division between legal and illegal use is spurious and one that is beginning to disintegrate.

Throughout the twentieth century legal drugs enjoyed a privileged position as a relatively safe and unproblematic culturally approved expression of leisure and pleasure. In recent decades they have faced increasing market competition from illicit drugs, however. This has been combined with a growing awareness of the dangers posed by legal drugs. A recent government report assessed alcohol and tobacco as more harmful than many widely used illegal drugs (House of Commons Science and Technology Select Committee 2006). The independent panel of drug specialists used a rating scale that covered physical harm, psychological harm and social harm. It placed heroin and cocaine at the top of the list; alcohol was ranked the fifth; and tobacco ninth – ahead of cannabis (eleventh), LSD (fourteenth) and ecstasy (eighteenth). The legal–illegal division between substances is not based on risk or harm, therefore, but is based on historical, economic and political imperatives.

While some illegal drugs may be considered less harmful than alcohol or tobacco, there are serious additional risks created by illegality. For example, when using an illegal substance the user is often unaware of the strength of the drug and risks overdose; has little idea of the purity or composition of the drug and risks consuming poisonous substances the drug may be mixed with; is forced to engage with a 'criminal' subculture to purchase his or her substance; must use the drug in secret to avoid detection; risks a criminal conviction and all its consequences; and faces social stigma and possible reprisal if his or her illegal substance use is discovered by friends, family or work colleagues. These significant risk factors are not caused by the pharmacological nature of the illegal drug itself but are caused by the social, legal and political context surrounding illegal drug use. The distinction, then, between legal and illegal substances is complex. The dominant discourse that presents illegal substances as inherently dangerous and deviant is reductionist and, at times, blatantly misleading.

The status of illegal substances is contained in the Misuse of Drugs Act 1971 that divides controlled substances into three categories, A, B and C:

- *Class A* includes ecstasy, LSD, heroin, cocaine, crack, magic mushrooms and amphetamine if it is prepared for injection. The penalties for possession of a Class A substance are up to seven years in prison and/or an unlimited fine. Supplying could result in life imprisonment and/or an unlimited fine.
- *Class B* includes amphetamines, methylphenidate (ritalin) and pholcodine. The penalties for possession are up to five years in prison and/or an unlimited fine. Supplying could result in up to 14 years in prison and/or an unlimited fine.
- *Class C* includes cannabis, tranquilizers, GHB (gamma hydroxybutyrate) and ketamine. The penalties for possession are up to two years in prison and/or an unlimited fine. Like Class B drugs, the penalties for supply are up to 14 years in prison and/or an unlimited fine.

It is now estimated over 11 million people in England and Wales have used an illegal substance. The greatest use is among young people – 45 per cent of 16–24-year-olds admit to having tried an illegal drug, with 15 per cent having used illegal drugs in the past month (Roe and Man 2006). It is argued that the widespread availability and use of illegal substances by young people across the UK suggest recreational illegal drug taking has become a 'normal' adolescent experience (Parker *et al.* 2002). The 'normal' and recreational nature of illegal substance use raises important questions about individual rights and freedom, as well as practical and ethical issues of policing and criminalizing large sections of society.

Some people who use substances develop difficulties and become 'substance misusers', causing harm to themselves, their friends/family and/or the wider community. It is estimated that around 3 per cent of those who take illegal substances could be classified as substance misusers or 'problem drug users' (Edmunds *et al.* 1998); the remaining 97 per cent are classified as recreational or experimental users. It is substance 'misuse' that attracts most attention. The perception of drugs, drug law and drug policy is largely based on the difficulties caused and faced by this small minority of substance misusers. The reasons why a small minority of substance users go on to develop drug problems is contested, but arguments centre on a range of factors, including pharmacological, psychological, social and legal conditions.

Proponents of the 'gateway theory' argue that exposure to so-called 'soft' drugs such as cannabis and ecstasy leads young people to use more dangerous 'hard' drugs, such as heroin and cocaine. This unsubstantiated theory, which has an appeal to prohibitionists, has largely been discredited (Pudney 2002). There is a growing realization that substance misuse is strongly associated with structural and environmental factors, such as social and economic exclusion and social disadvantage (Buchanan 2004). Any effort to tackle substance misuse should, therefore, incorporate robust strategies to tackle these underlying problems.

The UK drug strategy is dominated by a prohibition agenda primarily concerned with reducing the supply of drugs and strengthening deterrence, although the government has recently made substantial funds available through the Drugs Intervention Programme (DIP) initiative to get illegal drug users into treatment. The DIP (available for young people as well as adults) provides demanding coercive measures as part of new court orders to 'encourage' misusers to get 'treatment' and become drug free – or face serious court sanctions. Matching substance misusers to appropriate treatment and expecting them to achieve a rapid change of lifestyle – and to sustain that change over a period of time – may be too demanding for most substance misusers (particularly if the underlying causes of chronic substance misuse, such as unemployment, disadvantage, social exclusion, abuse and low self-esteem, are not adequately understood or addressed). The jury is still out on the effectiveness of coercive drug treatment tied into the criminal justice system (Norland *et al.* 2003; Hunt and Stevens 2004) and the nature of the connection between drugs and crime is not properly understood. Indeed, there may be no causal relationship between drugs and crime – they may be symptoms of deep-seated structural inequalities exacerbated by limited legitimate opportunities, in which drugs and crime become an alternative subcultural activity (Buchanan 2004).

The Drugs Act 2005 reinforces the government's determined stand on illegal substances. The Act enables the police to test offenders (aged 18 or over) who are suspected to be illegal substance misusers on arrest, rather than on charge, and gives provision for any person who tests positive for a Class A substance to be assessed by a drugs specialist. If the police suspect the offender has swallowed an illegal substance to avoid detection, he or she can now be held in police custody for up to 192 hours to recover the evidence. If the offender refuses without good cause to consent to an intimate body search, X-ray or ultrasound scan, the Act allows the court or jury to draw an adverse inference.

This tough approach towards illegal substance users isolates them and fuels hostility towards them. Further, the use of the criminal justice system by the USA and UK to tackle illegal substance use and misuse has resulted in severely overcrowded prisons that risk becoming silos for disadvantaged and damaged people who have a drug problem.

Untangling the mixed and contested messages concerning the different effects, risks and contexts of illegal and legal substance misuse makes it difficult to understand and engage with the problem of substance misuse. This is a complex area due to a range of issues, in particular: the relative normality of illegal drug use; the criminalization of millions of young people; the failure to distinguish between the use and misuse of illegal substances; the ignorance and fear surrounding illegal substances; the double standards concerning the cultural status and acceptance of legal substances; the imposition of coercive treatment measures; and the growing dependence on the criminal/youth justice system to tackle the problem.

Julian Buchanan

Related entries

Criminalization; Normalization; Resettlement; Social exclusion; Social harm; Subculture; Youth justice plans; Youth Matters.

Key texts and sources

Buchanan, J. (2004) 'Missing links: problem drug use and social exclusion', *Probation Journal* (special issue: 'Rethinking drugs and crime'), 51: 387–97.

Edmunds, M., May, T., Hearnden, I. and Hough, M. (1998) *Arrest Referral: Emerging Lessons from Research. DPI Paper* 23. London: Home Office.

House of Commons Science and Technology Select Committee (2006) *Drug Classification: Making a Hash of it? Fifth Report of Session 2005–6* (HC 1031) (available online at **www.publications. parliament.uk/pa/cm200506/cmselect/cmsctech/ 1031/1031.pdf**).

Hunt, N. and Stevens, A. (2004) 'Whose harm? Harm reduction and the shift to coercion in UK drug policy', *Social Policy and Society*, 3: 333–42.

Norland, S., Sowell, R.E. and Di Chiara, A. (2003) 'Assumptions of coercive treatment: a critical review', *Criminal Justice Policy Review*, 14: 505–21.

Parker, H., Williams, L. and Aldridge, J. (2002) 'The normalization of "sensible" recreational drug use: further evidence from the North West England Longitudinal Study', *Sociology*, 36: 941–64.

Pudney, S. (2002) *The Road to Ruin? Sequences of Initiation into Drug Use and Offending by Young People in Britain. Home Office Research Study* 253. London: Home Office.

Roe, S. and Man, L. (2006) *Drug Misuse Declared: Findings from the 2005/06 British Crime Survey*. London: Home Office.

SUMMARY JUSTICE

Summary justice can be used to refer to three quite distinct concepts. First, in Scotland the term is used to refer to non-jury criminal prosecutions and, in England and Wales, less commonly to prosecutions in the magistrates' court. Secondly, the term refers to methods of justice other than prosecution through the criminal courts and has recently been used to mean legal/semi-formal methods, such as civil orders and on-the-spot fines. Thirdly, it can refer to 'community punishment' (for example, by vigilantes).

In Scotland, summary prosecutions can take place in the sheriff ccourt (before a sheriff) or in the district court (before lay magistrates or a stipendiary magistrate). There are different maximum sentencing limits depending on the type of tribunal, the offence and the offender's record. The McInnes Report of 2004 recommended reforms to the summary justice system. The Criminal Proceedings (Reform) (Scotland) Act 2007 introduces reforms in this area, although the majority of its provisions are not yet in force.

In its second application, 'summary justice' has been promoted by the government in recent years. In a speech on the launch of the five-year strategy for crime in 2004 the Prime Minister said:

Summary justice through on-the-spot fines, seizure of drug dealers' assets, closure of pubs, clubs and houses that are the centre of drug use or disorder, naming and shaming of persistent

Anti-Social Behaviour offenders, interim Anti-Social Behaviour Orders will be rolled out … The purpose of the Criminal Justice System reforms is to re-balance the system radically in favour of the victim, protecting the innocent but ensuring the guilty know the odds have changed.

In relation to children and young people, the Department of Constitutional Affairs' paper, *Delivering Simple, Speedy, Summary Justice*, published in 2006, proposed a scheme that would be similar to the conditional cautioning regime for adults under Part 3 of the Criminal Justice Act 2003. The paper also mentioned developing restorative interventions for some first instances of minor offending. The general approach of the paper is to encourage the removal of cases from the court system where appropriate and to speed up court process.

Sally Ireland

Related entries

Anti-social behaviour; Caution; Criminal Justice Act 2003; Fixed-penalty notices (FPNs); Restorative cautioning; Sheriff courts.

Key texts and sources

Department for Constitutional Affairs (2006) *Delivering Simple, Speedy, Summary Justice*. London: Department of Constitutional Affairs (available online at **http://www.dca.gov.uk/publications/ reports_reviews/delivery-simple-speedy.pdf**).

Scottish Executive (2004) *The Summary Justice Review Committee: Report to Ministers* (the McInnes Report). Edinburgh: Scottish Executive (available online at **http://www.scotland.gov.uk/ Publications/2004/03/19042/34176**).

See the Office of Public Sector Information's website for the texts of the Criminal Justice Act 2003 (**http://www.opsi.gov.uk/acts/acts2003/20030044. htm**) and the Criminal Proceedings (Reform) (Scotland) Act 2007 (**http://www.opsi.gov.uk/ legislation/scotland/acts2007/20070006.htm**).

SUPERVISION ORDERS

The supervision order in England and Wales is a community sentence available for children and young people across the age range 10–17, in both the youth court and the Crown court. The order normally places the child or young person under the supervision of a youth offending team. There is no supervision order in Northern Ireland where the youth justice system has been reformed with a focus on restorative approaches and a youth conferencing system. Probation orders are available in the youth court, however. In Scotland, children are normally dealt with by children's hearings, although they may be made subject to compulsory 'supervision requirements' that differ from supervision orders (in England and Wales) in that they are reviewed, may be renewed or amended and lapse if not reviewed in one year.

Provisions to replace the supervision order (and other community orders) with a single menu-based community sentence – the youth rehabilitation order – are contained in the Criminal Justice and Immigration Bill 2006–7 to 2007–8.

The supervision order originated in the Children and Young Persons Act 1969. In basic form it placed a duty on the supervising officer (social worker or probation officer) to 'assist, advise and befriend' the child or young person who was, in turn, required to report when directed and notify the officer of changes of address. Subject to amendments during its history, a range of requirements or conditions could be attached to the order, including intermediate treatment. The supervision order played an important part in driving down custodial sentencing through the 1980s and early 1990s, at a time when juvenile justice teams across England and Wales were developing systems management approaches. A relatively short-lived but important form of order became available through the Criminal Justice Act 1988, known as the 'direct alternative to custody'. This could only be made at a point where a court considered the seriousness of the offence(s) had reached the custodial threshold and, in such cases, the court was required to state that it would have imposed a custodial sentence had it not made this type of supervision order. The 'direct alternative to custody' disposal was repealed by the Crime and Disorder Act 1998, leaving a gap that may have contributed, *inter alia*, to rising custodial sentencing thereafter. Many organizations have more recently pressed for the proposed youth rehabilitation order to be accompanied by a similar, and separate, intensive supervision and surveillance order that would have to precede a custodial sentence in most cases.

The supervision order emerged from a welfare-oriented approach and was closely related to the 'supervision order in care proceedings', both being made in a juvenile court dealing with both civil and criminal matters. The Children Act 1989 created the separate family proceedings courts and, later, the Criminal Justice Act 1991 replaced the (criminal) juvenile court with the youth court, bringing those aged 17 into its jurisdiction and amending the supervision order accordingly.

The Criminal Justice Act 1991 embodied the principle of proportionality, whereby supervision orders were only available for offences that were 'serious enough' to warrant a community sentence (with the 'direct alternative to custody' arguably being the exception). Henceforth the order has tended to be increasingly less welfare oriented, often accompanied by curfews, a stronger focus on risk and more robust standards and enforcement arrangements. Although the Crime and Disorder Act 1998 introduced a range of additional orders – including the action plan order and the reparation order – the courts have continued to make greater use of the supervision order, with or without additional requirements.

The Powers of Criminal Courts (Sentencing) Act 2000 consolidated all previous statute and provides for the supervision order in its current form. The overall length of an order can be up to three years. There is no minimum length although, in practice, orders are rarely made that are less than six months. A pre-sentence report is required where the order includes additional requirements. The order provides for a number of requirements – some of which can be combined – including to:

- participate in specified activities and attend places as directed either by the supervising officer or as specified by the court;
- reside at a particular place;
- make reparation for up to 180 days;
- refrain from certain activities;
- reside in local authority accommodation for up to six months or with a foster carer for up to one year (both of which involve the subject to be looked after by the local authority);
- receive treatment for a mental health condition;
- comply with educational arrangements approved by the local education authority; and
- comply with a programme of drug treatment (for those aged over 14 years).

Thus, the supervision order can be a short order with no additional requirements or an intensive longer order accompanied by electronically monitored curfew arrangements. Once in place, the National Standards for Youth Justice Services require that an 'intervention plan' be agreed that 'must' be based on the assessment of risk factors associated with the offending. In addition to any activities or restrictions arising from requirements made by the court, the national standards require supervision contact twice weekly for the first three months of an order, reducing thereafter. Enforcement of orders is also subject to national standards and, at present, the child or young person may be given a maximum of two formal written warnings for non-compliance before breach proceedings are instigated in court.

For courts, and pre-sentence report authors in particular, the very flexibility and range of the supervision order require a targeted approach that should adhere to the proportionality principle and seek to avoid the unnecessary use of additional requirements. Without this, there is some risk of the order being used to address welfare issues – that might be more appropriately met in other ways – or of requirements being attached that impose demands or restrictions on the child's/young person's liberty that are not commensurate with the seriousness of his or her offending.

Supervision orders can be imposed on more than one occasion, perhaps repeatedly. The repeated use of supervision orders might be characterized by increasingly restrictive or demanding requirements but, more importantly, requirements should suit the circumstances in each case. Prosecution for breaches of community orders has increased in recent years, and an approach based on helping children to comply, together with a careful balance between discretion and accountability, is advisable. In the context of a new menu-based sentence, it is crucial that this balanced approach is adopted by the courts, supervising officers and report authors, otherwise the use of inappropriate and/or premature custodial sentences could rise further.

Geoff Monaghan

Related entries

Alternatives to custody; Children's hearing system; Children and Young Persons Act 1969; Criminal Justice and Immigration Bill 2006–7 to 2007–8; Intermediate treatment (IT); Menu-based sentencing; National Standards for Youth Justice Services; Probation Service; Sentencing framework; Youth offending teams (YOTs).

Key texts and sources

Eadie, T. and Canton, R. (2002) 'Practising in a context of ambivalence: the challenge for youth justice workers', *Youth Justice*, 2: 14–27.

Nacro (2002c) *Supervision Orders – an Overview. Youth Crime Briefing.* London: Nacro.

Whyte, B. (2005) 'Youth justice in other UK jurisdictions: Scotland and Northern Ireland', in T. Bateman and J. Pitts (eds) *The RHP Companion to Youth Justice.* Lyme Regis: Russell House.

Youth Justice Board (2004a) *National Standards for Youth Justice Services.* London: Youth Justice Board (available online at **http://www.yjb.gov.uk/ Publications/Scripts/prodView.asp?idproduct= 155&eP=PP**).

SURE START

Sure Start is a multifaceted policy initiative to provide 'integrated early education, childcare, health and family support' services. The services are expected to improve young children's health and emotional development, thereby boosting their later achievements while simultaneously providing parents with affordable childcare to facilitate their return to/continuance in paid employment.

The government first proposed Sure Start as part of a suite of initiatives outlined in the consultation document, *Supporting Families* (Home Office 1998). The five chapters in the document were entitled 'Better services and support for parents' (including the Sure Start programme); 'Better financial support for families'; 'Helping families balance work and home'; 'Strengthening marriage'; and 'Better support for serious family problems' (including youth offending). Some £540 million was made available over three years to fund the programme across the UK. Initial funding was targeted on the most deprived local authority wards.

The underpinning rationale for Sure Start is that the early years of a child's life are critical to his or her future well-being and that investing in early years services, and providing parental support, enables children to succeed at school and 'in life' and enables problems to be tackled before they become entrenched. The benefits were projected as being relevant not only for individual families but also for society as a whole through reductions in a range of social problems, including truancy, drug abuse, crime and unemployment, and through improved achievement at school and later in the labour market. Some families were deemed to need more help than others, primarily because of deprivation as measured by poor educational achievement, poor health, overcrowded/unsuitable/insecure housing and/or unemployment. More integrated services were conceived as the most effective means of addressing such issues.

The *Supporting Families* consultation document emphasized the perceived relationship between early welfare provision for deprived families and later youth offending: 'Children who grow up in stable, successful families are less likely to become involved in offending. Helping parents to exercise effective care and supervision of their young children can achieve long-term benefits by reducing the risk that children will become involved in delinquent or offending behaviour.'

By the time the consultation document was issued, the government had already – through the Crime and Disorder Act 1998 – provided for the introduction of final warnings, parenting orders, child safety orders and local child curfews. These were referred to in Chapter 5 ('Better support for serious family problems') and reformulated as 'supporting families'.

Sure Start was expected to provide additional visits to every family with a new baby; an assessment of the needs of the child; and childcare advice for the parents. The programme was also designed to enhance parental employability by providing 'training for work' and help with literacy/numeracy. While Sure Start literature specifies that the services are for children from conception up to age 14 (up to 16 for those with special educational needs and disabilities), in practice its performance measures have concentrated on the progress of children under the age of 3 in 'workless households'.

By October 2006, 1,000 Sure Start centres were up and running – potentially accessible by 800,000 children – being rebadged as 'children's centres'. The target is to have 3,500 such centres by 2010. In 2006 the government announced an extension of the weekly free entitlement for 3 and 4-year-olds to 38 weeks a year, to be achieved by 2010. A pilot project providing free provision for 12,000 'disadvantaged' 2-year-olds in a number of local authorities was also announced. This is designed to increase the capacity of parents to return to the workplace.

The Department for Education and Skills-funded research programme, 'The Sure Start, Extended Schools and Childcare Group Research Programme', includes the National Evaluation of Sure Start initiatives. Early findings (November 2005) reported that, for most parents in programme areas, there were measurable improvements in parenting. For most

children there were small, but discernible, positive effects, such as fewer behavioural problems and better social skills. However a key finding was that there were continuing shortfalls in services reaching the families who needed them most. This triggered the publication of new planning, performance management and practice guidance for children's centres and local authorities. These specified that every centre must run a home-visiting and outreach programme for new parents – and evaluate the services provided – and provided a renewed emphasis on integrated working between agencies, allowing information about families to be more easily shared.

The Childcare Act 2006 significantly strengthens local authorities' responsibility for the performance of children's centres. The duty is placed on them to ensure there is sufficient childcare for parents in their area from April 2008. The Act also specifies how the Early Years Foundation Stage of the National Curriculum – that sets out learning arrangements for children from birth to 5 – should be implemented from September 2008, and it also defines the performance indicators for children's centres. The performance indicators now concentrate on assessing how successful centres are at 'reaching' the most disadvantaged groups. On a national level, the government's Public Service Agreement Targets (2005–8) include two targets for Sure Start:

1. *Outcomes for children*: there is an explicit expectation that 'stronger progress will be made' in the 20 per cent most disadvantaged areas.
2. *Childcare growth and take-up by lower-income families*: increasing the stock of childcare places and expanding provision throughout the working day.

While there is considerable evidence that adequately resourced, non-discriminatory and non-stigmatizing support services can improve the conditions of poor families in deprived areas, the specific impact of the Sure Start initiative remains unclear (with early findings showing limited effects). Research that highlights the potential negative effects on young children of spending substantial periods of time in day-care facilities appears to be overlooked.

Conversely, evidence that unemployment and poverty have significant negative impacts on children and families is emphasized (implying that parents should be active in the labour market). The long-term outcomes such as reduced youth offending, are even less certain and are unlikely to be attributed accurately to Sure Start given aetiological complexities and the myriad of other factors that impact on youth offending.

Sheena Doyle

Related entries

Children's trusts; Early intervention; Every Child Matters (ECM); Partnership working; Protective factors; Risk factors; Social exclusion; Social inclusion.

Key texts and sources

Home Office (1998) *Supporting Families*. London: Home Office.

Little, M. and Mount, K. (1999) *Prevention and Early Intervention with Children in Need*. Aldershot: Ashgate.

See also the websites of the National Evaluation of Sure Start (**www.surestart.gov.uk/ness**) and Sure Start (**http://www.surestart.gov.uk/**).

SURVEILLANCE

Surveillance refers to the oversight of suspicious people by official agencies, and the gathering of data, retrospectively or in real time, to monitor and/or regulate the movement or behaviour of particular individuals or groups of people.

Surveillance has not had a long history in youth justice and has traditionally been thought of – by youth justice workers and social workers, if not by the police – as having irredeemably malign associations. The term is not easily or directly associated with caring or punishment or with the achievement of lasting behavioural change. It has never fitted easily into traditional debates about welfare and justice and seemed in some initially inchoate way to represent something different

from both of them. Nonetheless, the colloquialism 'keeping an eye on', when applied to young people, has always had *potentially* benign connotations, evoking ideas of 'looking after' and 'watching over' someone for his or her own good or in his or her best interests. Youth justice workers in the past may well have done that, but without regarding it as surveillance.

Over the past 20 years, surveillance has become a more overt means of regulating young people's behaviour, and new scanning, monitoring, profiling and verification technologies have extended its forms. It is associated with the emergence of a techno-managerialist paradigm in criminal/youth justice that entails – more so than rehabilitative or punitive approaches to community supervision – the meticulous and (often) rapid regulation of behaviour. It also involves the gathering and processing of information over time to aid risk-based decision-making, whether in regard to specific individuals or to whole categories of people (for example, residents of a particular housing estate or an identified group of offenders, such as 'street robbers'). Police forces now have access to a range of integrated databases on both children/young people and adults that can be mined quickly for information on suspects, associates, crime patterns and 'hotspots'. Judgements can be made about individuals less on the basis of face-to-face contact and more on the basis of the 'digital selves' inscribed in databases.

Surveillance strategies for young people have largely emerged and evolved in three contexts – intensive supervision, enhancing detection and community safety. The intensification of community supervision programmes in the 1980s required closer contact with young offenders and tighter control over their locations and schedules. 'Tracking' – a method of intervention imported to England and Wales from Massachusetts in the USA – involved matching young offenders and support workers for a period of several weeks or months, during which the offender's use of time would be closely monitored to secure both immediate reductions in offending and to instil discipline in the longer term. Tracking was never widespread in the 1980s but was resurrected in the context of the Intensive Supervision and Surveillance

Programme (ISSP) – the first youth justice measure explicitly to proclaim surveillant intentions. Intensive mentoring schemes, within and without the ISSP, often resemble tracking but – semantically, at least – mentoring aspires to something much more constructive than surveillance.

The advent of electronic tagging sought to make monitoring a more integral feature of community supervision. It can be used separately or in combination with other measures as a sentence, for bail and for early release, and constitutes the surveillance element of the ISSP, alongside tracking and intelligence-led policing. Voice verification was a prototypical attempt to track the movement of offenders across several locations, which can be done in more precise and sophisticated ways with global positioning systems and mobile phone technology, the use of which was piloted with children and young people in England in 2004–5. This technology can also be used to monitor the perimeter of exclusion zones and, because spatial exclusion is an increasingly favoured means of dealing with young offenders, it may well have an auspicious future.

The use of public-space closed-circuit television (CCTV) has considerably increased the scale and scope of surveillance. All research studies show that young people are among the most intently surveilled of all target groups and, while CCTV seems less effective at deterring crime than originally envisaged, recorded images play an increased role in aiding detection. Fixed cameras are augmented by mobile units, hand-held cameras and even, in some cities, police helmet-mounted cameras, and can be linked to facial recognition systems. CCTV linked to public address systems is being piloted so that young people can be spoken to remotely from a control centre, increasing their awareness of being observed and enabling instructions to be given (to pick up litter or to stop fighting, for example). Powerless to prevent the spread of CCTV, young people have developed a variety of strategies for dealing with its presence, from the wearing of 'hoodies' to nihilistic exhibitionism.

The evolving police DNA database has been particularly controversial in respect of children and young people. In 2004 it became legally possible to retain a DNA sample taken at the point of arrest and, by January 2006, there were 24,000 children and young people on the database who had never been cautioned, charged or convicted. Inherent in this is great potential for racial discrimination, as proportionately more black and ethnic minority youngsters are arrested than white children and young people. The database may broaden in future, and DNA technology may one day produce rudimentary photofits of suspects. Knowing that their physical traces can be found and matched by forensic experts, some young offenders have already learnt to destroy potentially incriminating evidence (burning stolen cars, for example). Changed patterns of youth crime and new, improvised ways of evading surveillance may be the consequence of these developments.

Monitoring technologies now permeate many aspects of youth experience, from metal detectors to deter knife carrying, to random drug testing on the prolific offender and drug intervention programmes. Various sorts of scanning systems – fingers, face, iris and palm – are being used to verify and authenticate the identity of particular individuals, and thereby restrict or authorize access to particular physical spaces or resources. Such systems have been introduced into some schools to automate the process of borrowing library books and to identify – unobtrusively and ostensibly without stigma – those eligible for free school meals. Arguably, the worrying thing about these technologies – alongside the already ubiquitous CCTV in schools – is that they subtly normalize surveillance in young people's environments and may make them unduly accepting of the 'surveillance society' into which they are growing up.

Mike Nellis

Related entries

Community safety; Electronic monitoring; Enforcement; Exclusion orders; Intensive Supervision and Surveillance Programme (ISSP); Mentoring; 'Race' and justice; Risk management; Social harm.

Key texts and sources

Coleman, R. (2004) *Reclaiming the Streets: Surveillance, Social Control and the City.* Cullompton: Willan Publishing.

Garrett, P.M. (2004) 'The electronic eye: emerging surveillant practices in social work with children and families', *European Journal of Social Work*, 7: 57–71.

Gilbert, N. (2007) *Dilemmas of Privacy and Surveillance: Challenges of Technological Change.* London: Royal Academy of Engineering.

Lyon, D. (2006) *Theorising Surveillance: The Panopticon and Beyond.* Cullompton: Willan Publishing.

Nellis, M. (2004) 'The tracking controversy: the roots of mentoring and electronic monitoring', *Youth Justice*, 4: 77–99.

Penna, S. (2005) 'The Children Act 2004: child protection and social surveillance', *Journal of Social Welfare and Family Law*, 27: 143–58.

SYSTEMS MANAGEMENT

> Systems management is a strategic approach based on the belief that outcomes for individual young people and the way in which the youth justice system as a whole works can be changed by managing processes and targeting specific decision-making points within the system itself.

The book, *Out of Care* (Thorpe *et al.* 1980), comprised a damning critique of the juvenile justice system, one strand of which was aimed at the managers and practitioners in the system – police officers, social workers, probation officers, magistrates and social services administrators – and the decisions they were making. Thus, the researchers stated: 'Quite simply, cumulatively, these disparate bodies of professionals made the wrong decisions about the wrong children at the wrong time' (Thorpe *et al.* 1980: 3).

It was the emphasis on actual decision-making that was to become so powerful in subsequent juvenile justice practice. In short, if the decisions made about individual young people by the various professionals were wrong, the cumulative result was disastrous. Conversely, if enough of these decisions could be changed, then, in effect, the way in which the whole of the juvenile justice system operated could be improved and the outcomes for young people could be radically different. For example, if a decision is made to remand a young person in custody, then it increases the likelihood of an eventual custodial sentence. If the decision instead is to allow bail for the child (with or without conditions) in the community, then it is not only better for the young person in itself but it is also likely to *decrease* the prospect of an eventual custodial sentence and *increase* the chance of the young person receiving a community sentence. Therefore, if we begin to think about outcomes in the juvenile justice system as the product of a series of linked decisions, then changing decisions at crucial strategic points will ultimately produce change in the system as a whole. This is what came to be known as systems management thinking. Systems management is, therefore, a technique for changing system behaviour.

Much social work and juvenile justice practice in the 1970s was based on a predominant welfare philosophy. Welfarism underpinned work with young people, and there was little, if any, distinction between young people in social distress (welfare needs) and young people in trouble with the law (justice responses). Direct work with young people often mixed offenders and non-offenders, and the causes of social distress and offending were deemed to have the same root causes. At the same time, the courts retained powers to remove young people from home and to sentence them to residential care institutions or custody. The overall impact of this mix was that ever larger numbers of young people were drawn into the net of interventions by social workers, intermediate treatment staff and juvenile justice workers, and increasing numbers of young people were removed from home and placed in residential care institutions or sentenced to custody.

Research-based critiques of these outcomes were strident (Thorpe *et al.* 1980). Not only were these outcomes seen as being inimical to the best interests of young people – particularly those who ended up in residential care or custody – but the 'knowledge base' that underpinned such practice and justified these interventions was also, it was argued, deeply flawed. Moreover, particularly as far as young people who had offended were concerned, welfarism had been used to justify often free-ranging and quite intensive interventions that bore little or no relation to the seriousness of the offence/offending. These critiques hardened up and gradually formed what came to be known as 'new orthodoxy thinking'. Crucially, however, this new orthodoxy did not just offer a critique of the past but it also offered a vision for the future. This was a vision that recognized that much intervention with young people – arising out of court appearances – had a negative labelling effect and was potentially more harmful than beneficial (especially residential care and custody). Consequently, new orthodoxy thinking aimed to:

- promote diversion from the criminal justice system;
- limit intervention in accordance with the seriousness of the offence; and
- avoid the use of penal custody.

In the 1980s, it was the linking of new orthodoxy thinking with systems management techniques that became a powerful mixture in the hands of juvenile justice practitioners. This strategy was spectacularly successful to the extent that it quite rapidly brought about and sustained a significant growth in diversion and much reduced custodial sentencing with, notably, no evidence of any increase in the rate of juvenile offending.

In practice, for many workers in the juvenile justice system, new orthodoxy thinking and systems management were in tension with the reality of the lives of many of the young people they came into contact with, which were characterized by multiple deprivation and social exclusion. Many practitioners, therefore, balanced the former with the latter through sometimes quite intensive interventions, designed to minimize the negative consequences of involvement with the formal youth justice system, yet to maximize the positive outcomes for young people.

Kevin Haines

Related entries

Alternatives to custody; Diversion; Gatekeeping; Minimum necessary intervention; Partnership working; Penal welfarism; Proportionality; Remand management; Supervision orders.

Key texts and sources

Bell, C. and Haines, K. (1991) 'Managing the transition: implications of the introduction of a youth court in England and Wales', in T. Booth (ed.) *Juvenile Justice in the New Europe*. Sheffield: Joint Unit for Social Services Research.

Goldson, B. (1997) 'Children in trouble: state responses to juvenile crime', in P. Scraton (ed.) *'Childhood' in 'Crisis'?* London: UCL Press.

Haines, K. (1996) *Understanding Modern Juvenile Justice*. Aldershot: Avebury.

Haines, K. and Drakeford, M. (1998) *Young People and Youth Justice*. Basingstoke: Macmillan.

Thorpe, D., Smith, D., Green, C. and Paley, J. (1980) *Out of Care: The Community Support of Juvenile Offenders*. London: Allen & Unwin.

Tutt, N. and Giller, H. (1987) 'Manifesto for management – the elimination of custody', *Justice of the Peace*, 151: 200–2.

T

TARIFF

There are two distinct operational definitions of tariff: first, the minimum length of time a person must serve in custody – following a conviction for murder – before he or she becomes eligible for parole; and second, the notion that a hierarchy – or ladder – applies to the full range of sentencing options available to the courts, ranging from the least severe disposals (fines and discharges), through the mid-range (community orders) to the most severe sentences (custody).

If found guilty of murder, the court must impose a mandatory sentence 'to be detained during Her Majesty's pleasure' on any young person under the age of 18 years at the time the offence was committed (s. 90 of the Powers of Criminal Courts (Sentencing) Act 2000). Such a sentence is 'indeterminate' – not fixed in length as other sentences are – and is akin to the mandatory life sentence for adults. Such sentences have two components. The first part is the minimum period the young person must spend in custody – this is known as the 'tariff'. Once the young person has served his or her tariff, he or she remains in custody until the Parole Board decides to release him or her back into the community under licence – compulsory supervision/surveillance – which remains in force for life. The length of the tariff is set by the sentencing court and, in doing so, the judge must have regard to a statutory 'starting point' of 12 years, which may be varied up or down depending on the circumstances of the offence and the existence of aggravating or mitigating factors (s. 269 and Schedule 21 of the Criminal Justice Act 2003). The tariff element of an indeterminate prison sentence is, therefore, intended to reflect the appropriate amount of punishment or retribution, having regard to the relative seriousness of the crime committed.

In more general sentencing practice, the tariff refers to the notion that the range of sentencing options available to the courts forms a scale (or a ladder), with the least punitive or severe penalty at the bottom and the most punitive or severe at the top. More than this, however, the existence of the tariff implies that there is a link in sentencing between the seriousness of the offence and the severity of the penalty. The idea of the tariff, therefore, is explicitly linked to the sentencing aims of retribution and just deserts.

A further refinement of the existence of a tariff in the sentencing of young people is based on the idea of a 'stepping stone' mechanism – that is, that successive sentencing episodes result in a step up the tariff 'ladder'. Thus a first offence might normally be expected to attract a sentence at the bottom or lower end of the tariff and subsequent offences result in increasingly punitive sentences.

It is sometimes the case that young people are sentenced (often for a first offence or for a minor, less serious offence) to a relatively high-tariff sentence (a supervision order, for example) because the court is concerned – perhaps even for welfare-based reasons – to ensure that the young person receives intervention. On a subsequent court appearance, however, this 'good intention' can mean that the young person will receive a harsher penalty. This is known as the 'up-tariffing' effect and reflects the different (and sometimes contradictory) sentencing philosophies that are found in the youth court.

Kevin Haines

Related entries

Assessment framework; Dangerousness; Detention for public protection (DPP); Grave offences; Gravity factors (prosecution and sentencing); Just deserts; Proportionality; Retribution; Sentencing framework; Sentencing guidelines.

Key texts and sources

Easton, S. and Piper, C. (2005) *Sentencing and Punishment: The Quest for Justice.* Oxford: Oxford University Press.

Harrison, K. (2006) 'Community punishment or community rehabilitation: which is the highest in the sentencing tariff?', *Howard Journal*, 45: 141–58.

O'Mahony, D. and Haines, K. (1996) *An Evaluation of the Introduction and Operation of the Youth Court. Home Office Research Study 152.* London: Home Office.

Stafford, E. and Hill, J. (1987) 'The tariff, social inquiry reports and the sentencing of juveniles', *British Journal of Criminology*, 27: 411–20.

TRAINING SCHOOLS

A training school is a custodial institution (now defunct) for the detention of children and young people in Northern Ireland. Training schools emerged in the 1950s through the amalgamation of industrial and reformatory schools and were the equivalent of the 'approved schools' in England. From the mid-1990s the welfare and justice functions of training schools were separated, with the custodial institutions rebranded as Juvenile Justice Centres.

Training schools developed in Northern Ireland in the 1950s following the earlier recommendations of the Lynn Committee (1938), which had suggested the amalgamation of reformatories and industrial schools into a system of 'approved schools'. The Children and Young Person's (Northern Ireland) Act 1950 raised the age of criminal responsibility from 7 to 8 years and abolished reformatory and industrial schools, renaming them training schools. Training schools operated under the Training School Rules (Northern Ireland) 1952, which were in place until 1999.

Training school orders were the main custodial disposal available to juvenile courts under the Children and Young Persons (Northern Ireland) Act 1968. The Act also raised the age of criminal responsibility to 10 years. Training school orders were indeterminate in length and provided for a maximum of two years in custody. The actual length of custodial detention was determined by the training school manager, however, and, in many cases, this was dependent on whether or not the child was considered to have a stable home to go to following release. Training school orders did not take account of time spent on remand, and children could spend lengthy periods in custody for relatively minor offences. Children as young as 14 could be moved from a training school to Prison Service custody in a young offender centre or, in the case of girls, to Maghaberry Category A adult prison.

By the 1970s there were four training schools in Northern Ireland: Lisnevin in Millisle for Protestant and Catholic boys; Rathgael in Bangor for Protestant boys and girls; St Joseph's in Middletown for Catholic girls; and St Patrick's in Belfast for Catholic boys. In 1979 the report of the Children and Young Person's Review Group, chaired by Sir Harold Black, recommended the replacement of training schools by a single custodial centre for children, and that children should no longer be detained together for welfare and justice reasons.

Throughout the 1970s and 1980s there were mounting concerns among professionals and children's welfare organizations about the high numbers of children in custody (Convery 2002). Children's rights campaigners were particularly concerned about conditions in Lisnevin Training School, formerly a Borstal and modelled on a Category C prison (Kilkelly *et al.* 2002). The implementation of the Children (Northern Ireland) Order 1995 resulted in the separation of welfare and justice functions and the replacement of training schools with Juvenile Justice Centres (although this was achieved largely by separating each school into separate care and custodial 'wings') and renaming them).

Linda Moore

Related entries

Children in custody; Criminal Justice (Children) (Northern Ireland) Order 1998; Juvenile Justice Centre.

Key texts and sources

Convery, U. (2002) 'The use and nature of custody for children in the Northern Ireland criminal justice system.' Unpublished doctoral thesis, University of Ulster.

Convery, U. and Moore, L. (2006) *Still In Our Care: Protecting Children's Rights in Custody in Northern Ireland.* Belfast: Northern Ireland Human Rights Commission.

Department of Health and Social Services and Public Safety (2003) *A Better Future: 50 Years of Child Care in Northern Ireland 1950–2000.* Belfast: DHSSPS.

Kilkelly, U., Moore, L. and Convery, U. (2002) *In Our Care: Promoting the Rights of Children in Custody.* Belfast: Northern Ireland Human Rights Commission.

Northern Ireland Children and Young Persons Review Group (1979) *Legislation and Services for Children and Young People in Northern Ireland: Report of the Children and Young Persons Review Group* (the Black Report). Belfast: HMSO.

U

UNITED NATIONS COMMITTEE ON THE RIGHTS OF THE CHILD

> The United Nations Committee on the Rights of the Child is the international treaty-monitoring body for the United Nations Convention on the Rights of the Child. It normally meets three times a year in Geneva, Switzerland.

The States that have ratified the United Nations Convention on the Rights of the Child (UNCRC) elect the 18 members of the United Nations Committee on the Rights of the Child. Committee members act as independent individuals – not representatives of their countries – and are nominated for election on the basis of expertise in respect of children's issues. All the committee's members are adults. This has attracted criticism from children's rights activists in recent years, and there is mounting pressure from children in England and elsewhere for the committee – at least – to establish an international children's advisory group.

Two years after a government 'state party' ratifies the UNCRC it must submit an initial report to the committee for examination – outlining how it is applying the UNCRC – and, following this, each 'state party' must submit a periodic report to the committee every five years. The committee examines the 'state party' of children's rights in each country by requesting written evidence from government departments, non-governmental organizations (NGOs), national independent human rights institutions (such as children's commissioners) and children and young people themselves. It convenes a pre-sessional working group – with NGOs and others – ahead of its examination with state officials. Government officials are not permitted to take part in, or observe,

this working group, not least because in many countries of the world NGOs face serious threats from government. Even in so-called advanced democracies, openly criticizing the actions of government can bring negative consequences, such as withdrawal of funding. At the pre-sessional working group NGOs are able to suggest questions the committee may wish to put to government officials. There follows the state examination, with one or two of the committee members acting as a country rapporteur – their role is to lead the examination and the drafting of the committee's analysis and recommendations (known as 'concluding observations'). The committee issued its second set of concluding observations in respect of the UK in 2002 and is expected next to examine the UK's compliance with the UNCRC in 2008.

Every autumn the committee holds a day of general discussion and, in 1995, the specific theme under consideration was juvenile justice. The committee noted that 'state party' reports since 1991 (when it held its first examination) showed that:

special juvenile justice systems were often non-existent, that judges, lawyers, social workers or personnel in institutions were not given any special training and that information on fundamental rights and legal safeguards were not provided to children. For those reasons, and contrary to the Convention, deprivation of liberty was not used only as a measure of last resort or for the shortest period of time possible as called for in the Convention, nor were contacts with the family the rule; access to legal and other assistance was not provided and free legal aid was often not available

(United Nations Committee on the Rights of the Child 1995).

As with all treaty bodies, the committee issues 'general comments' that elaborate on the provisions and requirements of its principal human rights instrument. The latest 'general comment' in respect of the UNCRC was issued in February 2007, and it focuses on juvenile justice. It emphasizes that the juvenile justice system must safeguard the child's dignity at every point and underlines the UNCRC requirement that children should only be subject to judicial proceedings and custody as a very last resort. The aim of the juvenile justice system must be to meet the child's needs and to protect his or her best interests. The committee urges 'all professionals involved in the administration of juvenile justice [to] be knowledgeable about child development, the dynamic and continuing growth of children, what is appropriate to their well-being, and the pervasive forms of violence against children' (United Nations Committee on the Rights of the Child 2007).

Carolyne Willow

Related entries

Children's commissioners; Children's human rights; Criminal responsibility; Custody rate; Detention for public protection (DPP); Restraint; Secure training centres (STCs); Sentencing framework; United Nations Convention on the Rights of the Child (UNCRC).

Key texts and sources

United Nations Committee on the Rights of the Child (1995) *The Administration of Juvenile Justice* (available online at http://www.ohchr.org/english/bodies/crc/discussion.htm).

United Nations Committee on the Rights of the Child (2002) *Concluding Observations of the Committee on the Rights of the Child: United Kingdom of Great Britain and Northern Ireland.* Geneva: Committee on the Rights of the Child (available online at http://www.unhchr.ch/tbs/doc.nsf/(Symbol)/CRC.C.15.Add.188.En?Open Document).

United Nations Committee on the Rights of the Child (2007) *General Comment No. 10 (2007): Children's Rights in Juvenile Justice.* Geneva: Committee on the Rights of the Child (available online at http://www.ohchr.org/english/bodies/crc/comments.htm).

See also the websites of the Children's Rights Alliance for England ('Get ready for Geneva' web page) (www.getreadyforgeneva.org.uk) and the United Nations Committee on the Rights of the Child (http://www.ohchr.org/english/bodies/crc/).

UNITED NATIONS CONVENTION ON THE RIGHTS OF THE CHILD (UNCRC)

Children's human rights are set out in the United Nations Convention on the Rights of the Child (UNCRC), which was adopted by the United Nations General Assembly in 1989 and ratified by the UK government in 1991. The United Nations Committee on the Rights of the Child will next examine the UK's compliance with the convention in 2008.

The United Nations Convention on the Rights of the Child (UNCRC) is the second most widely ratified human rights treaty in the world, with only two states not yet formally accepting its obligations (the USA and Somalia). It was adopted by the United Nations General Assembly on 20 November 1989 and was formally ratified by the UK government on 14 December 1991. The UNCRC comprises 54 articles and it brings together children's economic, social and cultural, and civil and political rights. It is of central importance to youth justice policy and practice, both generally and specifically.

The general measures of the UNCRC cover the obligations on states to develop a children's human rights infrastructure and include the right to non-discrimination (Article 2); the primacy of the child's best interests (Article 3); the right to life and maximum development (Article 6); and the right to have the child's views given due weight in all matters affecting him or her (Article 12). The UNCRC also comprises a range of civil rights and freedoms, including the child's right to freedom of expression and association; the right to receive information; and the right to protection from all forms of violence, abuse, neglect and mistreatment. Similarly, provisions covering basic health and welfare include the child's right to an adequate standard of living and the right to the best possible health and healthcare services. Article 23 specifically relates to the rights of disabled children and young people to active participation in their community. The UNCRC also provides for children's rights with regard to education, leisure and cultural activities, including the right to education that helps develop the child's personality and talents (mental and physical abilities) and the right to rest and play. The provisions relating to special measures of protection include additional rights granted to children who are considered to be especially vulnerable, including young refugees, young workers, children affected by armed conflict, children subject to abuse and other forms of exploitation, and children in conflict with the law.

Articles 37 and 40 deal specifically with youth justice and give children the right to, *inter alia*, absolute protection from all forms of torture, cruel or inhuman or degrading treatment or punishment (this includes protection from capital punishment and indeterminate sentences). The articles also provide for the following:

- The right of detained children to be separated from adults.
- The rights of children in conflict with the law to legal representation and to have their cases heard before a court if their liberty is at risk.
- The right to be presumed innocent until proven guilty.
- The absolute right of privacy at all stages of youth justice proceedings.
- The right to be brought before a court or given a custodial sentence only as a very last resort.

The UK government has continued to retain two reservations to the UNCRC: one allowing it to detain children with adults in prison (Article 37c) and the other relating to immigration. Both reservations have attracted strong criticism nationally and internationally. The government claims that it plans to withdraw the Article 37c reservation on the basis that girls are no longer mixing with adult women in prison. However, recent reports from Her Majesty's

Chief Inspector of Prisons cite situations where girls and adult women continue to mix in prison – in healthcare, for example (Her Majesty's Inspectorate of Prisons 2006a, 2006b).

The UNCRC is to be read in conjunction with other human rights instruments. In juvenile justice, the two most important instruments are the United Nations Standard Mimimum Rules for the Administration of Juvenile Justice (the 'Beijing Rules') and the United Nations Guidelines for the Prevention of Juvenile Delinquency (the 'Riyadh Guidelines'). Together, these require United Nations member states to develop a distinct approach to preventing and tackling child offending, premised on meeting the child's needs and positive rehabilitation. Punishment and retribution have no place in these human rights standards.

The Council of Europe's Human Rights Commissioner has criticized UK youth justice policy, and the current incumbent, Thomas Hammarberg, issued a statement on youth justice in January 2007 that said:

Today, there are two very different approaches to juvenile crime. One is to lock up more and more young offenders, at an increasingly young age. The other trend – in the spirit of the UN Convention on the Rights of the Child – is to avoid criminalisation and to seek family-based or other social alternatives to imprisonment. I am arguing for the second approach ... In juvenile justice there should be no retribution.

When states ratify the UNCRC they are required to report periodically to the United Nations Committee on the Rights of the Child. The committee has twice examined the UK (in 1995 and in 2002), and the next examination is expected in 2008. Its concluding observations on the UK in October 2002 contain nine recommendations relating specifically to youth justice, including to:

- 'considerably increase' the minimum age of criminal responsibility;
- ensure children's privacy rights are protected at all stages of proceedings;
- use custody only as a very last resort; and
- ensure every child in custody has access to independent advocacy and a suitable complaints procedure.

The Children's Rights Alliance for England, a coalition of nearly 400 non-governmental organizations promoting the full implementation of the UNCRC, each year scrutinizes government progress in responding to the committee's recommendations. In November 2005 the alliance concluded that the government had made no progress whatsoever in the area of youth justice; indeed, it accused the UK government of 'tearing up the treaty' for children in trouble (Children's Rights Alliance for England 2005).

The Parliamentary Joint Committee on Human Rights has conducted an inquiry into the UK government's discharge of its obligations under the UNCRC (House of Lords/House of Commons Joint Committee on Human Rights 2003). Echoing the concerns of the United Nations Committee in 2002, its report calls for an increase in the age of criminal responsibility and a marked reduction in the use of custody, and it has since recommended the abolition of prison custody for children.

Two statutory bodies are significant in the protection of children's rights, as provided by the UNCRC: Children's commissioners and the Commission for Equality and Human Rights, established by the Equality Act 2006. The UNCRC is not justiciable, however, which means children cannot bring a case to court if they believe their rights have been breached. Neither is there any right of individual petition to the UN committee. However, the UK as a signatory to the UNCRC has accepted its provisions (subject to reservations), and all public authorities should be acting in a way that is compliant with its articles. The Vienna Convention on the Law of Treaties of 1969 – which entered into force in 1980 and is generally considered to reflect customary international law binding on all states – requires, in Article 26, that 'Every treaty in force is binding upon the parties to it and must be performed by them in good faith'.

It is imperative that all youth justice policy-makers and practitioners understand their detailed human rights obligations under the UNCRC.

Carolyne Willow

Related entries

Children First; Children in custody; Children's commissioners; Children's human rights; Comparative youth justice; Council of Europe; Criminal responsibility; Due process; Human Rights Act 1998; Informalism; Normalization; United Nations Committee on the Rights of the Child; United Nations Guidelines for the Prevention of Juvenile Delinquency; United Nations Standard Minimum Rules for the Administration of Juvenile Justice.

Key texts and sources

Children's Rights Alliance for England (2005) 'Government in breach of children's human rights – must do better', press release, 21 November. London: Children's Rights Alliance for England.

Children's Rights Alliance for England (2006) *The State of Children's Rights in England*. London: Children's Rights Alliance for England.

Hammarberg, T. (2007) 'It is wrong to punish the child victims?' (available online at http://www.coe.int/t/commissioner/Viewpoints/070108en.asp).

Her Majesty's Inspectorate of Prisons (2006a) *Report on an Unannounced Short Follow up Inspection of HMP/YOI Eastwood Park 7–9 March 2006 by HM Chief Inspector of Prisons*. London: Her Majesty's Inspectorate of Prisons.

Her Majesty's Inspectorate of Prisons (2006b) *Report on an Unannounced Short Follow up Inspection of HMP and YOI New Hall 20–23 March 2006 by HM Chief Inspector of Prisons*. London: Her Majesty's Inspectorate of Prisons.

Hodgkin, R. and Newell, P. (2002) *Implementation Handbook for the Convention on the Rights of the Child*. Geneva: Unicef.

House of Lords/House of Commons Joint Committee on Human Rights (2003) *The UN Convention on the Rights of the Child*. London: HMSO.

The United Nations Convention on the Rights of the Child is available online at http://www.unhchr.ch/html/menu3/b/k2crc.htm.

UNITED NATIONS GUIDELINES FOR THE PREVENTION OF JUVENILE DELINQUENCY

The United Nations Guidelines for the Prevention of Juvenile Delinquency (often referred to as the 'Riyadh Guidelines') were adopted by the United Nations General Assembly in 1990.

The United Nations Guidelines for the Prevention of Juvenile Delinquency operate within a framework of two other sets of international rules specifically governing juvenile justice: the United Nations Standard Minimum Rules for the Administration of Juvenile Justice 1985 (the 'Beijing Rules') and the United Nations Rules for the Protection of Juveniles Deprived of their Liberty 1990 (the 'JDL Rules' or the 'Havana Rules'). The guidelines should also be read alongside the United Nations Convention on the Rights of the Child.

The United Nations Guidelines for the Prevention of Juvenile Delinquency begin with the premise that 'the successful prevention of juvenile delinquency requires efforts on the part of the entire society to ensure the harmonious development of adolescents' (para. 2). Furthermore, a 'child-centred orientation should be pursued [whereby] … young persons should have an active role and partnership within society and should not be considered as mere objects of socialization or control' (para. 3). Paragraph 5 of the guidelines provides that 'official intervention' should be 'pursued primarily in the overall interest of the young person and guided by fairness and equity', underpinned by an 'awareness that, in the predominant opinion of experts, labelling a young person as "deviant", "delinquent" or "pre-delinquent" often contributes to the development of a consistent pattern of undesirable behaviour by young persons'. Paragraph 6 recommends that 'formal agencies of social control should only be utilized as a means of last resort'.

Separate but interrelated 'prevention' guidelines are provided with regard to the role of the family; the education system; the community and community-based services; the media; the broad corpus of social policy; and the law and the juvenile justice system. The overall approach emphasizes universal service provision and child-centredness. Paragraph 54 states: 'No child or young person should be subjected to harsh or degrading correction or punishment measures at home, in schools or in any other institutions.'

Finally, the guidelines encourage the exchange of research, policy development and practice experience at regional, national and international levels.

Barry Goldson

Related entries

Children's commissioners; Children's human rights; Council of Europe; Human Rights Act 1998; Informalism; Status offences; United Nations Convention on the Rights of the Child (UNCRC); United Nations Rules for the Protection of Juveniles Deprived of their Liberty; United Nations Standard Minimum Rules for the Administration of Juvenile Justice.

Key texts and sources

United Nations General Assembly (1990) *United Nations Guidelines for the Prevention of Juvenile Delinquency* (the Riyadh Guidelines) (available online at http://www.un.org/documents/ga/res/45/a45r112.htm).

UNITED NATIONS RULES FOR THE PROTECTION OF JUVENILES DEPRIVED OF THEIR LIBERTY

The United Nations Rules for the Protection of Juveniles Deprived of their Liberty (often referred to as the 'JDL Rules' or the 'Havana Rules') were adopted by the United Nations General Assembly in 1990.

The United Nations Rules for the Protection of Juveniles Deprived of their Liberty operate within a framework of two other sets of international rules specifically governing juvenile justice: the United Nations Standard Minimum Rules for the Administration of Juvenile Justice 1985 (the

'Beijing Rules') and the United Nations Guidelines for the Prevention of Juvenile Delinquency 1990 (often referred to as the 'Riyadh Guidelines'). The rules should also be read alongside the United Nations Convention on the Rights of the Child.

The rules are based on a number of core principles:

- Deprivation of liberty should be a disposition of 'last resort' and used only 'for the minimum necessary period'.
- Children and young people should only be deprived of their liberty in accordance with the principles, procedures and safeguards provided by international human rights standards, treaties, rules and conventions.
- In cases where children have their liberty restricted, small facilities are encouraged to enable individualized 'treatment' and the negative effects of incarceration should be avoided in larger penal institutions.
- Secure facilities should allow ready access and contact from family members and facilitate the child's/young person's reintegration into the community.
- Staff working with children and young people in detention should receive appropriate education and training, including child welfare and human rights.

It is important to note that the United Nations Rules for the Protection of Juveniles Deprived of their Liberty are not limited to penal institutions: they also apply in cases where children's/young people's liberty is restricted on the basis of welfare (secure accommodation) and health (secure psychiatric provision) interventions.

Barry Goldson

Related entries

Children in custody; Children's human rights; Hospital orders; Juvenile secure estate; Looked-after children (LAC); Secure accommodation; United Nations Convention on the Rights of the Child (UNCRC); United Nations Guidelines for the Prevention of Juvenile Delinquency; United Nations Standard Minimum Rules for the Administration of Juvenile Justice.

Key texts and sources

The United Nations Rules for the Protection of Juveniles Deprived of their Liberty are available online at http://www.ohchr.org/english/law/res 45_113.htm.

UNITED NATIONS STANDARD MINIMUM RULES FOR THE ADMINISTRATION OF JUVENILE JUSTICE

The United Nations Standard Minimum Rules for the Administration of Juvenile Justice (often referred to as the 'Beijing Rules') were adopted by the United Nations General Assembly in 1985. The rules provide guidance for the protection of children's rights in the development of separate and specialist juvenile justice systems.

The United Nations Standard Minimum Rules for the Administration of Juvenile Justice were a direct response to a call made by the Sixth United Nations Congress on the Prevention of Crime and the Treatment of Offenders that convened in 1980. The rules operate within a framework of two other sets of international rules specifically governing juvenile justice, both of which were adopted in 1990: The United Nations Guidelines for the Prevention of Juvenile Delinquency (the 'Riyadh Guidelines') and the United Nations Rules for the Protection of Juveniles Deprived of their Liberty (the 'JDL Rules' or the 'Havana Rules'). They should also be read alongside the United Nations Convention on the Rights of the Child.

Some of the core provisions of the United Nations Standard Minimum Rules for the Administration of Juvenile Justice include the following:

- *Rule 1.1:* 'Member States shall seek, in conformity with their respective general interests, to further the well-being of the juvenile and her or his family.'
- *Rule 1.3:* 'Sufficient attention should be given to positive measures that involve the full

mobilisation of all possible resources ... for the purpose of promoting the well-being of the juvenile, with a view to reducing the need for intervention under the law, and of effectively, fairly and humanely dealing with the juvenile in conflict with the law.'

- *Rule 2.1*: 'the following Standard Minimum Rules shall be applied to juvenile offenders impartially, without distinction of any kind, for example as to race, colour, sex, language, religion.'

- *Rule 4.1*: the age of criminal responsibility shall not 'be fixed at too low an age level, bearing in mind the facts of emotional, mental and intellectual maturity.'

- *Rule 5.1*: the juvenile justice system shall emphasize the well-being of the child and 'shall ensure that any reaction to juvenile offenders shall always be in proportion to the circumstances of both the offenders and the offence.'

- *Rule 8.1*: the child's 'right to privacy shall be respected at all stages in order to avoid harm being caused to her or him by undue publicity or by the process of labelling.'

- *Rule 13.5*: 'while in custody, juveniles shall receive care, protection and all necessary individual assistance... that they may require.'

- *Rule 19.1*: 'the placement of a juvenile in an institution shall always be a disposition of last resort and for the minimum necessary period.'

- *Rule 22.1*: 'professional education [and] in-service training... shall be utilised to establish and maintain the necessary professional competence of all personnel dealing with juvenile cases.'

Given the importance placed on juvenile justice by the international community, Unicef (1998: 2) has noted that 'it seems somewhat paradoxical that the rights, norms and principles involved are regularly ignored and seriously violated virtually throughout the world, on a scale that is probably unmatched in the field of civil rights implementation'.

Barry Goldson

Related entries

Children in custody; Children's human rights; Comparative youth justice; Council of Europe; Criminal responsibility; Diversion; Gender and justice; Human Rights Act 1998; Informalism; Labelling theory; Proportionality; 'Race' and justice; Status offences; United Nations Convention on the Rights of the Child (UNCRC); United Nations Guidelines for the Prevention of Juvenile Delinquency; United Nations Rules for the Protection of Juveniles Deprived of their Liberty.

Key texts and sources

Monaghan, G. (2005) 'Children's human rights and youth justice', in T. Bateman and J. Pitts (eds) *The RHP Companion to Youth Justice*. Lyme Regis: Russell House.

Unicef (1998) *Innocenti Digest: Juvenile Justice*. Florence: Unicef.

United Nations General Assembly (1985) *United Nations Standard Minimum Rules for the Administration of Juvenile Justice* (the Beijing Rules) (available online at **http://www.un.org/documents/ga/res/40/a40r033.htm**).

VICTIMIZATION

> Victimization refers to the processes associated with becoming a victim (of crime).

The concept of victimization can be used in at least two different ways. First, victimization relates to the processes of interaction that take place between people that result in the victimization of a person or persons who subsequently acquires the 'status' of victim. The interactional processes associated with the acquisition or non-acquisition of victim status and the impact that these processes have on an individual's identity have been relatively neglected in the study of victimization. Moreover, as Rock (2002) has observed, understanding victimization as an interactional process also requires analysis of when and how people define themselves as a victim; what it means for the person when victim status is recognized or not (and what significance is attached to it); and, finally, the point at which these processes might become problematic. Put simply, when do the processes of victimization result in an individual embracing a victim identity? Such questions constitute an important part of understanding the circumstances in which some people acquire victim status while others do not. This is particularly significant when the processes of victimization derive from relationships either within the family or within a child's or young person's immediate neighbourhood. Young people face added difficulties in these circumstances since the processes of victimization can damage other aspects of their relationship with their family or their neighbourhood, and this can result in them choosing not to report their victimization and thus their victim status being unrecognized.

Second, the concept of victimization refers to the ways in which becoming a victim of crime are not evenly distributed in society. In this context victimization is used to refer to the patterning of criminal victimization structured by age, class, gender and ethnicity. Criminal victimization survey data consistently reveal that younger people are much more likely to be victimized than older people; the poor and economically marginalized are much more likely to be victimized than the better-off; people from ethnic minorities are much more likely to be victimized than white people; and, in the context of street crime, men are much more likely to be victimized than women. When the picture of victimization is framed in this way it becomes clear that the young working-class black or minoritized male is *more likely* to be victimized, especially on the street, than any other category of person. Yet it is also the case that they are the *least likely* to be viewed as vulnerable *to* such victimization and *most likely* to be seen as the perpetrators *of* such victimization. Thus the empirical patterning of victimization would suggest that young, economically marginal males from ethnic minority groups belong to both 'victim' and 'offender' categories, often offending against each other.

Sandra Walklate

Related entries

Child abuse; Child prostitution; Children in custody; Demonization; Discrimination; Gender and justice; Left realism; Looked-after children (LAC); 'Race' and justice; Social harm; Street crime; Victimology; Victims.

Key texts and sources

Audit Commission (1986) *Misspent Youth: Young People and Crime.* London: Audit Commission.

Green, S. (2007) 'Crime, victimisation and vulnerability', in S. Walklate (ed.) *Handbook of Victims and Victimology.* Cullompton: Willan Publishing.

Miers, D. (1990) 'Positivist victimology: a critique. Part 2', *International Review of Victimology*, 1: 219–30.

Rock, P. (2002) 'On becoming a victim', in C. Hoyle and R. Young (eds) *New Visions of Crime Victims.* Oxford: Hart Publishing.

VICTIMOLOGY

Victimology is a sub-discipline of criminology concerned with understanding and explaining the patterning of criminal victimization.

Victimology draws together academics, activists and policymakers from different disciplinary backgrounds. This rather heady mixture frequently results in different political and policy perspectives being adopted by each of the groups of people who, nonetheless, all claim to be victimologists. There is some dispute as to who first coined the term 'victimology' but, as a discrete area of analysis, it emerged from attempts to understand how the mass victimization associated with the Holocaust could have occurred. Latterly it is possible to identify three distinct intellectual strands within victimological thought: positivist, radical and critical victimology.

Positivist victimology, according to Miers (1989), is preoccupied with the patterning of criminal victimization that was a product of interpersonal crime; forms of victimization in which the victim might have contributed to what happened to him or her and other factors that might contribute to the non-random nature of criminal victimization (for example, lifestyle). In positivist victimology the victim is taken as either being defined by the criminal law or by the self-evident nature of his or her suffering.

Radical victimology reflects a much wider understanding of the patterning of criminal victimization and is concerned to address the ways in which the state and the implementation of the law itself can render some people more likely to be victims than others. Here, the victim is conceived as a product of the way in which relations of power take their toll on some people more than others.

Critical victimology is a term with different meanings. For some, it is used to focus attention on the processes of interaction – between the 'victim' and the 'offender' – that result in victimization. For others, it is a term used to situate victimology squarely within the domain of sociology. Here critical victimology is concerned to understand how social processes produce both patterns of victimization that we can see (and, for example, are measurable by social surveys) and forms of victimization that are not so easily recognizable and measurable (such as, for example, victims of corporate fraud). It endeavours to capture the concerns of both positivist and radical victimology and to situate an understanding of the patterning of criminal victimization informed by critical realism. This means engaging with the processes – that go on 'behind our backs' – that contribute to the victims we see as well as to those we do not see (including the role of the state in those processes). For critical victimology it is important to challenge the use of the term 'victim' in and of itself and to develop a more subtle appreciation of when this term may or may not be applicable.

These different strands of victimological thought coexist with the campaigning voices of victimology that are themselves differently politically motivated. Taken together they contribute to what Rock (1986) has referred to as the discipline's 'catholic' nature.

Sandra Walklate

Related entries

Critical criminology; Social harm; Victimization; Victims.

Key texts and sources

Goodey, J. (2005) *Victims and Victimology.* Harlow: Longman.

Miers, D. (1989) 'Positivist victimology: a critique', *International Review of Victimology*, 1: 3–22.

Rock, P. (1986) *A View from the Shadows.* Oxford: Oxford University Press.

Spalek, B. (2006) *Crime Victims: Theory, Policy and Practice.* London: Palgrave.

Walklate, S. (2007) *Imagining the Victim of Crime.* Maidenhead: Open University Press.

VICTIMS

In common usage the term 'victim' connotes an individual who has suffered some kind of misfortune. Its more specific link with crime is now well established, however.

For many people working with victims of crime the term 'victim' is highly problematic. The feminist movement has been particularly critical of the term since its genealogy implicitly connects it with being female. In turn, this implies that the passivity and powerlessness often attributed to being a victim are, by definition, also associated with being female. Feminists express a preference for the term 'survivor' as this captures girls'/women's resistance to their structural powerlessness and potential victimization. However, the tension that exists with either being labelled a 'victim' or a 'survivor' is also problematic since each label fails to capture the processes of victimization. For example, it is possible that an individual – at different points in time and in relation to different events – can be an active victim, a passive victim, an active survivor, a passive survivor and all the experiential possibilities in between. From this point of view, the term victim is rather sterile. Moreover, there are other difficulties associated with the term.

The process in which an individual acquires the label of victim reflects social preoccupations with what Christie (1986) called the 'ideal victim'. For Christie, the 'ideal victim' is the victim of the 'Little Red Riding Hood' fairytale: a young, innocent female, out doing good deeds who is attacked by an unknown stranger. This ideal stereotype results in some people being viewed as 'deserving victims' – that is, acquiring the victim label very readily and easily – while other are labelled 'undeserving victims', who may never acquire the victim label. Many young offenders find themselves in this latter category. Indeed the power of such stereotyping contributes to the assumption that victims are 'good' and offenders are 'bad', as well as having the effect that it becomes very difficult to consider the extent to which offenders might also be victims. This latter effect has prompted

Carrabine and colleagues (2004: 117) to talk of a 'hierarchy of victimization'. At the bottom of this hierarchy would be the homeless person, the street prostitute, the drug addict – indeed, people for whom it is presumed that they expose themselves to victimization, making a claim to the label 'victim' very difficult.

The notion of a 'hierarchy of victimization' clearly suggests that some people are seen to have a much more legitimate claim to victim status than others. It also exposes the underlying politics associated with the processes that assign victim status to some individuals and groups and not others. In this respect it is interesting to note the difficulties faced by young offenders in officially acquiring victim status. Children are much more likely to be considered as victims because of the powerlessness associated with childhood – especially in the context of child abuse – but young offenders are much less likely to acquire victim status because of their offending behaviour. This is despite increasing evidence that there are links between the experience of abuse as a child and subsequent offending behaviour and, more generally, the experience of victimization common to many children and young people in trouble. Nevertheless, victim status is not so easily achieved for the young offender since he or she falls significantly short of the 'ideal victim' stereotype.

Sandra Walklate

Related entries

Child abuse; Child prostitution; Family group conferencing; Gender and justice; Mediation; Referral orders; Reparation; Restorative cautioning; Restorative justice; Restorative youth conferencing; Victimization; Victimology.

Key texts and sources

Carrabine, E., Iganski, P., Lee, M., Plummer, K. and South, N. (2004) *Criminology: A Sociological Introduction.* London: Routledge.

Christie, N. (1986) 'The ideal victim', in E.A. Fattah (ed.) *From Crime Policy to Victim Policy.* London: Macmillan.

Davies, P. (2007) 'Lessons from the gender agenda', in S. Walklate (ed.) *Handbook of Victims and Victimology.* Cullompton: Willan Publishing.

Rumgay, J. (2004) *When Victims Become Offenders. Occasional Paper*. London: Fawcett Society.

Walklate, S. (2003) 'Can there be a feminist victimology?', in P. Davies *et al.* (eds) *Victimisation: Theory, Research and Policy*. London: Palgrave.

VULNERABILITY

> Vulnerability refers to the state of being 'vulnerable' or being exposed to the risk of harm. In youth justice, vulnerability is particularly associated with the assessment of 'risk'.

The recognition of children and young people's vulnerability represents the contradiction between protection and punishment that often shapes criminal justice provision for young people. Young people under the age of 18 are, by definition, seen as being 'vulnerable' when they are the victim of, or a witness to, a crime, and may be entitled to special safeguarding/protective measures when giving testimony in court. Such measures might include the use of a video link, having a screen around the witness box and/or prerecording questioning. However, when the child or young person is the offender, a very different logic comes into play. The assessment and management of vulnerability form part of the assessment and management of risk, which is meant to inform the decision-making, recommendations and practice of youth offending team workers.

The main means by which youth offending teams identify and assess risk and vulnerability is through the formal tool, Asset. The 'core profile' of Asset contains a detailed section addressing vulnerability, as does the 'final warning profile'. The Youth Justice Board defines vulnerability as arising from the mental or physical health needs of the child/young person or his or her 'self-destructive' behaviours (including drug and alcohol abuse) or 'inappropriate behaviours'; the behaviour and activities of others – including bullying and neglect and physical, sexual or emotional abuse; and other circumstances that a child/young person might experience – such as housing problems, poverty, significant and troubling life events (for example, bereavement), the experience of incarceration and so on. The Youth Justice Board recommends that the level of vulnerability is assessed in accordance with the probability of actual harm.

There are at least two key problems with the concept of 'vulnerability' as it is typically framed in youth justice policy and practice. First, in the assessment tools there is little or no distinction between the concepts of 'vulnerability' and 'need'. Second, underpinning the management of 'risk' (of reoffending) and the assessment of vulnerability is a tautology. Thus the identification of 'vulnerabilities' is at once identified as 'risk factors' pertaining to the probability of future offending. In this respect, children and young people who are vulnerable might also be assessed as posing a greater level of risk of reoffending. The difficulty of this conflation of risk and vulnerability is that youth justice policy and practice tend to emphasize the risk of reoffending rather than vulnerability – unless and until such vulnerability is assessed in the context of statutory child protection. In this way, and in common with adult justice, much contemporary policy and practice are based on the translation of structurally derived socio-economic needs and vulnerabilities into individually centred criminogenic risks.

Jo Phoenix

Related entries

Assessment framework; Child abuse; Child poverty; Child prostitution; Children in custody; Mental health and young offenders; Protective factors; Risk factors; Risk management; Social exclusion; Victims.

Key texts and sources

Goldson, B. (2002b) *Vulnerable Inside: Children in Secure and Penal Settings*. London: Children's Society.

Hudson, B. (2003) *Justice in the Risk Society*. London: Sage.

WELFARE

The child's welfare is usually a paramount principle in child protection proceedings, but there are variable views and policies as to how far welfare is a relevant principle when dealing with children who have committed offences.

In England and Wales, s. 1(1)(a) of the Children Act 1989 provides that, when a court determines *any* question with respect to the upbringing of a child, 'the child's welfare shall be the court's paramount consideration'. Furthermore, when a court is considering making an order in child protection proceedings, it shall not do so 'unless it considers that doing so would be better for the child than making no order at all' (s. 1(5)). This has been described as a 'no non-beneficial order' principle.

Very similar legal provisions were enacted for Scotland in the Children (Scotland) Act 1995, s. 16(1) and (3). An important difference between the two jurisdictions, however, is that in Scotland the 'paramountcy of welfare' principle applies also (with some exceptions) to cases in the children's hearing system where an offence is the ground of the hearing. By contrast, welfare paramountcy is not a principle in offence-based cases in England and Wales, although the court is more generally required to 'have regard to the welfare' of youth court defendants (Children and Young Persons Act 1933, s. 44(1)). The approaches of both jurisdictions have strengths, but also weaknesses.

If welfare is a paramount consideration in offence-based cases, and a 'no non-beneficial order' principle also applies, then in principle it would seem that no compulsory action should be taken in respect of a socially 'well adjusted' child who commits an offence. Again, if two youths commit the same offence together, with similar culpability, but one has substantially greater welfare needs than the other, on welfare principles it would seem that the 'needy' youth should receive the greater intervention, but this would conflict with principles of proportionality and just deserts. Not surprisingly, therefore, research suggests that, in practice, the Scottish children's hearing system has not adopted a 'pure' welfare-paramountcy approach in offence-based cases (Bottoms 2002).

But a sharp separation of welfare and justice issues can also present problems. In effect the Crime and Disorder Act 1998 creates such a system in England and Wales, with 'welfare' considerations ostensibly paramount in the child protection system but 'justice' (or even retributive) considerations dominant in the youth justice system. Difficulties for this 'twin-track' system arise from the fact that juvenile offenders, especially persistent offenders, often have complex welfare needs (Goldson 2000c; Waterhouse *et al.* 2000). A twin-track system can, if applied mechanically, therefore quickly run into difficulties. For example, in one actual case in England a child had already received a final warning for an offence and then committed a further offence of bicycle theft. He had complex welfare needs, including emotional problems arising from being the victim of a serious sexual assault, and he was expected soon to give evidence at the Crown court trial of his assailant. According to the guidelines relating to the youth justice system in England and Wales, a post-final warning offence case should automatically be prosecuted in the youth court, but seminar discussions of this case with senior practitioners (including senior police officers) show that many would question the wisdom of such an approach, preferring to prioritize emotional support in readiness for the Crown court trial.

Historically, various combinations of 'welfare' and 'justice' principles have been applied to youth justice systems at different times. Some scholars have tried to resolve the debate by proposing some type of mixed system; one such suggestion was described as a 'just welfare' system. In more recent years, some advocates of restorative justice have argued that an approach grounded in restorative principles has the potential to transcend traditional welfare–justice debates, but others disagree.

Anthony Bottoms

Related entries

Children Act 1989; Children and Young Persons Act 1933; Children (Scotland) Act 1995; Children's hearing system; Crime and Disorder Act 1998; Just deserts; Persistent young offenders; Proportionality; Restorative justice.

Key texts and sources

Bottoms, A. (2002) 'The divergent development of juvenile justice policy and practice in England and Scotland', in M.K. Rosenheim *et al.* (eds) *A Century of Juvenile Justice.* Chicago, IL: University of Chicago Press.

Goldson, B. (2000c) '"Children in need" or "young offenders"? Hardening ideology, organisational change and new challenges for social work with children in trouble', *Child and Family Social Work*, 5: 255–65.

Harris, R. and Webb, D. (1987) *Welfare, Power and Juvenile Justice.* London: Tavistock.

Hill, M., Lockyer, A. and Stone, F. (eds) (2007) *Youth Justice and Child Protection.* London: Jessica Kingsley.

Waterhouse, L., McGhee, J., Whyte, B., Loucks, N., Kay, H. and Stewart, R. (2000) *The Evaluation of the Children's Hearings in Scotland: Children in Focus.* Edinburgh: Scottish Executive.

WELSH ASSEMBLY GOVERNMENT

The term 'Welsh Assembly Government' refers to the 'executive' arm of the National Assembly for Wales. Since its establishment in May 1999, the executive has been led by the Labour Party, either as a minority administration or in coalition with the Liberal Democrats, or – for two years – as a government with a one-seat majority, in a body of 60 members.

The Government of Wales Act 1998, which established devolved government, created a novel form of institution, structured as a 'corporate body', in which no formal separation existed between 'government' and 'opposition'. In practice, this distinction served mostly to blur lines of accountability rather than to create a new 'inclusive' politics. Once a majority coalition administration was created, 18 months into the first assembly term, opposition parties proposed that, in a *de facto* fashion, the institution should operate as far as possible on conventional parliamentary lines.

This position was confirmed, in *de jure* fashion, in the Government of Wales Act 2006. The new Act means that, as from the elections of May 2007, Welsh ministers are formally appointments of the Crown and provided with direct executive responsibilities in relation to many decisions that had previously fallen to the assembly as a whole.

The current position provides for an assembly government comprising of a First Minister and 12 further ministers. Since 2000, when the present First Minister, Rhodri Morgan, took office, the ministerial team has comprised a Cabinet of eight other ministers, together with four deputy ministers. As from May 2007, this was augmented by a new Law Officer – the Counsel General – of Cabinet rank, who may be an existing assembly member but who can be appointed from outside. In common with the gender balance in the assembly as a whole, the Cabinet has always included either four or five women ministers, covering all the major devolved responsibilities, such as health, education, finance, housing and local government. Unlike Scotland there is no separate Welsh criminal justice system and, as a result, the

Home Office retains responsibility for policing and the Prison and Probation Services.

In this context, youth justice has emerged as one of the most interesting constitutional areas. While the Youth Justice Board (YJB) remains an England *and* Wales body, a clear majority of youth offending team members in Wales – social workers, health workers, teachers, housing workers – are supplied by wholly devolved services. In this sense, the key services delivered in the youth justice system in Wales derive from authority and responsibility vested with Welsh ministers.

In recognition of this position, a particular way of working has evolved over the past eight years in which a separate All Wales Youth Offending Strategy (Welsh Assembly Government 2004) is overseen by a stakeholder board, jointly chaired by the Welsh Assembly Government Minister for Social Justice and the chair of the YJB. The strategy departs, in a series of significant ways, from the Home Office agenda. It emphasizes decarceration and community engagement; it favours diversionary strategies based on universal services; and it regards young people in trouble with the law as children first and offenders secondly. The strategy thus reflects the ideological preferences of the Welsh Assembly Government as a whole, in putting what First Minister Morgan has famously described as 'clear red water' between Labour in Wales and Westminster.

Mark Drakeford

Related entries

All Wales Youth Offending Strategy; Children First; Children's commissioners; Extending Entitlement (National Assembly for Wales).

Key texts and sources

Cross, N., Evans, J. and Minkes, J. (2003) 'Still children first? Developments in youth justice in Wales', *Youth Justice*, 2: 151–62.

Welsh Assembly Government (2004) *All Wales Youth Offending Strategy*. Cardiff: Welsh Assembly Government.

See the Office of Public Sector Information's website for the texts of the Government of Wales Act 1998 (http://www.opsi.gov.uk/acts/acts1998/ukpga_ 19980038_en_1) and the Government of Wales Act 2006 (http://www.opsi.gov.uk/acts/acts2006/ 20060032.htm).

WHAT WORKS

> With or without a question mark, the phrase 'What Works' is normally associated with the revival of the belief that some methods of intervention with offenders are relatively successful in reducing the risk of reoffending. It also derives from the government-supported movement – the 'new rehabilitationism' – to encourage the adoption of these methods, particularly in the Probation Service.

In 1974 the American journal, *The Public Interest*, published what became one of the most cited articles in criminological history: Robert Martinson's 'What works? Questions and answers about prison reform'. The article summarized the findings of a major review of 'the effectiveness of correctional treatment'. The review itself was commissioned by the New York State Governor's Commission on Criminal Offenders. It was completed in 1970, but its publication was delayed until 1975 because of official anxiety that the findings would erode confidence in the criminal justice system. Martinson and his colleagues examined 231 studies – covering a wide variety of interventions – conducted between 1945 and 1967. In terms of the impact of interventions on reoffending, the results they found were mainly negative, but arguably not so negative as to justify Martinson's famous conclusion: 'With few and isolated exceptions, the rehabilitative efforts that have been reported so far have had no appreciable effect on recidivism' (1974: 53). This was widely interpreted in Britain and elsewhere as meaning 'Nothing Works' and, despite reservations – later shared by Martinson himself – about whether this conclusion was justified, it quickly became the dominant view among practitioners and researchers. Buttressed by British studies that seemed to point in the same direction, pessimism prevailed at least until the early 1990s.

A few dissenting voices continued to argue that the messages from research were not as overwhelmingly negative as Martinson had claimed and, in 1990, Gill McIvor of the Social Work Research Centre at Stirling University published a review of *Sanctions for Serious or Persistent*

Offenders that reached different and much more positive conclusions. Drawing on more recent research, McIvor identified characteristics of interventions with offenders that were associated with improved prospects of a reduction in subsequent offending. These formed the basis for what, by the late 1990s, came to constitute the orthodoxy on 'what works'. Successful programmes, according to this interpretation of the research, were likely to be based in the community rather than run in institutions. The intensity and duration of intervention should be consistent with offenders' 'risk' of reoffending: the greater the risk, the more intensive the intervention should be. Effective interventions focus on needs and problems that are 'criminogenic' – associated with the participants' pattern of offending – and use active and participatory methods, reflecting the preferred learning style of most offenders. They are flexible enough to take account of the variety of offenders' problems and have, as a central aim, the improvement of participants' coping skills. They pursue this aim through the use of cognitive-behavioural methods designed to help offenders to think more clearly, to avoid acting impulsively and to consider the consequences of their actions. Successful interventions maintain 'programme integrity' in that their content and methods are relevant to, and compatible with, their stated aims and are delivered by well trained and well supported staff who are committed to the critical evaluation of their work. Unsuccessful interventions, according to McIvor's review of the research, are likely to lack all or some of these features, being, for example, open ended rather than time limited, without clearly stated aims or solely reliant on punishment as a means of promoting change.

Interested practitioners, managers and researchers organized a series of conferences on 'What Works' in Manchester in the early 1990s, in which they explored the implications for practice of the new, more optimistic account of what could be learnt from research, and these inspired an influential collection of papers edited by James McGuire and published in 1995. By then the Home Office was actively encouraging probation services to ensure that they were working in ways that were compatible with 'what works'. The phrase was no longer being posed as a question but as a matter of established fact, even though the evidence base in Britain was still very limited. Understandably, after almost 20 years of 'Nothing Works', probation managers and policymakers were eager to embrace research findings that conveyed a more positive message, and the Home Office published research in 1997 and 1998 that broadly supported the optimism of the time. The Probation Inspectorate also strongly supported the 'What Works' agenda, identifying good practice as practice that conformed to the criteria for effectiveness summarized above, the Inspectorate undertook its own research on how far probation services were running programmes based on 'what works' principles and found a considerable gap between rhetoric and reality: while 267 programmes of the approved kind were supposed to be running, only four could produce any real evidence that their interventions were effective. The report of this research, in identifying strategies for effective supervision, made clear that even programmes run on impeccable 'what works' lines needed to be backed by a broader effort to help offenders overcome problems arising from social, educational and economic stress and disadvantage (Underdown 1998). Contrary to what some civil servants in the Home Office apparently believed, cognitive-behavioural programmes focused on offending behaviour were not all that was required. Unfortunately some local managers came to share the civil servants' erroneous belief, leading a new Chief Inspector of Probation, Rod Morgan (later Chair of the Youth Justice Board), to complain in 2002 of 'programme fetishism'.

The Home Office identified a number of programmes that looked promising as 'pathfinders', which were to be given special support and were subject to external evaluation and which were conducted from 1999 as part of the ambitious Crime Reduction Programme (CRP). The programmes included, but were not restricted to, cognitive-behavioural approaches focused on offending behaviour; prisoner resettlement; basic skills; and enhancing community service. The programmes proved difficult to evaluate, partly because they were often difficult to implement:

drop-out rates were high and, in some cases, a high proportion of those who were meant to undertake the programme did not even start it. The quality of available data was often poor, and there were problems in identifying suitable comparison groups. Evaluation of programmes and other initiatives in youth justice – such as referral orders – encountered similar problems. The typical model adopted by the Youth Justice Board was of a national evaluation that collated and analysed data provided by local evaluators, but variations in method, research skills, resources and commitment at the local level meant that the data available for national analysis were inconsistent and incomplete. As a result, the findings from the evaluations were frustratingly inconclusive in both the adult and youth justice systems.

It was not surprising, then, that when the Home Office reviewed the overall results of the parts of the CRP that were concerned with reducing reoffending, it was much more cautious than it had been prior to the programme in claiming that we could be confident that we know 'What Works'. *Home Office Research Study* 291, published in December 2004 and subsequently revised, presented the findings that were then available from the CRP, as well as reviewing work from elsewhere (Harper and Chitty 2004). Its conclusion was that, while there was good evidence for the effectiveness of cognitive-behavioural programmes focused on offending, most of this came from abroad. Good British evidence on this or anything else was still lacking because of problems of implementation of the programmes and because of the use of 'suboptimal' research designs. The solution proposed was that future research should be conducted on a properly scientific basis, using randomized control trials. This is the method usually regarded as the 'gold standard' for research in medicine but, in practice, it has rarely been found feasible in the evaluation of social programmes.

Meanwhile a new approach to thinking about what works has begun to develop that stresses the importance of interpersonal relationships in interventions with people who offend, as one of the factors that can promote desistance from crime even when the statistical likelihood of this is low. For much of the history of social work and youth justice, practitioners more or less assumed that the quality of the direct relation-

ship between worker and client was important for the prospects of success, but this had tended to be forgotten in the enthusiasm for programmes, often implemented in a careless and mechanistic way (and contrary to the recommendations of the 'what works' research). Research on desistance – by (among others) Sue Rex and Shadd Maruna in England and Fergus McNeill in Scotland – reasserted the importance of the immediate personal relationship between the person helping and the person being helped. In other words, what mattered was not just what you did (implementing a programme according to an instruction manual) but how you did it – with care, respect, knowledge and commitment, or carelessly, impersonally and mechanistically. An example of research on young offenders that stressed the central importance of relationships of care and respect is the evaluation of the Freagarrach project which, while sharing some of methodological problems complained of in *Home Office Research Study* 291, concluded that Freagarrach had a positive impact on the offending careers of many of the young people with whom it worked, who were among the most persistent offenders in central Scotland (Lobley and Smith 2007).

David Smith

Related entries

Cognitive–behaviour programmes; Desistance; Effectiveness; Evaluative research; Positivism; Probation Service; Rehabilitation.

Key texts and sources

Harper, G. and Chitty, C. (2004) *The Impact of Corrections on Re-offending: A Review of 'What Works'. Home Office Research Study* 291. London: Home Office (available online at **www.home office.gov.uk/rds/pdfs04/hors291.pdf**).

Lobley, D. and Smith, D. (2007) *Persistent Young Offenders: An Evaluation of Two Projects.* Aldershot: Ashgate.

Lobley, D., Smith, D. and Stern, C. (2001) *Freagarrach: An Evaluation of a Project for Persistent Juvenile Offenders.* Edinburgh: Scottish Executive (available online at **www.scotland.gov. uk/Resource/Doc/156634/0042083.pdf**).

Martinson, R. (1974) 'What works? Questions and answers about prison reform', *The Public Interest*, 35: 22–54.

Maruna, S. (2001) *Making Good: How Ex-convicts Reform and Rebuild their Lives.* Washington, DC: American Psychological Association.

McGuire, J. (ed.) (1995) *What Works: Reducing Reoffending.* Chichester: Wiley.

McIvor, G. (1990) *Sanctions for Serious or Persistent Offenders: A Review of the Literature.* Stirling: Social Work Research Centre, University of Stirling.

McNeill, F. (2003) 'Desistance-focused probation practice', in W.-H. Chui and M. Nellis (eds) *Moving Probation Forward: Evidence, Arguments and Practice.* Harlow: Pearson Longman.

Raynor, P. and Robinson, G. (2005) *Rehabilitation, Crime and Justice.* Basingstoke: Palgrave Macmillan.

Rex, S. (1999) 'Desistance from offending: experiences of probation', *Howard Journal of Criminal Justice*, 36: 366–83.

Underdown, A. (1998) *Strategies for Effective Offender Supervision: Report of the HMIP What Works Project.* London: Home Office.

YOUNG OFFENDER INSTITUTIONS (YOIs)

Young offender institutions (YOIs) are specialist penal facilities usually managed by the Prison Service and designed for prisoners aged 15–20 years. Male 'juvenile' prisoners (15–17 years) are normally detained separately from 'young adult offenders' (18–20 years), although exceptions to this 'rule' have been known to apply with regard to female 'juvenile' prisoners.

At the end of August 2006 the number of under 21-year-old prisoners in England and Wales – either sentenced or remanded – stood at 11,672, 2,528 of whom were children ('juveniles'). Over the last ten years or more, the number of children and young people entering penal custody in England and Wales has increased very significantly. Approximately 85 per cent of 'juvenile' prisoners – the remaining 15 per cent being held in secure training centres and secure children's homes (secure accommodation) – and all 'young adult' prisoners are held in young offender institutions (YOIs). Although there are specific 'prison rules' governing these establishments, the regimes and conditions bear many similarities to those found in adult prisons.

For 'young adult' prisoners, an induction programme runs over the first few days following arrival in the YOI. This is designed to provide an opportunity for young prisoners to share any concerns they might have with prison personnel (particularly their 'personal officer'), to arrange education and/or training sessions and to settle the terms of a 'sentence plan'. There is greater regime differentiation from adult prisons for 'juvenile' prisoners. Induction is ostensibly more 'child centred' and individually tailored. 'Juvenile' prisoners are more rigorously assessed on arrival at the YOI and they are routinely provided with a 'first-night pack' that includes a telephone card and reading/writing materials. YOI staff are required to provide 'juveniles' with an opportunity to contact their families/carers within two hours of arriving at the YOI. The more detailed attention that focuses on the younger prisoners in YOIs is derived from a recognition of their particular vulnerabilities.

Indeed, since 2000 the Youth Justice Board (YJB) and the Prison Service have together implemented a programme of substantial reform designed to improve the conditions and treatment of 'juveniles' in penal custody. Institutional regimes must now be based on clear principles, and the YJB insists that there should be a structured and 'caring' environment in YOIs in order that 'juvenile' prisoners are kept safe and secure. As such, the YOIs that hold 'juveniles' have had centrally determined standards imposed on them; are classified as 'authorized' or 'accredited'; must operate and 'deliver' in accordance with 'contracting conditions'; are expected to provide 'placements' which are then 'purchased' or 'commissioned' by the YJB; and are subjected to more rigorous forms of monitoring and inspection.

Despite such reforms, the best efforts of the most motivated prison staff and reports of considerable improvement, Her Majesty's Chief Inspector of Prisons continues to raise serious and consistent concerns about the practices and regimes in some YOIs with regard to 'juvenile' and 'young adult' prisoners. Furthermore, in 2002 the Children's Rights Alliance for England (CRAE) undertook a detailed analysis of the conditions and treatment experienced by 'juvenile' prisoners, drawing on reports prepared by the Prisons Inspectorate. The results were problematic: widespread neglect in relation to physical and mental health; endemic bullying, humiliation and ill-treatment (staff on prisoner and prisoner on prisoner); racism and other forms of discrimination; the systemic invasion of privacy; long and uninterrupted periods of cell-based confinement; deprivation of fresh air and exercise; inadequate educational and rehabilitative provision; insufficient opportunities to maintain contact with family; poor diet; ill-fitting clothing in a poor state of repair; a shabby physical environment; and, in reality, virtually no opportunity to complain and/or make representations. According to the CRAE report, such negative and neglectful processes continue to define the conditions and treatment of many children and young people in YOIs in England and Wales, irrespective of recent reforms.

Prison Service staff working in YOIs undertake enormously challenging jobs with minimal training: they are effectively required to provide a service (to young prisoners and the community) for which they are singularly ill-equipped. There is mounting evidence of the social problems 'imported' into YOIs. 'Juvenile' and 'young adult' prisoners often experience damaged biographies, and increasing concerns are being raised about the mental health of many young prisoners – male and female. Such problems are additionally compounded by overcrowding, the inevitable strain on staffing and the frequent movement of 'young adult' and 'juvenile' prisoners around the YOI estate (unsettling young prisoners, fracturing relationships with staff, disrupting education and training programmes and producing inconsistent assessment, support and supervision). Furthermore, the Prison Reform Trust has reported that approximately 35 per cent of 'young adult' and 'juvenile' prisoners are held in YOIs over 50 miles away from their home areas, making visits from family and friends difficult if not impossible.

Girls and young women and black and minority ethnic young prisoners are particularly ill-served by YOIs. Despite repeated assurances from government ministers that all girls will be removed from YOIs, this has yet to be applied to 17-year-olds who continue to be held in five YOIs (Cookham Wood, Downview, Eastwood Park, Fosten Hall and New Hall). The limited number of specialist places for female 'juveniles' in YOIs inevitably compounds the problems relating to distance from home. Furthermore, it is not unknown for female 'juvenile' prisoners to be held on young adult wings. Racism also continues to permeate both male and female wings in YOIs. The publication, in June 2006, of the report of the inquiry into the circumstances that led to the death of Zahid Mubarek – a young Asian prisoner murdered by his racist cellmate at Feltham YOI – highlighted the depth and breadth of institutionalized racism in YOIs.

Against a backdrop of seemingly ever-increasing numbers of prisoners being held in YOIs in England and Wales, moribund conditions, human suffering and persistent failure when measured in terms of rehabilitation and recidivism, efforts to improve the treatment of society's youngest state prisoners and to enhance the 'performance' of YOIs seem as remote as ever.

Barry Goldson and John Muncie

Related entries

Children in custody; Deaths in custody; Family ties of young prisoners; Gender and justice; Juvenile secure estates; Mental health and young offenders; 'Race' and justice; Vulnerability.

Key texts and sources

Children's Rights Alliance for England (2002) *Rethinking Child Imprisonment: A Report on Young Offender Institutions.* London: Children's Rights Alliance for England.

Goldson, B. (2006a) 'Damage, harm and death in child prisons in England and Wales: questions of abuse and accountability', *Howard Journal of Criminal Justice*, 45: 449–67.

Her Majesty's Chief Inspector of Prisons (2006) *Annual Report of HM Chief Inspector of Prisons for England and Wales, 2004–2005.* London: HMSO.

Howard League for Penal Reform (2006) *Women and Girls in the Penal System.* London: Howard League for Penal Reform.

Youth Justice Board (2007) *Strategy for the Secure Estate for Children and Young People.* London: YJB (available online at **http://www.yjb.gov.uk/Publications/Scripts/prodView.asp?idproduct=270&eP=**).

See also the Zahid Mubarek Inquiry website (**http://www.zahidmubarekinquiry.org.uk/article.asp?c=374&aid=2848**).

YOUTH AND POLICING

Children and young people come to the attention of police services in a number of different guises: victims, witnesses, suspects and offenders. The emphasis here rests with the relations between the police and young people as suspects and offenders.

Public anxieties relating to 'anti-social behaviour', 'disorder' and 'youth crime' can be traced back to pre-industrial seventeenth-century society, whereas more recognizably 'modern' concerns originated and consolidated throughout the nineteenth century. The terms 'hooligan' and 'yob' (back slang for 'boy') each emerged in the late 1800s. Both expressions were widely used to describe young members of 'street gangs' in the burgeoning urban centres and developing cities of industrial Britain. Furthermore, a report compiled by the Howard Association on Juvenile Offenders in 1898 addressed the common concern that young people were becoming increasingly unruly, requiring more rigorous control. Indeed, many criminologists, sociologists and social historians have observed that policing young people, far from being a distinctive characteristic of modern times, has a much longer history – it is more accurately conceived as a perennial feature of industrial society rather than a present-day aberration.

Equally, historical analyses reveal that relations between the police and identifiable groups of young people (especially working-class males) are frequently characterized by tension and strain, particularly in the public sphere. It is the city centre, the shopping precinct, the bus station, the street corner, the local park – places of particular significance for young people 'hanging around' – where police–youth relations are shaped and defined. Numerous research studies have exposed 'proactive' methods of policing young people's public space, often underpinned by suppositions that groups of young people comprise a latent criminal presence and/or an intrinsic threat to social order.

It is important to locate the police–youth relation in historical context and to acknowledge its complexities, controversies and contested forms. It is equally important to note that the comparatively low age of criminal minority or criminal responsibility in *all* UK jurisdictions effectively means that expectations of the police – with regard to 'controlling' children and young people – are greater than those found elsewhere. Indeed, UK jurisdictions hold children to be criminally responsible at conspicuously young ages: 8 in Scotland; 10 in England and Wales and Northern Ireland. Other countries prefer to delay the formal criminalization of the young, and there is significant variation in the age of criminal minority – for example, 12 in Canada, the Netherlands and Turkey; 13 in France; 14 in Germany, Italy, Japan, New Zealand and Spain; 15 in Denmark, Finland, Norway and Sweden; and 18 in Belgium and Luxembourg. In other words, young people in the UK enter the orbit of the criminal justice system – thus the operational remit of the police – significantly earlier than their counterparts in most other western jurisdictions.

It follows that, once a child has reached the age of 8 or 10 in the UK, the police are vested with various statutory duties, powers and responsibilities. In England and Wales, for example, the Police and Criminal Evidence Act 1984 empowers a police officer to stop and search a child or young person for stolen or prohibited articles if the officer has 'reasonable grounds' to believe he or she will find such an article(s) as a result of the search. The same legislation also authorizes various powers of arrest, detention, questioning/interviewing under warrant, fingerprinting, photographing and charging, whereas the Bail Act 1976 provides for the granting or withholding of bail. The most significant legislation with regard to policing young people in England and Wales, however, is the Crime and Disorder Act 1998.

The Crime and Disorder Act 1998 is an extraordinarily wide-ranging statute substantially, although not exclusively, weighted towards 'tackling' youth crime, youth disorder and 'anti-social behaviour'. It is of particular significance with regard to the police–youth relation because it shifts the prime responsibility for crime prevention from the police to a police–local authority partnership. In this sense it provides statutory expression to the recommendations contained in the report of the Morgan Committee. The Morgan Committee was established in 1990 to consider multi-agency partnership approaches to 'crime prevention' and it formally reported in 1991. The Morgan Report observed that the term 'crime prevention' lent itself to narrow interpretation, implying that the police were solely responsible. The committee preferred the concept of 'community safety', arguing that it is open to wider application, thus encouraging greater participation from a number of key agencies in the 'fight against crime'. The Crime and Disorder Act 1998 applied this principle by imposing new duties on local authorities – in partnership with the police and other agencies – to reduce and ultimately prevent crime. The emphasis on 'joining up' services has since become a central feature of youth crime and disorder reduction strategies.

The infrastructure of the youth justice system in England and Wales has expanded very substantially since the implementation of the Crime and Disorder Act 1998 in April 2000. Youth offending teams are sizeable organizations, and the logic of youth crime prevention and community safety has penetrated the breadth of locally delivered services. Furthermore, 'youth disorder' and 'anti-social behaviour' have been systematically factored into the preventive imperative, resulting in a considerable extension of 'system reach'. Early intervention predicated on 'risk factors' and intensive intervention directed at 'persistent young offenders' are defining features of the 'new youth justice'. This is aptly expressed in the Association of Chief Police Officers' (ACPO) strategy for children and young people: 'never too early and never too late.'

The interventionist 'interagency policing' thrust of policy and practice is invariably presented in benign terms. The ACPO (2003) strategy, for example, defines the objective as 'working with partners to ... enable those children and young people at greatest risk to be identified at the earliest opportunity'. Alternative interpretations adopt a more circumspect and critical perspective, however, emphasizing the counterproductive tendencies of 'labelling' and stigmatization and raising concerns about crimi-

nalization, surveillance and human rights violations. Indeed, the question of policing children and young people in modern times assumes broad, opaque and certainly contested forms.

Perhaps the most controversial feature of the youth–police relation applies to the question of differential or selective policing. Police services throughout the world generally claim that their primary function is to prevent crime, to bring offenders to justice and to protect the law-abiding majority in a way that treats all sections of the community equally. Historical analyses of youth and policing, however, reveal that interventions are invariably mediated through the structural relations of social class, religion, 'race' and gender. Furthermore, research evidence provides that identifiable groups of young people (particularly male, working-class, black and minoritized youth) disproportionately experience unfavourable and discriminatory modes of police attention and intervention.

The history of the youth–police relation comprises continuity, change, complexity and contestation. The future of policing young people will almost certainly be characterized by further challenges and tensions. The Police Foundation is currently developing a major international initiative on the policing of children and young people that will ultimately complement work being undertaken by the Council of Europe. The initiative will no doubt cast light on the size and nature of such challenges and tensions.

Barry Goldson

Related entries

Anti-social behaviour (ASB); Community safety; Crime and Disorder Act 1998; Crime and disorder reduction (CDR); Criminal responsibility; Early intervention; Police and Criminal Evidence Act 1984 (PACE); 'Race' and justice.

Key texts and sources

ACPO (2003) *ACPO Strategy for Children and Young People.* London: Association of Chief Police Officers of England, Wales and Northern Ireland.
Goldson, B. and Muncie, J. (eds) (2006c) *Youth Crime and Justice: Critical Issues.* London: Sage.

Home Office (1991) *Safer Communities: The Local Delivery of Crime Prevention through the Partnership Approach* (the Morgan Report). London: Home Office.

Loader, I. (1996) *Youth, Policing and Democracy.* London: Macmillan.

Muncie, J. (2004) *Youth and Crime* (2nd edn). London: Sage.

Police Foundation (forthcoming) *Policing Children and Young People.* London: Police Foundation (available online at **http://www.police-foundation. org.uk/content/default.asp?PageId=619**).

YOUTH COURTS

The youth court is a specialized form of magistrates' court with jurisdiction in respect of children and young people aged 10–17. Cases are heard by magistrates or by a district judge. The youth court is not open to the general public and only those directly involved in the case will normally be permitted to attend. Youth courts are key institutions in the youth justice systems in England and Wales and in Northern Ireland. More recently, youth courts have been piloted in Scotland.

Most children and young people (aged 10–17) appearing in court in criminal proceedings in England and Wales and in Northern Ireland will have their cases dealt with in a youth court. Adult magistrates' courts may initially deal with specific cases involving children and young people, but only if they are tried with an adult. The youth court may also commit a child/young person to the Crown court for trial and/or sentence if the offence for which he or she is charged is very serious – grave offences – and the sentencing powers of the youth court are thought to be insufficient.

A hearing in the youth court is similar to one in the magistrates' court, although the procedure is often adapted to take account of the age of the defendant. The magistrates and district judges who sit in the youth court receive specialist training and have access to a youth court 'bench-book' that provides sentencing guidelines. Youth courts have a range of sentences

available to them and their powers extend to imposing custodial sentences – detention and training orders – for up to two years. In certain circumstances the press may attend court and report the proceedings, but they are not usually allowed to publish the defendant's name.

On 27 June 2002 the Scottish Executive launched a '10-point action plan' for addressing youth crime in Scotland. One of the commitments made in the action plan was to look at the feasibility of establishing a youth court to 'tackle' 16–17-year-old persistent young offenders. Accordingly, the Hamilton Youth Court was established on a 'pilot' basis in June 2003 to process 16–17-year-old 'offenders', with some flexibility to deal with 15-year-olds in certain circumstances. It has three distinctive features: a fast-track process; designated sheriffs to share the work in the youth court, to sustain relationships with young offenders after sentence, to monitor their progress and, if necessary, to amend sentences; and the capacity to 'roll up' all pre-existing charges in order to deal with all alleged offences committed in the same period at the same time. Following an evaluation of the Hamilton pilot, a second youth court was established in Airdrie in June 2004.

Barry Goldson

Related entries

Criminal Justice Act 1991; District judges; Juvenile courts; Magistrates; Sentencing framework; Sentencing guidelines; Youth diversion scheme.

Key texts and sources

McAra, L. (2006) 'Welfare in crisis? Key developments in Scottish youth justice', in J. Muncie and B. Goldson (eds) *Comparative Youth Justice: Critical Issues.* London: Sage.

Monaghan, G. (2000) 'The courts and the new youth justice', in B. Goldson (ed.) *The New Youth Justice.* Lyme Regis: Russell House.

Weijers, I. (2004) 'Requirements for communication in the courtroom: a comparative perspective on the youth court in England/Wales and the Netherlands', *Youth Justice*, 4: 22–31.

Whyte, B. (2003) 'Young and persistent: recent developments in youth justice policy and practice in Scotland', *Youth Justice*, 3: 74–85.

The Judicial Studies Board's document, *Youth Court Bench Book*, is available online at **http://www.jsboard.co.uk/magistrates/ycbb/index.htm**. See also the Magistrates' Association's 'Youth website' (**http://www.magistrates-association.org.uk/youth_site/youth_index.html**).

YOUTH DIVERSION SCHEME

The Northern Ireland Youth Diversion Scheme is a specialist unit in the Police Service which deals with young offenders. The scheme has been highly effective in managing to keep the number of young people prosecuted through the courts to a minimum.

The Police Service in Northern Ireland operates a Youth Diversion Scheme in which specialist officers review all cases involving young offenders (aged 10–17). The youth diversion officers are the main gatekeepers into the youth justice system. They have considerable discretion in terms of the recommendations they make to the public prosecutor and on how young offenders are dealt with.

When dealing with cases that come to the attention of the diversion scheme, there are four broad options available: first, 'no further action', in which case the young person is not processed any further than being referred to the scheme. This is most commonly used when there is insufficient evidence to establish that a crime was committed, or the offence and circumstances were so trivial that it is not considered worth pursuing. Second, the officer may give 'informed warning', which is an informal action and occurs where there is evidence that a crime has been committed but a warning is considered sufficient to deal with the matter. Such warnings are usually given to the young person and his or her parent(s) but they do not result in any formal criminal record for the young person – although a note of these warnings is kept for one year. Third, the police may decide to give a 'restorative caution' to the young person. This can only take place if the young person admits to the offence, there is sufficient evidence to prosecute and the young person and his or her parent(s) give informed consent to the caution. Police restorative cautions are recorded as part of a criminal record and kept for two and a half years and, should the young person reoffend, they may be cited in court. Fourth, the police can refer the case to the Public Prosecution Service for prosecution through the courts. This is usually reserved for more serious offences or where the young person has had previous warnings or prosecutions.

Typically, only about 10 per cent of cases dealt with through the Youth Diversion Scheme are referred for prosecution, and about 10–15 per cent are given restorative cautions. The majority (about 75–80 per cent) are dealt with informally through 'informed warnings' or no further police action is taken. In 2002–3, for example, only 5 per cent of cases dealt with by the Youth Diversion Scheme were prosecuted through the courts, 14 per cent were given formal cautions and 81 per cent were dealt with informally. There has been a general increase in the use of informal measures when dealing with young people who come to the attention of the police in Northern Ireland, and the proportion of cases given 'advice and warning' or no further police action has increased over the past 10 years.

Diverting young people away from the courts where possible is often a more effective response than formally prosecuting them. The police point to encouraging trends in reconviction data to support their policy, which show that only about 20 per cent of juveniles cautioned in Northern Ireland went on to reoffend within a one to three-year follow-up period (Mathewson *et al.* 1998), whereas about 75 per cent of those convicted in the juvenile courts were reconvicted over a similar period (Wilson *et al.* 1998).

David O'Mahony

Related entries

Diversion; Gatekeeping; Restorative cautioning; Systems management.

Key texts and sources

Mathewson, T., Willis, M. and Boyle, M. (1998) *Cautioning in Northern Ireland: A Profile of Adult and Juvenile Cautioning and an Examination of*

Reoffending Rates. Northern Ireland Office Research Findings 4/1998. Belfast: Northern Ireland Office.

O'Mahony, D. and Campbell, C. (2006) 'Mainstreaming restorative justice for young offenders through youth conferencing: the experience of Northern Ireland', in J. Junger-Tas and S. Decker (eds) *International Handbook of Juvenile Justice.* New York, NY: Springer.

Wilson, D., Kerr, H. and Boyle, M. (1998) *Juvenile Offenders and Reconviction in Northern Ireland. Northern Ireland Office Research Findings* 3/1998. Belfast: Northern Ireland Office.

See also the Criminal Justice System, Northern Ireland, website (**http://www.cjsni.gov.uk/index. cfm/area/information/page/youth_diversion**).

YOUTH INCLUSION AND SUPPORT PANELS (YISPs)

Youth inclusion and support panels (YISPs) aim to prevent anti-social behaviour and offending by 8–13–year-olds who are considered to be at 'high risk'. They are multi-agency partnerships – often including the police, local authority anti-social behaviour units, the Fire Service, schools, health agencies and social services departments – that offer early intervention based on assessed risk and need. Parenting support in the form of voluntary programmes is offered as part of a range of tailored interventions. The main emphasis of YISP work is to ensure that children and their families – at the earliest possible opportunity – can access mainstream public services and/or receive targeted intervention.

Following a successful 13-pilot area scheme that began in April 2003, funding is now available for the 122 youth inclusion and support panels (YISPs). The pilot areas – Barking and Dagenham, Birmingham, Ealing, Greenwich, Knowsley, Lancashire, Liverpool, Nottingham, Sheffield, Southwark, Tower Hamlets, Walsall and Wigan – have been evaluated and have received additional support to develop procedures and innovative practice that were intended to provide a best practice framework for all other YISPs.

Each YISP considers a report based on an Onset assessment and drawn up by the YISP 'key worker' examines the behaviour and circumstances causing concern and considers ways in which this might be improved. The report identifies the 'risk factors' and proposes 'protective factors' that might reduce risk. An 'integrated support plan' (ISP) is then drawn up with the child/young person and his or her family. The YISP decides the services that are needed; for how long the support will be required/available; and the agency/agencies that should provide the services. The key worker co-ordinates the implementation of the ISP. This intervention extends between three and six months and the plan is reviewed at regular intervals.

Due to the high eligibility thresholds for mainstream social services for children 'at risk', each YISP fills a gap whereby early intervention is provided instead of crisis intervention. The introduction of the Common Assessment Framework (CAF) (that omits the identification of 'criminogenic risk factors') alongside the Onset assessment (that does address those risk factors) puts YISPs in a strong position to become the hub of identified support for all children in support and in trouble. YISPs can work in both those assessment frameworks.

Some areas have expanded their YISP to include children and young people aged 14–17 because these areas have identified that the 'peak age' for first-time entrants to the youth justice system is 14 or 15. In these areas, the YISP has become the principal referral destination for all agencies identifying children and young people 'at risk' of anti-social behaviour and/or youth offending.

Peter Ashplant

Related entries

Actuarialism; Assessment framework; Early intervention; First-time entrants; Labelling theory; Positive Activities for Young People (PAYP); Protective factors; Risk factors; Risk management.

Key texts and sources

Beinhart, S., Anderson, B. and Lee, S. (2002) *Youth at Risk*. Swansea: Communities that Care.

McCarthy, P., Laing, K. and Walker, J. (2004) *Offenders of the Future? Assessing the Risk of Children and Young People Becoming Involved in Criminal and Antisocial Behaviour*. London: Department for Education and Skills.

Utting, D. and Langman, J. (2005) *A Guide to Promising Approaches*. Swansea: Communities that Care.

Youth Justice Board (2006k) *YISP Management Guidance*. London: Youth Justice Board.

YOUTH INCLUSION PROGRAMMES (YIPs)

Youth inclusion programmes (YIPs) were established in 2000 and are tailor-made programmes for 8–17-year-olds who are identified as being at 'high risk' of involvement in offending or anti-social behaviour. Young people on YIPs are identified through a number of different agencies, including youth offending teams, the police, social services, local education authorities or schools and the other local partners.

Youth inclusion programmes (YIPs) give young people somewhere safe to go where they can learn new skills, take part in activities with others and get help with their education and careers guidance. Positive role models – the workers and volunteer mentors – help to foster positive attitudes to education and direct children and young people away from crime.

The programmes operate in 110 of the most deprived/high-crime estates in England and Wales and focus their targeted interventions with between 50 and 80 young people in each designated area each year. In addition, YIPs offer 'diversionary' activities to around 150 young people in the local community.

Each project has the following aims. To:

- engage with a high proportion of the 'core group', especially children and young people deemed most 'at risk';
- address the risks identified by assessment using the Onset tool;
- increase access to mainstream and specialist services – especially in relation to education, training and employment – for the children and young people involved;
- prevent young people in the programme from entering the youth justice system and to reduce offending by young people already in the system; and
- intervene, not just on an individual level, but with communities and families (especially with the parents of children and young people in the 'core group').

Each YIP receives an annual grant from the Youth Justice Board through its local youth offending team and is required to find matched funding from local agencies to add to this. In many areas, programmes also obtain resources from other organizations (such as New Deal for Communities) that share the aim of supporting communities in relation to crime and anti-social behaviour reduction.

An independent national evaluation of the first three years of YIPs (Morgan Harris Burrows 2003) found the following:

- Arrest rates for the 50 young people considered to be most 'at risk' of crime in each YIP had been reduced by 65 per cent.
- For children and young people who had offended before joining the programme, 73 per cent were arrested for fewer offences after engaging with a YIP.
- For children and young people who had not offended previously but who were thought to be 'at risk', 74 per cent did not go on to be arrested after engaging with a YIP.

YIPs have a difficult task in ensuring that their targeted approach evidences the reduction of 'first-time entrants' to the youth justice system and prevents those in the early stages of criminal behaviour from reoffending. They have been exposed to critique in the context of wider concerns about actuarialism, early intervention and net-widening, and statistics recently published by the Youth Justice Board (2007d) reveal that the target to reduce the number of 'first-time entrants' to the youth justice system is 'at risk'. Furthermore, accusations of giving 'treats' to troublesome teenagers have also meant that the projects need to address their relationship with local people by encouraging positive participation by young people in community projects.

Peter Ashplant

Related entries

Actuarialism; Assessment framework; Early intervention; First-time entrants; Labelling theory; Mentoring; Net-widening; Positive Activities for Young People (PAYP); Protective factors; Risk factors; Risk management.

Key texts and sources

Morgan Harris Burrows (2003) *Evaluation of the Youth Inclusion Programme.* London: Youth Justice Board.

Youth Justice Board (2007d) *Annual Report and Accounts, 2006/07.* London: Youth Justice Board.

The Youth Justice Board's document, *Youth Justice System: Youth Inclusion Programme*, is available online at **http://www.yjb.gov.uk/en-gb/yjs/Prevention/YIP/**.

YOUTH JUSTICE AGENCY

The Youth Justice Agency carries out the Secretary of State's function for the provision of youth justice services under the Criminal Justice (Children) (Northern Ireland) Order 1998 and the Justice (Northern Ireland) Act 2002. Youth justice policy is separate from the functions of the agency and is one of the responsibilities of the Criminal Justice Directorate of the Northern Ireland Office. It is probable that the agency will come under the purview of a Department of Justice with the restoration of devolved government to Northern Ireland.

The Youth Justice Agency was launched as an executive agency of the Northern Ireland Office in April 2003. It replaced the former Juvenile Justice Board and it provides conferencing, a range of community-based services and custodial provision for children and young people who have offended across Northern Ireland. All the services delivered by the agency are subject to inspection and review by the Chief Inspector of Criminal Justice. Similarly, the same services may be subject to review by the Northern Ireland Commissioner for Children and Young People and the Northern Ireland Human Rights Commission. The agency is, therefore, regarded as part of both the criminal justice system and as a children's service.

The Youth Justice Agency aims to reduce youth crime and to build confidence in the youth justice system. It is managed by a board comprising the chief executive, two non-executive directors and four executive directors, each responsible for 'custodial services', the 'youth conference service', 'community services' or 'corporate services'.

The Custodial Services Directorate is responsible for Woodlands, the juvenile justice centre based in Bangor, Co. Down. Woodlands provides secure custody for up to 48 children aged between 10 and 17, male and female, remanded or committed under a juvenile justice centre order. The centre was purpose built as a direct consequence of the Criminal Justice Review in 2000. The review concluded that none of the existing secure/custodial facilities in Northern Ireland was suitable for children. Woodlands opened in 2007 and provides, in a secure setting, units for group living i.e. educational, training, medical, sport and leisure facilities. Although it remains an objective that Woodlands meets all youth justice custodial requirements, children under 18 may still be admitted to the young offenders centre managed by the Northern Ireland Prison Service.

The Youth Conference Service was introduced by the Justice (Northern Ireland) Act 2002, again as a direct result of the Criminal Justice Review. The service is designed to integrate restorative justice into the youth justice system by offering the child who has offended the opportunity to make reparation for his or her offence, to address his or her offending behaviour and to meet the needs of victims. The service employs trained co-ordinators to host conferences at which the child – accompanied by an appropriate adult – and the victim or victim representative may meet to devise a youth conference plan. The plan will be submitted to the Public Prosecution Service if the child was referred as a diversion from court, or to the youth court if the child was referred by the court. If the plan is accepted by the court, it becomes a youth conference order. Where, for whatever reason, the conference route is not followed by the court, a pre-sentence report may be sought from an officer of the Probation Board for Northern Ireland.

The Community Services Directorate is responsible for the delivery of a range of services within the agency's remit. These include schemes for the discharge of court orders and those for the prevention of offending by children. Through a network of community-based projects, provision is made for attendance centre orders, community responsibility orders and reparation orders. These projects also contribute to post-custody supervision and, further, will work voluntarily with children known to have offended with the aim of reducing reoffending. Community Services employ a systemic model of practice that seeks to address offending behaviour through work with families and in the community and by enhancing educational and employment opportunities. They are also responsible for a range of bail support services and work co-operatively with other agencies to deliver a strategy for youth crime prevention. The Corporate Services Directorate provides personnel, finance, communications and planning support to the agency.

The Youth Justice Agency is a comparatively young organization that is still working towards the complete integration of its services. There are degrees of overlap with other criminal justice organizations – probation and prisons being two referred to above – that need to be addressed. There are also new relationships to be established as the potential for increased political stability grows. The developing acceptability of policing may lead to an increase in reported offending by children, while local accountability might impact on methods of intervention. Youth justice in Northern Ireland remains a work in progress.

David Weir

Related entries

Children's commissioners; Criminal Justice (Children) (Northern Ireland) Order 1998; *Justice (Northern Ireland) Act 2002; Juvenile Justice Centre; Restorative youth conferencing.*

Key texts and sources

Criminal Justice Review Group (2000) *Review of the Criminal Justice System in Northern Ireland.* Belfast: HMSO (available online at **http://www.nio.gov.uk/review_of_the_criminal_justice_system_in_northern_ireland.pdf**).

See the Office of Public Sector Information's website for the texts of the Criminal Justice (Children) (Northern Ireland) Order 1998 (**http://www.opsi.gov.uk/is/si1998/19981504.htm**) and the Justice (Northern Ireland) Act 2002 (**http://www.opsi.gov.uk/acts/acts2002/20020026.htm**).

See also the Youth Justice Agency's website (**http://www.youthjusticeagencyni.gov.uk**).

YOUTH JUSTICE AND CRIMINAL EVIDENCE ACT 1999

The Youth Justice and Criminal Evidence Act 1999 received Royal Assent on 27 July 1999. The Act comprises two parts and it is Part 1 – 'Referrals to youth offender panels' – that is of primary significance in respect of youth justice.

Part 1 of the Youth Justice and Criminal Evidence Act 1999 provides for the referral order, the standard sentence imposed by the youth court or other magistrates' court in England and Wales for children who have been convicted of an offence or offences for the first time. Children who plead guilty to an offence – and in some cases an 'associated offence/s' (s. 15(2)) – are referred by the court to a youth offender panel (s. 2), unless the sentence for the offence is otherwise fixed by law (s. 1(1)(a)), *or* the court imposes a custodial sentence (s. 1(1)(b)), *or* the court deals with the case by means of an absolute discharge (s. 1(1)(c)). Children who have previously been bound over in criminal proceedings (s. 2(1)(c)), together with those who have been conditionally discharged by a court (s. 2(5)), will be treated as having a previous conviction and are *not* eligible for the referral order, although provisions of the

Criminal Justice and Immigration Bill 2006–7 to 2007–8 propose to reverse this.

When a child is referred to a youth offender panel, the court must specify the length of the order, which may extend from 3 to 12 months (s. 3(1)(c)). Youth offending teams are responsible for setting up the youth offender panels and for monitoring and recording the progress of children subject to referral orders. The panels establish a 'programme of behaviour' that the child is obliged to observe, and the programme is ostensibly informed by the three cornerstone principles of restorative justice: restoration to the victim; the reintegration of the child into law-abiding behaviour; and the child's assumption of responsibility for the consequences of his or her offence(s).

In short, Part 1 of the Act lays down the following:

* The circumstances in which the referral order is available to the court (ss. 1–5).
* The administrative arrangements for establishing panels (s. 6).
* The requirements for attendance at panel meetings (s. 7).
* The procedures for meetings between the child and the youth offender panel and the means by which the 'youth offender contract' setting out the 'programme of behaviour' should be established and monitored (ss. 8–9, 11–12 and 14).
* The action that is required – referral back to the court – should there be failure to agree a contract and/or the terms of the contract are breached (ss. 10 and 13 and Schedule 1).

In addition, the Home Office issued explanatory notes in order to 'assist the reader to understand the Act', and National Standards for Youth Justice Services (Youth Justice Board 2004) provide further guidance.

The compatibility of Part 1 of the Youth Justice and Criminal Evidence Act 1999 with international conventions, treaties, standards and rules is noteworthy. Although Part 1 does *not* provide for the avoidance of judicial proceedings as set out in Article 40.3(b) of the United Nations Convention on the Rights of the Child (UNCRC), it does offer the *potential* for a less adversarial and more child-centred approach to

practice by shifting emphasis from the formal court process to the comparatively unceremonious youth offender panel. Equally, youth offender panels should have sufficient capacity and flexibility to convene and operate expeditiously and to avoid unnecessary delay, consistent with Rule 20.1 of the United Nations Standard Minimum Rules for the Administration of Juvenile Justice (the 'Beijing Rules') and Article 40.2(b)(iii) of the UNCRC. Similarly, the youth offender panel is potentially well placed to ensure that the 'best interests of the child' comprise a 'primary consideration' (Article 3(1) UNCRC), particularly with respect to setting the terms of the 'youth offender contract' and its associated 'programme of behaviour'. This is also consistent with Rule 5 of the Beijing Rules that states: 'the juvenile justice system shall emphasise the well-being of the juvenile and shall ensure that any reaction to juvenile offenders shall always be in proportion to the circumstances of both the offenders and the offence.' The compatibility of referral order practice with Article 12 of the UNCRC will depend on the extent to which youth offender panels are effective in facilitating the active participation of the child in order that he or she may express his or her views (directly or indirectly) in all matters affecting him or her and in ensuring that, once such views are stated, they are given 'due weight'.

The Youth Justice and Criminal Evidence Act 1999 and the introduction of the referral order raise three core critical questions, however. First is the question of proportionality. The proportionality principle requires no more and no less than a fair and proportionate reaction in any case where a child is convicted of a criminal offence. By restricting the referral order to children at first conviction and by exposing such children to the wide-ranging powers available to the youth offender panel in setting the 'programme of behaviour' and the 'youth offender contract', the principle of proportionality is – at least potentially – compromised.

Second is the question of legal safeguards. Nowhere in Part 1 of the Act is there provision allowing for the child to be legally represented at the youth offender panel, and this places the child in a more vulnerable position than if he or she were being sentenced in court. The youth offender contract determines the extent of the restrictions that are to be applied to the child's liberty. This is precisely the issue that a legal representative would ordinarily address. Although s. 5 of the Act provides for the attendance of an 'appropriate person' at the youth offender panel and s. 7(3) allows for a person of the child's choice 'aged 18 or over' to attend (subject to the approval and agreement of the panel), neither such person is an adequate substitute for a professionally qualified legal advocate.

Third is the question of contracts. Section 8 (5) of the Act states that where a programme of behaviour is 'agreed between the offender and the panel, the panel shall cause a written record of the programme to be produced' and, once this record is signed by the child and a member of the panel, it takes effect as the terms of the youth offender contract. Bearing in mind the restrictions on the child's liberty that may be imposed by such 'contracts' – together with activities that the child may be obliged to undertake – both the ethics and justice of requiring a child (as young as 10) to sign such a contract are questionable. This is further compounded in view of the potential negative consequences of the child's 'failure to comply' with the conditions of the 'contract'.

Barry Goldson

Related entries

Children's human rights; Due process; Early intervention; Mandatory sentence; Net-widening; Proportionality; Referral orders; Restorative justice; United Nations Convention on the Rights of the Child (UNCRC); United Nations Standard Minimum Rules for the Administration of Juvenile Justice.

Key texts and sources

Crawford, A. and Newburn, T. (2003) *Youth Offending and Restorative Justice: Implementing reform in youth justice.* Cullompton. Willan.
Explanatory Notes to Youth Justice and Criminal Evidence Act 1999, available at: **http://www.opsi.gov.uk/ACTS/en1999/1999en23.htm**
Goldson, B. (2000d) 'Wither Diversion? Interventionism and the New Youth Justice', in B. Goldson (ed) *The New Youth Justice.* Dorset: Russell House Publishing.
Haines, K. (2000) 'Referral Orders and Youth Offender Panels: restorative Approaches and the New Youth Justice', in B. Goldson (ed) *The New Youth Justice.* Dorset: Russell House Publishing.
Youth Justice Board (2004) *National Standards for Youth Services.* London: Youth Justice Board, available at: **http://www.yjb.gov.uk/Publications/Scripts/prodView.asp?idproduct=155&eP=PP**
Youth Justice and Criminal Evidence Act 1999, available at: **http://www.opsi.gov.uk/acts/acts1999/19990023.htm**

YOUTH JUSTICE BOARD (YJB)

The Youth Justice Board (YJB) is a non-departmental public body that was established by the Crime and Disorder Act 1998. Board members – of which there can be between 10 and 12 – are appointed by the Home Secretary and have responsibility for monitoring the youth justice system across England and Wales and for providing advice to the government (the Home Secretary) on its operation.

The aim of the Youth Justice Board (YJB) is to prevent offending by children and young people. One of the main activities of the YJB is to identify ways of improving the effectiveness of the youth justice system. The board has promoted new approaches and has developed new programmes for addressing youth crime and youth justice. It also provides advice and guidance on effective practice to youth offending teams (YOTs) and to custodial and secure establishments, including the development of the Professional Certificate in Effective Practice and the publication of a series of effective practice guides (*Key Elements of Effective Practice*).

In 2000 the YJB developed a 'service-level agreement' with the Prison Service with regard to the provision of custodial 'placements' at young offender institutions. It also put agreements in place with local authorities to provide places in local authority secure children's homes (secure accommodation) and established contracts with the private sector in relation to secure training centres. The YJB issues grants to YOTs in order to develop specific initiatives in line with the board's aims (for example, funding for prevention programmes at one end of the spectrum and intensive supervision and surveillance programmes at the other). Such grants are conditional on satisfactory progress being made against the National Standards for Youth Justice Services and 'key performance indicators' set by the board.

During 2005–6 the YJB received income of £418 million, mainly as grant aid from the Home Office. It expended £401 million on youth justice programmes, of which 70 per cent was spent on the purchase of accommodation in the juvenile secure estate, despite the fact that custody accounts for only 6 per cent of all court disposals imposed on children and young people.

The YJB states that its core aims are to:

- prevent offending by children and young people so that fewer are criminalized;
- ensure that, when young people do offend, the manner and degree of intervention are proportionate to their welfare needs and/or their risk of reoffending or causing harm; and
- ensure that all children dealt with in the youth justice system, no matter what they have done, are treated equally and with respect.

However laudable these aims might be, some commentators have questioned how appropriate it is for the YJB to be located in the criminal justice sector – whether that be the Home Office or the newly established Ministry of Justice (Goldson 2000c; Allen 2006; Goldson and Muncie 2006b). Fundamental to the argument is that the essential outcomes for children pursued by the Department for Education and Skills – through the 'Every Child Matters' programme ('being healthy', 'staying safe', 'enjoying and achieving', 'making a contribution' and 'achieving economic wellbeing') – provide a more appropriate framework for organizing youth justice services than the Home Office, which is primarily concerned with public protection and domestic security. It is interesting to note that this line of argument has apparently found some favour with Prime Minister, Gordon Brown, who has recently vested joint responsibility for youth justice in the new Ministry of Justice and the Department for Children, Schools and Families.

The difficulties facing the future direction of the YJB are probably best demonstrated when one considers how its budget is spent. Despite the fact that the level of youth crime in England and Wales appears to be stable if not falling, the numbers of children and young people in penal custody have doubled over the past decade or more. Thus over 70 per cent of the YJB's budget – almost £300 million – is spent on detaining the 7,000 children and young people sent to custody each year. Furthermore, during 2006 the YJB distributed £45 million among YOTs to be spent on interventions with children and young people who had *not* yet formally entered the youth justice system. Such financial arrangements characterize the position the YJB finds itself in, with substantial funds made available at polar ends of the 'justice' spectrum but comparatively little spent on community-based programmes for children and young people in the youth justice system.

With the development of children's trusts in local authorities and the emergence of the Department for Children, Schools and Families in central government, there may be a strong argument for future 'prevention' funding streams going directly to local authorities rather than to YOTs, in line with the Every Child Matters agenda. This will free YOTs, under the direction of the YJB, to concentrate resources on children and young people in the criminal justice system.

Mike Thomas

Related entries

Children's trusts; Crime and Disorder Act 1998; Effectiveness; Every Child Matters (ECM); Juvenile secure estate; Key Elements of Effective Practice (KEEPs); National Standards for Youth Justice Services; Youth offending teams (YOTs).

Key texts and sources

Allen, R. (2006) *From Punishment to Problem Solving – a New Approach to Children in Trouble.* London: Centre for Crime and Justice Studies.

Goldson, B. (2000c) '"Children in need" or "young offenders"? Hardening ideology, organisational change and new challenges for social work with children in trouble', *Child and Family Social Work*, 5: 255–65.

Goldson, B. and Muncie, J. (2006b) 'Critical anatomy: towards a principled youth justice', in B. Goldson and J. Muncie (eds) *Youth Crime and Justice: Critical Issues.* London: Sage.

See the Office of Public Sector Information's website (**http://www.opsi.gov.uk/acts/acts1998/19980037. htm**) for the text of the Crime and Disorder Act 1998.

See also the Youth Justice Board's website (**http://www.yjb.gov.uk/en-gb/**).

YOUTH JUSTICE PLANS

Youth justice plans have to be completed annually by every youth offending team in England and Wales and submitted to the Youth Justice Board. The requirement is specified in s. 40 of the Crime and Disorder Act 1998. The 2007–8 submissions will mark the eighth round of plans.

The Youth Justice Board (YJB) is required to monitor and report on the performance of the youth justice system to the Home Secretary. One tool that is used to achieve this is the aggregate data compiled from the annual youth justice plans (the 'plans') submitted by every youth offending team (YOT) in England and Wales. The only exception to this is that local authorities rated as 3* or 4* (using the performance measures discussed below) are exempt from the statutory duty to submit a youth justice plan. The YJB uses this information in a number of ways, including for comparative analysis between YOTs; as an overview of the delivery challenges facing YOTs; and as a basis for YJB managers to engage with YOTs on a 'performance improvement agenda'.

The format and content of the plans are highly prescribed, and the requisite templates are published on the YJB website annually, with associated guidance on the method of completion. While the broad format of the plan remains constant, each year sees minor adjustments. An example of this is the new requirement for 2007–8 for YOTs to attach their 'youth crime prevention strategy' to the plan. The plan template has section headings that include 'Chair of the management board's summary'; 'Local planning environment'; 'Drivers of performance' (specified as 'governance and leadership', 'performance and quality systems', 'resources, people and organisation' and 'partnership working'); 'Delivery plan and action plan'; and 'Review and approval'. Plans must be acceptable to the YJB, and payment of centrally adminstered grants is contingent on this.

The 'Delivery plan' section of the plan requires reporting on performance of all the specified 'YOT themes'. The themes are prevent offending; intervene early; provide intensive community supervision; reduce reoffending; reduce the use of custody; enforce and enable compliance; detention and training order training plans; support young people engaging in education, training and employment; support access to appropriate accommodation; support access to mental health services; support access to substance misuse services; resettlement; provide effective restorative justice services; support parenting interventions; and ensure equal treatment regardless of race. A significant criticism of YOT targets is that they have tended to be 'process orientated' rather than 'outcome focused' – in other words, they tend to concentrate on (for example) the timely completion of reports rather than on measuring either the impact of or the quality of such reports.

In the formative years of the YJB and YOTs, planning and reporting requirements were developed essentially in isolation of other government department arrangements – even the reporting 'year' was different – making data analysis across a range of performance indicators virtually impossible. This has changed and there is now greater integration of YOT planning and performance monitoring with that of other services for children. An example of this is the YJB's current performance framework, which cross-references 'YOT themes' with YJB corporate targets and the 'Every Child Matters' (ECM) outcomes. For example, the YOT theme 'prevent offending' is linked to the YJB corporate target of 'Reduce the number of first time entrants to the Youth Justice System by 5% by March 2008 compared to the March 2006 baseline', and is further aligned with the ECM outcomes 'Stay safe' (safe from crime and anti-social behaviour in and out of school) and 'Make a positive contribution' (engage in law-abiding and positive behaviour in and out of school).

The performance management framework for local government includes the 'annual performance assessment' (APA), first introduced in 2005, which assesses a local authority's success at improving outcomes for children and young people. YOTs must now complete an APA template summarizing relevant performance data and this, along with their plan, will be used by APA inspectors. Selected YOT performance data ('prevention', 'recidivism', 'education, training and employment' and 'mental health services') now contribute to the performance of local councils. The overall score from these assessments informs the comprehensive performance assessment of councils, which is reported by the Audit Commission. The YJB provides additional YOT data on disposals and offences to the Audit Commission for these corporate assessments.

It is apparent that YOT performance and planning are highly regulated, and the YJB is keen to emphasize its robust overview of local performance and to take action where it is viewed as inadequate. However, the YJB's own corporate performance indicates unsatisfactory performance in many areas. The YJB *Annual Report and Accounts for 2006–7* sets out the YJB's key targets as:

- prevention – fewer first-time entrants (to the youth justice system);
- reduce reoffending; and
- reduce the use of custody.

For the first two, the target is deemed to be 'at risk' and, for the third, it concludes 'the target is highly unlikely to be met'. This provides a bleak assessment of the impact of the considerable resources that have been allocated to developing youth justice services in England and Wales. It remains to be seen whether the increasing focus on 'outcomes' for children rather than measuring the 'processes' they are subjected to, along with increasing integration into other children's services planning arrangements, will actually result in fewer children entering the youth justice system or, ultimately, having a custodial sentence imposed on them.

Sheena Doyle

Related entries

Audit Commission; Children's trusts; Effectiveness; Every Child Matters (ECM); Governance; Managerialism; Youth Justice Board (YJB); Youth offending teams (YOTs).

Key texts and sources

Audit Commission (2007) *Comprehensive Performance Assessment*. London: Audit Commission (available online at **http://www.audit-commission.gov.uk/cpa/index.asp?page=index.asp&area=hpcpa**).
Youth Justice Board (2007a) *Monitoring Performance: Youth Justice Plans*. London: Youth Justice Board (available online at **http://www.yjb.gov.uk/en-gb/practitioners/MonitoringPerformance/YouthJusticePlans/**).
Youth Justice Board (2007b) *Monitoring Performance: Performance Assessments of Children's Services*. London: Youth Justice Board (available online at **http://www.yjb.gov.uk/en-gb/practitioners/MonitoringPerformance/AssessingChildrensServices/**).

YOUTH LIFESTYLES SURVEY (YLS)

The Youth Lifestyles Survey (YLS) is a household cohort survey in England and Wales that uses questionnaires to measure the extent of self-reported active youth offending (in the past year) and to identify 'risk' and 'protective factors' for youth offending. The Home Office commissioned two sweeps of the YLS in 1992–3 and 1998–9.

The Youth Lifestle Survey (YLS) was first run in 1992–3 (Graham and Bowling 1995). The survey accessed 1,721 young people aged 14–25 and a 'booster sample' of 808 young people from ethnic minorities. A quarter of males and 1 in 8 females admitted offending in the past year, with 15 being the peak age for onset. However, female offending rates declined after this age, whereas male offending increased up to age 18 and levelled off into the mid-20s.

In 1998–9, the YLS ran its second sweep with 4,848 members of a broader age group, 12–30, in an attempt to gain a more complete picture of youth offending (Flood-Page *et al.* 2000). Key findings were that one fifth of the sample reported active offending, with the peak age for onset at 14 years. The second sweep focused more on serious offending (for example violence, burglary, car theft) and persistent offending (at least three offences in the past year). Risk factors for serious/persistent offending by 12–17-year-olds included drug use, truancy/school exclusion, poor parental supervision, delinquent peers and 'hanging around' in public (also identified as risk factors for active offending in the 1992–3 YLS). For 18–30-year-olds, drug use, leaving school without qualifications, previous school exclusion and delinquent peers statistically increased the risk of serious/persistent offending.

The YLS provides some support for the maturation thesis (although its authors have not made this claim) – female crime decreases after the mid-teens while male violent crime falls after the age of 18. If workplace crime is excluded, male property crime also falls in young adulthood, suggesting that boys 'grow out of crime' as they make the transition to adulthood.

The strengths of the YLS are the random and representative nature of its samples that serves to promote findings that are generalizable to the youth population; the mix of gender and ethnicity in the samples (avoiding accusations of androcentrism and ethnocentrism); the measurement of self-reported offending (which accesses the 'dark figure' of unreported/unrecorded crime); and the reliability/consistency of the risk and protective factor findings across the two surveys. The consideration of the role of protective factors – albeit limited to their influence on desistance – expands the surveys' foci from a narrow deficit-based approach to offending and risk.

However, the two sweeps are not directly comparable in terms of size or age range, which limits the scope to make valid comparisons across the studies. There are also different numbers of offences on the self-reported offending inventories for each study (23 in 1992–3; 27 in 1998–9), which further limits the validity of any cross-survey comparisons. The cross-sectional survey design inherently precludes the ability of the research teams from each survey to identify causal relationships between risk and protective factors and

offending, although it should be stressed that neither research team asserted causality in its reports, preferring to discuss risk factors as *correlated* with offending (a more valid and accurate approach). The YLS also prioritizes psychosocial risk factors to the neglect of a consideration of wider social-structural and political influences on offending. Additionally, there is no consideration of life histories or the role of life events on young people's offending, producing a somewhat static, quantitative methodology that makes for a narrow, prescribed range of risk factor findings and allows only a limited interpretation of these results.

Kevin Haines

Related entries

Crime statistics; Growing out of crime; Self-reported offending.

Key texts and sources

Flood-Page, C., Campbell, S., Harrington, V. and Miller, J. (2000) *Youth Crime: Findings from the 1998/99 Youth Lifestyles Survey. Home Office Research Study* 209. London: Home Office.
Graham, J. and Bowling, B. (1995) *Young People and Crime. Home Office Research Study* 145. London: Home Office.

YOUTH MATTERS

'Youth Matters' is the government's overarching policy for young people aged 13–19 in England, at the core of which is the aim to provide them with 'something to do, somewhere to go, and someone to talk to'.

The *Youth Matters* green paper was published in July 2005 and is an attempt to apply 'Every Child Matters' (ECM) principles to services for adolescents. It uses a children's trust partnership approach to take forward the joint planning and commissioning of a range of universal, specialist and targeted services for 13–19-year-olds. The expectation is that this will lead to the development of a holistic multi-agency service for young people underpinned by integrated governance, processes and front-line delivery. The effectiveness of the service will be measured in respect of how well it helps young people to achieve the best they can under each of the five ECM outcomes: 'being healthy'; 'staying safe'; 'enjoying and achieving'; 'making a positive contribution'; and 'achieving economic well-being'.

'Youth Matters' tries to address a number of problems: the variable availability and quality of youth service provision; the ineffectiveness of some local Connexions services; a lack of coherent support for young people through mainstream services; and a lack of co-ordinated support from both mainstream and targeted service providers, such as schools, youth offending teams or child and adolescent mental health services. When consulted, young people reported that they want the following: fewer worries about education, employment and personal safety; something to do with their free time; opportunities to learn new skills; and places to socialize with their friends.

Section 6 of the Education and Inspections Act 2006 places a duty on local authorities (the lead agency for children's trusts) to secure access to sufficient educational and/or positive leisure-time activities for the improvement of the well-being of young people aged 13–19. According to draft guidance on the duty, 'educational activities' can include homework clubs, out-of-school coaching, outdoor activity centres and/or volunteering. 'Recreational activities' can include sports, music, drama and visual arts. Certain activities may be made available through extended school services, while others will be provided/arranged through the local authority. The activities are meant to contribute to the young person's personal and social development.

The local authority should ensure that a variety of positive activities are available and that accessibility issues are resolved. Accessibility issues can include transport, opening hours, affordability and the range of choices available to meet the needs and preferences of young people. The draft guidance makes it clear that local authorities are expected to pay particular attention to the needs of 'harder-to-reach groups', including children in care/'looked after' children; black and minority ethnic young people; and young people in trouble. Although in

some ways similar to such targeted programmes as Positive Activities for Young People, the Youth Matters activities are available for *all* young people in a particular locality.

Bodies such as the Audit Commission and the Youth Justice Board support the provision of mainstream activities, presumably overseen by the children's trust, as well as targeted diversionary and youth crime prevention programmes. They argue that both need to remain in place despite the fact that they may be catering for some of the same young people, especially those 'at risk' of becoming involved in anti-social and criminal activity. Youth Matters introduces its own – multi-agency and local authority-led – Integrated Youth Support Service (IYSS) to target different 'at risk' groups of young people identified in the green paper: teenage parents; those with substance misuse or mental health problems; and those not involved in education, employment or training. This list of 'at risk' groups reflects other government priorities, but there is a recognition that many of the young people who may, for example, have dropped out of school may also end up in the youth justice system. However, it is not yet clear how the IYSS will work with youth crime prevention services.

The role of the Connexions Service is changing as the ECM programme develops, and Youth Matters proposes the establishment of a new Information, Advice and Guidance (IAG) service for 11–19-year-olds, working to a set of national quality standards. A draft version of these standards has been published in which the emphasis is on education, training and future employability. Out of 38 standards, only Standard 6 deals specifically with personal, social and health issues and Standard 11 refers to extra-curricular activities. Standard 14 states that IAG providers must be responsive to the needs of young people, including those 'at risk' and those in need of targeted support. Standard 18 lists criteria to ensure that IAG has links with such specialist services as the youth offending team and that it is able to help young people in trouble move into a 'successful' adulthood. IAG arrangements should be in place by 2008.

Recently the government announced that one of its core Youth Matters proposals would be abandoned due to prohibitive administrative costs. The 'youth opportunity card' was going to be made available to every 13–19-year-old in England, providing discounts at local shops or venues, or to pay for sports or other activities from accredited providers. No alternative policy has been put forward at the time of writing. However, the 'opportunity fund' (a local authority budget that can be spent on local projects at the discretion of young people) and a 'capital fund' (to promote ways to engage young people in helping the local authority decide what facilities to make available) are going ahead. Both are meant to pay particular attention to the needs and wishes of young people living in disadvantaged areas.

Finally, each local authority is to develop a 'local offer' for young people, and several have local 'youth offer' prospectuses available online. This document provides information on how young people can get involved locally; what activities are available and where to find them; how to access counselling and advice services; opportunities for volunteering; and the locations of youth work projects and places to meet their peers.

Lisa Payne

Related entries

All Wales Youth Offending Strategy; Children's trusts; Connexions; Every Child Matters (ECM); Partnership working; Positive Activities for Young People (PAYP); Positive Futures; Risk management.

Key texts and sources

Department for Education and Skills (2005c) *Youth Matters*. London: DFES (available online at **http://www.everychildmatters.gov.uk/_files/Youth %20Matters.pdf**).

Department for Education and Skills (2006d) *Quality Standards for Young People's Information, Advice and Guidance*. London: DFES (available online at **http://www.dfes.gov.uk/consultations/ conResults.cfm?consultationId=1435**).

Department for Education and Skills (2007b) *Statutory Guidance on Section 6 Education and Inspections Act (Positive Activities for Young People)*. London: DFES (available online at **http://www.dfes.gov.uk/consultations/conResults. cfm?consultationId=1432**).

See the Office of Public Sector Information's website (**http://www.opsi.gov.uk/ACTS/acts2006/2006004 0.htm**) for the text of the Education and Inspections Act 2006.

See also the Youth Matters website (**http://www. everychildmatters.gov.uk/youthmatters/**).

YOUTH OFFENDING TEAMS (YOTs)

Youth offending teams (YOTs) are multi-agency teams comprising personnel from health, education, police, probation (National Offender Management Service) and social services with responsibility for the provision of youth justice services in England and Wales.

Youth offending teams (YOTs) were established by the Crime and Disorder Act 1998 and became operational across local authorities in England and Wales during 2000. The Act placed a duty on local authorities – with responsibility for education and social services – together with chief officers of police/police authorities, chief officer's of probation/probation committees and health authorities to establish YOTs and to ensure that appropriate youth justice services were available in their area for children and young people aged 10–17 inclusive. Section 37 of the Crime and Disorder Act established the prevention of offending by children and young people as the principal statutory aim of the youth justice system. YOTs are one of the main vehicles for delivering this aim.

An interdepartmental government circular, issued in December 1998, outlined the services that YOTs are required to provide, including the provision of appropriate adult services; assessment and intervention work in support of final warnings; bail support and supervision services; services for the placement of children and young people on remand; pre-sentence reports to the courts; the supervision of children and young people sentenced to various court orders; and throughcare and post-release supervision services for children and young people sentenced to custody (Home Office *et al.* 1998a).

YOTs are not intended to 'belong' exclusively to any one department or agency. Indeed, each of the composite agencies was tasked with corporate responsibility to ensure that YOTs were established and adequately resourced. Ultimate responsibility, however, rests with the local authority chief executive.

YOTs may be seen as one of the most ambitious elements of the New Labour government's criminal/youth justice policy and have been held up as 'an excellent example of multi-agency, multi-disciplinary teams' (Department for Education and Skills 2004a). However, the extent to which YOTs have remained true to their original conception may be questioned.

YOTs are not a legal entity and, as such, they are unable to employ their own staff. They were established on the premise that all statutory partners would provide staff on the basis of (fixed-term) secondments. The Crime and Disorder Act 1998 does not prescribe roles for particular team members. Instead, all team members are expected to work flexibly, with work allocated according to their personal skills, experience and professional background. It is expected that staff who are seconded into the YOT from each of the partner agencies will eventually return to their 'parent' agencies, taking with them the experiences they have gained through working in a multi-agency environment. However, many YOTs have found increasing difficulties in replacing staff, with some questioning the commitment of partner agencies. Rather than providing staff, some agencies have found it easier to provide YOTs with the cash equivalent, leaving it to the YOT to determine what type of worker it 'buys in'. This has led to some YOTs losing the essence of their multi-agency ethos.

Of equal concern is the drift towards YOT intervention with children and young people outside the conventional youth justice system. Such an approach has been driven by the Youth Justice Board, which secured an additional £45 million in 2006 to be distributed among YOTs to be spent on 'preventive work'. Consequently an increasing amount of YOT time is now spent dealing with children who have not committed any criminal offence. Some YOTs have, therefore, struggled to establish a clear sense of identity, given the emphasis on 'prevention'. As the Every Child Matters agenda begins to bed down in local authorities, a clearer picture might emerge, with children's trusts assuming responsibility for the 'early intervention'/'prevention' agenda, leaving YOTs to concentrate on their core business of working with convicted young offenders.

In England the development of children's trusts has also led to opportunities to reconsider the governance arrangements for YOTs. While the majority may continue to be located in children's social services structures, others have found themselves part of a developing community safety framework or, more recently, part of a new alignment between the youth service and Connexions. As these developments take place it is critical that the YOT continues to recognize that it is the sole service responsible for juvenile offenders in England and Wales.

Mike Thomas

Related entries

Children's trusts; Community safety; Connexions; Corporatism; Crime and Disorder Act 1998; Crime prevention; Every Child Matters (ECM); Partnership working: Youth Justice Board (YJB).

Key texts and sources

Department for Education and Skills (2003) *Every Child Matters.* London: DFES (available online at **http://www.everychildmatters.gov.uk/_files/EBE7 EEAC90382663E0D5BBF24C99A7AC.pdf**).

Department for Education and Skills (2004) *Every Child Matters: Change for Children in the Criminal Justice System.* London: DFES (available online at **http://www.everychildmatters.gov.uk/_files/2F73 2FAF176ADC74EC67A78251B69328.pdf**).

Home Office, Department of Health, Welsh Office and Department for Education and Employment (1998a) *The Crime and Disorder Act: Inter-departmental Circular on Establishing Youth Offending Teams.* London: Home Office.

Souhami, A. (2007) *Transforming Youth Justice: Occupational Identity and Cultural Change.* Cullompton: Willan Publishing.

See the Office of Public Sector Information's website (**http://www.opsi.gov.uk/acts/acts1998/19980037. htm**) for the text of the Crime and Disorder Act 1998.

Z

ZERO TOLERANCE

Zero tolerance is the practice and/or policy of operating with little or no discretion in the control and punishment of behaviour defined as undesirable. Although the phrase has acquired a particular meaning in relation to domestic violence, racism and other forms of discrimination, in criminal/youth justice zero tolerance refers to the processes of intensive 'clamp down' – by the police and related criminal justice agencies – often targeted at minor street and other low-level offences and incivilities.

'Zero tolerance' is closely associated with the policing strategies adopted in the mid-1990s by Police Commissioner, William Bratton, in New York City. The logic to the strategy is that, by clamping down on (arresting and prosecuting) minor offences and incivilities – such as prostitution, drinking in public, underage drinking, graffiti, begging – potentially more serious crimes are 'nipped in the bud'.

'Zero tolerance' is also associated with the 'broken windows' thesis of neoconservative thinkers, J. Wilson and G. Kelling. Using the metaphor of a 'broken window', Wilson and Kelling asserted that, if a broken window in a building is not repaired, it conveyed a sense that no one cares or is in control, and this is likely to result in further broken windows. In this way, Kelling and Wilson claim that if low-level acts of crime and disorder go unchecked, the 'natural' order of a community breaks down and, as a consequence, more serious offenders are able to 'take over' the streets and public spaces.

There has been much discussion as to the efficacy of such a style of policing. As many of its advocates claimed, crime rates in New York City did drop dramatically in the period following the introduction of zero tolerance. The exact cause of this drop is disputed, however, as many American cities witnessed similar declines without adopting zero tolerance. In the UK, the idea that crime, disorder and anti-social behaviour can be reduced by targeting and prosecuting minor offences and incivilities – especially in relation to young people – has underpinned many of the youth justice policy reforms of the last two decades. Anti-social behaviour orders, for example, require a much lower threshold of evidence and permit more intensive policing of young people's public presence and behaviour.

Zero-tolerance policing has attracted a host of criticisms. Of particular concern is the way in which it can result in less accountable and heavier handed interventions that undermine the very notion of 'community policing'. More concerning, however, is that the individuals targeted by zero-tolerance initiatives are often those who are perceived to be 'outsiders'. Thus zero tolerance can result in the increased criminalization of already socially, economically and politically marginalized groups, including identifiable sections of the young and/or members of minority ethnic communities.

Jo Phoenix

Related entries

Administrative criminology; Anti-social behaviour (ASB); Authoritarianism; Criminalization; Early intervention; Institutionalized intolerance; Punitiveness; Social exclusion.

Key texts and sources

Cunneen, C. (1999) 'Zero tolerance policing: how will it effect indigenous communities?', *Indigenous Law Bulletin* (available online at **http://www. austlii.edu.au//cgibin/disp.pl/au/journals/ILB/ 1999/22.html?query=zero%20or%20tolerance% 20or%20policing#fn1**).

Dennis, N. (ed.) (1997) *Zero Tolerance: Policing a Free Society.* London: IEA Health and Welfare Unit.

Muncie, J. (1999) 'Institutionalised intolerance: youth justice and the 1998 Crime and Disorder Act', *Critical Social Policy*, 19: 147–75.

Wilson, J. and Kelling, G. (1982) 'The police and neighbourhood safety: broken windows', *Atlantic Monthly*, March: 29–38.

Directory of Agencies

Action for Prisoners Families (APF)

Head office address: Unit 21, Carlson Court, 116 Putney Bridge Road, London SW15 2NQ
Tel: 020 8812 3600
Fax: 020 8871 0473
Email: **info@actionpf.org.uk**
Website: **http://www.actionpf.org.uk/**

Action for Prisoners Families (APF) is the national federation of services supporting families of prisoners.

Adfam

Head office address: 25 Corsham Street, London N1 6DR
Tel: 020 7553 7640
Fax: 020 7253 7991
Email: **admin@adfam.org.uk**
Website: **http://www.adfam.org.uk/**

Adfam is a national organization working with, and for, families affected by drugs and alcohol.

Apex Scotland

Head office address: 9 Great Stuart Street, Edinburgh EH3 7TP
Tel: 0131 220 0130
Fax: 0131 220 6796
Email: **admin@apexscotland.org.uk**
Website: **http://www.apexscotland.org.uk/**

Apex Scotland aims to reduce reoffending by working with young offenders to help progress them towards employment, education or training.

Apex Trust

Head office address: St Alphage House, Wingate Annexe, 2 Fore Street, London EC2Y 5DA
Tel: 020 7638 5931
Fax: 020 7638 5977
Email: **jobcheck@jobcheck.com**
Website: **http://www.apextrust.com/**

The Apex Trust seeks to help people with criminal records to obtain appropriate employment by providing them with the skills they need in the labour market and by working with employers to break down the barriers to their employment.

ASBO Concern

Head office address: c/o K Falcon, 4 Chivalry Road, London SW11 1HT
Tel: 07890 285 558
Email: **info@asboconcern.org.uk**
Website: **http://www.asboconcern.org.uk/**

ASBO Concern is a campaigning alliance of organizations and individuals who are concerned about the use of anti-social behaviour orders. It aims to counteract what is sees as the scapegoating and stigmatizing of children, young people and other vulnerable groups and to campaign for properly funded youth services.

Association of Lawyers for Children (ALC)

Head office address: Julia Higgins, Administrator, PO Box 283, East Molesey, Surrey KT8 0WH
Tel: 020 8224 7071
Fax: 020 8941 7957
Email: **admin@alc.org.uk**
Website: **http://www.alc.org.uk/**

The Association of Lawyers for Children (ALC) is a membership organization that promotes justice for children and young people within the legal system in England and Wales. It lobbies for establishing properly funded legal mechanisms to enable all children and young people to have access to justice and against the diminution of such mechanisms.

Association of Youth Offending Team Managers (AYM)

Website: **http://www.aym.org.uk/**

The Association of Youth Offending Team Managers (AYM) was established in 2001 to promote the role and status of youth offending team managers and to agree policy initiatives that put young people at the centre of the youth justice system in England and Wales.

Barnardo's

Head office address: Tanners Lane, Barkingside, Ilford, Essex IG6 1QG
Tel: 020 8550 8822
Fax: 020 8551 6870
Email: **dorothy.howes@barnardos.org.uk**
Website: **http://www.barnardos.org.uk/**

Barnardo's is a major charity that believes that 'the lives of all children and young people should be free from poverty, abuse and discrimination'. It provides a range of services and has offices in England, Northern Ireland, Scotland and Wales.

British Youth Council

Head office address: The Mezzanine 2, Downstream Building, 1 London Bridge, London SE1 9BG
Tel: 0845 458 1489
Fax: 0845 458 1847
Website: http://www.byc.org.uk/

The British Youth Council promotes the active citizenship of young people and works with them to develop their skills and abilities to participate in decision-making and to control resources by encouraging them to work together and to take collective action. It has a membership of over 180 youth organizations and it comprises a network of over 400 local youth councils.

Care Commission (Scottish Commission for the Regulation of Care)

Head office address: Compass House,11 Riverside Drive, Dundee DD1 4NY
Tel: 01382 207100
Fax: 01382 207289
Website: http://www.carecommission.com/

The Care Commission was established in April 2002 – under the Regulation of Care (Scotland) Act 2001 – to regulate all child, adult and independent health care services in Scotland. It works to ensure that care service providers meet the Scottish Executive's National Care Standards and to improve the quality of care.

ChildLine

Head office address: Weston House, 42 Curtain Road, London EC2A 3NH
Tel: 0800 1111 (24-hour helpline for children and young people)
Website: http://www.childline.org.uk/

Launched in 1986, ChildLine is the UK's free 24-hour helpline for children in distress or danger. It is now part of the NSPCC and it is staffed by trained volunteer counsellors who advise and support children and young people.

Child Poverty Action Group (CPAG)

Head office address: 94 White Lion Street, London N1 9PF
Tel: 020 7837 7979
Fax: 020 7837 6414
Email: staff@cpag.org.uk
Website: http://www.cpag.org.uk/

The Child Poverty Action Group (CPAG) is the leading charity campaigning for the abolition of child poverty in the UK.

Child Rights Information Network (CRIN)

Head office address: c/o Save the Children, 1 St John's Lane, London EC1M 4AR
Tel: 020 7012 6866
Fax: 020 7012 6952
Email: info@crin.org
Website: http://www.crin.org/

The Child Rights Information Network (CRIN) is a global network that disseminates information about the United Nations Convention on the Rights of the Child.

Children Are Unbeatable! Alliance

Head office address: 94 White Lion Street, London N1 9PF
Tel: 0207 713 0569
Fax: 0207 713 0466
Email: **info@endcorporalpunishment.org**
Website: **http://www.childrenareunbeatable.org.uk/**

The Children Are Unbeatable! Alliance campaigns for the UK to be compliant with its human rights obligations by modernizing the law on assault to afford children the same protection as adults.

Children's Commissioner for England

Head office address: 1 London Bridge, London SE1 9BG
Tel: 0844 800 9113
Email: **info.request@11MILLION.org.uk**
Website: **http://www.childrenscommissioner.org**

The main function of the independent Office of the Children's Commissioner is to promote the views and interests of children in England. The commissioner might advise the government on the views and interests expressed and defined by children and young people.

Children's Commissioner for Northern Ireland (NICCY)

Head office address: Millennium House, 17–25 Great Victoria Street, Belfast BT2 7BA
Tel: 028 9031 1616
Email: **info@niccy.org**
Website: **http://www.niccy.org/**

The Northern Ireland Commissioner for Children and Young People (NICCY) aims to safeguard and promote the rights and best interests of all children and young people. Detailed powers are set out in legislation and are grouped under three main areas of work: 'Promoting children's rights'; 'Investigating complaints and initiating legal action'; and 'Commisioning research and inquiries'.

Children's Commissioner for Scotland

Head office address: 85 Holyrood Road, Edinburgh EH8 8AU
Tel: 0131 558 3733
Fax: 0131 556 3378
Email: **info@sccyp.org.uk**
Website: **http://www.sccyp.org.uk/**

Scotland's Commissioner for Children and Young People aims to promote and safeguard the rights of children and young people living in Scotland.

Children's Commissioner for Wales

Head office address: Oystermouth House, Phoenix Way, Llansamlet, Swansea SA7 9FS
Tel: 01792 765600
Fax: 01792 765601
Email: **post@childcomwales.org.uk**
Website: **http://www.childcom.org.uk/**

The Children's Commissioner for Wales aims to promote and safeguard the rights of children and young people living in Wales.

Children in Northern Ireland (CiNI)

Head office address: Unit 9, 40 Montgomery Road, Belfast BT6 9HL
Tel: 028 9040 1290
Fax: 028 9070 9418
Email: **info@ci-ni.org.uk**
Website: **http://www.ci-ni.org/**

Children in Northern Ireland (CiNI) is the umbrella organization for the children's sector in Northern Ireland.

Children in Scotland

Head office address: Princes House, 5 Shandwick Place, Edinburgh EH2 4RG
Tel: 0131 228 8484
Fax: 0131 228 8585
Email: **info@childreninscotland.org.uk**
Website: **http://www.childreninscotland.org.uk/**

Children in Scotland is the national agency for voluntary, statutory and professional organizations and individuals working with children and their families in Scotland.

Children in Wales

Head office address: 25 Windsor Place, Cardiff CF10 3BZ
Tel: 029 2034 2434
Fax: 029 2034 3134
Email: **info@childreninwales.org.uk**
Website: **http://www. childreninwales.org.uk**

Children in Wales is the national umbrella organization for those working with children and young people in Wales.

Children's Law Centre

Head office address: 3rd Floor Philip House, 123–137 York Street, Belfast BT15 1AB
Tel: 028 9024 5704
Fax: 028 9024 5679
Email: **info@childrenslawcentre.org**
Website: **http://www.childrenslawcentre.org/**

The Children's Law Centre uses the law to promote, protect and realize children's rights.

Children's Legal Centre

Head office address: University of Essex, Wivenhoe Park, Colchester, Essex CO4 3SQ
Tel: 01206 872 466
Fax: 01206 874 026
Email: **clc@essex.ac.uk**
Website: **http://www.childrenslegalcentre.com/**

The Children's Legal Centre is an independent national charity concerned with law and policy affecting children and young people. It provides legal advice and representation to children, their carers and professionals throughout the UK.

Children's Rights Alliance for England (CRAE)

Head office address: 94 White Lion Street, London N1 9PF
Tel: 020 7278 8222
Fax: 020 7278 9552
Email: info@crae.org.uk
Website: http://www.crae.org.uk/

The Children's Rights Alliance for England (CRAE) is an alliance of over 380 voluntary and statutory organizations committed to the full implementation of the United Nations Convention on the Rights of the Child.

Children's Rights Officers and Advocates (CROA)

Head office address: Suite 5J, North Mill, Bridgefoot, Belper, Derbyshire DE56 1YD
Tel: 01773 820100
Fax: 01773 820300
Email: info@croa.org.uk
Website: http://www.croa.org.uk/

Children's Rights Officers and Advocates (CROA) supports members and the children and young people they work with and is committed to the full implementation of the United Nations Convention on the Rights of the Child.

Citizens Advice Bureaux

Head office address: Myddelton House, 115-123 Pentonville Road, London N1 9LZ
Tel: 020 7833 2181
Fax: 020 7833 4371
Website: http://www.citizensadvice.org.uk/

All Citizens Advice Bureaux in England, Wales and Northern Ireland are members of the Citizens Advice service, which helps people resolve their legal, money and other problems by providing free information and advice and by seeking to influence policymakers.

CJScotland

Email: munro@cjscotland.org.uk
Website: http://www.cjscotland.org.uk/

CJScotland is an independently maintained website resource providing information about criminal justice in Scotland.

Community Safety Unit

Head office address: 4th Floor, Millenium House, Great Victoria Street, Belfast BT2 7AQ
Tel: 028 9082 8555
Email: info@communitysafetyni.gov.uk
Website: http://www.communitysafetyni.gov.uk/

The Community Safety Unit is a division of the Criminal Justice Directorate of the Northern Ireland Office.

Crime Concern

Head office address: 150 Victoria Road, Swindon SN1 3UY
Tel: 01793 863500
Email: **info@crimeconcern.org.uk**
Website: **http://www.crimeconcern.org.uk/**

Crime Concern is a national crime prevention charity whose work focuses largely, but not exclusively, on children and young people.

Criminal Cases Review Commission

Head office address: Alpha Tower, Suffolk Street Queensway, Birmingham B1 1TT
Tel: 0121 633 1800
Fax: 0121 633 1823
Email: **info@ccrc.gov.uk**

The Criminal Cases Review Commission is the independent public body set up to investigate possible miscarriages of justice in England, Wales and Northern Ireland. The commission assesses whether convictions or sentences should be referred to a court of appeal.

Criminal Justice Inspection Northern Ireland

Head office address: 6th/7th Floor, 14 Great Victoria Street, Belfast BT2 7BA
Tel: 028 9025 8000
Fax: 028 9025 8033
Email: **info@cjini.org**
Website: **http://www.cjini.org/**

Criminal Justice Inspection Northern Ireland is an independent statutory inspectorate, established under the Justice (Northern Ireland) Act 2002.

Criminal Justice Social Work Development Centre for Scotland

Head office address: 31 Buccleuch Place, Edinburgh EH8 9JT
Tel: 0131 651 1464
Fax: 0131 650 4046
Email: **CJSW@ed.ac.uk**
Website: **http://www.cjsw.ac.uk/cjsw/**

The centre is an independent national resource providing a range of services to those working in, or concerned about, criminal and youth justice social work services.

European Network of Ombudspersons for Children (ENOC)

Email: **post@barneombudet.no**
Website: **http://www.ombudsnet.org/enoc/**

Established in 1997, the European Network of Ombudspersons for Children (ENOC) links independent offices for children from 12 countries in Europe and aims to encourage the fullest possible implementation of the United Nations Convention on the Rights of the Child.

Extern

Head office address: Hydepark House, 54 Mallusk Rd, Newtownabbey BT36 4WU
Tel: 028 9084 0555
Fax: 028 9084 7333
Email: info@extern.org
Website: http://www.extern.org/

Extern is a charity that works directly with children, adults and communities affected by social exclusion throughout Ireland.

Families Outside

Head office address: 19a Albany Street, Edinburgh EH1 3QN
Tel: 0131 557 9800
Email: admin@familiesoutside.org.uk
Website: http://www.familiesoutside.org.uk/

Families Outside is a Scottish charity that aims to raise awareness of the needs of families affected by imprisonment.

Hibiscus

Head office address: 12 Angel Gate, 320 City Road, London EC1V 2PT
Tel: 020 7278 7116
Fax: 020 7837 3339
Email: fpwphibiscus@aol.com
Website: http://www.hibiscuslondon.org.uk/

Hibiscus, the 'Female Prisoners Welfare Project', caters specifically for the special needs of foreign national and British-based black and minority ethnic women in prison.

HM Inspectorate of Prisons

Head office address: First Floor, Ashley House, 2 Monck Street, London SW1P 2BQ
Tel: 020 7035 2136
Fax: 0207 035 2141
Website: http://inspectorates.homeoffice.gov.uk/hmiprisons/

Her Majesty's Inspectorate of Prisons (HMI Prisons) is an independent inspectorate that reports on the conditions for and treatment of those in prison, young offender institutions and immigration removal centres in England and Wales. It also inspects prisons in Northern Ireland, the Channel Islands, the Isle of Man and some 'Commonwealth-dependent territories'.

HM Prisons Inspectorate for Scotland

Head office address: Saughton House, Broomhouse Drive, Edinburgh EH11 3XD
Tel: 0131 244 8481
Fax: 0131 244 8446
Email: andrew.mclellan@scotland.gsi.gov.uk
Website: http://www.scotland.gov.uk/Topics/Justice/Prisons/17208

The main statutory responsibility of HM Prisons Inspectorate for Scotland is the regular inspection of individual penal establishments.

Home Office (Research Development and Statistics)

Head office address: Direct Communications Unit, Home Office, 2 Marsham Street, London SW1P 4DF
Tel: 020 7035 4848
Email: **public.enquiries@homeoffice.gsi.gov.uk**
Website: **http://www.homeoffice.gov.uk/rds/**

Research Development and Statistics (RDS) manages research and collects statistics in a number of areas, including crime, policing, justice, immigration, drugs and race equality.

Howard League for Penal Reform

Head office address: 1 Ardleigh Road, London N1 4HS
Tel: 020 7249 7373
Fax: 020 7249 7788
Email: **info@howardleague.org**
Website: **http://www.howardleague.org/**

The Howard League for Penal Reform is the most well established penal reform charity in the UK. It is entirely independent of government and is funded by voluntary donations.

Howard League for Penal Reform in Scotland

Head office address: 32A East Werberside, Edinburgh EH4 1SU
Tel: 07880 712893
Email: **admin@howardleaguescotland.org.uk**
Website: **http://www.howardleaguescotland.org.uk/**

The Howard League for Penal Reform in Scotland is an independent organization that seeks improvements to the criminal justice system in Scotland.

IncludeM

Head office address: 23 Scotland Street, Glasgow G5 8ND
Tel: 0141 429 3492
Fax: 0141 429 4519
Email: **enquiries@includem.co.uk**
Website: **http://www.includem.org**

IncludeM is a Scottish charity dedicated to redressing the social exclusion of the most vulnerable young offenders.

Include Youth

Head office address: Alpha House, 3 Rosemary Street, Belfast BT1 1QA
Tel: 028 9031 1007
Fax: 028 9024 4436
Website: **http://www.includeyouth.org/**

Include Youth was formed primarily as a campaigning organization working to enhance services for young people at risk of entering the care or criminal justice systems in Northern Ireland.

INQUEST

Head office address: 89–93 Fonthill Road, London N4 3JH
Tel: 020 7263 1111
Fax: 020 7561 0799
Email: **inquest@inquest.org.uk** for general inquiries
Website: **http://inquest.gn.apc.org/**

INQUEST is the only organization in England and Wales that provides a specialist, comprehensive advice and monitoring service in respect of deaths in custody (police stations, young offender institutions and other prisons, secure training centres, immigration detention centres and secure psychiatric institutions). It is particularly concerned with the deaths of children and young people, women, black people and people with mental health problems and in supporting the families of the bereaved.

International Centre for Prison Studies

Head office address: 3rd Floor, 26–29 Drury Lane, London WC2B 5RL
Tel: 020 7848 1922
Fax: 020 7848 1901
Email: **icps@kcl.ac.uk**
Website: **http://www.prisonstudies.org/**

The International Centre for Prison Studies aims to make the results of its academic research and projects widely available to groups and individuals, both nationally and internationally, who might not normally use such work.

IQRA Trust

Head office address: 20 East Churchfield Road, London W3 7LL
Tel: 020 8354 4460
Fax: 020 8354 4465
Email: **info@iqratrust.org**
Website: **http://www.iqratrust.org/**

The IQRA Trust is an independent Muslim educational charity that works in two distinct fields: 'education and information' and 'prisoners' welfare'.

Joseph Rowntree Foundation

Head office address: The Homestead, 40 Water End, York YO30 6WP
Tel: 01904 629241
Fax: 01904 620072
Email: **info@jrf.org.uk**
Website: **http://www.jrf.org.uk**

The Joseph Rowntree Foundation is one of the largest social policy research and development charities in the UK. It seeks to understand better the causes of social difficulties and to explore ways of overcoming them.

Justice

Head office address: 59 Carter Lane, London EC4V 5AQ
Tel: 020 7329 5100
Fax: 020 7329 5055
Email: **admin@justice.org.uk**
Website: **http://www.justice.org.uk/**

Justice is a law reform and human rights organization working to improve the legal system and the quality of justice.

Liberty

Head office address: 21 Tabard Street, London SE1 4LA
Tel: 020 7403 3888
Website: **http://www.liberty-human-rights.org.uk/**

Liberty (also known as the National Council for Civil Liberties) promotes the values of individual human dignity, equal treatment and fairness as the foundations of a democratic society and campaigns for fundamental human rights and freedoms.

Ministry of Justice (MoJ)

Head office address: Selborne House, 54 Victoria Street, London SW1E 6QW
Tel: 020 7210 8500
Email: **general.queries@justice.gsi.gov.uk**
Website: **http://www.justice.gov.uk/**

The Ministry of Justice's (MoJ) core responsibilities include youth justice and the sponsorship of the Youth Justice Board.

Nacro

Head office address: 169 Clapham Road, London SW9 0PU
Tel: 020 7582 6500
Fax: 020 7735 4666
Email: **communications@nacro.org.uk**
Website: **http://www.nacro.org.uk/**

Nacro is a national crime-reduction agency. Its Youth Crime section produces regular *Briefings* and it can help with planning, policy development and interagency working; project development and management; research, monitoring and evaluation; reviews and audits; training programmes; conferences; and information and advice, including a regular mailing of information about youth crime and justice.

National Association for Youth Justice (NAYJ)

Head office address: 4 Spring Close, Ratby, Leicester LE6 0XD
Tel: 0116 238 8354
Email: **NAYJKEN@aol.com**
Website: **http://www.nayj.org.uk/website/**

The National Association for Youth Justice (NAYJ) was established in Britain in 1994 following the merger between the National Intermediate Treatment Federation (NITFed) and the Association for Youth Justice (AYJ). The purpose of the NAYJ is to promote the rights of, and justice for, children in trouble, and it supports the publication of a journal: *Youth Justice: An International Journal* (published by Sage).

National Body of Black Prisoner Support Groups (NBBPSG)

Head office address: Valentine House, 1079 Rochdale Road, Blackley, Manchester M9 8AJ
Tel: 0161 740 3679
Fax: 0161 740 3206
Email: **info@nbbpsg.org**
Website: **http://www.nbbpsg.co.uk/**

The National Body of Black Prisoner Support Groups (NBBPSG) aims to encourage and promote the development of a nationwide network of support groups and services for black and minority ethnic offenders.

National Children's Bureau (NCB)

Head office address: 8 Wakley Street, London EC1V 7QE
Tel: 020 7843 6000
Fax: 020 7278 9512
Website: **http://www.ncb.org.uk/Page.asp**

The National Children's Bureau (NCB) is a charitable organization that acts as an umbrella body for organizations working with children and young people in England and Northern Ireland.

National Probation Service (NPS)

Head office address: NOMS Probation, 1st Floor, Abell House, John Islip Street, London SW1P 4LH
Website: **http://www.probation.homeoffice.gov.uk/output/page1.asp**

The National Probation Service (NPS) is a law-enforcement agency and public authority.

National Society for the Prevention of Cruelty to Children (NSPCC)

Head office address: Weston House, 42 Curtain Road, London EC2A 3NH
Tel: 020 7825 2500
Fax: 020 7825 2525
Email: **info@nspcc.org.uk.**
Website: **http://www.nspcc.org.uk/**

The purpose of the National Society for the Prevention of Cruelty to Children (NSPCC) is to end cruelty to children.

National Voice

Head office address: Central Hall, Oldham Street, Manchester M1 1JQ
Tel: 0161 237 5577
Fax: 0161 237 1441
Email: **info@anationalvoice.org**
Website: **http://www.anationalvoice.org/**

National Voice is an organization run for and by young people who are, or who have been, in care. It is committed to the rights of young people in and leaving care.

National Youth Advocacy Service (NYAS)

Head office address: Egerton House, Tower Road, Birkenhead, Wirral CH41 1FN
Tel: 0151 649 8700
Fax: 0151 649 8701
Email: **main@nyas.net**
Website: **http://www.nyas.net/**

The National Youth Advocacy Service (NYAS) is a UK charity providing children's rights and socio-legal services.

National Youth Agency (NYA)

Head office address: Eastgate House, 19–23 Humberstone Road, Leicester LE5 3GJ
Tel: 0116 242 7350
Fax: 0116 242 7444
Email: **nya@nya.org.uk**
Website: **http://www.nya.org.uk/**

The National Youth Agency (NYA) aims to advance youth work and to enable all young people to fulfil their potential within a just society.

NCH, The Children's Charity

Head office address: 85 Highbury Park, London N5 1UD
Tel: 020 7704 7000
Fax: 020 7226 2537
Website: **http://www.nch.org.uk/**

The NCH is one of the UK's leading children's charities with offices in England, Northern Ireland, Scotland and Wales.

Niacro

Head office address: Amelia House, 4 Amelia Street, Belfast BT2 7GS
Tel: 028 9032 0157
Fax: 087 0432 1415
Email: **niacro@niacro.co.uk**
Website: **http://www.niacro.co.uk/**

Niacro aims to contribute towards the creation of a society in which communities can live without fear of crime, and in which the rights and needs of everyone, including offenders, are equally respected.

No More Prison

Head office address: membership inquiries – c/o Dr Paul Mason, School of Journalism, Media and Culture Studies, Bute Building, Cardiff University, King Edward VII Avenue, Cardiff CF10 3NB
Email: **nomoreprison@aol.com**
Website: **http://www.alternatives2prison.ik.com/**

No More Prison is a membership organization committed to the abolition of prisons and it opposes the criminalization of young people.

Northern Ireland Human Rights Commission

Head office address: Temple Court, 39 North Street, Belfast BT1 1NA
Tel: 028 9024 3987
Fax: 028 9024 7844
Website: **http://www.nihrc.org/**

The Northern Ireland Human Rights Commission works to ensure that the human rights of everyone in Northern Ireland are fully and firmly protected in law, policy and practice.

Penal Reform International

Head office address: Unit 450, The Bon Marche Centre, 241–251 Ferndale Road, London SW9 8BJ
Tel: 020 7924 9575
Fax: 020 7924 9697
Email: **info@penalreform.org**
Website: **http://www.penalreform.org/**

Penal Reform International is an international non-governmental organization working on penal and criminal justice reform worldwide.

Police Foundation

Head office address: First Floor, Park Place, 12 Lawn Lane, London SW8 1UD
Tel: 020 7582 3744
Fax: 020 7587 0671
Email: **sue.roberts@police-foundation.org.uk**
Website: **http://www.police-foundation.org.uk/**

The Police Foundation is the only independent charity focused entirely on developing people's knowledge and understanding of policing and on challenging the Police Service and the government to improve policing for the benefit of the public.

Prison Reform Trust

Head office address: 15 Northburgh Street, London EC1V 0JR
Tel: 020 7251 5070
Fax: 020 7251 5076
Email: **prt@prisonreformtrust.org.uk**
Website: **http://www.prisonreformtrust.org.uk/**

The Prison Reform Trust aims to achieve a just, humane and effective penal system by inquiring into the workings of the system; by informing prisoners, staff and the wider public; and by influencing Parliament, government and officials towards reform.

Prisons and Probation Ombudsman for England and Wales

Head office address: Ashley House, 2 Monck Street, London SW1P 2BQ
Tel: 020 7035 2876
Fax: 020 7035 2860
Email: **mail@ppo.gsi.gov.uk**
Website: **http://www.ppo.gov.uk/**

The Prisons and Probation Ombudsman is appointed by the Home Secretary and investigates complaints from prisoners and those subject to probation supervision. The ombudsman is also responsible for investigating all deaths of prisoners, residents of probation hostels and immigration detainees.

Release

Head office address: 388 Old Street, London EC1V 9LT
Tel: 020 7729 5255
Fax: 020 7729 2599
Email: **ask@release.org.uk**
Website: **http://www.release.org.uk/**

Release offers a range of specialist services to professionals and the public concerning drugs and the law.

RESET

Head office address: Ground Floor, Hampton House, 20 Albert Embankment, London SE1 7SD
Tel: 020 7840 5615
Email: **info@reset.uk.net**
Website: **http://www.reset.uk.net/**

RESET is a diverse project with over 50 partners that aims to improve the resettlement process for young offenders.

Restorative Justice Consortium

Head office address: Suite 50, Albert Buildings, 49 Queen Victoria Street, London EC4N 4SA
Tel: 0207 653 1992
Fax: 020 7653 1993
Website: **http://www.restorativejustice.org.uk/**

The Restorative Justice Consortium was formed in 1997, bringing together a wide range of organizations with an interest in restorative justice.

Sacro

Head office address: 1 Broughton Market, Edinburgh EH3 6NU
Tel: 0131 624 7270
Fax: 0131 624 7269
Email: **info@national.sacro.org.uk**
Website: **http://www.sacro.org.uk/**

Sacro aims to promote community safety across Scotland through providing high-quality services to reduce conflict and offending.

Scottish Centre for Crime and Justice Research

Head office address: the centre has offices at each of the main participating universities
Website: http://www.sccjr.ac.uk

The Scottish Centre for Crime and Justice Research is a partnership between Glasgow, Stirling, Edinburgh and Glasgow Caledonian Universities in alliance with a wider consortium of individuals and groups aimed at promoting collaboration and enhancing research capacity.

Scottish Children's Reporter Administration (SCRA)

Head office address: Ochil House, Springkerse Business Park, Stirling FK7 7XE
Tel: 01786 459500
Fax: 01786 459532
Email: info@scra.gov.uk
Website: http://www.scra.gov.uk/

The Scottish Children's Reporter Administration (SCRA) is the national body responsible for the provision of care and justice systems for children. Its principal responsibilities are: to facilitate the work of children's reporters and to provide suitable accommodation for children's hearings.

Secure Accommodation Network

Website: http://www.secureaccommodation.org.uk/

The Secure Accommodation Network represents and promotes the work of secure children's homes in England and Wales.

Social Exclusion Task Force

Head office address: Social Exclusion Task Force, Cabinet Office, 4th Floor, Admiralty Arch, The Mall, London SW1A 2WH
Tel: 020 7276 1234
Email: setaskforce@cabinet-office.x.gsi.gov.uk
Website: http://www.cabinetoffice.gov.uk/social_exclusion_task_force/

The role of the Social Exclusion Task Force is to co-ordinate the government's policy responses to social exclusion.

SOVA

Head office address: 1st Floor, Chichester House, 37 Brixton Road, London   SW9 6DZ
Tel: 020 7793 0404
Fax: 020 7735 4410
Email: mail@sova.org.uk
Website: http://www.sova.org.uk/

SOVA is the leading charitable organization for voluntary services with offenders, ex-offenders and their families in England and Wales.

Unicef

Head office address: (UK office) Africa House, 64–78 Kingsway, London WC2B 6NB
Tel: 020 7405 5592
Fax: 020 7405 2332
Email: **info@unicef.org.uk**
Website: **http://www.unicef.org/**

Unicef is an international organization that is particularly concerned with children who are subjected to violence, exploitation and abuse, including children in conflict with the law.

Victim Support England and Wales

Head office address: Cranmer House, 39 Brixton Road, London SW9 6DZ
Tel: 020 7735 9166
Fax: 020 7582 5712
Email: **contact@victimsupport.org.uk**
Website: **http://www.victimsupport.org.uk/**

Victim Support helps people affected by crime.

Victim Support Northern Ireland

Head office address: 3rd Floor, Annsgate House, 70–74 Ann Street, Belfast BT1 4EH
Tel: 028 9024 4039
Fax: 028 9031 3838
Email: **info@victimsupportni.org.uk**
Website: **http://www.victimsupport.org.uk/vs_ni/contact/area_office.html**

Victim Support helps people affected by crime.

Victim Support Scotland

Head office address: 15–23 Hardwell Close, Edinburgh EH8 9RX
Tel: 0131 668 4486
Fax: 0131 662 5400
Email: **info@victimsupportsco.demon.co.uk**
Website: **http://www.victimsupportsco.org.uk/page/index.cfm**

Victim Support helps people affected by crime.

Voice

Head office address: Unit 4, Pride Court, 80–82 White Lion Street, London N1 9PF
Tel: 020 7833 5792
Fax: 020 7713 1950
Email: **info@voiceyp.org**
Website: **http://www.voiceyp.org/**

Voice is one of the UK's leading voluntary organizations working and campaigning for children and young people in public care.

YoungMinds

Head office address: 48–50 St John Street, London EC1M 4DG
Tel: 020 7336 8445
Fax: 020 7336 8446
Email: **enquiries@youngminds.org.uk**
Website: **www.youngminds.org.uk**

YoungMinds is a national charity committed to improving the mental health of all children and young people.

Youth Justice Agency of Northern Ireland

Head office address: 41–43 Waring Street, Belfast BT1 2DY
Tel: 028 9031 6400
Fax: 028 9031 6402/3
Email: **info@yjani.gov.uk**
Website: **http://www.youthjusticeagencyni.gov.uk/**

The principal aim of the Youth Justice Agency of Northern Ireland is to reduce youth crime and to build confidence in the youth justice system.

Youth Justice Board (YJB)

Head office address: 11 Carteret Street, London SW1H 9DL
Tel: 020 7271 3033
Fax: 020 7271 3030
Email: **enquiries@yjb.gov.uk**
Website: **http://www.yjb.gov.uk/**

The Youth Justice Board (YJB) oversees the youth justice system in England and Wales.

References

Abramson, B. (2006) 'Juvenile justice: the "unwanted child"', in E. Jensen and J. Jepsen (eds) *Juvenile Law Violators, Human Rights and the Development of New Juvenile Justice Systems*. Oxford: Hart Publishing.

ACPO (2003) *ACPO Strategy for Children and Young People*. London: Association of Chief Police Officers of England, Wales and Northern Ireland.

Adler, F. and Laufer, W.S. (eds) (2000) *The Legacy of Anomie Theory*. New Brunswick, NJ: Transaction Publishers.

Akers, R.L. (1985) *Deviant Behaviour: A Social Learning Approach*. Belmont, CA: Wadsworth.

Alcock, P., Craig, G., Dalgliesh, K. and Pearson, S. (1995) *Combating Local Poverty*. London: Local Government Management Board.

Alder, C. and Worrall, A. (2004) 'A contemporary crisis?', in C. Alder and A. Worrall (eds) *Girls' Violence: Myths and Realities*. Albany, NY: State University of New York Press.

Alexander, C. (2000) *The Asian Gang: Ethnicity, Identity, Masculinity*. Oxford: Berg.

Allen, C. (2005) 'The links between heroin, crack cocaine and crime: where does street crime fit in?', *British Journal of Criminology*, 45: 355–72.

Allen, R. (2006) *From Punishment to Problem Solving – a New Approach to Children in Trouble*. London: Centre for Crime and Justice Studies.

Amnesty International (2005) 'Public statement: Iran continues to execute minors and juvenile offenders' (available online at **http://www.amnestyusa.org/document.php?lang=e&id= 80256DD400782B84802570460056CF81**).

Armstrong, T.L. (ed.) (1991) *Intensive Interventions with High-risk Youths: Promising Approaches in Juvenile Probation and Parole*. Monsey, NY: Willow Tree Press.

Arvanites, T. and Defina, R. (2006) 'Business cycles and street crime', *Criminology*, 44: 139–64.

ASBO Concern (2005) *ASBOs: An Analysis of the First Six Years*. London: ASBO Concern (available online at **http://www.asboconcern.org.uk/**).

Ashford, M., Chard, A. and Redhouse, N. (2006) *Defending Young People in the Criminal Justice System* (3rd edn). London: Legal Action Group.

Ashton, J. and Grindrod, M. (1999) 'Institutional troubleshooting: lessons for policy and practice', in B. Goldson (ed.) *Youth Justice: Contemporary Policy and Practice*. Aldershot: Ashgate.

Audit Commission (1996) *Misspent Youth: Young People and Crime*. London: Audit Commission.

Audit Commission (2004) *Youth Justice 2004: A Review of the Reformed Youth Justice System*. London: Audit Commission.

Audit Commission (2007) *Comprehensive Performance Assessment*. London: Audit Commission (available online at **http://www.audit-commission.gov.uk/cpa/index.asp?page=index.asp&area=hpcpa**).

Audit Scotland (2001) *Youth Justice in Scotland: A Baseline Report*. Edinburgh: Audit Scotland.

Austin, J. and Krisberg, B. (1981) 'Wider, stronger and different nets: the dialectics of criminal justice reform', *Journal of Research in Crime and Delinquency*, 18: 165–96.

Bailey, S. and Williams, R. (2005) 'Forensic mental health services for children and adolescents', in R. Williams and M. Kerfoot (eds) *Child and Adolescent Mental Health Services*. Oxford: Oxford University Press.

Bainham, A. (2005) *Children – the Modern Law* (3rd edn). Bristol: Family Law.

Baker, K. (2005) 'Assessment in youth justice: professional discretion and the use of Asset', *Youth Justice*, 5: 106–22.

Baker, K., Jones, S., Roberts, C. and Merrington, S. (2003) *The Evaluation of the Validity and Reliability of the Youth Justice Board's Assessment for Young Offenders: Findings from the First Two Years of the Use of ASSET*. London: Youth Justice Board.

Bala, N., Hornick, J., Snyder, H. and Paetsch, J. (eds) (2002) *Juvenile Justice Systems: An International Comparison of Problems and Solutions*. Toronto: Thompson.

Bandalli, S. (2000) 'Children, responsibility and the new youth justice', in B. Goldson (ed.) *The New Youth Justice*. Lyme Regis: Russell House.

Barrow Cadbury Commission on Young Adults in the Criminal Justice System (2006) *Lost in Transition: Report*. London: Barrow Cadbury Trust.

Barry, M. (2006) *Youth Offending in Transition: The Search for Social Recognition*. London: Routledge.

Batchelor, S. (2002) 'The myth of girl gangs', in Y. Jewkes and G. Letherby (eds) *Criminology: A Reader*. London: Sage.

Batchelor, S. and Burman, M. (2004) 'Working with girls and young women', in G. McIvor (ed.) *Women Who Offend*. London: Jessica Kingsley.

Bateman, T. (2005a) 'Court reports', in T. Bateman and J. Pitts (eds) *The RHP Companion to Youth Justice*. Lyme Regis: Russell House.

Bateman, T. (2005b) 'Custody and policy', in T. Bateman and J. Pitts (eds) *The RHP Companion to Youth Justice*. Lyme Regis: Russell House.

Bateman, T. (2005c) 'Reducing child imprisonment: a systemic challenge', *Youth Justice*, 5: 91–105.

Bateman, T. (2006) 'Youth crime and justice: statistical "evidence", recent trends and responses', in B. Goldson and J. Muncie (eds) *Youth Crime and Justice: Critical Issues*. London: Sage.

Bateman, T. and Pitts, J. (2005) 'Conclusion: what the evidence tells us', in T. Bateman and J. Pitts (eds) *The RHP Companion to Youth Justice*. Lyme Regis: Russell House.

Bateman, T. and Stanley, C. (2002) *Patterns of Sentencing: Differential Sentencing across England and Wales*. London: Youth Justice Board.

Baumol, W.J., Panzar, J.C. and Wilig, R.D. (1982) *Contestable Markets and the Theory of Industry Structure*. New York, NY: Harcourt Brace Jovanovich.

Beck, U. (1992) *Risk Society*. London: Sage.

Becker, H.S. (1963) *Outsiders: Studies in the Sociology of Deviance*. New York, NY: Free Press.

Beer, J. with Stief, E. (1997) *The Mediator's Handbook*. Philadelphia, PA: Friends Conflict Resolution Programs.

Behan, B. (1958) *Borstal Boy*. Berkeley: Windhover.

Beinhart, S., Anderson, B. and Lee, S. (2002) *Youth at Risk*. Swansea: Communities that Care.

Bell, C. and Haines, K. (1991) 'Managing the transition: implications of the introduction of a youth court in England and Wales', in T. Booth (ed.) *Juvenile Justice in the New Europe*. Sheffield: Joint Unit for Social Services Research.

Berman, G. and Mansky, A. (2005) 'Community justice centres: a US–UK exchange', *British Journal of Community Justice*, 3: 5–14.

Bhabra, S., Hill, E. and Ghate, D. (2004) *Safer School Partnerships: National Evaluation of the Safer School Partnerships Programme*. London: Youth Justice Board and Department for Education and Skills.

Bind, J. and Gerlach, L. (2007) *Improving the Emotional Health and Wellbeing of Young People in Social Care*. London: National Children's Bureau.

Blair, T. (2004) 'Foreword', in *Confident Communities in a Secure Britain: The Home Office Strategic Plan, 2004–08*. London: HMSO.

Blyth, E. and Milner, J. (eds) (1996) *Exclusion from School: Inter-professional Issues for Policy and Practice*. London: Routledge.

Boswell, G. and Wedge, P. (2002) *Imprisoned Fathers and their Children*. London and Philadelphia, PA: Jessica Kingsley.

Bottoms, A. (1977) 'Reflections on the renaissance of dangerousness', *Howard Journal of Penology and Crime Prevention*, 16: 70–96.

Bottoms, A. (1995) 'The philosophy and politics of punishment and sentencing', in C. Clarkson and R. Morgan (eds) *The Politics of Sentencing Reform*. Oxford: Clarendon Press.

Bottoms, A. (2001) 'Compliance and community penalties', in A. Bottoms *et al.* (eds) *Community Penalties: Changes and Challenges*. Cullompton: Willan Publishing.

Bottoms, A., Brown, P., McWilliams, B., McWilliams, W., Nellis, M. with Pratt, J. (1990) *Intermediate Treatment and Juvenile Justice*. London: HMSO.

Bottoms, A., Gelsthorpe, L. and Rex, S. (2002) *Community Penalties, Change and Challenges*. Cullompton: Willan Publishing.

Bottoms, A. and Kemp, V. (2006) 'The relationship between youth justice and child welfare in England and Wales', in M. Hill et al. (eds) *Youth Justice and Child Protection*. London: Jessica Kingsley.

Bottoms, A. and McWilliams, W. (1979) 'A non-treatment paradigm for probation practice', *British Journal of Social Work*, 9: 159–202.

Bottoms, A. and Preston, R. (1980) *The Coming Penal Crisis*. Edinburgh: Scottish Academic Press.

Bottoms, A. and Stevenson, S. (1992) 'What went wrong? Criminal justice policy in England and Wales, 1945–70', in D. Downes (ed.) *Unravelling Criminal Justice*. London: Macmillan.

Bottoms, A. (2002) 'The divergent development of juvenile justice policy and practice in England and Scotland', in M.K. Rosenheim *et al.* (eds) *A Century of Juvenile Justice*. Chicago, IL: University of Chicago Press.

Bottoms, A., McClean, J.D. and Patchett, K.W. (1970) 'Children, young persons and the courts – a survey of the new law', *Criminal Law Review*, 368–95.

Bowles, R., Garcia Reyes, M. and Pradiptyo, R. (2005) *Safer Schools Partnerships*. London: Youth Justice Board (available online at **http://www.yjb.gov.uk/Publications/Scripts/prodView.asp?idProduct=269&eP=**).

Bowling, B. and Phillips, C. (2002) *Racism, Crime and Justice*. London: Longman.

Braithwaite, J. (1989) *Crime, Shame and Reintegration*. Cambridge: Cambridge University Press.

Braithwaite, J. (1993) 'Beyond positivism: learning from contextual integrated strategies', *Journal of Research in Crime and Delinquency*, 30: 383–99.

Braithwaite, J. (2002) *Restorative Justice and Responsive Regulation*. Oxford: Oxford University Press.

Britton, L., Chatrik, B., Coles, B., Craig, G., Bivand, P., Mumtaz, S., Burrows, R., Convery, P. and Hylton, C. (2002) *Missing Connexions: The Career Dynamics and Welfare Needs of Black and Minority Ethnic Young People at the Margins*. Bristol: Policy Press.

Brookman, F. and Pierpoint, H. (2003) 'Access to legal advice for young suspects and remand prisoners', *Howard Journal of Criminal Justice*, 42: 452–70.

Brown, A.P. (2004) 'Anti-social behaviour, crime control and social control', *Howard Journal of Criminal Justice*, 43: 203–11.

Brownlee, I. (1998a) 'New Labour – new penology? Punitive rhetoric and the limits of managerialism in criminal justice policy', *Journal of Law and Society*, 25: 313–25.

Brownlee, I. (1998b) *Community Punishment: A Critical Introduction*. London: Longman.

Buchanan, J. (2004) 'Missing links: problem drug use and social exclusion', *Probation Journal* (special issue: 'Rethinking drugs and crime'), 51: 387–97.

Buchanan, J. (2007) 'Understanding and engaging with problematic substance use', in S. Green *et al.* (eds) *Addressing Offending Behaviour: Context, Practice, Values*. Cullompton: Willan Publishing.

Buckley, H. and O'Sullivan, E. (2006) 'The interface between youth justice and child protection in Ireland', in M. Hill et al. (eds) *Youth Justice and Child Protection*. London: Jessica Kingsley.

Budd, T., Sharp, C., Weir, G., Wilson, D. and Owen, N. (2005) *Young People and Crime: Findings from the 2004 Offending, Crime and Justice Survey. Home Office Statistical Bulletin* 20/05. London: Home Office.

Bullock, S. and Jones, B. (2004) *Acceptable Behaviour Contracts: Addressing Antisocial Behaviour in the London Borough of Islington. Home Office Online Report* 02/04. London: Home Office (available online at **http://www.homeoffice.gov.uk/rds/pdfs2/rdsolr0204.pdf**).

Burke, L. (2005) *From Probation to the National Offender Management Service: Issues of Contestability, Culture and Community Involvement*. London: National Association of Probation Officers.

Burnett, R. and Appleton, C. (2004) *Joined-up Youth Justice: Tackling Youth Crime in Partnership*. Lyme Regis: Russell House.

Burnett, R. and Roberts, C. (eds) (2004) *What Works in Probation and Youth Justice: Developing Evidence-based Practice*. Cullompton: Willan Publishing.

Burney, E. (2005) *Making People Behave: Anti-social Behaviour, Politics and Policy*. Cullompton: Willan Publishing.

Burton, J. (1993) *The Handbook of Residential Care*. London: Routledge.

Byrne, D. (1998) *Complexity Theory and the Social Sciences*. London: Routledge.

Byrne, D. (1999) *Social Exclusion*. Buckingham: Open University Press.

Cadman, S. (2005) 'Proportionality in the youth justice system', in T. Bateman and J. Pitts (eds) *The RHP Companion to Youth Justice*. Lyme Regis: Russell House.

Campbell, A. (1984) *The Girls in the Gang: A Report from New York City*. Oxford: Blackwell.

Campbell, C., Devlin, R., O'Mahony, D., Doak, J., Jackson, J., Corrigan, T. and McEvoy, K. (2005) *Evaluation of the Northern Ireland Youth Conferencing Scheme. Northern Ireland Office, Research and Statistics Series*. Belfast: Northern Ireland Office.

Campbell, S. (2002) *A Review of Anti-social Behaviour Orders. Home Office Research Study* 236. London: Home Office Research, Development and Statistics Directorate (available online at **http://www.homeoffice.gov.uk/rds/pdfs2/hors236.pdf**).

Canton, R. and Eadie, T. (2005) 'Enforcement', in T. Bateman and J. Pitts (eds) *The RHP Companion to Youth Justice*. Lyme Regis: Russell House.

Carlile, A. (2006) *The Lord Carlile of Berriew QC: An Independent Inquiry into the Use of Physical Restraint, Solitary Confinement and Forcible Strip Searching of Children in Prisons, Secure Training Centres and Local Authority Secure Children's Homes*. London: Howard League for Penal Reform.

Carrabine, E., Iganski, P., Lee, M., Plummer, K. and South, N. (2004) *Criminology: A Sociological Introduction*. London: Routledge.

Carter, Lord (2006) *Legal Aid: A Market-based Approach to Reform* (available online at **http://www.legalaidprocurementreview.gov.uk/publications.htm**).

Carter, P. (2003) *Managing Offenders, Reducing Crime: A New Approach*. London: Home Office.

Cavadino, M. and Dignan, J. (2002) *The Penal System: An Introduction* (3rd edn). London: Sage.

Cavadino, P. and Gibson, B. (1993) *Bail: The Law, Best Practice and the Debate*. Winchester: Waterside Press.

Chakrabarti, S. (2006) 'ASBO-mania: from social and natural justice to mob rule.' BIHR lunchtime lecture, January (available online at **http://www.liberty-human-rights.org.uk/publications/ 3-articles-and-speeched/asbomania-bihr.PDF**).

Chamberlain, P. (1994) *Family Connections: A Treatment Foster Care Model for Adolescents with Delinquency*. Eugene, Oregon: Castalia Publishing.

Chapman, T. (2005) 'Group work with young people who offend', in T. Bateman and J. Pitts (eds) *The RHP Companion to Youth Justice*. Lyme Regis: Russell House.

Chesney-Lind, M. and Sheldon, R. (2004) *Girls, Delinquency and Juvenile Justice* (3rd edn). Belmont, CA: Wadsworth/Thomson.

Children's Commissioner for Wales (2003) *Annual Report*. Swansea: Children's Commissioner for Wales.

Children's Rights Alliance for England (2002) *Rethinking Child Imprisonment: A Report on Young Offender Institutions*. London: Children's Rights Alliance for England.

Children's Rights Alliance for England (2005) 'Government in breach of children's human rights – must do better', press release, 21 November. London: Children's Rights Alliance for England.

Children's Rights Alliance for England (2006) *The State of Children's Rights in England*. London: Children's Rights Alliance for England.

Christie, N. (1986) 'The ideal victim', in E.A. Fattah (ed.) *From Crime Policy to Victim Policy*. London: Macmillan.

Christie, N. (1993) *Crime Control as Industry*. London: Routledge.

Christie, N. (2004) *A Suitable Amount of Crime*. London: Routledge.

Chui, W.H. and Nellis, M. (2003) *Moving Probation Forward: Evidence, Arguments and Practice*. Harlow: Pearson.

Clarke, J. (1985) 'Whose justice? The politics of juvenile control', *International Journal of the Sociology of Law*, 13: 407–21.

Clarke, J. and Newman, J. (1997) *The Managerial State*. London: Sage.

Clinard, M.B. (ed.) (1964) *Anomie and Deviant Behaviour*. New York, NY: Free Press.

Cloward, R. and Ohlin, L. (1960) *Delinquency and Opportunity*. London: Routledge & Kegan Paul.

Coalter, F., Allison, M. and Taylor, J. (2000) *The Role of Sport in Regenerating Deprived Areas*. Edinburgh: Scottish Executive.

Cohen, A.K. (1955) *Delinquent Boys: The Culture of the Gang*. Glencoe, IL: Free Press.

Cohen, A.K. (1965) 'The sociology of the deviant act: anomie theory and beyond', *American Sociological Review*, 30: 5–14.

Cohen, P. (1997) *Rethinking the Youth Question*. Basingstoke: Macmillan.

Cohen, S. (1972) *Folk Devils and Moral Panics*. London: MacGibbon & Kee.

Cohen, S. (1979) 'The punitive city: notes on the dispersal of social control', *Contemporary Crisis*, 3: 339–63.

Cohen, S. (1980) *Folk Devils and Moral Panics*. London: Routledge.

Cohen, S. (1985) *Visions of Social Control: Crime, Punishment and Classification*. Cambridge: Polity Press.

Cohen, S. (2000) 'Some thoroughly modern monsters', *Index on Censorship*, 29: 36–43.

Cohen, S. (2002) *Folk Devils and Moral Panics: The Creation of Mods and Rockers*. London: Routledge.

Cole, M. (ed.) (2006) *Education, Equality and Human Rights* (2nd edn). London: Routledge.

Coleman, C. and Moynihan, J. (1996) *Understanding Crime Data*. Buckingham: Open University Press.

Coleman, R. (2004) *Reclaiming the Streets: Surveillance, Social Control and the City*. Cullompton: Willan Publishing.

Collier, P. (2005) *Managing Police Performance: Accountabilities, Performance Measurement and Control.* Swindon: Economic and Social Research Council (ESRC).

Commission for Social Care Inspectorate, Healthcare Commission, Her Majesty's Inspectorate of Constabulary, Her Majesty's Inspectorate of Probation, Her Majesty's Inspectorate of Prisons, Her Majesty's Crown Prosecution Service Inspectorate, Her Majesty's Inspectorate of Courts Administration and Office of Standards in Education (2005) *Safeguarding Children: The Second Joint Chief Inspectors' Report on Arrangements to Safeguard Children.* London: Department of Health Publications (available online at **www.safeguardingchildren.org.uk**).

Connelly, C. and Williamson, S. (2000) *Review of the Research Literature on Serious Violent and Sexual Offenders. Crime and Criminal Justice Research Findings* 46. Edinburgh: Scottish Executive Central Research Unit.

Convery, U. (2002) 'The use and nature of custody for children in the Northern Ireland criminal justice system.' Unpublished doctoral thesis, University of Ulster.

Convery, U. and Moore, L. (2006) *Still In Our Care: Protecting Children's Rights in Custody in Northern Ireland.* Belfast: Northern Ireland Human Rights Commission.

Corby, B. (2000) *Child Abuse: Towards a Knowledge Base.* Milton Keynes: Open University Press.

Corre, N. and Wolchover, D. (2004) *Bail in Criminal Proceedings* (3rd edn). Oxford: Oxford University Press.

Council of Europe (1987) *Social Reactions to Juvenile Delinquency* (Recommendation R (87) 20). Strasbourg: Council of Europe.

Council of Europe (2003) *New Ways of Dealing with Juvenile Delinquency and the Role of Juvenile Justice* (Recommendation R (2003) 20). Strasbourg: Council of Europe.

Crabbe, T. (2006) *Knowing the Score – Positive Futures Case Study Research: Final Report.* London: Home Office.

Crawford, A. (1999) *The Local Governance of Crime: Appeals to Community and Partnership.* Oxford: Oxford University Press.

Crawford, A. (2002) 'The governance of crime and insecurity in an anxious age: The trans-European and the local', in A. Crawford (ed.) *Crime and Insecurity: The Governance of Safety in Europe.* Cullompton: Willan Publishing.

Crawford, A. (2003) 'Contractual governance of deviant behaviour', *Journal of Law and Society,* 30: 479–505.

Crawford, A. (2007) 'Crime prevention and community safety', in M. Maguire et al. (eds) *The Oxford Handbook of Criminology.* Oxford: Oxford University Press.

Crawford, A. and Newburn, T. (2003) *Youth Offending and Restorative Justice: Implementing Reform in Youth Justice.* Cullompton: Willan Publishing.

Crime Concern (2006) *Be Part of Something.* London: Crime Concern.

Criminal Justice Review Group (2000) *Review of the Criminal Justice System in Northern Ireland.* Belfast: HMSO (available online at **http://www.nio.gov.uk/review_of_the_criminal_ justice_system_in_northern_ireland.pdf**).

Cross, N., Evans, J. and Minkes, J. (2003) 'Still children first? Developments in youth justice in Wales', *Youth Justice,* 2: 151–62.

Cross, N., Mair, G. and Taylor, S. (2007) *The Use and Impact of the Community Order and the Suspended Sentence Order.* London: Centre for Crime and Justice Studies.

Crown Prosecution Service (2004) *The Code for Crown Prosecutors.* London: Crown Prosecution Service (available online at **http://www.cps.gov.uk/publications/docs/code2004 english.pdf**).

Cunneen, C. (1999) 'Zero tolerance policing: how will it effect indigenous communities?', *Indigenous Law Bulletin* (available online at **http://www.austlii.edu.au//cgibin/disp.pl/au/ journals/ILB/1999/22.html?query=zero%20or%20tolerance%20or%20policing#fn1**).

Curtis, S. (1989) *Juvenile Offending: Prevention through Intermediate Treatment*. London: Batsford.

Davies, H. (1999) 'Managing juvenile remands and developing community-based alternatives to secure accommodation in Wales: towards a strategic approach', in B. Goldson (ed.) *Youth Justice: Contemporary Policy and Practice*. Aldershot: Ashgate.

Davies, M., Croall, H. and Tyrer, J. (2005) *Criminal Justice: An Introduction to the Criminal Justice System in England and Wales*. Harlow: Pearson.

Davies, P. (2007) 'Lessons from the gender agenda', in S. Walklate (ed.) *Handbook of Victims and Victimology*. Cullompton: Willan Publishing.

Davies, T., Nutley, S. and Smith, P. (2000) *What Works? Evidence-based Policy and Practice in Public Services*. Bristol: Policy Press.

Davis, A. (2003) *Are Prisons Obsolete?* New York, NY: Seven Stories Press.

Davis, H. and Bourhill, M. (1997) '"Crisis": the demonisation of children and young people', in P. Scraton (ed.) *'Childhood' in 'Crisis'?* London: UCL Press.

Davis, J. (1990) *Youth and Generation in Modern Britain: Images of Adolescent Conflict*. London: Athlone Press.

Dawson, P. (2005) *Early Findings from the Prolific and Other Priority Offenders Evaluation. Home Office Development and Practice Report* 46. London: Home Office.

Dawson, P. and Cuppleditch, L. (2007) *An Impact Assessment of the Prolific and Other Priority Offender Programme. Home Office Online Report* 08/07. London: Home Office.

Dean, M. (1999) *Governmentality: Power and Rule in Modern Society*. London: Sage.

de Boer-Buquicchio, M. (2005) Conference speech by the Deputy Secretary General of the Council of Europe, Berlin, 21 October, 'Raising children without violence' (available online at **http://www. coe.int/t/e/SG/SGA/documents/speeches/2005/ZH_21102005_Berlin.asp#TopOfPage**).

Defra (2004) *Guidance for Part 6, Anti-social Behaviour Act 2003*. London: Defra (available online at **http://www.defra.gov.uk/environment/localenv/pdf/asbact-guidance**).

Defra (2006a) *Fixed Penalty Notices: Guidance on the Fixed Penalty Notice Provisions of the Environmental Protection Act 1990, the Clean Neighbourhoods and Environment Act 2005, and Other Legislation*. London: Defra (available online at **http://www.defra.gov.uk/ environment/localenv/legislation/cnea/fixedpenaltynotices**).

Defra (2006b) *Issuing Fixed Penalty Notices to Juveniles: Guidance on Issuing Fixed Penalty Notices Contained within the Clean Neighbourhoods and Environment Act 2005*. London: Defra (available online at **http://www.defra.gov.uk/environment/localenv/ legislation/cnea/juveniles**).

de Haan, W. (1990) *The Politics of Redress: Crime, Punishment and Penal Abolition*. London: Unwin Hyman.

Dennis, N. (1993) *Rising Crime and the Dismembered Family*. London: Institute of Economic Affairs.

Dennis, N. (ed.) (1997) *Zero Tolerance: Policing a Free Society*. London: IEA Health and Welfare Unit.

Dennis, N. and Erdos, G. (1992) *Families without Fatherhood*. London: Institute of Economic Affairs.

Department for Constitutional Affairs (2006a) *Delivering Simple, Speedy, Summary Justice*. London: Department of Constitutional Affairs (available online at **http://www.dca.gov.uk/ publications/reports_reviews/delivery-simple-speedy.pdf**).

Department for Constitutional Affairs (2006b) *Making Sense of Human Rights: A Short Introduction*. London: Department for Constitutional Affairs.

Department for Culture, Media and Sport (1999) *Policy Action Team 10: Report to the Social Exclusion Unit – Arts and Sport.* London: HMSO.

Department for Education and Skills (2003) *Every Child Matters.* London: DFES (available online at **http://www.everychildmatters.gov.uk/_files/EBE7EEAC90382663E0D5BBF24C99 A7AC.pdf**).

Department for Education and Skills (2004a) *Every Child Matters: Change for Children in the Criminal Justice System.* London: DFES (available online at **http://www.everychild matters.gov.uk/_files/2F732FAF176ADC74EC67A78251B69328.pdf**).

Department for Education and Skills (2004b) *Guidance on Education-related Parenting Contracts, Parenting Orders and Penalty Notices.* London: DfES.

Department for Education and Skills (2005a) *Statutory Guidance on Interagency Cooperation to Improve the Well-being of Children: Children's Trusts* (available online at **http://www.every childmatters.gov.uk/_files/1200903D4F3C1396021B70D7146FAFEA.pdf**).

Department for Education and Skills (2005b) *Guidance on the Children and Young People's Plan* (available online at **http://www.everychildmatters.gov.uk/_files/58A771D2F683214 338B20DA1393F9B29.pdf**).

Department for Education and Skills (2005c) *Youth Matters.* London: DFES (available online at **http://www.everychildmatters.gov.uk/_files/Youth%20Matters.pdf**).

Department for Education and Skills (2006a) *Positive Activities for Young People: National Evaluation.* London: DfES.

Department for Education and Skills (2006b) *Youth Matters: Next Steps.* Norwich: HMSO.

Department for Education and Skills (2006c) *Joint Planning and Commissioning Framework for Children, Young People and Maternity Services* (available online at **http://www.everychild matters.gov.uk/_files/312A353A9CB391262BAF14CC7C1592F8.pdf**).

Department for Education and Skills (2006d) *Quality Standards for Young People's Information, Advice and Guidance.* London: DFES (available online at **http://www.dfes.gov.uk/ consultations/conResults.cfm?consultationId=1435**).

Department for Education and Skills (2007a) *Care Matters: Time for Change.* London: DfES.

Department for Education and Skills (2007b) *Statutory Guidance on Section 6 Education and Inspections Act (Positive Activities for Young People).* London: DFES (available online at **http://www.dfes.gov.uk/consultations/conResults.cfm?consultationId=1432**).

Department for Education and Skills and HM Treasury (2007) *Aiming High for Children: Supporting Families.* London: DfES and HM Treasury (available online at **http://www. policyhub.gov.uk/news_item/families_policy07.asp**).

Department for Education and Skills and Home Office (2006) *Parental Compensation Order Guidance (October 2006).* London: DfES and the Home Office (available online at **www.homeoffice.gov.uk/documents/parental-compensation-guid**).

Department of Health (1998) *Working Together to Safeguard Children: New Government Proposals for Inter-agency Cooperation* (consultation paper). London: HMSO.

Department of Health (1999) *Me, Survive, Out There? New Arrangements for Young People Living in and Leaving Care.* London: DoH (available online at **http://www.dh.gov.uk/en/ Publicationsandstatistics/Publications/PublicationsPolicyAndGuidance/DH_4010312**).

Department of Health (2001) *Children (Leaving Care) Act 2000: Regulations and Guidance.* London: DoH.

Department of Health (2006a) *Promoting the Mental Health and Psychological Well-being of Children and Young People: Report on the Implementation of Standard 9 of the National Service Framework for Children, Young People and Maternity Services.* London: Department of Health (available online at **http://www.dh.gov.uk/assetRoot/04/14/06/79/04140679.pdf**).

Department of Health (2006b) *Working Together to Safeguard Children: A Guide to Inter-agency Working to Safeguard and Promote the Welfare of Children.* London: HMSO.

Department of Health (2007) *Promoting Mental Health for Children Held in Secure Settings: A Framework for Commissioning Services.* London: Department of Health.

Department of Health and Social Services and Public Safety (2003) *A Better Future: 50 Years of Child Care in Northern Ireland 1950–2000.* Belfast: DHSSPS.

Diduck, A. and Kaganas, F. (2006) *Family Law, Gender and the State: Text, Cases and Materials* (2nd edn). Oxford: Hart Publishing.

Dignan, J. (2007) 'Juvenile justice, criminal courts and restorative justice', in J. Johnstone and D. Van Ness (eds) *Handbook of Restorative Justice.* Cullompton: Willan Publishing.

Ditchfield, J.A. (1976) *Police Cautioning in England and Wales.* London: HMSO.

Dodd, M. (2002) 'Children, the press – and a missed opportunity', *Child and Family Law Quarterly*, 103.

Doel, M. and Sawdon, C. (1999) *The Essential Groupworker.* London: Jessica Kingsley.

Downes, D. (1966) *The Delinquent Solution.* London: Routledge & Kegan Paul.

Downes, D. and Rock, P. (2007) *Understanding Deviance: A Guide to the Sociology of Crime and Rule-breaking* (5th edn). Oxford: Oxford University Press.

Drakeford, M. (1996) 'Parents of young people in trouble', *Howard Journal of Criminal Justice*, 35: 242–55.

Drakeford, M., Haines, K., Cotton, B. and Octigan, M. (2001) *Pre-trial Services and the Future of Probation.* Cardiff: University of Wales.

Drakeford, M. and McCarthy, K. (2000) 'Parents, responsibility and the new youth justice', in B. Goldson (ed.) *The New Youth Justice.* Lyme Regis: Russell House.

DTZ Consulting and Research and Heriot-Watt University (2006) *Use of Anti-social Behaviour Orders in Scotland: Report of the 2005/06 Survey* (available online at **http://www.scotland.gov.uk/Publications/2006/11/28153603/0**).

Dugmore, P. and Pickford, J. (2006) *Youth Justice and Social Work.* Exeter: Learning Matters.

Dunkel, F. (1996) 'Current directions in criminal policy', in W. McCarney (ed.) *Juvenile Delinquents and Young People in Danger in an Open Environment.* Winchester: Waterside Books.

Eadie, T. and Canton, R. (2002) 'Practising in a context of ambivalence: the challenge for youth justice workers', *Youth Justice*, 2: 14–26.

Earle, R. and Newburn, T. (2002) 'Creative tensions? Young offenders, restorative justice and the introduction of referral orders', *Youth Justice*, 1: 3–13.

Earle, R., Newburn, T. and Crawford, A. (2003) 'Referral orders: some reflections on policy transfer and what works', *Youth Justice*, 2: 141–50.

Easton, S. and Piper, C. (2005) *Sentencing and Punishment: The Quest for Justice.* Oxford: Oxford University Press.

Edmunds, M., May, T., Hearnden, I. and Hough, M. (1998) *Arrest Referral: Emerging Lessons from Research. DPI Paper* 23. London: Home Office.

Edwards, A. and Hughes, G. (2005) 'Comparing the governance of safety in Europe: a geo-historical approach', *Theoretical Criminology*, 9 (3): 345-363.

Edwards, L. and Griffiths, A. (2006) *Family Law* (2nd edn). Edinburgh: W. Green/Sweet & Maxwell.

Elliot, R., Airs, J., Easton, C. and Lewis, R. (2000) *Electronically Monitored Curfew for 10- to 15-year-olds – Report of the Pilot.* London: Home Office (available online at **http://www.homeoffice.gov.uk/rds/pdfs/occ-tagging.pdf**).

Etzioni, A. (1995) *The Spirit of Community.* London: Fontana.

European Forum for Restorative Justice (ed.) (2000) *Victim–Offender Mediation in Europe: Making Restorative Justice Work.* Leuven: Leuven University Press.

Evans, R. and Ellis, R. (1997) *Police Cautioning in the 1990s. Home Office Research Findings* 52. London: Home Office.

Evans, R. and Puech, K. (2001) 'Warnings and reprimands: popular punitiveness or restorative justice?', *Criminal Law Review*, 794–805.

Evans, R. and Wilkinson, C. (1990) 'Variations in police cautioning policy and practice in England and Wales', *Howard Journal of Criminal Justice*, 29: 155–76.

Fagan, F. and Zimring, F. (2000) *The Changing Borders of Juvenile Justice: Transfer of Adolescents to the Criminal Court.* Chicago, IL: University of Chicago Press.

Falconer, C. (2007) 'Human rights are majority rights.' The Lord Morris of Borth-y-Gest Memorial Lecture, 23 March, Bangor University.

Family Group Conference Service (2002) *Research Outcomes and Lessons Learned.* Essex: Essex County Council Family Group Conference Service.

Farmer, E., Moyers, S. and Lipscombe, J. (2004) *Fostering Adolescents.* London: Jessica Kingsley.

Farrall, S. (2002) *Rethinking What Works with Offenders: Probation, Social Context and Desistance from Crime.* Cullompton: Willan Publishing.

Farrall, S. and Calverley, A. (2006) *Understanding Desistance from Crime.* Maidenhead: Open University Press.

Farrant, F. (2006) *Out for Good: The Resettlement Needs of Young Men in Prison.* London: Howard League for Penal Reform.

Farrington, D.P. (1995) 'The development of offending and antisocial behaviour from childhood: key findings from the Cambridge Study in Delinquent Development', *Journal of Child Psychology and Psychiatry*, 36: 929–64.

Farrington, D.P. (1996) *Understanding and Preventing Youth Crime.* York: Joseph Rowntree Foundation.

Farrington, D.P. (2000) 'Explaining and preventing crime: the globalization of knowledge – the American Society of Criminology 1999 Presidential Address', *Criminology*, 38: 1–24.

Farrington, D.P. (2002) 'Developmental criminology and risk focused prevention', in M. Maguire *et al.* (eds) *The Oxford Handbook of Criminology* (3rd edn). Oxford: Oxford University Press.

Farrington, D.P., Ditchfield, J., Hancock, G., Howard, P., Jolliffe, D., Livingston, M. and Painter, K. (2002) *Evaluation of Two Intensive Regimes for Young Offenders. Home Office Research Study* 239. London: Home Office.

Feeley, M. and Simon, J. (1992) 'The new penology: notes on the emerging strategy of corrections and its implications', *Criminology*, 30: 449–74.

Feeley, M. and Simon, J. (1994) 'Actuarial justice: the emerging new criminal law', in D. Nelken (ed.) *The Futures of Criminology.* London: Sage.

Feilzer, M. and Hood, R. (2004) *Difference or Discrimination? Minority Ethnic People in the Youth Justice System.* London: Youth Justice Board.

Feld, B. (1991) 'Justice by geography: urban, suburban and rural variations in juvenile justice administration', *Journal of Criminal Law and Criminology*, 82: 156–210.

Ferraro, K. (1995) *Fear of Crime: Interpreting Victimisation Risk.* Albany, NY: State University of New York Press.

Ferrell, J. (1999) 'Cultural criminology', *Annual Review of Sociology*, 25: 395–418.

Ferrell, J., Hayward, K., Morrison, W. and Presdee, M. (2004) *Cultural Criminology Unleashed.* London: Glasshouse.

Ferrell, J. and Sanders, C. (1995) *Cultural Criminology.* Boston, MA: Northeastern University Press.

Fionda, J. (1998) 'The age of innocence? The concept of childhood in the punishment of young offenders', *Child and Family Law Quarterly*, 10: 77–87.

Fionda, J. (1999) 'New Labour, old hat: youth justice and the Crime and Disorder Act 1998', *Criminal Law Review*, 36–47.

Fionda, J. (2005) *Devils and Angels: Youth, Policy and Crime*. Oxford: Hart Publishing.

Flint, J. and Nixon, J. (2006) 'Governing neighbours: anti-social behaviour orders and new forms of regulating conduct in the UK', *Urban Studies*, 43: 939–55.

Flood-Page, C., Campbell, S., Harrington, V. and Miller, J. (2000) *Youth Crime: Findings from the 1998/99 Youth Lifestyles Survey. Home Office Research Study* 209. London: Home Office.

Follett, M. (2006) 'Crime reduction', in E. McLaughlin and J. Muncie (eds) *The Sage Dictionary of Criminology*. London: Sage.

Foucault, M. (1991) 'Governmentality', in G. Burchell *et al.* (eds) *The Foucault Effect: Studies in Governmentality*. Hemel Hempstead: Harvester.

France, A., Hine, J., Armstrong, D. and Camina, M. (2004) *The On Track Early Intervention and Prevention Programme: From Theory to Action*. London: Home Office.

France, A. and Homel, R. (eds) (2007) *Pathways and Crime Prevention: Theory, Policy and Practice*. Cullompton: Willan Publishing.

France, A. and Utting, D. (2005) 'The paradigm of "risk and protection focused prevention" and its impact on services for children and families', *Children and Society*, 19: 77–90.

Franklin, B. (2002) *The New Handbook of Children's Rights: Comparative Policy and Practice*. London: Routledge.

Friday, P. and Ren, X. (eds) (2006) *Delinquency and Juvenile Justice Systems in the Non-western World*. Monsey, NY: Criminal Justice Press.

Fry, E. (1994) *On Remand – Foster Care and the Youth Justice Service*. London: National Foster Care Association.

Fullwood, C. and Powell, H. (2004) 'Towards effective practice in the youth justice system', in R. Burnett and C. Roberts (eds) *What Works in Probation and Youth Justice: Developing Evidence Based Practice*. Cullompton: Willan Publishing.

Furlong, A. (2006) 'Not a very NEET solution: representing problematic labour market transitions among early school-leavers', *Work, Employment and Society*, 20: 553–69.

Gabbidon, P. and Goldson, B. (1997) *Securing Best Practice*. London: National Children's Bureau.

Garland, D. (1985) *Punishment and Welfare: A History of Penal Strategies*. Aldershot: Gower.

Garland, D. (1996) 'The limits of the sovereign state: strategies of crime control in contemporary society', *British Journal of Criminology*, 36: 445–71.

Garland, D. (1997) '"Governmentality" and the problem of crime', *Theoretical Criminology*, 1: 173–214.

Garland, D. (2001) *The Culture of Control: Crime and Social Order in Contemporary Society*. Oxford: Oxford University Press.

Garmezy, N. (1993) 'Vulnerability and resilience', in D. Funder and R. Parke (eds) *Studying Lives through Time: Personality and Development*. Washington, DC: American Psychological Association.

Garrett, P.M. (2004) 'The electronic eye: emerging surveillant practices in social work with children and families', *European Journal of Social Work*, 7: 57–71.

Gelder, K. and Thornton, S. (eds) (1997) *The Subcultures Reader*. London: Routledge.

Gelsthorpe, L. (1999) 'Youth crime and parental responsibility', in A. Bainham *et al.* (eds) *What is a Parent? A Socio-legal Analysis*. Oxford: Hart Publishing.

Gelsthorpe, L. and Morris, A. (1994) 'Juvenile justice, 1945–1992', in M. Maguire *et al.* (eds) *The Oxford Handbook of Criminology*. Oxford: Clarendon Press.

Gelsthorpe, L. and Sharpe, G. (2006) 'Gender, youth crime and justice', in B. Goldson and J. Muncie (eds) *Youth Crime and Justice: Critical Issues*. London: Sage.

Ghate, D. and Ramella, M. (2002) *Positive Parenting: The National Evaluation of the Youth Justice Board's Parenting Programme*. London: Policy Research Bureau for the Youth Justice Board.

Gibson, B. (2004) *Criminal Justice Act 2003: A Guide to the New Procedures and Sentencing*. Winchester: Waterside Press.

Gilbert, N. (2007) *Dilemmas of Privacy and Surveillance: Challenges of Technological Change*. London: Royal Academy of Engineering.

Gillespie, A. (2005) 'Reprimanding juveniles and the right to due process', *Modern Law Review*, 61: 1006–15.

Goffman, E. (1963) S*tigma: Notes on the Management of Spoiled Identity*. Englewood Cliffs, NJ: Prentice Hall.

Goldson, B. (1995) *A Sense of Security*. London: National Children's Bureau.

Goldson, B. (1997) 'Children in trouble: state responses to juvenile crime', in P. Scraton (ed.) *'Childhood' in 'Crisis'?* London: UCL Press.

Goldson, B. (1998) 'Re-visiting the "Bulger case": the governance of juvenile crime and the politics of punishment – enduring consequences for children in England and Wales', *Juvenile Justice Worldwide*, 1: 21–2.

Goldson, B. (ed.) (1999) *Youth Justice: Contemporary Policy and Practice*. Aldershot: Ashgate.

Goldson, B. (2000a) 'Youth Justice and Criminal Evidence Bill. Part 1. Referrals to youth offender panels', in L. Payne (ed.) *Child Impact Statements, 1998/99*. London: National Children's Bureau and Unicef.

Goldson, B. (ed.) (2000b) *The New Youth Justice*. Lyme Regis: Russell House.

Goldson, B. (2000c) '"Children in need" or "young offenders"? Hardening ideology, organisational change and new challenges for social work with children in trouble', *Child and Family Social Work*, 5: 255–65.

Goldson, B. (2000d) 'Wither diversion? Interventionism and the new youth justice', in B. Goldson (ed.) *The New Youth Justice*. Lyme Regis: Russell House.

Goldson, B. (2001) 'The demonisation of children: from the symbolic to the institutional', in P. Foley *et al.* (eds) *Children in Society: Contemporary Theory, Policy and Practice*. Basingstoke: Palgrave.

Goldson, B. (2002a) 'New punitiveness: the politics of child incarceration', in J. Muncie, G. Hughes and E. McLaughlin. (eds) *Youth Justice: Critical Readings*. London: Sage.

Goldson, B. (2002b) *Vulnerable Inside: Children in Secure and Penal Settings*. London: Children's Society.

Goldson, B. (2005a) 'Beyond formalism: towards "informal" approaches to youth crime and youth justice', in T. Bateman and J. Pitts (eds) *The RHP Companion to Youth Justice*. Lyme Regis: Russell House.

Goldson, B. (2005b) 'Child imprisonment: a case for abolition', *Youth Justice*, 5: 77–90.

Goldson, B. (2006a) 'Damage, harm and death in child prisons in England and Wales: questions of abuse and accountability', *Howard Journal of Criminal Justice*, 45: 449–67.

Goldson, B. (2006b) 'Fatal injustice: rampant punitiveness, child-prisoner deaths and institutionalised denial – a case for comprehensive independent inquiry in England and Wales', *Social Justice: A Journal of Crime, Conflict and World Order*, 33: 52–68.

Goldson, B. (2006c) 'Penal custody: intolerance, irrationality and indifference', in B. Goldson and J. Muncie (eds) *Youth Crime and Justice: Critical Issues*. London: Sage.

Goldson, B. (2007) 'New Labour's youth justice: a critical assessment of the first two terms', in G. McIvor and P. Raynor (eds.) *Developments in Social Work with Offenders: Research Highlights* 48. London and Philadelphia: Jessica Kingsley Publishers.

Goldson, B. and Chigwada-Bailey, R. (1999) '(What) justice for black children and young people?', in B. Goldson (ed.) *Youth Justice: Contemporary Policy and Practice.* Aldershot: Ashgate.

Goldson, B. and Coles, D. (2005) *In the Care of the State? Child Deaths in Penal Custody in England and Wales.* London: Inquest.

Goldson, B. and Jamieson, J. (2002a) 'Community bail or penal remand? A critical analysis of recent policy developments in relation to unconvicted and/or unsentenced juveniles', *British Journal of Community Justice*, 1: 63–76.

Goldson, B. and Jamieson, J. (2002b) 'Youth crime, the "parenting deficit" and state intervention: a contextual critique', *Youth Justice*, 2: 82–99.

Goldson, B., Lavalette, M. and McKechnie, J. (eds) (2002) *Children, Welfare and the State.* London: Sage.

Goldson, B. and Muncie, J. (2006a) 'Rethinking youth justice: comparative analysis, international human rights and research evidence', *Youth Justice*, 6: 91–106.

Goldson, B. and Muncie, J. (2006b) 'Critical anatomy: towards a principled youth justice', in B. Goldson and J. Muncie (eds) *Youth Crime and Justice: Critical Issues.* London: Sage.

Goldson, B. and Muncie, J. (eds) (2006c) *Youth Crime and Justice: Critical Issues.* London: Sage.

Goode, E. and Ben-Yehuda, N. (1994) *Moral Panics: The Social Construction of Deviance.* Cambridge, MA: Blackwell.

Goodey, J. (2005) *Victims and Victimology.* Harlow: Longman.

Gordon, D., Adelman, L., Ashworth, K., Bradshaw, J., Levitas, R., Middleton, S., Pantazis, C., Patsios, D., Payne, S., Townsend, P. and Williams, J. (2000) *Poverty and Social Exclusion in Britain.* York: Joseph Rowntree Foundation.

Graham, J. (1998) *Schools, Disruptive Behaviour and Delinquency: A Review of Research.* London: Home Office.

Graham, J. and Bowling, B. (1995) *Young People and Crime. Home Office Research Study* 145. London: Home Office.

Graham, P. (2004) *The End of Adolescence.* Oxford: Oxford University Press.

Green, P. and Ward, T. (2004) *State Crime: Governments, Violence and Corruption.* London: Pluto Press.

Green, S. (2002) 'The communitarian hi-jacking of community justice', *British Journal of Community Justice*, 1: 49–62.

Green, S. (2007) 'Crime, victimisation and vulnerability', in S. Walklate (ed.) *Handbook of Victims and Victimology.* Cullompton: Willan Publishing.

Greer, C. (2007) 'News media, victims and crime', in P. Davies *et al.* (eds) *Victims, Crime and Society.* London: Sage.

Guardian (2006) 'British girls among most violent in world', 23 January.

Guardian (2007) 'A temporary respite: jailing young people in ever larger numbers is not the answer to tackling youth crime', 19 February.

Hagell, A. (2004) *Key Elements of Effective Practice – Resettlement.* London: Youth Justice Board.

Hagell, A., Hazel, N. and Shaw, C. (2000) *Evaluation of Medway Secure Training Centre.* London: Home Office.

Hagell, A., Hazel, N. and Shaw, C. (2004) *Evaluation of Medway Secure Training Centre.* London: Policy Research Bureau (available online at **http://www.homeoffice.gov.uk/rds/pdfs/occ-medway.pdf**).

Hagell, A. and Newburn, T. (1994) *Persistent Young Offenders.* London: Policy Studies Institute.

Haines, K. (1996) *Understanding Modern Juvenile Justice.* Aldershot: Avebury.

Haines, K. (2000) 'Referral orders and youth offender panels: restorative approaches and the new youth justice', in B. Goldson (ed.) *The New Youth Justice*. Lyme Regis: Russell House.

Haines, K., Case, S., Isles, E., Rees, I. and Hancock, A. (2004) *Extending Entitlement: Making it Real*. Cardiff: Welsh Assembly Government.

Haines, K. and Drakeford, M. (1998) *Young People and Youth Justice*. Basingstoke: Macmillan.

Haines, K. and O'Mahony, D. (2006) 'Restorative approaches: young people and youth justice', in B. Goldson and J. Muncie (eds) *Youth Crime and Justice: Critical Issues*. London: Sage.

Hale, C. (1996) 'Fear of crime: a review of the literature', *International Review of Victimology*, 4: 79–150.

Hall, S. (1980) *Drifting into a Law and Order Society*. London: Cobden Trust.

Hall, S., Critcher, C., Jefferson, T., Clarke, J. and Roberts, B. (1978) *Policing the Crisis: Mugging, the State, and Law and Order*. Basingstoke: Macmillan.

Hall, S. and Jefferson, T. (eds) (1976) *Resistance through Rituals: Youth Subcultures in Post-war Britain*. London: Hutchinson.

Hallam, S. (2007) 'Evaluation of behavioural management in schools: a review of the Behaviour Improvement Programme and the role of behaviour and education support teams', *Child and Adolescent Mental Health*, 12: 106–12.

Halsey, K., Gulliver, C., Johnson, A., Martin, K. and Kinder, K. (2005) *Evaluation of Behaviour and Education Support Teams. Research Report* RR706. London: DfES.

Hammarberg, T. (2007) 'It is wrong to punish the child victims?' (available online at **http://www.coe.int/t/commissioner/Viewpoints/070108en.asp**).

Harper, G. and Chitty, C. (2004) *The Impact of Corrections on Re-offending: A Review of 'What Works'. Home Office Research Study* 291. London: Home Office (available online at **www.homeoffice.gov.uk/rds/pdfs04/hors291.pdf**).

Harris, R. and Timms, N. (1993) *Secure Accommodation in Child Care: Between Hospital or Prison or Thereabouts?* London: Routledge.

Harris, R. and Webb, D. (1987) *Welfare, Power and Juvenile Justice*. London: Tavistock.

Harrison, K. (2006) 'Community punishment or community rehabilitation: which is the highest in the sentencing tariff?', *Howard Journal*, 45: 141–58.

Hart, D. (2006) *Tell Them Not to Forget about Us: A Guide to Practice with Looked After Children in Custody*. London: National Children's Bureau.

Hart, D. and Howell, S. (2003) *Report to the Youth Justice Board on the Use of Physical Intervention within the Juvenile Secure Estate*. London: Youth Justice Board (available online at **www.yjb.gov.uk/engb/practitioners/Custody/BehaviourManagement/RestrictivePhysical Interventions/**).

Haydon, D. and Scraton, P. (2000) '"Condemn a little more, understand a little less": the political context and rights implications of the domestic and European rulings in the Venables–Thompson case', *Journal of Law and Society*, 27: 416–48.

Hayward, K.J. (2004) *City Limits: Crime, Consumer Culture and the Urban Experience*. London: Glasshouse.

Hayward, K.J. and Young, J. (eds) (2004) *Theoretical Criminology*, 8(3) (special edition on cultural criminology).

Hazel, N. (in press) *Cross-national Scoping Review of Policy and Practice in Juvenile Justice*. London: Youth Justice Board.

Hazel, N., Hagell, A., Liddle, M., Archer, D., Grimshaw, R. and King, D. (2002) *Detention and Training: Assessment of the Detention and Training Order and its Impact on the Secure Estate across England and Wales*. London: Youth Justice Board.

Healthcare Commission (2006) *Let's Talk About It: A Review of Healthcare in the Community for Young People who Offend*. London: Healthcare Commission.

Hearnden, I. and Millie, A. (2004) 'Does tougher enforcement lead to lower conviction?', *Probation Journal*, 51: 48–59.

Hebdige, D. (1979) *Subculture: The Meaning of Style*. London: Methuen.

Hedderman, C. and Hough, M. (2004) 'Getting tough or being effective: what matters?', in G. Mair (ed.) *What Matters in Probation*. Cullompton: Willan Publishing.

Heidensohn, F. and Gelsthorpe, L. (2007) 'Gender and crime', in M. Maguire *et al.* (eds) *The Oxford Handbook of Criminology*. Oxford: Oxford University Press.

Hendrick, H. (1990) *Images of Youth: Age, Class and the Male Youth Problem, 1880–1920*. Oxford: Clarendon Press.

Her Majesty's Chief Inspector of Prisons (2006) *Annual Report of HM Chief Inspector of Prisons for England and Wales, 2004–2005*. London: HMSO.

Her Majesty's Inspectorate of Prisons (2006a) *Report on an Unannounced Short Follow up Inspection of HMP/YOI Eastwood Park 7–9 March 2006 by HM Chief Inspector of Prisons*. London: Her Majesty's Inspectorate of Prisons.

Her Majesty's Inspectorate of Prisons (2006b) *Report on an Unannounced Short Follow up Inspection of HMP and YOI New Hall 20–23 March 2006 by HM Chief Inspector of Prisons*. London: Her Majesty's Inspectorate of Prisons.

Hibbert, P. (2005) 'The proposed extension of "naming and shaming" to the criminal youth court for breaches of ASBO's', *The Barrister*, 24 (available online at **http://www.barrister magazine.com/articles/issue24/pamhibbert.htm**).

Hill, M., Lockyer, A. and Stone, F. (eds) (2007a) *Youth Justice and Child Protection*. London: Jessica Kingsley.

Hill, M., Walker, M., Moodie, K., Wallace, B., Bannister, J., Khan, F., McIvor, G. and Kendrick, A. (2007b) 'More haste, less speed? An evaluation of fast track policies to tackle persistent youth offending in Scotland', *Youth Justice*, 7: 121–37.

Hillyard, P., Sim, J., Tombs, S. and Whyte, D. (2004) 'Leaving a "stain upon the silence": contemporary criminology and the politics of dissent', *British Journal of Criminology*, 44: 369–90.

Hillyard, P. and Tombs, S. (2004) 'Beyond criminology', in P. Hillyard *et al.* (eds) *Beyond Criminology: Taking Harm Seriously*. London: Pluto Press.

Hillyard, P. and Tombs, S. (2005) 'Beyond criminology', in P. Hillyard *et al.* (eds) *Criminal Obsessions: Why Harm Matters more than Crime*. London: Crime and Society Foundation.

Hine, J. and Celnick, A. (2001) *A One-year Conviction Study of Final Warnings*. London: Home Office.

HM Government (1998) *The Government's Response to the Children's Safeguards Review*. London: HMSO (available online at **http://www.archive.officialdocuments.co.uk/document/cm41/ 4105/4105.htm**).

HM Government (2005) *Statutory Guidance on Inter-agency Co-operation to Improve the Wellbeing of Children: Children's Trusts*. London: DfES.

HM Government (2006) *Working Together to Safeguard Children: A Guide to Interagency Working to Safeguard and Promote the Welfare of Children*. London: HMSO.

HM Government (2007) *Community Justice* (available online at **www.communityjustice.gov.uk**).

HM Prison Service (2005) *Change to Procedures set out in IG 54/1994* (Prison Service Instruction 22/05). London: HM Prison Service.

HM Treasury (2001) *Children at Risk: Cross-cutting Review*. London: HM Treasury.

Hodgkin, R. and Newell, P. (2002) *Implementation Handbook for the Convention on the Rights of the Child*. Geneva: Unicef.

Holdaway, S. (2003) 'The final warning: appearance and reality', *Criminal Justice*, 3: 351–67.

Hollin, C.R. and Palmer, E.J. (eds) (2006) *Offending Behaviour Programmes: Development, Application and Controversies*. Chichester: Wiley.

Holt, J. (1985) *No Holiday Camps: Custody, Juvenile Justice and the Politics of Law and Order.* Leicester: Association for Juvenile Justice.

Holt, P. (2000) *Case Management: Context for Supervision. Community and Criminal Justice Monograph 2.* Leicester: De Montfort University.

Home Affairs Committee (1993) *Juvenile Offenders (Sixth Report)* (HAC 441-I). London: HMSO.

Home Affairs Committee Inquiry (2007) *Young Black People and the Criminal Justice System.* London: House of Commons Home Affairs Select Committee.

Home Office (1960) *Report of the Home Office Departmental Committee on Children and Young Persons* (Cmnd 1191). London: HMSO.

Home Office (1968) *Children in Trouble* (Cmnd 3601). London: Home Office.

Home Office (1985) *The Cautioning of Offenders* (Circular 14/85). London: Home Office.

Home Office (1988) *Punishment, Custody and Community* (Cm 424). London: Home Office.

Home Office (1990) *Crime, Justice and Protecting the Public* (Cm 965). London: Home Office.

Home Office (1991) *Safer Communities: The Local Delivery of Crime Prevention through the Partnership Approach* (the Morgan Report). London: Home Office.

Home Office (1994) *The Criminal Histories of those Cautioned in 1984, 1988 and 1991. Home Office Statistical Bulletin* 8/94. London: Home Office.

Home Office (1997a) *No More Excuses: A New Approach to Tackling Youth Crime in England and Wales (Cn 3809).* London: HMSO (available online at **http://www.homeoffice.gov.uk/documents/jou-no-more-excuses?view=html**).

Home Office (1997b) *Tackling Delays in the Youth Justice System: A Consultation Paper.* London: Home Office.

Home Office (1998) *Supporting Families.* London: Home Office.

Home Office (2000) *The Crime and Disorder Act Guidance Document: Child Safety Order.* London: Home Office (available online at **http://www.homeoffice.gov.uk/documents/guidance-child-curfew?view=Binary**).

Home Office (2001a) *Criminal Justice: The Way Ahead.* London: Home Office.

Home Office (2001b) *Making Punishments Work: Report of a Review of the Sentencing Framework for England and Wales.* London: Home Office (available online at **http://www.homeoffice.gov.uk/documents/halliday-report-sppu/**).

Home Office (2001c) *Local Child Curfews Guidance Document: Working Draft.* London: Home Office (available online at **http://www.homeoffice.gov.uk/documents/guidance-child-curfew?view=Binary**).

Home Office (2002a) *Criminal Justice and Police Act 2001: Penalty Notices for Disorder – Police Operational Guidance.* London: Home Office.

Home Office (2002b) *Justice for All.* London: HMSO.

Home Office (2002c) *The Introduction of Referral Orders into the Youth Justice System: Final Report. Home Office Research Study* 242. London: Home Office.

Home Office (2003a) *'Cul-de-sacs and Gateways': Understanding the Positive Futures Approach.* London: Home Office.

Home Office (2003b) *Bind Overs: A Power for the 21st Century.* London: Home Office.

Home Office (2003c) *Reducing Crime – Changing Lives: The Government's Plans for Transforming the Management of Offenders.* London: HMSO.

Home Office (2003d) *Respect and Responsibility: Taking a Stand against Anti-social Behaviour.* London: Home Office (available online at **http://www.archive2.official-documents.co.uk/document/cm57/5778/5778.pdf**).

Home Office (2004a) *Best Practice Guidance for Restorative Practitioners.* London: Home Office (available online at **http://www.homeoffice.gov.uk/documents/rj_bestpractice.pdf?version=1**).

Home Office (2004b) *MAPPA Guidance*. London: Home Office.

Home Office (2004c) *Piloting Exclusion Orders and Satellite Tracking Technology under Provision of the Criminal Justice and Court Services Act 2000* (Circular 61/04). London: Home Office.

Home Office (2004d) *Prolific and Other Priority Offender Strategy: Prevent and Deter*. London: Home Office.

Home Office (2004e) *The National Reducing Re-offending Delivery Plan*. London: HMSO.

Home Office (2005a) *The Use of Penalty Notices for Disorder for Offences Committed by Young People Aged 16 and 17: Supplementary Operational Guidance for Police Officers*. London: Home Office.

Home Office (2005b) *Criminal Justice and Police Act 2001 (ss. 1–11) – Penalty Notices for Disorder for Offences Committed by Young People Aged 10 to 15: Police Operational Guidance*. London: Home Office.

Home Office (2005c) *Criminal Justice Act 2003: Implementation on 4 April* (PC 25/2005). London: Home Office.

Home Office (2005d) *Guidance on Offences against Children. Home Office Circular* 16/05. London: Home Office.

Home Office (2005e) *Police and Criminal Evidence Act 1984 (s. 60(1)(a), s. 60A(1) and s. 66(1)) Codes of Practice A-G 2005 Edition*. London: HMSO (available online at **http://police.homeoffice.gov.uk/operational-policing/powers-pace-codes/pace-code-intro/**).

Home Office (2005f) *Police and Criminal Evidence Act 1984 (s. 60(1)(a), s. 60A(1) and s. 66(1)): Codes of Practice A–G*. London: HMSO (available online at **http://police.homeoffice.gov. uk/operational-policing/powers-pace-codes/pace-code-intro/**).

Home Office (2005g) *Reducing Re-offending Delivery Plan*. London: Home Office Communication Directorate.

Home Office (2005h) *Use of Dispersal Powers*. London: Home Office.

Home Office (2006a) *MAPPA – the First Five Years: A National Overview of the Multi-agency Public Protection Arrangements, 2001–2006*. London: Home Office.

Home Office (2006b) *Police and Criminal Evidence Act 1984 (s. 66(1)) Codes of Practice C and H July 2006*. London: HMSO (available online at **http://police.homeoffice.gov.uk/operational-policing/powers-pace-codes/pace-code-intro/**).

Home Office (2006c) *Police and Criminal Evidence Act 1984 (s. 66(1)): Codes of Practice C and H*. London: HMSO (available online at **http://police.homeoffice.gov.uk/operational-policing/powers-pace-codes/pace-code-intro/**).

Home Office (2006d) *Positive Futures Impact Report: End of Season Review*. London: Home Office.

Home Office (2006e) *Respect and Dispersal Powers*. London: Home Office.

Home Office (2006f) *Respect Task Force and Action Plan 2006*. London: Home Office (available online at **http://www.homeoffice.gov.uk/documents/respect-action-plan**).

Home Office (2006g) *The Final Warning Scheme* (Circular 14/06). London: Home Office.

Home Office (2006h) *The NOMS Offender Management Model*. London: HMSO.

Home Office (2007) *Tools and Powers to Tackle Anti-social Behaviour*. London: Home Office.

Home Office, Department for Constitutional Affairs and the Attorney General's Office (2006) *Delivering Simple, Speedy, Summary Justice*. London: Department for Constitutional Affairs.

Home Office, Department for Constitutional Affairs and the Youth Justice Board (2004) *Circular: Parenting Orders and Contracts for Criminal Conduct or Anti-social Behaviour*. London: Home Office, Department for Constitutional Affairs and Youth Justice Board.

Home Office, Department of Health, Welsh Office and Department for Education and Employment (1998a) *The Crime and Disorder Act: Inter-departmental Circular on Establishing Youth Offending Teams*. London: Home Office.

Home Office, Lord Chancellor's Department, Attorney General's Office, Department of Health, Department for Education and Employment and Welsh Office (1998b) *Youth Justice: The Statutory Principal Aim of Preventing Offending by Children and Young People.* London: Home Office.

Home Office, Lord Chancellor's Department and Youth Justice Board (2002) *Referral Orders and Youth Offender Panels: Guidance for Courts, Youth Offending Teams and Youth Offender Panels.* London: Home Office (available online at **http://www.yjb.gov.uk/NR/rdonlyres/ 7A25AD98-8515-427F-8976-A6625789B54C/0/referral_orders_and_YOPs.pdf**).

Home Office, Youth Justice Board and Department for Educations and Skills (2004) *Prolific and Other Priority Offenders Strategy. Guidance Note 3: Prevent and Deter.* London: Home Office.

Homel, R. (2005) 'Developmental crime prevention', in N. Tilley (ed.) *Handbook of Crime Prevention and Community Safety.* Cullompton: Willan Publishing.

Hood, R. (1965) *Borstal Re-assessed.* London: Heinemann.

Hood, R. (1989) *The Death Penalty: A World-wide Perspective.* Oxford: Oxford University Press.

Hood, R. (2002) *The Death Penalty: A World-wide Perspective.* Oxford: Clarendon Press.

Hough, M., Allen, R. and Padel, U. (eds) (2006) *Reshaping Probation and Prisons: The New Offender Management Framework.* Bristol: Policy Press.

Hough, M., Clancy, A., McSweeney, T. and Turnbull, P.J. (2003) *The Impact of Drug Treatment and Testing Orders on Offending: Two-year Reconviction Results. Home Office Research Findings 184.* London: Home Office.

Hough, M. and Maxfield, M. (2007) *Surveying Crime in the 21st Century.* Cullompton: Willan Publishing.

Hough, M. and Mayhew, P. (1983) *The British Crime Survey. Home Office Research Study 76.* London: HMSO.

Hough, M. and Roberts, J. (2004) *Youth Crime and Youth Justice: Public Opinion in England and Wales.* Bristol: Policy Press.

House of Commons (1998) *The Crime and Disorder Bill [HL] [Bill 167 of 1997–1998]: Youth Justice, Criminal Procedures and Sentencing.* London: House of Commons.

House of Commons Science and Technology Select Committee (2006) *Drug Classification: Making a Hash of it? Fifth Report of Session 2005–6* (HC 1031) (available online at **www. publications.parliament.uk/pa/cm200506/cmselect/cmsctech/1031/1031.pdf**).

House of Lords/House of Commons Joint Committee on Human Rights (2003) *The UN Convention on the Rights of the Child.* London: HMSO.

Howard League for Penal Reform (1994) *Child Jails: The Case against Secure Training Orders.* London: Howard League for Penal Reform.

Howard League for Penal Reform (2006a) *Chaos, Neglect and Abuse: The Duties of Local Authorities to Provide Children with Suitable Accommodation and Support Services.* London: Howard League for Penal Reform.

Howard League for Penal Reform (2006b) *Women and Girls in the Penal System.* London: Howard League for Penal Reform.

Howarth, G., Kenway, P., Palmer, G. and Miorelli, R. (1998) *Monitoring Poverty and Social Exclusion.* York: Joseph Rowntree Foundation/New Policy Institute (and subsequent annual updates).

Hoyle, C., Young, R. and Hill, R. (2002) *Proceed with Caution: An Evaluation of the Thames Valley Police Initiative in Restorative Cautioning.* York: Joseph Rowntree Foundation.

Hucklesby, A. (2002) 'Bail in criminal cases', in M. McConville and G. Wilson (eds) *The Handbook of the Criminal Justice Process.* Oxford: Oxford University Press.

Hudson, B. (1987) *Justice through Punishment: A Critique of the 'Justice' Model of Corrections.* London: Macmillan.

Hudson, B. (1996) *Understanding Justice.* Buckingham: Open University Press.

Hudson, B. (2003) *Justice in the Risk Society.* London: Sage.

Hughes, G. (1998) *Understanding Crime Prevention: Social Control, Risk and Late Modernity.* Buckingham: Open University Press.

Hughes, G. (2007) *The Politics of Crime and Community.* Basingstoke: Palgrave.

Hughes, G. and Edwards, A. (2005) 'Crime prevention in context', in N. Tilley (ed.) *Handbook of Crime Prevention and Community Safety.* Cullompton: Willan Publishing.

Hughes, G. and Follett, M. (2006) 'Community Safety, Youth and the "Anti-Social"', in B. Goldson and J. Muncie (eds.) *Youth Crime and Justice: Critical issues.* London: Sage.

Hunt, N. and Stevens, A. (2004) 'Whose harm? Harm reduction and the shift to coercion in UK drug policy', *Social Policy and Society*, 3: 333–42.

Instance, D., Rees, G. and Williamson, H. (1994) *Young People Not in Education, Training or Employment in South Glamorgan.* Cardiff: South Glamorgan Training and Enterprise Council.

Jackson, S. (1999) 'Family group conferences and youth justice: the new panacea?', in B. Goldson (ed.) *Youth Justice: Contemporary Policy and Practice.* Aldershot: Ashgate.

Jamieson, J. (2006) 'New Labour, youth justice and the question of "respect"', *Youth Justice*, 5: 180–93.

Jeffs, T. and Smith, M. (1996) 'Getting the dirtbags off the streets: curfews and other solutions to juvenile crime', *Youth and Policy*, 53: 1–14.

Jewkes, Y. and Letherby, G. (2002) *Criminology: A Reader.* London: Sage.

Johnston, L. and Shearing, C. (2003) *The Governance of Security.* London: Sage.

Johnstone, G. and Van Ness, D. (2006) *Handbook of Restorative Justice.* Cullompton: Willan Publishing.

Jones, D. (2001) 'Misjudged youth: a critique of the Audit Commission's reports on youth justice', *British Journal of Criminology*, 41: 362–80.

Jones, R. (2006) *Mental Health Act Manual* (10th edn). London: Sweet & Maxwell.

Judicial Studies Board (2006) *Youth Court Bench Book* (2nd edn). London: Judicial Studies Board (available online at **http://www.jsboard.co.uk/magistrates/ycbb/index.htm**).

Junger-Tas, J. and Decker, S.H. (eds) (2006) *International Handbook of Juvenile Justice.* Dordrecht: Springer.

Kahan, B. (1994) *Growing Up in Groups.* London: HMSO.

Karp, D.R. and Clear, T.R. (eds) (2002) *What is Community Justice? Case Studies of Restorative Justice and Community Supervision.* London: Sage.

Keightley-Smith, L. and Francis, P. (2007) 'Final warning, youth justice and early intervention: reflections on the findings of a research study carried out in northern England', *Web Journal of Current Legal Issues* (available online at **http://webjcli.ncl.ac.uk/2007/contents2.html**).

Kemp, V., Sorsby, A., Liddle, M. and Merrington, S. (2002) *Assessing Responses to Youth Offending in Northamptonshire.* Research Briefing 2. London: Nacro.

Kemshall, H. (2003) *Understanding Risk in Criminal Justice.* Buckingham: Open University Press.

Kemshall, H. (forthcoming) 'Risks, rights and justice: understanding and responding to youth risk', *Youth Justice.*

Kemshall, H., Mackenzie, G., Wood, J., Bailey, R. and Yates, J. (2005) *Strengthening the Multi-agency Public Protection Arrangements.* Practice and Development Report 45. London: Home Office.

Kemshall, H., Marsland, L., Boeck, T. and Dunkerton, L. (2006) 'Young people, pathways and crime: beyond risk factors', *Australian and New Zealand Journal of Criminology*, 39: 339–53.

Kilbrandon Committee (1964) *Report on Children and Young Persons, Scotland*. Edinburgh: HMSO.

Kilkelly, U. (1999) *The Child and the European Convention on Human Rights*. Aldershot: Ashgate.

Kilkelly, U., Kilpatrick, R., Lundy, L., Moore, L., Scraton, P., Davey, C., Dwyer, C. and McAlister, S. (2004) *Children's Rights in Northern Ireland*. Belfast: Northern Ireland Commissioner for Children and Young People.

Kilkelly, U., Moore, L. and Convery, U. (2002) *In Our Care: Promoting the Rights of Children in Custody*. Belfast: Northern Ireland Human Rights Commission.

Kirby, M. and Fraser, M. (1998) *Risk and Resilience in Childhood: An Ecological Perspective*. Washington, DC: NASW Press.

Korczak, J. (1992) *The Child's Right to Respect*. University Press of America.

Lacey, M. (1988) *State Punishment: Political Principles and Community Values*. London: Routledge & Kegan Paul.

Lader, D., Singleton, N. and Meltzer, H. (2000) *Psychiatric Morbidity among Young Offenders in England and Wales*. London: Office for National Statistics.

Land, H. (1975) 'Detention centres: the experiment which could not fail', in P. Hall (ed.) *Change, Choice and Conflict in Social Policy*. London: Heinemann.

Laycock, G. and Tarling, R. (1985) 'Police force cautioning: policy and practice', *Howard Journal*, 24: 81–92.

Lea, J. and Young, J. (1984) *What is to be Done about Law and Order – Crisis in the Eighties*. Harmondsworth: Penguin Books.

Lea, J. and Young, J. (1993) *What's to be Done about Law and Order?* (2nd edn). London: Pluto Press.

Lee, M. (1998) *Youth, Crime and Police Work*. Basingstoke: Macmillan.

Lemert, E. (1967) *Human Deviance, Social Problems and Social Control*. Englewood Cliffs, NJ: Prentice Hall.

Lemert, E. (1970) *Social Action and Legal Change: Revolution within the Juvenile Court*. Chicago, IL: Aldine Press.

Lemert, E. (1972) *Human Deviance, Social Problems and Social Control*. Englewood Cliffs, NJ: Prentice Hall.

Liberty (2006) 'Senior government advisors question policies on ASBOs and "naming and shaming"' (press release). London: Liberty.

Liebmann, M. (ed.) (2000) *Mediation in Context*. London: Jessica Kingsley.

Liebmann, M. (2007) *Restorative Justice: How It Works*. London: Jessica Kingsley.

Lipscombe, J. (2006) *Care or Control? Foster Care for Children and Young People on Remand*. London: British Association for Adoption and Fostering.

Lipsey, M.W. and Wilson, D.B. (1999) 'Effective interventions with serious juvenile offenders', in R.E. Loeber and E.P. Farrington (eds) *Serious and Violent Juvenile Offenders*. London: Sage.

Lister, R. (2005) 'Investing in the citizen-workers of the future', in H. Hendrick (ed.) *Child Welfare and Social Policy*. Bristol: Policy Press.

Little, M. and Mount, K. (1999) *Prevention and Early Intervention with Children in Need*. Aldershot: Ashgate.

Lloyd, C. (1992) *Bail Information Schemes: Practice and Effect*. Research and Planning Unit Paper 69. London: Home Office.

Loader, I. (1996) *Youth, Policing and Democracy*. London: Macmillan.

Lobley, D. and Smith, D. (2007) *Persistent Young Offenders: An Evaluation of Two Projects*. Aldershot: Ashgate.

Lobley, D., Smith, D. and Stern, C. (2001) *Freagarrach: An Evaluation of a Project for Persistent Juvenile Offenders*. Edinburgh: Scottish Executive (available online at **www.scotland.gov.uk/Resource/Doc/156634/0042083.pdf**).

Local Government Association (1999) *Case Studies of the Local Government Role in Promoting Social Justice and Social Inclusion*. London: Local Government Association.

Lockyer, A. and Stone, F. (1998) *Juvenile Justice in Scotland: Twenty-five Years of the Welfare Approach*. Edinburgh: T. & T. Clark.

Lord, P., Wilkin, A., Kinder, K., Murfield, J., Jones, M., Chamberlain, T., Easton, C., Martin, K., Gulliver, C., Paterson, C., Ries, J., Moor, H., Stott, A., Wilkin, C. and Stoney, S. (2006) *Analysis of Children and Young People's Plans, 2006*. Slough: National Foundation for Educational Research (available online at **http://www.nfer.ac.uk/research-areas/ pims-data/summaries/analysis-of-cypp-2006.cfm**).

Lyon, C. (2000) *Loving Smack or Lawful Assault: A Contradiction in Human Rights and Law*. London: Institute for Public Policy Research.

Lyon, D. (2006) *Theorising Surveillance: The Panopticon and Beyond*. Cullompton: Willan Publishing.

Macpherson, Sir W. (1999) *The Stephen Lawrence Inquiry: Report of an Inquiry by Sir William Macpherson of Cluny* (Cm 4262-1). London: HMSO.

Magarey, S. (1978) 'The invention of juvenile delinquency in early nineteenth century England', *Labour History*, 34: 11–25.

Magistrates' Association (2004) *Magistrates' Court Sentencing Guidelines*. London: Magistrates' Association (available online at **http://www.jsboard.co.uk/downloads/acbb/ section2a.pdf**).

Mair, G. (1997a) 'Community penalties and the Probation Service', in M. Maguire *et al.* (eds) *The Oxford Handbook of Criminology*. Oxford: Oxford University Press.

Mair, G. (ed.) (1997b) *Evaluating the Effectiveness of Community Penalties*. Aldershot: Avebury.

Mares, D. (2000) 'Globalization and gangs: the Manchester case', *Focaal*, 35: 151–69.

Martinson, R. (1974) 'What works? Questions and answers about prison reform', *The Public Interest*, 35: 22–54.

Maruna, S. (2001) *Making Good: How Ex-convicts Reform and Rebuild their Lives*. Washington, DC: American Psychological Association.

Maruna, S. and Farrall, S. (2004) 'Desistance-focused criminal justice policy research' (introduction to a special issue on 'Desistance from crime and public policy'), *Howard Journal of Criminal Justice*, 43: 358–67.

Mathewson, T., Willis, M. and Boyle, M. (1998) *Cautioning in Northern Ireland: A Profile of Adult and Juvenile Cautioning and an Examination of Reoffending Rates*. *Northern Ireland Office Research Findings* 4/1998. Belfast: Northern Ireland Office.

Mathiesen, T. (1974) *The Politics of Abolition*. Oxford: Martin Robertson.

Mathiesen, T. (2000) *Prison on Trial*. Winchester: Waterside Press.

Matthews, R. (2005) 'The myth of the new punitiveness', *Theoretical Criminology*, 9: 175–201.

Matthews, R. and Young, J. (eds) (1986) *Confronting Crime*. London: Sage.

Matthews, R. and Young, J. (1992) *Rethinking Criminology: The Realist Debate*. London: Sage.

Matthews, R. and Young, J. (eds) (2003) *The New Politics of Crime*. Cullompton: Willan Publishing.

Matza, D. (1964) *Delinquency and Drift*. London: Wiley.

Matza, D. (1969) *Becoming Deviant*. Englewood Cliffs, NJ: Prentice Hall.

Maxwell, G. and Morris, A. (2002) 'The role of shame, guilt, and remorse in restorative processes for young people', in E.G.M. Weitekamp and H.-J. Kerner (eds) *Restorative Justice: Theoretical Foundations*. Cullompton: Willan Publishing.

May, M. (1973) 'Innocence and experience: the evolution of the concept of juvenile delinquency in the mid-nineteenth century', *Victorian Studies*, 17: 7–29.

Mayer, M., Haverkamp, R. and Levy, R. (eds) (2003) *Will Electronic Monitoring Have a Future in Europe?* Freiburg: Max Planck Institute.

McAra, L. (2005) 'Modelling penal transformation', *Punishment and Society*, 7: 277–302.

McAra, L. (2006) 'Welfare in crisis? Key developments in Scottish youth justice', in J. Muncie and B. Goldson (eds) *Comparative Youth Justice: Critical Issues*. London: Sage.

McAra, L. and McVie, S. (2007) 'Youth justice? The impact of system contact on patterns of desistance from offending', *European Journal of Criminology*, 4: 315–45.

McCarthy, P., Laing, K. and Walker, J. (2004) *Offenders of the Future? Assessing the Risk of Children and Young People Becoming Involved in Criminal and Antisocial Behaviour*. London: Department for Education and Skills.

McGillivray, A. (ed.) (1997) *Governing Childhood*. Aldershot: Dartmouth.

McGuire, J. (ed.) (1995) *What Works: Reducing Reoffending*. Chichester: Wiley.

McGuire, J. and Priestley, P. (1995) 'Reviewing "what works": past, present and future', in J. McGuire and P. Priestley (eds) *What Works: Reducing Offending Guidelines from Research and Practice*. Chichester: Wiley.

McIvor, G. (1990) *Sanctions for Serious or Persistent Offenders: A Review of the Literature*. Stirling: Social Work Research Centre, University of Stirling.

McKeaveney, P. (2005) *Review of 10–13 Year Olds Entering Custody*. Belfast: Youth Justice Agency.

McLaughlin, E., Muncie, J. and Hughes, G. (2001) 'The permanent revolution: New Labour, new public management and the modernization of criminal justice', *Criminal Justice*, 1: 301–18.

McNeill, F. (2003) 'Desistance-focused probation practice', in W.-H. Chui and M. Nellis (eds) *Moving Probation Forward: Evidence, Arguments and Practice*. Harlow: Pearson Longman.

McNeill, F. (2005) *Offender Management in Scotland: The First Hundred Years*. CJScotland (available online at **http://www.cjscotland.org.uk/pdfs/Offender%20management.pdf**).

McNeill, F. (2006) 'Community supervision: contexts and relationships matter', in B. Goldson and J. Muncie (eds) *Youth Crime and Justice: Critical Issues*. London: Sage.

Melrose, M. (2004) 'Fractured transitions: disadvantaged young people, drug taking and risk', *Probation Journal* (special issue on 'Rethinking drugs and crime'), 51: 327–42.

Melrose, M., Barrett, D. and Brodie, I. (1999) *One Way Street? Retrospectives on Childhood Prostitution*. London: Children's Society.

Merton, R.K. (1968) *Social Theory and Social Structure*. New York, NY: Free Press.

Mhlanga, B. (1997) *The Colour of English Justice: A Multivariate Analysis*. Aldershot: Avebury.

Miers, D. (1989) 'Positivist victimology: a critique', *International Review of Victimology*, 1: 3–22.

Miers, D. (1990) 'Positivist victimology: a critique. Part 2', *International Review of Victimology*, 1: 219–30.

Miller, J. (1991) *Last One Over the Wall: The Massachusetts Experiment in Closing Reform Schools*. Columbus, OH: Ohio State University Press.

Miller, J. (1998) *Last One Over the Wall: The Massachusetts Experiment in Closing Reform Schools* (2nd edn). Columbus, OH: Ohio State University Press.

Millie, A., Jacobson, J., McDonald, E. and Hough, M. (2005) *Anti-social Behaviour Strategies: Finding a Balance* (ICPR and Joseph Rowntree Foundation). Bristol: Policy Press.

Ministry of Justice (2007) 'Criminal Justice and Immigration Bill' (news release) (available online at **http://www.justice.gov.uk/news/newsrelease260607c.htm**).

Mizen, P. (2004) *The Changing State of Youth*. Basingstoke: Palgrave Macmillan.

Mizen, P. (2006) 'Work and social order: the "new deal" for the young unemployed', in B. Goldson and J. Muncie (eds) *Youth Crime and Justice: Critical Issues*. London: Sage.

Monaghan, G. (2000) 'The courts and the new youth justice', in B. Goldson (ed.) *The New Youth Justice*. Lyme Regis: Russell House.

Monaghan, G. (2005) 'Children's human rights and youth justice', in T. Bateman and J. Pitts (eds) *The RHP Companion to Youth Justice*. Lyme Regis: Russell House.

Moore, R. (2005) 'The use of electronic and human surveillance in a multi-modal programme', *Youth Justice*, 5: 17–32.

Moore, R., Gray, E., Roberts, C., Merrington, S., Waters, I., Fernandez, R., Hayward, G. and Rogers, R.D. (2004) *National Evaluation of the Intensive Supervision and Surveillance Programme: Interim Report to the Youth Justice Board*. London: Youth Justice Board for England and Wales.

Moore, R., Gray, E., Roberts, C., Taylor, E. and Merrington, S. (2006) *Managing Persistent and Serious Offenders in the Community: Intensive Community Programmes in Theory and Practice*. Cullompton: Willan Publishing.

Moore, S. and Smith, R. (2001) *The Pre-trial Guide: Working with Young People from Arrest to Trial*. London: Children's Society.

Morgan Harris Burrows (2003) *Evaluation of the Youth Inclusion Programme*. London: Youth Justice Board.

Morgan, R. (2004) *Children's Views on Restraint*. Newcastle: Office of the Children's Rights Director (available online at **www.ofsted.gov.uk/assets/Internet_Content/Shared_Content/Migration/crd/Restraint_crd.pdf**).

Morris, A. and Gelsthorpe, L. (2000) 'Something old, something borrowed, something blue, but something new? A comment on the prospects for restorative justice under the Crime and Disorder Act 1998', *Criminal Law Review*, 18–30.

Morris, A. and Giller, H. (1987) *Understanding Juvenile Justice*. London: Croom Helm.

Morris, A. and Maxwell, G. (1998) 'Restorative justice in New Zealand: family group conferences as a case study', *Western Criminology Review*, 1 (available online at **http://wcr.sonoma.edu/v1n1/morris.html**).

Morris, A. and McIsaac, M. (1978) *Juvenile Justice? The Practice of Social Welfare*. London: Heinemann.

Morrison, B. (1997) *As If*. London: Granta.

Muncie, J. (1990) 'Failure never matters: detention centres and the politics of deterrence', *Critical Social Policy*, 28: 53–66.

Muncie, J. (1996) 'The construction and reconstruction of crime', in J. Muncie and E. McLaughlin (eds) *The Problem of Crime*. London: Sage.

Muncie, J. (1999) 'Institutionalized intolerance: youth justice and the 1998 Crime and Disorder Act', *Critical Social Policy*, 19: 147–75.

Muncie, J. (2000) 'Pragmatic realism? Searching for criminology in the new youth justice', in B. Goldson (ed.) *The New Youth Justice*. Lyme Regis: Russell House.

Muncie, J. (2002) 'A new deal for youth? Early intervention and correctionalism', in G. Hughes *et al.* (eds) *Crime Prevention and Community Safety: New Directions*. London: Sage.

Muncie, J. (2004) *Youth and Crime* (2nd edn). London: Sage.

Muncie, J. (2005) 'The globalisation of crime control: the case of youth and juvenile justice', *Theoretical Criminology*, 9: 35–64.

Muncie, J. (2006) 'Governing young people: coherence and contradiction in contemporary youth justice', *Critical Social Policy*, 26: 770–93.

Muncie, J. and Goldson, B. (eds) (2006) *Comparative Youth Justice: Critical Issues*. London: Sage.

Muncie, J. and Hughes, G. (2002) 'Modes of youth governance: political rationalities, criminalisation and resistance', in J. Muncie *et al.* (eds) *Youth Justice: Critical Readings*. London: Sage.

Muncie, J., Hughes, G. and McLaughlin, E. (2002) *Youth Justice: Critical Readings*. London: Sage.

Munro, E. (2002) *Effective Child Protection*. London: Sage.

Murray, C. (1990) *The Emerging Underclass*. London: Institute of Economic Affairs.

Murray, C. (1994) *Underclass: The Crisis Deepens*. London: Institute of Economic Affairs.

Murray, J. and Farrington, D. (2005) 'Parental imprisonment: effect on boys' anti-social behaviour and delinquency through the life course', *Journal of Child Psychology and Psychiatry*, 46: 1269–78.

Nacro (2000a) *Proportionality in the Youth Justice System. Youth Crime Briefing*. London: Nacro.

Nacro (2000b) *The Detention and Training Order. Youth Crime Briefing*. London: Nacro.

Nacro (2002a) *Children who Commit Grave Crimes*. London: Nacro.

Nacro (2002b) *Looked After Children and Youth Justice: Anomalies in the Law. Youth Crime Briefing*. London: Nacro.

Nacro (2002c) *Supervision Orders – an Overview. Youth Crime Briefing*. London: Nacro.

Nacro (2003a) *A Failure of Justice: Reducing Child Imprisonment*. London: Nacro.

Nacro (2003b) *Children and Young People who Commit Schedule One Offences*. London: Nacro.

Nacro (2003c) *Pre-sentence Reports for Young People: A Good Practice Guide* (2nd edn). London: Nacro.

Nacro (2003d) *The Sentencing Framework for Children and Young People. Youth Crime Briefing*. London: Nacro.

Nacro (2004a) *Anti-social Behaviour Orders and Associated Measures. Part 2. Youth Crime Briefing*. London: Nacro.

Nacro (2004b) *Remands to Local Authority Accommodation. Youth Crime Briefing*. London: Nacro.

Nacro (2004c) *The Grave Crimes Provisions and Long Term Detention. Youth Crime Briefing*. London: Nacro.

Nacro (2004d) *The Referral Order: A Good Practice Guide* (2nd edn). London: Nacro.

Nacro (2005a) *A Better Alternative: Reducing Child Imprisonment*. London: Nacro.

Nacro (2005b) *A Handbook on Reducing Offending by Looked After Children*. London: Nacro.

Nacro (2005c) *Dangerousness in the Youth Justice System. Youth Crime Briefing*. London: Nacro.

Nacro (2005d) *Mental Health Legislation and the Youth Justice System. Youth Crime Briefing*. London: Nacro.

Nacro (2005e) *Out of Court: Making the Most of Diversion for Young People. Youth Crime Briefing*. London: Nacro.

Nacro (2005f) *Pre-sentence Reports and Custody. Youth Crime Briefing*. London: Nacro.

Nacro (2006a) *Appeals against Conviction and Sentence in the Youth Justice System. Youth Crime Briefing*. London: Nacro.

Nacro (2006b) *Reducing Custody: A Systematic Approach. Youth Crime Briefing*. London: Nacro.

Nacro (2006c) *Nacro Guide to the Youth Justice System in England and Wales*. London: Nacro.

Nacro (2006d) *Out of Court – Making the Most of Diversion for Young People (Recent Developments). Youth Crime Briefing*. London: Nacro.

Nacro (2006e) *Remand Fostering: Establishing a Service*. London: Nacro.

Nacro (2006f) *The Children (Leaving Care) Act 2000 – Implications for the Youth Justice System. Youth Crime Briefing*. London: Nacro.

Nacro (2006g) *The Dangerousness Provisions of the Criminal Justice Act 2003 and Subsequent Case-law. Youth Crime Briefing*. London: Nacro.

Nacro (2007a) *Some Facts about Children and Young People who Offend – 2005. Youth Crime Briefing*. London: Nacro.

Nacro (2007b) *Working in the Courts: Essential Skills for Practitioners in the Youth Justice System. Youth Crime Section Good Practice Guide Series.* London: Nacro.

National Audit Office (2001) *Education Action Zones: Meeting the Challenge – the Lessons Identified from Auditing the First 25 Zones. Report by the Comptroller and Auditor General* (HC 130 Session 2000–2001). London: HMSO.

National Audit Office (2004) *Youth Justice 2004: A Review of the Reformed Youth Justice System.* London: National Audit Office.

National Audit Office (2006) *Tackling Anti-social Behaviour: Report by the Comptroller and Auditor General* (HC 99 Session 2006–2007). London: Home Office.

National Children's Bureau (2006) *Interim Findings from the Research Study into the Developing Relationship between Youth Offending Teams and Children's Trusts* (available online at **http://www.everychildmatters.gov.uk/resources-and-practice/search/rs00012/**).

National Institute of Justice (2003) *Correctional Boot Camps: Lessons from a Decade of Research.* Washington, DC: US Department of Justice.

Neather, A. (2004) 'Fears haunting New Labour', *Evening Standard*, 5 April.

Nellis, M. (2004) 'The "tracking" controversy: the roots of mentoring and electronic monitoring', *Youth Justice*, 4: 77–99.

Newburn, T. (2003) *Crime and Criminal Justice Policy.* Harlow: Longman.

Newburn, T. and Reiner, R. (2004) 'From PC Dixon to Dixon PLC: policing and policing powers since 1954', *Criminal Law Review*, 601–18.

Newburn, T. and Shiner, M. (2005) *Dealing with Disaffection: Young People, Mentoring and Social Inclusion.* Cullompton: Willan Publishing.

Newburn, T. and Souhami, A. (2005) 'Youth diversion', in N. Tilley (ed.) *Handbook of Crime Prevention and Community Safety.* Cullompton: Willan Publishing.

Newburn, T. and Sparks, R. (eds) (2004) *Criminal Justice and Political Cultures: National and International Dimensions of Crime Control.* Cullompton: Willan Publishing.

Newman, J. (2001) *Modernising Governance.* London: Sage.

Nichols, G. (2007) *Sport and Crime Reduction: The Role of Sports in Tackling Youth Crime.* London: Routledge.

Nichols, G. and Crow, I. (2004) 'Measuring the impact of crime reduction interventions involving sports activities for young people', *Howard Journal of Criminal Justice*, 43: 267–83.

Norland, S., Sowell, R.E. and Di Chiara, A. (2003) 'Assumptions of coercive treatment: a critical review', *Criminal Justice Policy Review*, 14: 505–21.

Northern Ireland Children and Young Persons Review Group (1979) *Legislation and Services for Children and Young People in Northern Ireland: Report of the Children and Young Persons Review Group* (the Black Report). Belfast: HMSO.

Nutley, S., Walter, I. and Davies, T. (2007) *Using Evidence: How Research can Inform Public Services.* Bristol: Policy Press.

O'Brien, C. and Arkinstall, J. (2002) *Human Rights Act Project Database of Cases under the Human Rights Act 1998.* London: Doughty Street Chambers (available online at **http://www.doughtystreet.co.uk/hrarp/summary/index.cfm**).

Office for Standards in Education (2003) *Excellence in Cities and Education Action Zones: Management and Impact* (HMI 1399). London: Ofsted.

Office for the Commissioner for Human Rights (2005) *Report by Mr Alvaro Gil-Robles, Commissioner for Human Rights, on his Visit to the United Kingdom, 4–12 November 2004.* Strasbourg: Council of Europe.

O'Mahony, D. and Campbell, C. (2006) 'Mainstreaming restorative justice for young offenders through youth conferencing: the experience of Northern Ireland', in J. Junger-Tas and S. Decker (eds) *International Handbook of Juvenile Justice*. New York, NY: Springer.

O'Mahony, D., Chapman, T. and Doak, J. (2002) *Restorative Cautioning: A Study of Police Based Restorative Cautioning in Northern Ireland. Northern Ireland Office, Research and Statistical Series*. Belfast: Northern Ireland Office.

O'Mahony, D. and Doak, J. (2004) 'Restorative justice – is more better? The experience of police-led restorative cautioning pilots in Northern Ireland', *Howard Journal of Criminal Justice*, 43: 484–505.

O'Mahony, D. and Haines, K. (1996) *An Evaluation of the Introduction and Operation of the Youth Court. Home Office Research Study* 152. London: Home Office.

O'Malley, C. and Waiton, S. (2004) *Who's Anti-social? New Labour and the Politics of Antisocial Behaviour*. London: Institute of Ideas (available online at **http://www.instituteofideas.com/publications/index.html#occasional**).

O'Neill, T. (2001) *Children in Secure Accommodation: A Gendered Exploration of Locked Institutional Care for Children in Trouble*. London: Jessica Kingsley.

Orwell, G. (1954) *Nineteen Eighty-four*. London: Penguin Books.

PA Consultancy Group and MORI (2005) *Action Research Study of the Implementation of the National Offender Management Model in the North West Pathfinder*. London: Home Office.

Packman, J. (1975) *The Child's Generation: Child Care Policy from Curtis to Houghton*. Oxford: Blackwell.

Parent, D.G. (1995) 'Boot camps failing to achieve goals', in M. Tonry and K. Hamilton (eds) *Intermediate Sanctions in Over-crowded Times*. Boston, MA: Northeastern University Press.

Parker, H., Williams, L. and Aldridge, J. (2002) 'The normalization of "sensible" recreational drug use: further evidence from the North West England Longitudinal Study', *Sociology*, 36: 941–64.

Parsons, C. (1999) *Education, Exclusion and Citizenship*. London: Routledge.

Parton, N. (2006) *Safeguarding Childhood: Early Intervention and Surveillance in a Late Modern Society*. Basingstoke: Palgrave Macmillan.

Partridge, S. (2004) *Examining Case Management Models for Community Sentences*. London: Home Office.

Patrick, J. (1973) *A Glasgow Gang Observed*. London: Eyre Methuen.

Pawson, R. and Tilley, N. (1997) *Realistic Evaluation*. London: Sage.

Pearce, J. with Williams, M. and Galvin, C. (2002) *It's Someone Taking a Part of You*. London: National Children's Bureau.

Penna, S. (2005) 'The Children Act 2004: child protection and social surveillance', *Journal of Social Welfare and Family Law*, 27: 143–58.

Percy-Smith, B. and Weil, S. (2002) 'New deal or raw deal? Dilemmas and paradoxes of state interventions into youth labour markets', in M. Cieslik and G. Pollock (eds) *Young People in Risk Society*. Aldershot: Ashgate.

Philip, K. (2000) 'Mentoring: pitfalls and potential for young people', *Youth and Policy*, 67: 1–15.

Phoenix, J. (2002) 'Youth prostitution policy reforms: new discourse, same old story', in P. Carlen (ed.) *Women and Punishment: A Struggle for Justice*. Cullompton: Willan Publishing.

Phoenix, J. (2003) 'Rethinking youth prostitution: national provision at the margins of child protection and youth justice', *Youth Justice*, 3: 152–68.

Piacentini, L. and Walters, R. (2006) 'The politicization of youth crime in Scotland and the rise of the "Burberry court"', *Youth Justice*, 6: 43–61.

Pickford, J. (ed.) (2000) *Youth Justice: Theory and Practice*. London: Cavendish Publishing.

Pierpoint, H. (2004) 'A survey of volunteer appropriate adult services in England and Wales', *Youth Justice*, 4: 32–45.

Pierpoint, H. (2006) 'Reconstructing the role of the appropriate adult in England and Wales', *Criminology and Criminal Justice: The International Journal*, 6: 219–38.

Piper, C. (1999) 'The Crime and Disorder Act 1998: child and community "safety"', *Modern Law Review*, 62: 397–408.

Pitts, J. (1988) *The Politics of Juvenile Crime*. London: Sage.

Pitts, J. (1992) 'The end of an era', *Howard Journal of Criminal Justice*, 31: 133–49.

Pitts, J. (2000) 'The new youth justice and the politics of electoral anxiety', in B. Goldson (ed.) *The New Youth Justice*. Lyme Regis: Russell House.

Pitts, J. (2007) 'Violent youth gangs in the UK', *Safer Society: The Journal of Crime Reduction and Community Safety*, 32: 14–17.

Pitts, J. and Bateman, T. (2005) 'Youth crime in England and Wales', in T. Bateman and J. Pitts (eds) *The RHP Companion to Youth Justice*. Lyme Regis: Russell House.

Pitts, J. and Kuula, T. (2006) 'Incarcerating Young People: An Anglo-Finnish Comparison', *Youth Justice*, 5(3): 147-164.

Plotnikoff, J. and Woolfson, R. (2000) *Where Are They Now? An Evaluation of Sex Offender Registration in England and Wales. Police Research Series Paper* 126. London: Home Office.

Plummer, K. (1979) 'Misunderstanding labelling perspectives', in D. Downes and P. Rock (eds) *Deviant Interpretations*. Oxford: Martin Robertson.

Police Foundation (forthcoming) *Policing Children and Young People*. London: Police Foundation (available online at **http://www.police-foundation.org.uk/content/default.asp?PageId=619**).

Powell, H. (2004) *Crime Prevention Projects: The National Evaluation of the Youth Justice Board Crime Prevention Projects*. London: Youth Justice Board.

Pragnell, S. (2005) 'Reprimands and final warnings', in T. Bateman and J. Pitts (eds) *The RHP Companion to Youth Justice*. Lyme Regis: Russell House.

Pratt, J. (1987) 'A revisionist history of intermediate treatment', *British Journal of Social Work*, 17: 417–36.

Pratt, J. (1989) 'Corporatism: the third model of juvenile justice', *British Journal of Criminology*, 29: 236–54.

Pratt, J. (2003) 'Emotive and ostentatious punishment', *Punishment and Society*, 2: 417–39.

Pratt, J., Brown, D., Brown, M., Hallsworth, S. and Morrison, W. (eds) (2005) *The New Punitiveness*. Cullompton: Willan Publishing.

Priestley, P., McGuire, J., Flegg, D., Hemsley, V. and Welham, D. (1978) *Social Skills and Personal Problem-solving: A Handbook of Methods*. London: Tavistock.

Pudney, S. (2002) *The Road to Ruin? Sequences of Initiation into Drug Use and Offending by Young People in Britain. Home Office Research Study* 253. London: Home Office.

Pugh, G. (2005) *HMP/YOI Warren Hill: Visits and Family Ties Survey, 2004/5*. Ipswich: Ormiston Children and Families Trust.

Putnam, R. (2000) *Bowling Alone – the Collapse and Revival of American Community*. New York, NY: Simon & Schuster.

Quill, D. and Wynne, J. (1993) *Victim and Offender Mediation Handbook*. Leeds: Save the Children/West Yorkshire Probation Service.

Radzinowicz, L. and Hood, R. (1990) *The Emergence of Penal Policy*. Oxford: Clarendon Press.

Raynor, P. and Robinson, G. (2005) *Rehabilitation, Crime and Justice*. Basingstoke: Palgrave Macmillan.

Raynor, P. and Vanstone, M. (2002) *Understanding Community Penalties: Probation, Policy and Social Change*. Buckingham: Open University Press.

Respect Taskforce (2006) *Respect Action Plan*. London: Home Office (available online at **http://www.homeoffice.gov.uk/documents/respect-action-plan**).

Rex, S. (1999) 'Desistance from offending: experiences of probation', *Howard Journal of Criminal Justice*, 36: 366–83.

Rhodes, R.A.W. (1997) *Understanding Governance: Policy Networks, Governance, Reflexivity and Accountability*. Buckingham: Open University Press.

Richardson, N. (1991) *Justice by Geography II*. Knutsford: Social Information Systems.

Ridge, T. (2002) *Childhood Poverty and Social Exclusion: From a Child's Perspective*. Bristol: Policy Press.

Roberts, J. and Hough, M. (2005a) *Understanding Public Attitudes to Criminal Justice*. Maidenhead: Open University Press.

Roberts, J. and Hough, M. (2005b) 'Sentencing young offenders: public opinion in England and Wales', *Criminal Justice*, 5: 211–32.

Robinson, G. (2005) 'What works in offender management?', *Howard Journal of Criminal Justice*, 44: 307–17.

Rock, P. (1986) *A View from the Shadows*. Oxford: Oxford University Press.

Rock, P. (2002) 'On becoming a victim', in C. Hoyle and R. Young (eds) *New Visions of Crime Victims*. Oxford: Hart Publishing.

Roe, S. and Man, L. (2006) *Drug Misuse Declared: Findings from the 2005/06 British Crime Survey*. London: Home Office.

Rose, J. (2002) *Working with Young People in Secure Accommodation*. Hove: Brunner-Routledge.

Rose, N. (1989) *Governing the Soul*. London: Routledge.

Rose, N. (1996) 'Governing "advanced" liberal democracies', in A. Barry *et al.* (eds) *Foucault and Political Reason*. London: UCL Press.

Rose, N. (1999) *Powers of Freedom*. Cambridge: Cambridge University Press.

Rose, N. (2000) 'Government and control', *British Journal of Criminology*, 40: 321–39.

Rowlands, M. (2005) *The state of ASBO Britain – the Rise of Intolerance*. European Civil Liberties Network (available online at **http://www.ecln.org/**).

Rubenstein, M. (2006) *Discrimination*. London: Lexis Nexis Butterworths.

Rumgay, J. (2004) *When Victims Become Offenders. Occasional Paper*. London: Fawcett Society.

Russell, B. and Fry, E. (2005) 'In care and in trouble? The contribution family placement can make to effective work with young offenders', in A. Wheal (ed.) *The RHP Companion to Foster Care* (2nd edn). Lyme Regis: Russell House.

Rutherford, A. (1992) *Growing Out of Crime: The New Era*. Winchester: Waterside Press.

Rutherford, A. (1995) 'Signposting the future of juvenile justice policy in England and Wales', in Howard League for Penal Reform (ed.) *Child Offenders UK and International Practice*. London: Howard League for Penal Reform.

Rutherford, A. (2002a) 'Youth justice and social inclusion', *Youth Justice*, 2: 100–7.

Rutherford, A. (2002b) *Growing Out Of Crime – the New Era* (2nd edn). Winchester: Waterside Press.

Safer London Committee (2005) *Street Prostitution in London*. London: Greater London Authority.

Sampson, R.J. and Laub, J.H. (1993) *Crime in the Making: Pathways and Turning Points through Life*. Cambridge, MA: Harvard University Press.

Sampson, R.J. and Laub, J.H. (2005) 'A life-course view of the development of crime', *Annals of the American Academy of Political and Social Science*, 602: 12–45.

Sceats, S. (2007) *The Human Rights Act – Changing Lives*. London: British Institute of Human Rights.

Schoon, I. and Bynner, J. (2003) 'Risk and resilience in the life course: implications for interventions and social policies', *Journal of Youth Studies*, 6: 21–31.

Schur, E.M. (1973) *Radical Non-intervention: Rethinking the Delinquency Problem*. Englewood Cliffs, NJ: Prentice Hall.

Scottish Executive (1999) *Inclusive Communities*. Edinburgh: Scottish Executive.

Scottish Executive (2002a) *A Report by the Improving the Effectiveness of the Youth Justice System Working Group* (available online at **http://www.scotland.gov.uk/Publications/2002/12/16030/15870**).

Scottish Executive (2002b) *Scotland's Action Programme to Reduce Youth Crime* (available online at **http://www.scotland.gov.uk/Publications/2002/01/10601/File-1**).

Scottish Executive (2004) *The Summary Justice Review Committee: Report to Ministers* (the McInnes Report). Edinburgh: Scottish Executive (available online at **http://www.scotland.gov.uk/Publications/2004/03/19042/34176**).

Scottish Executive (2005) *The Mental Health of Children and Young People: A Framework for Promotion, Prevention and Care*. Edinburgh: Scottish Executive (available online at **http://www.headsupscotland.co.uk/documents/Framework_24Oct05.pdf**).

Scottish Executive (2007) *Criminal Proceedings in Scottish Courts, 2005/06. Statistical Bulletin, Criminal Justice Series*. Edinburgh: Scottish Executive (available online at **http://www.scotland.gov.uk/Publications/2007/03/21083652/0**).

Scraton, P. (ed.) (1987) *Law, Order and the Authoritarian State*. Milton Keynes: Open University Press.

Scraton, P. (1997a) 'Whose "childhood"? What "crisis"?', in P. Scraton (ed.) *'Childhood' in 'Crisis'?* London: UCL Press/Routledge.

Scraton, P. (ed.) (1997b) *'Childhood' in 'Crisis'?* London: UCL Press.

Scraton, P. (2007) *Power, Conflict and Criminalisation*. London: Routledge.

Scraton, P. and Chadwick, K. (1987) *In the Arms of the Law: Coroners' Inquests and Deaths in Custody*. London: Pluto.

Scraton, P. and Haydon, D. (2002) 'Challenging the criminalization of children and young people: securing a rights-based agenda', in J. Muncie et al. (eds) *Youth Justice: Critical Readings*. London: Sage/Open University.

Scraton, P. and Moore, L. (2005) *The Hurt Inside: The Imprisonment of Women and Girls in Northern Ireland* (rev. edn). Belfast: Northern Ireland Human Rights Commission.

Seddon, T. (2006) 'Drugs, crime and social exclusion: social context and social theory in British drugs-crime research', *British Journal of Criminology*, 46: 680–703.

Sellick, C. and Howell, D. (2003) *Innovative, Tried and Tested: A Review of Good Practice in Fostering*. London: Social Care Institute for Excellence.

Sentencing Commission for Scotland (2006) *The Scope to Improve Consistency in Sentencing*. Edinburgh: Sentencing Commission for Scotland (available online at **http://www.scottishsentencingcommission.gov.uk/publications.asp**).

Sentencing Guidelines Council (2006) *The Sentence. Newsletter Issue 4*. London: Sentencing Guidelines Council (available online at **http://www.sentencing-guidelines.gov.uk/docs/the_sentence_four.pdf**).

Sheldon, B. and Chilvers, R. (2001) *Evidence-based Social Care: A Study of Prospects and Problems*. Lyme Regis: Russell House.

Sherman, L.W., Gottfredson, D.C., MacKenzie, D.L., Eck, J., Reuter, P. and Bushway, S. (1997) *Preventing Crime: What Works, What Doesn't, What's Promising. Research in Brief.* Washington, DC: National Institute of Justice.

Sherman, L.W. and Strang, H. (2007) *Restorative Justice: The Evidence.* London: Smith Institute (available online at **www.smith-institute.org.uk/publications.htm**).

Sim, J. (2005) 'Abolitionism', in E. McLaughlin and J. Muncie (eds) *The Sage Dictionary of Criminology* (2nd edn). London: Sage.

Simon, J. (1995) 'They died with their boots on: the boot camp and the limits of modern penality', *Social Justice*, 22: 25–48.

Simon, J. (1997) 'Governing through crime', in G. Fisher and L. Friedman (eds) *The Crime Conundrum: Essays on Criminal Justice.* Boulder, CO: Westview Press.

Simon, J. (2001) 'Entitlement to cruelty: neo-liberalism and the punitive mentality in the United States', in K. Stenson and R. Sullivan (eds) *Crime, Risk and Justice.* Cullompton: Willan Publishing.

Sinclair, I. (2005) *Fostering Now – Messages from Research.* London: Jessica Kingsley.

Skinner, A. and Fleming, J. (1999) *Mentoring Socially Excluding Young People: Lessons from Practice.* Manchester: National Mentoring Network.

Smith, A. (2006) *Crime Statistics: An Independent Review (Carried out by the Crime Statistics Review Group for the Secretary of State for the Home Department, November 2006).* London: Home Office (available online at **http://www.homeoffice.gov.uk/rds/pdfs06/crime-statistics-independent-review-06.pdf**).

Smith, D. (1987) 'The limits of positivism in social work research', *British Journal of Social Work*, 17: 401–16.

Smith, D. (2002) 'Crime and the life course', in M. Maguire *et al.* (eds) *The Oxford Handbook of Criminology* (3rd edn). Oxford: Oxford University Press.

Smith, D. (ed.) (2004) *Social Work and Evidence-based Practice.* London: Jessica Kingsley.

Smith, D. (2006a) 'Youth crime and justice: research, evaluation and "evidence"', in B. Goldson and J. Muncie (eds) *Youth Crime and Justice: Critical Issues.* London: Sage.

Smith, D. (2006b) *Social Inclusion and Early Desistance from Crime. Report* 12. Edinburgh: Centre for Law and Society, University of Edinburgh.

Smith, R. (2003) *Youth Justice: Ideas, Policy, Practice.* Cullompton: Willan Publishing.

Smith, R. (2006) 'Actuarialism and early intervention in contemporary youth justice', in B. Goldson and J. Muncie (eds) *Youth Crime and Justice: Critical Issues.* London: Sage.

Smith, R. (2007) *Youth Justice: Ideas, Policy, Practice* (2nd edn). Cullompton: Willan Publishing.

Snacken, S. and Beyens, K. (1994) 'Sentencing and prison overcrowding', *European Journal on Criminal Policy and Research*, 2: 84–99.

Snyder, H. (2002) 'Juvenile crime and justice in the United States of America', in N. Bala et al. (eds) *Juvenile Justice Systems: An International Comparison of Problems and Solutions.* Toronto: Thompson.

Solanki, A.-R., Bateman, T., Boswell, G. and Hill, E. (2006) *Anti-social Behaviour Orders.* London: Youth Justice Board.

Souhami, A. (2007) *Transforming Youth Justice: Occupational Identity and Cultural Change.* Cullompton: Willan Publishing.

Spalek, B. (2002) *Islam, Crime and Criminal Justice.* Cullompton: Willan Publishing.

Spalek, B. (2006) *Crime Victims: Theory, Policy and Practice.* London: Palgrave.

Squires, P. (2006) 'New Labour and the politics of antisocial behaviour', *Critical Social Policy*, 26: 144–68.

Squires, P. and Stephen, D.E. (2005) *Rougher Justice: Anti-social Behaviour and Young People.* Cullompton: Willan Publishing.

Stafford, E. and Hill, J. (1987) 'The tariff, social inquiry reports and the sentencing of juveniles', *British Journal of Criminology*, 27: 411–20.

Stanley, C. (2005) 'The role of the courts', in T. Bateman and J. Pitts (eds) *The RHP Companion to Youth Justice.* Lyme Regis: Russell House.

Stein, M. (2004) *What Works for Young People Leaving Care?* Ilford: Barnardo's.

Stenson, K. (2000) 'Crime control, social policy and liberalism', in G. Lewis *et al.* (eds) *Rethinking Social Policy.* London: Sage.

Stenson, K. and Edwards, A. (2004) 'Policy transfer in local crime control: beyond naïve emulation', in T. Newburn and R. Sparks (eds.) *Criminal Justice and Political Cultures: National and International Dimensions of Crime Control.* Cullompton: Willan.

Stephen, D.E. (2006) 'Community safety and young people: 21st century homo sacer and the politics of injustice', in P. Squires (ed.) *Community Safety: Critical Perspectives on Policy and Practice.* Bristol: Policy Press.

Stephenson, M. (2007) *Young People and Offending: Education, Youth Justice and Social Inclusion.* Cullompton: Willan Publishing.

Stern, V. (1998) *A Sin against the Future: Imprisonment in the World.* London: Penguin Books.

Stevens, A. (2007) 'When two dark figures collide: evidence and discourse on drug-related crime', *Critical Social Policy*, 27: 77–99.

Stevens, M. and Crook, J. (1986) 'What the devil is intermediate treatment?', *Social Work Today*, 8 September: 10–11.

Stevenson, K., Davies, A. and Gunn, M. (2004) *Blackstone's Guide to the Sexual Offences Act 2003.* Oxford: Oxford University Press.

Stewart, J. (1995) 'Children, parents and the state: the Children Act 1908', *Children and Society*, 9: 90–99.

Stone, N. (2002) 'Shorter terms of Section 91 detention', *Youth Justice*, 2: 47–9.

Straw, J. and Michael, A. (1996) *Tackling Youth Crime: Reforming Youth Justice – a Consultation Paper on an Agenda for Change.* London: Labour Party.

Streib, V.L. (2003) 'The juvenile death penalty today: death sentences and executions for juvenile crimes, January 1973–September 2003' (available online at **http://www.deathpenaltyinfo.org/article.php?scid=27&did=203#execsus**).

Sudbury, J. (2004) 'A world without prisons: resisting militarism, globalized punishment and empire', *Social Justice*, 31: 9–30.

Sutherland, E.H. (1937) *The Professional Thief: By a Professional Thief.* Chicago, IL: University of Chicago Press.

Sutherland, E.H. (1947) *Principles of Criminology* (5th edn). Philadelphia, PA: Lippincott.

Sutherland, E.H. and Cressey, D.R. (1960) *Criminology.* Philadelphia, PA: Lippincott.

Tappan, P. (1949) *Juvenile Delinquency.* New York, NY: McGraw-Hill.

Thomas, S. (2003) *Remand Management.* London: Youth Justice Board.

Thomas, S. (2005a) 'Remand management', in T. Bateman and J. Pitts (eds) *The RHP Companion Guide to Youth Justice.* Lyme Regis: Russell House.

Thomas, S. (2005b) *National Evaluation of Bail Supervision and Support Schemes Funded by the Youth Justice Board for England and Wales from April 1999 to March 2002.* London: Youth Justice Board (available online at **http://www.yjb.gov.uk/Publications/Scripts/prodView.asp?idProduct=273&eP**).

Thomas, S. and Hucklesby, A. (2002) *Key Elements of Effective Practice for Remand Management.* London: Youth Justice Board.

Thomas, S. and Hucklesby, A. (2004) *Key Elements of Effective Practice – Remand Management.* London: Youth Justice Board (available online at **http://www.yjb.gov.uk/Publications/ Scripts/prodView.asp?idProduct=112&eP=PP**).

Thompson, N. (2006) *Anti-discriminatory Practice.* London: Palgrave Macmillan.

Thornton, D. (1984) *Tougher Regimes in Detention Centres.* London: Home Office.

Thorpe, D.H., Smith, D., Green, C.J. and Paley, J.H. (1980) *Out of Care: The Community Support of Juvenile Offenders.* London: Allen & Unwin.

Thrasher, F.M. (1927) *The Gang: A Study of 1,313 Gangs in Chicago.* Chicago, IL: University of Chicago Press.

Tierney, J.P., Grossman, J.B. and Resch, N.L. (1995) *Making a Difference: An Impact Study of Big Brothers Big Sisters.* Philadelphia, PA: Public/Private Ventures.

Tilley, N. (ed.) (2005) *Handbook of Crime Prevention and Community Safety.* Cullompton: Willan Publishing.

Tonry, M. (1996) 'Racial politics, racial disparities and the war on crime', in B. Hudson (ed.) *Race, Crime and Justice.* Aldershot: Dartmouth.

Tonry, M. (2004) *Punishment and Politics: Evidence and Emulation in English Crime Control Policy.* Cullompton: Willan Publishing.

Tonry, M. and Doob, A. (eds.) (2004) *Youth Crime and Youth Justice: Comparative and Cross-National Perspectives*: 'Crime and Justice' Volume 31. Chicago: Chicago University Press.

Tuckman, B. (1965) 'Developmental sequence in small groups', *Psychological Bulletin*, 63: 384–99.

Tutt, N. and Giller, H. (1987) 'Manifesto for management: the elimination of custody', *Justice of the Peace*, 151: 200–2.

Underdown, A. (1998) *Strategies for Effective Offender Supervision: Report of the HMIP What Works Project.* London: Home Office.

Unicef (1998) *Innocenti Digest: Juvenile Justice.* Florence: Unicef.

Unicef (2007) *Child Poverty in Perspective: An Overview of Child Well-being in Rich Countries.* Florence: UNICEF.

United Nations (1985) *United Nations Standard Minimum Rules for the Administration of Juvenile Justice.* New York, NY: United Nations.

United Nations Children's Fund (1998) *Innocenti Digest 3: Juvenile Justice.* Florence: Unicef International Child Development Centre (available online at **http://www.unicef-icdc. org/publications/pdf/digest3e.pdf**).

United Nations Committee on the Rights of the Child (1995) *The Administration of Juvenile Justice* (available online at **http://www.ohchr.org/english/bodies/crc/discussion.htm**).

United Nations Committee on the Rights of the Child (2002) *Concluding Observations of the Committee on the Rights of the Child: United Kingdom of Great Britain and Northern Ireland.* Geneva: Committee on the Rights of the Child (available online at **http://www.unhchr.ch/tbs/doc.nsf/(Symbol)/CRC.C.15.Add.188.En?OpenDocument**).

United Nations Committee on the Rights of the Child (2007) *General Comment No. 10: Children's Rights in Juvenile Justice.* Geneva: Committee on the Rights of the Child (available online at **http://www.ohchr.org/english/bodies/crc/comments.htm**).

United Nations General Assembly (1985) *United Nations Standard Minimum Rules for the Administration of Juvenile Justice* (the Beijing Rules) (available online at **http://www.un. org/documents/ga/res/40/a40r033.htm**).

United Nations General Assembly (1990) *United Nations Guidelines for the Prevention of Juvenile Delinquency* (the Riyadh Guidelines) (available online at **http://www.un.org/documents/ga/res/45/a45r112.htm**).

University of East Anglia in association with the National Children's Bureau (2007) *Children's Trust Pathfinders: Innovative Partnerships for Improving the Well-being of Children and Young People – National Evaluation of Children's Trust Pathfinders Final Report* (available online at **http://www.everychildmatters.gov.uk/resources-and-practice/IG00209/**).

Utting, D. and Langman, J. (2005) *A Guide to Promising Approaches.* Swansea: Communities that Care.

Valentine, G. (2006) *Public Space and the Culture of Childhood.* Aldershot: Ashgate.

Van Den Haag, E. (1975) *Punishing Criminals.* New York, NY: Basic Books.

Van Meeuwen, A., Swann, S., McNeish, D. and Edwards, S.S.M. (1998) *Whose Daughter Next? Children Abused through Prostitution.* Ilford: Barnardo's.

von Hirsch, A. (1976) *Doing Justice: The Choice of Punishments.* New York, NY: Hill & Wang.

von Hirsch, A. and Maher, L. (1998) 'Should penal rehabilitationism be revived?', in A. von Hirsch and A. Ashworth (eds) *Principled Sentencing: Readings on Theory and Policy.* Oxford: Hart Publishing.

Walgrave, L. (2004) 'Restoration in youth justice', in M. Tonry and A. Doob (eds) *Youth Crime and Youth Justice: Comparative and Cross National Perspectives.* Chicago, IL: University of Chicago Press.

Walker, A., Kershaw, C. and Nicholas, S. (2006) *Crime in England and Wales, 2005/06. Home Office Statistical Bulletin* 12/06. London: Home Office (available online at **http://www.homeoffice.gov.uk/rds/pdfs06/hosb1206.pdf**).

Walklate, S. (2003) 'Can there be a feminist victimology?', in P. Davies *et al.* (eds) *Victimisation: Theory, Research and Policy.* London: Palgrave.

Walklate, S. (2007) *Imagining the Victim of Crime.* Maidenhead: Open University Press.

Walsh, C. (1999) 'Imposing order: child safety orders and local child curfew schemes', *Journal of Social Welfare and Family Law,* 21: 135–49.

Walsh, C. (2002) 'Curfews: no more hanging around', *Youth Justice,* 2: 70–81.

Walter, I. (2002) *Evaluation of the National Roll-out of Curfew Orders.* London: Home Office (available online at **http://www.homeoffice.gov.uk/rds/pdfs2/rdsolr1502.pdf**).

Walters, R. (2003) *Deviant Knowledge: Criminology, Politics and Policy.* Cullompton: Willan Publishing.

Wargent, M. (2006) 'Contestability: is the model for NOMS "fit for purpose"?', *Vista,* 9: 162–8.

Waterhouse, L., McGhee, J., Loucks, N., Whyte, B. and Kay, H. (1999) *The Evaluation of the Children's Hearings in Scotland. Volume 3. Children in Focus.* Edinburgh: Scottish Executive Central Research Unit.

Waterhouse, L., McGhee, J., Whyte, B., Loucks, N., Kay, H. and Stewart, R. (2000) *The Evaluation of the Children's Hearings in Scotland: Children in Focus.* Edinburgh: Scottish Executive.

Webster, C. (2006) '"Race", youth crime and justice', in B. Goldson and J. Muncie (eds) *Youth Crime and Justice: Critical Issues.* London: Sage.

Webster, C. (2007) *Understanding Race and Crime.* Cullompton: Willan Publishing.

Webster, C., MacDonald, R. and Simpson, M. (2006) 'Predicting criminality? Risk factors, neighbourhood influence and desistance', *Youth Justice,* 6: 7–22.

Weijers, I. (2004) 'Requirements for communication in the courtroom: a comparative perspective on the youth court in England/Wales and the Netherlands', *Youth Justice,* 4: 22–31.

Welsh Assembly Government (2004) *All Wales Youth Offending Strategy*. Cardiff: Welsh Assembly Government.

Welsh Assembly Government (2005) *National Service Framework for Children, Young People and Maternity Services in Wales*. Cardiff: Welsh Assembly Government.

Welsh Assembly Government (2006) *Making the Connections – Delivering beyond Boundaries: Transforming Public Services in Wales*. Cardiff: Welsh Assembly Government.

Welsh Assembly Government Policy Unit (2000) *Extending Entitlement: Supporting Young People in Wales*. Cardiff: Welsh Assembly Government (available online at **http://www.ecoli inquirywales.org.uk/topics/educationandskills/policy_strategy_and_planning/extending_ entitlement/eepublications/supportyoungpeople?lang=en**).

Welsh Assembly Government/Youth Justice Board (2004) *All Wales Youth Offending Strategy*. Cardiff: Welsh Assembly Government and Youth Justice Board.

West, D. and Farrington, D. (1973) *Who Becomes Deliquent?* London: Heinemann.

West, D. and Farrington, D. (1977) *The Delinquent Way of Life*. London: Heinemann.

White, R. and Cunneen, C. (2006) 'Social class, youth crime and justice', in B. Goldson and J. Muncie (eds.) *Youth Crime and Justice: Critical Issues*. London: Sage.

Whitfield, D. (2001) *The Magic Bracelet: Technology and Offender Supervision*. Winchester: Waterside Press.

Whyte, B. (2003) 'Young and persistent: recent developments in youth justice policy and practice in Scotland', *Youth Justice*, 3: 74–85.

Whyte, B. (2005) 'Youth justice in other UK jurisdictions: Scotland and Northern Ireland', in T. Bateman and J. Pitts (eds) *The RHP Companion to Youth Justice*. Lyme Regis: Russell House.

Wilcox, A. (2003) 'Evidence-based youth justice? Some valuable lessons from an evaluation for the Youth Justice Board', *Youth Justice*, 3: 19–33.

Wilcox, A. and Hoyle, C. (2004) *The National Evaluation of the Youth Justice Board's Restorative Justice Projects*. London: Youth Justice Board.

Wilcox, A., Young, R. and Hoyle, C. (2004) *An Evaluation of the Impact of Restorative Cautioning: Findings from a Reconviction Study. Home Office Findings* 255. London: Home Office (available online at **http://www.homeoffice.gov.uk/rds/pdfs04/r255.pdf**).

Wilkins, L. (1964) *Social Deviance*. London: Tavistock.

Williams, B. (2005) *Victims of Crime and Community Justice*. London: Jessica Kingsley.

Williams, J.E. (1961) 'Report of the Interdepartmental Committee on the Business of the Criminal Courts', *Modern Law Review*, 24: 360–5.

Williams, R. and Richardson, G. (1995) *Together We Stand: The Commissioning, Role and Management of Child and Adolescent Mental Health Services: An NHS Health Advisory Service (HAS) Thematic Review*. London: HMSO.

Wilson, D., Kerr, H. and Boyle, M. (1998) *Juvenile Offenders and Reconviction in Northern Ireland. Northern Ireland Office Research Findings* 3/1998. Belfast: Northern Ireland Office.

Wilson, D., Sharp, C. and Patterson, A. (2006) *Young People and Crime: Findings from the 2005 Offending Crime and Justice Survey. Home Office Online Report* 17/06. London: Home Office (available online at **http://www.homeoffice.gov.uk/rds/offending_survey.html**).

Wilson, J.Q. (1975) *Thinking About Crime*. New York, NY: Vintage.

Wilson, J.Q. (1983) *Thinking about Crime*. New York, NY: Basic Books.

Wilson, J.Q. and Kelling, G. (1982) 'The police and neighbourhood safety: broken windows', *Atlantic Monthly*, March: 29–38.

Wilson, K., Sinclair, I., Taylor, C., Pithouse, A. and Sellick, C. (2004) *Fostering Success: An Exploration of the Research Literature in Foster Care. Knowledge Review* 5. London: Social Care Institute for Excellence.

Winterdyk, J. (ed.) (2002) *Juvenile Justice Systems: International Perspectives* (2nd edn). Toronto: Canadian Scholars Press.

Wootton, B. (1978) *Crime and Penal Policy: Reflections on Fifty Years' Experience.* London: George Allen & Unwin.

Worrall, A. and Hoy, C. (2005) *Punishment in the Community: Managing Offenders, Making Choices* (2nd edn). Cullompton: Willan Publishing.

Worth, S. (2005) 'Beating the "churning" trap in the youth labour market', *Work, Employment and Society*, 19: 403–14.

Yates, S. and Payne, M. (2006) 'Not so NEET? A critique of the use of NEET in setting targets for interventions with young people', *Journal of Youth Studies*, 9: 329–44.

Young, J. (1971a) 'The role of the police as amplifiers of deviancy', in S. Cohen (ed.) *Images of Deviance.* Harmondsworth: Penguin Books.

Young, J. (1971b) *The Drugtakers.* London: Paladin.

Young, J. (1994) 'Incessant chatter: recent paradigms in criminology', in M. Maguire *et al.* (eds) *The Oxford Handbook of Criminology.* Oxford: Oxford University Press.

Young, J. (1999) *The Exclusive Society.* London: Sage.

Young, J. and Matthews, R. (eds) (1992) *Issues in Realist Criminology.* London: Sage.

Youth Justice Agency (2007) *Attendance Centre Orders: A Guide for Young People and their Carers.* Belfast: Youth Justice Agency (available online at **http://www.youthjusticeagencyni.gov.uk/ community_services/court_services/**).

Youth Justice Board (2000a) *Analysis of the First Quarterly Returns Provided by the Youth Offending Teams in England and Wales.* London: Youth Justice Board.

Youth Justice Board (2000b) *Factors Associated with Differential Rates of Youth Custodial Sentencing.* London: Youth Justice Board.

Youth Justice Board (2000c) *National Standards for Youth Justice.* London: Youth Justice Board.

Youth Justice Board (2001) *Risk and Protective Factors Associated with Youth Crime and Effective Interventions.* London: Youth Justice Board.

Youth Justice Board (2003) *Referral Orders: Research into Issues Raised in 'The Introduction of the Referral Order into the Youth Justice System'.* London: Youth Justice Board.

Youth Justice Board (2004a) *National Standards for Youth Justice Services.* London: Youth Justice Board (available online at **http://www.yjb.gov.uk/Publications/Scripts/prodView.asp? idproduct=155&eP=PP**).

Youth Justice Board (2004b) *Guidance Document: Action Plan Order Drug Treatment and Testing Requirement as Part of an Action Plan Order or Supervision Order* (available online at **http://www.yjb.gov.uk/en-gb/practitioners/CourtsAndOrders/Disposals/Action PlanOrder/**).

Youth Justice Board (2004c) *Prolific and Other Priority Offenders Strategy Guidance for Youth Offending Teams.* London: Youth Justice Board (available online at **http://www.yjb. gov.uk/en-gb/practitioners/ImprovingPractice/PPO/**).

Youth Justice Board (2005a) *Mental Health Needs and Provision.* London: Youth Justice Board.

Youth Justice Board (2005b) *Risk and Protective Factors.* London: Youth Justice Board.

Youth Justice Board (2005c) *Strategy for the Secure Estate for Children and Young People: Plans for 2005/06 to 2007/08.* London: Youth Justice Board.

Youth Justice Board (2006a) *Criminal Justice Act 2003, 'Dangerousness' and the New Sentences for Public Protection: Guidance for Youth Offending Teams.* London: Youth Justice Board (available online at **http://www.yjb.gov.uk/Publications/scripts/prodView.asp?id product=209&eP=**).

Youth Justice Board (2006b) *Multi-agency Public Protection Arrangements: Guidance for Youth Offending Teams*. London: Youth Justice Board (available online at **http://www.yjb.gov.uk/publications/scripts/prodView.asp?idProduct=283&eP**).

Youth Justice Board (2006c) 'The secure estate for children and young people is nearing operational capacity.' News release, 8 August (available online at **http://www.yjb.gov.uk/en-gb/News/Secure+EstatePressures.htm?area=Corporate**).

Youth Justice Board (2006d) *Barriers to Engagement in Education, Training and Employment for Young People in the Youth Justice System*. London: Youth Justice Board.

Youth Justice Board (2006e) *Corporate and Business Plan, 2006/07–2008/09*. London: YJB (available online at **http://www.yjb.gov.uk/Publications/Scripts/prodDownload.asp? idproduct=301&eP**).

Youth Justice Board (2006f) *Courts and Orders* (available online at **http://www.yjb.gov.uk/en-gb/practitioners/CourtsAndOrders/**).

Youth Justice Board (2006g) *Individual Support Orders (ISO) Procedure: A Protocol to be Used and Adapted by YOTs when Managing ISOs*. London: Youth Justice Board.

Youth Justice Board (2006h) *Managing the Behaviour of Children and Young People in the Secure Estate: A Code of Conduct*. London: Youth Justice Board (available online at **www.yjb.gov.uk/en-gb/practitioners/custody/behaviourmanagement**).

Youth Justice Board (2006i) *Offences against Children*. London: Youth Justice Board.

Youth Justice Board (2006j) *Swift Administration of Justice*. London: Youth Justice Board (available online at **http://www.yjb.gov.uk/Publications/Scripts/prodView.asp?idProduct=47&eP=**).

Youth Justice Board (2006k) *YISP Management Guidance*. London: Youth Justice Board.

Youth Justice Board (2006l) *Youth Resettlement: A Framework for Action*. London: Youth Justice Board.

Youth Justice Board (2007a) *Monitoring Performance: Youth Justice Plans*. London: Youth Justice Board (available online at **http://www.yjb.gov.uk/en-gb/practitioners/MonitoringPerformance/YouthJusticePlans/**).

Youth Justice Board (2007b) *Monitoring Performance: Performance Assessments of Children's Services*. London: Youth Justice Board (available online at **http://www.yjb.gov.uk/en-gb/practitioners/MonitoringPerformance/AssessingChildrensServices/**).

Youth Justice Board (2007c) 'Government launches new guidance on the use of acceptable behaviour contracts' (available online at **http://www.yjb.gov.uk/en-gb/News/new Acceptable BehaviourContractsguidance.htm?area=Corporate**).

Youth Justice Board (2007d) *Annual Report and Accounts, 2006/07*. London: Youth Justice Board.

Youth Justice Board (2007e) *Position Statement on Sentencing Young People to Custody*. London: Youth Justice Board (available online at **http://www.yjb.gov.uk/engb/yjb/Media Centre/PositionStatements/sentencingchildrenandyoungpeopletocustody.htm**).

Youth Justice Board (2007f) *Strategy for the Secure Estate for Children and Young People*. London: YJB (available online at **http://www.yjb.gov.uk/Publications/Scripts/prodView.asp? idproduct=270&eP=**).

Youth Justice Board (2007g) *Youth Justice Annual Statistics, 2005/06*. London: Youth Justice Board (available online at **http://www.yjb.gov.uk/publications/Resources/Downloads/Youth%20Justice%20Annual%20Statistics%202005-06.pdf**).

Youth Justice Board (in association with Mediation UK) (2003) *Restorative Justice*. London: Youth Justice Board.

Zedner, L. (2004) *Criminal Justice*. Oxford: Oxford University Press.

Zehr, H. (2002) *The Little Book of Restorative Justice*. Intercourse, Pennsylvania: Good Books.

Index